Isaac Hughes Elliott

Record of the Services of Illinois Soldiers in the Black Hawk War,

1831-32

And in the Mexican War, 1846-8

Isaac Hughes Elliott

Record of the Services of Illinois Soldiers in the Black Hawk War, 1831-32
And in the Mexican War, 1846-8

ISBN/EAN: 9783337143589

Printed in Europe, USA, Canada, Australia, Japan

Cover: Foto ©ninafisch / pixelio.de

More available books at **www.hansebooks.com**

OF

ILLINOIS SOLDIERS

IN THE

BLACK HAWK WAR,

1831-32,

AND IN

THE MEXICAN WAR,

1846-8,

CONTAINING A COMPLETE ROSTER OF COMMISSIONED OFFICERS AND ENLISTED
MEN OF BOTH WARS, TAKEN FROM THE OFFICIAL ROLLS ON FILE
IN THE WAR DEPARTMENT, WASHINGTON, D. C.

WITH AN APPENDIX,

GIVING A RECORD OF THE SERVICES OF THE ILLINOIS MILITIA, RANGERS
AND RIFLEMEN, IN PROTECTING THE FRONTIER FROM THE
RAVAGES OF THE INDIANS FROM 1810 TO 1813.

PREPARED AND PUBLISHED BY AUTHORITY OF THE THIRTY-SECOND GENERAL ASSEMBLY,

By ISAAC H. ELLIOTT,

ADJUTANT-GENERAL OF THE STATE OF ILLINOIS.

SPRINGFIELD, ILL.:
H. W. ROKKER, STATE PRINTER AND BINDER.
1882.

Extract from Act of General Assembly, giving authority for this publication.

Forty-fifth—To the Adjutant-General, the additional sum of fifteen hundred dollars, for the preparation, printing and binding of the records of the services of the Illinois soldiers in the Mexican and Black Hawk wars, to be paid out of any money in the State treasury not otherwise appropriated, on the warrant of the Auditor of Public Accounts, drawn on vouchers of the Adjutant-General, approved by the Governor: *Provided*, that no part of this appropriation shall be paid for paper, which shall be furnished by the Secretary of State, out of paper obtained for the State under contract, of quality to be selected by the Governor.

Approved May 30, 1881. (See Laws 1881, p. 44.)

CONTENTS.

	PAGE.
Introductory	IX
Historical Memoranda.	
Black Hawk War	XI
Muster Roll Capt. Gholson Kercheval's company	XXIII
Mexican War	XXIV

BLACK HAWK WAR.

FIRST BRIGADE.

First Regiment.

Capt. John Bay's company	3
Capt. D. B. Russell's company	4
Capt. Achilles Coffee's detachment	5
Capt. Harrison Wilson's company	6
Capt. Joel Holliday's company	7
Capt. Achilles Coffee's company	8

Second Regiment.

Capt. George P. Bowyer's company	10
Capt. Wm. J. Stephenson's company	11
Capt. Obediah West's company	12
Capt. Charles Dunn's company	13
Capt. Jonathan Durman's company	14
Capt. Armstead Holman's company	14

Third Regiment.

Capt. Ardin Biggerstaff's company	16
Capt. John Onslott's company	17
Capt. James Hall's company	18
Capt. James N. Clark's company	19
Capt. Berryman G. Wells' company	20

Spy Battalion.

Capt. Wm. N. Dobbins' company	22
Capt. James Bowman's company	23

Detachments.

From Capt. W. S. Stephenson's company	25
From Capt. Charles Dunn's company	25
From Capt. Russell's company	26
From Capt. Arman's company	26
From Capt. West's company	26
From Capt. Holliday's company	26
From Capt. Bowyer's company	27

SECOND BRIGADE.

First Regiment.

Capt. Thomas B. Ross' company	28
Capt. Samuel Brimberry's company	29
Capt. Isaac Sanford's company	30
Capt. Robert Griffin's company	32
Capt. Jonathan Mayo's company	33
Capt. Royal A. Nott's company	34

CONTENTS.

PAGE.

Second Regiment.

Capt. Alex. M. Houston's company 36
Capt. John Arnold's company 37
Detachment of Capt. Elias Jordan's company 38
Detachment of Capt. Highsmith's company 38
Detachment of Capt. Barnes' company 39

Third Regiment.

Capt. Solomon Hunter's company 40
Capt. Champion S. Mading's company 41
Capt. John Haynes' company 42
Capt. William Thomas' company 43
Capt. Daniel Powell's company 44
Detachment of Capt. Powell's company 45

Spy Battalion.

Capt. John F. Richardson's company 46
Capt. Abner Greer's Company 47
Capt. John McCann's company 48

Detachments.

Adjutant Parmenter's 50
Of Capt. Hiram Roundtree's company 50
Of Capt. Hiram Kinade's company 50
Of Capt. Mayo's company 50
Of Capt. Earl Pierce's company 51
Of Capt. Bennett Howlin's company 51
Of Capt. Sol. Hunter's company 51
Of Capt. J. F. Richardson's company 51
Of Capt. Isaac Sanford's company 51
Of Capt. Wm. Highsmith's company 51
Of Capt. A. M. Houston's company 52
Of Capt. John Barnes' company 52
Of Capt. Abner Greer's company 53

THIRD BRIGADE.

First Regiment.

Capt. David Smith's company 54
Capt. William Gillham's company 55
Capt. William Gorden's company 56
Capt. George F. Bristow's company 57
Capt. S. T. Matthews', afterwards J. T. Arnett's company 57
Capt. Walter Butler's company 58

Second Regiment.

Capt. Hiram Roundtree's company 60
Capt. James Kincaid's company 61
Capt. Gershom Paterson's company 62
Capt. Aaron Bannon's company 63
Capt. Thomas Stout's company 64

Third Regiment.

Capt. Andrew Bankson's company 66
Capt. Wm. Adair's company 67
Capt. Josiah S. Briggs' company 68
Capt. James Thompson's company 69
Capt. Jacob Feman's company, afterward Capt. James Connor's company 70
Capt. James Burns' company 71

Fourth Regiment.

Capt. Bennett Nowlen's company 73
Capt. Ozias Hail's company 74
Capt. Jesse Claywell's company 75
Capt. Reuben Brown's company 76
Capt. Thomas Moffett's company 77
Capt. Henry L. Webb's company 78

Spy Battalion:

Capt. Allen F. Lindsey's company 80
Capt. Samuel Huston's company 81

WHITESIDE'S BRIGADE.

First Regiment.

Capt. Julius L. Barnsback's company 83
Capt. John Thomas' company 84
Capt. John Tate's company 85
Capt. Josiah Little's company 86

CONTENTS.

Second Regiment.

Capt. Thomas Chapman's company	88
Capt. Levi D. Boone's company	89
Capt. William G. Flood's company	90
Capt. Benjamin James' company	91
Capt. Jeremiah Smith's company	92

Third Regiment.

Capt. John Harris' company	93
Capt. Benjamin Barney's company	94
Capt. Elisha Petty's company	94
Capt. William B. Smith's company	95
Capt. Nathan Winter's company	96

Fourth Regiment.

Capt. M. G. Wilson's company	98
Capt. Wm. C. Rall's company	99
Capt. Abraham Lincoln's company	100

Fifth Regiment.

Capt. M. L. Covell's company	102
Capt. Robert McClure's company	105
Capt. J. C. Pugh's company	103
Capt. John G. Adams' company	104

Spy Battalion.

Capt. John Dawson's company	106
Capt. Thomas Carlin's company	107
Capt. John Dement's company	108

Odd Battalion.—Major James'.

Capt. Daniel Price's company	110
Capt. Peter Warren's company	111
Capt. Thomas Harrison's company	112

Odd Battalion.—Major Thos. Long's.

Capt. Jacob Ebey's company	113
Capt. Japhet A. Ball's company	114

Unattached Companies.

Capt. William Moore's company	116
Capt. John Winstanley's company	117
Capt. William T. Given's company	118
Capt. Erastus Wheeler's company	118
Capt. Samuel Smith's, late Jacob Fry's company	119
Capt. Thomas McDow's company	120
Capt. David Crow's company	121
Capt. L. W. Goodan's company	122

FOURTH BRIGADE.

Fortieth Regiment (Militia.)—Commanded by Col. John Strawn.

Capt. Geo. B. Willis' company	124
Capt. Robert Barnes' company	125
Capt. William M. Stewart's company	126
Capt. William Haw's company	127

INDEPENDENT REGIMENTS.

Col. Isaac B. Moore's Regiment.

Capt. John B. Thomas' company	128
Capt. Alexander Bailey's company	129
Capt. Eliakim Ashton's company	130
Capt. Morgan L. Payne's company	131
Capt. James Palmer's company	132
Capt. I. M. Gillespie's company	133
Capt. James Gregory's company	134
Capt. Corbin R. Hutt's company	135

Twenty-seventh Regiment—Militia.

Capt. Milton M. Maugh's company	136
Capt. Nicholas Dowling's company	138
Capt. Clack Stone's company	139
Capt. Charles McCoy's company	140
Capt. Benj. J. Aldenrath's company	141

VI   CONTENTS.

PAGE.

Capt. H. H. Gear's company	142
Capt. Samuel H. Scale's company	144
Capt. Jonathan Craig's company	145
Capt. Lambert P. Vansburgh's company	146

ODD BATTALIONS.

Major N. Buckmaster's Battalion.

Capt. Holden Seisson's company	148
Capt. Joseph Napier's company	149
Capt. Aaron Armstrong's company	189

Odd Battalion of Rangers.

Capt. Abner Eads'	152
Capt. David W. Barnes' company	151
Capt. Asel F. Ball's company	153

Companies in Odd Battalions.

Capt. John Sain's company	155
Capt. William McMurtry's company	159
Capt. Asel F. Ball's company	150
Capt. J. W. Kenney's company	158
Capt. Peter Butler's company	156
Capt. James White's company	167

Odd Companies Attached to Col Dodge's Regiment.

Capt. James Craig's company	162
Capt. Enoch Duncan's company	163

COMPANIES UNDER GEN. ATKINSON.

Capt. William Gordon's company	166
Capt. Cyrus Matthews' company	167
Capt. George McFadden's company	168
Capt. Samuel Smith's company	168
Capt. B. James' company	169
Capt. John Stennett's company	170
Capt. M. L. Covell's company	171
Capt. John S. Wilbourne's company	172
Capt. Solomon Miller's company	173
Capt. Elijah Iles' company	174

INDEPENDENT COMPANIES.

Capt. Jacob M. Early's company	176
Capt. Seth Pratt's company	177
Capt. Alexander D. Cox's company	178
Capt. James Walker's company	179
Capt. William Warwick's company	179
Capt. Alex. M. Jenkins' company	180
Capt. B. B. Craig's company	181
Capt. William C. Rall's company	182
Capt. Alexander White's company	183
Capt. Charles S. Dorsey's company	184
Capt. A. W. Snyder's company	184
Capt. Earl Pierce's company	186

COMPANIES SERVING PREVIOUS TO 1832.

1827—Capt. James M. Strode's company	187

Major N. Buckmaster's Battalion, 1831.

Capt. Solomon Miller's company	188
Capt. William Moore's company	190

MEXICAN WAR.

FIRST CALL—ONE YEAR VOLUNTEERS.

First Regiment—Col. J. J. Hardin.

	PAGE.
Field and Staff	194
Capt. Morgan's Co. A	195
Capt. Smith's Co. B	196
Capt. Fry's Co. C	197
Capt. McConnel's Co. D	198
Capt. Robertson's Co. E	200
Capt. Crow's Co. F	201
Capt. Wyatt's Co. G	202
Capt. Montgomery's Co. H	204
Capt. Prentiss' Co. I	205
Capt. Mower's Co. K	206

Second Regiment—Col. Wm. H. Bissell.

Field and Staff	229
Capt. Coffee's Co. A	229
Capt. Carder's Co. B	231
Capt. Baker's Co. C	232
Capt. Wheeler's Co. D	234
Capt. Lott's Co. E	235
Capt. Hacker's Co. F	236
Capt. Lemen's Co. G	238
Capt. Raith's Co. H	239
Capt. Miller's Co. I	241
Capt. Starbuck's Co. K	242

Third Regiment—Col. Ferris Foreman.

Field and Staff	266
Capt. Stout's Co. A	267
Capt. Freeman's Co. B	268
Capt. McAdam's Co. C	270
Capt. Bishop's Co. D	272
Capt. Seller's Co. E	274
Capt. Campbell's Co. F	276
Capt. Lawler's Co. G	277
Capt. Hicks' Co. H	279
Capt. Harvey's Co. I	281
Capt. McGinnis' Co. K	283

Fourth Regiment—Col. E. D. Baker.

Field and Staff	285
Capt. H. A. Roberts' Co. A	285
Capt. Garret Elkin's Co. B	287
Capt. J. C. Pugh's Co. C	289
Capt. Achilles Morris' Co. D	291
Capt. Daniel Newcomb's Co. E	293
Capt. Asa D. Wright's Co. F	294
Capt. Edward Jones' Co. G	296
Capt. John S. McConkey's Co. H	298
Capt. John C. Hurt's Co. I	300
Capt. Lewis W. Ross' Co. K	301

SECOND CALL (DURING THE WAR.)

First Regiment (Fifth Illinois)—Col. E. W. B. Newby.

Field and Staff	208
Capt. Bond's Co. A	208
Capt. Cunningham's Co. B	210
Capt. Turner's Co. C	212
Capt. Moses' Co. D	214
Capt. Hook's Co. E	216
Capt. Kinney's Co. F	218

Capt. Reed's Co. G.. 220
Capt. Hampton's Co. H.. 222
Capt. Niles' Co. I.. 224
Capt. Kinman's Co. K... 226

Second Regiment (Sixth Illinois)—Col. J. Collins.
Field and Staff.. 244
Capt. James Bowman's Co. A... 245
Capt. C. L. Wright's Co. B... 247
Capt. Harvey Lee's Co. C... 249
Capt. John Bristow's Co. D... 251
Capt. William Shepherd's Co. E... 253
Capt. David C. Berry's Co. F... 255
Capt. John M. Moore's Co. G.. 257
Capt. James Burns' Co. H... 259
Capt. Edward E. Harvey's Co. I... 261
Capt. John Ewing's Co. K... 263

INDEPENDENT COMPANIES.

Mounted Volunteers.
Capt. A. Dunlap's company.. 304
Capt. W. B. Stapp's company.. 307
Lieut. Lanphere's detachment... 309
Capt. M. K. Lawler's company... 309
Capt. Josiah Littell's company... 312

REGULAR ARMY ENLISTMENTS.

Fourteenth U. S. Infantry.
"E" company.. 314

Sixteenth U. S. Infantry.
"A" company.. 315
"G" company..315, 316

INTRODUCTORY

Although many years have elapsed since the close of the Mexican War, and a much greater period of time since the Black Hawk War, the archives in the Adjutant-General's office have shown no record of the services of our soldiers in either of these wars. In fact, excepting the meagre and occasional rolls of the militia and riflemen, deposited by Governor Edwards' heirs some years ago, there has been, until quite a recent date, no record of the service of any Illinois soldiers in this office prior to the late War of the Rebellion. The organization of the society of the "Veterans of the Mexican, Black Hawk and Florida wars," in 1874, revived an interest in this subject, and the members have, at their annual reunions since that date, agitated the subject with more or less effect, until they have, no doubt, largely aided in securing their demands in the present publication. In 1877, Hon. Cornelius Rourke, a member of the House of Representatives, from Menard county, offered a bill to authorize the Governor to employ a clerk to transcribe these records from the official rolls of the War Department. This, however, did not become a law. This bill was, no doubt, offered in response to the action of the "Mexican War Veteran Association," which, at the September meeting previous, held at Springfield, had passed the following resolution:

Resolved, That it is the sense of the Mexican War Veterans, now in session at the State capital, that a commission should be appointed by the next Legislature of Illinois, with instructions to procure from the archives at Washington, D. C., all information, statistical and otherwise, relative to the operations of the troops from Illinois, and that said information be placed on file in the Adjutant-General's office in this State.

The Legislature, in 1879, added to the general appropriation bill a section authorizing the Governor to appoint a clerk to go to Washington and transcribe all the records, of both volunteer and regular soldiers from Illinois, in the Black Hawk or Mexican wars, and appropriated the sum of five hundred dollars for the purpose. (Laws 1879, p. 30.) In pursuance of this act, Governor Cullom appointed Col. Ferris Foreman, of Vandalia, late the Colonel of the Third Regiment Illinois volunteers and the only surviving Colonel of the Mexican War, to that duty. Col. Foreman proceeded to Washington, and in his report to the Governor, under date of December 16, 1879, states that he was denied the privilege of access to the records by the Adjutant-General, under the standing orders and regulations of the War Department, and reported that it would be necessary to have a resolution passed by Congress before access could be had to the rolls on file in the War Department. After the Hon. Robert T. Lincoln became Secretary of War, Governor Cullom, who has always taken an active interest in the effort to obtain these records for the State, visited him in Washington, and on the personal solicitation of the Governor, Secretary Lincoln was induced to cause these rolls to be transcribed by clerks in the War Department, and correct copies of all such have been furnished by him to this office, and are published complete in this book.

The section of the appropriation bill passed in 1881, which authorizes this publication, was drawn up and offered by the Hon. Samuel H. Martin, a member of the Thirty-second General Assembly from White county, himself a Lieutenant in the Fourteenth United States Infantry during the Mexican War, and to whose efforts, as well as to the efforts of the Honorable Secretary of War and His Excellency the Governor, the merit of obtaining and publishing these records is largely due.

Before commencing the preparation of this publication, an advertisement was inserted in all the leading newspapers of the State, requesting all persons in possession of facts or any data concerning the service of the Illinois soldiers in the Black Hawk and the Mexican wars, to communicate the same to this office. Quite a general response was made to this request by the surviving veterans of both wars, and much interesting and valuable material has been thus accumulated in this office, the larger portion of which cannot, of course, be used in the limits of a publication like the present. The thanks, however, of this office are due to those who so kindly responded to our request, and their communications have all been carefully preserved among the files of this office for future historical reference, and will make a fund of valuable military information for the use of the historian of the future.

Believing the intention of the General Assembly mainly met in the publication of the complete rosters, the briefest possible introductory sketch is made of the prominent facts of the Black Hawk war, which is compiled from Edwards' History of the State of Illinois, and other trustworthy sources, including the correspondence before mentioned. This is followed by a short historical sketch of the part taken by the various commands of Illinois volunteers in the Mexican war, in which is included any honorable mention made of Illinois soldiers as shown by excerpts from the official reports and orders of the various Generals under whom they served, so far as the same appear in the official reports of these officers to the War Department at Washington. It is of course not intended to give an extended view of the operations of the war, therefore our memoranda is scrupulously confined to the actual service of our volunteers, and presents only such data as has been derived from official and other reliable sources, which is considered necessary to make intelligible the official rosters, and which we hope, when taken in connection with them, will make an enduring and reliable memorial of their services, thus more than fulfilling the wish of the General Assembly, who have neither appropriated for, nor expected the publication of, little else than the records as received from the War Department. Although this publication as it now stands is incomplete, particularly in the matter of the records of service in the Winnebago war, and the first campaign of the Black Hawk war, every effort has been made to obtain the desired information, both by correspondence with individuals and the War Department, and the work as presented gives the final result of the best efforts of this office to meet the expectations of the General Assembly.

HISTORICAL MEMORANDA.

THE BLACK HAWK WAR.

The rolls furnished from the War Department, and published in this volume, although by no means complete, show that the State of Illinois furnished one hundred and seventy-four companies of volunteer rangers and spies, which were actually mustered into the service of the United States for various periods of time, during the Black Hawk War. This, of course, does not include large numbers of the State militia, who were under arms, and performed services of greater or less importance, and whose names will remain forever unknown, many of whom were never actually mustered by any United States military officer, nor have any rolls or other account of their service been preserved.

That the public may understand the service of these companies, and the part performed by them in that most important, of any of the Indian wars of the West, we will give a brief sketch of the causes which led to, and the principal events which occurred in, the Black Hawk War. The causes which led to that war reach back to, and even before, the Winnebago or Sauk War of 1827, and are, as briefly stated by Edwards, in his History of Illinois, as follows:

"During Gov. Edwards' administration, as Executive of the State, the Indians upon the Northwestern frontier began to be very troublesome. The different tribes not only commenced a warfare among themselves, in regard to their respective boundaries, but they extended their hostilities to the white settlements. A treaty of peace, in which the whites acted more as mediators than as a party, had been signed at Prairie du Chien, on the 19th day of August, 1825, by the terms of which the boundaries between the Winnebagos and Sioux, Chippewas, Sauks, Foxes, and other tribes were defined, but it failed to keep them quiet. Their depredations and murders continued frequent, and in the summer of 1827 their conduct, particularly that of the Winnebagoes, became very alarming.

There is no doubt, however, that the whites, who at this period were immigrating in large numbers to the Northwest, and earnestly desired their removal further westward, purposely exasperated the Indians, at the same time that they greatly exaggerated the hostilities committed."—(Edwards' Hist. p. 218.)

A combination was soon formed by the different tribes of Indians under Red Bird, a chief of the Sioux, to kill or drive off all the whites above Rock river. This league, which included the Winnebagoes, Pottawotamies, and other tribes of the Northwest, commenced their offensive operations by killing two white men in the vicinity of Prairie du Chien, on the 24th day of July, 1827, and on the 30th of the same month they attacked two returning keel boats which had, on their upward trip, conveyed military stores to Fort Snelling, killing two of the crew and wounding four others, before they were repulsed. Governor Edwards, anticipating trouble, had, on the 14th day of July, issued an order to the commandants in Gen. Hanson's brigade, (located on the east side of the Illinois river), to detach one-fourth of their respective regiments, and be ready to meet any attack made by the Indians. On the same day he wrote to Col. Thomas M. Neale, of the Twentieth Regiment (from Sangamon county), to accept six hundred volunteers, who were to equip themselves, find their own subsistence, and continue in service thirty days, unless sooner discharged; to rendezvous the same at Fort Clark, and march with all possible expedition from there to Galena, to the assistance of the whites, as the Indians had threatened the settlers at the lead mines, near that place. The possession of these mines by the whites had always excited the serious jealousy of the Indians.

Under this call Col. Neale recruited one cavalry company, which was commanded by Capt. Edward Mitchell, and four companies of Infantry, commanded, respectively, by Captains Thomas Constant, Reuben Brown, Achilles Morris and Bowlin Green. The whole force under command of Col. Neale, (the other field officers are unknown except James D. Henry—Sheriff at the time of Sangamon County—Adjutant,) marched to Peoria, where the regiment was more fully organized, and from thence to Galena. Before their arrival, however, in the Indian country Red Bird and six of his principal warriors had surrendered, and the campaign being ended the volunteers returned to their homes. No rolls of these companies have been obtained, and if they were mustered into the United States service at all, the rolls were either never returned to the department, or have been mislaid.

While Col. Neale was recruiting and marching his regiment to Galena, the settlers there were not idle. A committee of safety had been formed and temporary defences were erected, and in pursuance of an order from Governor Edwards the miners were formed into companies and equipped for action, (the rolls of only one company of these militia have been furnished us, Capt. James M. Strode's, page 187.) These militia were placed under the immediate command of Gen. Henry Dodge, and formed an auxiliary force to the command of Brig.-Gen. Henry Atkinson, U. S. A., whose force consisted of six hundred regulars. Before the arrival of Col. Neale, these forces combining under Gen. Atkinson, marched into the Winnebago country and captured Red Bird, who, it appears by a letter of Gen. Street to Governor Edwards, voluntarily surrendered himself to the whites, coming into camp displaying a white flag. With Red Bird there also surrendered themselves six other Indians, including Black Hawk, who had not yet become famous. These Indians were retained in captivity several months, Red Bird dying during confinement; and some of them having been tried and convicted of complicity in the murder of white settlers, were executed on the 26th day of December, 1827. Black Hawk, against whom nothing could be proven, was acquitted, but it is alleged afterwards acknowledged his guilt and boasted of his connection with the murders for which he had been tried. With the death of Red Bird ended the Winnebago war. The tribe seemed to be thoroughly humbled by the result of the campaign, and although fears of further hostilities from them were for some time after entertained, they continued peaceable. In regard to the lands about which the difficulty originated, until the question of ownership could be adjusted amicably, they promised to keep away from the mines entirely, Gen. Atkinson promising them that "the next summer persons would come from their Great Father to consult with them about the matter."

"A talk was subsequently had with them in which they abandoned all the country south of the Wisconsin river. After this there was a general peace with the Indians throughout the western frontier." (Edwards' His. p. 224). In the meantime Governor Edwards did not cease his efforts to urge on the War Department the necessity of the entire removal of the Indians from the State, their presence being a constant menace, and their continued residence on lands which they had ceded being dangerous to the peace of the white settlers, who were constantly increasing in numbers, and whose animals the Indians did not hesitate to appropriate whenever opportunity offered. In October the Secretary of War informed the Governor that Governor Cass had been instructed to "take measures with regard to the removal of the Indians." But delays having occurred, and the Indians still remaining, on the 25th day of May, 1828, Governor Edwards wrote to Gen. Clark urging immediate action on the part of the Government. This he followed by a letter addressed to the Secretary of War, dated June 17th, in which he stated: "This grievance still continuing, and aggravated as it is by recent occurrences of which I am bound to presume you are informed, I feel it my duty to ask you what further in regard to this matter may be expected from the General Government." (Edwards' Hist. p. 226.)

Upon the urgent request of the Indians, and notwithstanding the earnest protest of the Governor (Edwards), twelve months additional time was given them in which to remove from the State. With regard to this delay and in a spirit of protest against the action of the Government in the premises, Governor Edwards wrote Gen. Clark, Indian agent at St. Louis, a letter, in the conclusion of which he used the following significant language: "If any act of hostility shall be committed on the frontiers, I will not hesitate to remove them on my own responsibility as Governor of the State." (Edwards' History, p. 227.)

As to the subsequent history of the causes which finally led to this outbreak, Edwards says:

About this time (1829) the President issued his proclamation, according to law, and, in pursuance thereof, all the country above the mouth of Rock river (the ancient seat of the Sauk nation) was sold to American families, and in the year following it was taken possession of by them. To avoid difficulty with the tribes another treaty, confirming previous ones, was made with the Sacs and Foxes, on the 15th of July, 1830, by the provisions of which they were to remove peacefully from the Illinois country. A portion of the Sacs, with their principal chief, Keokuk, at their head, quietly retired across the Mississippi. With those who remained in the village, at the mouth of Rock river, an arrangement was made by the Americans who had purchased the land, by which they were to live together as neighbors, the Indians still cultivating their old fields as formerly. Black Hawk, however, a restless and uneasy spirit, who had ceased to recognize Keokuk as chief, and who was known to be still under the pay of the British, emphatically refused either to remove from the lands or to respect the rights of the Americans to them. He insisted that Keokuk had no authority for making such a treaty, and he proceeded to gather around him a large number of the warriors and young men of the tribe, who were anxious to distinguish themselves as "braves," and, placing himself at their head, he determined to dispute with the whites the possession of the ancient seat of his nation. He had conceived the gigantic scheme, as appears by his own admissions, of uniting all the Indians, from the Rock river to the Gulf of Mexico, in a war against the United States, and he made use of every pretext for gaining accessions to his party.

In the meantime, on the 9th day of December, 1830, Hon. John Reynolds had been elected Governor of the State.

In pursuance of his declared intention of regaining possession of the ancient hunting grounds and the principal village of his tribe, in the month of April, 1831, Black Hawk recrossed the river, at the head of a force variously estimated at from three to five hundred braves of his own tribe, with from one to two hundred allies of the Pottawotamies and Kickapoos, bringing with them his women and children, with the avowed purpose of remaining.

Black Hawk immediately notified the whites that they must depart from the village, and they refusing to comply, their property was destroyed, and they suffered in person various indignities at the hands of the Indians. On the 30th of April, forty of these settlers sent a petition to Governor Reynolds, setting forth their grievances, and asking relief. Governor Reynolds, thus informed of the state of affairs, and believing that Black Hawk and his band were determined to retain possession of the country by force, resolved to effect their expulsion. A call was therefore made for volunteers (May 27, 1831,) and when it became known, the whole northwestern part of the State resounded to the clamor of war. No county south of St. Clair nor east of Sangamon was included in the call, which was limited to seven hundred men, who were to report within fifteen days' time, mounted and equipped, at the place of rendezvous, which was fixed at Beardstown, on the Illinois river. More than twice the number of men called for responded, and the Governor, finding so many willing and ready to go, decided to accept the services of the whole 1,600 men. They were moved to a camp two miles north of Rushville, and there organized into two regiments, and two battalions. One of the regiments elected James D. Henry, of Sangamon county, Colonel,* and the other elected Daniel Lieb, while Major Nathaniel Buckmaster was elected to command the "Odd Battalion." Major Samuel Whitesides was appointed by the Governor to the command of the "Spy Battalion," and the whole brigade was placed under the command of Hon. Joseph Duncan, then the member in Congress, and afterward Governor of the State, who was commissioned by Governor Reynolds as Brigadier General of militia. Colonels Enoch C. March and Samuel C. Christy were appointed quartermasters, while the Governor himself accompanied the expedition in his capacity of Commander-in-Chief of the militia of the State. They immediately (June 15th, 1831,) took up their march from camp near Rushville to Rock river, where they arrived on the 25th of June. Six companies of regular troops, which had been dispatched from Jefferson Barracks, under the command of Gen. Gaines, had arrived at Fort Armstrong a few days before, and had already had an unsatisfactory conference with Black Hawk, who declined to return across the river. Gen. Gaines met Governor Reynolds and his force at their encampment on the Mississippi, eight miles below the old Sac village, and after receiving the volunteers into the United States service, Gens. Gaines and Duncan concerted measures of attack. But the wily Black Hawk,

---

*Jacob Fry was Lieutenant-Colonel, and John T. Stuart Major.

no doubt well apprised of the number of the force which was ready to attack him, concluded not to risk an engagement, but on the night of the 25th had quietly recrossed the river, leaving his deserted camp and village to be peaceably taken possession of by the forces of the opposing Generals on the following morning. Out of vengeance, no doubt, for their disappointment at the escape of the Indians, and to remove future cause of dispute, the soldiers destroyed the village entirely by fire. As Governor Ford says in his history, "Thus perished this ancient village, which had been the delightful home of 6,000 to 7,000 Indians, where generation after generation had been born, had died and been buried." Gen. Gaines sent an order to Black Hawk requiring him and his band to return and enter into a treaty. They refusing to respond to the first invitation, a second and more peremptory mandate had the desired effect, and on the 30th day of June, 1831, Black Hawk and about thirty chiefs of the Sacs came, and in full council with Governor Reynolds and Gen. Gaines, signed an agreement, in which they agreed, among other things, that "no one or more shall ever be permitted to recross said river, to the usual place of residence, nor any part of their old hunting grounds east of the Mississippi, without permission of the President of the United States, or the Governor of the State of Illinois." The volunteer troops were then disbanded, and returned to their homes, while the subsistence gathered for their sustenance, was from time to time given by Gen. Gaines and the kind-hearted Governor to the Indians, who had, by their foolish invasion, rendered it impossible to raise any crop for that season, it being too late to plant any crop after the war had closed. Thus ended without bloodshed the first campaign of the Black Hawk war. Of the forces engaged therein, there are but the rolls of two companies, published herein, Capt. Solomon Miller's, from St. Clair county, and Capt. William Moore's, of the same county, both in Maj. Buckmaster's "Odd Battalion," (See pages 188, 190.)

1832—SECOND CAMPAIGN.

Notwithstanding the treaty, the trouble was not yet ended. In the spring of 1832 Black Hawk recrossed the Mississippi (April 6th) and commenced his march up Rock River Valley, accompanied by about five hundred warriors on horseback, while his women and children went up the river in their canoes. Gen. Atkinson, then stationed at Fort Armstrong, warned him against this aggression and ordered him to return, but this they refused to do, and went forward to the country of the Winnebagoes, with whom Black Hawk made arrangements to make a crop of corn, which reason he alleged to be the cause of the expedition. The Winnebagoes and Pottawotamies, however, both refused to yield to his solicitations to join him in a war against the whites.

On being informed of the movements of Black Hawk, Governor Reynolds (April 16th) called for a thousand mounted volunteers, from the central and southern parts of the State, to rendezvous at Beardstown, on the 22d of the same month. Daily accounts of the operations of the Indians were received. Judge Young, Col. Strode and Benjamin Mills wrote the Governor, urging speedy protection of the frontiers, as the inhabitants were in great danger. On receipt of this intelligence two hundred men (see pp. 151–4), under Major Stillman, were ordered to guard the frontier near the Mississippi, and two hundred (see Col. Johnson's regiment), under Major Bailey, the frontier between the Mississippi and the settlements on the Illinois. Such was the threatening aspect of affairs, that the call was extended to every part of the State. In the meantime eighteen hundred men had met at Beardstown, and were organized into a brigade of four regiments and an "odd" and a "spy" battalion. An election (April 28) for field officers, resulted in the election of Col. John Thomas to command the First Regiment, Col. Jacob Fry the Second Regiment, Col. Abram B. DeWitt the Third Regiment, Col. Samuel M. Thompson the Fourth Regiment* (in this regiment was Capt. Abraham Lincoln's† company—p. 100), while Major James D. Henry, of Sangamon county, was elected to command the Spy Battalion (p. 106), in which Captains John Dawson, Thomas Carlin and John Dement commanded the companies, and Major Thomas James to the command of the "Odd" Battalion (page 110). A part of the "Odd" Battalion under Maj. Long, consisting of the companies commanded by Capt. Jacob Eby and Capt. Japhet A. Ball, both from Sangamon county, was "detached for foot purposes." Eight companies, not attached to any regiment (pp. 116–122), also served in this brigade. Governor Reynolds, who also accompanied the expedition, placed Brigadier-Gen. Whiteside in the immediate command, while Cols. March and Christy, the efficient quartermasters in the campaign of 1831, were relied on to gather the supplies for the present campaign. William Thomas was appointed Brigade Quartermaster, while Capts. James B. Stapp and Joseph M. Chadwick were appointed to the general staff. Maj. James Turney, paymaster; Vital Jarrot, of St. Clair county, adjutant general, and Cyrus Edwards, ordnance officer, were appointed to their positions on the staff of the Commander-in-Chief.

On the 29th day of April, the army left camp near Beardstown and marched to the Mississippi river, at or near the present town

---

*George Carpenter, Esq., of Springfield, furnishes to us the commission of his father, the late Major Carpenter, as paymaster of this regiment, a copy of which we give:
"I do hereby certify that William Carpenter is duly appointed Paymaster in the Fourth Regiment on the detachment of mounted volunteers, called into the service of the United States. He is therefore required diligently and carefully to discharge the duties of said office. Given under my hand this 30th day of April, 1832.
"SAMUEL M. THOMPSON, Colonel Fourth Regiment Volunteers."

†William L. Wilson, who was a private in Capt. M. G. Wilson's company, of Thompson's regiment, of Whiteside's brigade, writes to this office from Rushville, under date of February 3, 1882, and after detailing some interesting reminiscences of Stillman's defeat, says: "I have during that time had much fun with the afterwards President of the United States, Abraham Lincoln. I remember one time of wrestling with him, two best in three, and ditched him. He was not satisfied, and we tried it in a foot-race, for a five dollar bill. I won the money and 'tis spent long ago. And many more reminiscences could I give, but am of the Quaker persuasion and not much given to writing."

The following discharge paper was found among the papers of the late Col. Wm. Carpenter, formerly Paymaster of Col. Thompson's regiment. The blank was filled in the handwriting of Capt. Lincoln:

"I certify that Lewis W. Farmer volunteered and served as a private in the company of mounted volunteers under my command, in the regiment commanded by Col. Samuel M. Thompson, in the brigade under the command of Gens. S. Whiteside and H. Atkinson, called into the service of the United States by the Commander-in-Chief of the militia of the State, for the protection of the northwestern frontier against the invasion of the British band of Sac and other tribes of Indians; that he was enrolled on the 21st day of April, 1832, and was *honorably discharged* on the 7th day of June thereafter, having served forty-eight days. Given under my hand, this 21st day of September, 1832

A. LINCOLN, Captain."

of Oquawka. On arriving at that place, and some delay occurring in the receipt of supplies, messengers were dispatched to Gen. Atkinson, at Fort Armstrong, who sent a boat loaded with provisions to the troops.

From here they marched up the river to the mouth of Rock river, where they were all received into the United States service by Gen. Atkinson. From this point the commanding general proceeded up the Rock river on a steamer, accompanied by a force of 400 regulars and an armament of cannon, while the volunteers under Gen. Whiteside marched through the swamps in the vicinity of the stream. They moved up Rock river without encountering savages until they arrived at the town of Dixon, on the evening of the 10th of May, where they found Majors Stillman and Bailey, who were at this place with their forces, where they had been directed to remain in their duty of protecting the frontier. Gen. Atkinson then sent out a scouting party of five men to confer with the chiefs of the Pottawotamies, and who, after getting lost, returned the third day afterward, reporting to have fallen in with some of Black Hawk's men who were encamped on a small stream known as Old Man's Creek, twelve miles above Dixon. Majors Stillman and Bailey having done but little service, besought the Governor to grant them the privilege of reconnoitering the enemy. Thereupon Governor Reynolds issued to them the following order: "Major Stillman: You will cause the troops under your immediate command, and the battalion under Major Bailey, to proceed without delay to the head of Old Man's Creek, where it is supposed there are some hostile Indians and coerce them into submission." On the following morning, May 14, 1832,) they started with 275 men (Stillman's Brigade. See page 151, for rolls of Bailey's command, afterward Fifth Regiment, pp. 102-5), and reached the Old Man's Creek without adventure, pursuing their course up that stream some fifteen miles, to Sycamore Creek. They dismounted for the purpose of passing the night. While engaged in camp duties, three Indians, bearing a white flag, came into camp, and were taken into custody. These

---

* From a memoranda kept by Major William Carpenter, paymaster of the Fourth regiment on this expedition, we subjoin the following as the distances marched by that command between different camps:

To Beardstown			50 miles.
" 1st	camp	over Illinois river	9 "
" 2d	"	Rushville	3 "
" 3d	"	Crooked Creek	25 "
" 4th	"	"	20 "
" 5th	"	Yellow Banks	18 "
" 6th	"	Camp Creek	30 "
" 7th	"	Rock River	20 "
" 8th	"	Cut bee tree	26 "
" 9th	"	Timber scarce, man shot himself	30 "
" 10th	"	Dixon	8 "
" 11th	"	Battle ground (Stillman's defeat)	25 "
" 12th	"	Return to Dixon's	25 "
" 13th	"	Express came to us about the murder	12 "
" 14th	"	Rock River—Capt. Gooden arrested	4 "
" 15th	"	One mile to good spring traveled	16 "
" 16th	"	Tishwakee	10 "
" 17th	"	Sycamore, here the scalps were trimmed	12 "
" 18th	"	Fox river timber	25 "
" 19th	"	Six miles from Paw-paw	20 "
" 20th	"	Two miles from the mouth of the river	20 "
		Then home in company with William Constant	110 "
		Total miles traveled	518

were soon followed by five more, who came near the camp, no doubt with the purpose of inviting an attack. In this they succeeded, and a party of Stillman's men immediately started in pursuit, while others followed as soon as they could mount, and soon three-fourths of the command had joined in an irregular chase across the prairie. The soldiers overtook and killed two of the Indians, and pursued the others to the edge of the forest. At this juncture Black Hawk, with about forty of his men, arose from an ambush, and with terrific yells charged on the assailants, who, in their turn, retreated in hot haste, followed by the infuriated savages. The fearful din caused by the retreating soldiers and their pursuers caused a stampede in the remainder of the force of the camp, and they all fled, in an inglorious panic, and in spite of the efforts of Major Stillman and others to rally them, the retreat was continued until they all reached the main force at Dixon. Major Perkins and Captain Adams, of Tazewell County, with about fifteen men, made a stand in which they somewhat checked the Indians, and thus saved the lives of many of the fugitives, who would otherwise have fallen victims to their pursuers. This rally cost the brave Adams his life, his body being found the next day near the dead bodies of two of the savages, whom he had undoubtedly slain before he himself was killed. As a result of the fight, eleven whites and seven Indians were killed, besides many wounded on both sides.

During the night of the battle, known since as "Stillman's Run," Governor Reynolds made a requisition for 2,000 men to be in readiness for future operations, while the utmost consternation spread throughout the State and Nation. Exaggerated reports of the numbers of the Indians, and the skill, ability, cunning and cruelty of Black Hawk, added much to the general alarm.

General Scott, with 1,000 United States troops, was immediately ordered to the Northwest, to superintend the future operations of the campaign.

When the news of Stillman's defeat reached the camp at Dixon, a council of war was held, and it was determined to return immediately to the battle field.

The next morning, after obtaining ten oxen from Col. John Dixon, which were slaughtered and issued to the men, without bread or salt, the whole force marched to the scene of the encounter. The dead were recovered, in most instances frightfully mutilated, and the fragments gathered together and buried; but although Major Henry and his men effectually scoured the surrounding country for miles in every direction, the enemy could not be found, and the whole force fell back to Dixon.

The new levies, under the call of Gov. Reynolds, were to meet, some on the 3d of June, at Beardstown, and the others on the 10th of the same month at Hennepin.

The men first recruited, now asked to be discharged, but the Governor appealing to their patriotism, they agreed to remain from 12 to 15 days longer, and the companies under Bailey (Covell's, McClure's, Pugh's and Adams'), with Stillman's battalion, (Captains Eads', Barnes' and Ball's companies) were organized into a regiment, known as the Fifth Regiment of Whiteside's Brigade, under Colonel James Johnson, and received into the service of the United

States, and one part ordered to Ottawa, for the defense of that place, while the other remained at Dixon to guard the stores, around which General Atkinson had caused embankments to be thrown.

On the 19th of May the whole army marched up the river in pursuit of the enemy, and on the evening of the same day received news of the massacre of several whites on Indian Creek, not far from Ottawa.

General Atkinson ordered Gen. Whitesde's and Col. Taylor (afterwards President of the United States) to continue the pursuit with the volunteers, while he, with the regulars, returned to Dixon. After following trails in several directions, which proved that the Indians had divided and left the immediate country for the north, and the troops expressing a determination to return to their homes, were brought to the mouth of Rock River, and there discharged on the 27th and 28th days of May, and thus the campaign ended without effecting any important results.

SECOND CAMPAIGN—1832.

On the requisition of Gen. Atkinson, the Governor called for 1,000 additional men, which were recruited out of the disbanded men for immediate service, for a term of twenty days, until the new levies should arrive. This regiment, which was filled without difficulty, organized by the election of Jacob Fry, as Colonel; James D. Henry, as Lieutenant-Colonel.

Although this regiment does not appear grouped together, as it should be, in this record, the companies, as well as can now be ascertained, were Capt. Samuel Smith's company (page 168), Capt. B. James' company (page 169), Capt. Elijah Iles' company (page 174) —(This company contained *private*

ABRAHAM LINCOLN,

who had been that day mustered out, with his company, as a captain, and reënlisted with many of his men in Capt. Iles' company, for this emergency service)—Capt. Alex. D. Cox's company (page 178), Capt. Wm. C. Ball's company (182), Capt. Alexander White's company (page 183), and Capt. A. W. Snyder's company (page 185). This regiment, after bravely guarding the imperiled frontier, was mustered out of the service on the 15th day of June, except Capt. Iles' company, which was discharged the 16th, and Capt. Snyder's discharged the 21st of June. This latter company had some severe skirmishing with the enemy, some seventy in number, near Kellogg's Grove, in which four of the Indians and two of the whites were killed.

On the 6th of June, Black Hawk, with about 150 warriors, made an attack on Apple River Fort, situated a quarter of a mile north of the present village of Elizabeth and twelve miles from Galena. Three messengers, on their way from Dixon to Galena, were fired upon when one-half mile from the fort, and one of them wounded, but all of them escaped to the fort. The inhabitants, alarmed at the shots, fled to the fort, which was invested, and a continual fire kept up for fifteen hours by the savages, who had taken possession of the dwellings of the whites, from which they fired through holes made for that purpose through the walls. The twenty-five men composing the garrison, made such a determined resistance that the savages, after having destroyed everything within their reach, departed, taking with them all the stock, provisions and movable property of the settlers. Only one man of the whites was killed, while the loss of the savages has never been ascertained. Col. Strode, of the militia, arrived the next day from Dixon with a force to their relief, but the enemy had made good his escape.

The savages having attacked and killed two men near Ft. Hamilton, five miles from Galena, Gen. Dodge, of Wisconsin, followed them, with the force under his command, and, overtaking them at Pecatonica, charged upon them and killed the whole number, with a loss of three men killed in his own force.

Capt. Stephenson, of Galena, and a part of his company, had a little skirmish with the enemy between Apple River Fort and Kellogg's Grove, and were repulsed by the Indians, who had taken shelter in a small grove, with the loss of three killed and the Captain and several others seriously wounded.

The new levies met as provided in the call, at Beardstown and Hennepin, but were afterward ordered to Fort Wilbourne, a small fortification on the south bank of the Illinois river, about a mile above Peru, which had been erected by Lieut. Wilbourne for the protection of the stores entrusted to his care by Col. March.

A promiscuous multitude of several thousands had assembled, among them many of the most prominent men in the State, and the selection of officers was a matter requiring great delicacy and tact. But after the organization of the companies, the captains of the several companies and the Governor agreed that the principal officers should be determined by an election, in which all the troops should participate. The brigades were organized, and on the 16th day of June Alexander Posey was elected General of the First, Milton K. Alexander of the Second, and James D. Henry of the Third. Gen. Atkinson received them into the service of the United States, and took the general command of the force thus organized, which amounted to 3192 men.

The Governor appointed to his staff, as Aids, Benjamin F. Hickman and Alex. F. Grant, James Turney, Adjutant General, and Col. E. C. March, Q. M. General. Besides the main army four battalions were organized for special purposes, commanded severally by Majors Bogart and Bailey, and Colonels Buckmaster and Dement.

The brigades were composed of three regiments each, commanded by officers of their own selection, but no rolls of the regimental field and staff, nor of the staff of the different brigade commanders are in the possession of this office, though supposed to exist among the records of the War Department at Washington, D. C.

In view of the disasters which threatened the northern frontier, the Governor ordered a chain of forts to be erected from the Mississippi to Chicago.

On the 17th day of June, Col. Dement, with his spy battalion of 150 men, was ordered to report himself to Col. Taylor at Dixon, while the main army was to follow. On his arrival at Dixon he was ordered to take position in Kellogg's grove, where, on the 25th day of June, he was visited by Mr. Funk, of McLean County, who, while on his way from the lead mines the night before, reported that a trail of about 300 Indians leading northward had been seen that day. A council of war, held that night, determined that Col. Dement and fifty picked men should reconnoiter the surrounding country the next day. At daylight the party sallied forth, and when within 300 yards of the fort discovered several Indian spies. Regardless of the cries of Col. Dement and Lieut.-Governor Casey, who accompanied him, and without waiting for direction, these undrilled and undisciplined men immediately charged on the foes, and recklessly following them, despite all efforts of Col. Dement to check them, were led into an ambush, and suddenly were confronted by 300 howling, naked savages under the command of Black Hawk in person. The sudden appearance of the savages created a panic among the whites, and each man struck out for himself in the direction of the fort, with a speed which equalled, if it did not excel, the alacrity with which they left it in the morning.

In the confused retreat which followed, five of the whites, who were without horses, were killed, while the remainder reached the fort, and dismounting, entered it, closely pursued by the enemy. The fort was vigorously assailed for over an hour by the savages, who were repulsed, and forced to retire, leaving nine of their number behind them, dead on the field, besides several others carried away wounded. No one in the fort was killed, but several wounded. Col. Dement received three shots through his clothing, but fortunately escaped unhurt. At 8 o'clock in the morning, messengers were sent fifty miles to Gen. Posey for assistance, and towards sundown that General and his brigade made their appearance, and no further attack was made on the fort by the savages. Gen. Posey started out in search of the enemy the next day, but the trail showed that they had pursued their favorite tactics of scattering their forces, and the pursuit was abandoned. The army continued its march up Rock river, near the source of which they expected to find the enemy. As provisions were scarce and difficult to convey for any distance, the command of Gen. Alexander, with a detachment under Gen. Henry and Maj. Dodge, was sent to Fort Winnebago, between Fox and Wisconsin rivers, to obtain supplies. Learning that Black Hawk was encamped on the Whitewater, Gen. Henry and Maj. Dodge started in immediate pursuit, leaving Gen. Alexander with his command in charge of the provisions to return to Gen. Atkinson. After several days' hard marches, and much suffering from exposure and lack of food, on the 21st day of July, the enemy were overtaken on the bluffs of the Wisconsin, and a decisive battle fought, in which Gen. Henry commanded the American forces, which consisted of Maj. Dodge's battalion on the right, Col. Jones, regiment in the center, and Col. Collins' on the left, with Maj. Ewing's battalion in the front, and Col. Fry's regiment in the rear as a reserve force. In this order they charged the enemy, and drove him from position after position with great loss, till the sun went down, leaving them victors, in the first important advantage gained over the enemy during the war.

In the morning it was discovered that the Indians had fled in the direction of the Mississippi river, leaving 168 dead on the field, and of their wounded, taken with them, twenty-five were found dead the next day on their trail, while Gen. Henry lost only one man killed and eight wounded. Litters were constructed for the wounded, and on the 23d of July, the army was again in motion, and after some difficulty on account of high water, reached Blue Mounds in safety, where they met Gen. Atkinson with the regulars, and the balance of the volunteer force. A return of the force at this time showed in Posey's brigade 200 effective men, Alexander's 850, in Henry's 300, while the regulars under Gen. Brady mustered 400 men; all told, the force mustered about 1,200 effective men,—though much reduced since the beginning of the campaign, still more than twice the number possessed by Black Hawk when in his best state of preparation, before any of the fights.

On the 25th the whole army was again put in motion, to try to find the Indians. Having spent two days in crossing the Wisconsin river, near Helena, on the 28th they came up with the trail of the Indians, the abandoned articles, and dead bodies strewed along the trail, showing them to be in a deplorable condition, and suffering for food. On the morning of the 2nd of August, the army reached the bluffs of the Mississippi, some distance, however, from the stream. The Indians had reached the river, and were making active preparations to cross. Some had already crossed, and some of the women and children had started down the river in canoes to Prairie du Chien, which they afterward reached in a starving condition. In this condition the Indians, when they arrived at the river, were attacked by a force under Capt. Throckmorton, who was on the steamer Warrior, and who, with a six-pound cannon, loaded with canister, destroyed many of the luckless fugitives, although they had displayed a white flag, which he refused to recognize. The fuel in the steamer having failed, it fell down the river to Prairie du Chien. Although he had killed twenty-three Indians and wounded many more, Capt. Throckmorton intended to return after wooding up, and finish the remainder. Before he could execute his intention, however, Gen. Atkinson had fallen on the unfortunate savages where they were encamped, at the mouth of the Bad Axe, a creek emptying into the Mississippi river, and had commenced a general battle, in which the Indians were completely routed, and suffered a loss of 150 killed, besides many drowned, and many more wounded. A large number of women and children lost their lives, owing to the fact that it was impossible to distinguish them from the men. [Davidson and Stuvé's Hist. 405.] The American loss was seventeen killed.

This battle virtually ended the war. Gen. Atkinson, with his whole force, and prisoners, [about fifty women and children], fell down the river to Prairie du Chien. On the 7th day of August, Gen. Winfield Scott, who, with nine companies of infantry, had been sent from Fortress Monroe, arrived, and assumed command. He had arrived with four of these companies at Chicago the day before, making the march of 1,800 miles in eighteen days, part of the way by steamer on the lakes, having left behind three companies, who had contracted Asiatic cholera at Detroit, at Fort Gratiot, forty miles from that city. This disease preyed to such an extent on the forces who came through, that they remained in Chicago until the latter part of the month before coming on to Fort Armstrong, their final destination. The volunteers now returned to Dixon, and were discharged on the 17th day of August. On the 27th Black Hawk, having been captured by some treacherous Winnebagoes, was delivered to the whites at Prairie du Chien, and he and his family were sent as hostages to Fortress Monroe, and there retained until June, 1833. In September, 1832, a treaty was made which ended the Indian troubles in this State, and although a few companies were detained a few weeks longer, the main body of the force returned to their homes in August, 1832.

Black Hawk, upon regaining his liberty, ever after conducted himself in a friendly manner to the whites. In 1837 he again visited Washington with a deputation of the chiefs of his tribe, on the invitation of the President, to settle differences which had occasioned a violent war with them and the Sioux. After his return he settled in what is now known as Lee county, Iowa. In the spring of 1838 he built himself a dwelling on the Des Moines river, 20 miles above its mouth. In this he moved his family, and prepared to farm and live after the manner of the whites. On a visit made to Burlington, the following autumn, he took cold, which brought on a disease which terminated his eventful life, and at the age of 72 Black Hawk was gathered to his fathers.

Perhaps no one of his race ever excelled Black Hawk in patriotism or love for his country. He fought an unequal battle for the home and the graves of his ancestors. In his last speech to the Americans he said: "Rock River was a beautiful country. I like my towns, my cornfields and the home of my people. I fought for it. It is now yours. It will produce you good crops."

A dispassionate view of the war and its causes will show that he had grievances, and when he had failed to redress them in a peaceable manner, had resorted to arms, because he thought it the only possible arbitrament.

Besides the companies of Capt. Joseph Napier [page 149], Capt. Holden Session [page 148] and Capt. James Walker [page 178], the latter from Walker's Grove, now Plainfield Township, in Will county, all of which were recruited within the limits of the then county of Cook; another company was organized for home defense within the city of Chicago, a muster roll of which is preserved in a book entitled "Early Chicago," by Hon. John Wentworth, being the third paper published by that gentleman on the early history of the city of Chicago. (No. 16, Fergus Hist. Phamplets).

MUSTER ROLL.

May 3, 1832.—We, the undersigned, agree to submit ourselves, for the time being, to Gholson Kercheval, Captain, and George W. Dale and John S. C. Hogan, First and Second Lieutenants, as commanders of the militia of the town of Chicago, until all apprehension of danger from the Indians may have subsided:

Richard J. Hamilton,
Jesse B. Brown,
Isaac Harmon,
Samuel Miller,
John F. Herndon,
Benjamin Harris,
S. T. Gage,
Rufus Brown,
Jeremiah Smith,
Heman S. Bond,
William Smith,
Isaac D. Harmon,
Joseph Lafromboise,
Henry Boucha,
Claude Lafromboise,
J. W. Zarley,
David Wade,
William Bond,
Samuel Ellis.

Jeddiah Wooley,
George H. Walker,
A. W. Taylor,
James Kinzie,
David Pemcton,
James Ginsday,
Samuel Debaif,
John Wellmaker,
Wm. H. Adams,
James T. Osborne,
E. D. Harmon,
Charles Moselle,
Francis Labaque,
Michael Ouilmette,
Christopher Shedaker,
David McKee,
Ezra Bond,
Robert Thompson.

THE MEXICAN WAR.

The volunteers from the State of Illinois performed such a conspicuous part in the war with Mexico, that it is necessary to give an epitome of the war, to be able to understand and appreciate the nature and value of their services, and render them the due credit which their importance demands.

On the 11th day of May, 1843, Congress passed an act, declaring that "By the act of the Republic of Mexico, a state of war exists between that Government and the United States." At the same time that body made an appropriation of ten million dollars to carry on the war, and authorized the President to accept fifty thousand volunteers.

This force, for convenience sake, to save transportation, and because of their already well-known familiarity with fire-arms, was drawn principally from the Southern and Western States. Illinois was called on for three regiments of infantry or riflemen, and the pay, with all allowances, placed at $15.50 per month to the private soldier. The militia of the State being then in an unorganized condition, Governor Ford issued a call for thirty full companies of volunteers of a maximum of eighty men, to serve for twelve months, and with the privilege of electing their own company and regimental officers.

The response to the call was enthusiastic in the extreme. Within ten days thirty-five full companies had organized and reported. By the time the place of rendezvous had been selected, (Alton), there had been seventy-five companies recruited,—each furious to go—of which the Governor (Ford) was compelled to select thirty companies —the full quota of the State—and the forty-odd unsuccessful companies were doomed to the disappointment of remaining at home. Of these thirty companies, were organized the *First* Regiment, Col. *John J. Hardin;* the *Second* Regiment, *Col. William H. Bissell,* and the *Third* Regiment, *Col. Ferris Foreman,* which were recruited during the months of April, May and June, and mustered into the United States service, at Alton, Ill., on the 2d day of July, 1846.

Hon. E. D. Baker, then a member of Congress from the Capital district, induced the Secretary of War to accept another regiment from this State, and thereupon the *Fourth* Illinois was organized and mustered into the service on the 18th day of July, 1846, and served in the same brigade with the Third Regiment until both were discharged.

The *First* and *Second Regiments* must be considered together, as their history is the same.

These regiments were transported separately down the Mississippi River and across the Gulf, and re-joined each other on the first day of August at Camp Erwin, near the old town of Victoria, on Weuloop river, and after marching together to San Antonio, Texas, they joined General Wool's army of the center. They left that city on the 26th day of September. Marching steadily along, they entered Santa Rosa on the 24th day of October with no opposition. Thence they marched to Monclova, thence to Parras, where the original idea of the march, the capture of Chihuahua, was abandoned.

After remaining at this place twelve days, General Wool started to intercept, if possible, Santa Anna's attack on Monterey, and on the 21st of December occupied Agua Nueva, thus completing a six weeks' march of about one thousand miles, which had been barren of results. In January, 1847, General Taylor proceeded from Saltillo and formed a junction with Gen. Wool. On the 22d day of February, 1847, was begun the battle of Buena Vista, which ended on the 23d, and resulted in a complete victory for the American forces, and in which these two Illinois regiments covered themselves with glory.

Concerning the conduct of the Illinois volunteers at the battle of Buena Vista, we quote from an extended report made by Major General Zach. Taylor, U. S. A., commanding, dated

"AGUA NUEVA, March 6, 1847.

"The First and Second Illinois and the Second Kentucky Regiments served immediately under my eye, and I bear a willing testimony to their excellent conduct throughout the day. The spirit and gallantry with which the First Illinois and Second Kentucky engaged the enemy in the morning, restored confidence to that part of the field, while the list of casualties will show how much these three regiments suffered in sustaining the heavy charge of the enemy in the afternoon. Captain Conner's Company of Texas Volunteers attached to the Second Illinois Regiment, fought bravely, its Captain being wounded and two subalterns killed. Colonel Bissell, the only surviving Colonel of these regiments, merits notice for his coolness and bravery on this occasion. After the fall of the field officers of the First Illinois and Second Kentucky Regiments, the command of the former devolved upon Lieutenant Colonel Weatherford, and that of the latter upon Major Fry. Regimental commanders and others, who have rendered reports, speak in general terms of the good conduct of their officers and men, and have specified many names, but the limits of this report forbid a recapitulation of them here. I may, however, mention * * * Lieutenant Colonel Weatherford, First Illinois Regiment, Lieutenant Colonel Morrison, Major Trail and Adjutant Whiteside (severely wounded), Second Illinois Regiment, and Major Fry, Second Kentucky Regiment, as being favorably noticed for gallantry and good conduct. * * * To Major Warren. First Illinois Volunteers, I feel much indebted, for his firm and judicious course, while exercising command in the city of Saltillo." (MSS. and doc. 1847, p. 139.)

From a return of troops engaged in the action of the 22d and 23d day of February, A. D. 1847, made by General Zachery Taylor to the Adjutant General of the Army, under date of March 6th, we quote as follows:

FIRST ILLINOIS.

Eight companies—1 Colonel, 1 Lieutenant Colonel, 8 Captains, 1 Adjutant, 18 Subalterns, 519 non-commissioned officers and privates. *Sick*—Two commissioned officers and 25 non-commissioned officers and privates, making an aggregate of 530 officers and privates.

SECOND ILLINOIS.

Eight companies—1 Colonel, 1 Major, 7 Captains, 1 Adjutant, 19 Subalterns, 496 non-commissioned officers and privates. Sick—Four commissioned officers, 40 non-commissioned officers and privates. Aggregate, 573 officers and privates.

From an official return of the killed, wounded and missing in battle of Buena Vista, we quote:

FIRST ILLINOIS FOOT.

Killed—One Colonel, one Captain, one Subaltern, 26 enlisted men. Total, 26.

Wounded—Two Subalterns, 16 enlisted men, missing, 3. Aggregate loss, 47.

SECOND ILLINOIS FOOT.

Killed—Two Captains, one Subaltern, 29 enlisted men.

Wounded—Two Captains, six Subalterns, 63 enlisted men. Missing, four enlisted men. Aggregate loss, 126.

With the exception of the sending out of an occasional foraging detachment no further service was performed by these two regiments during the war. They remained at Buena Vista until the latter part of May, when the following order was issued:

HEADQUARTERS, BUENA VISTA, }
May 28, 1847. }

Orders No. 302.

The term of service for which the First and Second Illinois regiments have engaged to serve the United States has nearly expired, and they are about to return to their homes. The General commanding takes this occasion to express his deep regret at the departure of those who have been so long under his immediate command, and who have served so well their country.

Few can boast of longer marches, greater hardships, or more privations, and none of greater gallantry on the field of Buena Vista. It was there that the General witnesses with infinite satisfaction their valor, which gave additional luster to our arms, and increased glory to our country. To their steadiness and firmness in connection with the Second Kentucky regiment of foot, in resisting the Mexicans at a critical moment, and when there were five to one against them, and as General Santa Anna said, "where blood flowed in torrents and the field of battle was strewed with their dead," we may justly ascribe a large share of the glorious victory achieved over 20,000 men. A great victory it is true ; but obtained at too great a sacrifice. Hardin, Zabriska, McKee, Woodward, Yell, Clay, and many others, fell leading their men to the charge. Their named and gallant deeds will ever be remembered by a grateful people. In taking leave of these regiments, the General cannot omit to express his admiration of the conduct and gallant bearing of all, and especially of Cols. Bissell and Weatherford and their officers, who have on all occasions done honor to themselves, and heroically sustained the cause of their country in the battle of Buena Vista. His best wishes will attend them to their homes, where they will be received with joy and gladness as the pride of their families and of their States.

By command of Brig.-Gen. WOOL.

IRWIN McDOWELL, Assistant Adjutant General.

These regiments were discharged at Camargo, Mexico, on the 17th day of June, 1847.

THE THIRD AND FOURTH REGIMENTS

were like the first two, brigaded together during their entire service. They were placed in Gen. Paterson's division, and marching from Matamoras to Tampico, formed part of Gen. Shields' force while he was in command of that city. On the 9th day of March, the Third and Fourth Regiments took part in the descent on Vera Cruz. Gen. Scott says in his report, dated Vera Cruz, March 14, 1847 : "I could not postpone the descent, successfully made on the 9th inst., for half of the surf boats, Brig.-Gen. Shields' brigade, (old volunteers from Tampico), or the wagons and teams, which were then behind. That General landed with the army, having a small part of one of his old regiments, (three companies of the Third Illinois Foot), and the New York regiment of new volunteers." (Mess. and Doc. 1847, p. 218.) Gen. Scott was mistaken in attributing to the Third Illinois credit due to the Fourth. Though both regiments took part in the expedition, it was companies "A," "F" and "G," of the Fourth Illinois, under the immediate command of Lieut.-Col. John Moore, who made the landing referred to, Capt. H. A. Roberts, of Co. "A," from Sangamon county, being the first man to place his foot on the enemy's soil.

In the battle of Cerro Gordo, the Third and Fourth were hotly engaged, and gained great credit for their bravery. Gen. Scott, in his report of that battle to the Secretary of War, under date of April 23, 1847, says:

> Early on the morning of the 18th, the columns moved to the general attack, and our success was speedy and decisive. * * * The Brigade so gallantly led by Gen. Shields, and after his fall, by Col. Baker, deserves high commendation for its fine behavior and success. Cols. Foreman and Burnett, and Maj. Harris (Fourth Illinois) commanded the regiments; Lieut. Hammond. Third artillery, and Lieut. Davis, Illinois volunteers, constituted the brigade staff. (Mess. and Doc. 1847, p. 263.)

Brig.-Gen. Twiggs, who was in the immediate command of all the advanced forces, in a report to the General-in-Chief, dated April 19, 1847, (the day following the battle), says:

> Of the conduct of the volunteer force under the brave Gen. Shields, I cannot speak in too high terms. After he was wounded, portions of the three regiments were with me when I arrived first at the Jalapa road, and drove before them the enemy's cannoneers from their loaded guns. Their conduct and names shall be the subject of a special report. (Mess. and Doc. 1847, p. 276.)

From the report of Maj.-Gen. Patterson, commanding the volunteer division at the battle of Cerro Gordo, under date of April 23, 1847, and made to the commanding General, we extract:

> "On the afternoon of the 17th, a rapid and continuous fire of artillery and infantry, announcing that the Second division of regulars was closely engaged with the left of the enemy's lines, I was instructed, and immediately directed the Third volunteer brigade, under Brig.-Gen. Shields, to proceed at once to its support. Before the brigade reached the position of that division, the action had ceased for the day; the night was, however, occupied in establishing several pieces of artillery upon a height adjacent to the "Cerro Gordo."
> Early on the morning of the 18th the brigade moved to turn the extreme left of the enemy's line, resting on the Jalapa road. This was done over rugged ascents and through dense chapparal, under a severe and continuous flank fire from the enemy. Brig.-Gen. Shields, whilst gallantly leading his command, and forming it for the attack of the enemy, posted in force in his front, fell severely wounded, and was carried from the field.
> Col. Baker, Fourth Illinois regiment, having assumed the command, the enemy's lines were charged with spirit and success by the Third and Fourth Illinois, and the New York regiment, under the respective commanders, Cols. Foreman and Burnett, and Major Harris. The rout now becoming general, the brigade pressed forward in rapid pursuit, leaving a sufficient force to secure the artillery, specie, baggage, provisions and camp equipage left in our hands."

Later in same report Gen. Patterson says: "The attention of the general-in-chief is particularly called to the gallantry of Brig.-Gens. Pillow and Shields, who were both wounded at the head of their respective brigades; and to Col. Baker, who led Shields' brigade during a severe part of the action, and during the pursuit; and Lieut. G. T. M. Davis, Illinois volunteer aid-de-camp to Shields' brigade."

The loss of both regiments is given in the official reports of killed and wounded, forwarded to the War Department after the battle, as follows:

Third Illinois—Killed, 1; wounded, 15; total, 16.
Fourth Illinois—Killed, 5; wounded, 43; total, 48.

This office is in receipt of a letter dated February 5, 1882, from Second Lieut. W. A. Tinney, of the Fourth Illinois volunteers, in which he says: "We stormed their fort and put the enemy to flight, taking about six thousand prisoners, and we captured Gen. Santa Anna's carriage, also his wooden leg, which I have in my possession."

The Third and Fourth Regiments were shortly afterward returned by vessels to New Orleans, where they were discharged from the 23d to the 25th days of May, 1847.

THE FIFTH REGIMENT,

which is known officially as the First Regiment, Illinois Volunteers "during the war" (the other regiments having been enlisted for "twelve months"), was called out, under the requisition made by the Secretary of War April 19th, 1847, for six thousand more volunteers to "serve during the war," to take the place of those whose term of enlistment was to expire. Of this call, but one regiment was assigned to the State of Illinois, which was organized June 8th, 1847, at Alton, Illinois, by the election of E. W. B. Newby as Colonel.

This regiment left Alton by steamer, for Fort Leavenworth June 14, and from thence marched across the plains to Santa Fe. In October, 1847, the first battalion with a part of a Missouri regiment marched to El Paso. The other battalion remained at Santa Fe, as a garrison. This regiment lost heavily by sickness and exposure in its long marches across the plains, but was engaged in no battles or skirmishes with the enemy. It was mustered out of the service at Alton, Illinois, from the 15th to the 18th day of October, 1848.

THE SIXTH REGIMENT,

otherwise known as the Second Regiment, enlisted "during the war," was organized out of the overflow of companies which were raised for the Fifth Regiment.

So much honor had been achieved by the four regiments sent out by this State the first year of the war, that their praise was on every lip, and the young and ambitious were ready to make any sacrifice to be able to go and fight the Mexicans. When the call was made for the Fifth Regiment it was difficult again for the Governor to select, as the men poured in by hundreds, and enough reported in ten days time to fill half a dozen regiments. Application was again made to the Secretary of War by Lieutenant Colonel Hicks and others for leave to organize another regiment. It was hard to refuse these veterans of Buena Vista and Cerro Gordo, and the permission was granted, and the regiment was organized at Alton, Illinois, on the 3d day of August, 1847, by the election of J. Collins as Colonel.

Shortly after the regiment was mustered into the United States service it was forwarded by steamer to New Orleans, and there divided into two battalions. Companies A, D, E, F and H, under command of Colonel Collins, being sent to Vera Cruz, where they arrived on the 31st day of August, 1847. They were shortly afterwards engaged in a skirmish with the guerrillas, but saw no further actual service, save the duties of camp and garrison life. The Second Battalion, under Lieutenant Colonel Hicks, consisted of Companies B, C, G, I and K, and was forwarded by vessel to

Tampico and there performed garrison duty until discharged. Both battalions, as the muster rolls show, lost heavily from sickness, incident to the climate, as might have been expected of raw and unacclimated men in so dangerous a climate. This regiment was mustered out on the 20th to the 25th days of July, 1848, at Alton, Illinois.

INDEPENDENT MOUNTED VOLUNTEERS.

The rolls furnished this office from the war office in Washington show that four independent companies of cavalry were mustered into the United States service during the Mexican war. All enlisted the second year of the war, and mustered in, as all troops were, under the second call, for "during the war." Of these, the first recruited,

CAPT. ADAM DUNLAP'S COMPANY,

was recruited during the month of May, 1847, at Rushville, at Schuyler county, and was mustered into the United States service in Alton, on the 21st day of the same month, its enlistment being authorized by the same order under which Col. Newby's regiment was recruited. This company was never engaged in any actual battle, but did considerable scouting service, and was in several skirmishes with the guerrillas and scouts of the enemy. This company also lost heavily, as did all the volunteers of that year, by sickness, several men having died while at Matamoras. It was finally discharged at Alton, Illinois, on the 7th day of November, 1848, having served eighteen months in all, being distinguished as the longest term of service of any company from this State in the whole war.

CAPT. WYATT B. STAPP'S COMPANY.

This company was recruited at Monmouth, in the month of June, 1847, and was mustered in at Quincy, Illinois, on the 10th day of August, 1847. It lost severely by sickness at Perote and Jalapa, and was finally returned to the States, without adventure of serious nature, and was mustered out at Alton on the 26th day of July, 1848, lacking fifteen days of serving one year from the date of muster.

FIRST LIEUT. GEORGE C. LANPHERE,

Of this company, returned home in the spring of 1848, to recruit for his company, and during the months of March, April, and May had recruited thirty-one men [page 309], who were never sent to the company, but were mustered out by order of the Secretary of War, at Jefferson Barracks, near St. Louis, Mo., June 28, 1848.

CAPT. MICHAEL K. LAWLER'S COMPANY.

During the month of August, 1847, Capt. Lawler, who was a veteran of the Black Hawk War, recruited an independent company of cavalry at Shawneetown, which was mustered into the United

States service at place of enrollment, on August 13, and forwarded to Mexico *via* the New Orleans route. Except the common experiences with fever, reptiles and insects, this company had no encounter with foes of any kind, and after some routine service, laborious but unimportant, was returned to place of enlistment, and mustered out on the 26th day of October, 1848.

CAPT. JOSIAH LITTLE'S COMPANY

was conspicuous as the last company received into the United States service, being mustered in at Alton on the 11th day of September, 1847. No record of its service has been received, and we can only add that it was mustered out at the same place July 25, 1848.

"REGULAR" ENLISTMENTS FROM ILLINOIS.

On the 11th day of February, 1848, Congress passed an act authorizing the President to raise ten new regiments for the Regular Army to be enlisted for "during the war." These regiments were all recruited prior to the 30th of September of the same year, and consisted of a regiment of Voltigeurs. eight regiments of Infantry, the Ninth, Tenth, Eleventh, Twelfth, Thirteenth, Fourteenth, Fifteenth and Sixteenth, and the Third regiment of Dragoons. These regiments were recruited at various stations all over the United States. Of these regiments the Twelfth, Thirteenth and Fourteenth regiments were recruited by Brig.-Gen. G. M. Brooke, at New Orleans, while the Fifteenth and Sixteenth were recruited by Lieut. Col. J. Erving, at Cincinnati. As will appear by the rolls published, Illinois furnished two companies for the Sixteenth and one company for the Fourteenth regiment, under this call. As to the history of these regiments we find that the Fourteenth regiment was brigaded with the Voltigeur regiment and the Eleventh Infantry, and under Brig.-Gen. Cadwalader was engaged in the battle of El Molino del Rey, on the 8th day of September, 1847. Concerning their conduct Major Gen. Worth, in his official report of the engagement, made to the Commander-in-Chief, dated Tacayuba, September 10th, 1847, says:

"I desire to bring the notice of the General-in-Chief to the gallantry and good conduct of Brig.-Gen. Cadwalader and his command, by which the most timely and essential service was rendered in supporting the attack, and following up the success. Such movements as he was directed to make were executed with zeal and promptness." (Mess. and Doc. 1847, p. 366.)

From a return of killed and wounded in this engagement accompanying this report, it appears that the Fourteenth regiment lost, Killed—1 Corporal. Wounded—1 Field Officer, 1 Captain, 3 Lieutenants, 2 Corporals and 16 Privates.

No official report of the service of the Sixteenth regiment is in possession of this office or at present accessible.

By General Order No. 25, A. G. O., June 8, 1848, the enlisted men of these two regiments, as well as others enlisted under the same act, were ordered to be mustered out, the Fourteenth at New Orleans, and the Sixteenth at Newport Barracks, Kentucky, which was done accordingly.

As several recruiting stations were opened in the Southwestern States, quite a number of Illinois men were recruited in the Regular Army proper, notably in the Fourth regiment. A member of this regiment, Mr. J. W. Thomson, of Princeton, Illinois, and a private of Company "A," has kindly furnished us an account of the services of his regiment in the Mexican war, but as we have no official statement of the names or number of the Illinois men scattered through these regiments, we forbear to publish this as well as some other interesting matter which we have concerning the services of the regular regiments in the Mexican war.

In closing this memoranda of the services of the Illinois soldiers in the Black Hawk and Mexican wars, we can not forbear to mention that in the voluminous correspondence this office has had with the survivors of these wars, the idea seems to be universally prominent with them that the General Government should, in the exercise of that spirit of patriotic gratitude, heretofore manifested in favor of the soldiers of the revolution and of the war of 1812, grant equally to these survivors some further recognition of their services in the way of a pension. While it is no part of our duty, in editing this record, to attempt to support, or further any propositions asking such action by Congress, we may be allowed to say, without subjecting ourselves to criticism, that there is something in the appearance of the letters of these old veterans of a generation gone before, which appeals to our liveliest sympathies. They almost unanimously ask in their quavering and palsied penmanship, that the General Government make some additional provision to secure them against want in their old age.

BLACK HAWK WAR.
1832.

FIRST BRIGADE.

FIRST REGIMENT.

CAPT. JOHN BAYS' COMPANY

Of Illinois Mounted Volunteers, called into the service of the United States by the Governor of the State of Illinois, by his order of the 15th of May, 1832, from the date of its enrollment to the 12th day of August, 1832, when mustered out of service.

Name and Rank.	Residence.	Enrolled	Remarks.
Captain. John Bays	Gallatin Co.	1832. June 16	Has two horses in service
First Lieutenant. William Robertson	"	"	Absent on furlough since August 9, 1832
Second Lieutenant. Daniel Wood	"	"	Absent on furlough since August 9, 1832
Sergeants.			
John Dawson	"	"	Detached from Co., on duty with main army.
Adran H. Davenport	"	"	Absent on furlough, by order of Brig.-Gen. Atkinson
John T. Brown	"	"	
Solomon McCloud	"	"	Absent on furlough since August 9, 1832
Corporals.			
Isaiah W. Pettigrew	"	"	Absent on furlough since August 9, 1832.
John Woods	"	"	Detached from Co., on duty with main army.
Thomas Smothers	"	"	Absent on furlough since August 9, 1832
Reuben Green	"	"	Detached from Co., on duty with main army.
Privates.			
Baker, Edmon	"	"	Absent on furlough since August 9, 1832
Bridges, James	"	"	
Bridges, Thomas L.	"	"	
Briant, John B.	"	"	Detached from Co., on duty with main army.
Brown, Daniel	"	"	On furlough since August 8, 1832
Brown, Samuel	"	"	Furloughed
Bays, David, Jr.	"	"	His horse lost, strayed or stolen
Cummons, William M	"	"	
Elder, John	"	"	Absent on furlough since August 9, 1832
Giles, Wm.	"	"	
Garner, Garrett	"	"	Detached on service with main army
Hargraves, Willis, Jr.	"	"	Detached from Co., on duty with main army.
Hargraves, Carter	"	"	
Henderson, Benj'min	"	"	
Hamons, Williams	"	"	
Hutson, John	"	"	Furloughed August 9, 1832
Johnson, William	"	"	Absent on surgeon's certif. since June 20, 1832
Kenrick, James	"	"	Absent on furl'h since July 16, '32; horse lost
Levil, Lewis	"	"	Absent on furlough
Mundine, Thomas S.	"	"	
McCaslin, James B.	"	"	His horse lost, strayed or stolen
Niswonger, Jefferson	"	"	Absent on furl'h since Aug. 9, '32; horse lost
Pruit, James	"	"	Furloughed Aug. 9, '32.
Robinnett, John	"	"	Furloughed Aug. 4, '32; his horse lost
Reed, Green	"	"	Furloughed Aug. 4, '32.

BLACK HAWK WAR.

Name and Rank.	Residence.	Enrolled	Remarks.
Sands, John	Gallatin Co.	June 16	Absent on furlough since August 9, 1832
Thorn, Alexander	" "	" "	Detached from Co., on duty with main army.
Tadlock, Green	" "	" "	At Fort Hamilton, by order of Captain
Vaughn, Thomas	" "	" "	Absent on furlough since July 16, 1832
Williams, Ebenezer.	" "	" "	" " Aug 9, 1832
Wrinkle, George	" "	" "	Furloughed; lost horse—b'ken down and left

I certify on honor that this muster roll exhibits the true state of the company under my command, and that the remarks set opposite the names of each officer and private are accurate and just.

    (Signed.) JOHN BAYS, Capt.,
            1st Reg't, 1st Brigade, Ill. Vol.

          DIXON'S FERRY, Aug. 12, 1832.

Mustered out of service by me, by order of Maj.-Gen. W. Scott, commanding N. W. army.
    (Signed.) Z. C. PALMER, Capt.,
            6th U. S. Inf., Com. Post.

STATE OF ILLINOIS,
GALLATIN COUNTY,

This day personally appeared before me, the undersigned, Justice of the Peace in and for said county, Joseph E. Watkins, and made oath that he commanded a company of mounted volunteers in the service of the United States, in the year 1832, and that among his company who did actually arrive on the 10th day of June at Hennepin, on Illinois river, was George Wrinkle, who was a member of his said company regularly enrolled. In testimony whereof I have set my hand and seal, this 5th June, 1834.
    (Signed.)   T. D. HEWITT, J. P.

Personally appeared before me, the subscriber, a Justice of the Peace in Gallatin county, Lieut. Wm. Robinson, of Capt. Bays' company, and made oath that Lee Hargraves served as a private in Capt. Bays' company from the 16th of June to the 12th of August, 1832; also as a wagon-master, and is entitled to traveling pay up to Wilbourn, and from Fort Dixon to the place of his discharge, home.
    (Signed.)   T. D. HEWITT, J. P.
EQUALITY, May 3, 1833.

CAPT. DAVID B. RUSSELL'S COMPANY

Of Mounted Volunteers of the State of Illinois, called into the service of the United States by the Governor of the State of Illinois, by his order of the 15th day of May, 1832, from the date of its enrollment to the 12th day of August, 1832, the time of its mustering out of service.

Name and Rank.	Residence.	Enrolled	Remarks.
Captain.		1832.	
David B. Russell	Gallatin Co.	June 16	Two horses in the service; lost one ax and spade in the water, $4.50.
First Lieutenant.			
William Pankey	" "	" "	
Sergeants.			
Geo. P. Keath	" "	" "	Absent on furlough
Claiborne Henders'n	" "	" "	
Thomas Pickering	" "	" "	
Stephen F. Mitchell	" "	" "	Detached from Co., on duty with main army.
Corporals.			
Jourdan Cook	" "	" "	Absent on furlough
Edward Hampton	" "	" "	Detached from Co., and on duty with main [army; reported himself Aug. 12, 1832.
Robert Mitchell	" "	" "	
Thos. Dodds	" "	" "	Detached from Co., and on duty with main army; reported himself Aug. 12, 1832.
Bugleman.			
Jesse Hall	" "	" "	Absent on furlough
Privates.			
Abney, Matthew	" "	" "	Absent on furlough
Blackman, Josiah	" "	" "	
Cotner, Duncan	" "	" "	Absent on furlough

FIRST BRIGADE.

Name and Rank.	Residence.	Enrolled	Remarks.
		1832.	
Cook, Cullen	Gallatin Co.	June 16	Detached from Co., on duty with main army;
Covington, John	"	"	Absent on furlough ....[Reported Aug. 12
Duncan, Thomas	"	"	Absent on furlough
Dunn, Squire	"	"	
Fleming, Zachariah	"	"	
Gaskins, William H.	"	"	Absent on furlough
Gulley, Thomas	"	"	
Griffin, John	"	"	" " granted on cert. of Surg.
Griffin, James S.	"	"	" "
Hope, James	"	"	" "
Harris, Aulsey	"	"	
Harris, Gillam	"	"	Furlough granted on Surgeon's certificate
Holland, James	"	"	Absent on furlough
Holmes, Jacob	"	"	" "
Hide, William	"	"	
Howell, John	"	"	" "
Howell, Riley	"	"	" "
Hull, John	"	"	
Hutchison, Wm. G.	"	"	
Ingram, Timothy	"	"	
Johnson, John J.	"	"	Absent on furlough; lost horse, bridle and
Pierson, Henry	"	"	..............[saddle; value, $68.50
Russell, John	"	"	Absent on furlough
Robinson, Mack	"	"	
Rood, Harvey	"	"	Absent on furlough
Rood, Ashby	"	"	
Smothers, John	"	"	Detached from Co., on duty with main army;
Shoat, Levi	"	"	Absent on furlough .....[Reported Aug. 12, '32
Stiff, Lewis	"	"	
Stanley, Thomas	"	"	
Waggoner, John	"	"	Absent on furlough

Muster roll of a detached part of Capt. Achilles Coffee's company, attached for the present to Capt. Russell's Company.

Name and Rank.	Residence.	Enrolled	Remarks.
Sergeants.		1832.	
Samuel Karnes, 2d	Gallatin Co.	June 16	
John Gardner, 3d	"	"	
William Chosier, 4th	"	"	
Privates.			
Abshear, Anderson	"	"	
Carder, James	"	"	
Hanse, Peter	"	"	
Karnes, George	"	"	
Karnes, John	"	"	
Karnes, James	"	"	
Martin, Jason	"	"	
Morris, Richmond	"	"	
Medlin, Needum	"	"	
Pryor, Anderson	"	"	
Spruil, Pleasant	"	"	
Stricklin, William	"	"	
Tong, Thomas	"	"	
Upchurch, John	"	"	
Upchurch, Thomas	"	"	
Upchurch, Jonathan	"	"	

I certify on honor this muster roll exhibits the true state of the detachment under my command, and that the remarks set opposite the name of each officer and private, so far as made from my knowledge, are accurate and true, and so far as made from information I believe to be accurate.

(Signed.)   DAVID B. RUSSELL, Capt.,
1st Regt., 1st Brigade Ill. Vol.

Mustered out of service by me, by order of Major-Gen. Scott, commanding N. W. army.

(Signed.)   Z. C. PALMER, Capt.,
6th U. S. Inft., Com. Post.

Dixon's Ferry, Aug. 12, 1832.

CAPT. HARRISON WILLSON'S COMPANY

Of Illinois Mounted Volunteers, commanded by Lieut. John Willis, called into the service of the United States by the Governor of the State of Illinois, by his order of the 15th of May, 1832, from the date of its enrollment to the 12th day of August, 1832, when mustered out of service.

Name and Rank.	Residence.	Enrolled	Remarks.
Captain.		1832.	
Harrison Willson...	Gallatin Co...	June 16	Detached from Co.; on duty with main army.
First Lieutenant.			
John Logston........	" "	" "	Absent on Surgeon's certif., June 20, 1832....
Second Lieutenant.			
John Willis............	" "	" "	Sword lost with baggage wagon, or stolen..
Sergeants.			
Charles Hood.........	" "	" "	
Robert Sidle.........	" "	" "	Absent on furlough, Aug. 5, 1832............
Solomon Brown......	" "	" "	Aug. 9, 1832............
Mastin Alexander...	" "	" "	Lost 1 blanket, $1....................
Corporals.			
Horatio Coffee	" "	" "	Lost 1 saddle, valued at $14.................
Isaac Crabtree......	" "	" "	Absent on furlough, Aug. 9, 1832............
William Keaton.....	" "	" "	Lost 1 bridle and 1 quilt, $4.............
Richard Tarlton.....	" "	" "	
Privates.			
Alexander, Rheubin.	" "	" "	
Barger, Richard A. S.	" "	" "	Lost 1 blanket.................
Burnet, Hiram.......	" "	" "	Absent on furlough, 9th Aug., 1832.........
Baker, James........	" "	" "	
Clack, John T........	" "	" "	Lost 1 mare, saddle, blankets, saddle-bags..
Cox, William.........	" "	" "	
Coop, William.......	" "	" "	Detailed from Co.; on duty with main army.
Caldwell, John......	" "	" "	
Davis, James M.....	" "	" "	
Davis, Francis.......	" "	" "	
Ellis, William........	" "	" "	Absent on furlough..................
Giberson, William...	" "	" "	Detailed on furlough.................
Hogan, Richard.....	" "	" "	
Holey, Henry........	" "	" "	Absent on furlough, Aug. 9, 1832. Lost a horse
Huston, Even........	" "	" "	Absent, and on duty with main army.........
Jones, Fountain W..	" "	" "	
Jacobs, Page.........	" "	" "	Absent on furlough, Aug. 9, 1832............
Kirkendal, Robert...	" "	" "	Lost 2 blankets..........................
Logston, Joseph.....	" "	" "	Absent on furlough, Aug. 9, 1832............
Pool, Orvel...........	" "	" "	
Peeples, James C....	" "	" "	
Scrogins, Barton....	" "	" "	
Taylor, Washington.	" "	" "	
Willis, Jacob.........	" "	" "	
Woodle, Andrew.....	" "	" "	

STATE OF ILLINOIS, } sct:
GALLATIN COUNTY. }

This 6th day of May, 1833, Captain Harrison Willson personally appeared before the undersigned, an acting Justice of the Peace in and for said county, and made oath that Mr. Alexander H. Hall, was enrolled in his (Willson's) company, as a volunteer in Gallatin county; that at Fort Wilbourn he was mustered into the service of the United States, in the war against the Sac Indians, on the 16th of June, 1832, in said company; that he, said Hall, was on the day after transferred to Gen. Posey's staff, as volunteer aid, and in a few days thereafter furloughed to return home, as he is informed.

(Signed.)   H. WILLSON, CAPT

Subscribed and sworn before me this 6th day of May, 1833.
(Signed.)   JAMES CALDWELL, J. P.

I certify on honor, that Wm. M. Wallace, Jno. McClernand and Mershall Rawlands volunteered as privates in Capt. Willson's company Ill. Militia and belonged to said company when it was organized at Fort Wilbourn. They afterwards were appointed on the staff and commissioned by the Governor, viz: Wallace as Brigade Paymaster, McClernand and Rawlins as Assistant Brigade Quartermasters. They served during the campaign and were mustered out at Fort Dixon, the 14th of August, 1832; they are at least entitled to private's pay.

(Signed.)   A. POSEY,
EQUALITY, May 4th, 1833.   late Brig.-Gen.

CAPT. JOEL HOLLIDAY'S COMPANY

1st Regiment, 1st Brigade of Illinais Mounted Volunteers, called into the service of the United States, on the requisition of Gen. Atkinson, by the Governor's proclamation, dated 15th May, 1832. Mustered out, Aug. 16, 1832.

Name and Rank.	Residence.	Enrolled	Remarks.
Captains.		1832	
James Caldwell	Gallatin Co		Resigned about the 19th of June
Joel Holliday	"	June 16	
First Lieutenant.			
Turner Cook	"	"	Absent on furlough, Aug. 5, 1832
Second Lieutenant.			
John J. Dean	"	"	Lost 1 pistol, wallet and saddle-bags
Sergeants.			
Benjamin Kinsall	"	"	
Robert R. Deull	"	"	
Quinzey Right	"	"	
Thos. V. Swearenger	"	"	
Corporals.			
David Kinsall	"	"	[tered out of service.
John Newman	"	"	Detached under Capt. Bays; supposed mus-
E. B. Puckett	"	"	Absent on furlough, July 1, 1832.
Benj Hubbs	"	"	Detached under Capt. Bays; supposed mus-[tered out of service.
Privates.			
Adams, John	"	"	Absent; I know not whether with or without
Bish, George	"	"	Absent on detached service [leave.
Barker, William	"	"	" "
Barker, Jesse	"	"	
Brown, Adonijah	"	"	
Bozarth, David	"	"	
Cusack, James	"	"	Absent; I know not whether with or without
Hays, Solomon	"	"	[leave.
Haskins, Jas. R	"	"	
Herod, Jno. W	"	"	Absent on furlough
Jones, Jonathan	"	"	
Luther, Ezra G	"	"	Lost 1 pair saddle-bags and wallet
Nelson, Stephen	"	"	
Powell, Thomas	"	"	Lost 1 horse on forced march
Quigley, Aaron	"	"	
Stiff, Richard	"	"	
Trousdale, James	"	"	
Thompson, Matthew	"	"	
Venson, Charles	"	"	

The following are supposed to be mustered out of service under Capt. Bays:

Name	Residence	Enrolled				Remarks
Privates.		1832				
Brown, James	Gallatin Co	June	16			Detached under Capt. Bays
Burris, Thomas	"	"	"	"	"	
Crissop, James	"	"	"	"	"	
Clayton, William	"	"	"	"	"	
Dunson, John	"	"	"	"	"	
Fouch, Levi	"	"	"	"	"	
Fouch, John	"	"	"	"	"	
Heraldson, William	"	"	"	"	"	
Hutchcraft, Elijah	"	"	"	"	"	
Johnson, Jas. B	"	"	"	"	"	
Morrow, Thomas	"	"	"	"	"	
Morrow, Forquer	"	"	"	"	"	
Patillo, Alexander	"	"	"	"	"	
Ralls, Nathaniel	"	"	"	"	"	
Sherwood, Hugh B	"	"	"	"	"	
Sherwood, Thomas	"	"	"	"	"	
Shoemaker, William	"	"	"	"	"	
Smith, Peter	"	"	"	"	"	
Sampson, William	"	"	"	"	"	
Westbrook, Samuel	"	"	"	"	"	
Williams, James	"	"	"	"	"	
Williams, Henry B	"	"	"	"	"	
Wood, Mason	"	"	"	"	"	

Name and Rank.	Residence.	Enrolled	Remarks.
Dake, Arnold B			Refused to march with company to Koskana.
Edwards, Phillip			" " "
Hughston, Jonathan			" " "
Keeny, Jonathan			" " "
Lafferty, William			" " "
Reynolds, Jas. L.			" " "
Tally, Amos			" " "

This company was enrolled by Capt. Jas. Caldwell, who commanded it until it entered the service of the United States, when he quit his command, and, in some three or four days after, the present Captain was elected. This company, individually at their own expense, furnished six days' rations for themselves when they marched from home to enter the service of the United States. They have each received but one-half bushel of corn as forage during the whole campaign, and the officers have drawn but one ration in kind per day. This company was mustered, and an election of officers had, on the 12th of May, 1832, marched for Fort Wilbourn June 1st, and was received into service June 16, 1832.

Capt. Archilaus Coffey's Company

Of the 1st Regiment, 1st Brigade Illinois Volunteers, called into the service of the United States, on the requisition of Gen. Atkinson, by the Governor's proclamation dated May 15, 1832. Mustered out, August 12, 1832.

Name and Rank.	Residence.	Enrolled	Remarks.
Captain.		1832	
Archilaus Coffey	Gallatin Co.	June 16	Furloughed at battle ground August 3.
First Lieutenant.			
Daniel Botright	"	"	Furl. on Surgeon's certificate July 15, 1832.
Second Lieutenant.			
Willis Stricklen	"	"	Furl. by Gen. Atkinson, from Prairie du Chien
Corporals.			
Wiley Roberts	"	"	Furloughed to return home, Aug. 9, 1832.
John Rhyon	"	"	"
David A. Grable	"	"	" attend sick, July 15, 1832.
Privates.			
Abner, Henry	"	"	Furl. on Surgeon's certificate July 15, 1832.
Barger, Isaac	"	"	Furloughed to return home Aug. 9, 1832.
Bond, George	"	"	" " " "
Bond, Stephen	"	"	" " " "
Coy, John	"	"	" " " "
Hall, Jonathan	"	"	" " " "
Hawkins, James	"	"	Furl. on Surgeon's certificate July 15, 1832.
Hedge, James	"	"	Furloughed to return home Aug. 9, 1832.
Isom, Richard	"	"	Furl. on Surgeon's certificate July 3, 1832.
Lewis, Abraham	"	"	Furloughed to return home Aug. 9, 1832.
Oldham, Thomas	"	"	Furl. Aug. 3; lost horse, saddle and bridle.
Pogue, James	"	"	
Richey, John P	"	"	Furloughed to return home Aug. 9, 1832.
Ryon, William	"	"	" " " "
Smith, John	"	"	" " " "
Smith, John H	"	"	
Whitesides, Thomas	"	"	Furl. on Surgeon's certificate July 15, 1832.
Ware, Robert	"	"	

Mustered out of service by Capt. Palmer:

Sergeants.		1832.	[Ferry, Aug. 12, 1832.
Samuel Ravney, 2d	Gallatin Co.	June 16	Mus. out under Capt. D. B. Russell, at Dixon's
John Garner, 3d	"	"	
Wm. Chosier, 4th	"	"	
Privates.			
Alshear, Anderson	"	"	
Carder, James K	"	"	
Hause, Peter	"	"	

FIRST BRIGADE.

Name and Rank.	Residence.	Enrolled	Remarks.
		1832.	
Karns, James........	Gallatin Co...	June 16.	
Karns, John..........	"	"	
Karns, George......	"	"	
Martin, Jason........	"	"	
Medling, Nedum.....	"	"	
Morris, Richmond...	"	"	
Prior, Anderson.....	"	"	
Strickland, William.	"	"	
Spruel, Pleasant.....	"	"	Mus. out under Capt. D. B. Russell, at Dixon's
Tongue, Thomas....	"	"	......................................[Ferry, Aug. 12, 1832.
Upchurch, John.....	"	"	
Upchurch, Jonathan	"	"	
Upchurch, Thomas..	"	"	

Supposed to have been mustered out with Col. Ewing's Regt., by Capt. Palmer:

		1832.	
Corporal.			
Gasaway, Hamilton.	Gallatin Co...	June 16	
Private.			
Carney, David.......	"	"	

Discharged:

		1832	
First Sergeant.			
Aden Warner........	Gallatin Co...	June 16	Discharged by Lieut. R. Anderson, A. I. Gen., [Aug. 16, 1832, by reason expiration service.
Privates.			
Cox, John.............	"	"	Dis. on Surg. certif. of disability, by Gen. At-......................................[kinson, June 18, 1832.
Fletcher, Wesley....	"	"	
Garret, William......	"	"	Dis. by Lieut. R. Anderson, A. I. Gen., Aug.
Strickland, Henry...	"	"	......................................[16, 1832; expiration service.

I certify on honor, that I have carefully examined this muster roll, and that I have this 25th day of Sept., 1832, signed this roll,—the Captain having called on me to certify as above, to the state of his company, and to account for the absence of the company from the place designated for being mustered out of the service of the United States. The company to be considered as having been mustered out on the same day its Regt. was mustered out.

      (Signed.)   ROBERT ANDERSON,
                  Lieut. and Ass't. Insp. Gen.

I certify that it was impossible for me to reach the place of mustering out, in consequence of the loss of my horse.
      (Signed.)   ARCHILAUS COFFEY, Capt.

Transportation furnished by the United States, from Galena to St. Louis, for all of the company who were furloughed after the battle of the 2d of August, 1832. This company was organized May 12th, 1832. Marched for the frontier May 26th, 1832. Mustered into the service of the United States June 16, 1832. Mustered out, Aug. 12, 1832.

SECOND REGIMENT.

CAPT. GEORGE P. BOWYER'S COMPANY

Of Mounted Volunteers of the State of Illinois, called into the service of the United States by the Governor of the State, by his order of the 15th day of May, 1832, from the date of its enrollment to the 7th day of August, 1832, the time of mustering out of service. Enrolled for 90 days.

Name and Rank.	Residence.	Enrolled	Remarks.
Captain. George P. Bowyer...	Franklin Co..	1832. June 16	Had two horses in service....................
First Lieutenant. Jacob Philips.........	" "	" "	....
Second Lieutenant. Thomas P. Moore...	" "	" "	Lost clothing, etc., valued at $9.50 ....
Sergeants.			
Thomas Adams, 1st..	" "	" "	Absent on furlough ....
Jacob Chark, 2d	" "	" "	
Edward Franklin, 3d	" "	" "	Left at Fort Hamilton, sick ....
Corporals.			
William Fleming, 1st	" "	" "	Bridle and tomah'wk lost, swim'g Pecatonica
William Akins, 2d ..	" "	" "	Coffee pot lost; value 62½ cents...............
Augustus Adams, 4th	" "	" "	Absent on furlough ....
Bugler. William Whittington	" "	" "	Absent on furlough ....
Privates.			
Adams, Benjamin...	" "	" "	
Bevers, Thomas.....	" "	" "	
Bowling, James	" "	" "	
Bowling, Benjamin..	" "	" "	Coffee and saddle-blanket lost; value $4.50...
Bowyer, Henry......	" "	" "	Bridle lo-t; value $2.00........................
Berry, John.........	" "	" "	Absent on furlough ....
Bailey, Jacob.......	" "	" "	
Browning, James ...	" "	" "	Transferred to Capt. West's company ....
Clampet, William....	" "	" "	
Cleveland, Evan.....	" "	" "	Saddle-blanket lost; value $2.50...............
Clark, John.........	" "	" "	Absent on furlough ....
Cleveland, Jesse....	" "	" "	
Clark, Reuben.......	" "	" "	
Due, John P.........	" "	" "	Absent on furlough ....
Dement, John	Fayette Co...	" "	Promoted to Major of Spy Bat., 1st Brig......
Dillingham, Vachel..	Franklin Co..	" "	
Estes, Absalom......	" "	" "	
Farris, James	" "	" "	
Gifford, Joseph.....	" "	" "	Absent on furlough ....
Hail, Thomas	" "	" "	Cloak and sack lost; value $7.00..............
Jourdan, Moses	" "	" "	Promoted Sergt.-Major; absent on furlough.
Jourden, Elijah......	" "	" "	
Jourden, James	" "	" "	Absent on furlough ....
Morgan, Nathaniel..	" "	" "	
Neal, Aaron.........	" "	" "	Transferred from Stephenson's Co.; on furl..
Plaisters, James	" "	" "	Absent on furlough ....
Redburn, Abraham..	" "	" "	
Robertson, Garrett..	" "	" "	Absent on furlough ....
Richardson, A. W....	" "	" "	
Scribner, John	" "	" "	Frying-pan and tin bucket lost; value $1.00..
Summers, James....	" "	" "	Sent to Fort Hamilton on duty; care of sick.
Summers, Noah	" "	" "	" " sick
Schoolcraft, James..	" "	" "	" " on duty; care of sick.
Slater, John.........	" "	" "	

Name and Rank.	Residence.	Enrolled	Remarks.
Whittington, Benj...	Franklin Co..	June 16	Tin bucket lost: value 37½ cents ....
Whittington, James.	"	"	Absent on furlough ....
Williams, Benjamin.	"	"	
Ward, William........	"	"	Blanket lost, valued at $2.50 ....
Western, Joseph	"	"	Transferred to Capt. Drennan's company....

I certify on honor that this muster roll exhibits the true state of the detachment under my command, and that the remarks set opposite the name of each officer and private are accurate and just.
        (Signed.)   GEO. P. BOWYER, CAPT.,
                                  2d Regt., 1st Brig. Ill. Vol.

                               DIXON FERRY, August 7, 1832.

Mustered out of service by me, by order of Maj.-Gen. Scott, commanding N. W. Army.
        (Signed.)   Z. C. PALMER, CAPT.,
                                  6th U. S. Inft. Com. Post.

STATE OF ILLINOIS, } ss.
FRANKLIN COUNTY.

I, George P. Bowyer, do solemnly swear that Jno. Slater and Alexander W. Richardson were regularly enrolled in the service of the United States in my company, at Fort Wilbourn, on June 16, 1832, and that they served the full period of time for which they were enrolled, and were regularly discharged at Fort Dixon, by Capt. Palmer, on a detached roll; and that they are justly entitled to full pay and allowance for said service (and, as I am informed, said detached roll was lost or mislaid).
                        (Signed.)   GEO. P. BOWYER, CAPT.
Subscribed and sworn to this 9th May, 1833.
                  (Signed.)   JOHN Y. DAVIS, J. P.

CAPT. WM. J. STEPHENSON'S COMPANY

Of Mounted Volunteers, called into the service of the United States by the Governor of the State of Illinois, by his order of the 15th day of May, 1832, from its enrollment to the 7th day of August, 1832, when mustered out of service. Enrolled for 90 days.

Name and Rank.	Residence.	Enrolled	Remarks.
Captain.		1832.	
Wm. J. Stephenson	Franklin Co..	June 16.	Gray mare lost in service; appraised at $65...
Second Lieutenant.			
Tramel Ewing.......	"	"	Absent on furlough ....
Sergeants.			
John P. Maddox.....	"	"	Absent on furlough ....
Anderson P. Corder.	"	"	Lost blanket in battle; appraised at $2 ....
Henry Hays..........	"	"	Lost horse and equipage; appraised $66.37½.
John T. Knox........	"	"	On duty at Apple River Fort ....
Corporals.			
Thos. Provence, 1st.	"	"	
Michael Rawlins, 2d.	"	"	
Musician.			
Walter B. Scates	"	"	Lost blanket, etc., in battle; appraised at $6..
Privates.			
Bobbitt, John........	"	"	Absent on furlough ....
Denning, Josiah B..	"	"	
Eubanks, Elisha.....	"	"	Discharged at Ft. Wilbourn; to rec. full pay.
Farris, Anderson P..	"	"	Lost horse, arms, blanket; appraised $84.50..
Garrett, Hezekiah ..	"	"	Absent on furlough ....
Garrett, Robert.....	"	"	" "
Gassaway, William.	"	"	
Hickman, Benj. F...	"	"	Appointed Governor's Aid, June 17, 1832......
Hays, John	"	"	Lost bridle in battle; appraised at $1.50.......
Hubbard, Wm. A....	"	"	
Hillen, Lewis	"	"	Lost blanket in battle; appraised $2.50........
Jones, Nathaniel	"	"	
Knox, Thomas.......	"	"	
Lynch, Larkin.......	"	"	
Maddox, Wm. P.....	"	"	Lost horse and equipage; appraised at $36.35.

Name and Rank.	Residence.	Enrolled	Remarks.
Miller, Andrew	Franklin Co.	June 16.	Blanket in battle; appraised at $2.50
Neal, Moses	"	"	Appointed Quartermaster Sergt. 2d Regt., 1st
Pope, Benj. W.	"	"	Absent on furlough....(Brig. Ill. Mounted Vol.
Rotramel, Henry	"	"	
Robertson, Andrew	"	"	
Rawlings, Ezekiel	"	"	On duty at Apple River Fort
Rea, Wilson	"	"	Discharged at Ft. Wilbourn; to rec. full pay.
Swafford, Harvey	"	"	Blanket in battle; appraised at $2.50
Silkwood, H. M.	"	"	Absent on furlough
Talbot, Benjamin	"	"	Absent on furl., or discharged at Ft. Wilbourn

I certify on honor that this muster roll exhibits the true state of the company under my command, and that the remarks set opposite the name of each officer and soldier are accurate and just.

(Signed.) WM. J. STEPHENSON, CAPT.,
of the 2d Regt., 1st Brig.

DIXON'S FERRY, Aug. 7, 1832.
Mustered out of service by me by order of Maj.-Gen. Scott, commanding N. W. army.
(Signed.) Z. C. PALMER, CAPT.,
6th U. S. Inft., Com. Post.

CAPT. OBEDIAH WEST'S COMPANY

Of Mounted Volunteers, called into the service of the United States by the Governor of Illinois, by his order of the 15th of May, 1832, from the date of its enrollment to the 6th day of August, 1832, when mustered out of service. (Company now under command of 1st Lieut. Robt. West, commanding.) Enrolled for 90 days.

Name and Rank.	Residence.	Enrolled	Remarks.
Captain.		1832.	
Obediah West	Franklin Co.	June 16	Absent on furlough
First Lieutenant,			
Robert West	"	"	
Second Lieutenant,			
Hugh Parks	"	"	Absent on furlough
Sergeants.			
Willie Scott, 1st	"	"	Horse lost in service
William Henry, 4th	"	"	Absent on furlough
Corporal.			
Moses Odum, 3d	"	"	
Privates.			
Browning, James	"	"	
Bradley, Pleasant	"	"	Absent on furlough
Beasley, Washington	"	"	" "
Franklin, Edward	"	"	
Groves, Isaac	"	"	
Hooker, Jabez	"	"	Absent on furlough
Henry, Augustus	"	"	" " horse lost in service
Joiner, Jiles	"	"	
Layman, Henry	"	"	
Meredith, Junior	"	"	
Murphy, William	"	"	
Provence, Albert	"	"	
Pulley, Thomas	"	"	Absent on furlough
Parks, Samuel	"	"	
Price, Richard	Pike Co.	"	Absent on furlough
Parks, Andrew	Franklin Co.	"	Tent cloth (private property) lost, value, $3.
Rich, William	"	"	
Rau, William	"	"	
Roper, Seth	"	"	
Springs, David H	"	"	
Worthen, Robert	"	"	
Ward, John	"	"	Absent on furlough
Ward, Dickson	"	"	
Watson, Robert	"	"	
Youngblood, Isaac	"	"	
Zacharias, George	"	"	

FIRST BRIGADE. 13

STATE OF ILLINOIS, } ss:
FRANKLIN COUNTY,

We, John Ewing, Col. of the 2d Regt., and Obediah West, Captain in said Regiment, do solemnly swear that John Cunningham was enrolled in Capt. West's company, at Fort Wilbourn, on the 16th of June, 1832, in the service of the United States, served up to 12th of August faithfully, but on account of being absent on detached service, was not mustered out of service with his proper company. We further state on oath that it is our opinion that said John is fully entitled to pay and all allowances for said service.

(Signed.)   JOHN EWING, COL.
(Signed.)   OBEDIAH WEST, CAPT.

Subscribed and sworn before me the 9th of May, 1833.
(Signed.)   JOHN T. DAVIS, J. P.

CAPT. CHARLES DUNN'S COMPANY

Of Mounted Volunteers, called into the service of the United States by the Governor of Illinois, by his order of May 15, 1832, from the date of its enrollment to August 13, 1832, the time of mustering out of service.

Name and Rank.	Residence.	Enrolled	Remarks.
Captain.		1832	
Charles Dunn	Pope Co	June 16	Two horses in service
First Lieutenant.			
Joseph Neal	"	"	Left at Fort Hamilton, sick
Second Lieutenants.			
John Raum	"	"	Promoted to Brig. Maj., June 16, '32, 1st Brig.
James H. McColugh	"	"	Elected and commis'd in place John Raum, [promoted June 16, 1832.
Sergeants.			
Jesse R. Pratt	"	"	Absent on furlough dated July 31, 1832
Andrew H. Drinnon	"	"	Appointed 1st Sergt., in place of Pratt, July [31, 1832; horse lost, strayed or stolen.
Corporals.			
James F. Johnston	"	"	Prom. Reg. Q. M. July 1, '32; mus. out as such
John Hamilton	"	"	U. S. halter lost
Jason B. Smith	"	"	Absent on furlough
Privates.			
Arnold, James	"	"	U. S. camp-ax lost
Anderson, William	"	"	
Bruce, David	"	"	
Bruce, Thomas	"	"	
Barr, William A	"	"	
Cowsert, Geo. W	"	"	Absent on furlough
Dobbins, John W	"	"	Left sick at Fort Hamilton
Hawley, Joshua S	"	"	U. S. halter lost
Hughes, Richard	"	"	
Harper, Joseph	"	"	U. S. halter lost
Hall, Thomas	"	"	U. S. tin bucket and camp-ax lost
Hodge, John P	"	"	
Kennedy, Jacob	"	"	U. S. halter lost
McCool, John	"	"	
Merow, John	"	"	
Paistly, William M	"	"	
Pearce, Daniel	"	"	Deserted July 20, 1832
Palmore, Willie R	"	"	
Palmore, Calvin H	"	"	U. S. hatchet lost
Pattello, Nathan	"	"	Absent on furlough
Pratt, Mathew Y	"	"	
Paisley, John	"	"	U. S. camp-ax, halter, bayonet-scabbard lost
Rose, James	"	"	
Slankard, Harrison	"	"	Horse lost, strayed or stolen
Smith, Hiram G	"	"	Absent on furlough
Wiley, Joseph	"	"	Left sick at Fort Hamilton
Whiteside, John	"	"	Absent on furlough dated July 31, 1832

Capt. Jonathan Durman's Company

Of Mounted Volunteers of Illinois, called into the service of the United States by the Governor of the State of Illinois, by his order of May 15, 1832, from the date of its enrollment to Aug. 12, 1832, the time of its mustering out of service.

Name and Rank.	Residence.	Enrolled	Remarks:
Captain. Jonathan Durman	Pope Co	1832 June 16	Two horses and one servant in service
First Lieutenant. Simon S. Bargar	"	"	
Second Lieutenant. Jacob Bunyard	"	"	
Sergeants.			
John B. Witt	"	"	
Thomas M. Ellis	"	"	
Green B. Veatch	"	"	
Alfred M. Hazel	"	"	
Corporals.			
John Lewis	"	"	
Thomas Matthews	"	"	
Privates.			
Anderson, Andrew	"	"	Left sick at Fort Wilbourn
Allen, Marshall	"	"	Horse lost in service
Bunty, Jesse	"	"	
Baily, James	"	"	
Bowman, David	"	"	Absent on furlough
Crawford, James	"	"	
Carlyle, William	"	"	Absent on furlough
Cowsent, Samuel	"	"	Ord. to Ft. Hamilton on duty; horse lost, shot
Davis, Colman	"	"	
Demick, Judetham C	"	"	
Dorset, William	"	"	
Holland, James	"	"	
Hobbs, Ezekial	"	"	Deserted July 20, 1832
Harlice, William	"	"	Left on duty at Ft. Wilbourn to attend sick
Hobbs, Christopher	"	"	Absent on furlough, granted on Surg's certif.
Jones, Alfred	"	"	
King, Anderson	"	"	
King, John	"	"	
Lewis, Joseph L	"	"	Absent on furlough
Lauderdale, John	"	"	
Martin, Isaac L	"	"	
Noaks, Abraham	"	"	Left sick at Fort Hamilton
Perrin, James	"	"	
Rancy, Robert R	"	"	Absent on furlough; horse lost in service
Slankard, Jacob	"	"	
Williams, John	"	"	Left at Fort Funk sick
Williams, James	"	"	" " "
Williams, Josiah	"	"	" to attend the sick
Williams, Isom	"	"	
Watkins, Isaac F	"	"	Left at Funk's Fort to attend the sick
Wallace, Squire	"	"	sick
West, Joseph	Franklin Co	"	Det. by cons'nt from Capt. West's Co.; att'ch'd to Capt. Durman's.

Capt. Holman's Company

Of Illinois Mounted Volunteers, called into the service of the United States by the Governor of the State, by his order of May 15, 1832, from the date of its enrollment to the 2d day of August, 1832, when mustered out of service.

Name and Rank.	Residence.	Enrolled	Remarks.
Captain. Armstead Holman		1832 June 15	
First Lieutenant. James Duncan		"	

FIRST BRIGADE.

Name and Rank.	Residence.	Enrolled	Remarks.
Second Lieutenant.		1832.	
Squire Howell		June 15	
Sergeants.			
O. H. Willey		"	
Joel Norris		"	
Abraham Duncan		"	One blanket lost in service
Wintfroy L. Crain		"	
Corporals.			
Manuel Hunter		"	
John Spiller		"	One horse lost in service
Willis Tiner		"	
James Norris		"	
Musician.			
Thomas C. Lowden		"	
Privates.			
Bold, Larry		"	
Crain, Noah		"	
Crain, Spencer		"	
Crain, Wm. B		"	
Crain, Manuel R		"	
Crain, Champ T		"	
Chittey, Alfred		"	
Daniel, Thomas		"	
Durock, Lewis		"	
Duncan, Wm. H		"	
Fisher, Thomas		"	
Fisher, Solomon		"	
Gulley, Isaac		"	One U. S. scabbard belt lost and one horse
Hail, Thos		"	
Hunter, George W		"	
Herring, Reuben		"	One horse lost in service
Hancock, Thomas		"	
Hindman, Wm		"	
Huffman, Westley		"	
James, Thomas		"	
Lastly, John		"	
Lewis, Isaac		"	
McAlley, Archibald		"	
Moake, Ezekiel		"	
Nelson, Morgan		"	
Nelson, James M		"	Furloughed (inability for service) June 20, '32.
Phenix, John		"	
Russell, James S		"	
Rowland, Wm		"	
Russell, Phillip J		"	
Rawls, Wm		"	
Rawls, Harris		"	
Ryburn, Byrd T		"	
Spiller, John B		"	
Stroud, Daniel		"	
Stroud, Levi		"	
Spiller, Martin B		"	
Stack, John		"	
Tarpley, Wm. H		"	
Tippey, James		"	
Tiner, Isham		"	One belt and tomahawk lost in service
Tiner, Joshua		"	
Williams, Tippo S		"	
Williams, David		"	
Yancey, Hiram		"	
Yancey, Wm. R		"	

THIRD REGIMENT.

Capt. Ardin Biggerstaff's Company

Of Mounted Volunteers of Illinois, called into the service of the United States by the Governor of Illinois, by his order of May 15, 1832, from the date of its enrollment to the 13th day of August, 1832, the time of mustering out of service. Enrolled for 90 days.

Name and Rank.	Residence.	Enrolled	Remarks.
Captain.		1832.	
Ardin Biggerstaff	Hamilton Co.	June 16	
First Lieutenant.			
Lewis Lane	"	"	
Second Lieutenant.			
Wesley W. Wiltes	"	"	On furlough
Sergeants.			
Wesley W. Gholston	"	"	On furlough
James M. Wilson	"	"	
James Allen, Sr.	"	"	One saddle lost; value $10
William Fuller	"	"	
Corporals.			
Joshua G. Weaver	"	"	One tent cloth lost on forc'd m'rch, val. $4.68¾
Benjamin I. Allen	"	"	
Grandville Gholston	"	"	
Solomon Skelton	"	"	Appointed 4th Corporal
Fifer.			
Elisha Everett	"	"	
Trumpeter.			
Adonijah G. Grimes	"	"	On furlough
Privates.			
Allen, John	"	"	
Allen, James, Jr	"	"	
Bryant, James H	"	"	
Bryant, William	"	"	
Blake, James	"	"	On furlough
Crouch, Adam	"	"	
Cook, Ellison	"	"	
Campbell, William	"	"	
Drew, William	"	"	Tent-cloth lost, escap'g from Ind's; also coat.
Everett, Elijah	"	"	
Gallaher, James F	"	"	Lost one bayonet bolt; supposed stolen
Gibson, John	"	"	
Hynes, Andrew S	"	"	
Johnson, Saml	"	"	On furlough
Jourdan, Jesse	"	"	
Jenkins, Thos. S	"	"	
Johnson, William	"	"	On furlough
Lowry, John	"	"	
Mayberry, David E	"	"	On furlough
Mayberry, Frederick	"	"	Discharged June 20, 1832, as sick
Morris, Daniel	"	"	Lost one bayonet and bayonet belt
Martin, Saml	"	"	On furlough
Moore, Jesse	"	"	"
Porter, Elbridge G	"	"	
Riley, William	"	"	
Riley, F. A.	"	"	
Richey, J. M	"	"	On furlough; lost horse in action, value, $100
Sexton, Charles	"	"	On furlough
Stull, Nicholas	"	"	
Steerman, N. D	"	"	

FIRST BRIGADE. 17

Name and Rank.	Residence.	Enrolled	Remarks.
Steerman, W. M.	Hamilton Co.	June 16	
Shelton, Joseph	"	"	Promoted to Major June 16, 1832; lost horse
Trotter, Archibald	"	"	
Trammel, Nicholas	"	"	
Thomason, Jos. F.	"	"	
Wheeler, Washingt'n	"	"	On furlough
Wheeler, John	"	"	

I certify on honor that this muster roll exhibits the state of the company under my command, and that the "remarks" set opposite the name of each officer and soldier are, to the best of my knowledge, accurate and just.
(Signed.) ARDIN BIGGERSTAFF, CAPT.,
Com. 2d Co., 2d Bat. 3d Regt., 1st Brig., Ill. Mounted Vol.
Station—Dixon Ferry. Date—Aug. 13, 1832.

CAPT. JOHN ONSLOTT'S COMPANY

Of the 3d Regiment of the 1st Brigade of Illinois Mounted Volunteers, called into the service of the United States, on the requisition of Gen. Atkinson, by the Governor's proclamation, dated ——, 1832; mustered out August 15, 1832, by order of Brig.-Gen. Atkinson.

Name and Rank.	Residence.	Enrolled	Remarks.
Captain.		1832.	
John Onslott	Clay Co.	June 16.	Elected Captain May 29, 1832
First Lieutenant.			
Trussey P. Hanson	"	"	Elected First Lieutenant May 29, 1832
Second Lieutenant.			
Alfred J. Moore	"	"	Elected Second Lieutenant May 29, 1832
Sergeants.			
Cyrus Wright	"	"	Appointed May 29, 1832
Elisha Bashford	"	"	" "
Arch. T. Patterson	"	"	[May 29, 1832
James Tompkins	"	"	Supposed disch'g'd by Gen. Scott; appointed
Corporals.			
Samuel Whiteley	"	"	Appointed May 29, 1832
Strother B. Walker	"	"	" "
Joseph Whiteley	"	"	" "
Francis Herman	"	"	
Privates.			
Ano, James T.	"	"	
Creek, Jefferson	"	"	
Cook, James	"	"	On furlough, by order of Col. Leech
Curbaugh, Sol. B.	"	"	
Chamberlin, Young	"	"	
Campbell, Augur	"	"	
Daniels, Levi	"	"	
Fitzgerald, A. S.	"	"	Broke down in service; furloughed Aug. 9, '32
Lethcoe, Joseph	"	"	
Logan, Russell	"	"	On furlough by order of Major Campbell
McDaniel, Hugh	"	"	Supposed discharged by Gen. Scott
McDaniel, Robert	"	"	
McGrew, John	"	"	On furlough, Aug. 9, 1832
McKenney, James	"	"	Broke down in service; furl. by Maj. Campbell
Moseley, Bennett W.	"	"	
Mortin, Perkey	"	"	Supposed discharged by Gen. Scott
Nicholson, John G.	"	"	
Nelson, James	"	"	On furlough by order of Col. Leech
Rogers, Isaac	"	"	
Rogers, Thomas	"	"	
Skief, Jesse	"	"	
Songer, Abram	"	"	
Stallings, Lockhard	"	"	
Sincoe, David	"	"	On furlough by order of Major Campbell
Sutton, John	"	"	On furlough, Aug. 1, 1832
Speaker, John	"	"	On furlough, Aug. 9, 1832

—2

Name and Rank.	Residence.	Enrolled	Remarks.
Tarter, Frederick....	Clay Co....	1832. June 16.	
Van Cleave, James...	"	"	
Walker, Isaac........	"	"	On furlough, Aug. 9, 1832
Wickersham, Jas. L.	"	"	On furlough, Aug. 1, 1832.
Whiteley, Martin....	"	"	

Took up line of March from Clay county June 2, 1832. Mustered into U. S. service June 16, 1832. Captain and other officers have drawn but one ration in kind each day, and but one-half bushel of corn for horse during the campaign, and eight days' rations to travel home on.

          (Signed.)   JOHN ONSLOTT, Capt.

On this 12th day of August, 1832.

Capt. James Hall's Company

Of Mounted Volunteers of Illinois, called into the service of the United States by the Governor of Illinois, by his order of May 15, 1832, from the date of its enrollment to August 13, 1832, the time of mustering out of service.

Name and Rank.	Residence.	Enrolled	Remarks.
Captain.		1832.	
James Hall	Hamilton Co..	June 16	One iron-gray horse lost; value, $100
First Lieutenant.			
John Burton	"	"	Absent on furlough
Second Lieutenant.			
John Townsand	"	"	Absent on furlough
Sergeants.			
Milton Carpenter....	"	"	Absent on furlough
Robert Witt	"	"	" " One mare stolen; value, $100
John M. Smith	"	"	
Alfred More..........	"	"	
Corporals.			
John Heard..........	"	"	Discharged ——, 1832, by Capt. Palmer
Charles Heard.......	"	"	[valued at $80
Keling T. Maulding..	"	"	Absent on furlough. One bay horse stolen.
Willis Atkinson......	"	"	
Bugleman.			
Clinton Hopkins.....	"	"	
Privates.			
Adair, Phillip........	"	"	
Bond, Elisha.........	"	"	
Burnett, John........	"	"	
Brown, Shearwood..	"	"	
Burress, Elijah		"	On furlough
Coffee, Thomas......	Hamilton Co..	"	Absent on furlough
Cannimore, Samuel.		"	
Coons, Martin		"	One bay horse lost, valued at $53
Davenport, James ..		"	Promoted June 16, 1832.....[lost, valued at $67
Fouch, John		"	One bay horse, saddle, bridle and blanket
Hungate, Charles ...	Hamilton Co..	"	
Hall, Joseph		"	
Hutson, Sanford	"	"	Absent on furlough
Hall, Thomas		"	One sorrel mare broke down, valued at $40.
Hauks, Thomas J....		"	
Johnston, Jesse		"	Discharged by Capt. Palmer on —— day
Krisel, Charles	Hamilton Co..	"	One gun lost on battle ground, valued at $15.
Krisel, John	"	"	Absent on furlough
Lane, Louis..........	"	"	
Lane, Levin..........	"	"	Promoted June 16, 1832, to Q. M.-Sergt.
Meredith, Frederick.	"	"	Absent on furlough
Monday, Samuel	"	"	
McBroom, Azariel...	"	"	Absent on furlough
McLaughlin, Wm....	"	"	
Morris, William		"	[valued at $71
Maulding, Ambrose.		"	On furlough. One bay mare, etc., stolen.

FIRST BRIGADE.

Name and Rank.	Residence.	Enrolled	Remarks.
		1832.	
Oglesby, Rhebin	Hamilton Co.	June 16	Horse, saddle, etc., stolen by Indians; furloughed.
Overturf, Adam		"	
Phelps, Charles	Hamilton Co.	"	
Pauley, Alexander	"	"	
Perry, William		"	
Prigmore, Willie		"	
Redrick, Jonathan	Hamilton Co.	"	Mare killed on forced march; valued at $63.
Rich, John		"	
Reynolds, Jeremiah		"	
Shealy, Moses	"	"	Mare, etc., stolen by Indians; valued at $94.
Schoolcraft, James		"	
Sims, Martin		"	[furloughed.
Townsand, Hiram	Hamilton Co.	"	Horse, saddle, etc., lost on forced march;
Tramel, Elijah		"	[loughed.
White, Snead	"	"	Mare, saddle, etc., stolen by Indians; furloughed.
Williams, Wiley	"	"	
Ward, Samuel	"	"	

I certify on honor that this muster roll exhibits true statement of the company under my command, and that the remarks set opposite the name of each officer and soldier are, to the best of my knowledge, accurate and just.

(Signed.)   JAMES HALL, CAPT.,
Com. 1st Co., 2d Bat, 3d Regt., 1st Brig. Ill. Mounted Vol.

Mustered out of service by me, by order of Major-General Scott, commanding the N. W. army.

(Signed.)   Z. C. PALMER, CAPT.,
6th U. S. Inft., Com. Post.

CAPT. JAMES N. CLARK'S COMPANY

Of 3d Regiment, 1st Brigade, Illinois Mounted Volunteers, called into the service of the United States on the requisition of Gen. Atkinson, by the Governor's proclamation dated May 15, 1832. Mustered out August 15, 1832.

Name and Rank.	Residence.	Enrolled	Remarks.
		1832.	
Captain.			
James N. Clark	Wayne Co.	June 16	Saddle, bridle and blanket lost
First Lieutenant.			
David Ray	"	"	One horse lost
Second Lieutenant.			
Jesse Laird	"	"	
Sergeants.			
Daniel Sumpter	"	"	On furlough August 10, 1832; lost saddle
William A. Howard	"	"	
Henry Oley	"	"	2d August, 1832, Ft. Dickson, to be discharged
Isaac Street	"	"	
Corporals.			
Joseph Walker	"	"	
John A. McWhartens	"	"	On furlough Aug. 3, 1832
Lewis Watkins	"	"	
Nathan E. Roberts	"	"	
Privates.			
Austin, Harris	"	"	
Austin, James B.	"	"	
Alexander, David	"	"	Discharged at Ft. Dickson, Aug. 2, 1832.
Bain, Robert	"	"	On furlough Aug. 9, 1832
Bradshaw, Greenup	"	"	
Bullard, Asa	"	"	Horse lost
Campbell, Joseph M.	"	"	
Clark, James	"	"	
Clark, William [H	"	"	
Dickerson, Younger	"	"	
Dolton, George	"	"	
Dolton, Andrew C.	"	"	

BLACK HAWK WAR.

Name and Rank.	Residence.	Enrolled	Remarks.
		1832.	
Farleigh, George	Wayne Co	June 16	
Fitzgerald, John F	"	"	Furloughed Aug. 8, 1832
Garrison, Joseph L	"	"	Left sick at Fort Wilbourn, June 19, 1832
Garrison, James	"	"	
Graham, William	"	"	
Hargrave, Jeremiah	"	"	
Harland, William	"	"	Furloughed August 9, 1832
Haws, Alfred	"	"	
Haws, Benjamin	"	"	
Hanson, John	"	"	Left at Fort Wilbourn, sick, June 19, 1832
James, Samuel	"	"	
Kenshalow, Peter	"	"	
Martin, David	"	"	
Martin, Nathan	"	"	
Mays, Andrew	"	"	
Mays, James	"	"	
McCullam, William	"	"	
Morris, Joseph	"	"	
Ray, Chesley	"	"	
Ray, Asa	"	"	
Rister, Jacob	"	"	Left at Fort Wilbourn, sick, June 19, 1832
Sanders, Fenton	"	"	
Sessions, Richard	"	"	
Slocumb, David D	"	"	Discharged at Fort Wilbourn, June 19, 1832
Smith, David	"	"	
Trotter, James	"	"	
Tyler, Johalen	"	"	On furlough Aug. 9, 1832
Walker, George	"	"	
Walker, Greenbury	"	"	
Warrick, Jefferson	"	"	
Warrick, James R	"	"	
Widdus, John G	"	"	On furlough Aug. 9, 1832
White, John L	"	"	
Bradshaw, Arthur	"	"	

James N. Clark elected Captain, May 12, 1832. David Ray elected 1st Lieut., May 12. Jesse Laird elected 2d Lieut., May 12, 1832.

From Wayne county took up line on June 1, 1832. Mustered into service June 16, 1832.

CAPT. BERRYMAN G. WELLS' COMPANY

Of the 3d Regiment, 1st Brigade of Illinois Mounted Volunteers, called into the service of the United States, on the requisition of Gen. Atkinson, by the Governor's proclamation dated May 15, 1832. Mustered out August 15, 1832.

Name and Rank.	Residence.	Enrolled	Remarks.
		1832.	
Captain.			
Benjamin G. Wells	Wayne Co	June 16	
First Lieutenant.			
John Brown	"	"	On furlough from Aug. 7
Second Lieutenant.			
James B. Carter	"	"	
Sergeants.			
Hugh Stewart	"	"	Absent by leave of Col. Leech
James G. Browner	"	"	
Leon Harrys	"	"	Furloughed Aug. 9
Riley T. Serratt	"	"	
Corporals.			
Robert S. Harriss	"	"	Furloughed Aug. 9
Ransom Harriss	"	"	
Albert Butler	"	"	
Elijah Harriss	"	"	On furlough Aug. 9
Drummer.			
Nathan Franklin	"	"	On furlough Aug. 9

FIRST BRIGADE.

Name and Rank.	Residence.	Enrolled	Remarks.
Trumpeter.		1832.	
Jonathan Wilsey	Wayne Co	June 16.	On furlough Aug. 9
Privates.			
Bird, John	"	"	
Beach, Justis	"	"	Absent by leave of Col. Leech
Browner, John	"	"	
Berry, John	"	"	
Cates, Robert D	"	"	
Cates, Robert	"	"	Horse, etc., lost
Cook, Howlet H	"	"	
Cook, James M	"	"	
Carter, Isaac	"	"	
Carter, William	"	"	Absent by leave of Col. Leech
Downer, Job	"	"	
Gasten, Robert R	"	"	
Hall, Jacob	"	"	Furloughed Aug. 9
Hodge-, Isaih	"	"	
Hodges, Isham	"	"	Absent Aug. 3 by leave of Col. Leech
Harland, James C	"	"	
Hart, Moses	"	"	Furloughed Aug. 9
Harriss, Joseph	"	"	Absent on leave to Galena; taken sick; went
Irvin, William	"	"	Furloughed June 25.....[home without leave.
Lock, Samuel	"	"	Absent on furlough; one horse, etc., lost
McCracken, Jon'th'n	"	"	One horse, etc., lost
Martin, Nathan	"	"	Absent from Aug. 3 by leave of Col. Leech
Neel, Samuel	"	"	
Neel, Andrew	"	"	
Neel, Henry	"	"	One horse, etc., lost
Phelps, Thomas	"	"	Absent by leave Aug. 3; one horse, etc., lost.
Smith, Nicholas	"	"	" " of Col. Leech; one musket
Stephenson, John G	"	"	Furloughed Aug. 9 ....[etc., lost in battle.
Shoemaker, Enoch	"	"	Absent by leave Aug. 3; one horse lost
Shoemaker, Hugh	"	"	
Stephenson, Job	"	"	
Snider, John W	"	"	Furloughed Aug. 9; one horse, etc., lost
Staton, Westley	"	"	Absent by leave of Col. Leech, Aug. 3
Turner, Fielding C	"	"	
Turner, James	"	"	
White, William	"	"	Horse, etc., lost
Wells, M. C	"	"	Absent on furlough Aug. 9
Young, Clement C	"	"	

Berryman G. Wells elected Captain, John Brown elected First Lieutenant, James B. Carter elected Second Lieutenant, May 12, 1832. Non-commissioned officers appointed same date.

SPY BATTALION.

Capt. William N. Dobbins' Company

Of Spy Battalion, 1st Brigade, of Illinois Mounted Volunteers, called into the service of the United States by the Governor's proclamation, dated April 19, 1832; mustered out August 16, 1832.

Name and Rank.	Residence.	Enrolled	Remarks.
Captain.		1832.	
William N. Dobbins	Marion Co...	June 16	Horse wounded, not fit for service; rifle lost.
First Lieutenant.			
Steven Yocam	" "	" "	Lost 1 U. S. halter.
Second Lieutenant.			
James Gray	" "	" "	On furlough August 11; horse killed.
Sergeants.			
John F. Draper	" "	" "	Absent by leave Aug. 11; lost 1 U. S. halter.
Alfred Ray	" "	" "	
Samuel Hull	" "	" "	Absent by leave August 11.
Daniel Mynes	" "	" "	
Corporals.			
Hamilton Furthing	" "	" "	Horse killed; lost 1 U. S. rope.
William B. Haddem	" "	" "	Absent by leave August 11.
William T. Booth	" "	" "	Lost 1 U. S. halter.
Joseph Gray	" "	" "	Absent by leave Col. Leech; horse killed.
Privates.			
Allen, Benjamin	" "	" "	Lost 1 U. S. halter.
Allen, John	" "	" "	Absent on furlough August 12.
Allman, David W.	" "	" "	Absent by leave August 11; horse lost.
Chandler, Wellas	" "	" "	" 11; killed.
Craig, William H.	" "	" "	Disch.; must'd out by Lieut. Depriest Aug. 3.
Craig, Samuel	" "	" "	Discharged; horse wounded; lost U. S. halt'r
Dunken, Green R.	" "	" "	" lost U. S. camp kettle.
Eagan, John	" "	" "	
Farmer, William	" "	" "	
Fields, Green	" "	" "	Disch.; horse killed; lost 1 U. S. coffee pot.
Field, Nathan	" "	" "	" lost 1 U. S. frying pan
Gaston, William	" "	" "	" horse killed; lost 1 U. S. coffee pot.
Gray, William	" "	" "	
Hill, William	" "	" "	
Hollen, James	" "	" "	Absent by leave Aug. 11; lost 1 U. S. halter.
Hutchison, Wm. G.	" "	" "	Discharged
Hays, Samuel H.	" "	" "	" ; horse killed.
Jones, John F.	" "	" "	Absent on furlough August 12.
King, Willa	" "	" "	Discharged; lost 1 U. S. frying pan.
King, William	" "	" "	" campkettle; horse kill'd
Lovel, James	" "	" "	Absent by leave August 11; horse killed.
Livenstone, Henry M	" "	" "	
McDaniel, Henry	" "	" "	Horse lost.
McGuire, John	" "	" "	Lost 1 U. S. halter.
McGee, William	" "	" "	
Mabry, Dudley H.	" "	" "	Horse killed; rifle-gun lost; also, U. S. halter
Marsh, William	" "	" "	Absent by consent Gen. Atkinson Aug. 4.
Nelms, Norflt B.	" "	" "	" leave August 11; horse killed.
Piles, Calven	" "	" "	Lost 1 U. S. halter; horse killed.
Phelps, Zadock	" "	" "	
Phelps, John	" "	" "	Absent on furlough July 20.
Richeson, James J.	" "	" "	Lost 1 U. S. halter.
Sterges, Jesse	" "	" "	Absent on furlough August 11.
Smith, Wellers	" "	" "	Discharged; horse killed.
Smith, John F.	" "	" "	

FIRST BRIGADE.

Name and Rank.	Residence.	Enrolled	Remarks.
		1832.	
Tompson, Bird M....	Marion Co...	June 16.	Absent by leave Aug. 12; horse killed..........
Uhls, John B.........	"	"	....
Williams, James....	"	"	Discharged; horse killed................
Warren, Asa.........	"	"	Absent by leave of Gen. Atkinson...........
Wright, Leven.......	"	"	Absent on furl. Aug. 11; lost 1 U. S. halter;
Young, Edward......	"	"	Discharged; horse killed.......[horse killed.

Company was organized in Marion county May 4, 1832. Marched, June 1, for Fort Wilbourn. Mustered into service June 17, 1832. Fourteen horses killed in battle at Kellogg's Grove, six wounded and three taken by the enemy, June 25, 1832.

James Eagan, left sick at Fort Wilbourn, to be discharged by Gen. Atkinson.
Issac Coppall,   "   "   "   "   "
Wm. Howell,   "   "   "   "   "

I certify that Young Burbee, a private of my company, was detailed as Hospital Steward, and served out his full term, and was mustered out on the field and staff muster roll of the Spy Battalion.

(Signed,)   WM. N. DOBBINS, CAPT.

CAPT. JAMES BOWMAN'S COMPANY

Of the Odd Battalion of Spies, 1st Brigade of Illinois Mounted Volunteers, called into the service of the United States, on the requisition of Gen. Atkinson, by the Governor's proclamation, dated May 15, 1832. Mustered out, Aug. 16, 1832.

Name and Rank.	Residence.	Enrolled	Remarks.
		1832	
Captain. James Bowman	Jefferson Co..	June 17	....
First Lieutenant. Franklin S. Casey...	"	June 16	Furloughed Aug. 7, 1832..................
Second Lieutenant. Green Deprist...	"	"	Supposed to be furloughed Aug. 3, 1832.........
Sergeants,			
Stephen C. Hicks...	"	"	Furloughed Aug. 17, 1832..................
Eli D. Anderson.....	"	"	Promoted 1st Serg't, *vice* Hicks, furloughed..
John R. Suterfield...	"	"	Supposed to be discharged August 12, 1832....
Littleton, Daniel.....	"	"	
Corporals.			
George Bullock......	"	"	....
James Bullock	"	"	....
Isaac S. Casey.......	"	"	Furloughed August 7, 1832................
Isaac Deprist	"	"	Supposed to be discharged August 3, 1832....
Privates.			
Anderson, H. S......	"	"	Promoted................
Atchison, Wash'ton.	"	"	Supposed to be discharged August 3, 1832....
Atchison, Ignatius..	"	"	" " " " ....
Bingeman, William..	"	"	" " " " ....
Bradford, Joseph....	"	"	" " " " ....
Bruce, Marcus D....	"	"	" " " " ....
Buffington, Philip C.	"	"	" " " " ....
Baugh, John.........	"	"	
Carpenter, Sam'l W.	"	"	
Casey, Zadock......	"	"	Promoted and furloughed July 2, 1832.........
Darnall, John........	"	"	Supposed to be discharged August 3, 1832 ....
Deweze, William ...	"	"	
Elkin, Gazaway.....	"	"	....
Elkin, Robert........	"	"	....
Faulkenby, Isaac....	"	"	
Gastin, Wm. D......	"	"	Sick in tent.............
Holder, Willis B.....	"	"	
Hays, William B.....	"	"	Furloughed Aug. 6, 1832................
Ham, James.........	"	"	
Harlow, Joel.........	"	"	
Isam, John...........	"	"	Furloughed Aug. 7, 1832................

Name and Rank.	Residence.	Enrolled	Remarks.
		1832.	
Kitrel, David	Jefferson Co.	June 16	Supposed to be discharged August 3, 1832
Martin, James C	"	"	" " " " " 12
Miner, James F	"	"	" " " " " 3
McBrien, John E	"	"	
Newby, Hezekiah	"	"	Supposed to be discharged August 12, 1832
Owens, Joshua	"	"	
Owens, Peter	"	"	" " " " "
Parish, Wiott	"	"	
Pace, George W	"	"	Furloughed July 10, 1832, to care for wounded
Rhea, James	"	"	
Reynolds, Jacob	"	"	Supposed discharged Aug. 12, 1832
Tarnison, William	"	"	Discharged Aug. 12, 1832

Dead:

		1832	
Allen, William	Jefferson Co.	June 16	Killed at Kellogg's Grove June 25
Black, James	"	"	
Band, James B	"	"	
Bradford, Abner	"	"	
Meek, Robert	"	"	Wounded (?)
Randolph, Marcus	"	"	Wounded at Kellogg's Grove; furl'd June 16.

I certify on honor that Zadock Casey volunteered in my company as a private, and proceeded to Fort Wilbourn, where, on June 17, 1832, he was promoted to Paymaster of the Spy Battalion, and served as such to the end of the Indian war. He is therefore entitled to traveling pay as a private to Wilbourn from this place.

(Signed.)   JAMES BOWMAN,
MOUNT VERNON, May 16, 1833.   late Captain.

Company organized May 28, 1832. Marched for Hennepin June 12, 1832.
12 horses killed at Kellogg's Grove, June 25, 1832.
  8 wounded   "   "
  5 missing   "   "
  4 wounded   "   Recovered.

Mustered into service at Wilbourn June 17, 1832. Drew only one-half bushel corn per horse, since mustered into service. Drew only one ration per day for self since mustered into service. Furnished 8 days' rations each at Springfield.

DETACHMENT.

Capt. William S. Stephenson's Detachment

Of Illinois Mounted Volunteers, called into the service of the United States by the Governor of the State, by his order of May 15, 1832, from the date of its enrollment to the 2d day of August, 1832, when mustered out of service.

Name and Rank.	Residence.	Enrolled	Remarks.
First Lieutenant.		1832.	
James G. Corder	Franklin Co.	June 16.	
Sergeant.			
Abraham Ray	"	"	
Corporals.			
James G. Trovillian	"	"	Horse killed in battle; saddle and bridle lost.
William Crawford	"	"	Horse lost; supposed stolen by Indians
Privates.			
England, William	"	"	
Flannagan, Jas. W.	"	"	Horse and saddle lost
Galloway, Robert	"	"	Horse shot in battle; saddle, bridle, etc., lost
Harrison, Benj. N.	"	"	Horse lost in battle; also saddle and bridle.
Hutson, John	"	"	Horse shot in battle
Herold, Lewis	"	"	Horse killed in battle; saddle-bags, etc., lost
Ice, James			
Jones, Whitman	"	"	Horse killed in battle
Kirkpatrick, William	"	"	
Kirkpatrick, Edward	"	"	
Mutton, Wilson L	"	"	
Newman, Clayton	"	"	
Piper, William	"	"	
Polk, John	"	"	Horse lost in battle; also saddle and bridle.
Taylor, John	"	"	
Williams, Milton	"	"	Horse killed in battle; saddle, bridle, etc., lost

Capt. Charles Dunn's Company, Second Regiment, First Brigade, detached part thereof:

Name and Rank.	Residence.	Enrolled	Remarks.
Sergeants.		1832	
William T. Walters	Pope Co.	June 16	
James Modglin	"	"	
Samuel Roper	"	"	
Corporal.			
Ransom King	"	"	
Privates.			
Barger, Abraham S.	"	"	
Crane, Elkin	"	"	
Cooper, David	"	"	
Dyke, John	"	"	
Fulkeson, James	"	"	
Lauderdale, William	"	"	Horse lost in service in forced march
Walters, Thomas, Jr.	"	"	
Walters, William H.	"	"	
Whiteside, William	"	"	

Capt. Russell's Company, First Regiment, First Brigade:

Name and Rank.	Residence.	Enrolled	Remarks.
Second Lieutenant. Edward Vinson	Gallatin Co.	1832. June 16	
Privates. Birchum, Joseph	"	"	Horse lost in service in forced march
Dunn, Isham	"	"	
Hill, Allen	"	"	
Hampton, David	"	"	
Wise, William	"	"	Horse lost in service in forced march

Capt. Arman's Company, Second Regiment, First Brigade:

Name and Rank.	Residence.	Enrolled	Remarks.
Corporals. Alexander McCorkle	Pope Co.	1832 June 16.	
Thomas W. Tanner	"	"	Mare lost in service in forced march
Bugler. John Castner	"	"	
Privates. Alexander, William	"	"	
Bennet, Richard	"	"	Mare and saddle lost in service
Bayless, William H.	"	"	Absent on furlough
Dyer, Joel	"	"	Horse rode down in forced march, and left
Holoman, James	"	"	Horse lost in service, and saddle left
McMurphy, John	"	"	
Tanner, John A	"	"	
Williams, William	"	"	Horse badly lamed in service, and left
Wallace, Sampson	"	"	

Capt. West's Company, Second Regiment, First Brigade:

Name and Rank.	Residence.	Enrolled	Remarks.
Sergeants. James Youngblood	Franklin Co.	1832 June 16.	
James Parker	"	"	
Corporals. Aaron Youngblood	"	"	
Martin Asbridge	"	"	
Obediah Rich	"	"	
Privates. Cane, John	"	"	
Finney, William	"	"	
Groves, William	"	"	
Gibbons, William	"	"	
Keaster, Lewis	"	"	
Keaster, George	"	"	
Murphy, John	"	"	
Welty, Jacob	"	"	Horse crippled in forced march; saddle left
Youngblood, Sol	"	"	
Youngblood, Jon'th'n	"	"	

Capt. Holiday's Company, First Regiment, First Brigade:

Name and Rank.	Residence.	Enrolled	Remarks.
Private. Mason Wood	Gallatin Co.	1832. June 16	

Capt. Bowyer's Company, Second Regiment, First Brigade:

Name and Rank.	Residence.	Enrolled	Remarks.
Corporal. John Suleven	Franklin Co..	1832 June 16	
Sergeant. Elijah Estes	"	"	
Privates. Aikins, Walter L. Estes, John Hutson, Owen McClain, Aikin	" " " "	" " " "	

SECOND BRIGADE.

FIRST REGIMENT.

Capt. Thos. B. Ross' Company

1st Regiment, 2d Brigade, of Illinois Mounted Volunteers, called into the service of the United States, on the requisition of Gen. Atkinson, by the Governor's proclamation, dated May 15, 1832. Mustered out August 15, 1832, by order of Brig.-Gen. Atkinson.

Name and Rank.	Residence.	Enrolled	Remarks.
Captain.		1832.	
Thos. B. Ross	Coles Co	June 18	
First Lieutenant.			
James Shaw	"	"	
Second Lieutenants.			
Isaac Lewis	"	"	Resigned July 25, 1832
Thomas Sconce	"	"	Promoted 2d Lieutenant July 25, 1832
Sergeants.			
James Shaw, 1st	"	"	
Daniel Needham, 2d	"	"	Horse lost in service
Thos. Barnham, 3d	"	"	Furl. from Ft. Dickson Aug. 13; app. 3d Sergt.
Silas M. Parker, 3d	"	"	Disch. f'm Ft. Coscanang on Surg. cer. July 19
Samuel Doty, 4th	"	"	
Corporals.			[Coscanang.
Van S. Castin, 1st	"	"	Sup. disch. under Capt. Brimberry; left at Ft.
James James, 2d	"	"	
John Barnham, 4th	"	"	Furl. from Ft. Dickson Aug. 13; horse lost....
Privates.			
Austin, Nathan	"	"	
Adams, John J	"	"	[Coscanang.
Ashman, Hezek'h N	"	"	Sup. disch. under Capt. Brimberry; left at Ft.
Brown, James G	"	"	Furloughed June 22, 1832, from Ft. Wilbourn.
Barker, Thomas	"	"	Prom. 3d Sergt. July 25; furl. Aug. 13, Ft. Wil.
Bracken, Jesse	"	"	
Baker, Mark	"	"	Furloughed August 13 from Ft. Dickson
Carrico, John	"	"	Left sick at Ft. Dickson
Canterbury, Reuben	"	"	[Coscanang.
Custin, Harman	"	"	Sup. disch. under Capt. Brimberry; left at Ft.
Chadwell, John	"	"	
Duty, William	"	"	"
Duty, Richard	"	"	
Easton, John W	"	"	Furloughed at Ft. Dickson August 13, 1832
Frust, Samuel	"	"	Horse lost in service
Frazier, William	"	"	[Coscanang.
Frost, Henry	"	"	Sup. disch. under Capt. Brimberry; left at Ft.
Gordon, Patrick	"	"	
Gastin, Gibson	"	"	" " "
Gately, John G	Sangamon Co	"	" " "
Hart, Jonathan	Coles Co	"	" " "

SECOND BRIGADE.

Name and Rank.	Residence.	Enrolled	Remarks.
		1832.	
Halfhill, Abram	Coles Co	June 18	
Hays, Thomas	"	"	Lost 1 pistol in service, worth $5
Kellogg, Samuel	"	"	Disch. f'm Ft. Coscanang on Surg. cer. July 19
Lester, Segier H	"	"	(Coscanang.
Logan, William	"	"	Sup. disch. under Capt. Brimberry; left at Ft.
Odell, Isaac	"	"	" " "
Phelps, Chas. D	"	"	
Parker, Nathaniel	"	"	
Parker, Benj., Jr	"	"	
Parker, Jonathan	"	"	
Riley, Thomas	"	"	
Sluder, Thomas C	"	"	
Scott, Andrew	"	"	
Stone, James H	"	"	
Shin, T. G. M	"	"	
Vincent, Obediah	"	"	
Vanwinkle, Green L	"	"	
White, William M	"	"	
Waldrope, John	Clark Co	"	
Williams, Henry	Coles Co	"	
Williams, Horace	"	"	Sick; furl. from Ft. Wilbourn June 22, 1832
Waldrope, William	"	"	Furloughed from Kellogg's Grove Aug. 11
Woodall, David	"	"	" " Ft. Williams June 22.
Young, John	"	"	

The company was organized and marched for the place of rendezvous on the 4th day of June, 1832. Drew one-half bushel corn per man, forage, while in service. One bucket, one ax, one coffee pot, two tin cups, two frying pans, two tin pans, public property, lost while in service.

(Signed.)   THOS. B. ROSS, Capt

N. B.—Two hundred and eighty rations have bee drawn for this company for traveling home from place of being mustered out of service.

(Signed.)   * THOS. B. ROSS, Capt.,

Capt. Samuel Brimberry's Company

1st Regiment, 2d Brigade of Illinois Mounted Volunteers, called into the service of the United States, on the requisition of Gen. Atkinson, by the Governor's proclamation dated May 15, 1832. Mustered out Aug. 15, 1832, by order of Brig.-Gen. Atkinson.

Name and Rank.	Residence.	Enrolled	Remarks.
First Lieutenant.		1832	
Philip B. Smith	Edgar Co	June 19	
Sergeants.			
James Adams	"	"	
William Craig	"	"	Ordered to Dixon; supposed mustered out
William Morgan	"	"	Absent by order Gen. Atkinson
John Morgan	"	"	Horse and equipage lost
Corporals.			
John Ripple, 1st	"	"	
John Young, 4th	"	"	
Privates.			
Anglin, Valentine	"	"	
Cronnick, Philip	"	"	
Crist, John	"	"	
Clapp, Joseph	"	"	
Charters, Duncan M	"	"	
Craig, Isaac N	"	"	Ordered to Dixon; supposed mustered out
Craig, Robert	"	"	" " "
Craig, Alexander	"	"	
Elledge, Isaac	"	"	Absent with leave; supposed mustered out
Ferrell, John	"	"	
Ferrell, William	"	"	
Goodman, William	"	"	
Grinder, Henderson	"	"	

Name and Rank.	Residence.	Enrolled	Remarks.
		1832.	
Henson, Robert	Edgar Co.	June 19	
Jones, Richard	"	"	
Jones, Thomas	"	"	Ordered to Dixon; supposed mustered out ..
Redmon, Greenbury	"	"	
Wells, Elijah	"	"	
Walls, James	"	"	
Williams, Samuel	"	"	Mare lost July 27, 1832
Wells, David A	"	"	

Moses Anglin and Joseph Andrews, privates of this company, were mustered into the service of the United States on the 19th day of June, 1832; mounted, armed and equipped, and on the 21st day of June were discharged by Brig.-Gen. Atkinson, being out of health. Their names were omitted on this muster roll by oversight, and they are fully entitled to pay to 21st of June, 1832.

(Signed.)   SAMUEL BRIMBERRY, Capt.,   (Signed.)
                                                   M. K. ALEXANDER,
                                                 Brig.-Gen. 2d Brig. Ill. Mil.

N. B.—The officers and men of this company have drawn only one ration each per day, and one-half bushel of corn forage each, during the campaign, and rations were furnished by each individual from home to Hennepin, on the Illinois river.

N. B.—This company was organized on the 10th day of May, 1832, and started from Paris, Edgar county, on the 4th day of June, 1832, to Hennepin, to rendezvous there on the 10th, by the Governor's orders. From there ordered to Wilbourn to rendezvous, on the 15th day of June, 1832. On the 17th were formed into regiment. On the 18th of June formed into a brigade, and on the 19th day of June, 1832, mustered into service.

Drew 10 days' traveling rations.

Capt. Isaac Sanford's Company

1st Regt., 2d Brigade of Illinois Mounted Volunteers, called into the service of the United States, on the requisition of Gen. Atkinson, by the Governor's proclamation dated May 15, 1832. This company was organized, etc., in Edgar county, May 10, 1832. Mustered out August 15, 1832, by order of Brig.-Gen. Atkinson.

Name and Rank.	Residence.	Enrolled	Remarks.
Captain.		1832.	
Isaac Sanford	Edgar Co.	June 19	
First Lieutenant.			
William Runyan	"	"	
Second Lieutenant.			
Aloysius Brown	"	"	Furloughed Aug. 4, 1832
Sergeants.			
Thomas J. Buntain	"	"	
George G. Boord	"	"	Mare and equipage lost
Charles Bodine	"	"	
Alfred VanHoutan	"	"	Furloughed Aug. 4, 1832; lost his horse
Corporals.			
John D. Bozeith	"	"	July 21, 1832, ordered to Dixon's Ferry
John Smith	"	"	" " " "
Wineson Robertson	"	"	
James Cummings	"	"	Furloughed Aug. 4, 1832
Privates.			
Allen, Harding C.	"	"	
Buntain, Andrew E.	"	"	July 21, 1832, ordered to Dixon's Ferry
Breeden, Fielder	"	"	
Bradshaw, Elias	"	"	July 21, 1832, ordered to Dixon's Ferry
Boord, Mezaldue H.	"	"	" " " "
Cupps, George W.	"	"	
Cowan, John	"	"	
Camp, Abisha	"	"	Mare lost, lamed and rendered useless
Cummings, John	"	"	Furloughed Aug. 4, 1832

SECOND BRIGADE.

Name and Rank.	Residence.	Enrolled	Remarks.
		1832.	
Davis, Abraham	Edgar Co.	June 19	Left sick at Fort Coscanang, July 10, 1832
Drummond, Henry	"	"	
Davis, James	"	"	July 21, 1832, ordered to Dixon's Ferry
Ewing, James	"	"	
Edwards, Allemus	"	"	July 21, 1832, ordered to Dixon's Ferry
Ewing, George	"	"	
Furnish, Thomas	"	"	July 21, 1832, ordered to Dixon's Ferry
Foster, Arthur	"	"	Furloughed Aug. 4, 1832
Foster, John	"	"	July 21, 1832, ordered to Dixon's Ferry
Fuller, John	"	"	" " "
Gillepcy, James	"	"	
Harding, George	"	"	
Hunter, Andrew	"	"	July 21, 1832, ordered to Dixon's Ferry
Hollingsworth, John	"	"	Lost one pistol, appraised at $3
Hunsacker, Benj'min	"	"	Furloughed Aug. 9, 1832
Hill, John	"	"	
Hawkins, James	"	"	
Hunter, Spencer R.	"	"	Sick
Jourdan, Hartwell	"	"	
Kehoe, Young	"	"	
Knight, John	"	"	
Knight, Joseph	"	"	
Lowery, Jacob D.	"	"	
Lewis, William	"	"	
Martin, Chas. K.	"	"	
Murphy, W. C.	"	"	July 21, 1832, ordered to Dixon's Ferry
McIntire, Lucius	"	"	Furloughed Aug. 4, 1832
McCully, Henry	"	"	
Montgomery, Wm.	"	"	
Morrison, David	"	"	
Martain, John	"	"	Name omit'd on original roll; on duty f'm start
Macy, Samuel	"	"	
Nolle, Thomas	"	"	July 21, 1832, ordered to Dixon's Ferry
Pownall, George C.	"	"	
Percell, James C.	"	"	Furloughed Aug. 4, 1832; lost horse and gun
Percell, Edward	"	"	
Ray, Martain	"	"	Furloughed Aug., 1832
Ray, Isaac	"	"	
Ray, Jesse	"	"	July 21, 1832, ordered to Dixon's Ferry
Ray, James	"	"	
Ray, William	"	"	Left at Dixon's Ferry, June 25, 1832
Ross, William	"	"	July 21, 1832, ordered to Dixon's Ferry
Reed, George	"	"	
Reed, William	"	"	
Ripple, Daniel	"	"	
Ripple, Michael	"	"	
Stump, Francis	"	"	
Taylor, Joseph	"	"	
Taylor, Gabril N.	"	"	
Ferrill, John	"	"	
VanHoutan, Isaac	"	"	
VanHoutan, Wm.	"	"	
Wilson, Larkin	"	"	
Wilson, Reason	"	"	

Record of events which may be necessary or useful for future reference at the War Department, or for present information:

N. B.—This company was organized on the 10th day of May, 1832, and started from Paris, Edgar county, on the 4th day of June, 1832, to Hennepin, to rendezvous there on the 10th, by the Governor's orders. From thence ordered to Wilbourn to rendezvous on the 15th day of June, 1832; on the 17th of June were formed into regiments; on the 18th of June formed into a brigade, and on the 19th day of June, 1832, mustered into service of the United States.

Rations have been drawn for the company at this place to return home, viz: Ten days, up to and including 25th day of August, 1832. I also believe, by information, that those men ordered to Dixon's are discharged under Capt. Brimberry.

Received, also, of the United States, 11 halters, 4 tent cloths; 3 of the best cloths have been returned, the other tent worn out or lost. All the halters worn out or lost.

All of which I certify on honor, at Dixon's Ferry, August 15, 1832.

(Signed.)   ISAAC SANFORD.

The officers and men of the company have drawn only one ration each per day, and one-half bushel corn forage each, during the campaign, and rations were furnished by each individual from home to Hennepin, on the Illinois river. All of which I certify on honor the 15th day of August, 1832.

(Signed.)   ISAAC SANFORD, Capt.

Capt. Robert Griffin's Company

Of the 1st Regiment, 2d Brigade. Illinois Mounted Volunteers, army of the United States, called into the service of the United States, on the requisition of Gen. Atkinson, by the Governor's proclamation, dated 1832; mustered out August 15, 1832, by order of Brig.-Gen. Atkinson.

Name and Rank.	Residence.	Enrolled	Remarks.
Captain. Robert Griffin	Edgar Co.	1832. June 19	Two buckets, ax, tub, lost, Mud Lake to Dixon
First Lieutenant. George Moke	" "	" "	One halter lost on the march
Second Lieutenant. Wm. N. Redman	" "	" "	Detailed to Dixon; supposed to be discharged
Sergeants.			
Jesse Raper	" "	" "	
George Phillips	" "	" "	Detailed to Dixon; supposed to be discharged
Edmund Minor	" "	" "	Absent with leave
George Redman	" "	" "	" " supposed to be discharged
Corporals.			
James McCoy	" "	" "	
Wm. P. Hicklin	" "	" "	Absent with leave; 1 horse lost
Wm. H. Faulkner	" "	" "	
Addison M. Qurvy	" "	" "	Absent with leave; supposed to be discharged
Privates.			
Alexander, Edmund	" "	" "	Absent without leave; supposed discharged.
Bryant, William	" "	" "	
Craig, John	" "	" "	Horse and equipments lost at Ft. Wilbourn.
Coe, James	Vermilion Co.	" "	Detailed to Dixon; supposed to be discharged
Clapp, Levi	Edgar Co.	" "	
Darnal, Wm.	" "	" "	Horse, etc., lost; disch. on Surgeon's certif.
Downs, Abraham	" "	" "	Absent without leave
Davis, Samuel	" "	" "	Furloughed August 13, 1832.
Dick, Ferdinand	" "	" "	Detailed to Dixon; supposed to be discharged
Elledge, William	" "	" "	" " Ft. Hamilton to hunt horses
Flood, William	" "	" "	
Fears, William	" "	" "	One camp kettle lost on forced march
Flack, James	" "	" "	Furlough
Furness, John	" "	" "	Detailed to Dixon; 1 horse lost
Green, William	" "	" "	
Harbaugh, Jacob	" "	" "	
Hensley, George W.	" "	" "	Equipage lost
Jones, Thomas	" "	" "	Absent without leave; supposed discharged
Lacksu, Tobias J.	" "	" "	
Lamb, Arthur	" "	" "	
May, William	" "	" "	Horse and equipage lost
Martin, Moses	" "	" "	Left at Fort Wilbourn, sick
Nobles, Jonathan B.	" "	" "	
Owsley, Henry	" "	" "	
Patterson, Jonathan	" "	" "	Detailed to Ft. Dixon; 1 horse, etc., lost
Packet, John	" "	" "	" " Dixon; supposed to be discharged
Parish, James	" "	" "	
Rockhold, Ezekiel	" "	" "	Horses and equipage lost
Stewart, Joseph H.	" "	" "	Detailed to Dixon; supposed to be discharged
Sizemon, Martin	" "	" "	Absent without leave
Southerland, R. B.	" "	" "	
Snyder, William	" "	" "	Horse and equipage lost
Smith, Samuel	" "	" "	
Tennery, Isaac H.	" "	" "	
Tennery, Patrick C.	" "	" "	
Thompson, John S.	" "	" "	Absent without leave
Tade, John	" "	" "	Detailed to Dixon; supposed to be discharged
Wayne, George W.	" "	" "	
Wright, Joseph	" "	" "	

N. B.—This company was organized on the 10th day of May, 1832, and started from Paris, Edgar county, on the 4th day of June, 1832, to Hennepin, to rendezvous there on the 10th, by the Governor's orders. From thence, ordered to Wilbourn, to rendezvous there on the 15th of June, 1832. On the 17th of June, were formed into Regiments. On the 18th of June, formed into Brigades; and, on the 19th day of June, 1832, mustered into service. Drew ten days' traveling rations.

N. B.—The officers and men of this company have drawn only one ration each per day, and one-half bushel of corn forage, each, during the campaign; and rations were furnished by each individual from home to Hennepin, on the Illinois river.

SECOND BRIGADE. 33

Capt. Jonathan Mayo's Company

Of the 1st Regiment, 2d Brigade, of Illinois Mounted Volunteers, called into the service of the United States, on the requisition of Gen. Atkinson, by the Governor's proclamation, dated ——, 1832; mustered out August 15, 1832, by order of Brig.-Gen. Atkinson.

Name and Rank.	Residence.	Enrolled	Remarks.
Captain. Jonathan Mayo	Edgar Co.	1832. June 19.	
First Lieutenant. Edward Y. Russell	"	"	Absent with leave, Aug. 4, 1832
Second Lieutenant. John S. McConkey	"	"	
Sergeants.			
James Buchannon	"	"	Appointed 1st Sergeant June 19, 1832
David Crozier	"	"	
Daniel Spencer	"	"	Horse lost
Joseph G. Barkley	"	"	Appointed 4th Sergeant June 19, 1832
Corporals.			
Simon Cameron	"	"	
Tracy Wheeler	"	"	
James Bailey	"	"	Ordered to Dixon's; supposed discharged
William N. Shaw	"	"	Appointed 4th Corporal June 19, 1832
Privates.			
Alexander, Wash'ton	"	"	
Bradley, John C	"	"	Horse lost
Burch, Newell	"	"	Supposed to be discharged; horse lost
Bond, William	"	"	" " " ; two horses lost
Bassford, Jonath'n S	"	"	Supposed to be discharged
Certer, Willard	"	"	
Dezar, George	"	"	
Dill, John	"	"	
Dill, Milton M	"	"	Supposed to be discharged
Doughertee, Thos. H	"	"	
Elder, Hugh M	"	"	
Evans, Thomas	"	"	
Buff, Calvin H	"	"	Absent with leave July 8, 1832
Hobbs, Thomas	"	"	" " " Aug. 4, 1832
Hobbs, Enos	"	"	
Jones, Samuel	"	"	
Lowry, Reuben	"	"	Horse lost
Lycan, Jacob J	"	"	
Morgan, Wells	"	"	
Martin, Enos	"	"	
Morgan, Thomas	"	"	
Montgonera, Alex	"	"	Supposed to be discharged
Matthews, John	"	"	
Pence, Emanuel	"	"	
Phillips, William	"	"	
Penson, Thomas	"	"	Absent with leave Aug. 4, 1832
Rhea, Robert M	"	"	
Rice, Hawkins	"	"	
Rice, Lewis	"	"	
Scott, Daniel	"	"	
Summerville, John	"	"	
Sprague, Harrison	"	"	Supposed to be discharged
Scott, Matthew R	"	"	
Scott, Joseph	"	"	
Sumpter, Alexander	"	"	Horse lost
Sumpter, Abraham	"	"	Supposed to be discharged; horse lost
Trimble, Green C	"	"	
Vance, William B	"	"	
Vance, Joseph	"	"	
Wilson, John	"	"	Horse lost
Wyatt, Augustus B	"	"	
Welch, Isaiah	"	"	Rifle bursted
Welch, Abraham	"	"	
Whalen, Patrick	"	"	Absent with leave, Aug. 4, 1832
Whitley, William	"	"	Transferred; appointed Hosp. Stew'd June 19

—3

Resigned:

Name and Rank.	Residence.	Enrolled	Remarks.
First Sergeant. Parker, Leonard B.	Edgar Co.	1832. June 19	Appointed Quartermaster June 19, 1832.

The officers and men of this company have drawn only one ration each per day, and one-half bushel of corn forage each during the campaign, and rations were furnished by each individual from Edgar county to Hennepin.
(Signed.)   J. MAYO, CAPT.

This company was organized at Paris, Edgar county, on the 10th day of May, 1832; took up the line of march for Hennepin on the 4th of June, the place where it was ordered to rendezvous, and reached that place on the 11th of June, and was mustered into the United States service at Wilbourn on June 19, 1832.

Ten days' rations are required, 8 drawn, 2 to be drawn.
(Signed.)   J. MAYO, CAPT.

William Whitley served till the 19th of July, when he engaged in the wagon train. He is entitled to pay till July 19, 1832.
(Signed.)   J MAYO, CAPT.

CAPT. ROYAL A. NOTT'S COMPANY

Of the 1st Regiment, 2d Brigade, of Illinois Mounted Volunteers, called into the service of the United States, on the requisition of General Atkinson, by the Governor's proclamation, dated 15th of May, 1832. This company was organized in Clark county, May 31, 1832. Mustered out August 15, 1832, by order of Brig.-Gen. Atkinson.

Name and Rank.	Residence.	Enrolled	Remarks.
Captain. Royal A. Nott	Clark Co	1832. June 19	
First Lieutenant. Daniel Poorman	"	"	
Second Lieutenant. George W. Young	"	"	July 21, 1832, ord'd to Dixon's; disch.; lost mare
Sergeants.			
Stephen Archer	"	"	
John Fears	"	"	
James Lockard	"	"	
Oliver C. Lawwill	"	"	
Corporals.			
William T. McClure	"	"	
James Dunlap	"	"	July 21, 1852, ordered to Dixon's; since disch.
Noah Beauchamp	"	"	
John W. Thompson	"	"	Lost sorrel mare, saddle, bridle and blanket.
Privates.			
Archer, Jesse K.	"	"	
Boone, Daniel	"	"	Lost horse; strayed away
Burk, Samuel	"	"	Lost horse; ordered to Dixon's; since disch.
Bostick, William	"	"	
Berry, George	"	"	
Bennett, Thomas F.	"	"	
Cooper, Theophelos	"	"	Lost his horse
Cowen, Joel	"	"	
Cooper, Chalkley I.	"	"	July 21, 1832, ord'd to Dixon's; disch.; lost mare
Crip, Jeremiah	"	"	
Chenewith, Martin L.	"	"	
DeHart, Alex. H.	"	"	July 21, 1832, ordered to Dixon's; discharged.
DeHart, Lorenzo D.	"	"	
Davis, Alhanan H.	"	"	Lost his mare
Davis, Daniel	"	"	
Dolsen, Samuel	"	"	Furloughed at Prairie du Chien Aug. 9, 1832.
Fleming, Andrew	"	"	July 1832, ordered to Dixon's; discharged.
Fanin, Ahalls	"	"	Horse worn out and left at Dixon's Ferry
Fears, Phineas	"	"	Lost his blanket

SECOND BRIGADE.

Name and Rank.	Residence.	Enrolled	Remarks.
		1832.	
Grove, Martin	Clark Co	June 19.	
Grant, John B.	"	"	
Henderson, James E.	"	"	
Henderson, Hez. A.	"	"	
Johnson, Sandford	"	"	
Kenny, Moses	"	"	July 21, 1832, ordered to Dixon's Ferry; disch.
Lafferty, Marshall	"	"	
Lathrop, Artemus	"	"	
McCabe, William	"	"	
McCabe, John	"	"	
McGuire, John	"	"	
Minor, Thomas	"	"	
Ogden, Benjamin	"	"	Sick and furloughed June 21, 1832
Ogden, Nehemiah	"	"	
Peters, Absalom O.	"	"	
Poorman, Samuel	"	"	July 21, 1832, ordered to Dixon's Ferry; disch.
Prero, Samuel	"	"	Furloughed at Prairie du Chien Aug. 7, 1832
Prero, Ira	"	"	
Payne, Ebenezer	"	"	July 21, 1832, ordered to Dixon's Ferry; disch.
Squires, Lyman R.	"	"	
Sharp, Elon	"	"	Lost his blanket
Shaw, James	"	"	
Stafford, Elijah	"	"	July 21, 1832, ordered to Dixon's Ferry; disch.
Van Winkle, John	"	"	Lost his blanket
Waters, John	"	"	Lost his horse
Wade, Thomas	"	"	
White, Thomas	"	"	Left his mare. etc., at Dixon's Ferry

This company of Volunteers assembled in Darwin, Clark county, Illinois, on the 31st day of May, 1832, and then and there elected officers, and from that place marched on the third day of June, 1832, and under the Governor's order rendezvoused at Hennepin, on the Illinois river, 11th day of June; next day marched and arrived at Fort Wilbourne, Lower Rapid, Illinois river, and the company was mustered into the United States service on the 19th day of said month of June, 1832. Rations have been drawn for the company at this place to return home, to-wit: fourteen days, up to and including the 28th day of August, 1832.

(Signed.)   ROYAL A. NOTT, CAPT.

AUGUST 15, 1832.

This company's officers and men have drawn one ration of provisions each per day only, and one peck of corn forage for horses each, and no more, during the campaign, and each individual furnished his own rations from home to Hennepin, on the Illinois river.

All of which I certify on honor.

(Signed.)   ROYAL A. NOTT,

AUGUST 15, 1832.   Commanding the Company.

1386804

SECOND REGIMENT.

Capt. Alex. M. Houston's Company

Of the 2d Regiment, 2d Brigade, of Illinois Mounted Volunteers, called into the service of the United States, on the requisition of Gen. Atkinson, by the Governor's proclamation, dated May 15, 1832. Mustered out August 15, 1832, by order of Brig.-Gen. Atkinson.

Name and Rank.	Residence.	Enrolled	Remarks.
Captain.		1832.	
Alex M. Houston	Crawford Co.	June 19	
First Lieutenant.			
Geo. W. Lagon	"	"	Leave of absence by Gen. Atkinson; Aug. 4.
Second Lieutenant.			
James Boatright	"	"	
Sergeants.			
O. F. D. Hampton	"	"	[Dixon, July 10; sup. furl. Ord. on command with baggage wagon to Ft.
Levi Harper	"	"	Leave of absence from Ft. Hamilton, Aug. 4.
David Porter	"	"	
James Cristy	"	"	
Corporals.			
Cornelius Doherty	"	"	[smith's Co.; discharged. Ord. to Ft. Dixon; sup. att'ch'd to Capt. High-
James F. Stark	"	"	[smith's Co; discharged.
Joseph Jones	"	"	Ord. to Ft. Dixon; sup. att'ch'd to Capt. High-
Rivers Heath	"	"	Furl. Ft. Wilbourn, return home, sick, June 21
Bugler.			
Francis Waldrop	"	"	
Privates.			
Baugher, Geo. W	"	"	[smith's Co.; discharged. Ord. to Ft. Dixon; sup. att'ch'd to Capt. High-
Brathares, Blanton	"	"	Furl. from Ft. Crawford to go home; app'ted
Bogard, John	"	"	[Corporal June 25.
Baker, Andrew	"	"	
Boatright, Alex	"	"	Furl. at Ft. Hamilton, to go home, Aug. 1.
Cruse, Samuel	"	"	
Danforth, Silas L	"	"	Furl. at Ft. Hamilton, to go home, Aug. 4.
Doughton, Geo. R	"	"	Ord. to Ft. Dixon; sup. att'ch'd to Capt. High-
Fitch, Edwin	"	"	[smith's Co.; discharged.
Fowler, Henry	"	"	
Goodwin, John	"	"	
Goodwin, Silas	"	"	
Grinton, Robert	"	"	
Hutton, John	"	"	[smith's Co.; discharged.
Hackett, Joseph	"	"	Ord. to Ft. Dixon; sup. att'ch'd to Capt. High-
Hackett, John A	"	"	App. Q. M. Sergt. July 10....[smith's Co.; dis.
Hawkins, William	"	"	Ord. to Ft. Dixon; sup. att'ch'd to Capt. High-
Houne, John	"	"	Absented himself July 6, 1832.
Kitchell, Wickliffe	"	"	Furl. to return home, July 10, at Ft. Cosgrum.
Kuykendall, James	"	"	[Dixon July 10; sup. furl.
Logan, Alex	"	"	Ord. on command with baggage wagon to Ft.
Lackey, Matthew	"	"	Absented himself July 6....[smith's Co.; dis.
McCoy, John	"	"	Ord. to Ft. Dixon; sup. att'ch'd to Capt. High-
Nelly, Johnson	"	"	
Porter, Robert	"	"	
Potter, Wm	"	"	[smith's Co.; discharged.
Pearson, Wm	"	"	Ord. to Ft. Dixon; sup. att'ch'd to Capt. High-
Pearson, Joseph	"	"	"
Pearson Edwin	"	"	"
Phelps, Zalmon	"	"	"

SECOND BRIGADE.

Name and Rank.	Residence.	Enrolled	Remarks.
		1832.	
Shaw, Samuel			Furl. at Ft. Dodge, to return home, Aug. 9....
Stewart, John			............[smith's Co.; discharged.
Vandeventer, Jno. F.			Ord. to Ft. Dixon; sup. att'ch'd to Capt. High-
Wilson, Vastin			Prom. Q. M. Sergt. June 20; ord. on command
Walters, Jacob			............[with baggage wagons; sup. dis.

Organized the 12th of May, 1832; marched from home on the 2d day of June, by order; mustered into service June 19, 1832; drew two days' rations from the 16th inst.; forage drawn during service, one-half bushel corn for each horse; officers drew one ration each.

CAPT. JOHN ARNOLD'S COMPANY

Of the 2d Regiment of the 2d Brigade of Illinois Volunteers, called into the service of the United States, on the requisition of Gen. Atkinson, by the Governor's proclamation dated May 15, 1832. Mustered out August 15, 1832. This company was organized in Wabash county, May 12, 1832.

Name and Rank.	Residence.	Enrolled	Remarks.
Captain.		1832.	
James Arnold	Wabash Co.	June 19	
First Lieutenant.			
George Danforth	" "	" "	
Second Lieutenant.			
Samuel Fisher	" "	" "	Absent with leave............
Sergeants.			
Mitchel C. Minnis	" "	" "	
Hiram Couch	" "	" "	
Mathias Leatherland	" "	" "	Absent with leave............
John A. Dodds	" "	" "	" " " lost mare; appraised at $50
Corporals.			
Solomon Frear	" "	" "	Absent with leave............
John Golden	" "	" "	" " " ....
Ira Keen	" "	" "	" " " ....
Wesley Woods	" "	" "	
Privates.			
Besley, James	" "	" "	Absent with leave............
Bass, Dolphin	" "	" "	
Buchannan, John W.	" "	" "	
Buchannan, Jos. O.	" "	" "	Absent with leave............
Buchannan, Henry R.	" "	" "	" " " lost mare; appraised at $52
Brines, Jefferson	" "	" "	
Dodds, Joseph M.	" "	" "	Absent with leave............
Godda, John	" "	" "	" " "
Garner, James	" "	" "	" " " lost horse; appraised at $60
Golden, William	" "	" "	" " "
Hull, Philip	" "	" "	
Hoyt, Jonathan S.	" "	" "	Absent with leave............
Hobbert, Henry	" "	" "	
Keen, Dennis	" "	" "	
Miller, Barton S.	" "	" "	Absent with leave............
McMillen, James	" "	" "	" " "
Ochletree, John	" "	" "	" " "
Parmeter, Isaac	" "	" "	
Pixley, Isaac	" "	" "	
Ridgely, William	" "	" "	Absent with leave............
Reel, Henry R.	" "	" "	" " " lost mare; appraised at $50
Sanford, Thomas	" "	" "	
Sanford, Jacob	" "	" "	
Smith, John O.	" "	" "	Absent with leave............
Turner, Abner	" "	" "	" " " lost mare; appraised at $65
Utter, John	" "	" "	
Vanderhoof, Philip	" "	" "	" " "
Woods, Jeremiah	" "	" "	

Name and Rank.	Residence.	Enrolled	Remarks.
		1832.	
Wear, Thomas	Wabash Co.	June 19.	Absent with leave
Wear, Harvey	" "	" "	" " " "
Winders, Warren	" "	" "	
Wright, Robbert	" "	" "	

N. B.—The absentees are supposed to have been mustered out of service at Fort Dickson, under Capt. Jordan.

DETACHMENT OF CAPT. ELIAS JORDAN'S COMPANY

Of the 2d Regiment, 2d Brigade, of Illinois Mounted Volunteers, called into the service of the United States, on the requisition of Gen. Atkinson, by the Governor's proclamation dated May 15, 1832. The company was organized in Wabash county, May 12, 1832. Mustered out August 15, 1832. Enlisted for 90 days.

Name and Rank.	Residence.	Enrolled	Remarks.
First Lieutenant.		1832.	
James Kennerly	Wabash Co.		
Second Lieutenant.			
John N. Barnett	" "		On furlough Aug. 7
Sergeant.			
James Grayson, 4th.	" "		
Corporal.			
Zach. Wilson, 2d	" "		On furlough Aug. 7
Privates.			
Barnett, Benj. F	" "		
Carlton, Robt	" "		
Campbell, Robert	" "		
Campbell, Patrick S.	" "		
Fortney, Daniel	" "		On furlough Aug. 7, and horse lost
Grayson, Wm	" "		
Hood, Albert	" "		On furlough Aug. 7
Levellett, Joseph	" "		
Painter, Joseph	" "		
Summer, Thomas	" "		
Summer, Joseph	" "		

DETACHMENT OF CAPT. HIGHSMITH'S COMPANY,

Organized May 1, 1832. Mustered out August 15, 1832.

Name and Rank.	Residence.	Enrolled	Remarks.
Sergeants.		1832.	
Beverly B. Piper, 1st	Crawford Co.		Elected 1st Sergeant June 22, 1832
John A. Christy, 4th	" "		
Corporal.			
Jackson James, 3d	" "		Elected 3d Corporal June 23, 1832
Privates.			
Attison, David M	" "		
Barrick, John	" "		
Condrey, James	" "		
Gregg, John	" "		

SECOND BRIGADE.

Name and Rank.	Residence.	Enrolled	Remarks.
		1832.	
Grise, Wm. R.	Crawford Co.		
Johnson, Hiram	"		
Levitt, William	"		
Myers, John L.	"		
Myers, Andrew W.	"		
Parker, John, Sr.	"		
Parker, Wm	"		
Simons, Robert	"		
Vaunriuch, Jacob	"		

I certify that Jason D. Jones was mustered into the service of the United States in my company on June 19, 1832, and was honorably discharged from the service by Gen. Atkinson, on June 20 or 21. His name was omitted from the muster-roll by oversight.

(Signed.)   ELIAS JORDAN, Capt.

Mustered into service June 19, 1832.

Detachment of Capt. Barns' Company

Of 2d Regiment, 2d Brigade of Illinois Mounted Volunteers, called into the service of the United States on the requisition of Gen. Atkinson, by the Governor's proclamation dated May 15, 1832. This company was organized in Lawrence county, Illinois, May 5, 1832. Mustered out August 15, 1832.

Name and Rank.	Residence.	Enrolled	Remarks.
		1832.	
Second Lieutenant.			
Daniel Morris	Lawrence Co.	June 19	Lost horse, reduced, worn out and left
Sergeants.			
John L. Bass, 1st	"	"	
Tho. McDonald, 2d	"	"	Lost horse, etc.; furloughed Aug. 7
Corporal.			
Jas. Buchanan, 2d	"	"	
Privates.			
Berton, Archibald	"	"	
Bass, Richard	"	"	
Crews, James	"	"	
Christy, Joseph R.	"	"	Furl. Aug. 2, to return with wounded men
Dunlap, Samuel	"	"	Promoted Adjutant July 9
Gallaher, Bonapart.	"	"	On extra duty at Beaughonan June 19
Gaddy, James	"	"	
Livingstone, John	"	"	
Moor, Edward	"	"	
Montgomery, John	"	"	Horse lost
Moaler, Peyton	"	"	Lost horse and equipage, and furloughed
McCleave, Benjamin	"	"	
Organ, Daniel	"	"	Lost mare; furl.; since disch'd; supposed to be must'd out under Capt. Highsmith
Lewis, Thomas T.	"	"	
Pollard, James W.	"	"	
Richards, Joshua	"	"	
Turner, Thomas I.	"	"	
Turner, John	"	"	
Turner, E. D. M.	"	"	
Taylor, George W.	"	"	
Walden, John	"	"	

This company was organized in Lawrence county, Illinois, on May 5, 1832. Marched from there June 2, 1832. Arrived at Springfield June 9. Mustered into U. S. service June 19, 1832.

THIRD REGIMENT.

Capt. Solomon Hunter's Company

Of 3d Regiment, 2d Brigade of Illinois Mounted Volunteers, called into the service of the United States, on the requisition of Gen. Atkinson, by the Governor's proclamation dated May 15, 1832. This company was organized in the county of Edwards May 5, 1832. Mustered out Aug. 15, 1832, by order of Brig.-Gen. Atkinson.

Name and Rank.	Residence.	Enrolled	Remarks.
Captain.		1832.	
Solomon Hunter	Edwards Co.	June 19	Sword broke and lost in service
First Lieutenant.			
William Carrabaugh	"	"	
Second Lieutenant.			
John S. Rotrammel	"	"	
Sergeants.			
Thomas Jaggers	"	"	Ordered to Dixon's Ferry July 21, '32; disch'd
Joseph McCreary	"	"	Left sick at Ft. Wilbourn June 20, 1832
John Hocking	"	"	
John Brown	"	"	Ordered to Dixon's Ferry July 21, '32; disch'd
Corporals.			
William H. Harper	"	"	
Zach. Bottinghouse	"	"	Furloughed Aug. 7, 1832
Hugh Mounts	"	"	
James N. Harper	"	"	Ordered to Dixon's Ferry July 21, '32; disch'd
Privates.			
Bottinghouse, Dani'l	"	"	Left sick at Fort Wilbourn. June 20, 1832
Birkett, Thomas	"	"	
Batson, William	"	"	Ordered to Dixon's Ferry July 21, '32; disch'd
Birkett, Samuel	"	"	
Charles, Solomon	"	"	Ord'd to Dixon's July 21, 32; disch'd; lost mare
Case, John	"	"	
Curtis, George	"	"	Ordered to Dixon's Ferry July 21, '32; disch'd
Chism, Elisha	"	"	
Dodd, Milton	"	"	Ordered to Dixon's Ferry July 21, '32; disch'd
Dorothy, Robert	"	"	
Everly, Nimrod	"	"	Ordered to Ft. Wilbourn June 25, '32; disch'd.
Emmerson, Alan	"	"	Promoted to Sergeant June 20, 1832.
Fortner, John	"	"	Left sick at Fort Wilbourn, June 20, 1832
Fortner, Henry	"	"	Left on foot at Ft. Wilbourn June 20, 1832
Frazer, Hiram	"	"	
Hamilton, William	"	"	Furloughed Aug. 7, 1832
Hensley, Charles	"	"	Left sick at Fort Wilbourn June 21, 1832
Hobson, Dison	"	"	Ordered to Dixon's July 21, 1832; since disch'd
Jones, William E.	"	"	
Jennings, James	"	"	
McKinney, William	"	"	Ordered to Dixon's Ferry July 21, 32; disch'd.
McCrackin, Hugh	"	"	Left sick at Fort Wilbourn June 20, 1832
Mebrose, William	"	"	Furloughed Aug. 4, 1832
Michels, Sumner	"	"	
Morris, Miles	"	"	Ordered to Dixon's July 6; disch'd; lost mare.
Morris, George	"	"	" " " " horse
Mifflin, William	"	"	" " " since discharged.
Moss, Moses	"	"	Furloughed August 4, 1832
Rice Mathew	"	"	
Robinson, John G.	"	"	Ordered to Dixon's July 21; disch'd; lost horse
Snell, William	"	"	
Skinner, Thomas W.	"	"	Ordered to Dixon's July 21, '32; since disch'd.
Truscott, William	"	"	
Thompson, Francis B	"	"	Furloughed July 15, 1832

Name and Rank.	Residence.	Enrolled		Remarks.
		1832		
Tait, John	Edwards Co.	June	19	Ordered to Dixon's July 21, 1832; since disch'd
Vincent, James	"	"		Disch'd at Ft. Wilbourn June 20, '32; disability
Vincent, Josiah	"	"		Ordered to Dixon's July 6, 1832; since disch..
Williams, Jonathan	"	"		Left sick at Fort Wilbourn July 20, 1832

The above named men ordered to Dixon's Ferry are said to have been discharged under Capt. E. Jordan.

This company was organized in Edwards county on the fifth day of May, 1832. Marched, according to Governor's order, for Hennepin, June 1, 1832. Was mustered into the service of the United States on the 19th of June, 1832. Each man of the company furnished six days' rations for himself and horse. The officers of said company drew one ration per day in kind, and the officers and men drew one-half bushel of corn as forage during the whole campaign.

CAPT. CHAMPION S. MADING'S COMPANY,

3d Regiment, 2d Brigade, of Illinois Mounted Volunteers, called into the service of the United States, on the requisition of Gen. Atkinson, by the Governor's proclamation, dated May 15, 1832. This company was organized and their officers commissioned May 5, 1832. Mustered out August 15, 1832, by order of Brig.-Gen. Atkinson.

Name and Rank.	Residence.	Enrolled		Remarks.
Captain.		1832.		
Champion S. Mading	Edwards Co.	June	19	1 horse left, on forced march, during battle..
First Lieutenant.				
William Curtis	"	"		Horse left, br'ke down; furl. Aug. 7 at P. Deesha
Second Lieutenant.				
Thomas Sanders	"	"		
Sergeants.				
James Hunt	"	"		
James Edmonson	"	"		Main spring U. S. gun broke
James Ellison	"	"		
John Edmonson	"	"		
Corporals.				
Sam'l Edmonson, 2d.	"	"		12 days' rations, from 15th Aug. for 21 men
Privates.				
Bogwood, David	"	"		
Cooper, John	"	"		Furloughed Aug. 7; 1 horse broke down
Garland, Joseph	"	"		
Greathouse, David	"	"		Furloughed Aug. 7; horse broke down
Hill, Starlin	"	"		Bayonet of U. S. gun lost
Mitchell, William	"	"		
Mounts, Stephen	"	"		
Pixley, Lewis	"	"		
Russell, Robert	"	"		Mainspring of U. S. gunlock broke
Rutherford, Josiah	"	"		
Shelby, David	"	"		
Shelby, E.	"	"		
Sames, L. B.	"	"		
Shores, William	"	"		
Spring, Henry	"	"		Furloughed Aug. 7; 1 horse broke down
Sterrit, John	"	"		
Waldrup, John	"	"		Furloughed Aug. 7, at battle-ground

Mustered out of service at Fort Dixon, under command of Capt. Jordan, of the 2d Regiment of 2d Brigade:

		1832		
Corporals.				
Bell, James, 1st	Edwards Co.	June	19	
Wilson, Elijah, 3d	"	"		
Bengaman, Wm., 4th.	"	"		

Name and Rank.	Residence.	Enrolled	Remarks.
Musician.		1832	
Drury, John	Edwards Co.	June 16	
Privates.			
Bennit, James	"	"	
Epney, Gordon	"	"	
Kelley, Milton	"	"	
Lay, Josiah	"	"	
Mading, Robt	"	"	
McKinney, Alfred	"	"	
Moore, Harrison	"	"	
Mays, Mathew	"	"	
Mounts, Joseph	"	"	
Shelby, Jonathan	"	"	
Thread, Robert	"	"	
Thread, James	"	"	
Underwood, Alex	"	"	
Warren, William R	"	"	

No rations only as privates drawn by any commissioned officer in my company; only one-half bu. of corn drawn by each man during the time of service; only one-half gallon of spirits drawn by the company; not one pound of baggage hauled or packed for any commissioned officer in my company.

This company was ordered to rendezvous at Hennepin June 10, and arrived the 11th, and was mustered into service the 19th.

Capt. John Haynes' Company

Of the 3d Regiment, 2d Brigade, Mounted Volunteers of Illinois, called into the service of the United States by the Governor's proclamation, dated May 15, 1832. Mustered out of service August 15, 1832.

Name and Rank.	Residence.	Enrolled	Remarks.
Captain.		1832.	
John Haynes	White Co.	June 19	
First Lieutenant.			
Thomas Fields	"	"	
Second Lieutenant.			
Reuben Emerson	"	"	Sup. disch. under Capt. Jordan; halter lost
Sergeants.			
Martin Johnson	"	"	Sup. disch. under Capt. Jordan; halter lost
Pliny H. Gawdy	"	"	Bucket, 1 pan and tin cup lost
John Robinson	"	"	Saddle and equipage lost
Robert Lowry	"	"	
Corporals.			
John Ponyman	"	"	Sup. disch. under Capt. Jordan; horse, saddle
John Heine	"	"	Sick (and bridle lost.
Leand'r W. McKnight	"	"	Sup. disch. under Capt. Jordon; horse, &c., lost
James Fields	"	"	
Privates.			
Berry, Edward	"	"	Sup. disch. under Capt. Jordan; halter lost
Barnet, Harvey	"	"	Furloughed on Aug. 7, 1832
Fields, William	"	"	Bayonet lost
Gott, Anthony	"	"	
Hunter, Philip P	"	"	
Hart, James W	"	"	
Hood, Henry	"	"	Halter lost
Johnson, Arthur L	"	"	Sup. disch. under Capt. Jordan; halter lost
Land, John	"	"	
Martin, Asa	"	"	Furloughed on Aug. 7, 1832
Moody, John	"	"	Supposed discharged under Capt. Jordan
Moore, William	"	"	Furloughed on Aug. 7, 1832; halter lost
McCan, Bartholom'w	"	"	

SECOND BRIGADE.

Name and Rank.	Residence.	Enrolled	Remarks.
McClarney, Robert..	White Co..	1832 June 19	Sup. disch. under Capt. Jordan; halter lost..
Nation, John.........	"	"	
Nation, Anderson....	"	"	Sup. disch. under Capt. Jordan; halter lost..
Nation, Thomas.....	"	"	" " horse lost...
Nucum, Joseph......	"	"	
Odd, John S.........	"	"	
Orr, James..........	"	"	
Parker, Joseph M...	"	"	
Parker, George C....	"	"	Bayonet lost.............................
Peacock, John......	"	"	
Porter, James.......	"	"	
Porter, William.....	"	"	
Patterson, Robert...	"	"	
Renshaw, Ebenezer.	"	"	Sup. disch. under Capt. Jordan; halter lost..
Teachner, Thad. R..	"	"	
Upton, John........	"	"	Furloughed Aug. 7, 1832; halter lost..........
Wrenwick, James...	"	"	Horse and halter lost.......................
Young, Ninian......	"	"	Supposed discharged under Capt. Jordan....

This company was organized in the county of White on May 12, 1832, and was mustered into the service of the United States on June 19, 1832.

CAPT. WILLIAM THOMAS' COMPANY

Of the 3d Regiment, 2d Brigade of Mounted Volunteers of Illinois, called into the service of the United States by the Governor's proclamation, dated May 15, 1832; mustered out on August 15, 1832.

Name and Rank.	Residence.	Enrolled	Remarks.
Captain. William Thomas....	White Co...	1832. June 19	
First Lieutenant, Henry Horn.........	"	"	
Second Lieutenant. Joel Rice.............	"	"	
Sergeants. Thomas Culbreth ...	"	"	
John M. Wilson......	"	"	Supposed discharged under Capt. Jordan....
Peter Miller..........	"	"	Furloughed Aug. 6, 1832; horse, etc., lost......
Enoch B. Hargrave .	"	"	Sup. disch. under Capt. Jordan; horse lost...
Corporals. Wesley Jameison...	"	"	
James B. Thomas ...	"	"	
William Null.........	"	"	
Green Bowen........	"	"	
Musician. William Greer.......	"	"	Furloughed Aug. 7 ....
Privates. Anderson, Bayles ...	"	"	Furloughed Aug. 6, 1832 ....
Byrd, John..........	"	"	Supposed discharged under Capt. Jordan....
Bowin, William.....	"	"	Furloughed Aug. 6, 1832.................
Bowin, Joshua	"	"	
Brown, Joseph......	"	"	
Clark, Benj..........	"	"	Supposed discharged under Capt. Jordan....
Chism, James.......	"	"	
Culbreth, Thomas, Jr	"	"	
Clyburn, James F...	"	"	Horse, etc., lost; sup. furl. under Capt. Jordan
Goodman, Joseph...	"	"	
Gardner, Thomas...	"	"	Supposed discharged under Capt. Jordan....
Goodwin, Miles.....	"	"	Sup. disch. under Capt. Jordan; horse lost...
Harman, Daniel.....	"	"	
Hargrave, Samuel..	"	"	Horse and equipage lost...................
Hogue, Lewis D.....	"	"	
Harman, John......	"	"	

Name and Rank.	Residence.	Enrolled	Remarks.
		1832.	
Jamison, John D. B.	White Co	June 19.	
Johnson, William	" "	"	Saddle lost.
Mears, James	" "	"	
Mears, Alexander	" "	"	Furloughed June 20, 1832; horse, etc., lost.
Mears, Mark	" "	"	Left sick at Fort Wilbourn June 20, 1832
Miller, William	" "	"	Furloughed Aug. 7, 1832.
Russel, Hiram A	" "	"	
Staley, Ezekiel	" "	"	Furloughed Aug. 7, 1832; horse, etc., lost.
Thomas, John	" "	"	
Vineyard, Joshua	" "	"	
Woods, Thomas	" "	"	
Wilson, William B.	" "	"	Furloughed Aug. 7, 1832.

This company was organized in the county of White county May 12, 1832. Marched, according to the order of the Governor, on May 29, 1832. Mustered into the service on June 19, 1832.

Capt. Daniel Powell's Company

Of 3d Regiment, 2d Brigade of Illinois Mounted Volunteers, called into the service of the United States, on the requisition of Gen. Atkinson, by the Governor's proclamation dated May 15, 1832. Mustered out Aug. 15, 1832.

Name and Rank.	Residence.	Enrolled	Remarks.
Captain.		1832.	
Daniel Powell	White Co	July 19.	
First Lieutenant.			
Joshua Blackard	" "	"	Furloughed at Coscannon by Gen. Atkinson.
Second Lieutenant.			
James Eubanks	" "	"	Ordered to Dixon; supposed to be disch'd
Sergeants.			
William Taylor	" "	"	Horse lost June 28, 1832.
Thos. M. Vineyard	" "	"	Furl. from Prairie du Chien by Capt. Powell.
Thos. Joyner	" "	"	Ordered to Dixon, and supposed discharged.
William Vickers	" "	"	
Corporals.			
Alex. McKinsey	" "	"	Furloughed August 6
John E. Ogburn	" "	"	Ordered to Dixon; supposed discharged.
Benjamin Rayney	" "	"	Ord. to Dixon; sup. disch'd; horse, etc., lost.
William Miller	" "	"	
Musician.			
Thomas Tary	" "	"	Ordered to Dixon; supposed discharged.
Privates.			
Askey, Elisha	" "	"	Ordered to Dixon; supposed discharged.
Briant, Henry	" "	"	Furloughed Aug. 6
Barnett, James	" "	"	
Burnett, David P	" "	"	
Butts, James W. G.	" "	"	
Brill, John A	" "	"	Furloughed Aug. 6.
Brill, Alfred L.	" "	"	
Bowers, Singleton	" "	"	
Bennett, Asa L	" "	"	Ordered to Dixon; supposed discharged.
Bri'nt, Daniel	" "	"	Furloughed Aug. 6
Chapman, William	" "	"	
Carson, John	" "	"	Horse and equipage lost Aug. 11.
Colbert, John	" "	"	Ordered to Dixon; supposed discharged.
Delap, John	" "	"	
Daviss, Isaac	" "	"	
Daviss, William	" "	"	
Everett, John	" "	"	Ordered to Dixon; supposed discharged.
Eubanks, James, Jr.	" "	"	" " " "
Gross, William	" "	"	
Garett, Peter	" "	"	Horse lost Aug. 13, 1832
Haskins, John	" "	"	Ordered to Dixon; supposed discharged.
Holland, Hezekiah	" "	"	

SECOND BRIGADE. 45

Name and Rank.	Residence.	Enrolled	Remarks.
		1832.	
Lewis, Jeremiah T. F.	White Co.	July 19.	
Lasiter, Eneus A.	"	....	
Marion, Bartholo'ew	"	....	Left sick at Wilbourn; on furlough June 20.
McNutt, Sidney	"	....	Ordered to Dixon; supposed discharged.
Netson, James	"	....	
Pearce, Moses	"	....	
Pearce, James	"	....	
Porter, Robert W.	"	....	Ordered to Dixon; supposed discharged.
Pool, Thomas	"	....	
Rogers, Reuben	"	....	Ordered to Dixon; supposed discharged.
Trousdale, Abner L.	"	....	
Tucker, Wooddy	"	....	
Todd, Thomas	"	....	
Trout, Daniel	"	....	
Vickers, Thomas	"	....	Horse and equipage lost
Vaugh, William H.	"	....	Furloughed Aug. 6
Vickers, Eli	"	....	Horse lost Aug. 15, 1832.
Waters, Thomas	"	....	Furl. Aug. 6; horse and equipage lost Aug. 6.
Williss, James	"	....	
Williams, Alexander	"	....	
Williss, Alfred	"	"	

DETACHMENT OF CAPT. DAVID POWELL'S COMPANY

Of Illinois Mounted Volunteers, called into the service of the United States by the Governor of the State, by his order of May 15, 1832, from the date of its enrollment to August 2, 1832, when mustered out of service at Dixon's Ferry.

Name and Rank.	Residence.	Enrolled	Remarks.
		1832	
Second Lieutenant.			
James Eubanks	White Co.	June 16.	
Third Sergeant.			
Thomas Joiner	"	"	Horse lost in service.
Corporals.			
John E. Ogburn	"	"	Horse lost in service.
Benj. Ranney	"	"	
Wm. Miller	"	"	Horse lost in service.
Privates.			
Askey, Elisha	"	"	
Bennett, Asa L.	"	"	
Colbert, John	"	"	Two blankets lost in service
Eubanks, James	"	"	
Everlet, John	"	"	
Gross, William	"	"	
Holland, Hezekiah	"	"	
Haskius, John	"	"	
Netson, James	"	"	Horse, saddle and bridle lost in service
McNutt, Sidney	"	"	Gun lost in service.
Porter, Robt. W.	"	"	
Rogers, Rueben	"	"	Horse, saddle and bridle lost in service
Terry, Thomas	"	"	One rifle gun lost in service.
Trousdale, A. L.	"	"	

SPY BATTALION.

Capt. John F. Richardson's Company,

Spy Battalion, 2d Brigade, Illinois Militia Mounted Volunteers, called into the service of the United States, on the requisition of Gen. Atkinson, by the Governor's proclamation dated May 15, 1832. Mustered out August 15, 1832, at Dixon's Ferry, Rock River, Illinois.

Name and Rank.	Residence.	Enrolled	Remarks.
Captain.		1832.	
John F. Richardson.	Clark Co	June 5	
First Lieutenant.			
Woodford Dulaney..			Furloughed and returned home Aug. 4, 1832..
Second Lieutenant.			
Justin Harlin........			Ret. home, furl., Aug. 4, from Prairie du Chien
Sergeants.			
Jacob Dolson........			Susp. from com'd June 29, at Prairie du Chien
John Wilson........			Lost horse, saddle and bridle, $78, July 15....
Asher V. Burwell....			Lost saddle and spancels, $18, August 1, 1832..
Robert Davidson....			Horse gave out; left at Ft. Winnebago, July 15
Corporals.			
Christian Jeffers....			
Nathan Hollenbach..			
Richard Ross.......			
George Wilson......			
Privates.			
Ashmore, Zeno A....			
Biggs, Samuel M....			Furn'd Martin L. Ashmore as subst. June 20..
Cooper, Franklin....			Lost horse and saddle July 4; sup. disch......
Chenowith, Martin F			Mustered out of service in Capt. Notts' Co....
Cooper, Theopolas..			" " " " "
Davidson, Daniel....			
Elliott, Aspano.....			Supposed to have been discharged............
Hadden, Andrew....			" " " "
Hadden, Samuel.....			" " " "
Hogue, Joseph......			
Johnson, George....			Supposed to be discharged...................
Kerr, John.........			
Locker, Conrad F...			Lost his horse; supposed to be disch. July 22.
Markle, Joseph W...			Supposed to have been discharged............
Nott, Stephen.......			
Prevo, Samuel......			Transferred to Capt. Notts' Co...............
Prevo, Ira..........			" " " "
Shaw, Nineveh.....			Appointed Adjutant June 18, 1832............
Sharp, Cyrus.......			
Thomas, Martin.....			
Taylor, Robert......			Deserted June 20; transferred from Co. roll..
Williams, James....			
White, Gideon B....			
White, Samuel......			Lost his gun and blankets (priv. prop.) July 12
White, Luther......			
White, Robert......			
Wheeler, Tarleton..			Lost his horse July 22; supposed to be disch.
Waters, John.......			Transferred to Capt. Notts' Co...............
Yocum, Alexander...			
Langham, Abel.....			Supposed to be discharged...................

Company was organized June 5, 1832, and marched from Fort Wilbourn June 9, 1832; mustered into the service of the United States, June 19, 1832.

SECOND BRIGADE.   47

My company furnished themselves with eight days rations while on their march from Clark county to Fort Wilbourn. The officers, while in service, have drawn but one ration per day, and no forage has been furnished. My company rations have been drawn for the company to return home, viz: twelve days, up to and including the 30th day of Aug., 1832.

(Signed.)   JOHN F. RICHARDSON, CAPT.

CAPT. ABNER GREER'S COMPANY,

Spy Battalion, of Illinois Mounted Volunteers, called into service of the United States, on the requisition of Gen. Atkinson, by the Governor's proclamation dated ——, 1832. Mustered out August 15, 1832.

Name and Rank.	Residence.	Enrolled	Remarks.
Captain. Abner Greer	Lawrence Co.	1832. May 5	Lost 1 pr. pistols worth $15—private property.
First Lieutenant. David D. Marney	"	"	Lost horse, etc., val. $94; on furlough Aug. 2.
Second Lieutenant. Aaron Wells	"	"	" " " " "
Sergeants.			
Ebenezer Z. Ryan	"	"	Furloughed at Fort Dodge, August 11
William R. Jackman	"	"	Lost horse and equipage valued at $70.50
Mason Jones	"	"	
Alex. H. Gilmore	"	"	Absent on furlough
Corporals.			
James Gadd	"	"	Lost horse, etc., valued at $91.; furloughed
Thomas B. Spencer	"	"	Furloughed to return home
Jeremiah Cawthorn	"	"	
Thomas J. England	"	"	Lost horse and equipage
Privates.			
Andrews, Silas	"	"	Lost horse and equipage; furloughed
Blizard, Thomas	"	"	" " "
Baird, James	"	"	
Baird, Proctor B	"	"	
Clubb, Eli	"	"	Furloughed Aug. 14, 1832.
Cooper, John	"	"	Lost horse; left on duty July 7
Dudley, Joshua	"	"	Furloughed Aug. 14, 1832.
Dickerson, George	"	"	Detached on duty July 19
Evans, William	"	"	Lost horse Aug. 7; furloughed
England, David	"	"	
Fyte, Moses	"	"	Furloughed Aug. 14.
Fyffe, Edward P	"	"	Left sick July 9.
Fish, Josiah	"	"	
Galaspie, William	"	"	
Gibbons, Harvey	"	"	
Jenady, Joseph	"	"	
Jackman, Bazel	"	"	Lost horse
Johnston, Abner	"	"	Furloughed Aug. 14.
Johnston, Robert	"	"	Detached June 20.
Kirkling, Williamson	"	"	Left on duty July 19.
Kellams, Gideon	"	"	Furloughed Aug. 12.
Lawler, William	"	"	Lost horse; left on duty July 19
Lackey, John O	"	"	Left on duty July 19.
Lackey, Thomas	"	"	Left sick July 19.
Neil, James	"	"	Furloughed August 14
Perkins, Thomas	"	"	Left sick July 19.
Pumphrey, Laonie	"	"	
Pollard, Edwin	"	"	
Rawlings, Nathan	"	"	Furloughed Aug. 14.
Richards, Newton	"	"	
Small, Thomas H	"	"	
Seeds, William	"	"	Lost horse and equipage
Selby, Josiah	"	"	Detailed on duty June 24.
Williams, John	"	"	Discharged July 19.
Young, Jacob	"	"	Lost horse and equipage
Young, Jonathan	"	"	

Thomas Spencer, a private of this company, was mustered into the service of the United States as a private of the company, mounted, armed and equipped, on the 19th of June, 1832, at Ft. Wilbourn. He served through the campaign and left the company in charge of a disabled man (T. B. Spencer) on the 10th and 11th of August, four or five days before the company was mustered out of service, and his name was omitted from this muster roll by oversight. He should have been mustered out of service upon this roll, and is fully entitled to pay during the full term of the company. To the truth of which I hereby certify on honor.

                                    (Signed,)   A. GREER,
    LAWRENCEVILLE, May 3, 1833.   Capt. com'd'g company.

    This company was organized and enrolled on May 5, 1832, and took up line of march for Ft. Wilbourn on June 2, and was mustered into the service of the United States June 19, 1832.

Capt. John McCann's Company

Of Spy Battalion, 2d Brigade, Illinois Mounted Volunteers, called into the service of the United States on the requisition of Gen. Atkinson, by the Governor's proclamation, dated 1832. Mustered out of the service of the United States Aug. 15, 1832.

Name and Rank.	Residence.	Enrolled	Remarks.
Captain.		1832.	
John McCann	White Co.	May 12.	
First Lieutenant.			
Samuel Slocumb			Furloughed at Prairie du Chien Aug. 7, 1832
Second Lieutenant.			
Walter Burress			Sword, belonging to U. S., lost
Sergeants.			
William Garrison			
Solomon Garrison			
Noah Staley			Furloughed at Prairie du Chein; horse lost.
James Keneda			Lost his horse and equipage
Corporals.			
Levi Wells			
William Stephens			
William Daniels			
Henry McCann			
Privates.			
Berry, George			Supposed to be discharged at Dixon's
Bailey, Alfred			Lost his horse and equipage
Britain, Joseph M.			
Blackledge, John			Sick
Blackwell, James C.			Supposed to be discharged at Dixon's
Cann, James			
Council, Willis			
Campbell, John			Lost his horse
Crowder, John			Furloughed at Prairie du Chien Aug. 7, 1832
Coonts, Thomas			
Edwards, Ambrose			
Evans, Jonathan			
Farley, Martin			Lost his saddle, bridle, blanket and halter
Farley, John			Supposed to be discharged at Dixon's Ferry
George, John			
George, Francis			Supposed to be discharged at Wilbourn
Goodman, James			Furloughed at Prairie du Chien Aug. 7, 1832
Hood, Allen			Supposed to be discharged at Dixon's
Hood, Anderson			
Hilyard, William			
Holderly, Dempsey			Lost his horse and equipage
Heasty, Daniel			Lost his horse
Hust, John			Lost his horse and equipage
Hamilton, Wm. S.			Supposed to be discharged at Wilbourn
Lindsey, Thomas J.			
Lowe, Thomas			
McMullin, Wilkerson			
Nevett, Wm. G.			Horse and equipage lost
Neslar, James			Supposed to be discharged at Dixon's
Parker, Wilson			
Robinson, Michael			Furloughed at Prairie du Chien Aug. 7, 1832
Robinson, Nich'l's A.			
Rippatoo, Burress			
Robinson, Aaron			
Stone, Thomas W.	White Co.		Supposed to be discharged at Dixon's Ferry
Smith, Slade			
Staley, George			Furloughed at Prairie du Chien August 7, 1832
Sutler, Rodolphus M.			Lost his horse and equipage

SECOND BRIGADE.

Name and Rank.	Residence.	Enrolled	Remarks.
		1832.	
Smith, Silas.........	....	....	Lost his horse and equipage..............
Wilson, Christopher.	....	....	" "
Williams, Hardy.....	....	....	Supposed to be discharged at Dixon's......

John C. Slocumb, of White county, volunteered, armed and equipped himself, and marched with the company from Carmi, took sick and was left at Fairfield, Wayne county. I am credibly informed, and believe, that said Slocumb afterwards reported himself for duty at Fort Wilbourn, and served there and as Wagon-Guard between Fort Wilbourn and Dixon's Ferry, when he was discharged early in August and returned home.

(Signed.)   WM. McHENRY,
              Major Spy Battalion.

This company enrolled under command of Wm. McHenry, Captain, May 12, 1832, and was mustered into the service of the United States June 19, 1832. John McCann was elected Captain in place of Wm. McHenry, promoted on June 18, 1832, and has commanded since.

DETACHMENTS.

A Detachment

Of Illinois Mounted Volunteers, under the command of Isaac Parmenter, Adjt. 2d Regiment, 2d Brigade, from the day of its enrollment to August 2, 1832, when mustered out of service, at Dixon's Ferry, Illinois.

Name and Rank.	Residence.	Enrolled	Remarks.
Adjutant.		1832.	
Isaac Parmeter	Wabash Co	June 16.	Adjutant 2d Regiment, 2d Brigade
First Lieutenant.			
Samuel Fisher	" "	" "	
Sergeants.			
Mathew Leatherland	" "	" "	
John A. Dodds	" "	" "	Lost his horse, etc., June 17, at Ft. Wilbourn.
Corporals.			
Solomon Frair	" "	" "	
John Golden	" "	" "	
Ira Keen	" "	" "	
Westley Wood	" "	" "	
Privates.			
Buchanon, Jos. O	" "	" "	
Buchanon, Henry K.	" "	" "	
Besley, James	" "	" "	
Bigley, William	" "	" "	
Dodds, Joseph M.	" "	" "	
Goddy, John	" "	" "	
Garner, James	" "	" "	Lost horse, etc., July 12, at Ft. Winnebago.
Golden, William	" "	" "	
Hoyt, Jonathan S	" "	" "	
McMullen, James	" "	" "	
Miller, Barton S	" "	" "	
Ochletree, John	" "	" "	
Reel, Henry R.	" "	" "	Lost horse, etc., July 21, at Rock River.
Smith, John O	" "	" "	
Turner, Abner	" "	" "	Lost horse, etc., June 17, at Ft. Wilbourn.
Utter, John	" "	" "	
Vanderhoof, Philip	" "	" "	
Wear, Thomas	" "	" "	
Wear, Harvey	" "	" "	

Capt. Hiram Roundtree's Company, 2d Regiment.

Name and Rank.	Residence.	Enrolled	Remarks.
Third Sergeant.		1832.	
Samuel Jackson	Montg'm'y Co.	June 16	
Private.			
Levi Booger		" "	Lost horse, on June 25, at Dixon's Ferry

Capt. Hiram Kinade's Company, 2d Regiment.

Name and Rank.	Residence.	Enrolled	Remarks.
		1832.	
Richard Rattan	Greene Co	June 17	Lost horse in service June 25, Dixon's Ferry
Daniel Rattan			
John C. Jordan			

Capt. Mayo's Company, 1st Regiment, 2d Brigade.

Name and Rank.	Residence.	Enrolled	Remarks.
		1832.	
Abraham Sumter	Edgar Co	June 16.	

SECOND BRIGADE.

Capt. Earl Peirce's Company, 2d Regiment.

Name and Rank.	Residence.	Enrolled	Remarks.
Brawdy, John C	Edgar Co	1832. June 16	Lost horse in service June 25, Dixon's Ferry.
Clark, William	"	"	
Harris, Abijah	"	"	
McCarty, Nathan	"	"	Lost horse in service, June 25, Dixon's Ferry.
Shire, Jonathan	"		

Capt. Bennett Howlin's Company, 4th Regiment, 3d Brigade.

Name and Rank.	Residence.	Enrolled	Remarks.
Jacob Gibson	Macoupin Co.	1832. June 17	

Capt. Solomon Hunter's Company, 3d Regiment, 2d Brigade.

Name and Rank.	Residence.	Enrolled	Remarks.
Everly, Nimrod	Edwards Co	1832 June 16	
Morris, Miles	"	"	Lost saddle in service July 4, at Rock River.
Morris, George	"	"	
Vincin, Josiah	"	"	

Capt. John F. Richardson's Company, Spy Battalion, 2d Brigade.

Name and Rank.	Residence.	Enrolled	Remarks.
Ashmore, Martin L		1832. June 16	Lost mare in service June 17, Ft. Wilbourn..
Ashmore, Zeno A		"	
Cooper, Franklin		"	Lost horse in service July 3, near Rock River
Johnson, George		"	" mare " July 6, on Rock River..

Capt. Isaac Sandford's Company, 1st Regiment, 2d Brigade.

Name and Rank.	Residence.	Enrolled	Remarks.
Davis, Abraham	Edgar Co	1832.	

CAPT. HIGHSMITH'S DETACHMENT

Of Illinois Mounted Volunteers, called into the service of the United States by the Governor of the State of Illinois, by his order of May 15, 1832, from the date of its enrollment to Aug. 2, 1832, when mustered out of service at Dixon's Ferry, Ill.

Name and Rank.	Residence.	Enrolled	Remarks.
Captain. Wm. Highsmith	Crawford Co	1832. June 16	Horse and saddle lost in service
First Lieutenant. Samuel V. Allison	"	"	
Second Lieutenant. John H. McMickle	"	"	Horse lost, July 15, 1832
Sergeants. Thomas Fuller, 2d	"	"	Horse and saddle lost
William McCoy, 3d	"	"	Saddle lost
Corporals. Nathan Highsmith, 1	"	"	
Martin Fuller, 2d	"	"	
John Lagon, 4th	"	"	

Name and Rank.	Residence.	Enrolled	Remarks.
Privates.		1832.	
Allison, John	Crawford Co.	June 16	
Allison, Samuel H	"	"	
Brimbery, John	"	"	
Carter, Benjamin	"	"	Horse and saddle lost
Easton, Thomas	"	"	
Garrison, Peter	"	"	
Johnston, John	"	"	
Kinney, George W.	"	"	
Lewis, James	"	"	Horse and saddle lost
Montgomery, And'w.	"	"	
Martin, Isaac	"	"	
Parker, John, Jr	"	"	Horse and saddle lost
Parker, Thomas N	"	"	
Phelps, Amos	"	"	
Stockwell, Thomas	"	"	
Rece, William	"	"	Horse, saddle and gun lost
Weger, James	"	"	Saddle lost.

Capt. A. M. Houston's Company, 2d Regt., 2d Brigade.

Name and Rank.	Residence.	Enrolled	Remarks.
Corporals.		1832	
Cornelius Doherty	Crawford Co.	June 16.	
Joseph Jones	"	"	
Privates.			
Baugher, George	"	"	
Donden, George R.	"	"	
Hacket, Joseph	"	"	
Hawkins, Wm	"	"	
McCoy, John	"	"	
Pearson, Joseph	"	"	
Pearson, Edward	"	"	Horse and saddle lost
Pearson, William	"	"	
Phelps, Zilman	"	"	Horse lost.
Vanderinder, John	"	"	

Capt. John Barns' Company, 2d Regt., 2d Brigade.

Name and Rank.	Residence.	Enrolled	Remarks.
Captain.		1832.	
John Barns	Lawrence Co.	June 16	Horse died in service July 4, 1832
First Lieutenant.			
Elijah Mays	"	"	Absent on furlough
Sergeants.			
James Nabb	"	"	Absent on furlough
Samuel Mundie	"	"	
Wm. Maso	"	"	
Corporals.			
A. S. Badollett	"	"	
Arthur Chenoweth	"	"	Absent on furlough
Joseph F. Darr	"	"	
Privates.			
Barns, Silas	"	"	
Bush, John	"	"	
Hunter, John T	"	"	Promoted to Quartermaster July 10, 1832
Lewis, Stephen S.	"	"	
Moore, Tilford	"	"	
Mullins, John R.	"	"	Horse and saddle lost
Organ, Daniel A	"	"	
Pea, Henry	"	"	
Pea, Samuel	"	"	
Pullis, John J	"	"	Absent on furlough
Rawlings, Frederick	"	"	Horse lost in service, and saddle.
Ruark, John W	"	"	
Ruark, Wm. F.	"	"	
Stewart, Joseph	"	"	Horse and saddle lost
Strother, Pendleton	"	"	Absent on furlough
Thompson, James	"	"	
Westfall, Isaac	"	"	Wounded; left at Hosp., at Dixon's, Aug. 2, '32

Capt. Abner Grear's Company, Spy Battalion, 2d Brigade.

Name and Rank.	Residence.	Enrolled	Remarks.
Privates.		1832.	
Andrews, Silas	Lawrence Co.	June 16.	
Cooper, John M	"	"	Left as attendant for Thompson; horse left..
Dickerson, George	"	"	
Fyffe, Edward P	"	"	
Kellams, Gideon	"	"	
Lackey, John O	"	"	
Lackey, Thomas	"	"	
Neil, James	"	"	
Pumphrey, Loami	"	"	
Selvy, Joseph			

THIRD BRIGADE.

FIRST REGIMENT.

Capt. David Smith's Company

Of Mounted Volunteers, called and mustered into the service of the United States by order of the Commander-in-Chief of the Militia of the State of Illinois, attached to the 1st Regiment, 3d Brigade, under the command of Brig.-Gen. Henry Atkinson, from June 1, 1832, to August 1, 1832, when mustered out of service. Distant from Atlas, Madison county, 300 miles.

Name and Rank.	Residence.	Enrolled	Remarks.
Captain.		1832.	
David Smith	Madison Co.	June 1.	
First Lieutenant.			
John Lee	"	"	On furlough
Second Lieutenant.			
John Umphrey	"	"	
Sergeants.			
S. I. Kendall	"	"	
James Sterett	"	"	
S. B. Gillhour	"	"	
W. B. Crowder	"	"	
Corporals.			
C. Subastian	"	"	
S. N. P. Elliott	"	"	
D. H. Fouquerer	"	"	
John Walker	"	"	
Privates.			
Brazil, S.	"	"	
Brown, U.	"	"	
Bangs, O.	Morgan Co.	"	Hospital Steward at Ottawa
Dunlap, R. M. C.	Madison Co.	"	
Drennan, C.	"	"	
Drennan, I.	"	"	
Dilliplain, I. P.	"	"	
Eakin, T.	"	"	
Harrison, W.	"	"	
Hart, A.	"	"	
Haynes, John	"	"	
Hewes, I.	"	"	
Kistler, W.	"	"	
Kellogg, E.	LaSalle Co.	June 29.	
Loman, T.	Madison Co.	" 1.	
Makun, I.	"	July 26.	
Nowland, John	"	"	
Peter, C.	"	"	
Pembroke, D.	"	"	
Rogers, D. B.	"	"	
Scott, John	"	"	
Summers, H. S	"	"	
Slayton, J. M	"	"	

THIRD BRIGADE. 55

Name and Rank.	Residence.	Enrolled	Remarks.
		1832	
Shaw, I. E	LaSalle Co	June 29	
Sprague, H. A	"	"	Sick at Ottawa
Sprague, G.	"	"	
Wood, S	Madison Co	" 1	
Wheeler, E	"	" 18	
Lowell, N	"	" 1	

CAPT. WILLIAM GILLHAM'S COMPANY

Of Mounted Volunteers, called and mustered into the service of the United States, by order of the Commander-in-Chief of the Militia of the State of Illinois, attached to the 1st Regiment of the 3d Brigade, under the command of Brigadier-General James D. Henry, from April 30, 1832. Mustered out at Fort Wilbourn Aug. 1, 1832.

Name and Rank.	Residence.	Enrolled	Remarks.
Captain.		1832.	
William Gillham	Morgan Co	April 30	
First Lieutenant.			
Robert H. McDow	"	"	On furlough
Second Lieutenant.			
James Etheal	"	"	
Sergeants.			
Daniel Clotfelter	"	"	
William Leib	"	"	
John Sergeant	"	"	On furlough
Aquilla Clarkson	"	"	
Corporals.			
Zadoc Riggs	"	"	
Samuel Vanslyke	"	"	
James Morris	"	"	
Isaac Graton	"	"	On furlough
Privates.			
Arnett, John	"	"	
Apple, John	"	"	
Avery, Joel	"	"	
Baker, John	"	"	
Bell, Alexander	"	"	Appointed Paymaster June 19, 1832
Clarkson, Kinza	"	"	
Clanton, Isaac	"	"	
Campbell, William	"	"	
Clarkson, Constant'e	"	"	On furlough
Carter, Vincin	"	"	
Duvall, Nicholas	"	"	
Garmon, George	"	"	
Gillham, James	"	"	Elected Lieut.-Col. June 19, 1832
House, H. W	"	"	On furlough
Halloway, James	"	"	
King, John	"	"	
Kemp, Emanuel	"	"	
Kemp, Murphy	"	"	
Lemon, H. H	"	"	
Murphy, Seth C	"	"	
Mathers, William	"	"	
McCullom, Robert	"	"	
McConnel, John	"	"	
Masters, Squire D	"	"	
Nichols, Clark	"	"	
Northcutt, Archabel	"	"	On furlough
Ovear, William	"	"	
Olney, Washington	"	"	Taken as wagoner; absent June 19, 1832
Piper, James	"	"	
Riggs, Henry L	"	"	
Ragfield, James	"	"	On furlough
Shelton, Scebert C	"	"	
Scott, Levi	"	"	
Smith, William R	"	"	

Name and Rank.	Residence.	Enrolled	Remarks.
Smith, George	Morgan Co	1832. April 30	
Simmons, Mastin G.	"	"	
Whitley, Alexander.	"	"	
Wilkison, Alexander	"	"	
Willson, Clinton	"	"	

Capt. William Gorden's Company

Of Mounted Volunteers of Illinois Militia, ordered into the service of the United States by the Governor of the State, on the requisition of Gen. Atkinson, of U. S. Army. Attached to 1st Regiment, 3d Brigade, in the year 1832. Mustered out of service July 29, 1832, 212 miles from place of enrollment. Mustered into service June 2, 1832.

Name and Rank.	Residence.	Enrolled	Remarks.
Captain. William Gorden		1832. April 30	
First Lieutenant, John Pickering		"	On furlough since July 19, 1832
Second Lieutenant. Thomas Askens		"	
Sergeants. Robert Dinsmore		"	
William York		"	On furlough since July 10, 1832
Sylvester Moss		"	
Benjamin Allen		"	
Corporals. Benjamin Murphy		"	On furlough since July 12, 1832
Loyd Aday		"	
Enoch Bramson		"	
John Dinsmore		"	
Privates. Allen, James G.		"	
Black, Thomas G.		"	
Boothby, Daniel		"	
Branson, Miram K.		"	Appointed Asst. Surgeon June 19, 1832
Coonrod, Woolery		"	On furlough since July 10, 1832
Davis, Hugh		"	
Drummond, Patter'n		"	
Dinsmore, Mathew		"	
Garret, Hiram		"	
Hardwick, Rice		"	On furlough since July 18, 1832
Jones, Daniel R.		"	" " " 19, 1832
Jones, William		"	
Johnson, James		"	
Kellogg, Orvill E.		"	On furlough since July 10, 1832
Keller, Joseph		"	
McGovern, Edward		"	Sent on express to Gen. Atkinson July 30, '32; [M. O. Aug. 2, '32.
Murphy, Dudley R.		"	
McDowell, Nelson		"	
Mills, William N.		"	
McCombs, Elijah		"	
Ogg, James		"	On furlough since July 19, 1832
Powell, Farington		"	
Powell, Henry		"	
Smith, Drury		"	
Strade, Malen		"	
Scott, Benjamin		"	
Slotten, Joseph		"	On furlough since July 26, 1832
Thomas, Manley		"	
Turner, William		"	
Williams, Elza		"	[M. O. Aug. 2, '32.
Weeks, Washington		"	Sent on express to Gen. Atkinson, July 20, '32.
Wood, Elisha K.		"	Appointed Surgeon June 18, 1832

THIRD BRIGADE. 57

Capt. George F. Bristow's Company

Of Mounted Volunteers, called and mustered into the service of the United States, by order of the Commander-in-Chief of the Militia of the State of Illinois, attached to the 1st Regiment under the command of Col. Samuel T. Matthews, of the 3d Brigade, commanded by Brig. Gen. James D. Henry, from May 21, 1832, for and during the term of 90 days from said date. Mustered out at Fort. Wilbourn Aug. 1, 1832.

Name and Rank.	Residence.	Enrolled	Remarks.
Captain. George T. Bristow	Morgan Co...	1832 May 21	
First Lieutenant. Stephen Henderson	" "	" "	On furlough
Second Lieutenant. Walter Ellis	" "	" "	
Sergeants. Allen Mattock George Thompson James V. Logston Asa L. Lane	" " " " " " " "	" " " " " " " "	
Privates. Brown, James Combs, John Constant, Archibald Clemens, Willey L. Carter, George Foster, Geo. W. Henry, Thomas Hopper, William S. Henderson, Nathan'l Hull, William	Ottawa. LaSalle Co. " " Morgan Co. " " " " " " " " " " " " " "	July 1 " " May 21 " " " " " " " " " " " " " "	 Deserted June 30, 1832 On furlough
Hicks, Henry W. Meeks, Allen Marshall, John Mackey, Daniel Moss, Isaac Ream, Michael Thompson, Oswell Turney, Russell Wilcox, John Warren, Ezekiel	Ottawa. LaSalle Co. Morgan Co. " " " " " " " " " " " " LaSalle Co. " "	July 1 May 21 " " " " " " " " " " " " July 1 " "	

Capt. S. T. Matthews',
afterwards
Capt. J. T. Arnett's Company

Of Mounted Volunteers, now under the command of 1st Lieut. D. B. McConnell, called and mustered into the service of the United States by order of the Commander-in-Chief of the Militia of the State of Illinois, belonging to the 1st Regiment, 3d Brigade. Mustered out August 1, 1832.

Name and Rank.	Residence.	Enrolled	Remarks.
Captain. S. T. Matthews	Morgan Co.	1832. May 5.	Promoted to Colonel June 19, 1832
First Lieutenant. N. H. Johnson	" "	" "	Appointed to Staff of Brigade June 20
Second Lieutenant. D. B. McConnell	" "	" "	Promoted to 1st Lieut. June 19, 1832
Sergeants. Josiah Gorham John Moss Sam'l P. Devone Moses R. Bennett	" " " " " " " "	" " " " " " " "	 Furloughed July 24, 1832 Furloughed July 3, 1832

Name and Rank.	Residence.	Enrolled	Remarks.
Corporals.		1832.	
John Sparks	Morgan Co.	May 5.	Furloughed July 18, 1832
Henry Moss	"	"	" " 24, 1832
L. B. Tankersby	"	"	
John Rusk	"	"	Furloughed July 18, 1832
Privates.			
Antle, Anderson	"	"	
Arnett, James	"	"	Promoted to Capt. June 19; resigned July 23.
Buchanan, Benj.	"	"	
Buchanan, Reuben	"	"	
Blair, James H	"	"	
Cassell, James	"	"	
Crane, Harvey	"	"	
Courtney, Robert C.	"	"	
Clayton, Madison	"	"	
Colton, John L.	"	"	
Durant, Samuel	"	"	
Devore, James H.	"	"	
Duncan, Wm.	"	"	
Deads, Phillip	"	"	
Deal, Isaac	"	"	Detailed for use of Brigade June 24, 1832
Evans, James	"	"	Promoted to Major June 19, 1832
Edwards, John	"	"	
Farris, Jonathan	"	"	
Graves, James H	"	"	Sick and discharged June 14, 1832
Gilmore, John	"	"	
Goodpaster, Madis'n	"	"	
Hawkins, Wm. B.	"	"	
Howard, Alanson	"	"	
Hurst, John	"	"	Furloughed July 18, 1832
Hobbs, Silas	"	"	
Hunter, Henry	"	"	
Henry, John	"	"	
Hook, Cornelius	"	"	Appointed to Staff of Brigade June 14
Holland, Berry	"	"	
Ingles, Darius	"	"	
Johnson, John	"	"	
Jarrod, Moses	"	"	
Jordan, Wm. L.	"	"	
Johnson, Abraham	"	"	
Lycock, Thomas	"	"	
Lamples, Jacob	"	"	Lost his horse
Lash, James	"	"	
Mounts, Matthias	"	"	Promoted to 2d Lieut. June 19, 1832
Million, Elijah F.	"	"	
McConnel, Murray	"	"	Appointed to Staff of Brigade June 19, 1832
Pitner, Alex	"	"	
Pitner, Montgomery	"	"	
Roberts, Milton B.	"	"	Appointed to Staff June 19
Richards, John	"	"	
Sweet, Dan'l	"	"	
Slocumb, John C.	"	July 14.	
Tolley, James	"	May 5.	Furloughed July 18, 1832
Turner, Jonathan	"	"	
Williams, David	"	"	Permitted to leave the company June 22, sick

Capt. Walter Butler's Company

Of Illinois Mounted Volunteers, in the service of the United States, under Brig.-Gen. H. Atkinson. Mustered out of service August 1, 1832.

Name and Rank.	Residence.	Enrolled	Remarks.
Captain.		1832.	
Walter Butler	Morgan Co.	June 4	
First Lieutenant.			
Thomas P. Ross	"	"	
Second Lieutenant.			
Fleming C. Maupin	"	"	

THIRD BRIGADE.

Name and Rank.	Residence.	Enrolled	Remarks.
Sergeants.		1832.	
Samuel Givens	Morgan Co.	June 4.	
Achilles Deatherage	"	"	
David Hart	"	"	
David Mackey	"	"	
Corporals.			
Nathan Hart	"	"	Appointed Q. M. Sergeant June 19, 1832
Henderson Vickens	"	"	
John L. Heffington	"	"	
William T. Nall	"	"	
Privates.			
Auston, Eli	"	"	Substitute for And. Wyatt
Beason, Henry	"	"	Substitute for Eli Auston
Brown, John	"	"	Furloughed June 24, during term of service
Brown, Joseph	"	"	Substitute for John Sappington
Clayton, Jesse	"	"	
Dougherty, John	"	"	
Davidson, David	"	"	
Fanning, George	"	"	
Fanning, Wushing'n	"	"	
Fanning, Abraham	"	"	
Groves, James	"	"	
Gilleland, Thomas	"	"	
Haynes, Bluford	"	"	
Hart, Anderson	"	"	
Harris, Thomas I.	"	"	
Hart, Charles	"	"	Furloughed June 24, during term of service
Kirby, James	"	"	
Keplinger, Isaac	"	"	
Murphy, Nimrod C.	"	"	
Minor, Samuel C.	"	"	Furloughed June 24, during term of service
Nall, John	"	"	
Norvell, Spencer	"	"	
Patterson, William	"	"	Substitute for Hiram Patterson
Porter, Ephriam	"	"	Jas. Hutcherson
Pryon, James	"	"	
Ray, Robert	"	"	Furloughed on July 10, 1832, for 25 days
Riggs, Archibald	"	"	Substitute for John Love
Ross, John W	"	"	Elected 1st Corporal June 19; N. Hart prom
Seamore, Edward	"	"	
Seamore, Richards'n	"	"	
Scott, James	"	"	
Stewart, Charles	"	"	
Talkington, William	"	"	
Wright, George	"	"	
Wiggs, Daniel	"	"	Substitute for John Still
Woods, John	"	"	
Weatherford, Wm	"	"	Appointed Adjutant June 19, 1832

SECOND REGIMENT

Capt. Hiram Roundtree's Company

Of 2d Regiment, 3d Brigade of Illinois Mounted Volunteers, called into the service of the United States on the requisition of Gen. Atkinson, by the Governor's proclamation dated May 15, 1832. This company was organized May 21, 1832, in Montgomery county, Illinois, Mustered out August 16, 1832.

Name and Rank.	Residence.	Enrolled	Remarks.
Captain.		1832.	
Hiram Roundtree...	Montg'm'y Co	June 20.	
First Lieutenant.			
John Kirkpatrick....	" "	" "	
Second Lieutenant.			
Thomas Philips	" "	" "	
Sergeants.			
Andrew K. Gray.....	" "	" "	
John Stone..........	" "	" "	
Samuel Jackson.....	" "	" "	Sent home sick from Korkenory July 9, 1832.
David B. Starr......	" "	" "	
Corporals.			
Spartan Grisham....	" "	" "	
Malaki Smith	" "	" "	
Thomas McAdams...	" "	" "	Permitted to return home another way.....
Thomas Edwards ...	" "	" "	
Privates.			
Aydlett, Clement C..	" "	" "	Discharged by order of Gen. Scott.........
Brown, John.........	" "	" "	Sent home sick from Korkenory, July 9, 1832.
Briggs, John........	" "	" "	
Burke, Joseph	" "	" "	
Berry, James M.....	" "	" "	
Booer, Levi W.......	" "	" "	Discharged by Gen. Scott; horse lost; val. $60
Coffey, Cleaveland..	" "	" "	
Copeland, David.....	" "	" "	
Carlew, John	" "	" "	
Cardwell, James	" "	" "	Sent home sick from Korkenory July 9, 1832.
Duncan, John	" "	" "	
Early, Thomas	" "	" "	
Evans, Thomas	" "	" "	
Forehand, Ammon..	" "	" "	
Griffith, William.....	" "	" "	
Gray, Thomas.......	" "	" "	Discharged at Helena July 28, 1832........
Gray, Alexander R..	" "	" "	
Hart, John	" "	" "	
Harkey, George.....	" "	" "	Sent home sick...........................
Holmes, John M.....	" "	" "	from Fort Wilbourn June 22.
Harkey, William	" "	" "	
Heady, Thomas W..	" "	" "	
Hughes, Thomas C..	" "	" "	Sent home by water; horse disabled; val. $60
Hannah, John	" "	" "	
Johnson, Alfred	" "	" "	
Jones, William	" "	" "	
Johnson, Jesse	" "	" "	
Johnson, Thomas...	" "	" "	
Lockerman, James..	" "	" "	
Long, John K........	" "	" "	[march after enemy.
McCurry, John	" "	" "	Sent to Galena sick; horse, etc., lost on forced
McPhaill, Malcolm..	" "	" "	
McCullock, David T.	" "	" "	

THIRD BRIGADE.

Name and Rank.	Residence.	Enrolled	Remarks.
		1832.	
Mansfield, Horace	Montg'm'y Co	June 20	Discharged by Gen. Atkinson
McCullock, Axrin	"	"	
McCullock, Robert	"	"	
McWilliams, John M.	"	"	Permitted to go home by water
McDavid, William	"	"	
Paisley, Samuel	"	"	
Potter, Thomas	"	"	............[march after enemy.
Potter, James	"	"	Sent to Galena sick; horse, etc., lost on forced
Rhodes, Jacob	"	"	Discharged by Gen. Scott
Rose, Willis	"	"	
Steel, Luke Sea	"	"	
Sturtevant, Thomas	"	"	Sent home June 22, as attendant on sick
Shirley, Zebedee	"	"	Permitted to go home before mustering out
Slater, John	"	"	Horse, etc., value $62, lost on forced march
Tennis, William M.	"	"	
Wilson, James	"	"	
Williams, David M.	"	"	
Williams, William S.	"	"	
Wilson, Joseph W.	"	"	Sent home by water, sick
Wood, Thomas	"	"	" sick from Ft. Wilbourn June 22
Williford, Thomas	"	"	Sent to Galena sick
Young, William	"	"	

This company was organized in Montgomery county, Illinois, May 21, 1832. Ordered to march June 4, and actually marched June 9, and was mustered into the service of the U. S. at Fort Wilbourn, June 20, 1832.

CAPT. JAMES KINCAID'S COMPANY,

2d Regiment, 3d Brigade of Illinois Mounted Volunteers, called into the service of the United States, on the requisition of Gen. Atkinson, by the Governor's proclamation dated May 15, 1832. Mustered out August 16, 1832.

Name and Rank.	Residence.	Enrolled	Remarks.
Captain,	Carrollton.	1832.	
James Kincaid	Greene Co.	June 19	Lost two horses on forced march
First Lieutenant.			
John Fry	"	"	
Second Lieutenant.			
Royal W. Pitts	"	"	Sick in quarters
Sergeants.			
John Link	"	"	
George Meldrum	"	"	
Henry Coonrod	"	"	
Christoph'r Dodgson	"	"	
Corporals.			
William McDorman	"	"	
Hugh Jackson	"	"	
John Coonrod	"	"	
Joseph M. Schuyler	"	"	Lost a horse
Privates.			
Bias, James	"	"	
Briggs, Thomas	"	"	Furloughed Aug. 12; lost a horse
Burton, Lemuel	"	"	2;
Coonrod, George	"	"	
Cook, Henry	"	"	
Cook, William	"	"	
Doughty, Felix	"	"	Lost a horse on forced march; sick in q'rt'rs.
Davis, Joshua	"	"	
Fry, Noah	"	"	
Finley, William	"	"	Furloughed August 2
Finley, Zuriah	"	"	
Green, Isaac R	"	"	Lost a horse
Harrison, Fielding	"	"	Furloughed Aug. 2
Johnson, John	"	"	
Jordan, John C	"	"	Discharged by order of Gen. Scott Aug. 2

Name and Rank.	Residence.	Enrolled	Remarks.
Johnson, Robert	Carrollton. Greene Co.	1832 June 19	Discharged June 22; ill-health
Lewis, William	"	"	
Link, Mathias L.	"	"	Lost a horse
Linder, George	"	"	
Mongold, John	"	"	
Mellon, David	"	"	
Noris, James L.	"	"	Discharged June 22; ill-health
Rattan, Hiram	"	"	Absent with leave
Rattan, Larkin	"	"	Lost a horse
Rattan, Jarvis B.	"	"	
Rattan, Littleton	"	"	Furloughed Aug. 2
Rattan, Daniel	"	"	Disch. by Gen. Scott, Aug. 2; lost a horse
Rattan, Richard	"	"	
Sterling, Morse	"	"	
Stone, Asa	"	"	
Standifer, Isreal	"	"	
Waggoner, David	"	"	
Woodman, Austin	"	"	Furloughed Aug. 12
Whitesides, John B.	"	"	
Whitesides, Wm. H.	"	"	" "

This company, May 6, 1832, received orders to march June 3d. Marched June 6th. Arrived at Fort Wilbourn, the appointed place of rendezvous, June 14th, and was mustered into service June 19th. This company found its own rations in full from the 6th of June to the 16th of June. Since the 16th of June nearly all the small rations have been furnished by the company. No forage has ever been issued to this company. No officer of this company has ever drawn more rations than a private.

N. B.—By small rations, we mean candles, soap and all other articles furnished for soldiers, except flour and pork.

CAPT. GERSHOM PATTERSON'S COMPANY

Of the 2d Regiment, 3d Brigade, of the Illinois Mounted Volunteers, called into the service of the United States, on the requisition of Gen. Atkinson, by the Governor's proclamation, dated May 15, 1832. This company was organized at the Rich Woodson, May 2, 1832. Mustered out Aug. 15, 1832, by order of Brig.-Gen. Atkinson.

Name and Rank.	Residence.	Enrolled	Remarks.
Captains.		1832.	
Alexander Smith	Greene Co.	June 19.	Resigned July 15, 1832
Gershom Patterson	"	"	Promoted Captain July 16, 1832
First Lieutenant.			
Jacob Baccus	"	"	Horse and saddle lost Aug. 9, '32, forc'd march
Second Lieutenant.			
Samuel Bowman	"	"	Killed in battle Aug. 2, 1832
Sergeants.			
Jonathan Cooper	"	"	Detailed on extra duty for Qr.-Master
Calvin Piggs	"	"	
James Novin	"	"	Lost horse; on furlough
Alexander Moore	"	"	
Corporals.			
John Reddish	"	"	
Alexander Lyberly	"	"	
Edmund Medford	"	"	Saddle lost in action
Robert Irwin	"	"	
Privates.			
Bonner, Alexander	"	"	On furlough from July 20, 1832
Bowm, John	"	"	" " August 7, 1832
Chowning, Robert	"	"	
Chapman, Thos. H.	"	"	
Carlin, Thomas	"	"	Lost horse, saddle and bridle, forced march.
Chisam, Alexander	"	"	
Clifford, Joseph	"	"	
Darnell, Isaac	"	"	Color bearer. Gun lost in battle
English, John N.	"	"	
McFaine, John	"	"	On furlough; lost horse, etc., forced march
Guffy, John	"	"	lost horse
Higgins, Phillonson	"	"	Lost horse, saddle and bridle, forced march.
Hamilton, Bush. W.	"	"	

THIRD BRIGADE. 63

Name and Rank.	Residence.	Enrolled	Remarks.
		1832.	
Higgins, John	Greene Co	June 19.	
McKinney, Joseph	"	"	On furlough from August 7, 1832
Moore, Seabourn I.	"	"	
Means, James	"	"	
Means, John	"	"	
Mannon, David	"	"	
Rice, Solomon	"	"	
Rusk, David	"	"	On furlough from August 7, 1832
Sears, Thomas	"	"	
Suttlemers, David	"	"	
Walden, Solomon	"	"	
Walden, John	"	"	

Resignation of Capt. Alexander Smith July 15, 1832. Samuel Bowman, 2d Lieut., fell in battle August 2, 1832. This company was organized May 2, 1832, and marched June 9, 1832, to Fort Wilbourn, and was mustered into service June 19, 1832. Gershom Patterson promoted to Captain July 16, 1832. Drawn eight days' rations for the purpose of taking the company to their respective homes. The company furnished their own provisions from the 9th to the 18th of June, 1832.

CAPT. AARON BANNON'S COMPANY

Of the 2d Regiment, 3d Brigade of Illinois Mounted Volunteers, called into the service of the United States, on the requisition of Gen. Atkinson, by the Governor's proclamation, dated May 15, 1832. This company organized, etc., in White Hall, Greene county, Illinois, June 5, 1832. Mustered out of service Aug. 16, 1832.

Name and Rank.	Residence.	Enrolled	Remarks.
Captain.		1832.	
Aaron Bannon	Greene Co	June 19	
First Lieutenant.			
Harvey Jarboe	"	"	
Second Lieutenant.			
Job Collins	"	"	
Sergeants.			
James C. Campbell	"	"	
Absolom Kitchens	"	"	
Uriah Allen	"	"	
James Doddy	"	"	Discharged on account of inability July 15
Corporals.			
Alexander W. Webb	"	"	Horse lost
Hezekiah Crawsby	"	"	
Job Phillips	"	"	
John Jones	"	"	
Privates.			
Bishop, John	"	"	
Breeden, Peter	"	"	
Brantly, Josiah	"	"	
Banon, William	Macoupin Co.	"	On extra duty
Conlee, Rheuben	Greene Co	"	Ordered on special duty June 22
Cartwright, Thomas	"	"	
Drummons, Benj	"	"	
Evelin, Frederick	"	"	
Evans, Joseph	"	"	
Fisher, Samuel A	"	"	Horse lost
Ford, James	"	"	
Goss, Sherman	"	"	
Hart, James	"	"	Horse lost
Hart, John F	"	"	
Han, Henry	"	"	
Hunter, Jesse	"	"	
Morrison, Haman	"	"	Furloughed June 22 from Ft. Wilbourn, sick
Magruder, Edmd. B.	"	"	
Manley, Gabriel	"	"	
McClanan, Jonatn. A	"	"	
Pope, George	"	"	Horse lost
Phillips, Edward	"	"	Furloughed June 22 from Ft. Wilbourn, sick
Rule, Alfred	"	"	Horse lost
Roe, Geo. W	"	"	

Name and Rank.	Residence.	Enrolled	Remarks.
		1832.	
Sprague, Ephriam	LaSalle Co.	June 20	Horse lost
Toops, John	"	June 19	"
Thompson, Beverly A	"	"	
Turman, John G	"	"	
Vineyard, Squire	"	"	
Walker, James	"	"	
Willis, James	"	"	Furloughed June 16 from Ft. Wilbourn, sick

Capt. Thomas Stout's Company,

2d Regiment, 3d Brigade, of Illinois Mounted Volunteers, called into the service of the United States, on the requisition of Gen. Atkinson, by the Governor's proclamation dated ———, 1832. This company organized May 5, 1832, in Bond county, Illinois. Mustered out August 16, 1832.

Name and Rank.	Residence.	Enrolled	Remarks.
Captain.		1832.	
John Stout	Bond Co.	June 19	
First Lieutenant.			
John Stropton	"	"	Absent with leave from Prairie du Chien
Second Lieutenant.			
John P. Hunter	"	"	
Sergeants.			
Austin R. Diamond	"	"	
Lewis Kerr	"	"	
Andrew W. Watson	"	"	
Wilson Carson	"	"	Absent with leave from Pra. du Ch.; horse l'st
Corporals.			
John N. Gilham	"	"	
Andrew Hawn	"	"	Absent with leave from Ft. Hamilton July 29.
Gideon B. Gilmore	"	"	Furloughed July 10th at Ft. Kuskenon
Alexander Steward	"	"	Horse lost
Privates.			
Black, William	"	"	
Bull, Duncan	"	"	
Barlow, Joseph	"	"	
Clanton, Chapman	"	"	Absent with leave from Prairie du Chien
Conry, Andrew	"	"	
Combs, James	"	"	Furloughed June 22, at Ft. Wilbourn
Combs, Westley	"	"	Deserted June 22, at Ft. Wilbourn
Cox, John	"	"	Discharged by order of Gen. Henry, June 22
Downing, James	"	"	
Ellis, Noah	"	"	
Ellison, Price	"	"	
Ellison, James	"	"	Absent with leave from Prairie du Chien
Enlow, James	"	"	Discharged by order of Gen. Scott, Aug. 3
Groen, George	"	"	
Green, James	"	"	Absent with leave from Prairie du Chien
Harper, Robert	"	"	
Harper, James	Putnam Co	"	
Hastings, Sutton	Bond Co.	"	
Hunt, Chas. W	"	"	
Hunter, Samuel	"	"	Discharged by order of Gen. Scott, Aug. 3
James, Benjamin	"	"	Attached to company 20th of June
Koonce, George	"	"	
Little, F. John	"	"	
Laxton, James	Sangamon Co	"	Absent with leave from Prairie du Chien
McCurty, Geo. W	Bond Co.	"	
Moody, Richard	"	"	Discharged by order of Gen. Henry June 22
Moore, James	"	"	
Moore, William	"	"	
McAdow, Samuel N	"	"	
Moody, John F	"	"	
McAdams, William	"	"	
McAdams, Wm. R	"	"	Absent with leave from Prairie du Chien
Nance, Webster	"	"	

THIRD BRIGADE.

Name and Rank.	Residence.	Enrolled	Remarks.
Nelson, Calvin C....	Bond Co....	1832. June 19	
Paisley, William....	"	"	Discharged July 26, at Helena
Pierce, Robert B....	Madison Co..	"	Attached to company June 20.
Pigg, Elijah........	Bond Co	"	
Perdien, Joshua G..	"	"	
Rice, William.......	"	"	
Stokes, Frederick...	"	"	
Stokes, William.....	"	"	
Stubblefield, Lewis.	"	"	Absent with leave from Ft. Hamilton Aug. 12.
Stubblefield, Wiatt..	"	"	
Stubblefield, Wm....	"	"	Absent with leave from Prairie du Chien.....
Sterling, John.......	"	"	
Sellers, Benjamin...	"	"	
Tailor, William T...	"	"	Furloughed from Ft. Hamilton Aug. 12.
White, Alexander R.	"	"	
White, Thomas N...	"	"	Furloughed from Ft. Wilbourn June 22.

THIRD REGIMENT.

Capt. Andrew Bankson's Company

Of the 3d Regiment, 3d Brigade, of Illinois Mounted Volunteers, called into the service of the United States, on the requisition of Gen. Henry Atkinson, by the Governor's proclamation dated May 15, 1832. Mustered out August 17, 1832, by order of Brig.-Gen. Atkinson. Enlisted for 90 days.

Name and Rank.	Residence.	Enrolled	Remarks.
Captain.		1832.	
Andrew Bankson	Clinton Co	May 23.	Absent with leave, July 24, 1832
First Lieutenant.			
Godfrey Ammons	"	"	Present commanding the company
Second Lieutenant.			
James J. Justice	"	"	
Sergeants.			
Henry L. Roper	"	"	Horse lost July 13, 1832
Elisha Phelps	"	"	
Allen Burton	"	"	Discharged on Surg. cert. July 21, 1832
Reubin T. Hawkins	"	"	
Corporals.			
Ephriam Phelps	"	"	
John Cartel	"	"	Disch. on Surg. cert. July 21, 1832; horse lost.
Meredith T. Nichols	"	"	On furlough; horse, etc., lost in battle
John T. Donaldson	"	"	" horse lost in battle
Privates.			
Alton, James	"	"	Discharged on Surg. cert. July 21, 1832. [horse
Blevins, Elijah	"	"	Disch. July 21, 1832, in consequence of loss of
Baker, William	"	"	On furlough Aug. 12, 1832; horse lost
Barcus, John	"	"	
Bradley, Joshua T.	"	"	Lost horse July 13, 1832
Bankson, James	"	"	Absent with leave July 24, 1832; horse lost
Briggs, Andrew	"	"	
Coles, Lewis	"	"	
Dunn, Jesse	"	"	
Edmunds, Levi	"	"	
Ellis, Joel	"	"	
Finch, Joshua	"	"	On furlough Aug. 2, 1832; disch. Aug. 4
French, William	"	"	
French, Richard E.	"	"	
Gates, John	"	"	
Hurst, Benjamin	"	"	Discharged on Surg. cert. July 21
Holland, James A.	"	"	
Hill, James	"	"	On furlough Aug. 2; discharged Aug. 4, 1832
Kelly, Charles D	"	"	
King, John	"	"	
King, Emanuel	"	"	
Lanson, James	"	"	
Logan, John B	"	"	
Mitchell, George	"	"	
McCully, Samuel	"	"	On furlough Aug. 12; lost horse on march
Martin, Peter	"	"	
Nichols, David A	"	"	Furloughed Aug. 12, 1832
Neely, Gilbert	"	"	
Neely, Harrison	"	"	
O'Harnett, John M.	"	"	Discharged on Surg. cert. July 10, 1832
Outhouse, James	"	"	Furloughed Aug. 12, 1832
O'Melvany, John	"	"	Sick in quarters; horse lost July 13, 1832
Parker, Hiram	"	"	Absent with leave July 26, 1832; horse lost
Petty, Anderson	"	"	
Phillips, Jesse	"	"	

Name and Rank.	Residence.	Enrolled	Remarks.
		1832.	
Phelps, Presley	Clinton Co.	May 23.	Discharged on Surg. cert. July 10
Petty, William	"	"	
Roper, John	"	"	
Rodgers, John	"	"	Absent with leave, Aug. 7, 1832; horse lost
Reeves, Thomas	"	"	
Rutledge, James	Morgan Co.	June 21.	Absent with leave Aug. 7; horse lost
Ray, Solomon	Clinton Co.	May 23.	Furloughed Aug. 12 and sick
Ray, Dabel	"	"	
Scott, William	"	"	Horse lost on forced march
Spencer, Daniel	"	"	Absent with leave Aug. 7
Segreaves, Henry	"	"	
Segreaves, William	"	"	
Short, William	"	"	
Smith, Benjamin	"	"	
Settles, Isaac	"	"	Absent with leave Aug. 7; sick
Sharp, Levi	"	"	
Talbut, William	"	"	Absent with leave July 24; horse lost
Talbee, Isaac D	Fayette Co.	June 21.	Horse lost at Mud Lake
White, George W	Clinton Co.	May 23.	Absent with leave July 24; horse lost
Walker, Jeremiah	"	"	
Yarborough, Amb'se	"	"	

The Clinton men started from Carlyle with six days' provisions and forage for their horses at their own expense, and the officers have not drawn any extra rations of any kind during the campaign, having only drawn one single ration for each day; the company only three rations of corn for their horses. The company was organized the 23d day of May, took up their march the 28th, and mustered into the service the 21st of June. The company being discharged, drew twelve days' rations. The officers only drew a single ration. Arrived at Fort Wilbourn on the 15th June, 1832.

(Signed.)   J. T. BRADLEY.

Capt. Wm. Adair's Company

Of the 3d Regiment, 3d Brigade, of Illinois Mounted Volunteers, called into the service of the United States, on the requisition of Gen. Henry Atkinson, by the Governor's proclamation, dated ———, 1832. Mustered out August 17, 1832.

Name and Rank.	Residence.	Enrolled	Remarks.
		1832.	
Captains.			
David Baldridge	Perry Co.	June 26	Resigned June 26, and appointed Adjutant
William Adair	"	"	Promoted Captain June 26, from the ranks
First Lieutenant.			
Jacob Short	"	June 19	Promoted, June 19, from 2d Lieutenant
Second Lieutenant.			
John Hansford	"	"	Promoted, June 19, from private; lost tent
Sergeants.			
Wm. C. Murphy	"	June 4.	Wounded in battle; left at Prairie du Chien
Anderson Bartley	"	"	
Albert B. Murphy	"	"	Lost tent
Frederick Williams	"	"	
Corporals.			
Abraham Cokenhour	"	"	Lost horse
Benjamin Hammock	"	"	Lost horse; furloughed Aug. 8
Robert Gillehan	"	"	
James M. Hogue	"	"	Furloughed Aug. 8
Privates.			
Anderson, Alexand'r	"	"	Discharged July 15 at Winnebago; surgeon
Anderson, Berry	"	"	Disch. June 23 at Wilbourn; surgeon's certif.
Brown, James	"	"	
Brown, James C	"	"	Furloughed Aug. 8
Brown, Payton	"	"	
Benson, Lewis	"	"	
Clark, John	"	"	Furloughed Aug. 8; lost horse
Crane, Joel	"	"	
Casey, Hiram	"	"	

Name and Rank.	Residence.	Enrolled	Remarks.
		1832.	
Crow, Robert	Perry Co	June 24.	Furloughed Aug. 8.
Dickson, John	"	"	Disch. June 23 at Wilbourn; surgeon's certif.
Earnest, Andrew	"	"	
Ford, Jesse	"	"	
France, Peter	"	"	
Garner, Francis	"	"	
Hawkins, Ausborn	"	"	
Hutchings, Eli J	"	"	
Hutching, ——	"	"	Died Aug. 3 of wounds received Aug. 2.
Hutching, William	"	"	Dead; left sick at Salt River June 14.
Huggins, James	"	"	
Hull, Zebedee	"	"	
Keath, Resin	"	"	
Keath, Bown	"	"	
McDowell, Thomas J	"	"	
Misenhammer, Pet'r	"	"	
Montague, James M.	"	"	Left sick at Prairie du Chien.
Pitchford, Samuel	"	"	Lost horse.
Pyle, Abner	"	"	Lost horse.
Petit, Jonathan	"	"	
Reece, Ephriam	"	"	
Rice, Abner L	"	"	
Terry, George	"	"	
Williams, Beverly	"	"	Discharged June 23 at Wilbourn.
Wells, Joseph	"	"	Disch. at Blue Mound, being wounded Aug. 10
Wells, Josiah	"	"	
Welks, Peter W	"	"	Furloughed Aug. 8.
Woodrum, Nicholas	"	"	
Washburn, John	"	"	
Wolf, Thomas	"	"	Furloughed Aug. 8.

Capt. Josiah S. Briggs' Company,

3d Regiment, 3d Brigade, of Illinois Mounted Volunteers, called into the service of the United States, on the requisition of Gen. Henry Atkinson, by the Governor's proclamation dated May 15, 1832. Mustered out August 17, 1832.

Name and Rank.	Residence.	Enrolled	Remarks.
Captain.		1832.	
Josiah S. Briggs	Randolph Co.	May 24	
First Lieutenant.			
John Morrison	"	"	
Second Lieutenant.			
John Thompson	"	"	Left at Winnebago with Col. Sharp; ord to [Galena; horse lost.
Sergeants.			
Robert Mann	"	"	
Francis S. Jones	"	"	
John Alcorn	"	"	
James Harmon	"	"	
Corporals.			
Andrew McFarlin	"	"	Horse lost.
John McFarlin	"	"	
Richard Bradley	"	"	" discharged at Winnebago July 15.
Samuel Hathorn	"	"	
Privates.			
Anderson, David	"	"	Supposed to be discharged at Casheonong.
Anderson, Thomas	"	"	
Barbour, James	"	"	Left to attend Saml. Barbour, sick at Ft. Win-
Batman, James	"	"	[nebago.
Burns, Samuel	"	"	
Brown, Samuel	"	"	
Campbell, Alexand'r	"	"	Furnished, July 25, Wm. Harper as substit'te;
Campbell, Samuel	"	"	[trans. to Capt. Lindsey's Co. July 25
Caldwell, Robert	"	"	Left at Prairie du Chien, sick.
Christie, Eneas	"	"	Left with Col. Sharp at Winneb. on det. serv.
Crawford, Samuel	"	"	Left at Prairie du Chien, sick.

THIRD BRIGADE.

Name and Rank.	Residence.	Enrolled	Remarks.
		1832.	
Clendenen, Wm. S.	Randolph Co.	May 24	Horse lost.............................
Gilbreath, Jno. R.	"	"	
Hathorn, John	"	"	Promoted Sergeant-Major June 21.......
Huey, John C.	"	"	
Hughes, John M.	"	"	
Harr, Sanford	"	"	
Jernigan, Bryant B.	"	"	
Jones, Moses	"	"	
Kilpatrick, Isaac A.	"	"	Left at Fort Hamilton, sick............
Lee, James F.	"	"	
Lee, John	"	"	Horse lost.............................
Lee, Thomas	"	"	
Lively, Joseph	"	"	
Laird, John	"	"	
Lively, James	"	"	
Murphy, David	"	"	
McHenry, John	"	"	
McDill, Samuel	"	"	
Morgan, Hiram	"	"	Left to attend sick at Prairie du Chien........
Maxwell, Samuel	"	"	horse lost
Oliver, Duritt	"	"	Left at Blue Mounds, sick............
Patterson, James H.	"	"	Left at Prairie du Chien, sick........
Pettit, Samuel	"	"	
Robinson, Richard	"	"	Horse lost.............................
Short, Thomas J.	"	"	Killed July 21.........................
Smith, Francis	"	"	
Swanwick, Francis	"	"	Left to attend the sick at Prairie du Chien...
Sadler, Benjamin	"	"	
Sheets, Firman	"	"	Horse lost.............................
Thomerson, George	"	"	
White, John	"	"	Wounded in battle Aug. 2, Prairie du Chien..
Woods, John	"	"	

This company enrolled and elected its officers on May 24, 1832. Marched, on May 27, 1832, for Beardstown, and was mustered into the service of the United States June 21, 1832.

CAPT. JAMES THOMPSON'S COMPANY

Of the 3d Regiment, 3d Brigade, of Illinois Mounted Volunteers, called into the service of the United States by the Governor's proclamation, dated ——, 1832. Mustered out August 17, 1832.

Name and Rank.	Residence.	Enrolled	Remarks.
		1832.	
Captain.			
James Thompson	Randolph Co.	June 4	
First Lieutenant.			
Samuel Barber	"	"	Absent, sick; left at Ft. Winnebago July 15...
Second Lieutenant.			
Wm. H. McDill	"	"	Absent; left at Prairie du Chien to take care of John White, wounded by Indians.
Sergeants.			
Moses W. Taggart	"	"	................[care of Robert Smith, sick.
Richard Lively	"	"	Absent; left above Prairie du Chien to take
Robert C. Jones	"	"	
Harmon Marlin	"	"	
Corporals.			
Archibald Crozier	"	"	
Robert Hamilton	"	"	....................[wounded by Indians.
James Thomson, Jr.	"	"	Absent; left to take care of Andr. McCormick.
William Pike	"	"	
Privates.			
Brown, John	"	"	
Brown, John C.	"	"	
Been, Allen	"	"	
Ball, Nelson	"	"	Discharged at Blue Mound on Surg. certif...
Bowerman, William	"	"	

Name and Rank.	Residence.	Enrolled	Remarks.
		1832	
Bilderback, Friend..	Randolph Co.	June 4.	
Crozier, Andrew	"	"	
Davis, Robert......	"	"	
Dukes, Martin	"	"	
Davis, Ishom F.....	"	"	
Foster, John........	"	"	
Gray, William	"	"	Lost his horse on forced march
Hathaway, Harvey..	"	"	
Harmon, Jacob......	"	"	
Hathaway, Milton ..	"	"	
Hughes, John.......	"	"	
Jones, Andrew	"	"	
Layne, Wiley	"	"	
Milligan, James	"	"	Discharged at Blue Mound on Surg. certif.
McBride, Absalom...	"	"	
McCormick, Andrew	"	"	Absent with leave; wounded in battle........
Murphy, Miller	"	"	
Marlin, Edward F. ..	"	"	Got his horse killed
Miller, Robert......	"	"	
McNeel, William ...	"	"	
Overton, Benj., Jr...	"	"	Present, sick
Patterson, John	"	"	Absent; left to take care of his brother James
Parks, William	"	"	Lost his horse; present, sick
Reed, James........	"	"	
Short, John	"	"	Discharged at Blue Mound on Surg. certif.
Steele, James.......	"	"	Absent on furlough since July 25
Steele, George......	"	"	Lost his horse
Smith, Robert R	"	"	Absent, sick; left near Prairie du Chien......
Taylor, John........	"	"	
Thomas, John W....	"	"	
Tindel, John........	"	"	
Vickers, Abel.......	"	"	
Wilcox, James......	"	"	
Wise, Enoch G	"	"	Horse drowned; got another, lost him........

This company was raised and organized on June 4, under the command of Gabriel Jones, Captain; James Thompson, 1st Lieut.; Samuel Barber, 2d Lieut. Marched on June 8, and was mustered into the service at Fort Wilbourn June 21, under Capt. James Thompson, Gabriel Jones having been elected Colonel.

Capt. Jacob Feaman's,
afterwards
Capt. James Conner's, Company

Of the 3d Regiment, 3d Brigade, of Illinois Mounted Volunteers, called into the service of the United States, on the requisition of Gen. Atkinson, by the Governor's proclamation dated —— 1832. Mustered out August 17, 1832.

Name and Rank.	Residence.	Enrolled	Remarks.
Captains.		1832.	
Jacob Feaman........	Randolph Co.	May 25.	Resigned July 25
James Corner	"	"	Promoted, July 25, from 1st Lieut. to Capt....
First Lieutenant.			
Mathew Gray	"	"	Promoted, July 25, from 1st Sergt. to Lieut...
Second Lieutenant.			
David Wright........	"	"	Pro. June 7 and left sick at Prairie du Chien.
Sergeants.			
Isaac Nelson........	"	"	Appointed, July 25
George Glenn.......	"	"	" June 22
Menard Maxwell	"	"	" 20
Joseph Orr..........	"	"	" Quartermaster Sergeant, July 26.

THIRD BRIGADE.

Name and Rank.	Residence.	Enrolled	Remarks.
Corporals.		1832.	
Patrick Faherty	Randolph Co.	May 25.	
James Whalen	"	"	
John Levett	"	"	Supposed discharged, Aug. 4, 1832.
Wiley Paschall	"	"	Horse lost or stolen.
Privates.			
Bond, Edward	"	"	
Brewer, Vincent	"	"	
Brightwell, John	"	"	
Brown, Allanson	"	"	Discharged, June 21, disability
Bogy, Lewis V	"	"	" July 15
Chapall, Elias	"	"	
Chaupine, Lewis	"	"	
Doris, Martin W	"	"	Promoted Paymaster, July 15.
Dugger, Flud	"	"	Left at Prairie du Chien to tend sick, Aug. 7
Drousse, Henry	"	"	
Davis, Michael	"	"	
Doza, Joseph	"	"	
Evens, William	"	"	
Fulton, William	"	"	
Hampton, Wilson	"	"	[on the 25th
Jones, Armstead	"	"	Wounded on July 21, and absent with leave
Jarrel, John	"	"	
Keemasa, Baptist	"	"	
Langton, Francis	"	"	Left sick at Mounds, July 25.
Lackopelle, Henry	"	"	
Levens, Henry	"	"	
Minard, Medard	"	/ "	Absent with leave, Aug. 7
Miers, James P	"	"	Detached to tend on Jones, July 25.
Mart, Ravelle	"	"	
Morrison, William	"	"	Absent with leave, Aug. 7
Mudd, Harrison	"	"	
Minard, Peter	"	"	Lost horse and pack-saddle on forced march
Onger, Ferdinand	"	"	
O'Hara, John	"	"	Discharged, July 15; disability
Phillips, Berrel	"	"	" "
Patterson, Bhenler	"	"	
Penncana, Baptist	"	"	Horse lost on or near Four Lakes
Pascal, Francis	"	"	
Roberts, Abram	"	"	
Reynolds, John	"	"	
Seymour, Grove	"	"	Supposed discharged, July 26, 1832
Vrain, Dometius F	"	"	Discharged, June 16; disability
Will, Joseph	"	"	
Winter, William	"	"	
Woolsey, Wash'ton	"	"	
Wilson, David E	"	"	Left at Prairie du Chien, sick
White, John	"	"	
Willmuth, Louis	"	"	

This company was organized at Kaskaskia, May 25, 1832, and was mustered into the service of the United States at Fort Wilbourn, June 21, 1832.

CAPT. JAMES BURNS' COMPANY

Of 3d Regiment, 3d Brigade of Mounted Volunteers, called into the service of the United States, on the requisition of Gen. Atkinson, by the Governor's proclamation dated May 15, 1832. Mustered into the service June 21, 1832. Mustered out August 17, 1832. Organized May 4, 1832.

Name and Rank.	Residence.	Enrolled	Remarks.
Captain.			
James Burns	Washing'n Co	May 4	
First Lieutenants.			
Andrew Lyons			Resigned June 28; does duty in line
William Wood			Lost horse; elected from 1st Corp, June 28; [lost tent.
Second Lieutenant.			
Cyrus Sawyers			Furl'd July 25; lost horse & tent on f'ced m'ch

Name and Rank.	Residence.	Enrolled	Remarks.
Sergeants.			
John D. Wood			Resigned June 21; promoted to Major
Henry Cherry			Absent with leave July 25
John H. Hood			Lost his horse; lost tent on forced march
Harvey Nevels			
Anthony Darter			Furloughed July 25; lost tent on forced m'ch
Corporals.			
John Mitchell			Broke bayonet
George Terrill			
Marquis G. Faulkner			Absent with leave Aug. 12; lost his horse
William Minson			Discharged July 15, on Surgeon's certificate.
Privates.			
Anderson, Samuel K.			Lost his blanket
Anderson, James			
Anderson, Alexand'r			
Andrew, Lyons			Absent with leave Aug. 12; lost his horse
Burns, John M.			" " " "
Burns, Samuel			" " " "
Burns, Robert			" " " "
Balch, Armstead B.			" " July 25
Casner, John			" " Aug. 12
Gilbreath, John W.			
Holly, Pleasant I. M.			
Rouse, Anthony M.			Absent with leave Aug. 5; lost his horse
Hutchens, Richard			Lost his horse; lost tent on forced march
Joiner, William			
James, Preston B.			Absent with leave July 25
King, William			" " "
Knight, John			" " Aug. 12
Lee, George W.			
Linch, Mathew K.			Absent with leave Aug. 12; lost his horse
Locke, James			
Livesay, Lorenzo D.			" " "
McMillen, Meredith S			Disch. July 25, being wounded July 21 in b'ttle
McElhannon, Jas. M.			Absent with leave July 25
Mitchell, Samuel C.			
Morgan, Solomon			
Morgan, Cary			Absent with leave July 25
Morgan, Benajah			
Pate, George W.			
Paterson, James			Absent with leave August 5
Pepper, Moseel D.			Appointed Surgeon's Mate June 21
Linyon, Edward			Absent with leave Aug. 12
Ramsey, James			
Thompson, James			Disch. July 25, being wounded July 21 in b'ttle
Tate, William			Absent; lost his horse & tent on forced m'ch
Underwood, David			
Underwood, James			Furloughed on Surgeon's certificate June 22.
Wells, Levi			
White, James R.			
White, Andrew			
White, James S.			
Wood, Charles H.			Lost his horse

FOURTH REGIMENT.

Capt. Bennet Nowlen's Company

Of 4th Regiment, 3d Brigade, Illinois Mounted Volunteers, called into the service of the United States, on the requisition of Gen. Henry Atkinson, by the Governor's proclamation dated May 15, 1832. Mustered out August 16, 1832.

Name and Rank.	Residence.	Enrolled	Remarks.
Captain.		1832.	
Bennet Nowlen	Macoupin Co.	June 19	
First Lieutenants.			
Jesse Scott	"	"	Resigned July 10, 1832
John Yowell	"	"	Elected 1st Lieut. July 12, 1832.
Second Lieutenant.			
John Allen	"	"	Furloughed August 14, 1832
Sergeants.			
Silas Harris	"	"	
George Sprouse	"	"	Discharged August 11, 1832
Cherry Peterson	"	"	
Daniel Huddlestun	"	"	
Corporals.			
Thomas McManus	"	"	Discharged August 11, 1832
Christopher Gilpin	"	"	
Thomas Grant	"	"	
Zachariah Stewart	"	"	
Privates.			
Adams, William C	"	"	
Bewford, Thomas	"	"	
Brawdy, Azariah	"	"	Furloughed June 20, 1832, on Surg. certificate.
Brown, Wiley	"	"	
Caudle, Isham	"	"	
Cummings, Thomas	"	"	
Cummings, Samuel	"	"	
Chapman, John	"	"	
Caudle, Thomas	"	"	
England, John	"	"	Horse lost.
Funderburk, Titus L.	"	"	
Gibson, Jacob	"	"	Discharged August 2, 1832
Hill, Wyat R.	"	"	
Hutton, Charles K.	"	"	
Hughs, Thomas	"	"	
Jordan, James	"	"	
Lair, Charles	"	"	Furloughed July 10, 1832
McCollum, Isaac	"	"	
McPoters, Harvy	"	"	
McKindley, Edward	"	"	
Nevins, John	"	"	Furloughed July 10, 1832
Powers, John H.	"	"	
Pruet, Isaac	"	"	
Record, John	"	"	Horse lost.
Richardson, Thomas	"	"	
Rush, William	"	"	Horse lost.
Richards, Edmund	"	"	
Sandridge, Hasting	"	"	Furloughed August 14, 1832
Snoll, Hardy	"	"	
Simmons, Joshua	"	"	

Name and Rank.	Residence.	Enrolled	Remarks.
Sharp, Isaac	Macoupin Co.	1832. June 19	
Snow, Obed	"	"	
Turner, Edmund L.	"	"	
Vincent, Joseph	"	"	

Company formed and elected Powell H. Sharp Captain, Bennet Nowlen 1st Lieut., and John Allen 2d Lieut., June 9, 1832. Marched June 11, 1832. Mustered into service June 19, 1832.

Powell H. Sharp promoted Lieut.-Colonel June 19, 1832. Bennet Nowlen promoted Captain June 19, 1832.

Capt. Ozias Hail's Company,

4th Regiment, 3d Brigade, of Illinois Mounted Volunteers, called into the service of the United States, on the requisition of Gen. Henry Atkinson, by the Governor's proclamation dated May 15, 1832. Mustered out August 16, 1832.

Name and Rank.	Residence.	Enrolled	Remarks.
Captain.		1832.	
Ozias Hail	Pike Co.	June 19.	
First Lieutenant.			
David Seeley	"	"	
Second Lieutenant.			
Robart Goodin	"	"	
Sergeants.			
Enoch Cooper	"	"	
Adam Harpool	"	"	
John McMullin	"	"	
Isaac Turnbaugh	"	"	
Josiah Sims	"	"	Discharged July 21
Corporals.			
Benjamin Shin	"	"	
John Battershell	"	"	Furloughed June 23.
William Cooper	"	"	
Isaac Dolbaugh	"	"	
John Crass	"	"	Discharged July 15.
Privates.			
Ames, Smith	"	"	
Alcorn, William	"	"	
Blair, Culverson	"	"	
Bradshaw, Elijah	"	"	
Blythe, John	"	"	Lost his horse
Bradshaw, Enoch	"	"	" " by forced march
Burcaloo, John	"	"	
Baker, Sylvanus	"	"	
Butler, Derns	"	"	
Buffenbarger, Wm.	"	"	
Butley, Frederick	Morgan Co.	"	Discharged June 22; lost his horse: wagoner
Cole, David	Pike Co.	"	" July 15.
Clark, Abnor	"	"	
Davis, Joshua	"	"	
Davis, William	"	"	
Foster, John	"	"	Left at Ft. Dickson sick; supp. disch'd Aug. 7
Franklin, Frederic	"	"	Left sick on the road June 12
Harpool, William	"	"	
Kinney, William	"	"	
McLain, Absalom	"	"	Furloughed June 23.
Miller, Calep	Pike Co.	"	
Miller, George	"	"	
Moore, David	"	"	
Melhizer, John	"	"	Horse lost.
McLain, Wm	"	"	Furloughed June 25.
Mitchell, William	Pike Co.	"	
Neeley, Burgess	"	"	
Neeley, John	"	"	Gun bursted.
Neeley, Samuel	"	"	

Name and Rank.	Residence.	Enrolled	Remarks.
		1832.	
Neeley, Thomas.....		June 19	Left sick at Wilbourn June 23.................
Nisenger, Rosen.....	Pike Co....	"	
Prior, James B.....	"	"	Discharged July 15; horse lost.................
Pulum, Benjamin...	"	"	
Shinn, John..........	"	"	
Spears, Harris......	"	"	
Stigney, Philip H...	"	"	
Turnbough, Joseph.	"	"	
Taylor, John M.....	"	"	
Yesley, Ebenezer...	"	"	

The above company volunteered and organized in Atlas, in Pike county, on June 4, 1832, and in pursuance of orders then received, marched immediately to rendezvous at Fort Wilbourn, where they arrived on June 17, and were mustered into service June 19, 1832.

CAPT. JESSE CLAYWELL'S COMPANY,

4th Regiment, 3d Brigade of Illinois Mounted Volunteers, called into the service of the United States, on the requisition of Gen. Atkinson, by the Governor's proclamation, dated May 15, 1832. Mustered out of service Aug. 16, 1832.

Name and Rank.	Residence.	Enrolled	Remarks.
Captain.		1832	
Jesse Claywell......	Sangamon Co	June 5.	Furloughed at Wisconsin river July 27.........
First Lieutenants.			
John H. Wilcoxson..	"	"	Elected 1st Lieut. July 11; sick at Hamilton..
Lowyel Cox	"	"	Resigned July 10.............................
Second Lieutenant.			
Rezen H. Constant..	"	"	Elected 2d Lieutenant July 11.................
Sergeants.			
Archibald Cass......	"	"	Elected 1st Sergeant July 11..................
Andrew Moore......	"	"	
Valentine R. Mallory	"	"	At Fort Crawford.............................
William S. Hussey..	"	"	Attending to a sick man......................
Corporals.			
Nathan Hussey, 1st.	"	"	Prom. Brig. Wagon Master June 21; lost horse
Robert L. Gott, 1st..	"	"	Attending to a sick man at Hamilton..........
William B. Hagan, 2d	"	"	
James C. Hagan, 3d.	"	"	
Harris'n McGary, 4th	"	"	Transferred to Capt. Earley's Co. June 20....
John McLemoor, 4th	"	"	
Privates.			
Anderson, Alexand'r	"	"	
Anderson, Lewis C..	"	"	
Anderson, James....	"	"	
Anderson, Wash'ton.	"	"	
Burns, John R........	"	"	
Barnet, William I....	"	"	
Barnet, William......	"	"	
Barnet, Hugh.........	"	"	
Brewer, John, Sr....	"	"	Furloughed July 10; also lost his horse.......
Brewer, John, Jr....	"	"	
Cass, Anderson B...	"	"	
Constant, Nathan E.	"	"	
Constant, Isaac......	"	"	
Crocker, Harvey....	"	"	
Currey, George......	"	"	
Copeland, John......	"	"	
Dooley, Jeremiah...	"	"	Discharged July 27 for disability.............
Dement, William....	"	"	Lost horse, saddle and bridle.................
Elliott, Haddon......	"	"	Furloughed by the Surgeon's certificate......
Elliott, Richard......	"	"	
Glenn, David A......	"	"	
Green, George.......	"	"	

Name and Rank.	Residence.	Enrolled	Remarks.
		1832.	
Helm, Guy	Sangamon Co	June 5.	
Hagan, Samuel C	"	"	
Hide, John	"	"	
Kelly, Jeremiah	"	"	Lost horse, saddle and bridle
Langston, James	"	"	
Lucas, Thomas	"	"	
McGary, Hugh	"	"	Transferred to Capt. Earley's Co. June 20.
Martin, Joseph	"	"	
Neucam, William T.	"	"	
Pickerel, Benj. F.	"	"	Transferred to Capt. Earley's Co. June 20.
Prim, Abraham	"	"	
Powel, John	"	"	
Powel, Hiram	"	"	Furloughed at Ft. Wilbourn June 20.
Rogers, William F	"	"	Lost his horse.
Riddle, James	"	"	
Snelson, John W	"	"	
Shearley, James	"	"	
Smith, Joseph I	"	"	
Smith, Philip	"	"	
Smith, Eliphas	"	"	Furloughed at Ft. Wilbourn June 20.
Stone, William A	"	"	
Stone, Caleb	"	"	
Turner, William	"	"	
Waldon, James	"	"	
Wilcox, Ephriam	"	"	
Young, Joseph R	"	"	Wound'd in battle at Mississ.; at Ft. Crawford

This company was organized June 5, 1832, marched for place of rendezvous on June 10, and was mustered into service June 20, 1832.

CAPT. REUBEN BROWN'S COMPANY

Of 4th Regiment, 3d Brigade, Mounted Illinois Volunteers, called into the service of the United States, on the requisition of Gen. Atkinson, by the Governor's proclamation, dated May 15, 1832. Mustered out Aug. 16, 1832.

Name and Rank.	Residence.	Enrolled	Remarks.
Captain.		1832	
Reuben Brown	Sangamon Co	June 20.	Commanding company; present, but sick
First Lieutenant.			
William Baker	"	"	
Second Lieutenant.			
Daloss Brown	"	"	On furlough during term enrollment, in con-[sequence of a wound.
Sergeants.			
Thomas Jones	"	"	
Saml. E. McKenzey	"	"	Promoted from private to Sergt. June 19, 1832.
Evan Morgan	"	"	Furl. during term of enroll.; cause, sickness.
Nathan Said	"	"	Furloughed Aug. 7, 1832, during term service.
Corporals.			
Jesse Said	"	"	
Reason Brown	"	"	
John Fegan	"	"	
James B. Jones	"	"	
Privates.			
Archer, Winston	"	"	
Baker, Thomas	"	"	
Baker, James	"	"	
Brown, Jerry	"	"	
Cutright, Peter	"	"	
Durboin, Edward	"	"	Joined from Capt. Warwick's Co. of Mounted [Volunteers Aug. 1, 1832, per certificate.
Delay, Stephen	"	"	
Duglass, Thomas	"	"	Furloughed Aug. 7, 1832, during term service.
Donaldson, Dudley	"	"	
Hendricks, Samuel	"	"	
Huggard, James	"	"	Furloughed Aug. 12, 1832, during term service.

THIRD BRIGADE. 77

Name and Rank.	Residence.	Enrolled	Remarks.
Larkin, Young	Sangamon Co	1832 June 20	
Lucas, Allen B	"	"	
Lucas, James	"	"	Deserted June 22, 1832, from Ft. Wilbourn, Ill.
Morgan, Thomas	"	"	
Martin, Rolley	"	"	Furl. during term of service; cause, sickness
McKinzey, Henry	"	"	
Pillman, James	"	"	
Poor, James H	"	"	Lost horse in service
Pike, John	"	"	
Porter, William	"	"	On furlough Aug. 7, during term of service
Read, James	"	"	Deserted June 22, 1832, from Ft. Wilbourn, Ill.
Spillars, Wm. H	"	"	Horse lost in service; furloughed August 7,
St. John, Joseph	"	"	..................[during term of service.
Stafford, Daniel S	"	"	
Trotter, George	"	"	
Williams, Isiah B	"	"	
Transferred.			
Baker, James	"	"	Trans. June 22, 1832, to Capt. Earley's Co

This company was organized in Sangamon county, Springfield, June 6, 1832. Arrived at headquarters, Ft. Wilbourne, June 15, 1832. Mustered into service June 20, 1832.

CAPT. THOMAS MOFFETT'S COMPANY,

4th Regiment, 3d Brigade, of Illinois Mounted Volunteers, called into the service of the United States on the requisition of Gen. H. Atkinson, by the Governor's proclamation. Mustered out August 16, 1832.

Name and Rank.	Residence.	Enrolled	Remarks.
Captain.		1832.	
Thomas Moffett	Sangamon Co.	June 4	Lost his horse
First Lieutenants.			
David Black	"	"	Resigned and went home July 10
Shadrack Campbell	"	"	Elected vice D. Black, resigned July 10, 1832
Second Lieutenant.			
James Watson	"	"	
Sergeants.			
John Oldfield	"	"	Lost his horse
Thos. Epperson	"	"	Elected vice Joseph Inslee; resigned July 10.
Joseph Inslee	"	"	Discharged by Gen. Atkinson June 29
George Lindsey	"	"	Elected vice T. Epperson; resigned July 10
Franklin Williams	"	"	Lost his horse
Wm. C. Stephenson	"	"	
Corporals.			
John Humphreys	"	"	
James Campbell	"	"	Horse lost
Nathan Ralston	"	"	
Jarret McKinney	"	"	
Cornet.			
Gersham Dorrence	"	"	
Saddler.			
John Ridgeway	"	"	
Farrier.			
Jesse H. Steel	"	"	
Trumpeter.			
Armstead Ables	"	"	Discharged by Gen. Atkinson July 10
David Duncan	"	"	Elected July 10 vice Armstead Ables, disch'd.
Privates.			
Armstrong, Hugh M.	"	"	
Atkinson, Bushrod	"	"	Furloughed August 11
Brazzle, William	"	"	

Name and Rank.	Residence.	Enrolled	Remarks.
		1832.	
Ball, Smith	Sangam'n Co.	June 4.	
Crain, Thomas	"	"	Discharged July 10 by Gen. Atkinson
Cooper, William	"	"	
Carmar, Walter	"	"	
Cabaniss, Zabulon P.	"	"	
Durham, Walter	"	"	
Duncan, Jo-eph W.	"	"	
Drennan, A. P.	"	"	Furloughed August 11
Elkin, Garret	"	"	June 18
Epperson, Thomas	"	"	Served as 2d Sergeant from June 29 to July 10
Enix, James	"	"	Lost one U. S. pistol
Forbus, R. A.	"	"	
Getsondiner, Jno. L.	"	"	
Glascock, Gregory	"	"	Lost his horse
Hill, John P.	"	"	Lost his horse
Latham, John	"	"	Furloughed on account of sickness June 19
Lowe, Richard	"	"	
Levi, John	"	"	Descended the Miss. river Aug. 8
Lane, Jacob	"	"	Horse missing
Langley, Robert	"	"	
McAllister, William	"	"	
Moore, Joseph	"	"	
Milts, William	"	"	
Norris, Joseph	"	"	
Paine, Barzilla	"	"	
Pulliam, Martin G.	"	"	Furloughed June 20 on account of sickness
Pierce, Philetus G.	"	"	Lost his horse
Peter, Samuel	"	"	Absent without leave June 23
Saunders, Presley	"	"	
Smith, Tillman	"	"	
Smith, John	"	"	Furloughed June 27 on account of sickness
Smith, Adam	"	"	Joined D. Earley's Spy company June 29
Stout, George	"	"	
Watson, Hiram	"	"	Lost his horse
Warnsing, John	"	"	Promoted Reg'l Surg. Mate June 22; horse lost

This company mustered into the service at Fort Wilbourn June 20, 1832; was enrolled and mustered preparatory to starting from home at Springfield, Ill., June 4, 1832.

Capt. Henry L. Webb's Company

Of Mounted Volunteers, called into the service of the United States by order of the Governor of the State, by his order of the 15th of May, 1832, until 3d August, 1832, when mustered out of service by order of Major-General Scott, commanding Northwestern army.

Name and Rank.	Residence.	Enrolled	Remarks.
		1832.	
Captain,			
Henry L. Webb	Alex'nder Co.	May 19	
First Lieutenant,			
Richard H. Price	"	"	Rifle lost swimming Rock River after Indians
Second Lieutenants,			
David H. Moore	"	"	Promoted Qu'rmaster Spy Bat. 3d Br. June 16
James D. Morris	"	June 16	Elected 2d Lt. June 16, when comm'n'd Corp. from the 19th of May, '32, until promoted
Sergeants.			
Owen Willis, 1st	"	May 19	
Quinton Ellis, 2d	"	"	
Aaron Atherton, Jr. 3	"	"	
Sam. Ath'ton Neal, 4th	"	"	
Corporals,			
Merritt Howell	"	"	
Aaron Anglin	"	"	
William Dickey	"	"	
Giles Whitaker	"	"	

Name and Rank.	Residence.	Enrolled	Remarks.
Privates.		1832.	
Anglin, William	Alex'nder Co.	May 19	
Anglin, James	"	"	
Bunch, Cader	"	"	
Burks, Hardin	"	"	
Brown, Berry	"	"	
Brooks, Benj.	"	"	
Caines, John	"	"	
Cannon, Tillman	"	"	
Dexter, Jeremiah	"	"	
Daniels, Solomon	"	"	
Eckols, Benjamin	"	"	
Harrison, Henry H.	"	"	
Harvill, Loudy	"	"	
Hargis, Resin	"	"	
Hughs, Franklin	"	"	
Hurgis, Turner	"	"	
Jeffers, John E.	"	"	Absent with leave.
Johnson, Henry K.	"	"	
Keneda, Thomas	"	"	
Keneda, Alexander	"	"	
Lackey, Alfred	"	"	
Lynch, Cyrus S.	"	"	Rifle lost swim'ing Rock River after Indians.
McCool, George	"	"	
McCool, Benjamin	"	"	
Meshow, William	"	"	
McCloud, Roderick	"	"	
Murphy, John	"	"	
Neale, George C.	"	"	
Post, Marcus	"	"	
Phillips, James	"	"	
Rice, Samuel F.	"	"	
Powell, Wm. S.	"	"	
Powell, Alanson	"	"	Prom. Q. M. Sergt. Spy Bat. 3d Brig. June 16.
Russell, Robert	"	"	
Smith, Enoch	"	"	
Taylor, James M.	"	"	
Thompson, Nathan M	"	"	
Townsend, James W.	"	"	
Townsend, John	"	"	
White, Samuel	"	"	

SPY BATTALION.

Capt. Allen F. Lindsey's Company

Of the Spy Battalion, 3d Brigade, Illinois Mounted Volunteers, called into service of the United States, on the requisition of Gen. Atkinson, by the Governor's proclamation dated May 16, 1832. Mustered out August 16, 1832.

Name and Rank.	Residence.	Enrolled	Remarks.
Captain. Allen F. Lindsey	Morgan Co	1832. June 19	Horse unfit for service, by forced marching.
First Lieutenant. William Scott	"		Sick in tent
Second Lieutenant. Isaac R. Bennett	"		One sorrel mare lost by forced marching
Sergeants. Martin Harding	"		One bay mare lost in service
Leftridge B. Lindsey	"		
Geo. W. Beggs	"		One bayonet scabbard lost in service
David Thomsberry	"		Furloughed July 25th at Casleman
Corporals. John Caldwell	"		One bayonet lost in service
Thos. R. Thompson	"		
John A. Creed	"		One mare lost on forced march; one bayonet-
Royal Flynn			[belt and scabbard.
Privates. Cox, Thomas	"		
Cooper, William			
Cumins, William	Sanganaw Cy		
Dick, John P	Morgan Co		Detailed by Brig. Qr. Master July 4, 1832
Fox, Madison	"		
Flynn, William	"		
Flynn, Zadock W	"		One bay mare lost in service
Garrett, Jesse B	"		Furloughed July 25th at Casleman
Hudspeth, John	"		
Hash, Philip	"		One bay horse and bayonet lost in service
Harper, William	"		Fransferred from Capt. Biggs' Co. July 25th
King, Daniel	Sanganaw Cy	June 22	
Lindsey, William	Morgan Co		
Lucas, William	"	June 22	One bay mare lost in service
Lucas, John	"		
Mathews, William	"		Furloughed July 25th at Casleman
Meeker, Usel	Sanganaw Cy	June 22	
Manchester, David	Morgan Co		
McDonald, Frederi'k	"	June 22	On detailed service
Olaker, Jacob	"		
Ogle, James A	"		
Plaster, Thomas	"		On detached service by Gov., July 4, 1832
Paschel, Samuel	"		
Poindexter, Micajah	"		Sick in tent; horse rendered unfit for service.
Ritchie, William	"		
Sims, Westley			[at Dixon's Ferry.
Shelton, David	Morgan Co		Discharged June 27, 1832, by Com.-in-Chief,
Taylor, James	"		Furloughed July 25th at Casleman
Thomas, James J	"		
Woldridge, Thomas	"		Absent with leave
Walker, James H	"		Mare, bayonet and scabbard lost in service
Yaple, Jacob			

This company was organized June 4, and was mustered into service on June 19.

Capt. Samuel Huston's Company,

Spy Battalion, 3d Brigade, of Illinois Mounted Volunteers, called into the service of the United States, on the requisition of Gen. Henry Atkinson, by the Governor's proclamation dated May 15, 1832. Mustered out Aug. 16, 1832, by order of Brig.-Gen. Atkinson.

Name and Rank.	Residence.	Enrolled	Remarks.
Captain.		1832.	
Samuel Huston	Fayette Co.	June 7	
First Lieutenant.			
John Watwood	"	"	Left Helena July 27; lost his horse July 23
Second Lieutenant.			
Henry Brown	"	"	
Sergeants.			
Payton R. Bankson	"	"	
Richard Auston	"	"	Lost his horse on the 11th of August
Hezekiah Thompson	"	"	
Isaac Fancher	"	"	Lost his horse on the 7th of August
Corporals.			
Benjamin Seals	"	"	Left sick on the 27th of July
Andrew I. Hickerson	"	"	
Alexander Fancher	"	"	Lost his horse on the 7th of August
Thomas Osbrooks	"	"	
Privates.			
Allen, John	"	"	
Austin, Philip L.	"	"	Furloughed at Helena on the 27th
Berry, Benjamin F.	"	"	
Beck, Paul	"	"	
Braswell, Richard	"	"	
Beal, James	"	"	
Browning, Harmon	"	"	Lost his horse on the 12th of August
Beasley, John	"	"	" " " " July
Brocket, Michael	"	"	
Browning, Joseph	"	"	
Baley, Henry P.	"	"	
Blundell, James	"	"	Left at Helena
Carson, James	"	"	
Cole, Eldridge	"	"	
Carter, Joseph	"	"	Sick in camp
Coventry, John W.	"	"	
Davis, Levi	"	"	Furloughed on the 24th of July
Doyle, A. P. H.	"	"	Sick in camp
Duncan, Thomas	"	"	
Enos, Charles	"	"	Lost his horse on the 16th of July
Flemming, Mordica	"	"	" " " " 10th of August
Freman, James	"	"	
Flemming, John	"	"	
Griffith, John	"	"	
Gillmore, Robert	"	"	
Herrington, John	"	"	Substituted for Wm. Linley from July 10
Hinton, Lewis	"	"	Furloughed on the 10th of July
Hickerson, Wash'n	"	"	
Hawkins, John B.	"	"	Left at Dixon in service
Harris, Zachariah	"	"	Furloughed on the 10th of July
Harris, Henry	"	"	
Johnson, Adaman	"	"	Lost his horse on the 27th of July
Jackson, William	"	"	
Kirkendal, William	"	"	Left at Helena on the 27th of July
Lawton, Henry	"	"	
Linley, William	"	"	Discharged by substitute on the 10th of July
Lowder, Gideon	"	"	
Lee, William H.	"	"	Left sick at Helena on the 27th of July
Miller, Henry	"	"	
Micks, John S.	"	"	Left in service at Dixon
McQuinter, Alex.	"	"	Furloughed on the 15th of July
Moore, Benjamin D.	"	"	
Nichols, William	"	"	
Neely, Bowling	"	"	
Pitcher, Payton I.	"	"	Lost his horse August 14
Porter, James	"	"	
Patten, James	"	"	
Parkhurst, Elijah	"	"	
Powell, Semore R.	"	"	
Prater, Alexander	"	"	

Name and Rank.	Residence.	Enrolled	Remarks.
		1832.	
Porter, Washington	Fayette Co.	June 7.	
Raybourn, Mitchell	"	"	
Remon, Frederick	"	"	Appointed Paymaster on July 10
Sears, John	"	"	
Smith, Jordan	"	"	
Smith, Henry	"	"	Lost his horse on the 14th of August
Smith, William	"	"	
Thompson, William	"	"	Lost horse on the 23d of July
Talby, James	"	"	
Trapp, John	"	"	
Welch, John	"	"	
Wakefield, John A.	"	"	
Wood, Anson	"	"	

Approved:

(Signed.)

H. ATKINSON,
Brig.-Gen. U. S. A.

This company was organized June 7, 1832, and received marching orders on the same day, and marched on the 9th and arrived at Fort Wilbourn on the 16th of June, and mustered into service June 19. This company found their own rations in full from the 8th to the 17th of June. Since the 17th of June till the present August 15th the company has found nearly all the small rations for itself.

This company was organized under the command of Capt. Wm. L. D. Ewing, at its first organization.

WHITESIDES' BRIGADE.

Regiments, Battalions and Companies commanded by Brigadier-General Samuel Whitesides.

FIRST REGIMENT.

CAPT. JULIUS L. BARNSBACK'S COMPANY

Of Mounted Volunteers, of the 1st Regiment of the Brigade under the command of Gen. Samuel Whitesides. Mustered out of the service of the United States at the mouth of Fox river, Illinois, May 28, 1832, distant 284 miles from the place of enrollment.

Name and Rank.	Residence.	Enrolled	Remarks.
Captain. Julius L. Barnsback.	Madison Co. Edwardsville.	1832. April 18	On furlough from May 18...............
First Lieutenant. Ryland Ballard......	"	"	In command of company from May 18 to 28..
Second Lieutenant. Jesse Bartlett........	"	"	....
Sergeants.			
Jacob Kinder.........	"	"	On furlough, sick.........................
Mathias Hanlan.....	"	"	On furlough...............................
Stephen Gaskill.....	"	"	....
Henry Armstrong...	"	"	On furlough, horse hunting.............
Corporals.			
Robert Murphy......	"	"	On furlough...............................
John E. Sharp.......	"	"	....
Isham M. Gillham...	"	"	....
Isaac McLane........	"	"	....
Privates.			
Armstrong, William.	"	"	On furlough, horse hunting.............
Armstrong, David...	"	"	....
Bartlett, Martin S...	"	"	Elected 1st Sergeant May 22, 1832......
Bartlett, Nicholas...	"	"	....
Barnsback, George.	"	"	....
Bowles, Austin......	"	"	....
Bowles, Stephen....	"	"	Absent on furlough ....
Burge, William......	"	"	....
Colyer, Charles......	"	"	Elected 4th Sergeant May 22, 1832......
Cox, Jacob B........	"	"	Absent, horse hunting..................
Dove, John..........	"	"	....
Day, Fauntleroy....	"	"	....
Ford, Aaron	"	"	Absent, sick...............................
Flinn, Joseph........	"	"	....
Guthrie, Henry......	"	"	....

Name and Rank.	Residence.	Enrolled	Remarks.
Gillham, John F	Madison Co. Edwardsville.	1832. April 18	
Hart, Henry	"	"	
Hart, John	"	"	
Hamilton, William	"	"	
Hood, Aaron	"	"	
Johnson, Charles W.	"	"	
Johns, James	"	"	Absent, sick
Knight, James	"	"	
Kell, William	"	"	
Merry, David W.	"	"	
Motley, Obediah C.	"	"	
Norman James	"	"	Absent, horse hunting
Page, Robert	"	"	
Ralph, William	"	"	
Seybold, Samuel	"	"	On furl., sick; appointed Ass't Q. M. April 28.
Scanland, Lewis W.	"	"	
Smith, Levi	"	"	
Smith, E. C.	"	"	
Semple, James	"	"	Appointed Judge Advocate May 1, 1832.
Van Hoozer, John	"	"	
Wall, John A	"	"	
Wall, David	"	"	
Weeks, Robert B	"	"	

Capt. John Thomas' Company

Of the 1st Regiment, commanded by Col. John Thomas, of the Brigade of Mounted Volunteer Militia from St. Clair county, Illinois, commanded by Brig.-Gen. Samuel Whitesides. Mustered out of the service of the United States, at the mouth of Fox river, Illinois, on May 28, 1832; distant 300 miles from the place of enrollment.

Name and Rank.	Residence.	Enrolled	Remarks.
Captains.		1832.	
John Thomas	Belleville	April 18.	Elected Col. of 1st Regt. on April 28
First Lieutenant.			
Gideon Simpson	"	"	Elected Capt. on April 28
Second Lieutenants.			
George Kinney	"	"	
Wm. S. Thomas	"	"	Elected 1st Lieut. on April 28
Sergeants.			
John W. Woods	"	"	Absent on furlough since May 19
Parker Adams	"	"	Elected 1st Sergt. since May 19
Prettyman Boyce	"	"	
James Nearen	"	"	
Enoch Bridges	"	"	
Corporals.			
John McDonald	"	"	
Andrew Terry	"	"	
James H. Ashby	"	"	
George West	"	"	
Privates.			
Abbott, Isaac			
Bird, John			
Casterline, Joseph O			
Crocker, Abner			Absent without leave.
Davis, James			
Enochs, Saml. B.			
Furgerson, Robt			
McHenry, Daniel			Joined the 4th Regt.; returned
Ogle, Benjamin			

WHITESIDES' BRIGADE.

Name and Rank.	Residence.	Enrolled	Remarks.
		1832.	
Roman, Richard	Belleville	April 18.	Appointed Surgeon in 1st Regt. on April 28.
Spann, Solomon			
Scott, Benjamin			
Scott, Chas			
Twiss, Wm			
Welker, Jos			

Daniel McHenry returned and served out his time in my Company.
(Signed.)   GIDEON SIMPSON, Capt.

Capt. John Tate's Company

Of Independent Riflemen of the 1st Regiment of the Mounted Brigade of Volunteers commanded by Brigadier-General Samuel Whitesides, in the service of the United States. Mustered out of service at the mouth of Fox river, Illinois, on May 28, 1832. Distance, 330 miles from the place of enrollment.

Name and Rank.	Residence.	Enrolled	Remarks.
Captain.	Belleville.		
John Tate	St. Clair Co.	April 18	
First Lieutenant.			
Joshua Hughes			
Second Lieutenant.			
Abram B. Vandigrif			
Sergeants.			
Jacob Miller			
Joseph Ogle			
William Tate			
George W. Hook			
Corporals.			
James Phillips			
Jacob Phillips			
William Woods			
Mathew Cox			
Privates.			
Ashlock, Robert			
Aspens, Charles			
Bear, Peter B.			
Bear, Bonham			
Blair, James			
Charles, James N.			
Dunlap, John			
Dingle, Atason			
Dun, Peter			
Edwards, I. C.			
Glass, George			
Higgins, Robert			
Higgins, Ichabod			Absent sick.
Holt, Christopher			
Hootes, Samuel			
Hootes, Anthony			Absent on furlough, sick.
Leach, Robert			Absent with brother.
Leach, A. H.			Absent, wounded.
Lyndon, Jefferson			
Lindon, Joseph			
McClintock, James			
Miller, Absalom			Absent without leave, May 1, 1832.
Million, John			
Owens, Hopson			
Owens, Charles			Absent, sick.
Owens, Ellit			
Phillips, Wm			
Patason, Horland			

Name and Rank.	Residence.	Enrolled	Remarks.
Perce, George			
Powers, James			
Rader, James			
Sample, James			
Skinner, Akerman			
Swillevant, Francis			
Smith, John			
Starkey, John			Promoted Major of 2d Batt. 1st Regt. April 28
Wood, Samuel			

Capt. Josiah Little's Company

Of the 1st Regiment, commanded by Col. John Thomas, of the Brigade of Mounted Volunteers of Illinois Militia, commanded by Brig.-Gen. Samuel Whitesides. Mustered out of the service of the United States at the mouth of Fox river, Illinois, on May 27, 1832. Distance from Madison county, place of enrollment, 284 miles.

Name and Rank.	Residence.	Enrolled	Remarks.
Captains.	Alton.	1832.	
Solomon Pruitt	Madison Co.	April 19.	Elected Capt. Apr. 19; elected Lt.-Col. Apr. 28
Josiah Little	" "	" "	
First Lieutenants.			
Josiah Little	" "	" "	Elected Captain April 28, 1832
William Arundell	" "	" "	
Second Lieutenant.			
Jacob Swegart	" "	" "	On furlough
Sergeants.			
Wm. Arundell	" "	" "	Elected 1st Lieut. April 28, 1832
Joseph Squire	" "	" "	" 1st Sergt. " " On furlough.
James R. Wood	" "	" "	
James Sanders	" "	" "	Sick and not present
Corporals.			
Thomas Akins	" "	" "	
John E. Hawkins	" "	" "	
Jno. Lawrence	" "	" "	
Isaiah Dunagan	" "	" "	
Privates.			
Barnet, Benj. F.			
Bridges, Madison			
Basy, Newton			On permit
Beck, Sandford			
Barr, Zachariah			
Chapman, Enoch			
Chapman, Jos.			
Cochran, Wm. C.			
Davis, William			On permit
Dickson, Thomas			
Dunagan, Jno. M.			
Edwards, Cyrus			
Eaves, William			On furlough
Fien, James			
Gillham, Marcus			On furlough
Gillham, Josiah R.			
Harris, Meeds A.			
Hodges, James H.			
Humes, Willis			
Harkleroad, Jno.			
Job, Samuel			
Job, Levi			On permit
Jones, Martin			
Jones, George			
Kirkendall, Wm.			
Kinyan, Edward			Sick and on permit
Linton, James			
Lee, Vincent			2d Sergt. April 28, 1832
More, Abel			On furlough
Pruitt, Solomon, Jr.			

Name and Rand.	Residence.	Enrolled	Remarks.
Palmer, Sam'l			
Roberts, Absalom			
Roberts, Elijah			
Rice, Elias			
Rose, Francis			
Roberts, Wm., Jr.			
Rogers, Jonathan			
Sanders, Shadrick			
Starkey, Russell			On permit.
Lowell, Lewis C.			Sick and not present.
Scarittlin, Stephen			
Sewill, Wm			Detailed to wait on sick
Smith, Elias			
Stent, Christopher			
Solomon, John			
Sterell, James			4th Sergt. to May 18; 1st from that time to 27.
Suels (?), William			
Wood, Jesse			3d Sergeant May 18, 1832
Walker, Philip V.			
Waddle, James			Sick and on permit.
Whitesides, Thomas			

SECOND REGIMENT.

CAPT. THOMAS CHAPMAN'S COMPANY

Of 2d Regiment, of the Brigade of Mounted Volunteers commanded by Brig.-Gen. Samuel Whitesides. Mustered out of service of the United States at the mouth of Fox river, on the Illinois river, in the State of Illinois, 250 miles from the place of enrollment in Greene county, on the 25th day of May, 1832.

Name and Rank.	Residence.	Enrolled	Remarks.
Captains.		1832.	[when elected Lieut.-Col. of 2d Regt.
Charles Gregory	Greene Co	April 20.	Commanded Co. from April 20 to April 30, 1832.
Thomas Chapman	"	"	Elected Captain April 30, 1832
First Lieutenant.			
Thomas Hill	"	"	Elected 1st Lieutenant April 30, 1832
Second Lieutenant.			
Levi Whitesides	"	"	Elected 2d Lieutenant April 30, 1832
Sergeants.			
Sherman Goss	"	"	Appointed 1st Sergeant April 30, 1832
Isaac Moore	"	"	" April 30, 1832
Henry Phillips	"	"	" April 30, 1832
Aaron Hart	"	"	" April 30, 1832
Corporals.			
Michael Hendrick	"	"	Appointed April 20, 1832
Samuel M. Pinkerton	"	"	" April 20, 1832
John F. Hart	"	"	" April 30, 1832
James H. Finley	"	"	
Privates.			
Burns, Martin	"	"	
Dunn, Squire	"	"	
Duff, John	"	"	Absent on furlough
Duff, Daniel	"	"	
Elmer, Elijah	"	"	
Elmore, George I.	"	"	
Elmore, Ralph	"	"	
Elmore, George R.	"	"	Absent on furlough
Garrison, Richard	"	"	
Gilleland, James	"	"	
Gilleland, William	"	"	
Hazlewood, George	"	"	
Hazlewood, Wyatt	"	"	
Philips, Israel	"	"	
Rule, Albert	"	"	Absent sick
Shelton, William	"	"	
Spencer, James R.	"	"	Sick and on furlough
Welch, Robert	"	"	
Wood, James	"	"	
Wiggins, Laban	"	"	

All the company were present except those marked absent and furloughed.

Capt. Levi D. Boone's Company

Of the 2d Regiment, commanded by Col. Jacob Fry, of the Brigade of Mounted Volunteers commanded by Brig.-Gen. Samuel Whitesides. Mustered out of the service of the United States at the mouth of Fox river, on the Illinois river, on May 28, 1832. Distance from place of enrollment, 210 miles.

Name and Rank.	Residence.	Enrolled	Remarks.
Captain. Levi D. Boone	Montg'm'y Co	1832. April 20	
First Lieutenant. James G. Hinman			
Second Lieutenant. Absalom Cress			
Sergeants.			
C. G. Blackberger			
Michael H. Walker			
Israel Foogleman			
William M. David			Absent on furlough
Corporals.			
John Prater			
Alex. T. Williams			
C. S. Coffey			
Newton Street			
Privates.			
Brown, James			
Briggs, Samuel L.			Absent on furlough
Brown, Harrison			
Blair, Cobbert			
Bennett, H. C.			Quartermaster
Cress, Peter			
Canins, G. W.			
Crabtree, John			
Duff, George E.			
Fanin, Michael			Lost a rifle-gun in service, appraised at $18
Griffith, William			
Grisham, James			
Hampton, Johnson			Absent by permission, to hunt horse
Hawkins, James			
Halbrock, Benjamin			
Hunt, Joshua			
Ishmael, Sam			
Jordan, William			
Knapp, Artisua H.			
Killpatrick, Eph.			
Kilingworth, Steph'n			
Ludwick, George E.			
Long, Robert A.			
McWilliams, John K			
Mansfield, Thos. J.			
Mayfield, William			
Michael, Barnabus			
Peacock, Samuel			
Rabb, Eli			
Rutledge, James M.			
Roberts, William			
Sherley, William D.			
Steel, Daniel			
Scrivener, Curtis			
Toedd, Thomas J.			
Turner, McKensie			
Williams, James B.			
Whitton, Easton			
Williams, Ben. R.			
Young, James			

Ben. R. Williams was discharged at Beardstown April 27, 1832, and not Hawkins. Williams was discharged solely because his horse was lost, and not for any offense or misconduct.

(Signed.)   LEVI D. BOONE, Capt.

Capt. Wm. G. Flood's Company

Of Mounted Volunteers, of the 2d Regiment of the Brigade commanded by Brigadier-General Samuel Whitesides. Mustered out of service of the United States at the mouth of Fox river, in the State of Illinois, on the 28th day of May, 1832. Distance, two hundred and fifty (250) miles from place of enrollment.

Name and Rank.	Residence.	Enrolled	Remarks.
Captain.		1832.	
Wm. G. Flood	Quincy	April 23	
First Lieutenant.			
Edward L. Pearson	"	"	
Second Lieutenant.			
Thomas Crocker	"	"	
Sergeants.			
Nathan Stringfield	"	"	On furlough
Granville Turner	"	"	
George W. Pollard	"	"	
Samuel E. Pierce	"	"	
Corporals.			
Richard S. Green	"	"	
Wm. Watson	"	"	
Elza D. Park	"	"	
John McDaniel	"	"	Sick and absent, by leave
Privates.			
Allen, Meredith	"	"	
Ames, Orestus	"	"	
Ames, Loring	"	"	
Bancroft, Amos	"	"	
Beebee, Erastus	"	"	
Browning, O. H	"	"	
Brown, George	"	"	
Boling, Lewis	"	"	
Beebee, David	"	"	
Burlingham, Sanford	"	"	
Caxe, George W	"	"	
Clark, James O	"	"	
Caldwell, John	"	"	
Doty, John	"	"	
Fortune, William	"	"	
Freeman, Elam S	"	"	Appointed Adjutant 2d Regiment
Furguson, Isaac	"	"	Absent on duty
Howard, John	"	"	Sick and absent
Holmes, Hiram	"	"	
Johnson, Thomas	"	"	
Kinney, Thos	"	"	Sick and absent; joined Co. at Yellow banks.
Laughland, J. W	"	"	
Lightfoot, Washint'n	"	"	
Malone, Andy	"	"	
Mast, Michael	"	"	
Miller, Henry W	"	"	
Moore, Daniel	"	"	
Pond, Hiram	"	"	
Parker, Samuel	"	"	
Popple, Simeon	"	"	
Pierce, Joshua	"	"	
Ralston, J. H	"	"	Absent on duty
Richardson, William	"	"	
Sheney, John	"	"	
Seehorn, Wiley V	"	"	
Shaw, Wm	"	"	Absent by sickness
Smith, Lewis M	"	"	
Streeter, Solomon	"	"	
Turner, Ebenezer	"	"	
Thompson, James	"	"	
Warrick, Jacob	"	"	
Wood, John	"	"	
Williams, Archibald	"	"	
Wilmot, Ben. R	"	"	

Capt. Benjamin James' Company.

Of the 2d Regiment, of Mounted Volunteers, commanded by Brig.-Gen. Samuel Whitesides. Mustered into the service of the United States at Beardstown, Illinois, on the 28th day of April, 1832, and mustered out of service on the 28th day of May, 1832, near Ottawa, at the mouth of Fox river, Illinois; distant 250 miles from place of enrollment. For 60 days.

Name and Rank.	Residence.	Enrolled	Remarks.
Captain. Benj. James	Bond Co	1832. April 17	
First Lieutenant. John McAdams	"	"	
Second Lieutenant. William Clouse	"	"	
Sergeants.			
A. C. Mackey	"	"	
James Johnston	"	"	
Thomas Price	"	"	
Ephriam M. Gilmore	"		
Corporals.			
Elisha Paine	"	"	
David H. Mills	"	"	
Amos Holbrooks	"	"	
Jordan Parker	"		
Privates.			
Anthony, Abraham	"	"	
Bradford, James	"	"	
Cruthis, William	"	"	
Dethero, George	"	"	
Durley, James	"	"	Prom. to Q. M. Sergt. of 2d Regt. April 30,'32.
Donee, Thomas C	"	"	
Downing, James	"	"	
Ellison, Elisha	"	"	
Galer, James C	"	"	
Gilmore, John M	"	"	
Gillispie, Josiah R	"	"	
Gill, Francis	"	"	
Glenn, Robert	"	"	
Gilham, Thomas C	"	"	
Gwyne, Hugh B	"	"	Absent on furlough
Hunter, David	"	"	
Harlin, William	"	"	
Hooper, James D	"	"	
Hooper, Thomas K	"	"	
Jones, Felix	"	"	
Lugg, Noah A	"	"	
Lucas, John	"	"	
Lyles, J. E	"	"	
McAdams, Jas	"	"	
McAdams, Jesse	"	"	
McAdams, Sloss	"	"	
McAdams, William	"	"	
Morgan, Jonathan	"	"	
Mills, A. O. H. P	"	"	
Mullican, James	"	"	
McClure, Eleazer	"	"	
Nicholas, Russell B	"	"	
Pender, Andrew	"	"	
Robinson, Lawson H	"	"	
Royer, Daniel	"	"	
Roberts, Calvert	"	"	Promoted Sergt. Major, April 30, 1832.
Sellers, Benjamin E	"	"	
Volentine, Jackson O	"	"	
West, John	"	"	
Wolard, James B	"	"	Appointed trumpeter, April 30, 1832.
Walker, James	"	"	
Walker, John T	"	"	

Capt. Jeremiah Smith's Company

Of the 2d Regiment, commanded by Col. Jacob Fry, of the Brigade of Mounted Volunteers of Illinois Militia, commanded by Brig.-Gen. Samuel Whitesides. Mustered out of the service of the United States, at the mouth of Fox river, on the 27th day of May, 1832. Place of organization, Whitehall, Greene county, Ill. Distance, 220 miles.

Name and Rank.	Residence.	Enrolled	Remarks.
Captain.		1832.	
Jeremiah Smith	Greene Co.	April 20.	Elected April 20, 1832.
First Lieutenant.			
James Allen	"	"	Elected April 20, 1832.
Second Lieutenant.			
Jacob Wagner	"	"	Elected April 20, 1832.
Sergeants.			
Andrew Guest	"	"	Elected April 20, 1832.
Gregory Doil	"	"	" "
Wm. Thompson	"	"	" "
Peter Thompson	"	"	" "
Corporals.			
Elihu Brown	"	"	Elected April 20, 1832.
Hardy Allen	"	"	" "
George Woods	"	"	" " on furlough
H. K. Stubblefield	"	"	
Privates.			
Broom, Wm	"	"	
Bundy, Horatio	"	"	
Baker, John	"	"	
Buman, Samuel	"	"	Disappeared from the day of enrollment
Crabtree, Benjamin	"	"	
Campbell, John G	"	"	Sick
Campbell, John	"	"	
Coats, Richard	"	"	
Carter, Harris	"	"	
Dunsworth, Chas	"	"	
Dollerhite, Jackson	"	"	
Fisher, James	"	"	
Godwin, Jacob	"	"	
Hodges, James	"	"	On furlough
How, David	"	"	
Hamilton, John	"	"	Sick
Hawkins, Bevis	"	"	On furlough
Lorton, Moritica D	"	"	
Lipincut, John	"	"	Deserted
Miller, John	"	"	
Monday, Samuel	"	"	
Williams, Wm	"	"	
Young, Robert	"	"	

THIRD REGIMENT.

Capt. John Harris' Company,

3d Regiment, commanded by Col. Abram B. Dewitt, of the Brigade of Mounted Volunteers of Illinois Militia, commanded by Brig.-Gen. Samuel Whitesides. Mustered out of the service of the United States, at the mouth of the Fox river, Illinois, May 27, 1832; distant 246 miles from Carlinville, the place of enrollment.

Name and Rank.	Residence.	Enrolled	Remarks.
Captain.			
John Harris	Carlinville, Macoupin Co.	1832. April 20.	
First Lieutenant.			
William G. Coop	"	"	
Second Lieutenant.			
Jeff. Weatherford	"	"	
Sergeants.			
Aquilla P. Peppedim	"	"	
John Lewis	"	"	
Wilford Palmer	"	"	
Travis Moore	"	"	
Corporals.			
Geo. W. Cox	"	"	
Henry H. Havren	"	"	
Samuel W. McVay	"	"	
Joshua Martin	"	"	
Privates.			
Allen, John	"	"	
Bayless, John	"	"	
Bayless, Rees	"	"	
Butler, James	"	"	Horse lost—strayed or stolen—value, $35.
Coop, John	"	"	Horse died from forced march; value, $68.
Coop, Ransom	"	"	
Driskell, Miles	"	"	
Davis, Thedorus	"	"	
English, Irum	"	"	
English, Levin N.	"	"	Appointed Q. M. Sergeant April 27, 1832.
Eallum, William	"	"	
Foss, Joseph	"	"	
Hill, Wyatt R.	"	"	
Hall, Oliver	"	"	
Hall, James T.	"	"	Horse gave out on forced march; value, $40.
Harris, Robert	"	"	
Matthews, Geo.	"	"	
McVay, Healy W.	"	"	
Miller, Alexander B.	"	"	
Powell, John	"	"	
Rhea, Henry D.	"	"	
Richardson, Larkin	"	"	
Solomon, Lewis	"	"	
Thurman, Thomas	"	"	
Weatherford, Hardin	"	"	
Wall, Richard	"	"	

Captain Benjamin Barney's Company

Of the 3d Regiment, commanded by Col. Abram B. Dewitt, of the Brigade of Mounted Volunteers commanded by Brig.-Gen. Whitesides. Mustered out of the service, at the mouth of Fox river, on May 27, 1832. Distant 250 miles from the place of enrollment.

Name and Rank.	Residence.	Enrolled	Remarks.
Captains.	Atlas,	1832.	
William Ross	Pike Co	April 20.	Captain from April 20th to 28th, 1832
Benjamin Barney	"	"	1st Lieut. to the 28th, then elected Captain
First Lieutenant.			
Israel N. Bert	"	"	Elected April 28, 1832
Second Lieutenant.			
Lewis Allen	"	"	Elected April 28, 1832
Sergeants.			
Bridge Whitten	"	"	Elected April 28, 1832
Hawins Judd	"	"	" "
Eli Hubbard	"	"	" "
Hansel G. Horn	"	"	" "
Corporals.			
Allen B. Lucas	"	"	Elected April 28, 1832
Mathias Bailey	"	"	" "
William Mallory	"	"	" " absent on furlough
Jesse Luster	"	"	" " horse strayed or stolen
Privates.			
Allen, Jonathan B			
Adney, William			Absent on furlough
Blair, William			
Bush, Alfred			
Card, Joseph			
Coffee, Meredith W			
Davis, Robert			Appointed Sergeant-Major April 29, 1832.
Gall, Joseph			
Garrison, Louis A			
Haze, Robert			
Hull, David			
Haskins, Eliphalet			
Kannada, Charles			
Lay, Willis			
Lewis, Chidister B			
Love, Samuel W			
Lucas, Jesse			
McAtee, John			
McAtee, Andrew			Appointed Paymaster April 29, 1832.
Marrow, Richard			
Meredith, Adair C			Horse, valued at $60, strayed or stolen
Mize, Samuel P			
O'Neil, James			
Perkins, John			
Prewitt, St. Clair			
Swiney, Emery			
Shipman, Stephen			Left sick, on the march
Tolbert, Lindsay			
Wilson, Austin			
Wells, Lucius			

Capt. Elisha Petty's Company

Of the 3d Regiment, commanded by Col. Abraham B. Dewitt, of the Brigade of Mounted Volunteers of Illinois Militia, commanded by Brig.-Gen. Samuel Whitesides. Mustered out of the service at the mouth of Fox river May 27, 1832. Distance, 250 miles from place of enrollment.

Name and Rank.	Residence.	Enrolled	Remarks.
Captain.	Atlas,	1832.	
Elisha Petty	Pike Co	April 20	Elected April 28, 1832
First Lieutenant.			
James Ross	"	"	Elected April 28, 1832
Second Lieutenant.			
John W. Birch	"	"	Elected April 28, 1832

WHITESIDES' BRIGADE.

Name and Rank.	Residence.	Enrolled	Remarks.
Sergeants.	Atlas,	1832.	
Joab Brooks	Pike Co	April 20	Elected April 28, 1832
Gillham Bailey	"	"	" "
Joel Harpole	"	"	" "
Cornelius Jones	"	"	" "
Corporals.			
William Kinman	"	"	Elected April 28, 1832
William Gates	"	"	" "
Ira Shelly	"	"	" "
James Woosley	"	"	" "
Privates.			
Andrews, Ira	"	"	
Buchalew, Garet	"	"	
Bailey, Caleb	"	"	
Coleman, Franklin P.	"	"	
Cavender, Joseph	"	"	
Decker, Harrison	"	"	
Edwards, Thomas	"	"	Horse, valued at $70, broke down on march
Fugate, Benj.	"	"	
Greer, James	"	"	
Grimshaw, Edwin	"	"	
Hubbard, Appolis	"	"	
Hume, Berry	"	"	Horse, valued at $65, strayed or stolen
Jackson, Francis	"	"	
Jeffers, Samuel	"	"	
Kinman, Sims	"	"	
Kinman, Hiram	"	"	
Kinney, Thomas	"	"	
Lynch, William	"	"	
McLintock, Joseph	"	"	Gun, val. $18, bursted; fired by com'nd of Col.
Main, Solomon	"	"	
More, Thomas	"	"	
Mays, Mathew	"	"	
Parkis, Owen	"	"	
Riggs, Samuel	"	"	
Triplet, Nathaniel C.	"	"	
Wadsworth, William	"	"	

Capt. William B. Smith's Company

Of the 3d Regiment, commanded by Col. Abraham B. Dewitt, of the Brigade of Mounted Volunteers commanded by Brigadier-General Samuel Whitesides. Mustered out of the service of the United States at the mouth of Fox river, on the Illinois River, on May 27, 1832, being 200 miles distant from place of enrollment.

Name and Rank.	Residence.	Enrolled	Remarks.
Captain.	Morgan Co.	1832.	
William B. Smith	Jacksonville	April 21	
First Lieutenant.			
Starkey R. Powell	"	"	Lost horse on march; appraised at $60
Second Lieutenant.			
Willie Myers	"	"	
Sergeants.			
Samuel Givens	"	"	
Richard Nelson	"	"	
Peter Barker	"	"	
Wingate I. Numens	"	"	
Corporals.			
Abraham N. Mills	"	"	Gun bursted while firing, by order; value, $20
Thomas Shepherd	"	"	
Felix Ray	"	"	
London C. Ragan	"	"	
Privates.			
Black, William	"	"	Lost his horse on march; appraised at $45
Bennel, Gabriel E.	"	"	

Name and Rank.	Residence.	Enrolled	Remarks.
Bristow, Thomas	Jacksonville	1832. April 21	
Chapman, Isaac	"	"	
Connell, Murray Mc	"	"	Appointed Adjutant of 3d Regt. April 27,1832.
Deaton, Robt. H.	"	"	Farrier of the "
Dewitt, Abraham B.	"	"	El'ct'd and app'ted Col. 3d " " "
Flynn, Zadick W.	"	"	
Holland, Berry	"	"	
Hardin, John J.	"	"	High private
Hall, Aquilla	"	"	
Laughrey, John	"	"	
McCall, Arris	"	"	
McKee, James	"	"	
Miller, William	"	"	
Orre, Richard	"	"	Left sick on the march, and furl'd at Dixon's.
Orear, George	"	"	Appointed Quartermaster 3d Regt. April 27,'32
Potts, Joel	"	"	
Provines, James	"	"	
Plasters, Lemmon	"	"	Detailed into service of Commander-in-Chief
Roberts, William	"	"	
Runsdell, Charles	"	"	
Smith, George	"	"	Left sick on march; furl'ed at Dixon's Ferry.
Smith, Laurence	"	"	Detailed by Quartermaster-Gen. as cook.
Smith, Thomas	"	"	Furl'd to attend sick at Dixon's Ferry.
Willson, James	"	"	

Capt. Nathan Winters' Company

Of the 3d Regiment, commanded by Colonel Abram B. Dewitt, of the Brigade of Mounted Volunteers of Illinois commanded by Brig.-Gen. Samuel Whitesides. Mustered out of the service of the United States, at the mouth of Fox river, on the 27th day of May, 1832. Distance, 215 miles from place of enrollment.

Name and Rank.	Residence.	Enrolled	Remarks.
Captain. Nathan Winters	Brown and Morgan Cos.	1832. April 21.	Elected April 21, 1832
First Lieutenant. John D. Pinson	"	"	Elected April 21, 1832
Second Lieutenant. John L. Kirkpatrick	"	"	Elected April 21, 1832
Sergeants.			
Leander J. Walker	"	"	Elected April 21, 1832
William D. Johnson	"	"	" " "
David Grattan	"	"	" " "
Thomas J. Cox	"	"	" " "
Corporals.			
Asa C. Earle	"	"	Elected April 21, 1832
Bird Smith	"	"	" " "
James F. New	"	"	" " "
George W. Sawyer	"	"	
Privates.			
Asher, William	"	"	
Adams, James	"	"	
Axby, John	"	"	Horse lost, valued at $40
Beall, Alexander	"	"	$70 Elected Major April 29, 1832
Beasley, Benjamin	"	"	Absent on furlough
Black, Jefferson	"	"	
Bell, Arthur	"	"	
Brown, Cornelius	"	"	
Carson, John	"	"	
Cox, William G.	"	"	
Crisp, Benjamin	"	"	
Campbell, James G.	"	"	
Cooper, Asa	"	"	
Coultis, William	"	"	
Campbell, David	"	"	
Dew, Joseph	"	"	Detailed as a wagoner

Name and Rank.	Residence.	Enrolled	Remarks.
Dixon, Thomas	Brown and Morgan Cos..	1832. April 21.	Detailed as a wagoner.
Forsyth, Johnson	"	"	
Fink, Presley	"	"	
Fulton, John	"	"	
Gillham, Thomas M.	"	"	
Greene, William H.	"	"	
Holmes, Curtis	"	"	
Hobson, John	"	"	
James, Henry	"	"	
Johnson, Samuel	"	"	Detailed into service of Commander-in-Chief
Little, Yancy	"	"	
Moore, David	"	"	
McGee, James	"	"	
Neal, Robert D.	"	"	Detailed as a wagoner.
Powell, Elijah	"	"	
Rue, David W.	"	"	
Riggs, James B.	"	"	
Sawyer, James	"	"	
Wells, Albert	"	"	Horse lost, valued at $70.
Wilcher, Stephen	"	"	

FOURTH REGIMENT.

Capt. M. G. Wilson's Company

Of the 4th Regiment, commanded by Samuel M. Thompson, of the Brigade of Mounted Volunteers commanded by Brig.-Gen. Samuel Whitesides. Mustered out of the service of the United States, at the mouth of Fox river, May 28, 1832; distant 220 miles from place of enrollment.

Name and Rank.	Residence.	Enrolled	Remarks.
Captain.		1832.	
Moses G. Wilson	Rushville, Ill.	April 23.	Elected Major April 30, 1832
First Lieutenant.			
Alex. Hollingsworth	"	"	Lost horse May 22, 1832; award
Second Lieutenant.			
Harvey Skiles	"	"	
Sergeants.			
John B. Watson	"	"	Appointed Adjt. of 4th Regt. April 30, 1832
G. W. P. Maxwell	"	"	1st Sergt. April 30; resign'd May 19
Saml. Hollingsworth	"	"	Elected Captain April 30, 1832
I. G. Randall	"	"	Resigned May 19, 1832
Corporals.			
Ava. Hollingsworth	"	"	Resigned April 30, 1832
James Martin	"	"	Appointed 1st Corporal April 30, 1832
David Frayner	"	"	" 2d Sergeant
L. B. Skiles	"	"	" 3d Corporal " "
Privates.			
Abbott, Thomas	"	"	Furloughed (sick) May 19, 1832
Abbott, A.	"	"	" (to attend sick) May 19, 1832
Bogart, Samuel	"	"	Appointed 1st Sergt. May 19, 1832; lost horse.
Burnett, William	"	"	
Butler, George	"	"	
Cox, William	"	"	Appointed 4th Corporal April 30, 1832
Collins, Elijah	"	"	Detailed on extra duty
Dunlap, Adam	"	"	Appointed 1st Surgeon's Mate April 30, 1832
Frakes, James	"	"	
Guinn, William	"	"	
Harrison, G. H.	"	"	
Hollingsworth, Abe.	"	"	
Hollingsworth, John	"	"	
Holliday, I. S.	"	"	
Hobart, Chauncey	"	"	Appointed 4th Sergeant April 30, 1832
Hills, Gamaliel	"	"	
Horney, Nowlen	"	"	Lost horse May 22, 1832
Hills, Ishmael	"	"	
Horney, Samuel	"	"	Appointed Quartermaster April 30, 1832
Justus, G. W.	"	"	
Kirkham, Ezra	"	"	Lost horse May 22, 1832
Lockhart, William	"	"	
Lane, Rutherford	"	"	Lost horse May 22, 1832
McFadden, John	"	"	Appointed 3d Sergeant May 19, 1832
Murphy, Robert	"	"	Detailed on extra duty
Morgan, John	"	"	
Moore, Willis	"	"	
Naught, George	"	"	
Riley, Daniel	"	"	Lost horse May 22, 1832
Reno, Jonathan	"	"	Appointed 2d Corporal April 30, 1832
Riley, Caleb	"	"	
Skiles, Benjamin	"	"	
Wilson, Wm. L.	"	"	
Wallace, Moses	"	"	
Wright, Henry	"	"	
Williams, Eli	"	"	
Young, William	"	"	Lost horse May 22, 1832

Capt. Wm. C. Ralls' Company

Of the 4th Regiment of Mounted Volunteers, commanded by Col. Samuel M. Thompson, of the Brigade of Mounted Volunteers commanded by Brig.-Gen. Samuel Whitesides. Mustered out of the service of the United States at the mouth of Fox river May 28, 1832; distant from the place of enrollment, 220 miles.

Name and Rank.	Residence.	Enrolled	Remarks.
Captain.		1832.	
Wm. C. Ralls	Rushville, Ill.	April 23	
First Lieutenant.			
James Blackburn		"	Resigned and returned home May 13, 1832
Second Lieutenant.			
John Stumet		"	Promoted to 1st Lieutenant May 13
Sergeants.			
John M. Jones		"	
George W. Penney		"	
James Hunter		"	
James P. Hinney		"	Promoted to 2d Lieutenant May 13
Corporals.			
Theodore Jourdon		"	
Stephen H. St. Cyr.		"	
Jeremiah White		"	
Alfred W. McHatton		"	Appointed Sergeant-Major May 18
Privates.			
Ballard, Noah B			Sick and furloughed May 26
Bryant, Rosnel			
Briscoe, John			
Boothe, James			
Coonrod, Jefferson			
Combs, Stephen			
Crawford, John D			
Chapman, Johnston	Rushville, Ill.	April 23	
Dewit, Gabl			
Davis, John			
Edmondson, David			
Earnest, Aaron			Detailed in wagon service
Glenn, Robert H			
Gay, Lewis			
Hayden, Thomas			
Hambaugh, Stephen			Appointed 4th Sergeant May 13
Hill, James			
Ives, Joll			
Killion, Michael			Sick and furloughed May 26
Morris, William			
Moore, Daniel			
McKee, William			
Owen, Luke			
Palmer, Benj			
Rose, Wm. B			
Richardson, Jacob			
Richardson, Aaron			
Redick, Thos			
Starr, John H			
Sellars, Thomas			
Seaward, Luster			
Till, Fleming			Sick and furloughed May 10
Van Winkle, Alex			
Vandeventer, Corn's			Furloughed May 26
Vanvatter, John			Sick and furloughed May 19
Wilkerson, Jacob			Appointed 4th Corporal May 18
Wilson, Benj			

CAPT. ABRAHAM LINCOLN'S COMPANY

Of 4th Regiment of Mounted Volunteers, commanded by Brig.-Gen. Samuel Whitesides. Mustered out of the service of the United States at the mouth of Fox river, May 27, 1832.

Name and Rank.	Residence.	Enrolled	Remarks.
Captain.		1832	
Abraham Lincoln...	Sangamon Co	April 21	
First Lieutenants.			
Samuel M. Thomps'n	"	"	Resigned April 30,'32; Col. 4th Regt. Ill. Vol...
Second Lieutenant.			
John Brannan.......	"	"	
Sergeants.			
John Armstrong.....	"	"	
Tavner B. Anderson.	"	"	
George W. Foster...	"	"	Transferred to a foot company April 29,1832...
Obediah Morgan....	"	"	
Corporals.			
Thomas Comb.......	"	"	
John Plasters........	"	"	Resigned May 20, and served as private since
William F. Berry....	"	"	
Alexander Trent....	"	"	
Privates.			
Alexander, Urbin...			Absent on extra duty............
Armstrong, Pleasant			
Anderson, Isaac....			
Armstrong, Hugh...			Promoted to 1st Lieut. April 30
Barnette, Clardey..			
Crete, Valentine....			
Cox, Henry.........			
Cox, Wm...........			
Clemment, James...	Richland	April 21	
Clary, Royal........			
Cummins, William ..			
Clary, William.....			
Carman, Merritt M .			
Dutton, Samuel.....			
Dobson, Joseph.....			
Drake, Nathan......	Beardstown..	April 29	
Erwin, John........	Sangamon Co	April 21	Promoted 3d Sergt. vice G. W. Foster, Apr. 29
Elmore, Cyrus.....			
Elmore, Travice....			
Farmer, Lewis W...			
Foster, William.....			Transferred to a foot company April 29.....
Green, William.....			
Guliher, Isaac......	Dixon's Ferry	May 19	
Houghton, John H..	Sangamon Co	April 21	
Hadley, Henry.....			
Holmier, Joseph....			
Hoheimer, Wm.....			Absent on furlough..............
Heaverer, Jacob....			
Jones, Richard.....			Promoted from the ranks May 2, color-bearer
Jones, John........			Absent without leave.............
Kirkpatrick, Wm...			Promoted from the ranks April 30
King, Allen........			
Lamb, Evan T.....			
Lane, John Y.....			
Lane, Richard.....			
Long, Thomas.....			
Mathews, Bordry...			
Meeker, Usli.......			
Mounce, John.....			Absent without leave.............
Marshall, Wm.....			
Pierce, Thomas....			
Pierce, Calvin.....			
Pierce, Elijah.....			
Patter, Royal......			
Pantier, David M...			Absent on furlough.............
Pierce, Charles....			
Plaster, Michael....			Absent without leave.............
Plunkett, Robert S..			
Rankin, David.....			Transferred to foot company May 19, 1832.....
Rutledge, John M...			
Rutledge, David...			

Name and Rank.	Residence.	Enrolled	Remarks.
Sulivan, Eph			
Sulivan, Charles			
Simmons, James			
Sprouce, Wm. T.			Prom'd f'm ranks May 2; guns'h field and staff.
Tebb, Samuel			
Tibb, Joseph			
Warburton, George			
Yardley, James			

FIFTH REGIMENT.

CAPT. M. L. COVELL'S COMPANY

Of Mounted Volunteers, belonging to the 5th Regiment, commanded by Col. James Johnson, of the Brigade of Mounted Volunteers of Illinois Militia commanded by Brig.-Gen. Samuel Whitesides. Mustered out of the service of the United States at the mouth of Fox river, Illinois, on May 27, 1832; distance 130 miles from place of enrollment.

Name and Rank.	Residence.	Enrolled	Remarks.
Captain. M. L. Covell	Bloomington.	1832. April 23.	
First Lieutenant. Asahel Gridley	"	"	Absent with leave
Second Lieutenant. Moses Baldwin	"	"	Absent with leave
Sergeants.			
Baley H. Coffee	"	"	Absent with leave
Isaac Murphy	"	"	" "
David Simmons	"	"	" "
Charles Gates	"	"	" "
Corporals.			
Charles Vezay	"	"	Absent with leave
Henry Miller	"	"	" "
Reuben Dodson	"	"	
James Durley	"	"	Absent with leave
Privates.			
Brown, Thomas	"	"	
Busick, Henry	"	"	Absent with leave
Copes, William	"	"	" "
Conger, Benjamin	"	"	
Dimmet, William	"	"	
Davenport, Isaiah	"	"	
Davis, Alexander	"	"	Absent with leave
Draper, Joseph	"	"	Killed in battle May 14, 1832
Ellis, Martin C.	"	"	Absent with leave
Funk, John	"	"	
Gilpin, Samuel	"	"	" "
Gates, Stephen F.	"	"	
Hurbert, Mathew	"	"	
Hurbert, Robert A.	"	"	Absent with leave
Harris, Robert F.	"	"	" "
Hatten, John	"	"	" "
Isham, John	"	"	" "
Johnson, Charles	"	"	" "
Kimber, Baley	"	"	" "
Landy, John	"	"	
McCullough, William	"	"	
McKee, William	"	"	Absent with leave
Oatman, Clement	"	"	
Orrendorff, James	"	"	Absent with leave
Provo, Francis	"	"	
Phillips, James	"	"	
Paul, James	"	"	Absent with leave
Rutledge, Thomas	"	"	" "
Simpson, Timothy	"	"	" "
Toliver, John	"	"	" "
Vittito, John	"	"	" "
Vandoler, Jesse	"	"	" "
Windham, Reuben	"	"	" "
Wiley, George	"	"	" "
Young, Anderson	"	"	" "
Young, Briant	"	"	

Capt. Robert McClure's Company

Of Mounted Volunteers, belonging to the 5th Regiment, commanded by Col. James Johnson, of the Brigade of Mounted Volunteers of Illinois Militia commanded by Brig.-Gen. Samuel Whitesides. Mustered out of service of the United States, at the mouth of Fox river, Illinois, on May 27th, 1832; distance 130 miles from the place of enrollment.

Name and Rank.	Residence.	Enrolled	Remarks.
Captain. Robert McClure	McLean Co.	1832. May 4.	
First Lieutenant. John H. S. Rhodes	"	"	
Second Lieutenant. Thomas Glenn	"	"	
Sergeants.			
Chaney Thomas	"	"	
Charles S. Dorsey	"	"	
Eli Frankeberger	"	"	
James G. Reyburn	"	"	
Corporals.			
David Maxiell	"	"	
Levi Danley	"	"	
John W. Brown	"	"	
Owen Chaney	"	"	
Privates.			
Ashburn, Jesse	"	"	
Benson, John	"	"	
Benson, James	"	"	
Baker, Elliott H.	"	"	
Barr, James	"	"	
Baker, Jonathan	"	"	
Bomington, Joseph	"	"	
Burns, Wm	"	"	
Bowman, Thadius	"	"	
Ball, Henry	"	"	
Blair, Wm	"	"	
Copes, Jacob	"	"	
Chaney, Ebenezer	"	"	
Damal, Bundren	"	"	
Davis, Davis	"	"	
Dixon, Elisha	"	"	
Davidson, John E.	"	"	
Ewing, Phineas	"	"	
Fordico, John	"	"	
Hamley, Henry	"	"	
Hamilton, Absalom	"	"	
Howard, Madison	"	"	
Harrison, Henry H.			Served 5 days, pilot, Dixon to mouth of Fox.
Lane, Harrison	McLean Co.	May 4.	
Lundy, Nicholas	"	"	
Miller, Anderson	"	"	
McCord, Thomas A.	"	"	
Moore, Josiah	"	"	
Martin, Mathew	"	"	
Oatman, Jesse	"	"	
Patrick, Allen	"	"	
Rogers, Thomas	"	"	
Ruth, Nathan	"	"	
Scott, Martin	"	"	
Wright, William G.	"	"	

Capt. I. C. Pugh's Company

Of Mounted Volunteers, belonging to the 5th Regiment, commanded by Col. James Johnson, of the Brigade of Mounted Volunteers of Illinois Militia commanded by Brig.-Gen. Samuel Whitesides. Mustered out of the service of the United States, at the mouth of Fox river, in the State of Illinois, on May 27, 1832; distance 150 miles from the place of enrollment.

Name and Rank.	Residence.	Enrolled	Remarks.
Captain. James Johnson	Macon Co. Decatur, Ill.	1832. April 24.	Promoted May 16, 1832, to Colonel
First Lieutenant. William Warnick	"	"	Absent with leave
Second Lieutenant. I. C. Pugh	"	"	Promoted to Captain May 16, 1832
Sergeants. John D. Wright	"	"	Absent on extra duty
James A. Ward	"	"	Promoted to 2d Lieutenant May 16
Walter Bowles	"	"	Absent with leave
Joseph Hauks	"	"	
Corporals. Henry M. Gorm	"	"	
Stephen R. Shepherd	"	"	
Geo. Copperberger	"	"	Absent with leave
James Milton	"	"	Killed in battle
Privates. Adams, William	"	"	Absent with leave
Bell, Alexander W.	"	"	
Black, Abraham	"	"	
Butler, Elisha	"	"	Absent with leave
Black, Jacob	"	"	" " "
Clifton, John	"	"	" " "
Cox, William	"	"	" " "
Clifton, Josiah	"	"	
Dickey, Jesse	"	"	Wounded
Dewees, Sam. B	"	"	
Davenport, Thomas	"	"	Absent with leave
Ennis, James	"	"	
Hauks, John	"	"	
Henderson, John	"	"	Absent with leave
Herrod, James	"	"	
Hooper, Obediah	"	"	" " "
Hauks, William	"	"	
Hooper, William	"	"	" " "
Ingram, Kinian	"	"	
Lane, Jacob	"	"	Absent on extra duty
McCall, Daniel	"	"	
Miller, James	"	"	
Miller, Sam	"	"	
Miller, William	"	"	
Manley, John	"	"	
Murphy, John	"	"	
Querry, James	"	"	
Simpson, Asher	"	"	
Steward, David H.	"	"	Absent on extra duty
Smallwood, Geo. D.	"	"	
Smith, Robert	"	"	
Troxel, Sam	"	"	
Williams, John	"	"	Absent with leave

Capt. John G. Adams' Company

Of Mounted Volunteers, belonging to the 5th Regiment, commanded by Col. James Johnson, of the Brigade of Mounted Volunteers commanded by Brig.-Gen. Samuel Whitesides. Mustered out of the service of the United States at the mouth of Fox river, in the State of Illinois, on May 17, 1832.

Name and Rank.	Residence.	Enrolled	Remarks.
Captain.		1832.	
John G. Adams	Pekin, Ill	April 27	Killed in battle May 14, 1832
First Lieutenant.			
Benj. Briggs	"	"	Absent on escort of family
Second Lieutenant.			
Jno. O. Hyde	"	"	Able for duty
Sergeants.			
Michell Reeder	"	"	Able for duty
James Wright	"	"	Escaped in battle, by orders
Seth Wilson	"	"	Able for duty
John Ford	"	"	"
Corporals.			
Henry Cline	"	"	Able for duty
Conaway Rhodes	"	"	On duty
Hartside Hittle	"	"	"
D. Hanger	"	"	On escort of family
Privates.			
Alexander, David	"	"	On duty
Alexander, David	"	"	Appointed Paymaster
Berry, Phenis	"	"	On duty
Ballard, Jacob	"	"	"
Briggs, Thomas	"	"	"
Bemis, Eli	"	"	On furlough
Baxter, Samuel	"	"	On escort of family
Barlow, Jno. M	"	"	On furlough
Council, Redick	"	"	On duty
Cullum, Green	"	"	"
Cline, William	"	"	"
Coffey, John	"	"	"
Craig, Orison	"	"	"
Conner, James	"	"	"
Carter, Daniel	"	"	On furlough
Crain, Jas. W	"	"	Appointed Adjutant
Dunbough, Pinkney	"	"	On duty
Drum, Abner	"	"	"
Date, Jesse	"	"	On furlough
Evans, D. S	"	"	Deserted May 16, 1832
Gordon, Geo	"	"	On duty
Hughes, Geo. W	"	"	"
Haynes, Jonathan	"	"	"
Hendricks, Wm. A	"	"	"
Henson, Samuel	"	"	"
Harper, William	"	"	"
Helme, Jonathan	"	"	On furlough
Judy, Jas	"	"	Deserted May 16, 1832
Kreeps, David	"	"	Killed in battle May 14
Lewis, Bazwell	"	"	On furlough
Laudes, Joseph	"	"	On duty
Morgan, Reese	"	"	"
McJenkins, Hugh	"	"	On escort of family
Maxwell, Ferdinand	"	"	On duty
McCann, Stephen T	"	"	On furlough
Mendinall, Zadock	"	"	Killed in battle May 14, 1832
McKnight, Alex	"	"	Furlough
Orendorff, Benj	"	"	On duty
Paisley, Robt	"	"	"
Paul, John	"	"	On escort of family
Perkins, Isaac	"	"	Killed in battle May 14
Ryon, Will	"	"	On duty
Reeder, Joseph	"	"	"
Rickey, Samuel	"	"	On furlough
Ramsey, Wm	"	"	On duty
Summer, Jas	"	"	On furlough
Shoemaker, Elmore	"	"	On duty
Stout, Samuel	"	"	"
Williamson, Chapan	"	"	"

SPY BATTALION.

Capt. John Dawson's Company

Of Mounted Volunteers, composing one of Spy Battalion, commanded by Major James D. Henry, in the service commanded by Brig.-Gen. Samuel Whitesides. Mustered out May 28, 1832.

Name and Rank.	Residence.	Enrolled	Remarks.
Captain.		1832.	
John Dawson	Sangam'n Co.	April 21.	
First Lieutenant.			
Wm. Dickrell	"	"	
Second Lieutenant.			
John Hornback	"	"	
Sergeants.			
Corbin C. Judd	"	"	
Harrison McGary			
John Brewer			
John Retherford			On parole
Corporals.			
Thos. J. Knox			
John Wright			
Seymour Vanmeter			
Hugh McGary			
Privates.			
Brown, James			
Bracken, John			
Black, Joseph			
Bridges, John			
Burch, Benjamin			Promoted to 2d Surg. Mate of Batt. April 26.
Barney, Lewis			
Burrett, Hugh			On parole
Brundage, Solomon			
Clark, William			
Cherry, Benjamin			
Churchill, Lewis			
Crane, William			
Dernon, Archelas			
Dickerson, David		April 21.	Trans. from com'y of Capt. Goodwin May 1.
Evans, Samuel			In place of John Critz
Foster, Squire			
Green, George			
Glasscock, Geo. W.		April 21.	Trans. from com'y of Capt. Goodwin May 1.
Garrard, Joseph F.			
Hornback, Jesse			
Harrison, Jesse M.			Promoted to Paymaster's Sergeant April 26.
Hughes, Robert			
Iles, Elijah			Trans. from Capt. Goodwin's com'y May 1
Jones, Edward		April 21.	
Killyon, Michael			
Kelly, Jeremiah			
Killyon, Jacob			In place of Wm. Johnson
Keys, John		April 21.	Trans. from com'y of Capt. Goodwin May 1.
Kelly, Wm.			
Lucas, Geo. B.			
Lobb, Wm.			
Martin, John			
Monlaud, Zachariah			
Minor, Joel			
Martin, Jacob			

Name and Rank.	Residence.	Enrolled	Remarks.
		1832.	
Musick, John			
Martin, Jefferson			
Morgan, Zaduck		April 30.	
Matheny, Lorenzo D.		" 21.	Trans. from com'y of Capt. Goodwin May 1
Oliphant, Ethelb'rt J.		" 21.	
Powell, Alphred			
Potts, Wm. L.		April 21.	Trans. from Capt. Goodwin's com'y May 1
Pugh, Jonathan H.		" 30.	
Roger, John			
Reulpo, John			
Ridgway, John			Discharged May 3
Read, James M.			
Reid, James F.		April 21.	Trans. from com'y of Capt. Goodwin May 1
Royborn, Joseph			
Strader, John C.			
Strickland, Clemons.			
Smith, James			
Stone, Calohill			
Short, Wm. B.		April 28.	
Stewart, John		" 21.	Trans. from com'y of Capt. Goodwin May 1
Sanders, Presley A.			
Scoggins, John			
Turley, Charles			On parole
Taylor, James		April 21.	Trans. from com'y of Capt. Goodwin May 1
Venus, Adam			
Wade, Samuel			
Williams, Jacob			
Wages, Joseph			
White, Wm.			
Ward, John			Discharged at Beardstown April 30
Warwick, Jacob G.			On parole
Warwick, Montg'm'y			Promoted to Q. M. April 26, and on parole

Capt. Thomas Carlin's Company

Of the Odd Battalion of Spies, commanded by Major James D. Henry, of the Brigade of Mounted Volunteers of Illinois commanded by Brigadier-General Samuel Whitesides. Mustered out of the service of the United States of America at the mouth of Fox river of the Illinois river on May 27, 1832; distant 230 miles from place of enrollment.

Name and Rank.	Residence.	Enrolled	Remarks.
Captain.		1832	
Thos. Carlin	Carrollton	April 20	
First Lieutenant.			
Jesse V. Mounts	"	"	
Second Lieutenant.			
George D. Laurens	"	"	
Sergeants.			
Mearel E. Rattan	"	"	Appointed Sergeant-Major April 28, 1832
David Thurston	"	"	
James Gilliland	"	"	Attached to Capt. Chapman's Co. about Apr. 28
Harrison Boggess	"	"	Lost horse night of May 22, 1832, by stampede
Corporals.			
Lewis B. Edwards	"	"	
Josiah Ashlock	"	"	
William Cook	"	"	
William Finley	"	"	
Privates.			
Abner, Joshua	"	"	
Ashlock, John	"	"	
Banning, Williamson	"	"	
Bogers, Preston	"	"	Appointed 3d Sergt. April 28, 1832
Courtney, John	"	"	
Cook, John	"	"	
Carlin, James	"	"	
Crabb, Edward	"	"	

Name and Rank.	Residence.	Enrolled	Remarks.
Crane, Silas	Carrollton	April 20	
Dulaney, William H.	"	"	Appointed Surg. 2d Regt. April 30, Col. J. Fry
Dawdy, Howell	"	"	
Eldred, Elan	"	"	Appointed 1st Sergt. April 28, 1832
Eldred, Silas	"	"	
Edwards, Talbert	"	"	
Finley, Zuriah	"	"	
Gilliland, William	"	"	Attached to Capt. Chapman's Co. April 20, 32.
Gibbs, Valentine A.	"	"	
Hoskins, William	"	"	
Hill, Jonathan	"	"	
Huitt, John, Jr.	"	"	
Hess, Samuel	"	"	Lost horse May 16, after forced m'ch to Dixon's
Herrick, Rheuben	"	"	
Hopper, Thomas	"	"	
Jackson, John	"	"	
King, Robert	"	"	
Linder, Joseph	"	"	
Linder, George	"	"	
Moore, James	"	"	
Moore, David	"	"	
Pinkerton, William	"	"	
Pinkerton, John F	"	"	
Pinkerton, Henry B.	"	"	
Rattan, Larkin	"	"	
Reno, Philamon	"	"	
Reddish, John	Rock Island	May 10	
Short, James	Carrollton	April 20	
Scott, John W.	Beardstown	" 26	Det'hed on Exp. April 21; rejoined Co. May 15
Scott, Thomas D.	"	" 26	
Spencer, Roswell H	Rock Island	May 8	
Tunnel, Luther	"	" 10	Lost horse night of May 22, affright of horses
Tunnel, William	"	" 10	
Thackston, Starlin	Carrollton	April 20	
Whiteside, William H	"	"	
Whiteside, John B.	"	"	
Williams, John C	"	"	Never appeared after enrollment
Woodson, Joseph	Beardstown	April 26	App. Surg. to Spy Bat., Maj. Henry, April 28

Capt. John Dement's Company

Of the Odd Battalion of Spies, commanded by Maj. James D. Henry, of the Brigade of Mounted Volunteers of Illinois Militia commanded by Brig.-Gen. Samuel Whitesides. Mustered out of the service of the United States, at the mouth of Fox river, near Ottawa, on the 28th of May, 1832; distant from the place of enrollment 240 miles. Organized in Fayette county.

Name and Rank.	Residence.	Enrolled	Remarks.
Captain. John Dement	Fayette Co. Vandalia, Ill	1832. April 20.	
First Lieutenant. Dem's'y Yarborough	"	"	
Second Lieutenant. Abraham Starns	"	"	
Sergeants. William Bradford	"	"	
Jos. Hickman	"	"	
Henry B. Roberts	"	"	
Joel Thomas	"	"	
Corporals. Wyatt B. Stapp	"	"	
T. N. Gains	"	"	
Isaac D. Taulbee	"	"	
A n os Eakle	"	"	

Name and Rank.	Residence.	Enrolled	Remarks.
Privates.	Fayette Co.	1832.	
Alley, James	Vandalia, Ill.	April 20.	
Allen, Madison	"	"	
Blackwell, Robert	"	"	Sent on express May 15, 1832
Conner, Edward	"	"	
Coventry, John W	"	"	
Cole, Eldridge	"	"	
Duncan, Thomas	"	"	
Doolin, Daniel	"	"	
Dimond, G. W.	"	"	
Duncan, Matthew	"	"	Promoted April 26, 1832, to Surg. Foot Bat'llon
Evans, Horatio	"	"	
Enos, Josiah	"	"	
Ewing, John	"	"	Sent on express May 15, 1832
Glass, Rody	"	"	
Ginger, M. C.	"	"	
Green, Robert	"	"	
Hockett, Wm. I.	"	"	
Harrington, John	"	"	
Hawkins, John B.	"	"	
Hickerson, Geo. W.	"	"	
Jones, Thomas	"	"	
Johnson, Henry	"	"	
Lee, Wm. H.	"	"	
Leak, James P.	"	"	
Moore, Benj. D	"	"	
Morrison, Wm. L. E.	"	"	Appointed Adjt. of Spy Battalion April 26, '32.
Noris, Coleman	"	"	Sick, and sent to Rock Island
Posey, John F.	"	"	Appointed Q. M. Sergt. Spy Bat. April 26, 1832.
Phelps, A. J.	"	"	
Patterson, Jas.	"	"	
Ryal, Nelson	"	"	
Sanburn, Nathl.	"	"	
Shrader, L. O.	"	"	
Snyder, John	"	"	
Shirley, John	"	"	
Smith, Wm.	"	"	
Smith, John, Jr.	"	"	
Scroggins, Henry	"	"	
Stapp, James T. B.	"	"	
Whitfield, Bryand	"	"	
Wiley, Henry	"	"	
Wakefield, John A.	"	"	Sent on express May 15, 1832
Whitlock, James	"	"	Appointed Q. M. to Maj. James' Odd Bat.
Walker, Harvey H.	"	"	
Yarborough, E.	"	"	

I certify that the above roll, with the annexed remarks, is correct, to the best of my knowledge, upon honor. (Signed.) JOHN DEMENT, Capt.

ODD BATTALION.

Capt. Daniel Price's Company,

Belonging to an Odd Batallion of Mounted Vonunteers, commanded by Brig.-Gen. Samuel Whiteside. Mustered out of the service of the United States, at the mouth of Fox river, Illinois, on May 28, 1832; distance from place of enrollment 275 miles.

Name and Rank.	Residence.	Enrolled	Remarks.
Captain. Daniel Price	Shelby Co Shelbyville	1832. April 24.	Elected April 24, 1832; on John Sacket's horse
First Lieutenant. William Williamson	"	"	On furlough; elected April 24, 1832
Second Lieutenant. Hiram M. Trimble	"	"	Elected April 24, 1832
Sergeants.			
Len Mosley	"	"	Elected April 24, 1832
Elizer Briggs	"	"	
William Price	"	"	" " "
Mathew McNear	"	"	
Corporals.			
Gideon Walker	"	"	On Pleasant Gordon's horse
Isaac Daniel	"	"	On furlough; on Beelin's horse
John Green	"	"	On Ben Walden's horse
William Moore	"	"	
Privates.			
Austin, Hugh	"	"	
Ball, George	"	"	Lost his horse; on Pleasant Dotson's horse
Cochran, John	"	"	
Daniel, William	"	"	On Daniel Price's horse
Daniel, Amon	"	"	John Reise's horse
Daniel, Wiley B	"	"	On I. T. Sandford's horse
Daniel, Jeremiah	"	"	On I. B. Henry's horse; on furlough
Douthat, David	"	"	On John Renshaw's horse
Elliott, David	"	"	
Frazer, Gran B	"	"	On Francis Gordon's horse
Green, Washington	"	"	
Green, William	"	"	
Howard, Jonathan B	"	"	
Harper, William	"	"	
Hoosong, James	"	"	
Johnson, Isaac M	"	"	On S. Scribner's horse
Lee, George	"	"	
Mosley, John	"	"	
McLavi, Joseph	"	"	
Poe, Abner	"	"	
Pardue, John	"	"	On S. Sherrill's horse
Richardson, Wm. A	"	"	Appointed Asst. Q. M., May 5, 1832, to Odd Bat.
Scribner, Thomas	"	"	
South, James	"	"	
Smith, William	"	"	On Witt Robinson's horse
Smith, Wesley	"	"	On Mr. Graves' horse
Smith, David	"	"	His gun stolen; on Allen Bent's horse
Strong, Solomon S	"	"	On Absalom Hezzer's horse
Sherrill, William	"	"	On Thomas Stutz's horse
Templeton, William	"	"	
Welch, Charles	"	"	On Francis Jordan's horse

Capt. Peter Warren's Company

Of the Odd Battalion of Mounted Volunteers commanded by Brig.-Gen. Samuel Whitesides. Mustered out of the service of the United States, at the mouth of Fox river, Illinois, on May 28, 1832; distant from the place of enrollment, 275 miles.

Name and Rank.	Residence.	Enrolled	Remarks.
Captain. Peter Warren.........	Shelbyville, Shelby Co ..	1832. April 24	Elected April 24, 1832; on I. Culter's horse....
First Lieutenant. Archibald Wynns...	" ..	"	Elected April 24, 1832 ....
Second Lieutenant. Robert T. Brown	" ..	"	Elected April 24, 1832 ....
Sergeants.			
Isaac M. Shell	" ..	"	Elected; on I. Culter's horse—pressed.........
John McGuire	" ..	"	" horse gave out, l'ft on Gen. Daisey's
Levi Gorles	" ..	"	" [horse.
John Perryman.......	" ..	"	" on Isaia L. Kortman's horse.........
Corporals.			
Thomas Hall..........	" ..	"	Elected..
William Headen.....	" ..	"	App'd Surgeon of the Odd Battal. May 5, 1832.
John Abbott	" ..	"	Elected 2d Corporal May 6, 1832; on furlough.
Thomas Lay	" ..	"	App'd 2d Corporal May 22, 1832; E. Ellis' horse
James Davis..........	" ..	"	On G. Todd's horse ....
Enos Ellis..............	" ..	"	On John Smith's horse ....
Privates.			
Bergerman, John ...			
Bell, Alfred	Shelbyville,	....	On furlough; on G. Todd's horse..............
Casey, Levi	Shelby Co ..	April 24	....
Curry, Nathan.......			
Cuink, James........			On furlough; lost horse; on J. Reese's horse.
Dowthat, James.....	Shelbyville,		
Dixon, Lawson	Shelby Co ..	April 24	On John Patub's horse...........................
Dixon, Robert S.....	" ..	"	
Elam, Joel			On John Storm's horse ....
Frazier, Albert			On furlough...
Fleming, John.......	Shelbyville,		
Fleming, Jacob L...	Shelby Co ..	April 24	On Abraham Teluck's horse ....
Graves, William.....			On Free Sexton's horse ....
Greer, James	Shelbyville, Shelby Co ..	April 24	
Graham, Mortilus...	" ..	"	On Thomas Puiz's horse.........................
Gorden, George	" ..	"	App'd Surg'n's Mate May 5, '32; lost his horse
Hale, John.......... ..	" ..	"	On Barkley Lottz's horse ....
Hill, John	" ..	"	On G. Stucker's horse............................
Hall, John P..........	" ..	"	On John Hale's horse..............................
Johnston, James W.	Shelbyville,		
Johnston, Isaac O...	Shelby Co ..	April 24	On John Hill's horse...............................
Johnston, Henry	" ..	"	
May, Thomas........	" ..	"	
More, Peyton........	" ..	"	
Owens, William P...	" ..	"	On furlough; on William Harrison's horse ...
Penyman, Jacob			
Parks, Samuel.......			
Rankin, Samuel.....			Horse left; on Mr. Young's horse; on furlo'gh
Robinson, David M..	Shelbyville,		
Ruther, James.......	Shelby Co ..	April 24	On furlough, lost his horse.......................
Roberds, William D.	" ..	"	On Jas. Cockran's horse..........................
Simpson, John			On furlough; lost his horse ....
Smith, James.......	Shelbyville,		
Sulivan, Dempsey F.	Shelby Co ..	April 24	On Peter Warren's horse ....
Stamp, Annias.......	" ..	"	On John Rice's horse..............................
Vaughan, George A.			On Jacob Elliott's horse...........................
Vaughan, James W.			Appointed Armorer Odd Battalion May 5, 1832
Woolen, Edward....	Shelbyville, Shelby Co ..	April 24	On Richmond Web's horse.......................
Williams, Thomas H.	" ..		

Capt. Thomas Harrison's Company.

Of the Odd Battalion commanded by Thomas James, Major, composing part of the Brigade of Mounted Volunteers commanded by Brig.-Gen. Samuel Whitesides. Mustered out of service of the United States, at the mouth of Fox river on the Illinois river, on May 28, 1832; distance 350 miles from the place of enrollment.

Name and Rank.	Residence.	Enrolled	Remarks.
Captain,	Waterloo,	1832.	
Thomas Harrison...	Monroe Co....	April 28	Entit'd to pay 1st Lt. April 19-28; app'd Capt..
First Lieutenant.			
Edward T. Morgan..	''	April 19	Entit'd to pay private Apr. 19-28; elect'd 1st Lt.
Second Lieutenant.			
Thomas McRoberts.	''	''	Entit'd to pay private Apr. 19-28; elect'd 2d Lt.
Sergeants.			
James Moor..........	''	''	Entit'd to pay private April 19-28; app't'd Adjt.
Thomas Taylor......	''	''	
Felix Clark..........	''	''	
John Strong..........	''	''	
Corporals.			
William McMoore...	''	''	
Pendleton Hill......	''	''	
Wm. McNabb........	''	''	
Henry Hartlin.......	''	''	
Farriers,			
Johnston, Nathan C.	''	''	App. Farrier Apr. 19; May 18 app. Sergt.-Maj.
Miller, William......	''		
Whitelock, James...	Beardstown..	April 30	
Cornelius, J. M. Mc..	Waterloo, Monroe Co....	April 19	Tr. May 9 another Reg.; Surg's Mate 1st Reg.
Privates.			
Bond, Shadrach B..	''	''	
Baird, Scipio........	''	''	Appointed Quartermaster May 18, 1832........
Birch, John..........	''	''	
Birch, Fielder.......	''	''	
Brooks, Stephen....	''	''	
Clark, George.......	''	''	
Carr, Solomon......	''	''	
Easten, Stephen....	''	''	
Fisher, Gramer......	''	''	
Haskins, Moses.....	''	''	Entit'd pay priv. Apr. 19-28; app. Brig. Trump'r
Horin, Michael......	''	''	Appointed Paymaster April 28, 1832..........
James, John..........	''	''	On furl.; app. Sergt.-Maj. Apr.28; resig'd May 18
Kidd, John...........	''	''	
Lacey, Caleb.........	''	''	
Livers, Joseph.......	''	''	
McDaniel, John.....	''	''	Appointed 1st Sergeant April 28, 1832..........
Morgan, William....	''	''	
Moor, J. Milton......	''	''	Appointed Brigade Color Bearer April 28, 1832
Modglin, John.......	''	''	
McNabb, James.....	''	''	
McCulah, James.....	''	''	
Nowlin, Henry.......	''	''	
Neff, Henry..........	''	''	
Needles, James B...	''	''	
Preston, James......	''	''	
Ramsey, William....	''	''	
Rogers, John.........	''	''	
Right, John..........	''	''	
Snider, Solomon R..	''	''	
Smith, Calvin.......	''	''	
Shook, Michael.....	''	''	
Starr, Ashbridge....	''	''	
Todd, Edward.......	''	''	
Trail, Xerxes F......	''	''	
Triplett, Nimrod....	''	''	
Wyatt, R. M..........	''	''	

ODD BATTALION.

Capt. Jacob Ebey's Company

Of Mounted Men (detached for foot purposes). One of the companies of the Odd Battalion, commanded by Major Thomas Long, now in the service of the United States, commanded by Brig.-Gen. Samuel Whitesides. Mustered out of service on May 25, 1832, at the mouth of Fox river, 175 miles from Springfield.

Name and Rank.	Residence.	Enrolled	Remarks.
Captain.		1832.	
Jacob Ebey	Sangamon Co	April 21	
First Lieutenant.			
Edward Shaw	"	"	In hospital.
Second Lieutenant.			
Winslow M. Neal	"	"	
Sergeants.			
Thomas I. Marshall	"	"	Appointed Q. M. Sergt. April 29, 1832.
Davis Meredith	"	"	
James B. Goble	"	"	
David S. Collins	"	"	
Corporals.			
Reese Williams	"	"	
James E. Haws	"	"	
Harmon Renshaw	"	"	Promoted to 1st Sergeant April 29, 1832.
Wiley Blunt	"	"	
Privates.			
Attwood, Wm. C	"	"	
Bashaw, Jackulin	"	"	
Byers, James D	"	"	
Boyd, John	"	"	
Brown, Joseph	"	"	
Byer, Jesse	"	"	
Carver, James	"	"	
Clark, Philip	"	"	
Clark, Isaac	"	"	
Catha, George	"	"	
Collins, John	"	"	
Deimin, Joseph	"	"	
Dickson, Henry	"	"	Promoted 3d Corporal April 29, 1832.
Davis, John	"	"	
Ferril, Milton	"	"	
Foster, George W	B e dstown	April 29	
Graham, Samuel	Sangamon Co	April 21	
Graft, John	Rock Island	May 10	Entered as mark'd; never afterw'ds appeared
Harper, James	Sangamon Co	April 21	
Hamilton, Fred'k A	"	"	
Hatan, Daniel	"	"	
Hillis, John	"	"	
Hazlet, William	"	"	
Hinkle, Jacob	"	"	
Hedrick, Stephen	"	"	
Herndon, Felix	"	"	
Hash, Alfred	Beardstown	April 28	Entered as mark'd; never afterw'ds appeared
Jones, Granbury B	Sangamon Co	April 21	
Milton, George	"	"	
McClies, Daniel	"	"	
Martin, William	"	"	

Name and Rank.	Residence.	Enrolled	Remarks.
		1832.	
McMenus, Lawrence	Sangamon Co	April 21	
Newhouse, John G..	"	"	
Rusett, William D..	"	"	
Rutlege, James			
Rittenhouse, Obed'h	Beardstown..	April 29	Absent without leave, May 17, 1832.
Sherril, Thomas	Sangamon Co	April 21	
Stout, Thomas			
Scovle, Samuel B.	Beardstown..	April 29	
Taylor, James			
Vancel, Adam	Sangamon Co	April 21	In hospital.
Woolverton, Ulrich.	"	"	
Whitmore, John	"	"	In hospital.
Wright, John H	Beardstown..	April 28	Entered as mark'd; never afterw'ds appeared

CAPT. JAPHET A. BALL'S COMPANY

Of Mounted Men (detached for foot purposes), one of the companies of the Odd Battalion commanded by Major Thomas Long. Mustered out of the service on May 28, 1832.

Name and Rank.	Residence.	Enrolled	Remarks.
Captain.		1832.	
Japhet A. Ball	Sangamon Co	April 21.	
First Lieutenant.			
Alexander D. Cox...	"	"	
Second Lieutenant.			
John McCormack...	"	"	
Sergeants.			
Joseph W. Duncan..	"	"	
James McCormack..	"	"	
Wm. F. Cox	"	"	
Charles Day	"	"	
Corporals.			
Harvey Graham	"	"	
John M. Barns	"	"	
Thos. I. Clark	"	"	
Richard Cox	"	"	
Privates.			
Averill, Henry	"	"	
Brunsfield, John	"	"	In hospital.
Blue, Barnabas M..	"	"	
Ball, John	"	"	
Bagley, John D	"	"	
Coleman, Jonathan.	"	"	
Cook, Thomas	"	"	
Donner, William	"	"	
Galton, Thomas	"	"	
Gatlin, William	"	"	
Gately, John	"	"	
Hazlet, Joseph	"	"	
Hulton, John	"	"	
Hause, Salmon W	"	"	
Hampton, Samuel C	"	"	On extra duty.
Howard, Abram	"	"	
Jones, Lewis C	"	"	
Ketchum, Daniel	"	"	
Kendall, John	"	"	
Lauterman, Abram.	"	"	
McKinney, Thos. L.	"	"	
Massee, Elder	"	"	
Mitts, William	"	"	
Menicks, Morris R..	"	"	
McCormack, Wm	"	"	
Mitts, Jesse	"	"	
Patton, Robert	"	"	

Name and Rank.	Residence.	Enrolled	Remarks.
Spears, Nathan H	Sangamon Co	1832. April 21	
Smith, Charles	"	"	
Sexton, Robert B	"	"	
Swearingter, Thos	"	"	In hospital
Tempe, Garret	"	"	
Terry, John	"	"	In hospital
Vincent, John	"	"	
Ward, James	"	"	
Wright, Moses	"	"	
Waters, Daniel	"	"	

COMPANIES NOT ATTACHED TO REGIMENTS.

Capt. William Moore's Company

Of the Brigade of Mounted Volunteers commanded by Brig.-Gen. Samuel Whitesides. Mustered out of the service of the United States at the mouth of Fox river, Illinois, on May 28, 1832; distant from place of enrollment, 330 miles.

Name and Rank.	Residence.	Enrolled	Remarks.
Captain.		1832.	
William Moore	St. Clair Co.	April 18.	
First Lieutenant.			
Isaac Griffin	"	"	
Second Lieutenant.			
A. T. Fike	"	"	
Sergeants.			
Aaron Land	"	"	Sick; absent
Pleasant N. Dupee	"	"	
Nehemiah McMillion	"	"	
Elijah Herring	"	"	
Corporals.			
John Land	"	"	Absent; with the sick
Jonathan Crane	"	"	On furlough
Jarvis M. Jackson	"	"	Absent with leave
George Land	"	"	
Privates.			
Angle, David	"	"	Absent
Alexander, Julius	"	"	
Brown, Wm. G	"	"	Appointed Paymaster to 1st Regt., on Apr. 28.
Brooks, Benjamin	"	"	
Baker, John T	"	"	
Cunningham, Wm. J.	"	"	
Chisney, Benjamin	"	"	
Campbell, Wm	"	"	
Cook, James	"	"	
Cook, Wm	"	"	
Edwards, John	"	"	
Everett, Jesse J	"	"	
Fike, Nathan	"	"	
Gaskill, Samuel	"	"	
Jackson, Lorenzo D.	"	"	
Johnson, John	"	"	
Hickman, George	"	"	
LaCroix, Rene M	"	"	
Moore, Jonathan	"	"	
McDaniel, Benjamin	"	"	
Pate, Jeremiah	"	"	
Reynolds, Thomas	"	"	
Taylor, Charles	"	"	
Thompson, L. D	"	"	
Tracewell, Edward	"	"	
Vodon, Harrison	"	"	
Wright, Wm	"	"	
Ward, Henry	"	"	
Whitesides, John	"	"	

CAPT. JOHN WINSTANLEY'S COMPANY

Of the Brigade of Mounted Volunteers commanded by Brig.-Gen. Samuel Whitesides. Mustered out of the service of the United States, at the mouth of Fox river, Illinois, on May 28, 1832; distant from the place of enrollment 330 miles.

Name and Rank.	Residence.	Enrolled	Remarks.
Captain. John Winstanley....	St. Clair Co. Belleville	1832. April 18	
First Lieutenant. Aaron Stookey	"	"	
Second Lieutenant. David Snier..........	"	"	Absent sick..........
Sergeants.			
Thomas H. Kimber..	"	"	Absent with leave..........
Joseph McAdams....	"	"	
James W. McMurty..	"	"	Absent with leave..........
George Higgins......	"	"	
Corporals.			
Narcisse Pincinneau	"	"	
Joseph McMurty ..	"	"	
James R. Grigeory..	"	"	
George P. Dyke......	"		
Privates.			
Brumly, Thomas	"	"	Absent sick..........
Barthume, Alexis ...	"		
Brock, Bayley			
Blackwell, John A ..			Appointed Quartermaster April 29 .
Coon, Thomas........	Belleville	April 18	
Carr, Joseph........			Absent with leave..........
Carr, James........			
Decoto, Jno. Baptiste	Belleville	April 18	
Eastwood, Jacob Q..			
Hendricks, Elijah A.	"	"	
Hughes, Watson	"	"	
Hay, Richard			
Jarrot, Vital	Belleville	April 18	
Jarrot, Francis			
Leaird, Jarrot	Belleville	April 18	
Long, Thomas......			Absent with leave..........
LeCompte, Louis....			
McBride, Thomas....	Belleville	April 18	Absent with leave..........
Macomson, Wm. B ..			
Mitchell, Wm....			Appointed Surgeon's mate April 29.
Menard, Peter			
Mecker, Ambrose....			
Orr, William........			
Pincinneau, Laurent	Belleville	April 18	Interpreter..........
Pincineau, Louis....			
Roach, David........			
Smith, Samuel......	Belleville ...	April 18	
Smith, Valentine ...	"		
Snyder, Adam W			April 29, appointed Adjutant 1st Regiment....
Stubblefield, John...			Armorer
Tetter, Philip......			
Tetter, Solomon.....			
Walker, Gilla			Absent with leave..........
Woods, John........			
Whiteside, Joseph ..			
Wildy, Rudolph.....			
Wemet, Louis........			Appointed interpreter ....

Capt. William T. Givens' Company

Of the Brigade of Mounted Volunteers commanded by Brig.-Gen. Samuel Whitesides. Mustered out of the service of the United States of America, at the mouth of Fox river, on the 27th day of May, 1832, being 220 miles from place of enrollment.

Name and Rank.	Residence.	Enrolled	Remarks.
Captain. William T. Givens	Franklin, Morgan Co.	1832. April 21.	
First Lieutenant. Walter Butler	"	"	
Second Lieutenant. Thomas Wright	"	"	
Sergeants.			
Jacob Talkington	"	"	
James Pryon	"	"	
Joseph Reynolds	"	"	
Asa Johnson	"	"	
Corporals.			
James Thomas	"	"	
James Bryan	"	"	
John Nall	"	"	
Jasper Roland	"	"	
Privates.			
Buchanan, Reuben	"	"	Furloughed and sent back on April 28; sick
Burnett, Freeman	"	"	
Clayton, William C.	"	"	
Clayton, John	"	"	
Clayton, William H.	"	"	Furl. and returned home April 28; sick
Deatherage, George	"	"	
Greer, Robert	"	"	
Gibson, William	"	"	Detailed as wagoner on April 20, 1832
Haynes, Lewis	"	"	
Jackson, Brice B.	"	"	
McDonnell, Fredrick	"	"	Detailed into service of Q. M. April 27, 1832
Reynolds, Samuel	"	"	
Sollers, William	"	"	
Smith, Jacob	"	"	
Tannohill, Alford	"	"	
Thomas, Joseph	"	"	
Van Winkle, Hiram	"	"	
Vickers, Henderson	"	"	
Wiggs, Daniel	"	"	[on April 29, 1832.
Weatherford, Wm.	"	"	Elected and appointed Lieut.-Col. 3d Regt.

Capt. Erastus Wheeler's Company

Of the Brigade of Mounted Volunteers commanded by Brig.-Gen. Samuel Whitesides. Mustered out of the service of the United States, at the mouth of Fox river, Illinois, on the 28th day of May, 1832; distance from place of enrollment, 295 miles; enrolled for 60 days

Name and Rank.	Residence.	Enrolled	Remarks.
Captain. Erastus Wheeler	Troy	1832. April 18	
First Lieutenant. John W. Lusk	"	"	
Second Lieutenant. Richard R. Randle	"	"	

WHITESIDES' BRIGADE.

Name and Rank.	Residence.	Enrolled	Remarks.
Sergeants.		1832.	
William Tindall	Troy	April 18	
W. Torrence	"	"	On furlough
John Montgomery	"	"	
Wm. G. Martin	"	"	
Corporals.			
Josiah T. Randle	"	"	
Milton Gingles	"	"	
Henry H. West	"	"	
Benj. Stephenson	"	"	
Privates.			
Adams, O. M	"	"	
Beers, Henry	"	"	
Carey, Thomas	"	"	On furlough
Cochran, Hugh E	"	"	
Cleveland, Lorin	"	"	
Cason, John	"	"	
Dugger, Alfred	"	"	
Gracey, Jas. T	"	"	
Gillespie, Joseph	"	"	
Herrington, Charles	"	"	
Holman, Nathaniel	"	"	
Hamilton, Samuel	"	"	
Howard, Abraham	"	"	
Journey, Ninian E	"	"	
Lusk, Marquis	"	"	
McCullock, Samuel	"	"	
McElroy, James	"	"	
McMahan, Robert	"	"	
Montgomery, Wm	"	"	
Owens, John	"	"	
Otwell, Ceylon Y	"	"	
Pritchett, John	"	"	On furlough
Pearce, Robert B	"	"	
Powell, Arkansas	"	"	
Robinson, Allen	"	"	
Randle, Peter W	"	"	App'd Surg's Mate in Spy Bat., April 26, 1832
Shields, G. R	"	"	Appointed Sergeant-Major April 28, 1832
Shields, Alexander	"	"	
Stice, Chas	"	"	On furlough
Steele, Jesse	"	"	Appointed Brigade Paymaster April 26, 1832
Starr, Wm. E	"	"	
Vanhouser, Valent'e	"	"	
Voyles, Abel	"	"	
Walker, John L	"	"	
Yates, Elijah	"	"	

CAPT. SAMUEL SMITH'S COMPANY,

formerly

CAPT. JACOB FRY'S,

Of the Brigade of Mounted Volunteers commanded by Brig.-Gen. Samuel Whitesides. Mustered out of the service of the United States, at the mouth of Fox river, Illinois, on the 27th day of May, 1832; distant 230 miles from the place of enrollment.

Name and Rank.	Residence.	Enrolled	Remarks.
Captains.	Carrollton,	1832.	
Jacob Fry	Greene Co.	April 20.	Elected Col. April 30, 1832
Samuel Smith	"	"	
First Lieutenants.			
Samuel Smith	"	"	Elected Capt. April 30, 1832
E. D. Baker	"	"	
Second Lieutenant.			
E. D. Baker	"	"	Elected 1st Lieut. April 30, 1832
Mathias S. Link	"	"	

Name and Rank.	Residence.	Enrolled	Remarks.
Sergeants.		1832.	
Mathias S. Link	Greene Co.	April 20	Elected 2d Lieut. April 30, 1832
Frederick Atchison	"	"	
David Miller	"	"	
T. J. Brown	"	"	
Corporals.			
Martin Rigsby			Absent with leave
John Miller			
Abner P. Hill			
David Buson			
Privates.			
Atchison, Fielden			
Adcock, Isam			
Burton, Lemuel			
Brown, Erving D.			
Crane, Harvy			
Campbell, Nicholas			Appointed 1st Corporal May 8
Deeds, Philip			
Emerson, Henry			
Goan, Shedrick			
Hobson, John			
Lee, Archibald			
Lee, Richard G.			
Link, David	Greene Co.	April 20	
Lee, William			
Milton, David			
Miller, Lemuel			
Medkiff, David			
Nix, Elisha			
Nix, Joseph			
Powell, Dempsey			
Poindexter, Harris'n	Greene Co.	April 20	
Piper, Israel			
Renna, Wm. C.			
Smith, Aaron			
Sanders, George			
Samuel, Thomas			Deserted
Scott, Benj. F.			
Scott, James D.			
Thomason, Spencer			
Thomason, William			
Tucker, James			
Tunnel, Luther	Greene Co.	April 20	
Tunnel, William	"	"	Transferred to Spy Battalion May 10
Trearney, James			In the staff
Vandiver, Ervin			
West, T. A.			
Watton, Thomas R.			
Whittle, Wyatt			
Wallace, Wm. P.			Absent with leave
Wood, Squire	Greene Co.		Elected 1st Sergt. May 13

Capt. Thomas McDow's Company

Of the Brigade of Mounted Volunteers commanded by Brig.-Gen. Whitesides. Mustered out of the service of the United States, at the mouth of Fox river, Illinois, on May 27, 1832; distant 250 miles from the place of enrollment.

Name and Rank.	Residence.	Enrolled	Remarks.
Captain.		1832.	
Thomas McDow	Greene Co.	April 20	
First Lieutenant.			
James Whitlock	"	"	
Second Lieutenant.			
Silas Crain	"	"	Absent on furlough

Name and Rank.	Residence.	Enrolled	Remarks.
Sergeants.		1832.	
Thos. Briggs	Greene Co.	April 20	
B. F. Massey	"	"	
Jas. Burke	"	"	Absent on furlough
Jas. Whitehead	"	"	
Corporals.			
Josiah Dunn	"	"	
Wm. Phillips	"	"	
Jas. Walden	"	"	
Privates.			
Brown, Hezekiah	"	"	
Boren, Daniel	"	"	
Clifton, Thos.	"	"	
Clark, Squire	"	"	
Cowan, Matthew	"	"	
Costly, Daniel	"	"	
Dobbs, John	"	"	Absent on furlough
Erwin, Alfred	"	"	
Ferguson, James	"	"	
Fleming, Edward	"	"	
Green, Royal P.	"	"	
Hurd, William	"	"	Absent on furlough
Jamison, John M.	"	"	
Lofton, Ben	"	"	Absent on furlough
Lakin, Joseph	"	"	
Latham, Robert	"	"	
Means, John	"	"	
Morris, Lewis	"	"	
McCommack, John	"	"	
Means, Lewis	"	"	
Medford, Garrison	"	"	Absent without leave
Nairn, Wm	"	"	
Northam, Wm	"	"	Absent on furlough
Rouden, Wm. H.	"	"	
Swan, William	"	"	
Sutton, John D.	"	"	Absent on furlough
Saxton, Washington	"	"	
Thornton, Anderson	"	"	Absent without leave
Webb, Geo. W.	"	"	

CAPT. DAVID CROW'S COMPANY

Of the Brigade of Mounted Militia Volunteers commanded by Brig.-Gen. Samuel Whitesides, United States Army. Mustered out of the service of the United States at the mouth of Fox river, on the Illinois, on the 27th day of May 1832; distant 250 miles from the place of enrollment.

Name and Rank.	Residence.	Enrolled	Remarks.
Captain.		1832.	
David Crow	Quincy, Ill.	April 20	
First Lieutenant.			
Christopher Howard	"	"	
Second Lieutenant.			
Elijah G. Lillard	"	"	
Sergeants.			
Jno. Crawford, 1st	"	"	
George Campbell, 2d	"	"	Sick and present
John F. Battell, 3d	"	"	
James Crawford, 4th	"	"	
Corporals.			
Daniel Harty	"	"	
Coleman Talbert	"	"	
Jno. Fletcher	"	"	Furloughed
Jeremiah Stone	"	"	

Name and Rank.	Residence.	Enrolled	Remarks.
Privates.		1832.	
Beatty, Robert	Quincy, Ill.	April 20	
Campbell, Clayborn	"	"	
Campbell, Joseph	"	"	
Crow, Isaac	"	"	
Dunlap, David	"	"	
Edwards, Andrew	"	"	
Hatton, James	"	"	
Hillory, Alexander	"	"	
Hines, Wm	"	"	
Harty, Abram	"	"	
Lang, John	"	"	Furloughed
Lewis, Jno	"	"	
McCoy, Joseph	"	"	Furloughed
McCoy, Robins	"	"	
Points, John	"	"	"
Payne, Stephen O	"	"	
Riddle, Ebenezer	"	"	
Ruddle, John	"	"	Ret'd home from Henderson river on May 8
Shephard, Jno	"	"	
Smith, Elisha	"	"	
Smith, Stedman	"	"	
Southward, Wm	"	"	
Williams, Benj	"	"	Furloughed; lost horse at Camp Dixon
Worrell, Atwell	"	"	

Capt. L. W. Goodan's Company

Of the Brigade of Mounted Volunteers, commanded by Gen. Samuel Whitesides. Mustered out of the service of the United States at the mouth of Fox river, Illinois, on May 28, 1832.

Name and Rank.	Residence.	Enrolled	Remarks.
Captain.		1832.	
L. W. Goodan	Springfield	April 20	
First Lieutenant.			
John Reed	"	"	
Second Lieutenant.			
Wm. Cantrell	"	"	
Sergeants.			
Alford Wood	"	"	
Hiram Watson	"	"	
John Ridge	"	"	
Milton Humes	"	"	
Corporals.			
John Kline	"	"	
Wm. Smith	"	"	
Jairus B. Jones	"	"	Furloughed, sick, on May 19, 1832; reduced
Geo. E. Cabenness	"	"	
Moses Brunts	"	"	Made Corporal May 19, 1832
Privates.			
Archey, Vincon			
Archey, Michael			
Baker, John	Springfield	April 21	
Brunfield, Moses	"	"	
Brassle, Robert	"	"	Furloughed, sick
Brink, David M	"	"	
Bunts, Simoon			
Brown, John B			
Baker, James	Springfield	April 21	Wagon Master from May 1
Crow, William	"	"	
Carpenter, William	"	"	Appointed Paymaster April 30, 1832
Calhoun, John	"	"	
Constant, Wm	Springfield	April 21	Appointed Surgeon's Mate, 4th Regt., April 29
Chilton, Mathias	"	"	Furloughed, sick
Devenport, Wm	"	"	
Darrow, Jesse			

WHITESIDES' BRIGADE. 123

Name and Rank.	Residence.	Enrolled	Remarks.
		1832.	
Dawson, Charles....			
Ditson, Simon......			
Dotson, Jesse.......			
Dickison, D.........	Springfield...		Joined the Spies on May 1.
Easters, Asa.......		April 21	Sick.
Erby, Jacob M......	"		Appointed Surgeon of 4th Regiment April 30.
Foster, Nathaniel...			
Goode, Daniel......			
Garet, Joseph......			Joined the Spies on May 1.
Glasscock, George..			
Hurst, John........	Springfield...	April 21	
Henry, James D....	"	"	Appointed Major of the Spies on April 28, 1832
Hamilton, Samuel...			
Iles, Elijah.........			Joined the Spies on May 1.
Jones, Noah........	Springfield...	April 21	On furlough, horse muster.
Jones, James.......			
Jones, Edward.....			Joined the Spies on May 1.
Kindle, M. C.......	Springfield...	April 21	
King, Rheubin.....			
Kirk, Jack.........	Springfield...	"	Joined my company on May 1.
Keys, John........			Joined the Spies on May 1.
McCollister, Wm ...	Springfield...	April 21	
McKinsey, Samuel..	"	"	
Mann, Uriah.......			
Mason, Noah.......			
Malugon, Samuel...			
Malugon, Zaciah....			
Morris, Achalis.....	Springfield...	April 21	Private; elected Lt. Col. of 4th Reg. April 30.
McCoy, Joseph.....			
Matheny, L. D.			Joined the Spies on May 1.
Neale, T. M........			Sick; absent by leave.
Neale, Samuel O....		April 21	
Olesshart, E. P.....			Joined the Spies on May 1.
Potts, William.....			
Queenston, Richard.	Springfield...	April 21	
Robison, George....	"	"	
Ramer, Samuel.....			
Rutlage, John B....			
Richardson, Daniel.			
Rolston, Joseph....			
Richardson, Robert.			
Rusk, B. O.........	Springfield...	April 21	On extra duty from May 1.
Radford, Reuben...			
Reed, James F......			Joined the Spies on May 1.
Sims, Benjamin.....	Springfield...	April 21	
Said, Jesse.........			
Steel, William......			
Sherill, Thomas.....	Springfield...	April 21	Joined my company on May 18.
Sanders, P. A......			Joined the Spies on May 1.
Stewart, John T....			
Sherell, James.....			
Thomas, Harden....		April 21	
Taylor, James......			Joined the Spies on May 1.
Welch, Jefferson...	Springfield...	April 21	
Wills, James Q.....	"	"	
Wells, William E...	"	"	

FOURTH BRIGADE.

FORTIETH REGIMENT.

Capt. Geo. B. Willis' Company

Of Mounted Volunteers belonging to the 40th Regiment, 4th Brigade, 1st Division of Illinois Militia, commanded by Col. John Strawn, called into the service by the Governor of Illinois, and mustered out of service of the United States, at Hennepin, Putnam county, on June 18th, 1832.

Name and Rank.	Residence.	Enrolled	Remarks.
Captain. George B. Willis	Putnam Co. Hennepin	1832. May 21	
First Lieutenant. Timothy Perkins	"	"	
Second Lieutenant. Samuel D. Laughlin	"	"	
Sergeants.			
James D. Laughlin	"	"	
Thomas Wafer	"	"	
Anthony Turk	"	"	
Samuel Mann	"	"	
Corporals.			
Elisha G. Powers	"	"	By leave of Capt., went with team for U. S. [June 15.
Linas B. Skeels	"	"	
Solomon Perkins	"	"	
Maron Dimic	"	"	
Privates.			
Brigham, Sylvester	"	May 21	
Blanchard, Roswell	"	" 31	
Burrow, John	"	" 21	
Benson, Lewis B	"	"	On foot
Chamberlain, O. G	"	"	
Cole, John	"	" 24	
Corse, Christopher	"	" 31	
Carey, Abijah	"	"	On foot
Carey, Ellas	"	"	On foot; 6 days off duty
Delong, Henry	"	" 21	Returned, sick, June 6th; not yet fit for duty.
Dunlary, James G	"	" 24	
Daniels, Henry	"	" 21	Six days off duty
Durley, Williamson	"	" 31	On font [for U. S. June 15.
Doolittle, Joel	"	"	On foot; by leave of Capt. went with team
Dimic, Elijah	"	"	On foot; six days off duty
Davis, Alex	"	" 21	Horseman; 12 days off duty
Forristel, James G	"	"	
Griffin, John	"	"	
Gunn, Aaron	"	"	On foot
Hart, Matthias B	"	"	

FOURTH BRIGADE.

Name and Rank.	Residence.	Enrolled	Remarks.
Harper, James	Hennepin	May 21	Left for the main army June 14
Hall, John	"	" 26	
Hoskins, William	"	"	
Ham, Wm. H.	"	" 21	On foot
Hendricks, John	"	"	No service rendered
Janess, John	"	"	On foot; taken up for stealing, and run away
Kellerman, Michael	"	" 26	
Leeper, Robert A.	"	" 21	
Leeper, Charles	"	"	Had leave to team for U. S., but did not do it.
Laughlin, Alex. M.	"	"	One day off duty
Laughlin, Thos. W.	"	"	
McCormas, David	"	"	Horseman; 6 days off duty
Mosely, Roland	"	" 31	On foot
Moore, John	"	" 23	
Morris, William	"	" 26	
Philips, Elijah	"	" 21	Killed by Indians on Bureau June 18
Prunk, Daniel	"	" 31	On foot
Rexford, Joseph W.	"	" 21	
Ross, James G.	"	"	On foot
Roth, Solomon	"	" 31	By leave Capt., went with team for U.S. June 15
Roth, Leonard	"	" 31	On foot; 6 days off duty
Shepherd, Nelson	"	"	
Simpson, John H.	"	" 31	
Tompkins, Claud. L.	"	"	No service rendered
Taylor, Adam	"	"	
Willis, James W.	"	"	
Williamson, John	"	"	
Wilmouth, Geo. P.	Bureau Co.	" 23	Enlisted in the U. S. service
Williams, John	Hennepin	" 21	On foot; 6 days off duty
Williams, Curtis	"	"	
Warnock, Hugh	"	"	On foot
Zenor, Harsin K.	"	"	

CAPT. ROBERT BARNES' COMPANY

Of Mounted Volunteers belonging to the 40th Regiment, 4th Brigade, and 1st Division, of Illinois Militia, called by the Governor and Commander-in-Chief; was mustered into the service of the United States by Col. John Strawn, at Columbia, on May 20, 1832, and mustered out of service at Hennepin, Putnam county, Illinois, on June 18, 1832; distance, 25 miles from home.

Name and Rank.	Residence.	Enrolled	Remarks.
Captain.		1832.	
Robert Barnes	Columbia	May 20	
First Lieutenant.			
William M. Neal	"	"	Lost 4 days
Second Lieutenant.			
John Weir	"	"	
Sergeants.			
James Dever	"	"	
James Hall	"	"	Lost 4 days
James N. Reeder	"	"	"
Nathan Owen	"	"	
Corporals.			
Beletha Griffith	"	"	
William Gallaher	"	"	Lost 4 days
James Harris	"	"	
Morgan Buckingh'm	"	"	Lost 4 days
Privates.			
Burt, Joseph			
Burt, William	Crow Creek	May 30	Lost 4 days
Bird, John	"	"	
Bird, Robert	Columbia	May 20	
Byrns, William	"	"	Lost 4 days
Barnhart, Hiram	"	"	on foot
Barnhart, Peter	"	May 26	

Name and Rank.	Residence.	Enrolled	Remarks.
		1832.	
Babb, Benjamin	Columbia	May 20	
Bullman, Joshua	"	May 30	Lost 4 days
Cassel, Henry K	"	May 20	Lost 20 days
Dawdy, Howell	"	"	
Davis, Milton			
Davis, William	Crow Creek	May 30	Lost 4 days
Davis, William W	"		
Darnell, John	"	May 20	
Earther, George	Columbia	"	Broke his leg May 30
Edwards, Stanton	"	"	No duty
Forbes, William	"	"	Lost 4 days
Hendrick, William A	"	"	
Hendrick, John P	"	"	Lost 13 days
Hawkins, Samuel	Crow Creek	"	Lost 10 days
Hamilton, David	Columbia	"	Lost 4 days
Hiff, Robert	"	May 30	
Johnston, John	"	June 5	No duty
Kemp, John	"	May 20	Lost 4 days
Keys, Elmer	"	"	"
McGuire, Philip	"	"	
Phillips, Joseph	"	"	
Russell, Lemuel	"	"	Lost 4 days
Sawyer, Jordan	"	"	
Smally, Jacob	"	May 30	
Swan, Elisha	"	June 5	Lost 4 days
Statler, David	"	May 20	Said he must plough
Shaw, George H	"	"	No duty

CAPT. WILLIAM M. STEWART'S COMPANY

Of Mounted Volunteers, attached to the 40th Regiment, 4th Brigade and 1st Division of Illinois Militia commanded by Col. John Strawn; called and mustered into the service of the United States, by order of the Commander-in-Chief of the Militia of the State of Illinois, on May 21, 1832, and mustered out of the service of the United States at Hennepin, Putnam county, Illinois, on June 18, 1832

Name and Rank.	Residence.	Enrolled	Remarks.
Captain.		1832.	
William M. Stewart	Hennepin	May 21	
First Lieutenant.			
Mason Willson	"	"	
Second Lieutenant.			
Livingston Roberts	"	"	
Sergeants.			
William Myers	"	"	
James S. Simpson	"	"	
Jonathan F. Wilson	"	"	
Joseph S. Warnock	"	"	
Corporals.			
William Patten	"	"	
Moses G. Williams	"	"	
William Walkup	"	"	
Privates.			
Bird, William	"	"	
Bird, John	"	"	
Brock, Aquilla	"	"	Dismissed by officers; served 3 days
Coats, Benjamin	"	"	
Dugan, Robert	"	"	
Ellis, Peter	"	"	
Gunn, Daniel	"	"	
Galaher, Thomas, Sr	"	"	
Holterbrand, Isaac	"	"	
Hunt, Richard	"	"	
Haily, Washington	"	"	Dismissed by officers; served 3 days
Jones, David	"	"	
Knox, Adam	"	"	

FOURTH BRIGADE.   127

Name and Rank.	Residence.	Enrolled	Remarks.
		1832.	
Knox, Lewis	Hennepin	May 21	
Letts, David	"	"	
Richie, David	"	"	
Ramsey, John L	"	"	
Sturdwin, Madison	"	"	
Stewart, William	"	"	
Stewart, James T	"	"	
Stephenson, Adison	"	"	Adison Stevenson rendered only 10 days.
Thompson, David	"	"	
Thompson, Aaron	"	"	
Thomas, Franklin	"	"	
Willis, Stephen D	"	"	
Willson, Alexander	"	"	

CAPT. WM. HAWS' COMPANY

Of Mounted Volunteers, belonging to the 40th Regt., 4th Brigade and 1st Division Illinois Militia, commanded by Col. John Strawn; called into service by the Governor of Illinois, and mustered out of service at Hennepin, on the Illinois river, State of Illinois, on June 18, 1832.

Name and Rank.	Residence.	Enrolled	Remarks.
Captain.		1832.	
William Haws	Hennepin	May 2	
First Lieutenant.			
James Garvin	"	"	
Second Lieutenant.			
Wm. M. Hart	"	"	
Sergeants.			
Thomas Gunn	"	"	
George Hilterbrand	"	"	
Jacob Greenawalt	"	"	Deserted
John Hunt	"	"	
Corporals.			
John Hart	"	"	
William Kincade	"	"	
Wm. Knox	"	"	
Wm. Lathrop	"	"	
Privates.			
Allen, Hiram	"	"	
Ash, Reuben	"	"	
Ash, Joseph	"	"	
Boyle, Abner	"	"	
Dent, George	"	"	
Glenn, Thomas	"	"	
Graves, Obed	"	"	
Glenn, Samuel	"	"	
Harmon, Asael	"	"	
Hart, Wm	"	"	
Healey, Hartwell	"	"	
Isaac, Elias	"	"	
Loyd, John	"	"	
Martin, George	"	"	
Neal, Little	"	"	
Stout, Hosa	"	"	
Stacey, Julius	"	"	
Winters, Christoph'r	"	"	
Whitacre, Aaron	"	"	
Wilson, Garrison	"	"	

INDEPENDENT REGIMENTS.

COL. MOORE'S REGIMENT.

Capt. John B. Thomas' Company

Of Volunteer Mounted Gunmen of Vermilion county, Illinois, called for by the Executive of said State, and received and mustered into service by Col. Isaac R. Moore, on May 23, 1832, and remained in service until June 23, 1832, both days inclusive.

Name and Rank.	Residence.	Enrolled	Remarks.
Captain.			
John B. Thomas			
First Lieutenant.			
William Nox			
Second Lieutenant.			
Gabriel G. Rice			
Sergeants.			
James C. McGee			
Richard F. Giddens			
Mijamin Byers			
John Q. Deakin			
Corporals.			
John R. Jackson			
William O. Neal			
William Trimmel			
David Moore			
Privates.			
Atwood, William			
Buoy, Laban			
Coddington, John			
Cox, John			
Cook, Michael			
Cunningham, Wm			
Creamer, Lewis			
Chandler, William			
Conner, Stephen B			
Deer, Thomas			
Fuller, Abner			
Gill, George			
Humphreys, Enoch			
Ham, William			
Harris, James			
Jones, Crawford H			
Judy, Henry			
Jackson, Hiram			
Jackson, Elijah			
Jose, Michael H			
Lane, John			

INDEPENDENT REGIMENTS.

Name and Rank.	Residence.	Enrolled	Remarks.
		1832.	
McGee, John			
McDonald, Henry			
Newell, Hugh			
Newell, David			
Newell, Wilson			
Reed, John A			
Reese, Morgan			
Shockey, Henry			
Shampaign, John B			
Standford, Philip M			
Smith, Jefferson			
Thomas, Joseph			
Tombs, Edwin B			
Wright, Jesse B			
Wilson, Henry			
Wilson, Hiram			
Wilson, John M			

We certify that Benjamin Tatam volunteered, mounted, armed and equipped and entered the service of the United States, on May 23, 1832, in Capt. Thomas' Company, but by consent of Col. Moore he was transferred and served part of the time in Capt. Ashton's Company, but rejoined this company and was mustered out of service with it; that he served the full term of 32 days; his name was omitted from this muster roll by oversight, and that he is entitled to pay and allowances with the rest of the company.

(Signed,)   JOHN B. THOMAS, Capt.
(Signed,)   ISAAC R. MOORE, Col.

CAPT. ALEXANDER BAILEY'S COMPANY

Of Mounted Gunmen, belonging to Col. I. R. Moore's Regiment of Illinois Volunteers. Mustered into the service on May 23, 1832. Mustered out June 23, 1832.

Name and Rank.	Residence.	Enrolled	Remarks.
		1832.	
Captain.			
Alex. Bailey			
First Lieutenant.			
George Ware			
Second Lieutenant.			
G. S. Hubbard			
Sergeants.			
Noah Sapp			
Asa Duncan			
Isaiah M. Treat			
Ralph Martin			
Corporals.			
Robert Osbern			
John Leneeve			
Obediah Leneeve			
William Martin			
Privates.			
Andrews, A. P			
Angle, Jacob			
Blair, William			
Bailey, David			
Blount, William			
Beckwith, George M			
Bowman, James			
Burbridge, Wm			
Botts, Feeling			
Crider, Archibald			
Canady, Wm			
Cunningham, James			
Canady, Watson			
Duncan, Alfred			
Deck, John			

Name and Rank.	Residence.	Enrolled	Remarks.
		1832.	
Ekler, Jacob			
Enos, Joab			
Foster, William			
Fitch, John R			
Gurthery, Michael			
Gilbert, Othnial			
Gilbert, Sylvester			
Hor, Warren			
Hall, James			
Hinkle, Josiah			
Hill, Robert			
Jennings, Soame			
Kelly, Asahel			
Knight, David			
King, James R			
Layton, Thomas			
Luman, Amos			
Loveless, Joseph R			
More, William			
Miller, Abraham K			
Oliver, Bushrod			
Ogg, Thomas			
Piper, John			
Russell, Samuel			
Skinner, John			
Shobore, Isadore			
Skinner, James			
Scott, Notly C			
Scott, John			
Vanvickle, Enoch			
Watson, John R			
White, James			
Willson, Robert P			
Wiles, Sanford			
Young, Scott			
Young, John			

CAPT. ELIAKEM ASHTON'S COMPANY

Of Mounted Riflemen, belonging to Col. Moore's Regiment of Vermilion Volunteers of the State of Illinois. Entered service on May 23, 1832, and remained in actual service until June 23, 1832, both days inclusive.

Name and Rank.	Residence.	Enrolled	Remarks.
Captain.			
Eliakem Ashton			
First Lieutenant.			
Wm. Mackin			
Privates.			
Brown, John			
Bryant, R. H			
Best, David			
Huntsman, Jarvas			
Hays, George J			
Hays, Hiram			
Kester, John			
Moner, Christopher			
Mann, Samuel			
McCann, Wilson B			
Mills, Elijah			
Mann, William			
Mansfield, Robert			
Mackey, Elias			
Nokes, Amos			
Potts, John			
Riddle, James			
Roll, Edw			
Shipp, Elias			

Name and Rank.	Residence.	Enrolled	Remarks.
Turner, James			
Turner, Daniel			
Ventiones, George W			
Wilson, Wm			
Williams, David T			

Capt. Morgan L. Payne's Company

Of Mounted Volunteers commanded by Major Nathaniel Buckmaster, commanding at Fort Payne, on the DuPage river, and stationed for the protection of the frontier between Ottawa and Chicago, in the county of Cook, in the State of Illinois; 135 miles from Danville, Vermilion county, State aforesaid, where recruited. Mustered out of service July 25, 1832.

Name and Rank.	Residence.	Enrolled	Remarks.
Captain.		1832.	
Morgan L. Payne	Danville	May 12	
First Lieutenants.			
Noah Ginion			Served as 1st Lt. to June 22, then resigned
John Black			Served as private to June 23, then elect'd 1st Lt
Second Lieutenant.			
Thos. McConnell			
Sergeants.			
Jonathan Pratt			Served as 1st Sergt to June 21, then as private.
Jacob Glass			Served as private to June 23, then as 1st Sergt.
Squire L. Payne			" " 22, " " 2d
John Cook			
Phillomon Spicer			
Corporals.			
Greenville Groves			
John Cassel			
Joseph Spicer			
Joshua Fleming			
Privates.			
Brown, Wm			Killed by the enemy on June 16, 1832
Bevens, James			
Cotten, Wm			
Coffee, Randolph R			
Collins, John			
Douglass, Cyrus			
Elliott, John			
Elliott, Nathan			
Furguson, Asa			
Fisher, Wm			
Hays, Bennett			Three days on express to Fort Wilbourn
Howell, John			
Kinny, Miram H			
Lucus, Presly			
Lucus, John			
Lucus, Reason			
Lyons, John			
Morgan, Evan S			
Morgan, John			
McBride, John	Danville	May 12	
O'Neal, Samuel			
Parkeson, Samuel			
Rutledge, Leander			
Stephens, John			
Stephens, Solomon			
Stephen, Isaac			
Springer, Levi			
Thompson, James			
Underwood, Wm			
Vankirk, Joseph			
Waters, John			
Wilson, Hardy			

Capt. James Palmer's Company

Of Mounted Volunteers, in Vermilion county, State of Illinois, called into service by order of the Executive of said State, from May 23, 1832, until June 23, 1832, both days inclusive.

Name and Rank.	Residence.	Enrolled	Remarks.
Captain.			
James Palmer			
First Lieutenant.			
John Light			
Second Lieutenant.			
Joseph Jackson			
Sergeants.			
Bluford Runyon			
Marcus Snow			
David Macumson			
Thomas Froman			
Corporals.			
Henry Streight			
Washington Lusher			
Abner M. Williams			
David Morgan			
Musicians.			
William H. Parkers'n			
Noah Delay			
Privates.			
Allen, Jared			
Atwood, Green			
Bandy, William			
Bandy, Washington			
Brown, John H			
Bensyl, John			
Banta, Solomon			
Currant, William			
Currant, Martin			
Cloe, Alexander			
Chandler, James			
Cline, Jesse			
Cravins, James C			
Dunn, Ferrel			
Delay, Henry			
Delay, Jacob			
Delay, Isaac			
Fielder, Charles			
Foley, Francis			
Fithian, William			
Fry, Jona. W			
Going, John			
Griffith, Stephen			
Gebhart, William			
Hale, Elijah B			
Henderson, Ely			
Jenkins, Malachi			
Kinkenon, William P			
Kenedy, Franklin			
Kizer, Andrew			
Lewis, David			
Love, William			
Lewis, Solomon			
Lambert, James			
Lenman, William			
Lizer, David C			
Malory, D. W. C			
Morgan, Joseph			
Macumson, Samuel			
Mendenhall, Ely			
Oiler, Abraham			
Phelps, Jonathan			
Payne, Henry B			
Prince, Francis			
Reynolds, Davis			

INDEPENDENT REGIMENTS.

Name and Rank.	Residence.	Enrolled	Remarks.
Rock, James			
Rutlage, Peter S			
Simpson, George		?	
Thomas, John			
Wooden, Elmore			
Yount, Jonathan			

Capt. I. M. Gillispie's Company

Of Volunteers of Mounted Militia, commanded by Col. I. R. Moore. Mustered into service May 23, 1832, and remained in service until June 23, 1832—both days inclusive.

Name and Rank.	Residence.	Enrolled	Remarks.
Captain.		1832.	
I. M. Gillispie		May 23	
First Lieutenant.			
Barnet Wever		"	
Second Lieutenant.			
Edwin Stanfield		"	
Sergeants.			
George Lewis		"	
James Adams		"	
Andrew Davis		"	
Corporals.			
Locklin Madden		"	
Wm. Nugent		"	
Elza Hoskins		"	
I. B. Prebble		"	
Privates.			
Bugely, Nicholas		"	
Brackall, Martin		"	
Bosely, Wm. M		"	
Don Carlens, John		"	
Don Carlos, Archelus		"	
Don Carlos, Wm		"	
Evans, Jonathan		"	
Foster, Samuel		"	
Freeman, James		"	
Gallion, Abram		"	
Gephart, Emanuel		"	
Howell, John		"	
Houghman, Jos. N		"	
Lyons, John H		"	
Millikan, Baptist		"	
Morgan, Thos		"	
Morgan, Achelis		"	
Morgan, Levi		"	
Mayfield, Stephen		"	
Ritter, John		"	
Rowe, William		"	
Swearengen, Isaac		"	
Swank, Richard		"	
Swank, William		"	
Swank, David		"	
Swisher, Anthony		"	
Yeager, C. F		"	
Yoke, Charles		"	

Capt. James Gregory's Company

Of Mounted Riflemen, belonging to Col. I. R. Moore's Regiment of Illinois Volunteers. Entered the service May 31, 1832, and remained in the service until June 23, 1832.

Name and Rank.	Residence.	Enrolled	Remarks.
Captain. James Gregory			
First Lieutenant. Wm. E. Williams			
Second Lieutenant. James Goodwin			
Sergeants. Jas. Cunningham			
Jas. Harnies			
Privates. Acton, James			
Bell, Elias B		†	
Cook, Stephen			
Collins, James			
Conner, Luke			
Cook, Isaac			
Evans, Thomas J			Tr. f'm Capt. Bailey's Co.; whole time, 31 days
Eccleston, Harry			
Farmer, Enoch			
Fuget, Bracston M			
Goodwin, Thomas			
Gilbert, James			
Jackson, Alexes			
James, Jesse			
Leaman, Jacomiah J			
Mace, Daniel			
McNeal, Benjamin			
Musgave, James			
McCoons, Thomas			
Morris, Thomas			
McCart, Edward			
McCart, John			
Staley, Jacob			
Stephenson, John			
Smith, Zion			
Sigler, George			
Watson, Charles M			
White, David			
Wilkenson, Jacob			

The men in this company, unless otherwise stated in "Remarks," each served 24 days.

Capt. Corbin R. Hutt's Company

Of Mounted Riflemen, belonging to Col. I. R. Moore's Regiment of Illinois Volunteers. Mustered into service May 23, 1832, and remained in service until June 23, 1832, both days inclusive.

Name and Rank.	Residence.	Enrolled	Remarks.
Captain. Corbin R. Hutt			
First Lieutenant. William Jeremiah			
Second Lieutenant. John A. Green			
Sergeants. Levin Watson			
Alex. McDonnell			
Jacob Hammer			
Moses Vest			

INDEPENDENT REGIMENTS.

Name and Rank.	Residence.	Enrolled	Remarks.
Privates.			
Anderson, Hiram			
Alexander, Wash't'n			
Brown, Hiram			
Brown, David			
Cole, Edward			
Cole, John			
Crusor, Robert			
Chitty, Ferguson			
Ellis, Henry Lee			
Foley, William			
Frazier, John			
Hathaway, Isaac			
Howard, Phillip			
Hammer, John			
Lowdowsky, Isaac			
Lacey, Moses			
Lacey, Willie			
McDowell, John B.			
Rheuby, John			
Scott, Fielding L.			
Smith, Luke			
Todd, Samuel			
Williams, Samuel			
Williams, William			
Wheat, John			
Yilkey, Joseph A.			

TWENTY-SEVENTH REGIMENT.

CAPT. MILTON M. MAUGH'S COMPANY

Of the 27th Regiment of Illinois Militia, called into the service of the United States by the Governor's order dated May 15, 1832. Mustered for discharge Sept. 6, 1832, and mustered out Sept. 8, 1832.

Name and Rank.	Residence.	Enrolled	Remarks.
Captain.		1832.	
Maughs, Milton M...	....	May 19	....
First Lieutenants.			
Moses Swan	....	"	Resigned June 8................
Wm. Johnson.......	....	June 9	....
Second Lieutenant.			
Mathew Johnson....	....	May 29	
Sergeants.			
John Turney.......	....	May 19	Resigned July 8................
John C. Bond	....	July 9	
Thomas Spriggins ..	....	May 19	
John D. Bell	....	"	
William Johnson....	....	May 24	Elected 1st Lieut. June 9.......
Joseph Walker	....	June 11	Discharged Aug. 1.
Corporals.			
A. M. Wallen.......	....	May 19	Joined Mounted Rangers.......
John G. Hulett	....	June 6	
James Jones........	....	May 19	
Absolom McCorm'ck	....	"	Absent Sept. 6 without leave....
Chas. T. Saunderson	....	"	Transferred to Capt. Gear's company ....
Musicians.			
Abel Procter.......	....	"	
Greenleaf Warren...	....	"	Absent without leave Sept. 6....
Privates.			
Alston, John.......	....	"	
Anderson, J. C.....	....	"	
Avery, David	....	May 25	
Avery, William	....	"	
Binninger, Jacob...	....	May 19	
Barnett, Leo L.....	....	"	Discharged July 30..............
Birdsell, Renphus...	....	"	
Britt, Leroy.......	....	"	
Blakely, J. P.......	....	"	Absent without leave from June 1........
Bass, George	....	"	Transferred June 9.
Brown, A	....	May 20	Absent without leave from June 1........
Brown, Julius......	....	"	" " " " 10.
Brice, G. W........	....	"	
Bond, John C.......	....	June 27	Appointed 1st Sergt. July 9.....
Bond, Wm. B.......	....	"	
Blundell, Wm	....	May 23	Sick................................
Beaty, James.......	....	Aug. 16	
Brock, Aquilla.....	....	Aug. 26	
Crow, Albion T....	....	May 19	Absent with leave Sept. 6.......
Culleran, T. B......	....	May 21	Attached to artillery Co. July 10........
Cook, Pleasant.....	....	May 19	Discharged July 13.
Cooy, Samuel......	....	May 21	" " " " 10.
Digney, Barney	....	May 20	
Davis, B. G. F......	....	"	Absent without leave from July 1........
Davis, B. G	....	"	" " " " " June 1........
Davenport, James...	....	"	
Dickinson, John L..	....	May 19	" with leave Sept. 6 ....

INDEPENDENT REGIMENTS. 137

Name and Rank.	Residence.	Enrolled	Remarks.
		1832.	
Dillon, Levi		May 20	Absent without leave June 1
Dooling, John		May 21	
Davidson, George		May 24	Hospital Steward
Dame, J. H.		May 19	
Drummond, Rob't H.		Aug. 16	
Freth, Isaiah		May 21	
Farnsworth, Terra B		May 19	Absent with leave Sept. 6
Fore, Joseph		" "	" " "
Fanley, Jacob		" "	" " "
Fanchette, Alex		" "	" without leave from June 20
Fultz, Frederick		July 5	" Sept. 6 with leave
Foreman, Moses		July 28	" from Sept. 6 with leave
Gray, Patrick		May 19	
Gruwell, John		May 24	Attached to Mounted Volunteers June 1
Gillham, Lemuel		" "	Discharged July 27
Hunt, Benson		May 19	
Hendley, Esbrey		" "	
Hulett, John G		" "	Appointed Corporal June 6
Imns, Abraham		" "	Absent without leave from June 10
Igo, Lewis		May 24	
Igo, William		" "	" " "
Igraham, John		May 25	" " " June 1
Journey, James		May 19	" " " May 20
Joslin, John		June 25	
Kelly, J		May 19	Absent without leave from June 1
Klean, Michael		June 23	" Sept. 6 with leave
King, John H		July 7	" without leave from Aug. 1
Lovell, Timothy		May 19	Transferred to Capt. Gear's Co. July 1
Lytle, William K		" "	Absent Sept. 6 with leave
Lepage, Clement		" "	
Lockwood, Ezekeil		" "	Detached to join artillery company
Manichael, Baptiste		" "	
Maughs, Henry		" "	
Maughs, D. H. T.		" "	
Maughs, James K		June 23	
McDuff, Wm		May 19	
McClair, P		May 20	Discharged July 29
Miller, Preston N		May 19	" June 4
Maxwell, J. J		May 20	Absent without leave from May 24
McAllister, Lem. S.		May 24	
McRayney, Daniel		May 20	Discharged June 11
Martin, Elkins		May 21	
Perregon, Wales		May 19	Sick
Paul, John		July 5	
Patterson, John B		May 26	Omitted in former rolls
Rice, Sylvester		May 19	Absent without leave from June 1
Rice, Thomas		May 20	
Rice, James		May 21	
Roberts, John		May 19	Discharged June 1
Rickman, Francis		" "	Absent Sept. 6 with leave
Rose, Pleasant		May 20	Discharged Aug. 4
Robedeaux, Lawr'ce		May 19	
Stukey, John		May 20	
Stewart, James B		May 19	
Smith, Wm		" "	Sick
Smith, Orlando		" "	Discharged June 27
Smith, James		" "	Absent without leave from June 26
Smith, Wm., 2d		May 20	Joined rifle company June 1
Smith, N		July 25	
Spears, Robert W		May 21	
Stoner, B		May 19	
Stephenson, Wm		May 20	Absent without leave from June 20
Saunett, Francis		" "	" " " 1
Sagan, Peter		May 19	" " " July 1
Strait, John		May 20	" " " Sept. 6
Shaw, Wm		" "	
Scribner, E		" "	Discharged May 25
Saucer, Robt		May 26	Joined Rangers June 26
Sherman, O. P.		May 20	Absent without leave from June 1
Shaw, John		" "	
Sincour, Jacob		June 25	Absent without leave from July 24
Shirmer, Philip		May 19	Omitted in former rolls
Slayton, T		" "	Absent without leave from June 1
Tharp, John		" "	
Taylor, James		" "	Absent Sept. 6 with leave
Turney, John		July 9	
Templeton, Robt		May 21	Absent Sept. 6 with leave
Usher, M. H		May 20	
Vansand, John		" "	Discharged July 27

Name and Rank.	Residence.	Enrolled	Remarks.
		1832	
Willard, Henry		May 21	
Webb, Thos. J.		May 19	Transferred June 6 with leave
Walker, James		"	Discharged Aug. 1
Wells, Guilford		"	Absent without leave from June 1
Walker, Joseph		"	Appointed Sergeant; discharged Aug. 1
Wood, Jeremiah		May 21	Absent Sept. 6 with leave
Young, Lewis		May 16	By a transfer from Mounted Rangers
Young, Hiram		May 21	Discharged June 27

CAPT. NICHOLAS DOWLING'S COMPANY

Of Artillery, 27th Regiment, Illinois Militia, called into service of the United States by the Governor's order, dated May 15, 1832, and now mustered for discharge this Sept. 6, 1832.

Name and Rank.	Residence.	Enrolled	Remarks.
Captains.		1832.	
I. R. B. Gardenier		May 19	By request acted as comd't of Co. until July
Nicholas Dowling		July 15	[14, 1832, when he resigned.
First Lieutenant.			
G. W. Campbell		May 19	
Second Lieutenant.			
Charles Gratiot		May 19	
Third Lieutenant			
Leonard Goss		June 26	Detached to the staff
Sergeants.			
Nicholas Dowling		May 19	Elected Captain July 15, 1832
S. Gridley		July 15	
Z. Bell		May 19	
Daniel Argent		"	
George Ferguson		July 15	
Corporals.			
A. M. Delong		May 19	
N. Barber		"	
Michael Byrne		July 15	Lost his blanket
T. T. Davis		"	
Musician.			
Wm. Blair		July 15	Drew no arms nor blanket from company
Privates.			
Byrne, Michael		May 19	Appointed Corporal July 8, 1832
Byrne, Philip		"	Sick
Brush, R. W.		June 30	
Coligan, P.		"	
Cullum, C. B.		July 8	
Drum, Thos.		May 19	
Davis, T. T.		"	Appointed Corporal July 15, 1832
Ellis, P.		July 16	Drew no arms nor blanket from Co.
Ferguson, George		May 19	Corporal from May 25 to July 25, when appointed Sergeant
Farley, I. P.		"	
Graham, Robert		"	
Gridley, S.		"	Corporal until July 15, 1832, when he was appointed Sergeant.
Garner, T.		"	
Gray, M.		June 20	
Gray, B.		"	
Hempested, Wm.		June 30	On extra duty in ordnance department
Lockwood, Ezekial		"	
Mitchell, A.		July 14	
Mitchell, J.		"	Furloughed; drew no arms nor blanket
Nevelle, E.		June 16	
Nutting, Josiah		July 16	Drew no arms nor blanket from company
Powell, R. B.		May 19	
Reed, Samuel		June 30	Furloughed
Roberts, I.		June 14	
Roundtree, S.		July 8	Drew no arms nor blanket from company

Name and Rank.	Residence.	Enrolled	Remarks.
		1832	
Sayre, S. L.		May 19	
Stahl, F.		June 20	
Smead, H.		May 25	Sick
Sharp, C. P.		May 19	Discharged June 3, 1832.
Taylor, Robert		"	"
Towmer, Wm.		May 27	
Vanbuskirk, J.		July 16	
Weather, John		May 19	
Wann, Daniel		"	

Capt. Clack Stone's Company

Of the 27th Regiment, Illinois Militia, called into the service of the United States by the Governor's order, dated May 15, 1832. Mustered out September 6.

Name and Rank.	Residence.	Enrolled	Remarks.
Captain.		1832.	
Clack Stone		May 25	
First Lieutenant.			
Heber Morris		"	
Second Lieutenant.			
Samuel Jimmerson		"	
Sergeants.			
George Lowry		"	Quit June 15, with leave.
Jefferson Clark		June 15	
Privates.			
Armstrong, John		June 25	
Armstrong, David		"	
Bean, Joseph		"	
Bean, Charles		"	Absent June 26 to July 16, on public duty.
Clark, David		"	Quit June 20; discharged.
Cook, Horace		"	" with leave.
Crane, Westley		June 23	
Crane, Thomas		July 13	
Fowler, Daniel		May 25	Quit June 25, with leave.
Hack, Washington		"	
Hack, John, Jr.		"	Quit August 13, with leave.
Hack, James		"	
Hack, John, Sr.		"	
Hack, Milton		"	
Hitt, Thadeus		"	
Hulett, Samuel		"	
Howard, Stephen P.		"	Killed in battle June 18.
Immerson, John B.		"	
Johnson, Robert B.		"	
Johnson, Wm., Jr.		"	
Kerkley, James B.		"	Discharged July 16.
Kilyan, Thomas		"	
Knox, John		July 13	
Lee, Jesse		May 25	
Lawhoon, William		"	Discharged June 25.
Morris, Nath'l		"	
Milligan, David		"	
Murdock, Fergus I.		"	
Milligan, Hezek		"	
Murdock, John		"	
Matthews, Granville		"	
Nutting, Josiah		"	Wounded and sent to hospital June 25.
Rittenhouse, Obed'h		"	Quit June 15, with leave.
Rollings, Ezekiel		July 16	" Aug. 16, "
Tart, Benjamin		May 25	" June 26, "
Thacher, Alfred		"	" June 20, "
Van Vaultingburg, H.		"	
Vanbuskirk, Jesse		"	Quit June 20, with leave.

Name and Rank.	Residence.	Enrolled	Remarks.
		1832	
Wooton, Daniel		June 19	
Wooton, Moses		May 25	
Williams, Richard			
White, Ambrose			

CAPT. CHARLES McCOY'S COMPANY

Of Infantry, 27th Regiment of Illinois Militia, called into the service of the United States by the Governor's order, dated May 15, 1832, and was mustered for discharge this 6th day of September, 1832.

Name and Rank.	Residence.	Enrolled	Remarks.
Captain.		1832.	
Charles McCoy	Jo Daviess Co.	May 27	Drew no rations for himself or servant; had a servant three months.
First Lieutenant.			
James M. Miller	"	"	Drew one month's rations only
Second Lieutenant.			
Jesse Yount		"	Drew one month's rations only
Sergeants.			
P. Thomas January		"	Discharged July 25
Dennison Billings		"	Entitled to twenty-four rations
Hezekiah Young		"	" " " "
John Tyree		"	" " " "
Corporals.			
John W. Smallwood		"	Entitled to twenty-four rations
William Barnhouse		"	" " " "
Jefferson Crawford		"	" " " "
John Brown		"	" " " "
Privates.			
Barker, Allen			Entitled to twenty-four rations
Blundrett, James		May 27	Discharged August 20
Baker, Sylvester		May 29	Drew no rations
Coffman, Abram		May 27	Entitled to twenty-four rations
Curtis, Horace		"	" " " "
Cottle, Oliver		"	
Curtis, Henry		"	
Eversoul, Chris'pher		"	Entitled to twenty-four rations
Field, William		July 1	
Gossett, Joseph		May 27	Entitled to twenty-four rations
Gillett, Benoni R.		"	Drew no rations
Green, Andrew I		"	Entitled to twenty-four rations
Gilbert, Braxton		July 1	Entitled to eighteen rations
Grontjean, James		May 27	Drew no rations
Hindman, John		"	
Igo, Lewis		July 1	
Lillipon, Vichel		"	Entitled to eighteen rations
Langet, Francis		May 27	Entitled to twenty-four rations
Lewis, Lawson		"	
McGehee, Evan		"	
Miller, Vincent B		"	Entitled to twenty-four rations
McNair, Thomas		May 29	Drew no rations
Marlow, Rudolph		July 1	
Nicholson, John R.		May 27	Discharged Aug. 20
Ogan, Irwin		"	Entitled to twenty-four rations
Phelps, George		July 1	Entitled to eighteen rations
Rand, Allen		May 27	Entitled to twenty-four rations
Reed, John		July 1	Entitled to eighteen rations
Richey, Milton		May 27	Discharged Aug. 20
Shultz, Christopher		"	Discharged Aug. 28
Stewart, Wm. M.		"	Transferred to staff July 4
Stewart, John		July 1	
Town, Warren		May 27	Entitled to twenty-four rations
Tessott, Daniel		"	" " " "
Tyree, Jacob		"	" " " "

INDEPENDENT REGIMENTS.   141

Name and Rank.	Residence.	Enrolled	Remarks.
Vaughan, Peyton....	....	July 1	....
Wolcott, John	....	May 27	Entitled to twenty-four rations ....
Young, Robert R	....	" "	....
Young, Wm. C.	....	" "	....
Yount, Benjamin M.	....	" "	....
Yount, George	....	" "	....

Capt. Benjamin J. Aldenrath's Company

Of Infantry of the 27th Regiment of Illinois Militia, called into the service of the United States by the Governor's proclamation dated May 15, 1832, and was mustered for discharge on the 6th of September, 1832.

Name and Rank.	Residence.	Enrolled	Remarks.
Captain.		1832.	
Benj. J. Aldenrath..	JoDaviess Co	May 18	....
First Lieutenant.			
John C. Robinson...	....	" "	
Second Lieutenants.			
Daniel P. Price......	....	" "	Resigned June 2............
James Simonds......	....	June 10	Elected 2d Lieut. June 9..........
Sergeants.			
James Simonds......	....	May 18	....
Joseph Campbell....	....	" "	Absent without leave May 26..........
Barnett Whittimore.	....	" "	
Mynot Selleman.....	....	" "	Absent without leave June 10..........
Samuel Moore.......	....	June 21	
George F. Smith....	....	June 26	Absent from August, with arms, blankets, etc.
Corporals.			
Noah Thomas.......	....	May 18	Joined horse company July 1..........
Charles McGee......	....	" "	Absent without leave June 19..........
Enoch Thomas......	....	" "	
Samuel Love........	....	" "	
Privates.			
Billings, James......	....	" "	
Beasley, Ephraim...	....	" "	Quit June 19..........
Bilto, Charles........	....	" "	Quit May 27..........
Brophy, Thomas....	....	" "	Shot-bag returned........
Chandler, Nathaniel	....	" "	Quit May 27.
Chaney, Osborn.....	....	" "	Did no duty; return'd no arms or accoutrem's
Courts, Walter......	....	" "	Quit June 19, with leave........
Carroll, Nicholaus..	....	" "	
Case, Aaron..........	....		
Crosby, Cyrus.......	....	July 3	
Cord, Stephen.......	....	May 24	Quit June 3; returned no gun, blanket, etc...
Dickerson, George H	....	May 18	Quit July 1..........
Duncan, John.......	....	" "	
Dyas, William.......	....	" "	
Dyas, John..........	....	" "	
Dyas, David.........	....	" "	
Dooley, Linville.....	....	June 10	
Fortune, William....	....	May 18	
Faherty, William....	....	" "	
Faherty, John.......	....	" "	
Fullerton, John V...	....	June 18	
George, Alexander..	....	May 18	
George, Lewis.......	....	" "	
George, Stephen....	....	" "	
Gentel, Perret.......	....	June 10	Drew no rations..........
Guthray, Thomas...	....	" "	Discharged July 23..........
Grafford, Lewis E...	....	July 3	
Gocky, Gabriel......	....	May 23	Quit June 2..........
Hathaway, Samuel..	....	July 16	Joined after mustering into service..........
Hanniman, Thomas.	....	May 18	
Hinman, Nelson.....	....	" "	Absent without leave May 18..........
Hoozer, Jacob.......	....	June 18	

Name and Rank.	Residence.	Enrolled	Remarks.
		1832.	
Harrison, Daniel		June 25	
Hubbard, Thomas		July 11	
Hubbard, Goodrich		"	
Hubbard, William		"	
Hugell, Thomas		May 20	Quit June 1
Kenney, Patrick		May 18	
McGulpin, Samuel		May 28	Quit June 7
Moffitt, Benj. F.		May 18	Joined Horse Co. June 1; returned no arms.
McCausland, David		May 19	
McKinney, Patrick		June 18	
Minett, Toosus		May 23	Quit June 1
Moore, Samuel		May 18	
Phillis, John		"	Quit June 10
Quinliven, Dennis		"	Absent without leave
Quinliven, Mark		June 24	
Ross, Thomas L		May 18	
Stevner, Lewis		"	Quit May 28
Skinner, Thomas H.		"	Gave certif. for 1 mo. serv.; ret'd no arms, etc.
Shannon, Daniel		"	Absent without leave
Stockton, Thomas B		May 20	Disch. June 19, by order of Col. Strode
Smith, George F		May 19	
Thomas, John		May 18	Over age
Thomas, Enos			
Williams, Wm		"	
Williams, John		"	Absent without leave
Williams, James		"	
Whalon, John		"	Quit June 1
Ware, Reuben S		May 19	Two blankets not returned
Young, Joseph S		June 7	Quit July 17.

Capt. H. H. Gear's Company

Of Infantry of the 27th Regiment, Illinois Militia, called into service of the United States by general order, dated May 15, 1832, and now mustered for discharge this 6th of September, 1832.

Name and Rank.	Residence.	Enrolled	Remarks.
Captain.		1832.	
H. Hezekiah Gear	JoDaviess Co	May 19	
First Lieutenant.			
J. W. Foster		"	
Second Lieutenant.			
Alesworth Baker		"	
Sergeants.			
Fountain Matthews			Retained one blanket and lost one blanket
William Alloway			
B. Service		June 10	Arms not retain'd, 1 rug, 2 kettles; abs'nt, sick
John K. Robinson		June 14	Abs'nt, furl.; furnish'd arms, etc; abs'nt, leave
Corporals.			
Francis Sheverell		May 27	
Zelo Corey			
Timothy Lovell		July 1	
James Howerton		May 19	
Privates.			
Baganell, Charles		June 5	Deserted July 12; carried off U.S. musket, &c.
Boxley, William		May 27	Killed in battle July 1
Bass, George		July 31	
Bias, Joseph		June 1	Refuses to deliver U. S. musket
Bryan, Leonard		"	Servant to Capt. Legate, U. S. A.; disch. July 16
Bennett, G. W. B.		June 5	Deserted July 6; carried off U.S arms
Bachelor, William		May 19	June 12, & blanket
Cardinalle, Parish		"	Musket returned; one blanket not returned.
Campbell, Hamilton		"	One musket returned
Cardinalle, Eustace		"	One musket and one blanket returned

INDEPENDENT REGIMENTS.

Name and Rank.	Residence.	Enrolled		Remarks.
		1832.		
Craig, Martin		May	19	Discharged June 7
Chapman, A. C		"		June 15
Cole, J		"		Deserted June 7
Carrigan, Charles		June	5	" June 6; carried off 2 robes, 1 musket
Dodge, John		July	17	Detailed for extra duty, Hosp. Cook, July 17.
Deslain, Thomas		June	1	
Downey, Antoine		May	19	Deserted June 12
Dement, William		June	10	
Elgin, F. C		May	19	Discharged June 7
Gray, J. H				
Guest, Samuel		May	27	Deserted with blanket June 15
Gorton, William		May	19	" June 12; absent without leave June 12
Hudson, M. W		"		Lost one U. S. musket.(to Sept. 6; lost musk't
Hollman, Jesse		July	17	Found his own arms and equipments
Hallett, Moses		June	22	
Howell, J. W		June	5	Deserted July 6, and took off 1 U.S. musket..
Hughs, Peter		May	27	" June 10, and took off his blanket
Kirkpatrick, J. F		May	19	Abs'nt without leave; joined Capt. Craig's Co.
Lestrange, Patrick		May	25	
Laport, Toulouse		May	27	Absent without leave July 16; present Sept. 6
Lepold, M		May	19	Musket and accoutrements returned
Long, A		"		Discharged June 7
Long, M		"		
Means, Jacob		"		Furnished own arms; rec'd 1 robe, not ret'ed
McBride, Felix		"		Discharged July 25
Marstin, J		July	31	
Massey, H		June	22	Detailed as an artificer
Mitchell, James		June	21	Absent without leave; never mustered
McDonald, J		June	5	Deserted June 12; took musket and blanket.
Mitchell, Augustus		June	21	Absent without leave; never mustered
Messmore, George		May	19	Discharged June 10
Nigh, Edmund		June	22	
O'Neil, John		May	19	Blanket not returned; 2 months hosp. attend.
Ontio, Peter		"		Absent without leave; his arms taken July 12; returned 26th; paid by Dan'l Warm, $13.25..
Pelott, William		July	31	Furnished his arms and equipments
Primer, John B				
Rice, ——		June	22	Deserted July 6th
Robinson, M. C		May	19	Furnished his arms and equipments
Rhoads, Henry		May	27	
Randleman, Jacob		July	22	
Stuart, John		May	27	One musket returned; 1 blanket not returned
Scott, Samuel		June	10	Discharged August 5
Sincere, Michael		June	22	
Snider, S		May	19	Discharged June 7
Simmons, Silas G		June	5	Deserted July 12; took musket and buf. robe.
Saunderson, Chas. F		July	1	Deserted July 6; took musket and buf. robe.
Thatcher, Alfred		June	27	Furnished his own arms and equipments
Truegate, Benjamin		June	22	Discharged August 7
Truegate, Meredith		"	"	
Toulouse, J		May	27	
Tooley, Henry		May	19	Deserted June 7
Urie, Samuel		June	5	Returned musket and equipment
Urie, John				
Vaughn, Amos		May	19	
Williams, John				
Williamson, S. N		June	22	Absent without leave July 16
Webb, Thomas J		July	31	
Young, William		May	19	Discharged June 7

Capt. Samuel H. Scales' Company

Of Infantry, of the 27th Regiment of Illinois Militia, called into the service of the United States by the Governor's order dated May 15, 1832, and now mustered for discharge this 6th day of September, 1832.

Name and Rank.	Residence.	Enrolled	Remarks.
Captain.		1832.	
Samuel H. Scales	JoDaviess Co.	June 16	
First Lieutenant.			
John L. Soals		"	
Second Lieutenant.			
George Wells		"	
Sergeants.			
James Smith		"	
John B. Woodson		"	Quit June 16
William Davis		"	
John Nevib		"	Quit June 16
Corporals.			
Richard Willis		"	
Robert Hendrix		"	
Samuel Cory		"	
Emerson Chapman		"	
Privates.			
Brock, Elias		"	Drew no rations
Cook, Harris		"	
Charles, Elijah		"	Quit June 16
Davis, Noah		"	
Davis, John		"	
Davis, Jonathan		"	
Frost, Benjamin		July 22	
Gibson, Julius		June 16	
Hendrix, James		"	
Hale, David		"	Drew no rations
Hawkins, James L.		"	Quit June 16
House, William		"	
Lytchtenberger, Cyr.		"	
Lytchtenberger, Con		"	Quit June 15
McMath, William		"	
Miller, Geo. B.		"	
McKee, John		"	
Roberts, John		"	
Streeter, John		"	
Shook, Samuel		"	
Smitch, Isaac		"	
Streeter, Joshua		"	
Walbridge, Hiram		"	
Wood, John		"	
Wood, George		"	
Woods, William		"	
Wadhams, William		"	
Wadhams, John		"	
Woodcock, James S.		"	Quit June 16

INDEPENDENT REGIMENTS. 145

Capt. Jonathan Craig's Company

Of Infantry of the 27th Regiment of Illinois Militia, called into the service of the United States by the Governor's order of May 15, 1832, and now mustered for discharge, this 6th day of September, 1832; enrolled for three months and twenty days.

Name and Rank.	Residence.	Enrolled	Remarks.
Captain.		1832.	
Jonathan Craig	JoDaviess Co.	May 19	
First Lieutenant.			
Thomas Kilgore		"	
Second Lieutenant.			
Robert C. Bourne		"	
Sergeants.			
John Furlong		"	
Tarlton F. Brock		"	
Joseph Claig		"	
Nathan White		"	
Corporals.			
Lewellyn Brock		"	
Hiram Morrison		"	
William Caradiff		"	
Philip Rice		"	
Privates.			
Boy, John		"	
Bruno, Peter		"	Drew a blanket; did not return it; with leave
Brock, Elisha		"	
Bowman, Benjamin		"	Quit July 6, with leave
Brady, Bernard		"	
Buster, Robert B.		"	
Biggs, William		June 27	
Bilto, Charles		July 12	
Campbell, John		May 19	
Coyle, Peter		"	
Coyle, James		"	
Dalton, William		"	Quit June 19, with leave
Dowling, Robert		July 18	
Dean, Elias		May 19	
Dugan, Patrick		June 27	
Dugan, John		"	
Fine, John		May 19	Quit July 5, with leave
Furlong, Walter		"	
Farrar, Robert		July 26	
Frost, Benjamin		May 19	Quit July 23, with leave
Foley, James		"	Quit July 4, with leave
Graham, Thomas		"	Dismissed July 6, with leave
Gilroy, Patrick		"	
Haines, Martin		"	
Kilgore, John		"	
Kirtley, J. W.		July 16	
Kelley, James		May 19	
Leary, Thomas		"	
Liddle, George		"	
Langford, William		"	
Lynch, Bernard		"	
McDermit, James		"	
Meara, Michael		"	
McCabe, James		"	
Maple, John L.		July 14	
Morrison, William		July 19	
Moore, Thomas		May 19	
Miller, Edward		June 27	
Murray, Keaven		"	
McNabb, Edward		"	
McNair, David		"	Quit July 20, with leave
O'Leary, Peter		July 6	
Parkinson, John		May 19	
Richardson, Fount'n		"	
Rice, James		"	
Roberts, James		July 14	
Rice, Henry		July 26	
Smith, Abner		May 19	
Sherrill, Adam		June 27	

-- 10

Name and Rank.	Residence.	Enrolled	Remarks.
		1832.	
Townsend, John		May 19	Drew blanket and did not return it............
Tobin, Bartlett		" "	
Vanbuskirk, Jesse		July 19	
Willis, Noah		July 2	

STATE OF ILLINOIS,
November 10, 1832.

I certify that James M. Strode was, on September 6 last, Colonel of the 27th Regiment of Illinois Militia, acting in said office; said company was in service under my order, and their service was necessary in the defence of the country last summer.

(Signed.)   JOHN REYNOLDS.
Commander-in-Chief Illinois Militia.

CAPT. LAMBERT P. VANSBURGH'S COMPANY

27th Regiment of Illinois Militia, called into the service of the United States by the Governor's order, dated May 15, 1832, and now mustered for discharge this 6th day of September, 1832.

Name and Rank.	Residence.	Enrolled	Remarks.
Captain.		1832.	
L. P. Vansburgh		May 18	
First Lieutenant.			
John W. Blackstone		June 20	
Second Lieutenant.			
Henry Cavener		May 18	Joined Mounted Vol. with permiss'n, June 20.
Sergeants.			
Zack Hillyard		June 20	
Thomas L. Potter		May 19	Joined Mounted Vol. with permiss'n, June 20.
John W. Blackstone		" "	Elected 1st Lieut. June 20
Elias Griggs		" "	Joined Mounted Vol. with permiss'n, June 20.
Alex. M. Neville		" "	
Wm. Tomlinson		June 20	
Wm. Mattox		" "	
Corporals.			
Thomas Reed		May 18	Joined Mounted Vol. with permiss'n, June 20.
Wm. P. Ravandaugh		" "	
Edmund Mattox		June 20	
Wm. Tomlinson		May 18	Appointed Sergeant June 20
James Arwin		" "	Joined Mounted Vol. with permiss'n, July 9.
Privates.			
Ashbrook, Chas. C.		" "	
Ammeman, Josh		" "	Joined Mounted Vol. with permiss'n, June 20.
Austin, Hiram		July 13	Furloughed
Beard, Samuel		May 18	Absent from July 9.
Ballard, John H		" "	Joined Mounted Vol. with permiss'n, June 20.
Ballard, Bartholo'ew		" "	
Broody, Israel		" "	Absent since June 20.
Brown, William		June 20	
Broody, Washington		May 18	Absent since June 20.
Crothers, Hamilton		June 20	
Cunningham, Wm		May 18	Sick in hospital
Cunningham, John		" "	
Crigan, John		" "	Absent with leave July 9, sick
Clary, Patrick		" "	
Craghead, John		" "	Absent with leave June 20, sick.
Dooly, Lindley		" "	
Davenport, James		" "	" " " "
Divin, David		" "	
Donall, Jonathan		" "	Joined Mounted Vol. with permiss'n, June 20.
East, William		" "	
Fulton, W. J		" "	Absent since June 20.
Fugate, Preston		" "	

INDEPENDENT REGIMENTS. 147

Name and Rank.	Residence.	Enrolled	Remarks.
		1832.	
Funtress, Eleanzer..		June 20	
Gallager, Patrick...		May 18	Absent since June 20
Hullgate, Weston...		"	Discharged July 13
Hoffman, Zack......		"	Discharged July 9
Humes, Thompson..		"	
Huling, Samuel......		"	Joined Mounted Vol. with permiss'n, June 20.
Harden, Isam S.....		"	
Hays, James........		July 10	Furloughed
Ingraham, Alphs....		May 18	
Johnson, Wm.......		July 6	Sick in hospital
Jourden, E.........		May 18	Joined Mounted Vol. with permiss'n, June 20.
Karnes, Patrick....		"	
Knowland, Hardin..		June 20	
Larkin, James......		May 18	Absent with leave July 9, sick
Lawhorn, Willin....		June 20	
Mattox, Wm........		May 18	Appointed Sergeant June 20.
Mattox, Edmund...		"	Appointed Corporal June 20.
Murphy, Richard...		"	
McKaney, Daniel...		June 29	
Obanion, George....		May 18	
Orm, Alexander.....		June 20	Absent since July 9
O'Brian, Wm.......		May 18	Discharged June 20.
Palmer, John.......		"	Absent since June 20, sick
Phalen, Lawrence..		June 27	
Ragan, John		May 18	Absent since June 20, sick
Ritter, Jacob.......		"	
Robinson, Benj.....		"	" " " "
Ruggle, Edmund L..		June 20	
Stevens, George W..		May 18	Joined Mounted Vol. with permiss'n, June 20.
Smith, Wm.........		June 20	Absent since July 9
Scott, George......		"	Sick in hospital
Sain, Philip........		July 13	Furloughed
Thompson, Willis...		May 18	Joined Mounted Vol. with permiss'n, June 20.
Tracey, Charles.....		"	" " " " "
Thomas, John C....		July 2	
Williams, John.....		May 18	Absent since June 20
Wilson, Henry M...		"	
Whittle, Levi.......		"	
Walker, Samuel.....		June 26	
Wright, Hezekiah...		"	

ODD BATTALIONS.

ODD BATTALION COMMANDED BY MAJOR N. BUCKMASTER.

CAPT. HOLDEN SEISSION'S COMPANY

Of Mounted Volunteers, in the service of the United States, in defense of the Northern frontier of the State of Illinois, against the Sac and Fox Indians, from the county of Cook, in said State, in the year 1832. Mustered out August 15, 1832.

Name and Rank.	Residence.	Enrolled	Remarks.
Captain, Holden Seission	Cook Co.	1832. July 23	
First Lieutenant, Robert Stephens	"	"	
Second Lieutenant, William H. Bradford	"	"	
Sergeants,			
James Sayres	"	"	
Uriah Wentworth	"	"	
John Cooper	"	"	
Abraham Franciss	"	"	
Corporals,			
Armstead Runyan	"	"	
Thomas Coons	"	"	
Edward Poor	"	"	
Cornell's C. VanHorn	"	"	
Privates,			
Barlow, William	"	"	
Cox, Joseph	"	"	
Clarke, Timothy B.	"	"	
Clarke, Barrett	"	"	
Clarke, William	"	"	
Chapman, William	"	"	
Crandell, David	"	"	
Crandell, Alva	"	"	
Darling, Enoch	"	"	
Fleming, Samuel	"	"	
Frame, Patterson	"	"	
Franciss, Thomas	"	"	
Friend, John	"	"	
Friend, Aaron	"	"	
Gougar, William	"	"	
Gougar, John	"	"	
Gougar, Nicholas	"	"	
Gougar, Daniel	"	"	
Haight, Daniel	"	"	
Henderson, Silas	"	"	

ODD BATTALIONS. 149

Name and Rank.	Residence.	Enrolled	Remarks.
		1832.	
Johnson, Alfred	Cook Co.	July 23	
Johnson, Joseph	"	"	
Johnson, James	"	"	
Lampseed, Peter	"	"	
Lemsis, Peter	"	"	
Lamfear, Selah	"	"	
More, Aaron	"	"	
Maggard, Daniel	"	"	
McDeed, John	"	"	
McDeed, James	"	"	
Mack, Daniel	"	"	
Maggard, Benjamin	"	"	
Mathews, James	"	"	
Norman, Joseph	"	"	
Pettijohn, George	"	"	
Poor, Anderson	"	"	
Rowley, Calvin	"	"	
Rodgers, William	"	"	
Rice, Rufus	"	"	
Robb, Daniel	"	"	
Scott, Wm. H	"	"	
Scott, Lucius	"	"	
Smith, David	"	"	
Stephens, Oren	"	"	
Turner, O. L.	"	"	
Van Horne, Abrah'm	"	"	
Van Horne, Simon C.	"	"	
Wares, Aaron	"	"	
Wilson, John	"	"	

I certify on honor that the company of Mounted Volunteers, under the immediate command of Capt. Holden Scission, was organized for temporary purposes on the 23d of July, 1832, by the advice and consent of Major-General Scott, for the protection of the frontier, in Cook county, State of Illinois. Which organization was recommended and approved by the said Major General Scott (in consequence of the mustering two companies out of service which constituted part of the guard for the protection of that frontier under my command); that this organization was necessary for the protection of the frontier; that said company should be in service, and that they did actually perform the service, as mentioned in said roll, up to the 13th of August, 1832, under my command as Major of an Odd Battalion, wherein said company formed a part.

Given under my hand, at Edwardsville, August 19, 1833.

(Signed.)   N. BUCKMASTER,
                                       Major Commanding.

I certify that, at the time mentioned in the muster roll of Capt. Scission's Company of Mounted Volunteers, the above named Nathaniel Buckmaster was legally acting as Major in an Odd Battalion, including said company, and commissioned by me in that office, and, judging from the certificates of said Major Buckmaster and Capt. Seission, I have no doubt said company served as stated in said roll; and I state further, that the service of said company was necessary in the defense of the country, as stated above.

(Signed.)   JOHN REYNOLDS,
               Governor, and Commander-in-Chief Illinois Militia.

AUGUST 20, 1833.

CAPT. JOSEPH NAPIER'S COMPANY

Of Mounted Volunteers, in the service of the United States, in defence of the northern frontier of the State of Illinois against the Sac and Fox Indians, from the county of Cook in said State, in the year 1832. Mustered out Aug. 15, 1832.

Name and Rank.	Residence.	Enrolled	Remarks.
		1832.	
Captain. Joseph Napier	Cook Co.	July 19	
First Lieutenant. Alanson Sweet	"	"	

Name and Rank.	Residence.	Enrolled	Remarks.
Second Lieutenant. Sherman King	Cook Co.	1832. July 19.	
Sergeants.			
S. M. Salisbury	"	"	
John Manning	"	"	
Walter Stowell	"	"	
John Napier	"	"	
Corporals.			
T. E. Parsons	"	"	
Lyman Butterfield	"	"	
J. P. Bladget	"	"	
Nelson Murray	"	"	
Privates.			
Ament, Anson	"	"	
Ament, Calvin	"	"	
Barber, William	"	"	
Clarke, Dennis	"	"	
Fox, George	"	"	
Foster, Caleb	"	"	
Fox, John	"	"	
Gault, William	"	"	
Geddiens, Josiah H.	"	"	
Hawley, Peres	"	"	
Harrison, Edmund	"	"	
Hobson, Bailey	"	"	
Langdon, Daniel	"	"	
Peck, P. F. W.	"	"	
Parsons, T.	"	"	
Paine, Uriah	"	"	
Paine, Christopher	"	"	
Stevens, John	"	"	
Stevens, John, Jr.	"	"	
Scott, Williard	"	"	
Stowell, Augustine	"	"	
Stowell, Calvin M.	"	"	
Sweet, Richard M.	"	"	
Walstcoat, Seth	"	"	
Wilson, Henry T.	"	"	
Wicoffe, Peter	"	"	

I certify on honor that the company of Mounted Volunteers under the immediate command of Capt. Joseph Napier was organized for temporary purposes on July 19, 1832, by the advice and consent of Major-General Scott, for the protection of the frontier in Cook county, State of Illinois, which organization was recommended and approved by the said Major-General Scott (in consequence of the importance of mustering two companies out of service which constituted a part of the guard for the protection of that frontier under my command); that this organization was necessary for the protection of the frontier; that said company should be in service, and that they did actually perform the service, as mentioned in said roll, up to the 13th of August, 1832, under my command as Major of an Odd Battalion wherein said company formed a part.

Given under my hand at Edwardsville, August 19, 1833.

(Signed.)   N. BUCKMASTER,
                                                   Major Commanding.

I certify that at the time mentioned in the muster roll of Capt. Joseph Napier's Company of Mounted Volunteers, the above named Nathaniel Buckmaster was legally acting as Major in an Odd Battalion including said company, and commissioned by me in that office, and judging from the certificate of Major Buckmaster and Capt. Napier, I have no doubt said company served as stated in said roll; and I further state that the service of said company was *necessary* in the defence of the country, as stated above.

(Signed.)   JOHN REYNOLDS,
August 20, 1833.   Gov. and Com.-in-Chief Ill. Mil.

I further certify that the United States furnished no forage for the within company, and the said company was in service when I was mustered out of service on Aug. 13, 1832.

(Signed.)   N. BUCKMASTER,
                                                   Major Commanding.

ODD BATTALION OF RANGERS.

CAPT. ABNER EADS' COMPANY

Of Mounted Rangers. Enrolled at Peoria, Illinois, by virtue of an order from the Commander-in-Chief of the Militia of the State of Illinois, to Brig.-Gen. Josiah Stillman. Mustered into the service of the United States April 23, 1832. Discharged June 28, 1832.

Name and Rank.	Residence.	Enrolled	Remarks.
Captain.		1832.	
Abner Eads		April 23	
First Lieutenant.			
William A. Stewart		"	
Second Lieutenant.			
John W. Caldwell		"	
Sergeants.			
Aquilla Wren		"	Promoted to Quartermaster Sergt. May 17 '32
Hiram M. Curry		"	
Edwin S. Jones		"	
John Hinkle		"	
Corporals.			
William Wright		"	
John Stringer		"	
John Hawkins		"	
Thomas Webb		"	
Privates.			
Bristol, John E.		"	
Brown, Harrison		"	
Cooper, Jeremiah		"	
Clifton, John		"	
Carle, Stephen		"	
Conner, Joseph H.		"	
Cox, Jefferson		"	
Cox, John		"	
Clark, Ebenezer		"	
Cleaveland, Hiram		"	
Caldwell, Alexander		"	
Doty, James		"	
Dodge, John B.		"	
Eads, William		"	
Love, Elias		"	
Moffat, Alvah		"	
Moats, Jacob		"	
Moore, Sylvanus		May 8	
Miner, Harris		May 3	
Owen, John C.		"	
Phillis, Joseph		April 23	
Redick, George		"	
Ridgeway, David		"	
Root, Lucas		"	
Ross, David		"	
Ross, John		"	
Reed, Thomas B.		"	
Reed, Simon		"	
Sharp, Francis		"	
Smith, Rice		"	
Talifero, Jefferson		"	
Trial, William D.		"	
Thurman, Johnson T.		"	
Thomas, Henry		May 1	
Wood, William L.		April 23	

Capt. David W. Barnes' Company

Of Mounted Volunteer Rangers under the command of Brig.-Gen. Isaiah Stillman, acting as Major for the Battalion, according to the orders of the 19th of April, 1833, received from the Commander-in-Chief of this State, and entered into the service of the United States against the hostile band of Sac and Fox tribes of Indians, on the 21st day of April, 1832, and discharged out of service at Lewistown, Fulton county, on the 25th day of June, 1832.

Name and Rank.	Residence.	Enrolled	Remarks.
Captain.		1832	
David W. Barnes	Fulton Co	April 21	
First Lieutenant.			
Thos. W. Clark	"	"	
Second Lieutenant.			
Asa Langford	"	"	
Sergeants.			
Seth Hilton, 1st	"	"	Sergeant 30 days after being private 35 days.
Josiah Marchant, 1st	"	"	" " " balance 1st Sergt. vice Hilton
Reding, Putman	"	"	Wounded in battle on Sycamore C'k May 14..
David C. Murray	"	"	
Frederick Wachel	"	"	
Corporals.			
John Holcomb, 1st	"	"	Paid passage home of R. Putman, w'nded; $4
Medad Comstock, 2d	"	"	
Bird W. Ellis, 3d	"	"	Minor; killed in bat'l; disch. drawn to father
Hazel Putman, 3d	"	May 14	Prom. 3d Corp. May 15, vice B.W.Ellis, killed..
John W. Ward, 4th	"	April 21	
Bugler.			
Jodisah Moore	"	"	
Privates.			
Anderson, Joseph	"	"	Discharged at Canton May 30, 1832, sick
Bybee, Alfred	"	"	
Babitt, Jacob	"	"	
Barker, William	"	May 9	
Brown, Elijah	"	April 21	
Baughman, Samuel	"	"	
Brink, Henry	"	"	
Chein, Charles	"	"	
Cooper, Owen J.	"	"	
Chase, Wheaton	"	"	
Childs, Tyrus M.	"	"	Killed in battle May 14; disch. in favor of wife
Depriest, Charles C.	"	May 9	
Dalton, Avery	"	May 30	
Dehart, William	"	April 21	Discharged May 21, 1832
Ellis, Absalom	"	"	
Farris, David	"	"	
Farris, Jeremiah	"	"	
Farris, Joseph B.	"	"	Killed in battle May 14, 1832
Hoocky, David	"	"	
Huff, John	"	"	
Hilton, Seth	"	"	
Jones, Ahriah	"	"	
Jones, Williston	"	"	
Maxwell, Alex H.	"	"	
Marchant, Josiah	"	"	Prom.; served 1st Sergt. 30 days, vice S. Hilton
Miles, Christopher	"	"	
Nichols, John G.	"	June 2	
Pennington, Stephen	"	"	
Putman, Hazel	"	May 9	
Richards, Henderson	"	April 21	
Rice, Benjamin	"	"	
Smith, Asa	"	"	
Shesin, Isaac	"	"	
Swann, Isaac	"	"	
Strickland, Isaac	"	May 9	
Shirlock, Zachariah	"	"	
Watchell, Henry	"	April 21	
Woolf, Jacob C.	"	"	
Watkins, Fountaine	"	"	
Wilcockson, Samuel	"	"	

ODD BATTALIONS. 153

I certify on honor that this muster roll exhibits the true state of Capt. David W. Barnes' Company of Mounted Volunteer Rangers, in the Battalion commanded by Major Isaiah Stillman, for the periods herein mentioned; that the remarks set opposite the name of each officer and soldier are as nearly accurate and just, and exhibit in every particular the true state of the company, as possible.

(Signed.)   D. W. BARNES, CAPT.

Date, Lewistown, Fulton Co., Ill., Aug. 30, 1832.

Stationed as Rangers.

CAPT. ASEL F. BALL'S COMPANY

Of Mounted Volunteers, under the command of Brig.-Gen. Stillman, acting as Major for the Battalion according to the orders of the 16th of April, 1832, received from the Commander-in-Chief of this State, and entered into the service of the United States, Lewistown, Fulton county. Mustered out June 25, 1832.

Name and Rank.	Residence.	Enrolled	Remarks.
Captain.		1832.	
Asel F. Ball..........	Fulton Co....	April 28	Amount of property lost in battle $35.50.......
First Lieutenant.			
William D. Baldwin..	"	May 15	
Second Lieutenant.			
David S. Baughman	"	April 28	Amount of property lost in battle $75.00.......
Sergeants.			
William Miner, 1st..	"	April 28	Amount of property lost in battle $7.25.....
John Walters, 2d....	"	"	Killed in battle May 14th, 1832; amt. lost $21....
Joseph L. Sharp, 2d.	"	May 15	Appointed 2d Sergt. on 15th of May..........
John Heinford, 3d...	"	April 28	Amount of property lost in battle $26...........
John Thompson...	"		
Corporals.			
Thomas J. Welsh....	"	May 15	
Francis Irwin	"	"	
Thomas, Walters....	"	April 28	Amount of property lost in battle $9.37½......
Hugh Finley..........	"	"	" " " $10.25....
Musician.			
Jonathan Cazad.....	"	May 15	
Privates.			
Arrington, Ethelbert	"	April 28	Amount of property lost in battle $30.50.......
Austin, Nathan	"	"	" " " $24.87........
Anderson, George...	"	May 15	
Brush, John..........	"	"	
Barker, William.....	"	"	
Cary, Almon.........	"	"	
Denis, Thomas.......	"	"	
Dunawin, Levering.	"	April 28	Amount of property lost in battle $12.62 .....
Ellis, James..........	"	"	" " " $12.25....
Fouts, Elmsby.......	"	"	" " " $5.25 ....
Freeman, Moses F .	"	May 15	
Foster, James M....	"	"	
Foster, Harvey.....	"	"	
Garner, Denyson....	"	April 28	
Howard, Zachius....	"	"	Amount of property lost in battle $9.00 .....
Hoxton, Williamson	"	"	" " " $5.50 .....
Harness, Seton......	"	May 15	
Hendricks, Price....	"	"	
Harwick, Henry.....	"	"	
Hill, William.........	"	"	
Langford, Thomas ..	"	April 28	Property lost in battle $17, horse killed $75.00
Lanpersel, Sumn....	"	May 15	
Laswell, James......	"	"	
Morris, Thomas.....	"	April 28	Prop. lost in battle $11.00; disch. May 25 '32.
Maxfield, Andrew H	"	"	" $36.75; 1 horse, $40.00......
Murphy, Adam	"	May 15	
Morgan, James......	"	"	
Scovel, Norman......	"	April 28	Amount of property lost in battle, $25.75 .....
Walling, Ebenezer..	"	"	" " " $21.12½ ....
Whipple, Sylvester..	"	"	
Walters, John	"	"	Amount of property lost in battle, $6.75 ....
Wilson, Charles.....	"	May 15	
Yunt, Jacob..........	"	"	

I certify that the above return roll of all of the Mounted Volunteers under my command is a correct return, and of all the property lost in battle, and otherwise, by the said Volunteers, and who have duly certified on oath before an acting Justice of the Peace.
(Signed.) ASEL F. BALL, CAPT.
Lewistown, Fulton county, June 26, 1832

I certify on honor that I have carefully examined this muster roll of the above named Battalion and find it correct.
(Signed.) THOS. W. TAYLOR,
Brig.-Major 53d Ill. Mil.,
acting Adjt. for above named Bat.
Lewistown, Fulton county, Ill., June 26, 1832.

ILLINOIS VOLUNTEERS.

I certify that John Walters volunteered and served service as a second Sergeant in a company of mounted Rangers under my command, ordered on the 16th day of April, for the protection of the Northern Frontier, in the Battalion command of Major Isaiah Stillman; that he was enrolled on the 28th day of April, 1832, and was killed in battle while in the line of duty, on the 14th day of May thereafter, having served sixteen days.
Given under my hand this 26th day of June, 1832.
(Signed.) ASEL F. BALL, CAPT.
Amount of property lost in battle on the night 14th of May, $21.

STATE OF ILLINOIS, }
SCHUYLER COUNTY. }

Asahel F. Ball and David W. Barnes, being duly sworn, depose and saith that Jane R. Walters is the lawful wife of John W. Walters, deceased.
Sworn and subscribed before me.
(Signed.) H. FELLOWS, (Signed.)
Justice Peace
D. W. BARNES,
ASEL F. BALL,

The paymaster will pay whatever may be due me on the within contents, to Asel F. Ball, who is hereby authorized to receive and receipt for the same.
Dec. 26th, 1832.
her
(Signed.) JANE R. + WALTERS,
Witness, mark.
JOSIAH MOORE, { SEAL } Relict of JOHN WALTERS, deceased.
THOMAS U. CLARK.
(Signed.)

COMPANIES IN ODD BATTALIONS.

Capt. Sain's Company

Of the Odd Battalion of Mounted Rangers, called into the service of the United States, on the requisition of Gen. Atkinson, by the Governor's proclamation, dated 30th of May, 1832. Mustered out September 4, 1832.

Name and Rank.	Residence.	Enrolled	Remarks.
Captain.		1832.	
John Sain	Fulton Co.	June 7	
First Lieutenant.			
Livings Burrington	"	"	
Second Lieutenant.			
Elijah Wilcoxson	"	"	Detached on extra duty Aug. 27
Sergeants.			
Lewis M. Ross	"	"	Detached on extra duty Aug. 27
Jerry Farris	"	"	
William Hummell	"	"	
Cyrus P. Fellows	"	"	
Corporals.			
Patrick H. Hart	"	"	
S. Harrington	"	"	Furloughed from 20th of Aug. to this date
Doctor Eccles	"	"	
James Carter	"	"	
Privates.			
Allrea, Nathan	"	"	Sick; furloughed on the 22d Aug
Barnes, David W	"	"	
Babbit, Jacob	"	"	Horse crippled Sept. 27
Bartley, Joseph	"	"	Sick; furloughed on the 24th Aug
Barker, William	"	"	
Bybee, Alfred	"	"	Furloughed; unable to march on 27th Aug
Comstock, Medad	"	"	Detached on extra duty
Cary, Alamaran	"	"	
Cooper, Owen I	"	"	
Chaw, Silas	"	"	
Doud, John	"	"	
Emerson, Reuben	"	"	Horse left near Winnebago swamp
France, John	"	"	
Franklin, Able	"	"	Detached on extra duty
Foster, James M	"	"	
Farris, David	"	"	Sick on the 27th Aug
Griffin, William	"	"	
Harris, John	"	"	
Hull, Jess	"	"	Horse lamed and left on 27th Aug
Hull, William	"	"	
Johnson, Hiram	"	"	
Kendrick, Price	"	"	Detailed on extra duty on 20th Aug
Long, Madison	"	"	
Long, Ranson	"	"	
Long, Lewis	"	"	
Long, William	"	"	Detached on extra duty the 20th Aug
Langford, Thomas	"	"	Detached on the 1st Sept. to find lost horse
Lancaster, John	"	"	
Morgan, James	"	"	
Manar, Antoin	"	"	Detached to find lost horse on the 20th Sept.
McKim, John H	"	"	
Maxwell, Alexander	"	"	
Nichols, John	"	"	
Phelps, William	"	"	

Name and Rank.	Residence.	Enrolled	Remarks.
		1832.	
Shaw, Zachariah....	Fulton Co....	June 7	
Shain, Charles.......	"	"	
Smith, Asa....	"	"	Detailed to fined lost horse 1st Sept......
Spencer, Oliver......	"	"	Detached on extra duty on the 20th Aug.....
Ulmore, Daniel......	"	"	Detailed with sick horse on the 27th Aug.....
Vandyke, Minard....	"	"	
Wolf, David.........	"	"	Detailed with sick horse on the 27th Aug.....
Wilcoxson, Samuel.	"	"	
Welch, Thomas J....	"	"	Detached to find lost horse on 28th Aug......
Westerfield, A. M....	"	"	
Yount, Jacob........	"	"	

It appears from certificates accompanying muster-roll that Jesse B. Wilcoxson volunteered as a Mounted Ranger on the 7th of June, 1832, and served as a private in the company commanded by Capt. John Sain, and that he was honorably discharged therefrom on the 4th day of September, 1832.

Capt. William McMurtry's Company

Of the Odd Battalion of Mounted Rangers, called into the service of the United States, on the requisition of Gen. Atkinson, by the Governor's proclamation, dated May 30, 1832. Mustered out September 4, 1832.

Name and Rank.	Residence.	Enrolled	Remarks.
		1832.	
Captain, William McMurtry..	Knox Co....	June 24	
First Lieutenant, George G. Lattimore	"	"	
Second Lieutenant, Turner R. Rountree.	"	"	
Sergeants.			
Edward Martin......	"	"	
Benjamin Brown....	"	"	
Josiah Vaughn......	"	"	
James McMurtry....	"	"	
Corporals.			
Edward Fuqua.......	"	"	
James H. Rountree.	"	"	
Thomas Maxwell, Jr.	"	"	
Obediah Fuqua......	"	"	
Privates.			
Adcock, Edmund....	"	"	
Adkins, Jesse........	"	"	
Bell, Peter..........	"	"	
Brown, James	"		
Barber, Franklin B..	"	June 25	
Brown, Wilson......	"	"	
Brown, Alfred......	"		
Brown, George......	"	Aug. 19	
Brown, Joshua......	"	Aug. 20	
Bell, Henry.........	"	June 25	
Criswell, Jas McM...	"	June 24	
Criswell, Ebnr......	"		
Corban, William.....	"	June 25	
Coy, Erbin.........	"	June 24	
Davis, Solomon......	"	June 25	
Fuqua, Daniel......	"	June 24	
Frakes, Alexander..	"	June 25	
Ferguson, James....	"		
Fraker, John.... ...	"	"	
Gillett, Luster T....	"	"	
Goff, James.........	"	"	
Hunt, Zachias.......	"	"	
Hilton, William......	"	"	

ODD BATTALIONS.

Name and Rank.	Residence.	Enrolled	Remarks.
		1832.	
Hendricks, Robt. K.	Knox Co.	June 25	
Holiday, Joseph	"	Aug. 6	
Jennings, Berryman	"	June 24	
Jennings, Theodore.	"	"	
Jones, Reese	"	Aug. 6	
Lewis, William	"	June 25	
McKee, Thomas W.	"	June 24	
McMurtry, John	"	"	
McGehee, James	"	"	
Maxwell, Thomas, Sr	"	"	
Maxwell, James	"	"	
Miles, John	"	"	
McCallister, Thos C.	"	June 25	
McCallister, ——	"	"	
Miles, Daniel	"	Aug. 21	
Miles, Elisha	"		Sick 1st September, Henderson Block House
Norton, John	"	June 25	
Nevett, James	"	"	
Osbourn, Andrew	"	June 24	
Osbourn, Stephen	"	"	
Owen, Parnick	"	"	
Pennington, Simeon.	"	"	
Rountree, John D	"	"	
Robinson, John P	"	"	
Row, Joseph	"	"	
Rice, Jonathan	"	June 25	
Robertson, Alexan'r.	"	"	
Stillings, Josiah	"	"	
Vaugh, John	"	June 24	
White, Samuel S.	"	"	
Wallace, Joseph	"	"	
Williams, Calvin	"	June 25	
Williams, William	"	Aug. 6	

Capt. Asel F. Ball's Company

Of the Odd Battalion of Mounted Rangers, called into the service of the United States, on the requisition of Gen. Atkinson, by the Governor's proclamation dated 20th May, 1832. Mustered out Sept. 4, 1832. For 90 days.

Name and Rank.	Residence.	Enrolled	Remarks.
Captain.		1832.	
Asel F. Ball	Fulton Co.	July 27	
First Lieutenant.			
Thomas W. Clark	"	"	
Second Lieutenant.			
Asa Langford	"	"	On furlough Aug. 28 for six days
Sergeants.			
William Avery	"	"	
William Hill	"	"	On furlough Aug. 28 for six days
William Crosby	"	"	
Absalom Maxwell	"	"	
Corporals.			
Hiram Sanders	"	"	Detailed to find horse Sept. 1st
John Miller	"	"	
James R. Sharp	"	"	
Jesse Walden	"	"	
Privates.			
Anderson, Joseph	"	"	
Ashby, William	"	"	
Bradshaw, James	"	"	Furloughed Aug. 26 for six days
Brown, John	"	"	
Baldwin, William D.	"	"	
Cole, Henry	"	"	
Cozea, Jonathan	"	"	
Dorris, Josiah	"	"	

Name and Rank.	Residence.	Enrolled	Remarks.
		1832.	
Dorris, Thomas	Fulton Co.	July 27	
Deprist, Charles C.	"	"	
Dixon, Hiram	"	"	Furloughed Aug. 26 for 6 days
Enos, Horace B	"	"	
Grim, David	"	"	
Harness, Seaton	"	"	
Harrison, Samuel	"	"	
Laleiker, Frederick	"	"	
Lichfield, Lenard	"	"	
Long, Weir	"	"	
Murry, David C	"	"	Furl'd Aug. 11; thrown by horse; sh'lder b'kn
McGehee, Allen	"	"	
Maxwell, Abner	"	"	Furloughed Aug. 5 for 6 days; supposed sick
McGehee, Stephen	"	"	
Purtle, Peter	"	"	
Purvin, Hozy	"	"	
Richards, Henders'n	"	July 7	
Strickland, Isaac	"	"	
Shaw, John	"	"	
Sharp, Joseph L	"	"	
Thaxton, Williamson	"	July 27	

Capt. J. W. Kenney's Company

Of an Odd Battalion, commanded by Major Bogart, called into the service of the United States on the requisition of Gen. Atkinson, by the Governor's proclamation dated May 20, 1832. Mustered out Sept. 4, 1832.

Name and Rank.	Residence.	Enrolled	Remarks.
Captain.		1832.	
John W. Kenney	R'k Island Co	May 20	
First Lieutenant.			
Joseph Danforth	"	"	
Privates.			
Davis, Thomas	"	"	
Danforth, Manly	"	"	
Danforth, Samuel	"	July 1	
Kenney, Samuel	"	May 20	
Kenney, Thomas	Adams Co	June 12	On furlough
McGee, Gentry	R'k Island Co	May 20	
McNeal, Henry	"	"	
McNeal, Neel	"	July 1	
Maskal, James	"	May 20	
Smith, Martin	"	"	
Sams, Wm. H	"	July 1	
Thompson, Joel	"	May 20	
Thompson, Wm	"	"	
Wells, Ira	"	"	
Wells, Eri	"	"	
Wells, Asaph	"	"	
Wells, Nelson	"	"	
Wells, Hannah	"	"	
Wells, Joel, Jr	"	"	
Wells, Joel, Sr	"	"	
Wells, Luke, Sr	"	"	

ODD BATTALIONS. 159

Capt. Butler's Company

Of the Odd Battalion Mounted Rangers, called into the service of the United States, on the requisition of Gen. Atkinson, by the Governor's proclamation dated May 20, 1832. Mustered out September 4, 1832.

Name and Rank.	Residence.	Enrolled	Remarks.
Captain.		1832.	
Peter Butler	Warren Co.	June 11	
First Lieutenant.			
James McCalen	"	"	
Second Lieutenant.			
John Wilson	McDon'u'h Co	"	
Sergeants.			
Abraham Dover	"	"	
Asa Cook	"	"	
Erastus S. Denison	Warren Co.	"	Sick at Yellow Banks August 30.
John Vernater	"	"	
Corporals.			
Josiah Osborn	"	"	
Lewis F. Temple	McDon'u'h Co	"	
Benjamin Tucker	Warren Co.	"	Sick at Yellow Banks September 1.
Daniel Cranshaw	Hancock Co.	"	
Privates.			
Ambrose, Ezekiel	"	"	Sick at Yellow Banks August 25.
Allen, Ezra G	Warren Co.	"	
Butler, Ira F. M	"	"	Sick at Yellow Banks August 1.
Booth, Moses	McDon'u'h Co	July 13	
Campbell, James M.	"	June 11	
Clark, David	"	"	
Coffman, Jacob	"	"	
Cranshaw, Isaac	"	"	
Carter, Thomas	"	"	
Cranshaw, Paschal	Hancock Co.	June 29	
Cartwright, Dunias B	Warren Co.	June 11	Sick at Yellow Banks August 20.
Caldwell, James J	"	"	
Cash, William	Hancock Co.	June 29	Detached on extra duty September 1.
Davidson, John	Warren Co.	July 2	Sick at Yellow Banks August 6.
Denison, William H.	"	June 11	
Ferington, Orsemus.	McDon'u'h Co	"	
Gibson, Andrew	Warren Co.	"	
Hardisty, John	McDon'u'h Co	"	
Hays, Peter	"	"	
Hays, Nathaniel	"	"	
Hendricks, John	Warren Co.	"	
Hogus, Samuel L	"	"	
Jarves, Fields F	"	"	
Jackson, John	McDon'u'h Co	"	
Jones, Lace	"	"	
Jones, Berry	"	"	
Jones, John	"	"	
Kirkland, Zacheriah	"	"	
Lathrope, John	"	June 28	
McGuffies, James J.	Hancock Co.	June 11	
McCoy, John	Warren Co.	"	
Morris, Isaac	McDon'u'h Co	"	
Osborn, Larkin	"	"	
Paxton, William S	Warren Co.	"	
Penceno, Paschal	"	"	Sick at Yellow Banks September 1, 1832.
Quinn, John	"	"	
Richey, Adam	"	"	
Richey, Thomas	"	"	Sick at Yellow Banks September 1.
Richey, John D	"	"	
Russell, John L	McDon'u'h Co	"	
Stice, Robert L	Warren Co.	"	Sick at Yellow Banks August 20.
Smart, Josiah	"	"	
Smith, Paschal H	McDon'u'h Co	"	
Smith, Charles A	Warren Co.	"	
Sacket, William	McDon'u'h Co	"	
Southward, William	"	July 2	
Stark, William	Warren Co.	June 11	
Tetherow, David	McDon'u'h Co	"	Sick at Yellow Banks August 30.

Name and Rank.	Residence.	Enrolled	Remarks.
		1832.	
Tetherow, George	McDon'u'h Co	June 11	Sick at Yellow Banks August 30
Tomberlin, Fount'n C	"	"	
Vertrees, Isaac	Warren Co.	"	
Williams, Amos	"	"	

Capt. James White's Company

Of the Odd Battalion of Mounted Rangers, called into the service of the United States on the requisition of Gen. Atkinson. Mustered out of the service of the United States September 5th, 1832.

Name and Rank.	Residence.	Enrolled	Remarks.
Captain.		1832.	
James White	Hancock Co.	April 30	
First Lieutenant.			
John Reynolds	"	"	Furloughed Sept. 2, for 3 days
Second Lieutenant.			
James Miller	"	"	
Sergeants.			
A. S. Foot, 1st	"	"	
Amasah Doolittle, 2d	"	July 16	
William White, 3d	"	April 30	
John Vance, 4th	"	"	
John Robinson, 5th	"	"	
Corporals.			
Gabriel Long		"	
Samuel Gooch		"	
George Wilson		"	
Anabel Whiting		"	
Privates.			
Atherton, John R		July 16	Sick at Fort Spillman on Sept. 1
Buckanan, George		"	
Brown, Enoch D		"	
Burnet, William		"	
Barber, Samuel		"	
Coon, David		April 30	Furloughed on Aug. 30, up to this day
Clark, Johnson		July 16	
Clark, Johnson, Jr		"	
Cheney, Richard		"	Sick on Sept. 1; Musician
Carponter, Joseph		"	
Doolittle, Briar		"	
Donald, Jonathan		"	
Delong, Perry			
Enslen, Squire D			
Felt, Cyrus		April 30	
Gregg, John			
Goodwin, Samuel		July 16	
Gray, James		"	
Horner, John		"	
Harper, George W		"	
Higgins, Wm		"	
Hickason, Wm		"	
Hickason, Elisha		"	
Hill, Davis		"	
Kennedy, Nathan		"	
McNitt, Benjamin		"	
Miller, William		April 30	Sick Aug. 28, 1832
Moffitt, James, 1st		May 17	
Moffitt, James, 2d		July 16	
Moffitt, John		"	
Middleton, George		"	
Moore, Abraham		July 16	
Smith, Andrew F		April 30	Thrown from horse; shoulder dislocated
Spillman, Hezekiah		July 16	
Stevens, Isaac		"	Sick Aug. 30
Tongate, Jeremiah		"	

Name and Rank.	Residence.	Enrolled	Remarks.
		1832.	
Thompson, Daniel..		July 16	
Tanner, James......			
Vance, Samuel.....		April 30	
Williams, Levi.....			
White, Joseph......		July 16	
White, Alexander...		April 30	2d Sergeant.
White, Hugh.......		July 16	Furloughed; detailed to guard Indian pris'rs
White, Edward.....		"	
Wilson, Hugh......			
Wilson, William....		April 30	
Willes, Thomas.....		July 16	
Wallace, James.....		April 30	
Wallace, William...		July 16	

ODD COMPANIES.

COMPANIES ATTACHED TO COL. DODGE'S REGIMENT.

Capt. James Craig's Company

Of Mounted Volunteers of JoDaviess county, State of Illinois, called into service by the Governor on May 26, 1832, and by order of Gen. Atkinson, U. S. Army, attached to the command of Col. Henry Dodge, and now mustered by Lieut. Gardner, by order of Gen. Atkinson, to be discharged Sept. 14, 1832.

Name and Rank.	Residence.	Enrolled		Remarks.
Captain.		1832.		
James Craig	JoDaviess Co.	May	26	Two horses and boy
First Lieutenant.				
H. T. Camp	"	"		Rode Bush's horse
Second Lieutenants.				
Leonard Goss	"	May	20	Resigned June 26; horse lost, appraised at $60
Orn Smith	"	July	1	Served as private from June 1
Sergeants.				
Whites'ds Horgess, 1	"	May	20	Deserted with gun
James B. Ketler, 1st.	"	June	1	
John McDonald, 2d	"	May	20	Disch. for intemp'nce June 1; took 2 blankets
Isaac M. Reynolds, 2d	"	"	26	Rode Capt. Estes' horse
Albert Henry, 3d	"	June	1	Rode R. Shores' horse
A. M. Wallace, 4th	"	May	20	Disch. to go to Cincln. Aug. 15; took gun, etc.
James Temple, 4th	"	Aug.	15	
Corporals.				
David Morrison	"	May	26	Rode R. Shores' horse
George Sparks	"	"	"	Rode F. C. Kirkpatrick's horse
Benj. Sutton	"	"	"	Absent July 20; rode public horse
Sam'l Warren	"	"	"	Rode A. Kent's horse
Privates.				
Armstrong, James	"	May	20	Discharged for intemperance July 4
Avery, Azel	"	June	1	to go to Fort Clark July 13
Avery, Elias P.	"	May	26	Rode D. Avery's horse
Bernard, John	"	"	"	
Bush, Michael	"	"	"	Rode E. Brotherlen's horse
Boles, John	"	"	"	
Bivins, John	"	"	"	Transferred to hospital; 2d Surg., July 7
Bass, George	"	"	"	Discharged for intemperance July 4
Covel, Peter	"	June	1	July 12 stayed at Fort Winnebago
Chaney, Osborne	"	"	"	
Collins, William	"	June	20	Absent with leave
Crane, Thomas	"	Sept.	1	
Charles, Elijah	"	June	16	
Dolton, William	"	"	"	
Davis, D. R.	"	Aug.	15	
Davidson, L. V.	"	May	26	
Delereon, Bazell	"	June	1	June 29 disch. to go to Selkirk's; acted as spy
Detandeberaty, M	"	"	20	Trans. to Capt. E. Duncan's company Aug. 15

ODD COMPANIES. 163

Name and Rank.	Residence.	Enrolled	Remarks.
		1832.	
Enlow, Enoch	JoDaviess Co.	July 1	Rode G. Bass' horse
Foley, James	"	June 20	" J. Furlong's horse
Flack, John	"	July 1	
Howell, Jesse	"	May 26	Disch. for disobedience of orders July 13
Howell, Wm.	"	"	Joined Jones' company in M. T. July 16.
Hercleroad, G. W.	"	"	Killed by Indians at Apple River June 24
Head, N. T.	"	June 1	Rode G. White's horse
Hawkins, Jas. L.	"	" 16	
Jordan, Thomas	"	" 1	Rode Grey's horse
Kirkpatrick, F. C.	"	May 26	Rode J. Kitler's horse to July 20, then his own
Kirkpatrick, Jas. G.	"	"	Rode Lockwood's horse
Kirkpatrick, F. W.	"	"	Rode Brotherlin's horse
Kirkpatrick, Wm. M.	"	"	Captain of Spy company
Kirkpatrick, J. S.	"	"	Absent with leave; retains gun, powder horn.
Kirkpatrick, John F.	"	"	Rode Hillyard's horse
Langworthy, Edw'd	"	July 1	Disch. Aug. 12; gone to M.T.; rode Flint's horse
Langworthy, James	"	May 26	Rode T. B. Farnsworth's horse
Lictenberger, Conr'd	"	June 16	
Moffatt, Joseph	"	" 26	56 rations due him
Moffatt, Francis	"	" 1	Discharged July 13 to go to Fort Clark
Montgomery, John	"	" 1	" " 5; rode Eades' horse
McColister, Reuben	"	" 1	" " 13; " Ketter's horse
McNair, David	"	May 26	Rode H. H. Gear's horse
Mann, Harvey	"	July 1	
Mitchell, Isaac	"	Aug. 1	Absent with leave
McKinney, Charles	"	June 1	" without leave Aug. 1
Nevil, John		" 16	
Osborn, Abraham		July 1	Rode H. H. Gear's horse
Parishon, Eustach		June 1	Disch. June 29; acted as spy; rode pub. horse
Porter, James C.		July 1	Rode Mullet's mule
Quinliven, Dennis		May 26	Rode public horse
Swan, Moses		July 1	Rode John Taylor's horse
Stevens, Sam'l F.		June 1	Disch. Jul. 29; gone to Quincy; rode pub. horse
Sancer, Robt.		"	July 24 absent without leave
Stocton, Isaac		"	Aug. 16 transferred to Capt. Duncan's Co
Stocton, William		"	
Smith, Orlando		"	Deserted June 10 with gun and 2 blankets
Sanderson, F. C.		" 6	" July 1 " " blanket
Thomas, John		May 26	
Thomas, Noah		July 1	Rode Hogan's horse
Thompson, Willis		May 26	Rode A. Philco's horse
Tracy, Charles		July 1	Rode Hillyard's horse
Upton, Robert		May 26	Rode Dubois' horse
Webb, T. J.		"	Disch. July 4 for intemp'nce; rode pub. horse
White, Garey		June 1	
Woodson, John B.		" 16	
Woodcock, James S.		" 16	

John Nevil, Elijah Charles, John B. Woodson, Jas. S. Woodcock, J. L. Hawkins and Conrad Lictenberger were detached from the company under my command to act as spies in the neighborhood of Scale's Fort, on the east fork of Fever river.

Capt. Enoch Duncan's Company

Of Mounted Riflemen, maintained in the service of the United States under the command of Col. H. Dodge, by order of Brig.-Gen. H. Atkinson, U. S. Army. Mustered for discharge by Lieut. J. R. B. Gardiner, U. S. Army, Sept. 14, 1832, by order of Brig.-Gen. H. Atkinson.

Name and Rank.	Residence.	Enrolled	Remarks.
Captains.		1832.	
James W. Stephens'n		May 19	Elected Major June 26
Enoch Duncan		June 26	
First Lieutenants.			
James K. Hammett		May 19	Resigned June 4
Alex. Kerr		June 4	" " 26
Harvey Cavanaw		Aug. 13	
James L. Kirkpatrick		June 26	Resigned Aug. 13

Name and Rank.	Residence.	Enrolled		Remarks.
		1832.		
Second Lieutenants.				
Alexander Kerr		May	19	Elected 1st Lieut. June 4
Enoch Duncan		June	4	" Captain " 26
D. S. Harris		June	26	
Sergeants.				
John Foley		May	19	Private since June 4
Fred Stahl		"		Has not done duty as Sergeant from June 4
Job Alcot		"		
John Mathews		"		
James Temple		June	4	On leave
Musicians.				
Jonathan Gallagher		June	7	On leave
S. D. Scot		May	19	"
Privates.				
Anderson, Wm. S		"		
Armstrong, Abner		"		On furlough
Atchison, Marcus		"		
Bennett, William		"		
Bohannon, Isaiah		"		On furlough
Brophy, John		"		
Bennett, Thomas		"		
Boggess, William		"		On furlough
Burbridge, Benjamin		"		Discharged July 19
Bennett, Charles R		"		On furlough
Bain, John		"		
Blair, William		"		Absent on leave, sick
Barnet, H. C		Aug.	12	
Cavanaw, Harvey		May	19	Elected 1st Lieut. Aug. 13
Coates, John		"		On furlough
Collins, William		"		
Cook, G. M		"		
Cooper, A		"		Discharged Aug. 12
Coates, Thomas		"		On furlough
Cormack, John		"		
Chastee, Samuel		"		On furlough
Coyle, Peter		"		
Caldwell, William		"		On furlough
Chichester, Thomas		"		Discharged July 19
Darley, William		"		Killed while on express May 19
Downs, Daniel D		"		
Duncan, Enoch		"		Elected 2d Lieut. June 4
Davis, D. R		"		Transferred to J. Craig's company
Dennison, Joseph		"		On furlough
Davidson, V. L		May	25	"
Dudley, Wm		May	19	
Dudley N		June	28	
Dixon, Fred		May	19	
Eames, Charles		"		
Eames, George		"		Killed in battle June 17
Furr, Chas		"		
Fields, Solomon		"		
Gleason, Isaac		"		
Garrison, E		"		
Gruell, John		"		
Green, Wm. B		"		On furlough
Gilbert, Hayden		"		
Ham, Mathias		"		
Harris, D. S		"		Elected 2d Lieut. June 26
Hodges, H. W		Aug.	12	
Harris, Kuler		May	19	On furlough
Hays, James		"		Discharged July 19
Hoops, George		"		
Hammond, N. I		"		Discharged July 26
Hood, Alexander		"		On furlough
Howard, Stephen P		"		Killed in battle June 17
Imus, Alfred		"		
Imus, Charles		"		
Job, Ira B		"		
Jonas, William		"		
Jourdan, James		"		
Jourdan, I. B		"		
Jourdan, William		"		
Kerns, Patrick		"		
Kirkpatrick, I. L		Aug.	16	
Kirkpatrick, Jesse I		May	19	
Koons, John		"		On furlough

ODD COMPANIES.

Name and Rank.	Residence.	Enrolled	Remarks.
		1832.	
Lukes, J		May 19	June 25 quit, by honorable discharge
Lovell, Michael		"	June 17, killed in battle
Massey, H. L		"	
Mineclear, I. B		"	
Morrison, Wm. H		"	
McNulty, John		"	On furlough
McCabe, John		"	
McDonnell, John		"	
Mann, Harvey		"	Transferred to Capt. J. Craig's Co. July 1
McNair, Alexander		"	Horse killed in battle
McBride, William		"	On furlough
McKenney, Charles		"	"
Meeker, Jonathan		"	
Mulliken, John D		"	
Oliver, Solon		"	
Phillo, Addison		"	Appointed Surgeon
Putnam, H		"	
Pease, H. H		"	
Prigg, G		"	
Reed, Thomas		"	
Stocton, Isaac		Aug. 15	
Stocton, William		"	
Swan, A. C		May 19	
Stout, B. F		"	
Shull, Jesse W		"	
Smith, Malcomb		"	On furlough; wounded in battle
Smith, Vincent		"	
Shore, Richard		"	
Shipton, John		"	
Shipton, Jesse		"	
Shauance, Thos		"	
Sublett, Thos		"	
Snyder, F		"	
Snyder, S		"	
Shanley, Thomas		"	
Shannon, D		"	
Sinoker, Samuel		"	On detached service; ordnance officer
Tinan, Dennis		"	
Thomas, V. I		"	Discharged July 15
Taylor, Mason		"	
Temple, James		"	Sergeant from June 4
Thrailkill, John		"	On leave
Vance, Samuel		"	Quit June 19
Vance, William		"	
Williamson, Samuel		"	
Williams, Freeman		"	
Whitesides, Mac		"	
Whitesides, Abram		"	
Whitesides, Jno. B		"	
Whooten, Daniel		"	On furlough
Wallace, James M		"	
Wheeler, Loring		"	
Welch, Edwin		"	Sick; wounded on express
Winters, J. D		"	On leave
Young, Lewis		"	

COMPANIES UNDER BRIG.-GEN. ATKINSON.

Capt. William Gordon's Company,

A company of Mounted Volunteers of Illinois Militia, organized as a company of Spies, by order of Brig.-Gen. Atkinson, of the U. S. Army. The non-commissioned officers and privates having been taken from the lines of other companies in the service, and the officers having been appointed by Gen. Atkinson, and continued in the service as a Spy Company, during the period stated. Mustered out at Dixon's, August 14, 1832.

Name and Rank.	Residence.	Enrolled	Remarks.
Captain.		1832.	
William Gordon	St. Louis, Mo.	June 22	
First Lieutenant.			
Peter Menard	Peoria, Ill.	"	
Second Lieutenant.			
William Morrison	Kaskaskia	"	
Sergeants.			
William Murphy	Pinckneyville	"	
Francis Swanwick	Kaskaskia	"	
William Myers	"	"	
Samuel Crawford	"	"	
Corporals.			
Medard Menar		"	
Louis Wilmot	Peoria	"	
Robert Murphy	Kaskaskia	"	
Robert Caldwell	"	"	
Privates.			
Adams, Levi	"	"	
Banson, Lewis	"	"	
Brown, John	"	"	
Champine, Lewis	"	"	
Doza, Joseph	"	"	
Hill, Lewis	"	"	
Jones, Slaughter	"	"	
Jerrard, Francis	"	"	
Kinion, James	"	"	
Kimmansa, Baptist	"	"	
Lynch, James	"	"	
Omelvany, John	"	"	
Pepper, L	"	"	
Pamiguvi, Baptist	"	"	
Paschal, Francis	"	"	
Smith, Francis	"	"	
Sachappelle, Henry	"	"	
White, John	"	"	

Capt. Cyrus Mathews' Company

Of Foot Volunteers, in the service of the United States under Brig.-Gen. Atkinson. Mustered out at Fort Wilbourn August 1, 1832.

Name and Rank.	Residence.	Enrolled	Remarks.
Captain.		1832.	
Cyrus Mathews	Morgan Co	June 2	On furlough since July 23, 1832
First Lieutenant.			
William Hunter	" "	" "	
Second Lieutenant.			
W. R. Lindsay	" "	" "	Resigned June 23, 1832
Sergeants.			
William Barker	" "	" "	
M. Q. Dennis	" "	" "	
Thomas Shepherd	" "	" "	
W. C. Harris	" "	" "	
Corporals.			
A. B. Shepherd	" "	" "	
Enos Hobbs	" "	" "	
Wiley Scribner	" "	" "	Elected 2d Lieutenant June 23, 1832
R. S. Anderson	" "	" "	
Privates.			
Anderson, J. S.	" "	" "	
Busy, Thomas	" "	" "	
Bones, John	" "	" "	
Carson, Thomas	" "	" "	
Carson, James	" "	" "	
Crowly, C. W.	" "	" "	
Dickens, A. C.	" "	" "	
Foster, William	" "	" "	
Grimsley, William	" "	" "	
Grimsley, Fielding	" "	" "	Absent driving team, haul'g provis. for army
George, Francis	White Co		
Hamilton, William S.			
Holland, Berry		June 2	
Horton, William	Morgan Co	" "	
Hart, Josiah	" "	" "	
Haymes, J. L.	" "	" "	
Humphrey, B.	" "	" "	
Huston, J. C.	" "	" "	
Joiner, Peter	" "	" "	
Kurkendall, I.	" "	" "	
Lutes, Daniel	" "	" "	
Loflin, Thomas	" "	" "	
Lynch, J. H.	" "	" "	
McGinnis, L.	" "	" "	
Myers, William M	" "	" "	
Morris, William	" "	" "	
Moss, Isaac	" "	" "	
Ragen, L. B.	" "	" "	On furlough
Rodes, Joseph	" "	" "	
Row, G. W.	" "	" "	Elected 3d Corporal June 23, 1832
Row, John	" "	" "	
Rose, Samuel	" "	" "	
Reed, John A.	" "	" "	
Sammons, Edin	Morgan Co	June 2	
Stinson, M. L.	" "	" "	
Taylor, William	" "	" "	On furlough
Webb, William	" "	" "	

Capt. George McFadden's Company

Of Mounted Volunteers, in the service of the United States under Brig.-Gen. Atkinson. Mustered out of service of United States June 29, 1832.

Name and Rank.	Residence.	Enrolled	Remarks.
Captain. George McFadden	LaSalle Co.	1832. May 24	
First Lieutenant. W. F. Walker	"	"	On command.
Second Lieutenant. Oliver Bangs	"	"	
Sergeants.			
H. A. Sprague	"	"	
Alex. K. Owen	"	"	On command by order of Gen. Atkinson
John Combs	"	"	
George A. Sprague	"	"	
Corporals.			
Henry Hicks	"	"	
S. Bartholomew	"	"	On command by order of Gen. Atkinson
Ezekiah Warren	"	"	On command.
Samuel Warren	"	"	
Privates.			
Armstrong, Will	"	"	
Broomfield, Benj	"	"	
Beresford, John	"	"	
Beresford, James	"	"	Killed by Indians June 24, 1832.
Brown, James	"	"	
Brown, Charles	"	"	
Gonsoles, Peter	"	"	
Galloway, James	"	"	On furlough since May 24.
Hogoboom, Richard	"	"	On command by order of Gen. Atkinson
Hogoboom, John	"	"	
Kimball, Russell	"	"	
Lewis, Will	"	"	On command by order of Gen. Atkinson
Morgan, J. W.	"	"	
Morgan, Josiah	"	"	On command by order of Gen. Atkinson
Richey, Will, Sr	"	"	" " "
Richey, Will, Jr	"	"	
Bucker, John	"	"	
Sprague, Abel	"	"	On command by order of Gen. Atkinson
Sprague, Ephriam	"	"	
Shaw, Josiah E.	"	"	
Walker, George	"	"	On command by order of Gen. Atkinson
Warren, Daniel	"	"	
Workman, John	"	"	
Wilcox, John	"	"	

Capt. Samuel Smith's Company

Of Illinois Mounted Volunteers, called into the service of the United States under the command of Brig.-Gen. H. Atkinson. Mustered out June 15, 1832, by order of Brig.-Gen. Atkinson. Enrolled for 20 days.

Name and Rank.	Residence.	Enrolled	Remarks.
Captain. Samuel Smith	Greene Co.	1832. May 27	
First Lieutenant. James D. Scott	"	"	
Second Lieutenant. Jacob Waggoner	"	"	

Name and Rank.	Residence.	Enrolled	Remarks.
Sergeants.			
Thomas Briggs	Greene Co.	May 27	
Frederick Atchison	"	"	Absent with leave
Fielden Atchison	Morgan Co.	"	
Squire Wood	Greene Co.	"	On special duty as Wagon Master
Corporals.			
George Sanders	"	"	On furlough
Harrison Poindexter	"	"	
R. G. Lee	"	"	
Vincent Lee	"	"	
Privates.			
Adcock, Isam		"	
Burns, Martin	Greene Co.	"	On furlough
Barnet, Benj. F.	Madison Co.	"	
Burton, Lemuel	"	"	
Baker, John	Greene Co.	"	On furlough
Boggus, Preston	"	"	
Bonner, A. V.	Madison Co.	June 8	
Clark, Squire	"	May 27	
Cook, William	Greene Co.	"	
Crabb, Edward	"	"	
Dun, Squire	"	"	Absent on leave
Delany, H.	"	"	Appointed Surgeon May 30, 1832
Doll, Gregory	"	"	On furlough
Dansworth, Chas. W.	"	"	Absent with leave
Fisher, James	"	"	On furlough
Fry, Jacob	"	"	Promoted Colonel May 31, 1832
Gilliland, James	"	"	On furlough
Hopper, Thomas	Greene Co.	"	Absent with leave
Hill, Jonathan	"	"	On furlough
Link, Mathias S.	"	"	
Link, David	"	"	
Laxton, Washington	"	"	
Lakin, Joseph	"	"	
Leighton, Jonathan	Morgan Co.	"	Promoted Surgeon's Mate May 31, 1832
Moore, Isaac	Greene Co.	"	Absent with leave
Massey, Benj. F.	"	"	
Metton, David	"	"	
Meeker, Ambers M.	St. Louis, Mo.	"	
Piper, Israel	Greene Co.	"	On furlough
Reddish, John	"	"	
Smith, Jeremiah	"	"	
Scott, John W.	"	"	Promoted to Paymaster May 31, 1832
Story, S. S.	Shelby Co.	"	Disch. June 10, 1832, by order of Gen. Atkinson
Tourney, James	Greene Co.	"	Horse absent
Whitesides, Levi T.	"	"	
Whitesides, Wm. H.	Madison Co.	"	
Whitesides, John B.	Greene Co.	"	
Whitlock, James	"	"	
Walden, James	"	"	
Walden, Thos. R.	"	"	Promoted Q. M. Sergt. May 31, 1832
Walker, Gideon	Shelby Co.	"	

Capt. B. James' Company

Of Illinois Mounted Volunteers, in the service of the United States, under the command of Brig.-Gen. H. Atkinson. Mustered out of the service of the United States by order of Brig.-Gen. Atkinson, this 15th day of June, 1832. Enrolled for 20 days. Distant 250 miles from the place of enrollment.

Name and Rank.	Residence.	Enrolled	Remarks.
Captain.		1832.	
Benjamin James	Bond Co.	May 27.	Horse killed in the service
First Lieutenant.			
Calvert Roberts	"	"	Absent with leave
Second Lieutenant.			
W. D. Shirley	"	"	

Name and Rank.	Residence.	Enrolled	Remarks.
Sergeants.		1832.	
Sloss McAdams	Bond Co.	May 27	Absent with leave; horse absent
James Downing	"	"	
John W. West	"	"	Absent with leave.
James Prior	"	"	Horse absent.
Corporals.			
James Walker	"	"	
Wm. Corruthers	"	"	
G. W. Conyer	"	"	
Benjamin Holbrooks	"	"	
Privates.			
Anthony, Abraham	"	"	Absent with leave.
Coffey, Cleavlin S.	"	"	
Duff, G. D.	"	"	
Glen, Robert	"	"	Absent with leave.
Gill, Francis	"	"	
Griffith, William	"	"	
Gillispie, Joseph R.	"	"	
Holdbrooks, Amos	"	"	
Lynch, William	"	"	
Lyles, Elbert	"	"	
Mills, Andrew P.	"	"	
Mills, Daniel H.	"	"	
McAdams, James	"	"	
McAdams, William	"	"	Appointed Sergeant-Major 31, 1832
Royer, Daniel	"	"	
Sellers, Benjamin E.	"	"	
Voluntine, Jackson O	"	"	
Walker, John T.	"	"	Absent with leave.

Capt. Stennett's Company

Of the Odd Battalion of the Brigade of Mounted Rangers, called into the service of the United States, on the requsition of Gen. Atkinson, by the Governor's proclamation, dated May 30, 1832. Mustered out on Sept. 4, 1832.

Name and Rank.	Residence.	Enrolled	Remarks.
Captain.		1832.	
John Stennett	Schuyler Co	June 6	
First Lieutenant.			
Daniel Mathoney		"	
Second Lieutenant.			
Joel Pennington		"	Absent on furlough from Aug. 27 to this date.
Sergeants.			
John B. Smith		"	
Samuel L. Dark		"	
Norris Hobert		"	
Philip Horney		"	
Corporals.			
Robart Martin		"	
Eli Williams		"	
James Bell		"	
Isaiah Price		"	Absent on furlough from Aug. 27 up to date.
Privates.			
Allen, William		"	Absent on furlough from Aug. 27 up to date.
Brown, William		"	
Briscow, Isaac		"	
Bristow, Mathew C.			
Briggs, Elias		June 26	
Brakewell, Charles		June 6	Sick on the way home.
Busan, Jesse			
Friend, Abel		"	
Glen, Fielding T.		Aug. 1	
Golston, Benjamin		June 6	
Howard, James			

Name and Rank.	Residence.	Enrolled	Remarks.
		1832.	
Hartley, Eli............	....	June 6	On furlough from Aug. 27, up to this date.....
Hunter, Jesse........	....	"	
Holiday, Sandford...	....	"	
Harrison, George H.	....	July 18	
Horney, Samuel.....	Schuyler Co	June 6	Appointed Q. M. of the Battalion on June 15.
Isaac, Allen.........	....	"	
Jones, John M.......	....	July 18	
Kennett, William....	Schuyler Co	June 6	
Luster, Jesse........	....	Aug 1	Absent on extra duty......................
McGeeby, William..	....	June 6	
McKee, William.....	Schuyler Co	June 6	
McKee, James.......	....	"	
Matheny, Daniel, Jr.	....	"	
Martin, Richard D...	....	"	
O'Neil, Simon P.....	....	"	Detailed on extra duty...................
Osburn, Joseph.....	....	"	On furlough, arm dislocated...........
Pennington, Riggs...	....	"	
Pennington, S. O....	Schuyler Co	Aug. 1	
Pennington, Riley...	"	June 6	
Peckingham, Peter.	....	"	
Penningham Wesley	Schuyler Co	Aug. 1	
Pettigrew, George M.	"	June 6	
Rice, Nicholas......	"	"	
Rose, Stephen.......	"	"	
Rose, John S........	"	"	
Rigg, William T.....	"	"	
Smith, George.......	"	"	
Smith, Samuel......	"	"	
Smith, Hugh........	"	"	
Sallie, Oliver P......	"	"	
Stewart, Samuel....	"	"	
Tallis, Joel..........	"	"	
VanWinkle, John...	"	"	
Williams, Mervin....	"	"	
White, Jeremiah....	"	Aug. 1	

Capt. M. L. Covell's Company

Of Mounted Volunteers (Rangers), being an Odd Detachment under the direction of the Col. of McLean County, under the command of Brig.-Gen. Atkinson. Mustered out of the service of the United States at Bloomington, Illinois, on August 3, 1832, at the place of enrollment.

Name and Rank.	Residence.	Enrolled	Remarks.
		1832.	
Captain.			
M. L. Covell.........	Bloomington.	June 3	....
First Lieutenant.			
Wm. Dimmet........	"	"	Absent with leave.......................
Second Lieutenant.			
Richard Edwards...	"	"	....
Sergeants.			
Benjamin Depew....	"	"	....
John Vittito.........	"	"	....
Stephen F. Gates....	"	"	....
George Wiley........	"	"	....
Corporals.			
Robert F. Harris....	"	"	....
John Toliver........	"	"	Served 30 days, then employed substitute....
Harrison Flesher....	"	July 3	Served 30 days as substitute for John Toliver
Charles Vezay......	"	June 3	....
John J. McGraw....	"	"	....

Name and Rank.	Residence.	Enrolled	Remarks.
Privates.		1832.	
Atherton, Henry	Bloomington.	June 3	
Benson, Thomas	"	"	
Busick, Henry	"	"	
Britton, Elijah	"	"	
Britton, Nathan	"	"	
Cox, Henry	"	"	Served as substitute for George Spaur
Carlock, Reuben	"	"	
Carlock, George	"	"	
Cheney, Jonathan	"	"	
Davis, Alexander	"	"	
Downs, Lawson	"	"	
Draper, Reuben	"	"	
Foster, William	"	"	
Gaylord, Horace	"	"	
Gridley, Asahel	"	"	
Gibbs, Elias	"	"	
Glenn, John P	"	"	
Harbert, Joseph A	"	"	
Harbert, Hez. M	"	"	
Harbert, Hiram	"	"	
Harper, William	"	"	
Johnson, James	"	"	
Lane, Harrison	"	"	
Lundy, Amos	"	"	
Merryfield, Rolla	"	"	
Martin, Franklin	"	"	
Mullin, John A	"	"	
Oatman, Clement	"	"	Taken sick July 27, 1832
Provo, Franklin N	"	"	
Patton, John	"	"	
Rook, Frederick	"	"	
Ruth, Nathan	"	"	
Spaur, George	"	"	Employed substitute for 18 days
Scott, Martin	"	"	Absent with leave
Vincent, William	"	"	
Vandoler, Jesse	"	"	
Wyatt, L. M	"	"	Absent with leave
Wright, James C	"	"	
Washburn, Thos. C	"	"	
Young, Briant	"	"	

Capt. John S. Wilbourn's Company

Of Illinois Infantry, in the service of the United States under command of Brig.-Gen Atkinson. Mustered out June 9, 1832.

Name and Rank.	Residence.	Enrolled	Remarks.
Captain.		1832.	
John S. Wilbourn		May 22	
First Lieutenant.			
William Chase		"	
Second Lieutenant.			
James H. Blackman		"	
Sergeants.			
P. J. O'Connor		"	
David Edgar		"	
Privates.			
Bonner, Alexand'r V		"	
Bertrand, Charles		"	
Byas, Jesse		"	
Carver, James		"	
Crosier, James		"	
Davis, Aaron		"	
Davis, John		"	
Greene, William		"	
Harper, John		"	

ODD COMPANIES.   173

Name and Rank.	Residence.	Enrolled	Remarks.
		1832.	
Hill, William		May 22	
Hash, Alfred		"	
Hays, James		"	
Howard, Abraham		"	
King, Allan		"	
Mullan, Joseph B		"	
Morgan, Lewis		"	
Manard, Antonio		"	
Morgan, John		"	
Moss, William		"	
Plasters, Lemond		"	
Rouse, Isaac M		"	
Smedley, John J		"	
Stuart, Enoch		"	
Trent, Martin S		"	Sick
Taylor, E. S.		"	
Young, Achriel		"	

Capt. Solomon Miller's Company

Of Mounted Volunteers, called into the service of the United States on a requisition o Gen. Atkinson on the Governor of the State of Illinois, and under the command of Gen. Atkinson. Mustered out at Belleville, St. Clair Co., on Aug. 2, 1832.

Name and Rank.	Residence.	Enrolled	Remarks.
Captain.		1832.	
Solomon Miller	St. Clair Co.	April 27	
First Lieutenant.			
Jacob S. Stout	"	"	
Second Lieutenant.			
William H. Phillips	"	"	
Sergeants.			
Enoch Luckey	"	"	
Lewis Doyle	"	"	
James Petitt	"	"	
Robert Higgins	"	"	
Corporals.			
George Higgins	"	May 30	
Nathaniel Smith	"	April 27	
Boneham Beer	"	May 30	
Benjamin I. Smith	"	April 27	
Farrier.			
Thomas Ervin	"	"	
Saddler.			
John D. Hughes	"	"	
Armorer.			
Michael Randleman	"	"	
Trumpeter.			
John W. Johnson	"	"	
Privates.			
Beer, William	"	"	
Carroll, William	"	"	
Callehan, Vance	"	"	
Collier, William	"	"	
Cornoyer, Narcisse	"	"	
Dunn, John	"	"	
Eastwood, Daniel L.	"	"	
Franklin, John A	"	"	
Fike, Benjamin	"	"	
Fike, Ausby	"	"	
Gonville, Lawrence	"	"	

Name and Rank.	Residence.	Enrolled	Remarks.
		1832.	
Gaskill, Samuel	St. Clair Co.	May 30	
Hughes, Robert	"	April 27	
Holcomb, Joel	"	"	
Hill, William	"	"	
Hill, James	"	"	
Jarrot, Vital	"	June 5	In service of Governor.
Jackson, Jarvis M.	"	May 30	
Koen, John	"	April 27	
Krupp, John	"	"	
McMurtrie, George	"	"	
Macculley, John	"	"	
O'Harro, Charles	"	"	
Phelps, Michael	"	"	
Patterson, Samuel	"	"	
Payne, George W.	"	"	
Quick, Daniel P.	"	"	
Quick, George C.	"	"	
Reynolds, Robert	"	"	
Rogers, Samuel	"	"	
Reames, Jesse	"	"	
Stout, William	"	"	
Stubblefield, John	"	May 30	
Short, William B.	"	April 27	
Scott, James	"	"	
Taylor, Charles	"	"	
Taylor, John	"	"	
Vertrees, John	"	"	
Vannosdal, Benjam'n	"	"	
Watson, William	"	"	
Walker, Gilley	"	May 30	
Wilson, Edward	"	April 27	
Whitesides, Samuel	"	"	

NOTE.—There is a discrepancy in dates relative to the service of this company, which requires correction before it can be paid. The date of enrollment appears generally to have been April 27, 1832, whilst Gov. Reynolds' certificate says that it was called out by him under Gen. Atkinson's requisition of May 29 last.

Paymaster-General's Office, Aug. 16, 1832.

CAPT. ELIJAH ILES' COMPANY

Of Illinois Mounted Volunteers, in the service of the United States, under the command of Brig.-Gen. H. Atkinson. Mustered out of service June 16, 1832.

Name and Rank.	Residence.	Enrolled	Remarks.
Captain.		1832.	
Elijah Iles	Sangamon Co	May 27	
First Lieutenant.			
Jesse M. Harrison	"	"	
Second Lieutenant.			
Henry B. Roberts	Fayette Co.	"	
Sergeants.			
George W. Glasscock	Sangamon Co	"	
Zachariah Millugent	"	"	
James A. Ward	Macon Co.	"	
Benjamin Birch	Sangamon Co	"	
Corporals.			
Alexander Trent	"	"	Absent on furlough; no horse.
G. W. Foster	"	"	No horse.
G. W. Diamond	Fayette Co.	"	
Jesse Darrow	Sangamon Co	"	Horse absent.
Privates.			
Archer, Michael	"	"	
Alley, James	Fayette Co.	"	Absent, sick.

ODD COMPANIES.

Name and Rank.	Residence.	Enrolled	Remarks.
		1832	
Bell, A. W............	Macon Co....	May 27	....
Brents, Moses........	Sangamon Co	"	....
Brannan, John......	"	"	....
Cole, Eldridge.......	"	"	....
Crow, William.......	"	"	....
Churchill, Lewis....	"	"	
Coventry, John......	Fayette Co...	"	....
Dickinson, David...	Sangamon Co	"	....
Dewees, Samuel B..	Macon Co....	"	....
Esles, Asa............	Sangamon Co	"	....
Earley, Jacob M.....	"	"	
Ebey, Jacob..........	"	"	....
Garret, Joseph F....		"	
Ginger, Miles........	Fayette Co...	"	....
Gateley, John J......	Sangamon Co	"	No horse................................
Graft, John..........	JoDaviess Co	"	Absent with leave; no horse..........
Hickerson, G. W.....	Fayette Co...	"	
Henry, James D.....	Sangamon Co	"	Elected Major; promoted Lieut. Col. May 31..
Harrington, John....	Fayette Co...	"	Absent with leave..........................
Hanks, Joseph.......	Macon Co....	"	....
Hankins, John.......	Fayette Co...	"	....
Johnson, Henry.....	"	"	
Kirkpatrick, John...	Sangamon Co	"	....
Keys, John...........	"	"	
Kirkpatrick, William	"	"	Appointed Quartermaster May 31, 1832......
Kendall, John J......	"	"	Absent with leave; no horse................
Lincoln, A............		"	
Letcher, John........		"	Deserted June 1; no horse..................
Long, Thomas.......	Sangamon Co	"	....
Lane, Jacob..........	Macon Co....	"	
Mauly, John..........	"	"	No horse.....................................
McAlister, Wm......	Sangamon Co	"	Absent with leave..........................
Mason, Noah.........	"	"	
McCoy, Joseph......	"	"	....
Matheny, Lorenzo D	"	"	....
Millugent, Samuel..	"	"	
McAlister, John.....	"	"	No horse.
McJenkins, Hugh...	Tazewell Co.	"	....
Morris, Achilles.....	Sangamon Co	"	....
Neale, Winston M...	"	"	
O'Neal, Samuel......	"	"	....
Oliphant, E. P.......	"	"	Appointed Adjutant May 31, 1832..........
Pierce, Thomas......	"	"	....
Potts, William L....	"	"	....
Pickerell, William S.	"	"	
Patterson, Joseph..	Fayette Co...	"	|..
Paul, John...........	Tazewell Co.	"	....
Querry, James.......	Macon Co....	"	....
Rutledge, James....	Morgan Co...	"	Absent with leave; no horse...............
Rutledge, John B...	Sangamon Co	"	Appointed Surgeon May 31, 1832 ....
Reid, James F.......	"	"	....
Rusk, Benjamin.....	"	"	....
Saunders, Presly A.	"	"	
Stuart, John T.......	"	"	
Shirley, John........	Fayette Co...	"	Absent with leave..........................
Taulbee, Isaac.......	"	"	....
Wright, John D.....	Macon Co....	"	
Welch, Jefferson.....	Sangamon Co	"	Absent with leave; no horse...............
Ward, James M......	"	"	No horse ....

INDEPENDENT COMPANIES.

Capt. Jacob M. Earley's Company

Of Mounted Volunteers, mustered out of the service of the United States by order of Brig.-Gen. Atkinson, U. S. Army, on White Water river of Rock river, on July 10, 1832.

Name and Rank.	Residence.	Enrolled	Remarks.
		1832.	
Captain. Jacob M. Earley	Sangamon Co	June 16	
First Lieutenant. G. W. Glasscock	"	"	Hunting horse with leave
Second Lieutenant. B. D. Rusk	"	"	
Sergeants.			
Zachariah Malugin	"	"	
Noah Mason	"	"	
Jacob Eby	"	"	Absent on furlough since June 29, 1832
W. M. Neale	"	"	Remained at Dixon's without leave
Corporals.			
R. M. Wyatt	Madison Co	"	
M. H. Brentz	Sangamon Co	"	
William Crow	"	"	Absent horse hunting since June 29, 1832
Henry Johnson	Fayette Co	"	
Privates.			
Bailey, David	Tazewell Co	"	
Baker, John		June 21	
Brewer, John	Sangamon Co	"	
Climon, James	Vermilion Co	"	Hunting horse
Darrow, Jesse	Sangamon Co	June 16	Absent with leave, horse hunting
Fanchier, G. B.	Coles Co	"	
Gilbert, R. J.		"	
Henry, James D.	Sangamon Co	"	Promoted from the ranks
Hubbard, G. S.	Vermilion Co	"	
Harrison, George		June 21	
Harrington, John	Fayette Co	"	
Johnston, John D.	Coles Co	June 16	Hunting horse
Lincoln, A	Sangamon Co	"	
Loveless, J. R.	"	"	
Morris, Achilles	Sangamon Co	June 16	
McJenkins, Hugh	Tazewell Co	"	Absent with leave from enrollment
Matheny, L. D.	Sangamon Co	"	
McCoy, Joseph	"	"	Absent with leave, horse hunting
McGarey, Hugh	"	"	
McGarey, Harrison	"	"	
McRoberts, Samuel	Vermilion Co	"	
Neal, Samuel O	Sangamon Co	"	
Paul, John	"	"	Absent with leave from date of enrollment
Pickerel, Wm. S.	"	"	Left sick at Dixon's since June 25, 1832
Potts, Wm. L.	"	"	Hunting horse
Pickerel, B. F.	"	"	
Reed, James F.	"	"	Hunting horse
Rutledge, James	Morgan Co	June 21	
Stephenson, John L.	Sangamon Co	June 16	
Smith, Adam	"	"	Hunting horse with leave
Strawbridge, Wm.	"	June 21	
Stout, George	"	"	
Spencer, Roswell H.	R'k Island Co	"	
Stuart, John T.	Sangamon Co	June 16	
Warrick, Montgom'y	"	"	
Warrick, John C.	"	"	

Capt. Seth Pratt's Company

Of Illinois Volunteer Militia, stationed at Fort Armstrong, Rock Island, Illinois. In the service of the United States from April 21, 1832, to June 3, 1832, when mustered out.

Name and Rank.	Residence.	Enrolled	Remarks.
Captain.		1832.	
Seth Pratt		April 21.	Commanding company
First Lieutenant.			
John M. Crabtree		"	For duty
Second Lieutenant.			
Joseph Leister		"	For duty
Sergeants.			
Simpson Stewart		"	
William B. Sisk		"	
Elihu Sparks		"	
Abraham Crabtree		"	
Corporals.			
James Stockton		"	
George Yates		"	
James Kellar		"	
James Curry		"	
Thomas Burton		"	Appointed Drum Major April 29, 1832
Fifer.			
James Carr		"	
Privates.			
Acton, Golman		"	
Bradbury, Nathan		"	
Brantly, Henry		"	
Birdsell, Clark		"	
Booth, Isaac		"	
Brock, Daniel		"	
Bradley, Amos		"	
Bradshaw, John		"	Dismissed May 12, 1832; claimed as a deserter
Bohvare, John H		"	Sent to hospital sick May 10, 1832; furloughed.
Castlebury, Berry		"	
Cooper, Stephen L		"	
Davis, John		"	
Ford, Henry		"	
Foster, William		"	On detached service with army May 19, 1832
Gulliher, Isaac		"	
Hamilton, Parnell		"	
Hunly, Harrison		"	
Hopper, William		"	
Jackson, Alfred		"	
Leighton, Jonathan		"	Appointed Ass't Surgeon April 29, 1832
Long, Nicholas		"	
Low, James M		"	
Lawrence, Iredell		"	
Langston, Martin		"	
Langston, Larkin B		"	On detached service with army May 19, 1832
Letcher, John		"	
Melton, Henry		"	
McConnell, Francis		"	
McDaniel, Frederick		"	On detached service with army May 19, 1832
New, James		"	
Overstreet, Wm. C		"	
Pervine, John		"	
Pointer, William		"	
Russ, Jonathan		"	
Smothers, Andrew		"	
Schmick, Isaac		"	
Smith, Samuel		"	
Wells, Samuel		"	

Capt. Alexander D. Cox's Company

Of Illinois Volunteers, in the service of the United States. Mustered out June 15, 1832, at Fort Wilbourn.

Name and Rank.	Residence.	Enrolled	Remarks.
Captain. Alexander D. Cox...		1832. May 28	
First Lieutenant. Joseph W. Duncan..		"	
Second Lieutenant. Thomas T. Clark....		"	
Sergeants.			
Charles Day.............		"	
William F. Cox..........		"	
Richard Cox.............		"	
Robert Patten............		"	
Corporals.			
Harvey Graham.......		"	
John M. Barnes........		"	
James McCormick....		"	
Daniel Waters.........		"	
Privates.			
Atwood, William C...		"	
Byas, James D........		"	
Byas, Jesse............		June 12	Joined my company on June 12, 1832...
Foster, William......		May 28	
Hedrick, Stephen....		"	
Hutton, John..........		"	
Hamilton, Frederick		"	
Hays, John.............		"	
Hays, Harrison.......		"	
Hays, Jonathan......		"	
Hays, James..........		"	
Massee, Elder........		"	
Snyder, Solomon R.		"	
Tompkins, Alfred....		"	
Wright, Moses.......		"	

Capt. James Walker's Company

Or Detachment of Mounted Volunteers, called into the service of the United States by the Governor of the State of Illinois, and by his order of June 19, 1832, from the date of its enrollment to the 12th of August, 1832, when mustered out. Mustered out at Fort Walker, on DuPage river.

Name and Rank.	Residence.	Enrolled	Remarks.
Captain. James Walker........	Cook Co.....	1832. June 25	
First Lieutenant. Chester Smith.......	"	"	
Second Lieutenant. George Hollenboch.	"	"	
Sergeants.			
William Lee...........	"	"	
Edmund Weed	"	"	
Chester Ingersoll....	"	"	
Corporals.			
Elisha Fish	"	"	
Rueben Flagg........	"	"	
Peter Watkins.......	"	"	

ODD COMPANIES.

Name and Rank.	Residence.	Enrolled	Remarks.
Musician. Edward A. Rogers	Cook Co.	1832. June 25	
Privates.			
Ament, Edward G.	"	"	
Ament, Hiram	"	"	
Ament, Anson C.	"	"	Absent, on furlough till expiration
Clark, David K.	"	"	
Covell, Thomas R.	"	"	
Curtis, Elisha	"	"	
Fountain, Samuel	"	"	
Gilston, James	"	"	
Jones, Henry	"	"	
Smith, Ralph	"	"	
Watkins, Benj. T.	"	"	
Watkins, Peter, Jr.	"	"	
Wooley, Jeddiah	"	"	
Wooley, Thomas	"	"	
Walkeley, Henry	"	"	

CAPT. WILLIAM WARNICK'S COMPANY

Of Mounted Volunteer Rangers, ordered out by the Governor, for the protection of the frontier of Macon county, Illinois. Mustered out of the service of the United States at Decatur, Illinois, on September 24, 1832.

Name and Rank.	Residence.	Enrolled	Remarks.
Captain. William Warnick	Decatur	1832. June 4	Officers and privates found own rations, arms and ammunition.
First Lieutenant. J. C. Pugh	"	"	
Second Lieutenant. E. Freeman	"	"	
Sergeants.			
F. G. Paine	"	"	
J. H. Johnson	"	"	
A. M. Wilson	"	"	
R. Law	"	"	
Corporals.			
J. Smith	"	"	
A. Travice	"	"	
J. Brown	"	"	
J. Miller	"	"	
Privates.			
Arnold, A.	"	"	
Alsup, Thomas	"	"	
Burrell, N.	"	"	
Brown, M.	"	"	
Butler, E.	"	"	
Church, T. G. D.	"	"	
Cunningham, H.	"	"	
Cunningham, J.	"	"	
Davis, J.	"	"	
Edwards, J.	"	"	
Farris, J.	"	"	
Hall, A.	"	"	
Howell, D.	"	"	
Hooper, W.	"	"	
Hendline, A.	"	"	
Hall, D.	"	"	
Ingram, L.	"	"	
Johnson, R.	"	"	
Jackson, L.	"	"	
Lowry, J.	"	"	

Name and Rank.	Residence.	Enrolled	Remarks.
		1832.	
Mounce, S	Decatur	June 4	
McMennamy, J. H	"	"	
Newcomb, D	"	"	
Owen, T	"	"	
Paine, M	"	"	
Paine, Mason	"	"	
Piatt, J. A	"	"	
Smith, A. W	"	"	
Sinnett, S	"	"	
Stevens, J	"	"	
Slatten, Benjamin	"	"	
Travis, F	"	"	
Widick, S	"	"	
Ward, William	"	"	
Wilson, T. F	"	"	
Warnick, James	"	"	
Warnick, J	"	"	
Walker, J	"	"	
Wheeler, R	"	"	

CAPT. ALEX. M. JENKINS' COMPANY

Of Illinois Volunteers, called out on the requisition of Gen. H. Atkinson, by the Governor's proclamation dated ——, 1832, and regularly mustered into the service of the United States by Lieut. J. R. Gardine, U. S. A., on July 13, 1832, and now mustered for discharge this 10th day of August, 1832, by N. W. Army Special Orders No. 45 of 1832, by Lieut. J. R. Gardine, U. S. A.

Name and Rank.	Residence.	Enrolled	Remarks.
Captain.		1832.	
Alexan'r M. Jenkins	Jackson Co	June 16	Horse shoes, $1; $1 due Bennett for care horse
First Lieutenant.			
James Herald	"	"	Horse shoes, $1
Second Lieutenant.			
Silas Hickman	"	"	
Sergeants.			
Milton Ladd	"	"	
John D. Owings	"	"	Horse shoes, $1
Mathias Hagler	"	"	Lost 1 blanket in the service, appraised at $3.
Aaron Quillman	"	"	Horse shoes, $1
Corporals.			
Binningson Boone	"	"	
Daniel House	"	"	Horse shoes, $1
John Logan	"	"	2
Jacob Schwartz	"	"	
Cornet.			
Wm. M. Bowring	"	"	
Privates.			
Burkley, David	"	"	Lost his horse, appraised at $45
Blacker, James		"	Absent, sick
Blacker, David		"	
Casey, Henry	Jackson Co	"	Horse shoes, $1
Casey, John	"	"	
Cram, Squire	"	"	
Creath, Hiram	"	"	
Clark, John G	"	"	Lost 1 blanket in the service, appraised at $3.
Camron, James	"	"	Horse shoes, $1
Deason, James A	"	"	
Deason, William	"	"	
Delaplain, John	Randolph Co	"	Horse shoes, $1
Davis, Joseph	"	"	Absent, sick
Davis, Ralph	Jackson Co	"	Horse shoes, $1
Davis, Samuel	"	"	
Etherton, James	"	"	

ODD COMPANIES.   181

Name and Rank.	Residence.	Enrolled	Remarks.
		1832.	
Gardner, Robert R..	Jackson Co..	June 16	
Griffith, Geo. F......	"	"	
Hagler, Paul..........	"	"	Horse shoes, $1................
Huff, O. M............	"	"	
Hinson, Nicholas....	"	"	Horse shoes, $1................
Hagler, Edmund....	"	"	
Holden, John........	"	"	Horse shoes, $1................
Ireland, Alexander..	"	"	
Logan, James.......	"	"	
Logan, John, 2d.....	"	"	Horse shoes, $1; Dr. J. Logan was app'd Surg.
Lorrels, Walker.....	"	"	
Lafferty, Alexander.	"	"	Bridle-bit, 50c...........
Owings, James F....	"	"	Horse shoes, $1.........
Orton, William......	"	"	
Richards, John......	"	"	
Sorrels, James......	"	"	
Shumaker, William..	"	"	
Timmons, James M.	"	"	
Teague, Hezekiah..	"	"	
Taylor, Richard R...	"	"	
Vote, Gilbert D......	"	"	
Vansel, George......	"	"	Horse shoes, $1 ....
Walker, Nathan D...			" " Detached service...........
Wood, Wilson D.....	"	"	

I certify that this muster roll exhibits the true state of Capt. A. M. Jenkins' Company of Illinois Militia, in the service of the United States for the period herein mentioned; that the "Remarks" set opposite the name of each officer and soldier are accurate and just, and that the recapitulation exhibits in every particular the true state of the company.
(Signed.)   A. M. JENKINS,
Capt. Command'g the Co.

The company marched, by order of th Colonel, to the Wisconsin, while Gen. Atkinson, with the main army, lay at Helena, and while there tendered our service to him to pursue the Indians, but were ordered by him to return to Fort Hamilton, to guard the provisions, as we had been ordered to do by Col. Holmes.
The company have drawn, while in service, 97½ bushels of corn.

Capt. B. B. Craig's Company

Of Illinois Mounted Volunteers, called into the service of the United States, on the requisition of Gen. Atkinson, by the Governor's proclamation dated May 12, 1832, and regularly mustered into the service by Lieut. J. R. B. Gardiner July 13, 1832, and was mustered for discharge this August 10, 1832, by Northwestern Army Special Order No. 45, of 1832.

Name and Rank.	Residence.	Enrolled	Remarks.
Captain.		1832	
B. B. Craig............	Union Co....	June 19	Horse, etc., appraised at $79, lost in service..
First Lieutenant.			
William Craig........	"	"	
Second Lieutenant.			
John Newton........	"	"	Horse, etc., appraised at $70, lost in service..
Sergeants.			
Samuel Moland......	"	"	
Solomon David......	"	"	
Hezekiah Hodges...	"	"	Absent on furlough................
John Rendlemen....	"	"	Horse, etc., appraised at $85, lost in service..
Corporals.			
Joel Burker..........	"	"	
Adam Cauble........	"	"	
Martin Ury..........	"	"	
Jeremiah Irvine.....	"	"	
Privates.			
Barringer, Aaron....	"	"	Saddle, etc., appraised at $17, lost in service.
Barringer, John.....	"	"	
Corgan, John........	"	"	
Cheser, Mathew.....	"	"	Horse, etc., appraised at $64.50, lost in service
Ellis, Daniel.........	"	"	
Farmer, William....	"	"	
Farmer, Thomas....	"	"	

Name and Rank.	Residence.	Enrolled	Remarks.
		1832.	
Fisher, Moses	Union Co.	June 19	
Goodin, Abraham	"	"	Absent on furlough
Gavin, William G.	"	"	
Gramer, Hiram	"	"	
Gramer, William	"	"	
Hancock, Lot. W.	"	"	Saddle, etc., appraised at $10, lost in service.
Hill, Daniel P.	"	"	
Huntsucker, Jackson	"	"	
Lance, Peter	"	"	
Lance, Andrew	"	"	Horse, etc., appraised at $87, lost in service.
Langley, John	"	"	
Liveley, Moses	"	"	
Lingle, A. W.	"	"	
Murphy, John	"	"	
McCall, P. W.	"	"	Horse, etc., appraised at $67.50, lost in service
Morris, John	"	"	
McIntosh, Nimrod	"	"	
McIntosh, John A.	"	"	
Miller, Solomon	"	"	
McElyea, Thomas	"	"	
Morgan, James	"	"	
McLean, Washingt'n	"	"	
McGraw, Elijah	"	"	
Penrad, John	"	"	
Parmer, John	"	"	Horse, etc., appraised at $43, lost in service.
Quillman, John	"	"	
Rumsey, W. H.	"	"	Horse, etc., appraised at $126, lost in service.
Shepherd, Elijah	"	"	" " $40, "
Salmons, Daniel	"	"	" " $87, "
Staten, Preston I.	"	"	
Vincent, John	"	"	
Wright, Jesse	"	"	Horse, etc., appraised at $37, lost in service.

CAPT. WM. C. RALLS' COMPANY,

Illinois Mounted Volunteers, mustered out of the service of the United States by order of Brig.-Gen. Atkinson, June 15, 1832.

Name and Rank.	Residence.	Enrolled	Remarks.
Captain.		1832.	
William C. Ralls	Schuyler Co.	May 27	
First Lieutenant.			
Radford M. Wyatt	Monroe Co.	"	
Sergeants.			
John M. Jones	Schuyler Co.	"	
Samuel M. Pierce	Adams Co.	"	
Stephen A. St. Cyr	St. Louis, Mo.	"	
S. G. Bond	Monroe Co.	"	
Privates.			
Briscoe, John	Schuyler Co.	"	
Brooks, Stephen	Monroe Co.	"	
Beebe, Erastes	Adams Co.	"	
Crawford, John D.	Schuyler Co.	"	
Coonrod, Jefferson	"	"	
Chapman, Johnston	"	"	
Eves, Joel	"	"	
Johnston, James W.	Shelby Co.	"	Lost his horse
Johnston, Thomas	Adams Co.	"	
Kirkland, Ezra	Schuyler Co.	"	
Lane, Ruthford	"	"	
Moore, Daniel	"	"	
Morris, William	"	"	
Melvan, Andrew	Missouri	"	
Owens, Luke	Schuyler Co.	"	
Richardson, Jacob	"	"	
Richardson, Aaron	"	"	
Trail, Xerxes F.	Monroe Co.	"	
Turner, Eben	Adams Co.	"	
Wilkerson, Jacob	Schuyler Co.	"	

Capt. Alexander White's Company

Of Mounted Volunteers, called into the service of the United States by the order of the Governor of the State of Illinois, and served from May 26 to June 15, 1832.

Name and Rank.	Residence.	Enrolled	Remarks.
Captain.		1832.	
Alexander White....		May 26	
First Lieutenant.			
Tolbert Shipley......		"	
Sergeants.			
Ebenezer Higgins...		"	
John Waggoner......		"	
Ent. Perkins.........		"	
John O. Smith		"	
Corporals.			
Hugh Wilson		"	
William Wallace		"	
Amzi Doolittle.......		"	
Privates.			
Atherton, John R....		"	
Brewer, Thomas		"	
Buchannan, George.		"	
Bradley, Hezekiah P		"	
Cash, William		"	
Clark, Johnson, Sr..		"	
Clark, Johnson, Jr..		"	
Compton, Jacob.....		"	
Driskel, Riley.......		"	
Franklin, Wm. F....		"	
Forrest, John M.....		"	
Goodwin, Samuel ...		"	
Hibbert, Davidson..		"	
Higgins, William....		"	
Higgerson, Elisha ..		"	
Hickerson, Wm. D..		"	
Kenedy, Mathase...		"	
Lincoln, Abraham ..		"	
Maffett, John........		"	
Middleton, George ..		"	
Marfettt, James		"	
Moore, Abraham....		"	
McKee, John.........		"	
Mutchler, Benjamin		"	
Owens, Joshua		"	
Owens, Thomas H...		"	
Perkins, Wm. G.....		"	
Perkins, Andrew H.		"	
Sailors, William		"	
Spillman, Hezekiah.		"	
Stephens, Isaac		"	
Turner, Andrew.....		"	
Thompson, Daniel..		"	
Willis, Thomas......		"	
White, Hugh.........		"	
White, Edward......		"	
Wilson, James.......		"	
Wilson, Thomas.....		"	

STATE OF ILLINOIS, }
   Adams Co.

Alexander White, being duly sworn, states that he is the person whose name appears on this muster-roll as Captain; that Lewis Ray was a private in said company, and entered the service on May 26, 1832, and continued in the service until the company was mustered out of service, and his name was omitted from the muster-roll by accident or inadventure, and not by design.

                   (Signed.)   ALEXANDER WHITE.

CAPT. CHARLES S. DORSEY'S COMPANY

Of Mounted Volunteers, called into service by the order of the Governor of Illinois, on June 8, 1832, for one month, ending on July 9.

Name and Rank.	Residence.	Enrolled	Remarks.
Captain. Charles S. Dorsey		1832. June 8.	
First Lieutenant. Thaddeus Bowman.		"	
Second Lieutenant. William Burns		"	
Sergeants.			
James Harvey		"	
John H. Reed		"	
Jonathan Reed		"	
Peter Cline		"	
Corporals.			
Peter P. Scott		"	
A. W. Vanmeter		"	
Wm. Holland		"	
James McClure		"	
Privates.			
Bennington, Robt.		"	
Bennington, Thomas		"	
Bandy, Reuben		"	
Bird, Jas.		"	
Bennington, Joseph.		"	
Conley, Levi P.		"	
Huddleson, Abrah'm		"	
Huddleson, Benj.		"	
Holland, Lawson		"	
Heath, William		"	
McCorkle, Rich. B.		"	
Reed, William T.		"	
Shields, Thomas L.		"	
Thomas, Hanson		"	
Wilson, William		"	

STATE OF ILLINOIS, Nov. 20, 1832.

I certify that said Chas. L. Dorsey was the Captain commanding said company of Mounted Volunteers; that it was necessary that said company should be employed for said period, while the excitement occasioned by the affair of Major Stillman continued. Said company ranged on the portion of Tazewell county, and prevented the settlers from leaving their homes.

(Signed.)   JOHN REYNOLDS,
Com.-in-Chief, Ill. Militia.

CAPT. A. W. SNYDER'S COMPANY

Of Mounted Volunteers. Mustered out of service on June 21, 1832, at Dixon's Ferry, Rock river, Illinois.

Name and Rank.	Residence.	Enrolled	Remarks.
Captain. Adam W. Snyder	St. Clair Co.	1832. May 27	Horse and arms lost in battle June 16, 1832. (Not true. See note at end.)
First Lieutenant. Jas. Winstanley	" "	"	
Second Lieutenant. John T. Lusk	Madison Co.	"	

ODD COMPANIES.

Name and Rank.	Residence.	Enrolled	Remarks.
Sergeants.		1832.	
Nathan Johnston	Monroe Co..	May 27	
Solomon Spurr	St. Clair Co..	"	
James Taylor	" "	"	
Josiah R. Gillam	Madison Co..	"	
Corporals.			
H. Hartline	Monroe Co..	"	Gun lost in battle June 16, 1832
Benj. McDaniel	St. Clair Co..	"	Killed on June 16, and horse lost
Robt. B. Pierce	Madison Co..	"	
Thos. Cook	St. Clair Co..	"	
Privates.			
Abbott, Isaac	" "	"	Horse killed June 16
Ashby, J. W.	" "	"	
Adams, Orlen M.	Madison Co..	"	On express
Brooks, Benjamin	St. Clair Co..	"	On command
Baker, John T.	" "	"	
Cornelius, I.M.McTy	Monroe Co..	"	Gun lost June 16 in battle
Cleveland, Loren	Madison Co..	"	Died in service June 12, 1832
Dikes, George P.	St. Clair Co..	"	
Gillespe, Joseph	Madison Co..	"	
Hendricks, Elijah A.	St. Clair Co..	"	Sick; absent
Herrington, Charles.	Madison Co..	"	On furlough
Hamilton, Wm.	" "	"	
Hill, Pendleton	Monroe Co..	"	
Harrison, Henry	Putnam Co..	"	
Hall, John	LaSalle Co..	"	On furlough
Jarrott, Francis	St. Clair Co..	"	
Kinney, George D.	" "	"	
Lusk, Marcus	Madison Co..	"	
Lawrence, John	" "	"	
Lamsett, Pier	LaSalle Co..	"	On command
Makenson, Wm. B.	St. Clair Co..	"	Killed June 16 in battle
McElroy, Jas. E.	Madison Co..	"	On command
Motley, O. C.	" "	"	
McClain, Isaac	" "	"	On furlough
Moore, John M.	Monroe Co..	"	
McMoore, William	" "	"	
McCalaugh, Samuel.	Madison Co..	"	Delivered to civil authority June 13, 1832
Menard, Pier	Randolph Co.	"	Absent without leave
Needles, James B.	Monroe Co..	"	
Otwell, Ceylon G.	Madison Co..	"	
Owens, Lewis	Randolph Co.	"	Absent without leave
Randle, Josias	Madison Co..	"	On furlough
Right, William	St. Clair Co..	"	
Roman, Richard	" "	"	
Randle, Richard R.	Madison Co..	"	On command
Right, John	Monroe Co..	"	
Smith, Levi	Madison Co..	"	
Scott, Charles	St. Clair Co..	"	
Stephenson, Benj.	Madison Co..	"	
Shields, George B.	" "	"	
Sample, James	" "	"	
Scott, Benj	St. Clair Co..	"	Killed June 16, 1832
Spencer, Russell H.	R'k Island Co.	"	
Thomas, John	St. Clair Co..	"	Promoted to Major
Thomas, W. S.	" "	"	
Teter, Solomon	" "	"	
Teter, Philip	" "	"	
Torence, Wm. W.	Madison Co..	"	
Whiteside, Joseph	St. Clair Co..	"	
Whitesides, Samuel.	" "	"	
Woods, John	Madison Co..	"	
Welker, Joseph	St. Clair Co..	"	Gun lost June 16 in battle
Wilderman, Levi	" "	"	
Wheeler, Erastus	Madison Co..	"	On command
West, Henry H.	St. Clair Co..	"	
Whitten, B.	Pike Co.	"	On command; gun lost in battle June 16
Wells, Lucius	" "	"	" "
Wells, John	R'k Island Co.	"	

Note as to Captain's horse: I was informed by the Major of the regiment, and various other officers and soldiers, that this statement was entirely untrue.

(Signed.) T. P. ANDREWS,
Paymaster U. S. A.

EDWARDSVILLE, ILL.,
December 14, 1832.

CAPT. EARL PIERCE'S COMPANY

Of the Illinois Volunteers in the service of the United States.

Name and Rank.	Comm'ncem't of service.	Term'n of serv'e	Remarks.
Captain.	1832.	1832.	
Earl Pierce	June 18	Aug. 16	
First Lieutenant.			
Banford Morris			
Second Lieutenant.			
Loring Ames			
Sergeants.			
A. Westfall			
P. Haynes			
William Smith		Aug. 7	
Reuben Turner		Aug. 16	
Corporals.			
William Carter			
J. Black			
P. Morris		Aug. 7	
J. Hanks			
Privates.			
Bridgewater, A			
Black, A			
Billington, C. M			
Benedict, D			
Benedict, J			
Brawelle, J. C		Aug. 2	
Brooks, H		Aug. 16	
Bateman, Henry			
Chapman, G. W			
Childers, G			
Clark, W		Aug. 2	
Dodd, C		Aug. —	
Dickerson, J			
Denson, B			
Furguson, S			
Feet, A			
Gillingswater, E			
Hansucker, D			
Hedrick, A			
Harrison, H			
Homes, Hol		Aug. 16	
Harris, A			
Howard, A			
Jacobs, H			
Jeffers, J. E			
Lyell, J			
McCarty, N		Aug. 2	
Payne, S. O			
Peter, J			
Roulston, J. H			
Roberts, J			
Shun, J		Aug. 2	
Shipman, Wm. M			
Shaw, L		June 16	
Tully, H			
Williams, G. W			
Whitehall, George			
Warrick, J		Aug. 16	
Walker, J. D			

COMPANIES IN SERVICE PREVIOUS TO 1832.

Capt. James M. Strode's Company

Of Galena Mounted Volunteers, commanded by General Henry Dodge, and serving under the command of Brig.-Gen. Henry Atkinson, of the United States Army, on the Wisconsin, from August 26, 1827, to September 16, 1827.

Name and Rank.	Residence.	Enrolled	Remarks.
Captain. James M. Strode	Galena, Ill.	1827. Aug. 26.	
First Lieutenant. John Larrison	"	"	
Second Lieutenant. Joseph Payne	"	"	
Sergeants.			
Moses B. Vance	"	"	
Charles Gear	"	"	
Samuel Matthews	"	"	
Jas. L. Kirkpatrick	"	"	
Corporals.			
Charles C. Deprist	"	"	
John Ware	"	"	
John Loughary	"	"	
Privates.			
Alexander, Matthew	"	"	Serving from Aug. 26, 1827, to Sept. 2, 1827
Blake, Page	"	"	
Bono, John	"	"	
Cooper, Jeremiah	"	"	
Dempsey, John	"	"	
East, H. E. W.	"	"	
Hall, Richard	"	"	
James, Benjamin	"	"	
Kirkpatrick, Wm. M.	"	"	
Kirkpatrick, John L.	"	"	
Kirkpatrick, Rich. H.	"	"	
Kirkpatrick, Fran. C.	"	"	
Pixley, John	"	"	
Phillis, Joseph	"	"	Serving from Aug. 26, 1827, to Sept. 2, 1827
Palmer, James	"	"	
Rankin, Wm. S.	"	"	
St. John, Willis	"	"	Serving from Aug. 26, 1827, to Sept. 2, 1827
Searles, A. D.	"	"	
Scott, Lyman	"	"	
Scott, Franklin J.	"	"	
Scott, George	"	"	
Shults, John R.	"	"	
Shannon, Daniel	"	"	
Thomas, Arthur	"	"	
Turley, John	"	"	Serving from Aug. 26, 1827, to Sept. 2, 1827
Vibert, Henry	"	"	
Williams, David	"	"	

BATTALION UNDER COMMAND OF MAJOR N. BUCKMASTER.

1831.

Capt. Solomon Miller's Company

Of the Odd Battalion of Mounted Volunteers of the State of Illinois, commanded by Major Nathaniel Buckmaster, employed in the service of the United States by order of the Governor and Commander-in-Chief of the Militia of the State of Illinois, from June 2, 1831, to July 2, 1831, day of its disbandment and discharge at Rock river, 300 miles from the company's rendezvous.

Name and Rank.	Residence.	Enrolled	Remarks.
Captain.		1831.	
Solomon Miller	Belleville	June 2	
First Lieutenant.			
John Winstanley	"	"	
Second Lieutenant.			
Samuel B. Chandler	"	"	
Sergeants.			
David Angle	"	"	
Enoch Luckey	"	"	
Robert Higgins	"	"	
Stephen Brooks	"	"	
Corporals.			
David Phillips	"	"	
William Tate	"	"	
Solomon Span	"	"	
Isaac Hendrick	"	"	
Privates.			
Blackwell, John H.	"	"	Appointed Q. M. Sergt. June 19, 1831
Barker, Amos T.	"	"	
Brewer, Wm. M.	"	"	
Clampitt, Samuel	"	"	
Coon, Thomas	"	"	
Carr, William	"	"	
Doyle, Lewis	"	"	
Davis, James	"	"	
Demint, William	"	"	Joined the Spies June 19, 1831
Edwards, Ninian W.	"	"	
France, William	"	"	
Gardner, Stephen	"	"	
Hartwell, Stephen A.	"	"	Joined the Spies June 19, 1831
Holt, Jacob	"	"	
Higgins, Ichabod	"	"	
Horn, Abner	"	"	
Hill, Jonathan	"	"	
Higbee, Charles	"	"	Appointed Surgeon June 19, 1831
Krupp, John	"	"	Appointed Armorer June 19, 1831
King, Ambrose	"	"	
Lacey, Caleb	"	"	Joined the Spies June 19, 1831
Lard, Robert A.	"	"	
Lemming, Thomas	"	"	Joined the Spies June 19, 1831
McDowell, Garrett	"	"	
McMurty, George	"	"	

ODD COMPANIES.

Name and Rank.	Residence.	Enrolled	Remarks.
		1831.	
Moore, Jacob	Belleville	June 2	
Miller, Absalom	"	"	Sick; absent on furlough
Null, Henry L	"	"	
Owen, Hopson	"	"	
Owen, Josiah	"	"	
Petitt, James	"	"	
Phillips, John	"	"	
Scott, John B	"	"	
Scott, William	"	"	
Smith, Nathaniel	"	"	
Smith, John, Sr	"	"	
Smith, John, Sr	"	"	
Smith, Daniel B	"	"	
Stooky, Aaron	"	"	
Skinner, Akeman	"	"	
Skinner, Thomas	"	"	
Sulivan, Francis	"	"	
Swaggart, Samuel	"	"	Joined the Spies June 19, 1831
Stubblefield, John	"	"	
Taylor, John	"	"	
Threefall, John	"	"	
Threefall, William	"	"	
Touchette, Francis	"	"	
Visno, Joseph	"	"	
Wood, John	"	"	
Woods, William	"	"	
Wildy, Rodolph	"	"	
Whitesides, Samuel	"	"	Joined the Spies June 19, 1831

CAPT. AARON ARMSTRONG'S COMPANY

Of Mounted Volunteers, commanded by Major Nathaniel Buckmaster, commanding a Battalion, and stationed for the protection of the frontier between Ottawa and Chicago, at Fort Walker, in the county of Cook, in the State of Illinois, 290 miles from Edwardsville, Madison county, where recruited. Mustered out of service July 26, 1832.

Name and Rank.	Residence.	Enrolled	Remarks.
Captains.		1832.	
Nath'n'l Buckmaster	Madison Co	June 2	Captain to June 20, when promoted
Aaron Armstrong	"	"	1st Lieut. until June 20, 1832, when prom. Capt.
First Lieutenant.			
Jacob Swaggart	"	"	2d Lieut. until June 20, when prom 1st Lieut.
Second Lieutenant.			
William Tindall	"	"	Orderly until June, 20, 1832, when prom. 2d Lt.
Sergeants.			
Samuel B. Gillam	"	"	
John P. Dyo	"	"	
Henry Beer	"	"	
Nicholas Felker	"	"	
Corporals.			
Martin Bridges	"	"	
Calvin Kinner	"	"	
Wm. McAninch	"	"	
George Milton	"	"	
Privates.			
Atkins, Aber			Private to June 20, when, promoted to staff
Adams, Washing'n F			
Armstrong, Wm			
Ayres, David			
Brewer, Rice			
Bensell, Chas. E			Disch'd extra duties of Ass't Quartermaster
Doncy, Robert			
Day, Philip S			
Fruit, Franklin			

Name and Rank.	Residence.	Enrolled	Remarks.
		1832.	
Goodwin, Abner			
Gillam, John F			1st Corp. to June 20; then Armorer to Battal'n
Gillam, Isom M			2d " " " promoted to staff ..
Gillam, Wm			Private to " " " "
Hank, Daniel			
Hart, Henry			
Hart, Pleasant			
Howard, Abram			
Johns, James			
Jackson, Lon			
Johnson, Chas			Disch'd extra duty of Wagonmaster to Bat'l'n
Kennedy, George F			Priv. to June 20, when app'd Adjutant "
McFarland, William			
Murphy, Robert			
Mahwron, John			
Piper, William			
Rico, George			
Smith, Asa G			
Sampson, Peter			
Swaggart, Samuel			
Shirtlofft, John			
Thompson, William			
Taylor, Elijah			
Vincent, John			
Waddle, George			
Whittington, James			
Washburn, John A			
Wethers, Enoch B			Private to June 20, when promoted to staff...
Wright, David			2d Sergt. to June 20, when prom. Q. M. to Bat.

The horses used in this service by George Milton, Pleasant Hart, John A. Washburn James Johns, Abram Howard and Henry Beer were the property of N. Buckmaster, who is to receive the wages for the same from the U. S. Government.

Capt. William Moore's Company

Of the Odd Battalion of Mounted Volunteers of Illinois, commanded by Major Nathaniel Buckmaster, employed in the service of the United States by order of the Governor and Commander-in-Chief of the Militia of Illinois, from June 2, 1831, to July 2, 1831, the day of its disbandment and discharge at Rock Island, 300 miles distant from company rendezvous.

Name and Rank.	Residence.	Enrolled	Remarks.
Captain.		1831.	
William Moore	Belleville	June 2	Pay due as 3d Lieut. from 2d to 18th June, and elected Capt. June 19, 1831.
First Lieutenant.			
Benjamin Chesney	"	"	Pay due as private from June 2; elected 1st Lieutenant June 19, 1831.
Second Lieutenant.			
William F. Hill	"	"	Pay due as private from June 2; elected 2d Lieutenant June 19, 1831.
Sergeants.			
Aaron Land	"	"	Pay due as private from June 2; elected 1st Sergeant June 19, 1831.
William Nichols	"	"	Pay due as private from June 2; elected 2d Sergeant June 19, 1831.
William Million	"	"	Pay due as private from June 2; elected 3d Sergeant June 19, 1831.
Charles S. Moore	"	"	Pay due as private from June 2
Corporals.			
Walcott A. Strong	"	"	Pay due as private from June 2
David Young	"	"	" " "
Franklin J. Scott	"	"	" " "
Samuel Gaskell	"	"	
Privates.			
Anderson, James	"	"	
Anderson, Stinson H	"	"	
Adams, William	"	"	
Brown, Hiram	"	"	

ODD COMPANIES.

Name and Rank.	Residence.	Enrolled	Remarks.
		1831.	
Brown, William G...	Belleville	June 2	Appointed Paymaster-General of detachment (June 2, 1831.
Brown, Alfred.......	"	"	
Bradsby, Richard..	"	"	Joined the Spies June 19...
Briggs, Josiah.......	"	"	
Basey, Edmund.....	"	"	
Coleman, Jesse	"	"	
Crane, Lewis W.....	"	"	
Crocker, William...	"	"	
Clemson Eli B.......	"	"	Absent on furlough
Davis, Robert.......	"	"	
Enocks, David......	"	"	
Enocks, Samuel.....	"	"	
Fike, John J.........	"	"	
Fike, A..............	"	"	
Griffin, George.....	"	"	
Galbreath, Undrell B	"	"	
Hipes, Joseph	"	"	
Hodge, James.......	"	"	
Herring, Elijah......	"	"	
Herring, Abner......	"	"	
Jackson, John.......	"	"	
Jones, John J........	"	"	
Kinney, Geo. D......	"	"	
Lane, Thomas.......	"	"	
Long, Thomas.......	"	"	Absent on furlough
LaCroux, Rene M...	"	"	
Larame, Lewis	"	"	Absent; sick
Mitchell, William D.	"	"	
Macom, Peter	"	"	
Macom, George	"	"	
McNabb, Laoni	"	"	
Mitchell, William....	"	"	
Manage, Louis	"	"	
Ogle, Joseph........	"	"	
Payne, Geo. W......	"	"	
Pea, James	"	"	Attached to the wagons
Russell, William.....	"	"	
Reynolds, Thomas..	"	"	
Rittenhouse, Elijah.	"	"	
Russell, James	"	"	
Russell, John H.....	"	"	
Russell, Isaac P.....	"	"	
Roman, Richard....	"	"	Appointed Surgeon's Mate June 19, 1831
Seymore, Grove.....	"	"	
Scott, Felix.........	"	"	
Tracewell, Edward..	"	"	
Thomas, Charles....	"	"	
Vernor, Zenas H	"	"	
Virgin, Hiram	"	"	
Woods, Lewis	"	"	
Woods, John W.....	"	"	
Wilson, John	"	"	
Williamson, A.......	"	"	
Winters, Joshua.....	"	"	
Whiteside, Joseph..	"	"	Absent on furlough

It is presumed this company was fully organized by the election of the officers and non-commissioned officers on June 19, 1831.
(Signed.)
J. BLISS,
Major, and Mustering Officer.

MEXICAN WAR.

1846-8.

MEXICAN WAR.

FIRST REGIMENT.

FIELD AND STAFF OF THE FIRST REGIMENT

Of late Col. J. J. Hardin's Illinois Foot Volunteers, commanded by Col. William Weatherford, called into the service of the United States by the President, under act of Congress approved May 13, 1846, for the term of twelve months. From the 28th day of February, 1847 (when last mustered), to the 17th day of June, 1847, when discharged.

Name and Rank.	Place of Enlistment.	Enrolled	Remarks.
Colonels.		1846	
John J. Hardin	Alton, Ill	June 30	Killed in battle at Buena Vista, Feb. 23, 1847..
Wm. Weatherford	"	June 25	Elected at Buena Vista, Feb. 26, vice Hardin.
Lieutenant-Colonel.			
Wm. B. Warren	"	June 25	Elected from Major, at Buena Vista, Feb. 26..
Major.			
Wm. A. Richardson	"	June 26	Elected from Capt. Co. "E," at Buena V.,Feb.26
Adjutants.			
Benj. M. Prentiss	"	June 18	Appointed from 1st Lieut. Co. "A," Alton, Ill..
Wm. H. L. Wallace	"	June 22	........[June 30; elected Capt. Co. "I," Sept. 14.
Surgeons.			
James H. White	"	June 23	Transferred at Buena Vista, in March.........
C. Payton	Little R'k, Ark	June 20	....
Assistant Surgeon.			
Chris. B. Zalviskie	Alton, Ill	June 26	Transferred at Panas, Mex., in December....
A. A. Q. Ms.			
John Scanland	"	June 27	Appointed from 1st Lieut. Co. "F," Nov. 1.
William Erwin	"	June 18	................[Transferred to Co. "F," Dec. 31.
A. A. C. S.			
George S. Myers	"	June 26	....
Sergeant-Major.			
Edward A. Giller	"	June 23	....
Q. M. Sergeants.			
Thomas Smothers	"	June 25	Died at New Orleans July 27 ....
Wm. Osman	"	June 22	....
Principal Musicians.			
Austin W. Fay	"	June 22	Killed in battle at Buena Vista, Feb. 23, 1847..
Levi Bixby	"	June 19	Reduced to ranks and trans. to Co. "B," Nov. 1.
Jerome Gibson	"	June 19	....
John Aug. Stemple	"	June 18	App. at Agua Neuva, Mex., vice Fay, killed..
Levi Bixby	"	June 19	Reduced to ranks, and transferred Nov. 1....

FIRST REGIMENT.

Company "A."

Name and Rank.	Place of Enlistment.	Enrolled	Remarks.
Captain.		1846.	
James D. Morgan	Alton, Ill.	June 18	
First Lieutenant.			
William Y. Henry	"	"	
Second Lieutenant.			
James Evans	"	"	
George T. M. Davis	"	"	Detached serv., Aid-de-Camp to Gen. Shields
Sergeants.			
John Archer	"	"	
Edward Everett	"	"	Absent, wounded; on furl'gh at San Antonio.
Ephraim B. Wood	"	"	
John W. Burns	"	"	On furl'h in Q. M. Dep't, by order Gen. Taylor
Corporals.			
George Evans	"	"	
Lewis W. Sweet	"	"	
John P. Brook	"	"	
Jno. T. Congers	"	"	
Privates.			
Arnold, Abraham	"	"	
Beck, Jacob	"	"	Deserted
Beck, Joseph	"	"	
Beers, Lewis	"	"	
Bush, Daniel B	"	"	
Cunningh'm, Oliver H	"	"	On furl'h in Q. M. Dep't, by order Gen. Taylor
Croes, William N	"	"	
Cassady, William	"	"	
Cooper, Wendell B	"	"	
Cooper, Benjamin	"	"	
Collett, Leon	"	"	
Cassill, Joseph	"	"	
Congers, Enoch W	"	"	
Downard, Jordan	"	"	Died at Saltillo March 15
Ewing, Charles L	"	"	
Finney, William	"	"	
Grimm, George	"	"	
Gramper, Joseph	"	"	
Grant, Richard	"	"	
Gladdish, Leander J	"	"	
Hoyt, John W	"	"	On furl'h in Q. M. Dep't, by order Gen. Taylor
Hoffman, Isaac	"	"	
Humphrey, Charles	"	"	
Hoag, Alamer	"	"	
Houck, Thomas L R	"	"	
Innman, Andrew	"	"	
Jordan, James B	"	"	
Jordan, Wesley	"	"	
Jordan, Harrison	"	"	
Jordan, William J	"	"	
Jordan, Miles	"	"	
Johnson, Smith	"	"	
Jenkins, Jesse H	"	"	
Konkle, Philip	"	"	
Knapp, Charles R	"	"	Died at Saltillo May 17
Lewis, Zachariah	"	"	
Littlefield, August P	"	"	
Lawrence, Jasper	"	"	
Meekempson, John S	"	"	
Mills, Elisha	"	"	
Meir, Francis	"	"	
Miller, William A	"	"	
McCoy, John	"	"	On furl'h in Q. M. Dep't by order Gen. Taylor
McNeil, Daniel C	"	"	
McLess, Henry	"	"	
Owen, John F	"	"	Died at Saltillo, March 11
Pounds, Benjamin A	"	"	Discharged for disability, at N. Orl'ns, Nov.—
Pounds, Joseph M	"	"	
Parsons, Jeremiah	"	"	
Pounds, Samuel	"	"	
Piper, Albert R	"	"	
Peake, Joseph H	"	"	

Name and Rank.	Place of Enlistment.	Enrolled	Remarks.
		1846.	
Painter, Joseph	Alton, Ill	June 18	
Roberts, John J	"	"	
Rupright, Martin	"	"	
Renoud, John F	"	"	
Rossell, James	"	"	
Renck, Andrew J	"	"	
Richter, Ferdinand	"	"	
Ramsey, James	"	"	
Rust, George	"	"	
Slott, Handford	"	"	
Short, James	"	"	
Smith, Marinus G	"	"	
Slouse, Michael	"	"	Absent, sick, at Presido, Rio Gr. from Oct. 16
Shepherd, Hedrick	"	"	
Shepherd, Oan	"	"	
Shear, Michael	"	"	
Sellon, William H	"	"	
Sellon, Charles J	"	"	
Tuttle, Abner J	"	"	
Vight, William S	"	"	On furl'h in Q. M. Dep't, by order Gen. Taylor
Vandenburg, John W	"	"	
Wren, Thomas	"	"	
Wade, George W. D	"	"	
Wolte, Frederick	"	"	
Webb, John B	"	"	
Williman, Joseph	"	"	

This company was mustered out June 17, 1847, at Camargo, Mexico.

Company "B."

Name and Rank.	Place of Enlistment.	Enrolled	Remarks.
Captain.		1846.	
M. P. Smith	Alton, Ill	June 19	
First Lieutenant.			
Patrick Higgins	"	"	
Second Lieutenants.			
William A. Clark	"	"	
Elias B. Zabriska	"	June 25	
Sergeants.			
Authar Perry	"	June 19	
Abraham Peters	"	"	
Chauncey H. Snow	"	"	
Alfred Wrose	"	"	
Corporals.			
Patrick Mehan	"	"	
L. M. Mathews	"	"	
Geo. Mackenzie	"	"	
Geo. P. Wilmot	"	"	
Musicians.			
D. M. Burdick	"	"	
Levi Bixby	"	"	Promoted from private, by Col. Weatherford
Privates.			
Anderson, Wm. O	"	"	
Burk, Patrick	"	"	Sick in hospital, Saltillo
Blanchard, James A	"	"	
Burkholder, John	"	"	
Burr, Thos. J	"	"	
Bisbee, John	"	"	
Boneby, John D	"	"	
Conover, Peter	"	"	
Clemens, Patrick	"	"	
Crane, Henry	"	"	

… FIRST REGIMENT. …

Name and Rank.	Place of Enlistment.	Enrolled	Remarks.
		1846.	
Chandler, Bradley..	Alton, Ill.....	June 19	On detached serv. in Q. M. Dept. from Aug. 8
Dilly, Junius.........	"	....	
Dolan, Peter.........	"	....	"
Edson, James T.....	"	....	"
Ells, Simeon L......	"	....	"
Fitch, Leroy D......	"	....	"
Finton, Michael.....	"	....	"
Gavin, Thomas......	"	....	" Sick in hospital, Saltillo................
Garregus, Edw'd D.	"	....	"
Gun, Hiram..........	"	....	"
Griffin, Dennis......	"	....	" To be Dishon. disch. by order of Gen. Wool.
Gorman, Thomas...	"	....	"
Gitty, James.........	"	....	"
Howland, John......	"	....	"
Hodge, William.....	"	....	"
Huzey, Edward.....	"	....	"
Half, Michael........	"	....	"
Krebbs, Geo. W.....	"	....	"
Kirkham, Solomon..	"	....	"
Murry, Patrick......	"	....	"
Malone, John........	"	....	"
Mains, Philip........	"	....	"
Moore, Thomas S...	"	....	" On furlough in Q. M. Dept. from May 20.....
Orouke, James......	"	....	"
Quinn, Francis......	"	....	"
Pratt, Joseph H.....	"	....	" On furlough in Q. M. Dept. from May 20.....
Riley, Thomas.......	"	....	"
Richards, B. A......	"	....	"
Smith, John L.......	"	....	"
Sullivan, Jeremiah .	"	....	"
Scary, Barney.......	"	....	"
Tyler, O. C...........	"	....	"
Underhill, Geo. W...	"	....	" On furlough in Q. M. Dept. from May 20.....
Wright, Edward.....	"	....	"
White, Thomas P...	"	....	" Sick in hospital, Saltillo................
Woolworth, S. T.....	"	....	"
Died.			
Thomas Diley.......	"	....	" Died at General Hospital, Saltillo, March 10..

This company was discharged June 17, 1847.

COMPANY "C."

Name and Rank.	Place of Enlistment.	Enrolled	Remarks.
		1846.	
Captain.			
Noah Fry.............	Alton, Ill....	June 23	
First Lieutenant.			
William C. Rainey..	"	"	
Second Lieutenants.			
Solomon S. Chester.	"	"	On furlough from May 24 ....
Joshua C. Winters..	"	"	
Sergeants.			
John J. Sears........	"	"	
Elihu Boan...........	"	"	
Edwin Parks.........	"	"	
Wm. McGovran.....	"	"	
Corporals.			
Rufus Cleaveland...	"	"	
James H. Brock.....	"	"	
William C. Rainey..	"	"	
Wilson Whitlock....	"	"	Appointed Corporal March 18................
Edward McGovran..	"	"	

198   MEXICAN WAR.

Name and Rank.	Place of Enlistment.	Enrolled	Remarks.
Privates.		1846.	
Attebery, William T.	Alton, Ill	June 23	
Attebery, Stephen C	"	"	
Allen, Jas. V	"	"	
Allen, Andrew J	"	"	
Ashlock, Jas. M	"	"	Discharged on Surgeon's certificate March 22
Bowman, Calvin L	"	"	
Bandy, James T	"	"	
Bandy, Elihu	"	"	
Bandy, Richard T	"	"	
Blackshor, William	"	"	
Ballow, George	"	"	
Barnard, Andrew J	"	"	
Barnett, Jno. B	"	"	
Conway, Silas P	"	"	
Cade, James R	"	"	
Conner, George	"	"	
Clark, Hiram	"	"	
Cochran R. K. F	"	"	
Dennis, Matthew Q	"	"	
Fisher, Elihu	"	"	
Ferguson, William B	"	"	
Fitch, George C	"	"	
Goodwin, Jno. M	"	"	
Gillam, Larkin	"	"	
Hughs, Jno. W	"	"	
Houser, Thompson	"	"	
Hudson, James	"	"	On furlough in Q. M. Dept from May 15
Kirgin, Jno. M	"	"	
Knapp, Cyrus, Jr	"	"	
Long, William A	"	"	
Leonard, Jno	"	"	
Laton, Charles	"	"	
Leonard, Jacob W	"	"	
Murry, James	"	"	
Martin, George	"	"	
Moore, Uriah	"	"	
Morrow, George W	"	"	Discharged on Surgeon's certificate April 7.
Neece, Alfred W	"	"	
Poindexter, Lawr'ce	"	"	
Porter, William A	"	"	
Powel, Elija	"	"	
Robbins, James A	"	"	
Roe, David	"	"	
Record, James S	"	"	
Sloan, Asa	"	"	
Swinden, Jno	"	"	
Skeen, Henry W	"	"	
Stoddard, Jno. L	"	"	
Spofford, Thomas	"	"	
Stone, Craven	"	"	
Stone, Noah M	"	"	
Stephens, David	"	"	On furlough in Q. M. Dept. from May 24
Tunnel, Martin L			
Taylor, Walter			
Watson, Hiram			
Witt, Morrill			On furlough in Q. M. Dept. from May 15

This company was mustered out June 17, 1847, at Camargo, Mexico.

Company "D."

Name and Rank.	Place of Enlistment.	Enrolled	Remarks.
Captain.		1846	
John L. McConnel	Alton, Ill	June 25	
First Lieutenant.			
Samuel R. Black	"	"	
Second Lieutenants.			
James E. Dunlap	"	"	
Nathan D. Hatfield	"	"	

FIRST REGIMENT.

Name and Rank.	Place of Enlistment.	Enrolled	Remarks.
Sergeants.		1846.	
Hugh Fee	Alton, Ill	June 25	
John T. Longley	"	"	
John C. Barr	"	"	
Thomas J. Moss	"	"	
Corporals.			
John Selby	"	"	
P. L. N. Dustin	"	"	
Thomas Turley	"	"	
John Grogan	"	"	
Musician.			
Edward Hines	"	"	On furlough in Capt. Mear's Co. Mounted Volunteers, at Saltillo, May 29.
Privates.			
Adkin, George W	"	"	
Bennett, Isaac R	"	"	
Bennett, William	"	"	
Bozarth, John C	"	"	
Bozarth, A. Johnson	"	"	
Brown, George S	"	"	
Brown, Nathan	"	"	
Bryant, James	"	July 9	
Bryant, Thomas	"	June 25	
Bobbett, Wm. C	"	"	
Barr, Oliver P	"	"	
Christy, James S	"	"	
Carter, John	"	"	
Cobbs, Edward	"	"	
Clayton, Wm	"	"	
Dixon, James	"	"	
Dean, John	"	"	
Ellison, Robt	"	"	
Fuller, John	"	"	
Goodheart, John	"	"	
Huoy, George I	"	"	Extra duty (Hosp. Steward) at a post of more than 4 Co's, from July 4, order Col. Hardin.
Huoy, James S	"	"	
Hurry, David	"	"	
Howard, Henderson	"	"	
Hopper, John	"	"	On furl. in Q.M. Dept., at Saltillo, from May 17.
Ingalls, Alphonso	"	"	
Kennett, Thomas F	"	"	
Kennett, Frank D	"	"	
Kercher, Valentine	"	"	
Kershaw, Albert	"	"	
Knight, Ezekiel	"	"	
Lewis, Wm. M	"	"	
Lessley, A. S	"	"	
Lorner, Beat	"	"	
Martin, Benj. F	"	"	
McConnel, C	"	"	
McCormick, Isham	"	"	
Neeley, James	"	"	
Ogle, John W	"	"	
O'Neil, Patrick	"	"	
Olds, Daniel	"	"	Died in Hospital at Saltillo, March 29.
Pullman, Wm. E	"	"	
Price, David	"	"	
Puryear, John F	"	"	
Redding, Enoch	"	"	
Reeder, Levi	"	"	
Stewart, James	"	"	
Shoff, John D	"	"	
Stoker, Jacob R	"	"	
Simms, Wm. W	"	"	
Sorrels, Peter	"	"	
Sorrels, Thomas	"	"	
Servance, Preston	"	"	
Taylor, Wm	"	"	
Thornley, James	"	"	
Tefft, Willis	"	"	
Weathers, George	"	"	
Winningham, A. J	"	"	
Warner, William	"	"	
White, John	"	"	
Whitaker, Wm	"	"	

This company was mustered out June 17, 1847, at Camargo, Mexico.

Company "E."

Name and Rank.	Place of Enlistment.	Enrolled	Remarks.
Captain. G. W. Robertson	Alton, Ill.	1846. June 26	
First Lieutenant. Allen Persinger	"	"	
Second Lieutenants. George S. Myers	"	"	
John T. May	"	"	
Sergeants. George W. Calvert	"	"	
Francis R. McElroy	"	"	
Luke P. Allphin	"	"	
James Coakenour	"	"	
Corporals. Robt. A. Lawler	"	"	
Moses Littaker	"	"	
Reuben Allphin	"	"	
William Petefish	"	"	
Musician. James H. Carden	"	"	
Privates. Allphin, Wm. R.	"	"	
Billings, Jonathan	"	"	
Black, John, Sr.	"	"	Killed by the enemy near Cessalvo, Feb. 24.
Black, John, Jr.	"	"	
Beach, Cyrus	"	"	
Brooks, William	"	"	
Bennett, Lemuel	"	"	
Berry, George G.	"	"	
Curry, Isaac	"	"	
Curtis, George W.	"	"	
Crane, Goodsell	"	"	
Clarkson, Franklin B	"	"	
Carter, Irvin F.	"	"	
Davis, Moses W.	"	"	
Dalton, Franklin	"	"	
Doyle, James	"	"	
File, Henry	"	"	
Garrett, John	"	"	
Gray, Hiram H.	"	"	
Gray, George L.	"	"	
Gillett, Leonard M.	"	"	Disch. by reason of having re-vol'd to serve [dur'g war in Capt. Mear's Co.
Horney, Leonidas	"	"	
Harris, James H.	"	"	
Harris, William	"	"	
Hewitt, Allen O.	"	"	
Ishmael, George N.	"	"	
Jones, Anderson	"	"	
Jones, Walter	"	"	Disch. on Surg.'s certif, Mar. 15, by Gen. Wool
Jacobs, Daniel	"	"	
Koch, Isaac	"	"	
Littaker, Joseph H.	"	"	
Littaker, Rowland G	"	"	
Lee, John P.	"	"	
Luttrell, Benjamin	"	"	
Luttrell, James H.	"	"	
Lawler, Joseph T.	"	"	
Lansdon, Richard	"	"	
McClelland, Daniel	"	"	
Ogden, Jonathan B.	"	"	
Rose, Isaac	"	"	
Riccardson, Wm.	"	"	
Richardson, W. R.	"	"	
Stapleton, Wm.	"	"	
Strahan, James	"	"	
Smotherman, Thos.	"	"	
Smith, Charles	"	"	
St. John, Wm. H.	"	"	
Stephenson, Wm.	"	"	Died of wounds rec'd at Buena Vista, Mar. 25.
Thompson, John B.	"	"	
Turner, Berry	"	"	

FIRST REGIMENT.   201

Name and Rank.	Place of Enlistment.	Enrolled	Remarks.
Thorp, Levitus M.	Alton, Ill.	1846. June 26	
Vantossell, F. M.	"	"	
Wilson, James O.	"	"	
Wilson, Thomas	"	"	

This company was discharged June 17, 1847, at Camargo, Mexico.

Company "F."

Name and Rank.	Place of Enlistment.	Enrolled	Remarks.
Captain.		1846.	
Albion T. Crow	Alton, Ill.	June 27	
First Lieutenant.			
John Scanland	"	"	
Second Lieutenants.			
Robt Buzan	"	"	
Francis Ryan	"	"	
Sergeants.			
John P. McKibbin	"	"	
John Hughs	"	"	
Alonzo D. Frazer	"	"	
George Reed	"	"	
Corporals.			
John J. Ross	"	"	
Alfred M. Jarbo	"	"	
Henry Inglekink	"	"	
Henry L. Thompson	"	"	
Musician.			
Jesse Dreeser	"	"	
Privates.			
Ball, Joseph	"	"	
Birch, Luman P.	"	"	
Backman, John	"	"	
Brush, A. W.	"	"	
Curry, Daniel	"	"	On furlough Buena Vista, order Gen. Wool.
Campbell, James R	"	"	
Cavanaugh, Joseph	"	"	
Donner, Levi	"	"	
Daugherty, Austin	"	"	
Evan, Evans	"	"	
Edle, John	"	"	
Farra, Samuel C.	"	"	On furlough Buena Vista, order Gen. Wool.
Fuller, William	"	"	
Funk, Hezekiah	"	"	
Griffith, Samuel C.	"	"	
Harper, Lafayette	"	"	
Hohl, Nicholas	"	"	
Harper, William	"	"	
Hobbs, William A.	"	"	
Isbel, John K	"	"	
Kinkade, John	"	"	
Labadie, Louis	"	"	
McClure, James A.	"	"	
Moss, Isaac W.	"	"	
Maple, John M.	"	"	
Martin, Samuel	"	"	
McBride, Archibald	"	"	
McIntosh, John	"	"	
McGinnis, James	"	"	
McLeavy, Francis	"	"	
Noble, Nelson	"	"	
Phillips, Liman D.	"	"	
Pierce, Ira M.	"	"	

Name and Rank.	Place of Enlistment.	Enrolled	Remarks.
Pase, Peter	Alton, Ill	1846. June 27	
Poterfield, Isaac M.	"	"	
Robe, William	"	"	
Ross, John	"	"	
Slater, George	"	"	
Shepherd, Roland G	"	"	
Shean, Daniel	"	"	
Schlosser, Conrad	"	"	
Taggart, William	"	"	
Taylor, Andrew J	"	"	
Upton, Michael	"	"	
Wetzel, Augustus	"	"	
Waddle, William A	"	"	

Discharged:

Name and Rank.	Place of Enlistment.	Enrolled	Remarks.
Alexander, Henry	Alton, Ill	1846. June 27	Discharged May 31, order Gen. Wool
Brown, Job	"	"	" " " " " "
Brown, David	"	"	" " " " " "
Bender, Elias	"	"	" May 28 " " "
Campbell, Thomas	"	"	" " " " " "
Crane, Nelson R	"	"	" " " " " "
Crum, Henry	"	"	" " " " " "
Dignan, Dominick	"	"	" " " " " "
Decker, Alonzo	"	"	" " " " " "
Davison, Thomas H	"	"	" " " " " "
Herald, Robert	"	"	" " " " " "
Hitchcock, Thomas	"	"	" " " " " "
Kirtley, Francis	"	"	" " " " " "
Lockhart, William	"	"	" " " " " "
Lacock, John M	"	"	" " " " " "
Murray, James	"	"	" " " " " "
Mohan, James	"	"	" " " " " "
Peterman, Charles	"	"	" " " " " "
Patten, Harrison	"	"	" " " " " "
Parker, William	"	"	" " " " " "
Rock, Francis	"	"	" May 31 " " "
Shriver, John	"	"	" May 28 " " "
Spencer, Ephriam	"	"	" " " " " "
Vandergrift, Howard	"	"	" " " " " "
Vandergrift, James	"	"	" " " " " "
Musician. Gilbreath, Victor	"	"	" " " " " "

This company was discharged on June 17, 1847 at Camarago, Mexico.

Company "G."

Name and Rank.	Place of Enlistment.	Enrolled	Remarks.
Captain. William J. Wyatt	Alton, Ill	1846. June 25	
First Lieutenant. Jas. H. Wetherford	"	"	
Second Lieutenants. Isaac S. Wright	"	"	
Jas. M. Wood	"	"	
Sergeants. J. B. Duncan	"	"	
George W. Evans	"	"	
Dolphin F. Drew	"	"	
Jas. L. Wyatt	"	"	

FIRST REGIMENT.

Name and Rank.	Place of Enlistment.	Enrolled	Remarks.
Corporals.		1846.	
James A. Summer	Alton, Ill.	June 25	
Abraham Grimsley	"	"	
Jas. L. Nichols	"	"	
Ananias D. Sevier	"	"	
Musician.			
Jas. Persor	"	"	
Privates.			
Ashbaugh, G. P.	"	"	
Allen, G. W.	"	"	
Bellows, C. S.	"	"	
Brown, Elisha	"	"	
Buchanan, Jas.	"	"	
Clayton, J. S.	"	"	
Clayton, Elias	"	"	
Conner, J. F.	"	"	
Cowden, J. W.	"	"	
Carver, Thos. W.	"	"	
Carver, G. W.	"	"	
Coen, Jas.	"	"	
Cox, Beaverly	"	"	Died at Saltillo, in hospital, March 12
Dean, W. R.	"	"	
Davenport, P. E.	"	"	
Detherage, Colmor	"	"	
Dodson, Benjamin	"	"	
Edwards, Thos.	"	"	
Fulling, Frederick	"	"	
Fanning, A. P.	"	"	
Fanning, J. M.	"	"	
Foss, S. J.	"	"	
Gunnels, J. D.	"	"	
Henry, William	"	"	
Henry, E. R.	"	"	
Hart, J. L.	"	"	
Hart, Josiah	"	"	
Hill, Isaac	"	"	
Harris, Joseph	"	"	
Hague, J. W.	"	"	On furl'h in Q.M. Dep't at Saltillo, from May 15
Haynes, Baxter	"	"	
Hopper, S. F.	"	"	
Jones, Edward	"	"	
Joiner, Thomas	"	"	
Lorge, Adam	"	"	
Matthews, R. D.	"	"	
Moore, Travice	"	"	
Miner, A. S.	"	"	
McCollum, J. S.	"	"	
McCormac, A. L.	"	"	
McAvoy, William	"	"	
Piercy, Z. R.	"	"	
Pettyjohn, Thos.	"	"	
Pulliam, E. C.	"	"	
Phillips, H. M.	"	"	
Rogers, R. W.	"	"	
Rogers, J. W.	"	"	
Russel, W. L.	"	"	
Russel, Jas.	"	"	
Rigg, G. W.	"	"	
Ruffner, Jacob	"	"	
Saunderson, S. T.	"	"	
Sharp, John	"	"	
Sharp, H. H.	"	"	
Swere, Abraham	"	"	
Smitherman, Jas.	"	"	
Shipherd, W. A.	"	"	
Vanote, William	"	"	
Ward, E. D.	"	"	
Ward, Jas.	"	"	
Winsor, Jesse	"	"	
White, Jno.	"	"	
Witt, Enoch	"	"	
Wright, A. J.	"	"	

This company was discharged June 17, 1847, at Camargo, Mexico.

Company "H."

Name and Rank.	Place of Enlistment.	Enrolled	Remarks.
Captain.		1846.	
Samuel Montgomery	Alton, Ill.	June 25	
First Lieutenant.			
Hezekiah Evans	"	"	
Second Lieutenants.			
Thomas H. Flynn	"	"	
Thomas R. Roberts	"	"	
Sergeants.			
John C. Dinsmore	"	"	
William Lower	"	"	
Elam J. Gaither	"	"	
John M. Delapp	"	"	
Corporals.			
Ezekiel Flynn	"	"	
John Fisher	"	"	
Wm. N. Shibley	"	"	
Erastus L. Gillham	"	"	
Musician.			
Remus G. Morris	"	"	Discharged on Surg. certif. March 17, 1847.
Privates.			
Allen, Joseph	"	"	
Atkinson, Elias	"	"	
Burch, William	"	"	
Burch, Tilman	"	"	
Burch, Milton	"	"	
Black, Thomas B.	"	"	
Beard, Isaac	"	"	
Beaird, Thomas	"	"	
Breeding, Wesley	"	"	
Brackett, John H.	"	"	
Cary, Dawson	"	"	
Crinion, William	"	"	
Chistison, Luther	"	"	
Carr, Calvin	"	"	
Beckman, Oliver P.	"	"	
Dawdy, Alanson	"	"	
Dunsmore, George	"	"	
Evans, Jackson	"	"	
Evans, James J.	"	"	
Hulett, Joseph	"	"	
Hanback, William	"	"	
Hamilton, Jacob B.	"	"	
Hamilton, Adam	"	"	
Horrald, Alfred	"	"	
Hodge, James	"	"	
Harkins, Abram	"	"	
Jelison, Milertiap	"	"	
Kemp, James F.	"	"	
Low, Edgar M.	"	"	Disch. on acc't of re-enrollment May 22, 1847.
Lewis, William	"	"	
Lynn, James	"	"	
Little, Michael	"	"	
Langston, Matthew	"	"	
Lankford, William	"	"	
Martin, Caleb	"	"	
Mans, John	"	"	
Moore, John	"	"	
Morris, Jacob	"	"	
Maupin, George	"	"	
Northent, Edward	"	"	
Pike, Eli			
Peneger, William			
Pentzer, Daniel			
Reyon, Christopher			
Roe, William			
Summers, John W.			
Six, William			

FIRST REGIMENT.

Name and Rank.	Place of Enlistment.	Enrolled	Remarks.
		1846.	
Smith, Thomas			
White, Thomas			
Zimmerman, Jas. N.			
Zimmerman, Thom's			

This company was discharged on June 17, 1847, at Camargo, Mex.

COMPANY "I."

Name and Rank.	Place of Enlistment.	Enrolled	Remarks.
Captain.		1846.	
Benjamin M. Prentiss	Alton, Ill.	June 18	
First Lieutenant.			
Edmund S. Holbrook	"	June 22	
Second Lieutenants.			
Wm. H. L. Wallace	"	"	Adjutant of Regiment from Sept. 15, 1846.
John Reddick	"	"	
Sergeants.			
George S. Fisher	"	"	
John Bending	"	"	
Joseph E. Skinner	"	"	
Moses Osman	"	"	
Corporals.			
Alonzo Perkins	"	"	Absent on furl'h in Q. M. Dep't from May 30,'47
Levi Jackson	"	"	" " " " " " 31,'47
William M. McCay	"	"	Appointed from private at Saltillo Mar 23, 18—
Lindsey H. Carr	"	"	
Harley W. Clay	"	"	Died at Saltillo, Mexico, March 23, 1847.
Musicians.			
Wilson L. Smith	"	"	
Salmon Z. Powers	"	"	
Privates.			
Atwood, William C.	"	"	
Bowen, Aaron, 2d	"	"	
Baker, Schuyler	"	"	
Boyd, David P.	"	"	
Black, Philip	"	"	Absent on furl'h in Q. M. Dep't, from May 28.
Bates, William W.	"	"	
Bleekely, Joseph	"	"	
Cameron, Thomas	"	"	Died at Saltillo, Mexico, April 5, 1847.
Claude, Frederick E.	"	"	
Clay, Levi	"	"	
Dewitt, George N.	"	"	Absent on furl'h in Q. M. Dep't from May 28.
Dickson, Wilburn F.	"	"	
Errickson, Errick	"	"	
Evans, Abraham L.	"	"	
Falston, Benjamin G	"	"	Absent, sick at Port Lavaca, Tex., from Aug. 3
Gibson, William L.	"	"	Absent on furl'h in Q. M. Dep't from May 26.
Goodell, Rossell E.	"	"	
Gillett, Nicholas	"	"	
Handcock, Armig'l W	"	"	
Haughterling, Chas.	"	"	Absent on furl'h in Ord'n'ce Dep. from May 29
Hopper, Rowland	"	"	
Hollaker, Goll	"	"	
Hollaker, Donut	"	"	
Hoes, Peter	"	"	
Harris, Edward	"	"	
Hausman, David	"	"	
Howlet, Robert W.	"	July 9	
Kelley, William	"	June 22	Absent on furl'h in Q. M. Dep't from May 26.
Kelley, Edward P.	"	"	
Lawrence, Augustus	"	"	
Lynch, John W.	"	"	
Maleure, John	"	"	

MEXICAN WAR.

Name and Rank.	Place of Enlistment.	Enrolled	Remarks.
		1846.	
Mitchell, Bradford C	Alton, Ill.	June 22	
Matthews, Geo. W...	"	"	
Morrell, John	"	"	
Morse, Evander	"	"	
Miller, Joseph	"	"	
Martin, Robert B	"	"	
Mattiese, Nicholas	"	"	
Mulkin, Ezra	"	"	
McCarty, Timothy	"	"	
McDonald, John T	"	"	
Napier, Dwight	"	"	
Nichol, John P	"	"	Absent on furl'h in Q. M. Dep't from May 27.
Ordway, Edson	"	"	
Pitzer, James F	"	"	
Pratt, Christopher M	"	"	
Reddick, Joseph	"	"	
Rider, Charles	"	"	
Rouse, Charles R	"	"	Absent on furl'h in Q. M. Dep't from May 30. 26.
Story, Joseph	"	"	
Strong, William	"	"	
Shope, Emanuel	"	"	
Skinner, William B	"	"	
Stewart, James	"	"	
Shilliker, Johannus	"	"	
Stauffer, Nicholas	"	"	
Teeters, David	"	"	
Thompson, Daniel L	"	"	
Taylor, John	"	"	
Taylor, James T	"	"	
Van Orten, James	"	"	
Woolcot, Alford	"	"	
Woodberry, Benj. F.	"	"	
Williams, William	"	"	
Webb, James	"	"	
Willnor, John	"	"	

This company was discharged at Camargo, Mexico, June 17, 1847.

Company "K."

Name and Rank.	Place of Enlistment.	Enrolled	Remarks.
Captain.		1846.	
Lyman Mower	Alton, Ill	June 18	
First Lieutenant.			
Wm. Erwin	"	"	On detached service Q. M. Dept
Second Lieutenants.			
Samuel M. Parsons	"	"	On detached service with Col. Churchill, [Insp.-Gen. U. S. A.
Mathew Moran	"	"	
Sergeants.			
Joshua Herrindan	"	"	
Frederick Hailborn	"	"	
Augustus Tilford	"	"	
Dewitt C. Davis	"	"	
Corporals.			
Samuel Scott	"	"	
Chas. Banks	"	"	
Benj. VanVrankin	"	"	
Geo. D. Slack	"	"	Wounded in battle Buena Vista, Feb. 23, 1847.
Musicians.			
John Helms	"	"	
Augustus Stemple	"	"	On detached service; appointed principal Musician March 1.

Name and Rank.	Place of Enlistment.	Enrolled	Remarks.
Privates.		1846.	
Atley, Simon	Alton, Ill	June 18	
Asant, Phillip	"	"	
Baker, David	"	"	
Bruner, Henry	"	"	
Brennan, Michle C.	"	"	
Bunker, George C.	"	"	
Battleman, Lewis	"	"	
Cline, William	"	"	
Carle, James	"	June 28	
Carlin James	"	June 18	
Devoe, Edward	"	"	
Dolson, David	"	June 28	
Durling, John H.	"	June 18	
English, Isaac	"	June "	
Ellering, Harmon	"	"	Sent to San Antonio, from Presidio, Rio Grande, Jan. 3, 1847; sick, and not officially heard of since.
Elam, Stephen	"	"	
Franks, Abraham	"	"	
Fuller, Tina P.	"	"	
Fowk, Charles	"	June 28	
Gardner, Eliacune	"	June 18	
Gardner, John	"	"	
Guinnip, Lyman	"	June 28	
Groves, Jonathan	"	"	
Groves, Luther	"	"	
Hyde, Michle	"	June 18	
Handy, Austin	"	June 28	
Johnson, Nelson	"	June 18	
Lathrop, Cyrus	"	June 28	
Myers, Charles	"	June 18	
Miller, John	"	"	
Miller, Jacob	"	"	
McCarty, Michle	"	"	On furlough from May 28, 1847, in Q. M. Dept.
Olmstead, Wm. P.	"	"	
Osmand, Christian	"	"	
Phettiplace, George	"	"	
Porter, Henry	"	"	On furlough from May 28, 1847, in Q. M. Dept.
Phinisy, Wm	"	"	
Rowe, Ed. L.	"	"	
Roth, Fredrick	"	"	
Rikow, Fredrick	"	"	Wounded in battle at Buena Vista, Feb. 23
Robinson, W. H. H.	"	"	
Shrader, Frederick	"	"	
Steinhouse, Aug	"	"	
Secomb, Harmon	"	"	
Temple, John H.	"	June 28	
Warlan, John	"	"	
Wenter, Frederick	"	June 18	
Waters, Samuel	"	"	
Wells, John	"	"	On furlough from May 15, 1847, in Q. M. Dept.
Walker, James	"	"	
Wise, John	"	"	

Discharged:

		1846.	
Burroughs, Francis	Alton, Ill	June 18	[Mounted Vols. during war, May 28, 1847. Disch. by reason of joining Capt. Mear's Co.
Black, Adam	"	"	" " " " "
Upperman, George	"	"	" " " " "
Willett, Freeman	"	"	" " " " "
Weaver, Frederick	"	"	
Carney, Franklin	"	"	Disch. by reason of having hired to Maj. Butler, Paymaster U. S. A., June 3.

This company was discharged on June 17, 1847, at Camargo, Mexico.

FIRST REGIMENT.

THE FIELD AND STAFF

In the 1st Regiment of Illinois Foot Volunteers, commanded by Colonel E. W. B. Newby, called into the service of the United States by the President, under the act of Congress approved May 13, 1846, at Alton, Ill. (the place of general rendezvous), on the 8th day of June, 1847, to serve for the term of during the war with Mexico, from the date of enrollment, unless sooner discharged. From the 30th day of June, 1848, (when last paid), to the 16th day of October, 1848. The Regiment was organized by Col. Newby, at Alton, Ill., in the month of June, 1847.

Name and Rank.	Place of Enlistment.	Enrolled	Remarks.
Colonel. Edw'd W. B. Newby.	Alton, Ill	1847. June 8	Elected from Capt. in Newby's Co. "D" at Alton, Ill., June 8, 1847.
Lieutenant-Colonel. Hend'n P. Boyakins.	"	"	Elected from private in Turner's Co. "C" at Alton, Ill., June 8, 1847.
Major. Israel B. Donalson..	"	"	Elected from Capt. in Donalson's Co. "K" at Alton, Ill., June 8, 1847.
1st Lt. and Adjutant. William H. Snyder..	"	"	1st Lieut. in Hook's Co. "E." Discharged at Alton, Oct. 14.
2d Lt. and A. A. Q. M. Rich'd N. Hamilton..	"	July 16	2d Lieut. in Kenny's Co. "F"...... ....
Surgeon. Daniel Turney......	Appointed by the President	" 13	....
Assistant Surgeon. James D. Robinson.	Appointed by the President	" 13	Absent with leave from Oct. 7 to report at N. Y.
Act. Asst. Surgeon. Thomas B. Lester ...	Alton, Ill.....	Oct. 8	Is private in Co. "C." empl'y'd by Col. at Santa Fe Oct. 8, 1847, till Oct. 3, 1848.
Sergeant-Major. John H. White.......	"	Mch. 6, '48	Appointed from Sergt. in Co. "B" Mar. 6, *vice* Tappan, reduced.
Q. M. Sergeants. Charles R. Slade .... Geo. F. Bull..........	" "	Jun. 8, '47 Fb. 17,'48	Died at Santa Fe Feb. 9................................ App'd from private Feb. 17, *vice* Slade, dec'd..
Principal Musicians. Thos. W. Pace....... John L. Kiser........	" "	Mch. 6,'48 "	App'd from Co. "C," *vice* Case, reduced....... " "K." *vice* Maynard, reduced..

COMPANY "A."

Name and Rank.	Place of Enlistment.	Enrolled	Remarks.
Captain. Thomas Bond.......	Alton, Ill.....	1847. May 22	....
First Lieutenants. John B. Roper...... Henry Richardson..	" "	" "	Discharged by resignation May 20, 1848........ Elected from private, *vice* Roper, resigned...

FIRST REGIMENT.

Name and Rank.	Place of Enlistment.	Enrolled	Remarks.
Second Lieutenants.		1847.	
Alex. H. Johnson	Alton, Ill.	May 22	
Levi Edmunds	"		
Sergeants.			
William Willcocks	"		
Henry A. Neely	"		Sick in hospital at Alton, from Oct. 4
William White	"		
Morris'n I. O'Hornett	"		Appointed from Drummer, Oct. 1
Corporals.			
John L. Smith	"		
Joseph Gordon	"		
Wesley Myatt	"		
Elijah Anderson	"		
Fifer.			
Jesse Kirkham	"		
Privates.			
Abbott, Charles W	"		
Affick, John M	"		
Bowles, Thomas	"		Sick in hospital at Alton, from Oct. 4
Bellardy, Melcher	"		
Bukema, Cornelius	Ottawa, Ill.	Feb., '48	Joined, a recruit, Aug. 16
Clark, James M	Alton, Ill.	May, '47	
Clark, Thomas	"		
Carroll, John	Ottawa, Ill.	Mar., '48	Joined, a recruit, Aug. 16
Cox, George	"		
Duncan, James	Alton, Ill.	May, '47	
Determann, Joseph	"		
Enington, James	"		Sick in hospital at Alton, from Oct. 4
Epla, William	Ottawa, Ill.	Mar., '48	Joined, a recruit, Aug. 16
Fisher, David	Alton, Ill.	May, '47	
Fisk, Norman	Ottawa, Ill.	Mar., '48	Joined a recruit, Aug. 16
Greer, William	Alton, Ill.	May, '47	
Guithouse, Chris. H.	"		Detached as Hosp. Steward Oct. 28, 1847
Green, Charles	Ottawa, Ill.	Mar., '48	Joined, a recruit, Aug. 16
Greenlee, Elihu	Belleville, Ill.	Feb., '48	
Hockelberg, John	Alton, Ill.	May, '47	
Hammond, Charles B	"		
Hill, Thomas F	"		
Hughes, Arthur	"		
Hutton, James	"		
Hutton, Henry	"		
Hale, Washington	"		
Hunt, Joel I	Belleville, Ill.	Feb., '48	Joined, a recruit, Aug. 16
Hartmann, Tamerl'e	Ottawa, Ill.	Mar., '48	" " "
Hough, Levi	"		
Jarvis, Alfred M	Alton, Ill.	May, '47	
Johanning, Bernard	"		
Kopemann, Clemens	"		
Kennie, Sylvanus	Ottawa, Ill.	Mar., '48	Joined, a recruit, Aug. 16
Lifert, Henry	Alton, Ill.	May, '47	
Lubbers, Bernard	"		
Lane, Nathaniel	Ottawa, Ill.	Mar., '48	Joined, a recruit, Aug. 16
Murray, Patrick	Alton, Ill.	May, '47	
Miles, Thomas	"		
Myatt, Albert	Belleville, Ill	Feb., '48	Joined, a recruit, Aug. 16
Morgan, Comfort	Ottawa, Ill.		
Nicholson, Wil'mson	Alton, Ill.	May, '47	
Newton, Jabez B	"		
Page, Michael	"		
Poll, Josiah	"		
Pine, Daniel	Ottawa, Ill.	Mar., '48	Joined, a recruit, Aug. 16
Phillips, Joseph D	Belleville, Ill.	Feb., '48	" " "
Phillips, Francis	"		
Ranney, William	Alton, Ill.	May, '47	
Slade, Joseph A	"		
Sharp, Anderson	"		
Stites, Isaac	"		
Shields, George T	"		
Scott, William	"		
Siebenburgen, H	"		
Sharp, Wm. H	Belleville, Ill.	Feb., '48	Joined, a recruit, Aug. 16
Town, David	Ottawa, Ill.	Mar., '48	
Wall, Wm. A	Alton, Ill.	May, '47	
Wall, James	"		
Warner, John	Ottawa, Ill.	Feb., '48	Joined, a recruit, Aug. 16
Weddle, Sylvester	Belleville, Ill.		

—14

Discharged:

Name and Rank.	Place of Enlistment.	Enrolled	Remarks.
Bullard, Henry	Alton, Ill	1847. May 22	[heard from since; supposed deserted.
Ballard, Jesse	"	"	Left sick at Ft. Leavenworth July 15, '47; not
Briggs, Andrew	"	"	Discharged July 24, 1847; disability
Briggs, Arabia	"	"	" July 13, 1847; "
Dougherty, Nathan'l	"	"	" June 10, 1848; "
Gibson, William	"	"	" July 13, 1847; "
Huey, James M	"	"	" Apr. 10, 1848; "
Huey, Jefferson	"	"	" June 10, 1848; "
Lona, Charles	"	"	Left sick July 13, 1847; supposed discharged.
Martin, William	"	"	Discharged July 24, 1847; disability
Schonefeld, Bernard	"	"	" June 10, 1848; "
Toole, Theodore	"	"	" July 24, 1847; "
Vogt, John P	"	"	" Mar. 18, 1848; "

Died:

Name and Rank.	Place of Enlistment.	Enrolled	Remarks.
Sergeants.		1847.	
Story, John W	Alton, Ill	May 22	Died at Point of Rocks, Aug. 26, 1848.
Hull, James M	"	"	Died at Albuquerque, N. M., April 24, 1848.
Corporals.			[heard from since; supposed died.
Posey, Jabez H	"	"	Left sick at Ft. Leavenworth July 15, '47; not
Todd, Squire S	"	"	Died at Albuquerque, N. M., Feb. 24, 1848
Isaacs, Harris	"	"	" " Feb. 27, 1848
Buck, Andrew	"	"	Died at Santa Fe, N. M., March 1, 1848
Dunlap, James H	"	"	Died at Albuquerque, N. M., April 10, 1848
Privates.			
Allen, Elias	"	"	Died at Ft. Leavenworth July 10, 1847
Ammons, Felix	"	"	Died at Santa Fe, N. M., Oct. 9 1847
Cox, Theodore R	"	"	Left sick at Ft. Leavenworth; supposed died.
Ensley, William	"	"	Died at Santa Fe, N. M., Nov. 3, 1847
Findley, Preston	"	"	Died at Albuquerque, N. M., April 10, 1848
Gullick, John M	"	"	Died at San Miguel Aug. 11, 1848
Heeman, Henry	"	"	Died at Albuquerque, N. M., June 7, 1848
Huey, Joseph M	"	"	" " March 8, 1848
Holley, Williamson	"	"	" " Feb. 26, 1848
Hull, Joseph F	"	"	Died at Santa Fe, N. M., Nov. 19, 1847
Hobener, Louis	"	"	Died Aug. 18, 1847, *en route* for Santa Fe.
Morton, Oliver	"	"	Died at Ft. Leavenworth June 27, 1847
Morrison, Joshua	"	"	Died at Santa Fe, N. M., Nov. 21, 1847
Matsler, John A. I	"	"	Died at Albuquerque, N. M., March 8, 1848
Outhouse, John	"	"	Died at Santa Fe, N. M., Oct. 14, 1847
Posey, Jubelee	"	"	Died at Lexington, Mo., June 24, 1847
Pierson, Isrom	"	"	Died at Santa Fe, N. M., Sept. 20, 1847
Reeves, George W	"	"	" " Feb. 1, 1848
Shields, W. A	"	"	Died at Albuquerque, N. M., Feb. 14, 1848
Petree, George	"	"	Died at Ft. Leavenworth July 14, 1847

This company was mustered out Oct. 16, 1848, at Alton, Ill.

Company "B."

Name and Rank.	Place of Enlistment.	Enrolled	Remarks.
Captain.		1847.	
J. M. Cunningham	Alton, Ill	May 28	
First Lieutenants.			
Benj. F. Furlong	"	"	Disch. by resign'n Mar. 6, by ord. Col. Newby
Wm. M. Eubanks	"	"	Was 1st Sergt. from enrollment until Mar. 7.
Second Lieutenants.			
Robt. M. Hundley	"	"	
Danl. R. Pulley	"	"	

FIRST REGIMENT.

Name and Rank.	Place of Enlistment.	Enrolled	Remarks.
Sergeants.		1847.	
Miles A. Dillard	Alton, Ill	May 28	Was private from enrollment till Mar. 11
Joseph W. Benson	"	"	
Larken M. Riley	"	"	
Augustus M. Henry	"	"	Appoin'd from private Aug. 30, 1848, *vice* Sergt. Norris, deceased.
Corporals.			
John G. Boles	"	"	Was private from enrollment till May 26, 1848.
George Q. North	"	"	
Silas M. Calvert	"	"	
Wm. D. Durham	"	"	
Musicians.			
Jesse A. McIntosh	"	"	
Henry Sykes	"	"	
Privates.			
Ables, Sandy P	"	"	
Anderson, Jas. M	"	"	
Baker, John	"	"	
Baker, Robt	"	"	
Bandy, Wm. P	"	"	
Baine, Isaac	"	"	
Barber, John B	"	"	
Bradley, Mathew	"	"	
Buckner, Jas. D	"	"	
Cox, Joseph	"	"	
Clark, Benj	Santa Fe, N.M	Jul. 13, '48	
Davis, Thos. M	Alton, Ill	M'y 28, '47	
Daniel, Reuben	"	"	
Drummond, John G	"	"	
Drummond, William	"	"	
Duff, John	"	"	
Duff, Andrew D	"	"	
Eaton, Benjamin	"	"	
Eason, Abner	"	"	
Greene, Thomas	Santa Fe, N.M	Jul. 13, '48	
Hays, Harvey L	Alton, Ill	M'y 28, '47	
Harris, John L	"	"	
Herring, Joseph	"	M'y 30, '47	Joined by transfer from Co. "H," Nov. 1, 1847.
Huffman, John W	"	M'y 28, '47	
Jones, Edmund	"	"	
Kelley, Robert R	"	"	
Kelley, Alex	"	"	
Lipsey, Wm. H	"	"	
Lowry, Jas. H	"	"	
Mares, Samuel	"	"	
McAnnelly, Matthew	"	"	
McCoy, Jas. M	"	"	
McKenney, Thos. J	"	"	
McNeill, Benj. F	"	"	
Miller, Isaac	"	"	
Miller, Wm. H	"	"	
Mitchell, John P	"	"	
Norris, John C	"	"	
Newsom, Frederick	"	"	
Odum, Briton	"	"	
Odum, Wm. L	"	"	
Payne, Peter M	"	"	
Pierce, William	Ottawa, Ill	Feb. 3, '48	Joined, a recruit, Aug. 1
Rawlings, David	Alton, Ill	M'y 28, '47	
Rose, Alfred J			
Russell, Jas. H	"	"	
Reed, James	Alton, Ill	M'y 28, '47	Joined by transfer from Co. "E," June 3, 1847.
Richardson, Fred'k	Ottawa, Ill	Fb. 14, '48	Joined, a recruit, Aug. 1
Sands, William	Alton, Ill	M'y 28, '47	
Stacks, Benj. J	"	"	
Shearer, Thos. W	"	"	
Swafford, Jas	"	"	
Smith, William	"	"	
Sisney, Geo. W	"	"	
Sanders, Luke	"	M'y 30, '47	Joined by transfer from Co. "H," Nov. 1, 1847.
Sells, Abram H	Ottawa, Ill	Mar. 3, '48	Joined, a recruit, Aug. 1
Tippy, Abram	Alton, Ill	M'y 28, '47	
Turney, Fayette	Santa Fe, N.M	Oc. 20, '47	
West, Hezekiah	Alton, Ill	M'y 28, '47	
West, John	"	"	
Woods, Thomas	"	"	
Whitlock, John	"	"	
Warren, Jas. M	"	"	

Name and Rank.	Place of Enlistment	Enrolled	Remarks.
		1847.	
Wiggs, Robt.	Alton, Ill.	May 28	
Wiley, Evan T.	"	"	
Wiley, Benj. L.	"	"	
Youngblood, John	"	"	

Discharged:

Name and Rank.	Place of Enlistment	Enrolled	Remarks.
		1847.	
Avery, Noah W.	Alton, Ill.	May 28	Disch. by reason of Surg. cert. Mar. 18, 1848
Bowyer, Horace L.	"	"	" " " " "
Cagle, Timothy	"	"	" " " " " May 26, 1848
Erwin, Robt. P.	"	"	" " " " " Mar. 18, 1848
Garrett, Hezekiah	"	"	" " " " " May 26, 1848
Lewis, Wm. W.	"	"	" " " " "
Pinckum, Owen	"	"	" " " " " Oct. 13, 1847

Died:

Name and Rank.	Place of Enlistment	Enrolled	Remarks.
Sergeant.		1847.	
Norris, James C.	Alton, Ill.	May 28	Died on march f'm Santa Fe, N.M., Aug. 30, '48.
Corporal.			
Askew, Wm. G.	"	"	Died at Santa Fe, N. M., May 25, 1848
Privates.			
Daniel, Nathan	"	"	Died at Santa Fe, N. M., Feb. 15, 1848
Davis, Elihu	"	M'y 30,'47	Joined Co. "H" Nov.,'47; died at Santa Fe in '48
Gaines, Joseph M.	"	M'y 28,'47	Died at Louis Lopez, N.M., Dec. 14, 1847
Keel, Ira	"	"	" " Santa Fe, N. M., Oct. 18, 1847
Mooneyham, Cal. I.	"	"	" " " " " Jan. 9, 1848
Norris, Henry C.	"	"	" " " " " Oct. 14, 1847
Odum, John L.	"	"	" " " " " May 9, 1848
Pike, John H.	"	"	" " Louis Lopez, N. M., Nov. 15, 1847
Ryan, William	"	"	" " Alton June 3, 1847

Transferred:

Name and Rank.	Place of Enlistment	Enrolled	Remarks.
		1847.	
Carlisle, Alex. M.	Alton, Ill.	May 28	Trans. to Co. "H" Nov. 1; order of Col. Newby
Newman, Wm. J.	"	"	" " " " " " " "
Wimms, Meredith	"	"	" " " " " " " "

This company was discharged Oct. 11, 1848, at Alton, Ill.

Company "C."

Name and Rank.	Place of Enlistment.	Enrolled	Remarks.
Captain.		1847.	
Vantrump Turner	Alton, Ill.	May 21	
First Lieutenant.			
Isham N. Haynie	"	"	
Second Lieutenants.			
Levi Wright	"	"	
Benj. F. Marshall	"	"	
Sergeants.			
Jesse M. Wade	"	"	
Longin J. Wnorowski	"	"	
James S. Martin	"	"	
Joseph Wham	"	"	

FIRST REGIMENT. 213

Name and Rank.	Place of Enlistment.	Enrolled	Remarks.
Corporals.		1847.	
James N. Barr	Alton, Ill	May 21	Private from enrollment to June 9, 1848
James Nelson	"	"	
Dwyer Tracey	"	"	
James M. B. Gaston	"	"	Private from enrollment to Feb. 6, 1848
Musicians.			
Cornelius N. Breese	"	"	Private from enrollment to March 5, 1848
Wm. N. Haynie	"	"	
Privates.			
Anglin, James G	"	"	
Adams, Nathan	"	"	
Anderson, James S	"	"	
Allman, Richard S	"	"	Sick in Hospital at Alton, from Oct. 11
Ashton, George W	"	"	
Buckhout Peter	"	"	
Beasley, Augustus W	"	"	
Beasley, Wm	"	"	
Barbee, Joseph A	"	"	
Bundy, Alexander	"	"	
Bundy, Wm. K	"	"	
Bundy, Isaac	"	"	
Blackburn, Barney L	"	"	
Cox, Oliver H. P	"	"	
Cutchin, Milton	"	"	
Chasteen, James M	"	"	
Denton, James W	"	"	
Elliott, Andrew	"	"	
Elston, William	"	"	
French, Marshall	"	"	
Hill, James McD	"	"	
Jones, Dennis G	"	"	
Jones, Jasper N	"	"	
Jackson, Wm	"	"	
King, Edmund	Belleville, Ill.	Feb., '48	Joined, a recruit, Aug. 14, 1848
Lester, Thomas B	Alton, Ill	May, '47	Act. Surg. with detachments of 3 and 5 Co's, [from Oct. 8, 1847, to Oct. 4, 1848.
Lester, John J	"	"	
Lewis, Wm. J	"	"	
Lature, Lewis	"	"	
Marshall, James A	"	"	
McColgan, Hamilton	"	"	
Mifford, Jacob C	"	"	
Morgan, William C	"	"	
McGuire, Joseph F	"	"	
Middleton, Geo. W	"	"	
Middleton, Pleasant	Belleville, Ill.	Mch., '48	Joined, a recruit, Aug. 14, 1848
Milliron, Ira A	Alton, Ill	May, '47	
McGregor, John	Ottawa, Ill	Feb., '48	Joined, a recruit, Aug. 14, 1848
Neel, Thomas	Alton, Ill	May, '47	
Nell, Wm. C	"	"	
Nelson, John R	"	"	
Parker, James	"	"	
Parryman, James L	"	"	
Pettus, Thomas G	"	"	
Roach, Wm. C	"	"	
Rainey, Samuel	"	"	
Rolan, Wm. E	"	"	
Richie, George D	Ottawa, Ill	Jan., '48	Joined, a recruit, Aug. 14, 1848
Songer, Wm. F	Alton, Ill	May, '47	
Smith, Solomon	"	"	
Smith, William	"	"	
Tully, John	"	"	
Torrence, John S	"	"	
Thomas, Charles	"	"	
Tyler, Joseph R	"	June, '47	
Vaughn, John P	"	May, '47	
Wham, John McN	"	"	
Wham, Robert McM	"	"	
Wham, Benj. A	"	"	
Winn, David A	"	"	
Walsh, Joshua B	"	"	
Wallis, Elijah	"	"	
White, John W	"	"	
Winn, John	Ottawa, Ill	Dec., '47	Joined, a recruit, Aug. 14, 1848

Died:

Name and Rank.	Place of Enlistment.	Enrolled	Remarks.
Corporal.		1847.	
James Cooper	Alton, Ill	May 21	Died at Santa Fe, N. M., Feb. 4, 1848
Privates.			
Baker, James	"	"	Died at Fort Leavenworth, July 14, 1847
Brazol, William	"	"	" " Aug. 19, 1847
Bass, William H	"	"	" Santa Fe, N. M., Jan. 11, 1848
Collins, John W	"	"	" *en route* to Santa Fe, N. M., July 14, 1847
Cheely, Fountain L	"	"	" at Santa Fe, N. M., Nov. 22, 1847
Easley, Robert	"	"	" *en route* to Santa Fe, N. M., Aug. 5, 1847
Jones, William W	"	"	" at Santa Fe, N. M., Sept. 29, 1847
Vaughn, Uriah	"	"	" Albuquerque, N. M., April 25, 1848
White, James H	"	"	" Santa Fe, N. M., Jan. 22, 1848
Wadkins, Joseph	"	"	" Fort Leavenworth, July 15, 1847

Discharged:

Name and Rank.	Place of Enlistment.	Enrolled	Remarks.
Corporal.		1847.	
Jesse Ray	Alton, Ill	May 21	Disch., disabil'y, Las Vegas, N. M., June 9, '48.
Privates.			
Bethard, John	"	"	Disch., disabil'y, Las Vegas, N. M., June 8, '48
Cox, James M	"	"	" " Albuquerque,N.M.,Apr.11, '48
Jones, Alexander	"	"	" " Santa Fe, N. M., Mch. 20, '48
Minard, Lorenzo	"	"	" " Albuquerque,N.M.,Apr.11, '48
Ray, Andrew	"	"	" " Las Vegas, N. M., June 8, '48
Whitlock, John M	"	"	" expir'n serv.,Santa Fe.,N.M.,Aug.14, '48
Wilson, Hartwell G	"	"	" " Las Vegas,N.M.,Aug.18,'48
Young, Zachariah	"	"	" disabil'y, Santa Fe, N. M., June 11, '48

Transferred:

Name and Rank.	Place of Enlistment.	Enrolled	Remarks.
Musician.		1847.	
Thomas W. Pace	Alton, Ill	May 21	App. Drum Maj. Mch. 5; trans. field and staff.
Private.			
Hend'son P. Boyakin	"	"	Elected Lieut.-Colonel June 8, 1847

This company was discharged at Alton, Ill., Oct. 13, 1848.

Company "D."

Name and Rank.	Place of Enlistment.	Enrolled	Remarks.
Captains.		1847.	
Edward W. B. Newby	Alton, Ill	May 22	Elected Col. of Regiment, at Alton, June 8, '47
John C. Moses	"	"	Was 1st Sergt. from enrollment to June 9
First Lieutenant.			
George A. Keith	"	"	
Second Lieutenants.			
James H. Easley	"	"	
Sam'l B. Alexander	"	"	
Sergeants.			
William E. Oscar	"	"	Was private from enrollment to June 9
Thomas B. Love	"	"	
Emesley Harris	"	"	
James T. Brooks	"	"	

FIRST REGIMENT.

Name and Rank.	Place of Enlistment.	Enrolled	Remarks.
Corporals.		1847.	
Alexander Parker.	Alton, Ill.	May 29	
Thomas M. Roberts	"	"	
Calvin H. Wilson	"	"	Was private from enrollment to December 4.
Thomas Dragoo	"	"	
Musicians.			
Eli Dennis	"	"	
Mathew Johnson	"	"	
Privates.			
Angle, Joshua	"	"	
Adams, Thomas D	"	"	
Briscoe, William H	"	"	
Bass, George W	"	"	
Burk, George J	"	"	
Berry, William C	"	"	
Baker, Jacob	"	"	
Barker, Comfort W	"	"	
Coppage, Joseph W	"	"	
Clark, George W	"	"	
Carter, Joseph R	"	"	
Dolton, John W	"	"	
Davis, George W	"	"	
Emery, John T	"	"	
Forsythe, William	"	"	
Fuller, Bradford	"	"	
Glenn, Samuel R	"	"	
Gibson, Thomas	"	"	
Grant, Hardin H	"	"	
Giddings, George H	"	"	
Gaston, William	"	"	
Hansell, Nathaniel	Ottawa, Ill.	"	Joined, a recruit, August 1, 1848.
Higgins, Clark B	Alton, Ill.	"	
Hunt, William	"	"	
House, John	"	"	
Hills, Richard	"	"	
Heddleton, John	"	"	
Ingles, Noah	"	"	
Ishmael, William S	"	"	
King, James M	"	"	
Kendrick, George W	"	"	
Kelly, Isaac			
Lake, Myron	Ottawa, Ill.	Feb., '48	Joined, a recruit, August 1, 1848.
Lomax, John	Alton, Ill.	May, '47	
McCauly, Andrew	"	"	
McMeans, John	"	"	
McLane, John E	"	"	
Nix, Jasper L	"	"	
Parker, Orlando M	"	"	
Parker, Newborn P	"	"	
Preston, Lyman	"	"	
Preston, James H	"	"	
Pitchford, William H	"	"	
Roberts, Silas H	"	"	
Rainey, Abram C	"	June, '47	
Starks, John	"	May, '47	
Smith, James J	"	"	
Smith, John	"	"	
Simons, David B	"	"	
Steel, James M	"	"	Was Corporal from enrollment to Dec. 4.
Shober, John L	"	"	
Taulbee, Daniel	"	"	
Taylor, John H	"	"	
Vanwey, Charles	"	"	
Wilson, Cavil K	"	"	
Woods, Joseph	"	"	
Wells, James F	"	"	
Watts, John	"	"	
White, Edmond R	"	"	
Walker, John M	"	"	
Died:			
Angel, Thomas	Alton, Ill.	May, '47	Died at Santa Fe, N. M., Sept. 28, 1847
Bostick, John	"	"	" Jemez, N. M., May 28, 1848
Green, Augustus	"	"	Died near Albuquerque, N. M., Nov. 9, 1847
Huffman, Samuel	"	"	" at Santa Fe, N. M., Oct. 15, 1847
McDiggins, John	"	"	" Fort Leavenworth June 27, 1847
Nowles, John	"	"	" Santa Fe, N. M., May 17, 1848
Putnam, Johnson K	"	"	" " " October 16, 1847
Phillips, Joseph H	"	"	" " " " 18, 1847

Discharged:

Name and Rank.	Place of Enlistment.	Enrolled	Remarks.
		1847.	
Bennett, Hiram	Alton, Ill	May 22	Disch., disabil'y, at Ft. Leavenw'th, Aug. 19, '47
Bowen, John M	"	"	" " at Santa Fe, May 29, 1848.
Davis, Hiram	"	"	Drummed out of servce at Santa Fe June 14, '48
Harriss, John	"	"	Disch., disability, at Santa Fe, March 20, 1848.
Hamilton, Horatio J.	"	"	" " at Las Vegas, June 8, 1848.
Langly, James R	"	"	" at Santa Fe, expiration serv., Aug. 10.
Lewis, Jacob	"	"	" disabil'y, at Ft. Leavenw'th, Aug. 21, '47
Nunn, Henry	"	"	" at Santa Fe, expiration serv., Aug. 10.
Phillips, James G.	"	"	
Raymond, Charles L.	"	"	" disability, at Santa Fe, March 8, 1848.
Studdy, John J	"	"	" Ft. Leavenw'th, Aug. 24, '47
Salmon, H. P	Ottawa, Ill	Jan., '48	" at Santa Fe, expiration serv., Aug. 10.
Taylor, William	Alton, Ill	May, '47	" disability, at Santa Fe, May 29, 1848.
Vansickle, Samuel B.	"	"	" at Las Vegas, June 8
Waldon, Eli W	"	"	" at Santa Fe, expiration serv., Aug. 10.

This company was discharged at Alton, Illinois, October 12, 1848.

Company "E."

Name and Rank.	Residence.	Enrolled	Remarks.
Captains.		1847.	
G. W. Hook	Alton, Ill.	May 26	
First Lieutenant.			
William H. Snyder	"	"	
Second Lieutenants.			
Enoch Lucky	"	"	
John T. Damron	Marion, Ill.	"	Died at Santa Fe, N. M., Dec. 28
Robert Beer	Belleville, Ill	"	Sergeant from enrollment to Dec. 28
Sergeants.			
William H. Bennett	"	"	
William S. Flemming	"	"	
Thomas J. Aliff	"	"	
James A. Etter	"	"	
Corporals.			
Rand'lph C. Goddard	Marion, Ill.	"	
John A. Parker	Belleville, Ill	"	
Augustus K. Askey	Marion, Ill.	"	
John A. J. Bragg	Belleville, Ill	"	
Musicians.			
Benjamin F. Jones	"	"	
Stephen Cooper	"	"	
Privates.			
Boyd, William R	"	"	
Bonham, James	"	"	
Briggs, Charles	"	"	
Brazewell, George A	"	"	
Badgly, Abijah	"	"	
Beattie, Francis H	"	"	
Beavers, Charles W	"	"	
Bullock, John W	Marion, Ill	"	
Burns, Elijah	"	"	
Badger, Chester	Ottawa, Ill.	Feb., '48	Joined, a recruit, Aug. 5
Belle, George	"	Jan., '48	" " "
Beeler, Isaiah	"	Feb., '48	" " "
Collard, John C. C.	Belleville, Ill	May, '47	
Carlisle, James W	"	"	
Cookingham, Uri J	"	"	
Carroll, Hezekiah	"	"	
Cobrenger, Joseph	"	"	
Crocker, George W.	"	"	
Due, John P	"	"	

FIRST REGIMENT.

Name and Rank.	Place of Enlistment.	Enrolled	Remarks.
		1847.	
Deobalt, John	Belleville, Ill	May 26	
Dietrich, Andrew	"	"	
Dingle, Jonathan	"	"	
Damron, Walt. M. C.	Marion, Ill.	"	
Drew, William	Belleville, Ill	"	
Epperson, Richard	Marion, Ill.	"	
Fitzgerald, James	Belleville, Ill	"	
Goddard, William E.	Marion, Ill.	"	
Gibbons, John	Belleville, Ill	"	
Harlow, Thomas F.	"	Feb., '48	Joined, a recruit, Aug. 5
Heath, William H.	"	May, '47	
Hendricks, Thomas J	"	"	
Hawkins, General L.	"	"	
Jones, George W.	Ottawa, Ill	Feb., '48	Joined, a recruit, Aug. 5
Kable, Nicholas	Belleville, Ill	May, '47	
Koekler, Henry	"	"	
Kimble, John	"	"	
Keeler, Francis	Ottawa, Ill	Mar., '48	Joined, a recruit, Aug. 5
Lacey, Franklin	Belleville, Ill	May, '47	
Lunceford, Isaac	"	"	
Longdow, Andrew	Las Vegas, NM	July, '48	Joined, a recruit, July 13.
Lawrence, George	Belleville, Ill	Feb., 48	" " Aug. 5
McKenzie, Elijah	Las Vegas, NM	July, '48	" " July 10
Mottzfelt, John	Belleville, Ill	Feb., '48	" " Aug. 5
Majors, Huling	"	May, '47	
Peck, John Q. A.	"	"	
Polson, Richard	"	"	
Rung, Jacob	"	"	
Reed, James	Marion, Ill.	"	Transferred to Co. "B" June 27, 1847.
Russell, Robert R.	Belleville, Ill	"	
Springs, Samuel	Marion, Ill.	"	
Springs, Josephus	"	"	
Shefter, George T.	Belleville, Ill	"	
Stilson, Leonard	Ottawa, Ill.	Dec., '47	Joined, a recruit, Aug. 5.
Stattman, Franklin	Belleville, Ill	Feb., '48	" " "
Smith, Oziel G.	"	Feb., '48	
Sterrick, Charles T.	"	May, '47	
Triplett, William	"	"	
Talbott, Jesse	"	"	
Whitesides, Joseph F.	"	"	
Woolley, William A.	"	"	
West, Frederick	"	"	
Wheeler, Martin	"	"	
Warton, Samuel	"	"	
Whitney, David	Ottawa, Ill.	Mar., '48	Joined, a recruit, Aug. 5
Webb, Adams	Belleville, Ill	Mar., '48	" " "
Weisenbach, George	"	Mar., '48	

Died:

Corporals.		1847.	
Andrew J. Davis	Belleville, Ill	May 26	Died at Las Vegas, N. M., April 13
Josiah Mullen	"	"	" " " Feb. 9
Privates.			
Allen, Thomas J.	"	"	Died at Las Vegas, N. M., Feb. 19
Brown, Franklin J.	Marion, Ill.	"	" Santa Fe, Sept. 27
Berry, Charles B.	Belleville, Ill	"	" " Nov. 7
Bragg, William	"	"	" Las Vegas, " Feb. 9
Crocker, Jesse W.	"	"	" Santa Fe, " Oct. 19
Campbell, Aaron J.	Marion, Ill.	"	" Fish C'k, *en route* for Santa Fe, July 20
Crabb, Thomas H.	Belleville, Ill	"	" Alton, Ill., June 11, 1847
Earl, Francis M.	"	"	" Santa Fe, N. M., Oct. 15
Gascil, Thomas	"	"	" " " Dec. 30
Lively, William	"	"	" " " Dec. 12
Maxwell, John	"	"	" " " Feb. 7
Turner, William	"	"	" Cedar Sp'gs, *en route* Santa Fe, Aug. 28
Vandyde, Theodore	"	"	" Santa Fe, N. M., Jan. 12

Discharged:

Name and Rank.	Place of Enlistment.	Enrolled	Remarks.
Sergeant.		1847.	
Thomas J. Ward	Marion, Ill.	May 26	App'd July 7; disch., disability, Las Vegas, N. M
Privates.			
Buckner, William O.	"	"	Disch., disability, at Las Vegas, N. M., April 26
Case, Coe W.	Belleville, Ill	"	" " Santa Fe, " May 27.
Hurley, Tilman	"	"	" " Las Vegas, " April 26
Layman, Jackson	"	"	" " Ft. Leavenworth, July 7.
Morray, James B.	Marion, Ill.	"	" " " "
McDaniel, Abednego	"	"	" " Las Vegas, N. M., April 26
Roberts, Lewis L.	Santa Fe, N. M	Nov. 27	" exp. service, " Aug. 18, '48
Swift, John W.	Belleville, Ill	May 26	" disability, " April 26
Stephenson, William	Marion, Ill.	"	" " " "
Spaunhorst, Frederic	Belleville, Ill	"	" " " "
Vanorsdoll, Knowles	"	"	" " Ft. Leavenworth, July 7.

Deserted:

		1847.	
Christian, William	Belleville, Ill	May 26	Deserted June 16, 1847, at Alton, Ill.
Farquer, John W.	"	"	" " 19, " "
Lincoln, Robert	"	"	" April 13, 1848, at Jefferson B'cks, Mo

This company was mustered out on Oct. 14, 1848, at Alton, Ill.

COMPANY "F."

Name and Rank.	Place of Enlistment.	Enrolled	Remarks.
Captain.		1847.	
Thos. B. Kinney	Alton, Ill.	May 31	
First Lieutenants.			
Murray F. Tuley	"	"	Disch. by resignation, at Santa Fe, Aug. 15.
Alban V. Morey	"	"	Elected f'm 1st Sergt. Aug. 19, *vice* Tuley res'd
Second Lieutenants.			
R. N. Hamilton	"	"	Detached serv., Act. A. Q. M. from July 16, '47.
James M. Hunt	"	"	Disch. by resignation, at Santa Fe, Aug. 15.
John A. Knights	"	"	Elected from Sergeant Aug. 19.
Sergeants.			
William Forsyth	"	"	Appointed from private Aug. 19.
Geo. E. Brinsmaid	"	"	Was Corporal from enrollment to June 2, '47.
Charles C. P. Holden	"	"	Promoted from Corporal Aug. 19.
Albert S. Woodford	"	"	Appointed from private Aug. 19.
Corporals.			
Geo. Hewitt	"	"	
Davenport Morey	"	"	
Asa H. Cochran	"	"	
James Rote	"	"	Appointed from private Aug. 19.
Fifer.			
Charles Styles	"	"	
Privates.			
Anderson, Ashley	"	"	
Brunker, Brabson W	"	"	
Bour, John M.	"	"	
Burns, John	"	"	
Barnum, Nelson	"	"	
Case, Geo. W.	"	"	
Danforth, Richm'd S	"	"	
Foster, James	"	"	
Gregg, William P.	"	"	

Name and Rank.	Place of Enlistment.	Enrolled	Remarks.
		1847.	
Gurrad, John P	Alton, Ill	May 31	
Griffith, Amos N	"	June 14	
Gardner, Joseph	"	May 31	
Herrick, Lyman	"	"	
Hall, Harvey	"	"	
Huntington, Seth P.	"	"	
Huntley, Daniel	"	"	
Halleck, Alanson	"	"	
Hagan, Edward	Ottawa, Ill	Jan, '48	Joined, a recruit, Aug. 1
Johnson, Iver	Alton, Ill	May, '47	
Kratzer, Frederick	"	"	
Lahr, Henry	"	"	
Lord, Rufus	Ottawa, Ill	Feb., '48	Joined, a recruit, Aug. 1
Matthews, Wm	Alton, Ill	May, '47	
Mudge, Wm	"	"	
Morrison, Morris H.	"	"	
Morrison, Joshua	Ottawa, Ill	Feb., '48	Joined, a recruit, Aug. 1
McCully, David A	Alton, Ill	May, '47	
Martin, Wm	"	"	
McClain, Wm	"	"	
Michael, Theophilus	"	"	
Napier, Dwight	Ottawa, Ill	Jan., '48	Joined, a recruit, Aug. 1
Ramsden, James V.	Alton, Ill	May, '47	(no individual disch. made.
Rodholtz, Nicholas	"	"	Left boat on pas'ge down Missouri riv., Oct. 2;
Riley, Thomas	Ottawa, Ill	Feb., '48	Joined, a recruit, Aug. 1
Stroh, Gotrich	Alton, Ill	May, '47	
Seidler, Augustus H.	"	"	
Snight, Henry	"	"	
Thornton, Freeman.	"	"	
Tappin, Alex. H	"	"	
Utho, Christopher F.	"	"	
Wiley, Adam	"	"	
Watson, Wm. A	"	"	
Warren, Wm. E	"	"	
Warren, June	"	"	
Warren, James	"	"	
Williams, Juno	"	"	
Young, James C	"	"	

Discharged:

		1847.	
Sergeant. John D. Goodrich	Alton, Ill	May 31	Disch. by expir'n of serv. Aug. 9, '48, Santa Fe.
Drummer. George Cannon	"	"	Disch. by expir'n of serv. Aug. 9, '48, Santa Fe.
Privates. Brown, Erastus D	"	"	Disch. July 20, '47, Ft. Leavenworth; disabil'y
Backman, Peter	"	"	" by expir'n of serv. Aug. 11, '48, Santa Fe.
Eberhard, August	"	"	" Mar. 5, '48, at Santa Fe; disability
Emory, Stephen	"	"	" by expir'n of serv. Aug. 9, '48, Santa Fe.
Huginin, James R	"	"	" " " 11 "
Hipwell, John W	"	"	" " " 9 "
Kensling, Jacob	"	"	
Loring, Lorenzo D	"	"	" Feb. 9, '48, at Santa Fe; disability
Martin, Orange C	"	"	" Mar. 19, '48, " " "
Morteller, George	"	"	" Mar. 20, '48, " " "
Morgan, James D	"	"	" by expir'n of serv. Aug. 9, '48, Santa Fe.
Maynard, Lorenzo D	"	"	" " " "
McCormack, Chas. J	"	"	" " " Aug. 11, '48 "
Fage, Phineas	"	"	
Rolph, John S	"	"	Left sick at Las Vegas; supposed discharged
Reinhard, Valentine	"	"	Disch. by expir'n of serv. Aug. 9, '48, Santa Fe.
Shepard, Julius C	"	"	" " " "
Shaw, Julius C	"	"	" " " "
Seacon, Thomas	"	"	" July 5, '48, at Santa Fe; disability
Strebel, John W	"	"	" Mar. 6, '48, " " "
Vantassel, Levi R	"	"	" by expir'n of serv. Aug. 9, '48, Santa Fe.
Wilson, James	"	"	" Oct. 10, '47, at Santa Fe; disability
Whitbeck, Seymour.	"	"	" July 15, '47, " " "

Died:

Name and Rank.	Place of Enlistment.	Enrolled	Remarks.
		1847.	
Allen, James H	Alton, Ill	May 31	Died at Sabinal, N. M., Dec. 10 1847
Black, Wm. H	"	June 14	" Santa Fe, Oct. 9, 1847
Croft, Robert	"	May 31	" Ft. Leavenworth, 1847
Daniels, Wm	"	"	" en route to Santa Fe, Aug. 19. 1847
Godfrey, James H	"	"	" at Santa Fe, Jan. 29, 1848
Hattendorf, Hendr'k	"	"	Drowned in the Miss. river, June 11, 1847
Pratt, Spencer	"	"	Died at Santa Fe, Sept. 19, 1847
Pool, Edgar	"	"	" " Sept. 30, 1847
Styles, Jeremiah	"	"	" " Nov. 3, 1847
Wheat, John W	"	"	" " Sept. 29, 1847

Deserted:

Name and Rank.	Place of Enlistment.	Enrolled	Remarks.
Sergeant.		1847.	
Luther G. Hager	Alton, Ill	May 31	Deserted at Alton, June 12, 1847
Privates.			
Freeman, Alexander			Deserted at Alton, June 17, 1847
Martin, Daniel			Deserted en route to Santa Fe, July 26, 1847

This company was mustered out Oct. 18, 1848, at Alton, Ill.

Company "G."

Name and Rank.	Place of Enlistment.	Enrolled	Remarks.
Captain.		1847.	
Henry J. Reed	Alton, Ill	June 1	
First Lieutenant.			
Relly Madeson	"	"	
Second Lieutenants.			
James Tebay	"	"	
Simon Lundry	"	"	
Sergeants.			
Clement L. Lakins	"	"	Appointed Sergt. Aug. 9, vice Mosten
Ceap. H. Washburn	"	"	
Hiram M. Morse	"	"	Promoted from Corporal Aug. 9
Henry Berklin	"	"	
Corporals.			
Mason B. Kelly	"	"	Appointed from private Aug. 9
William A. Clements	"	"	" " " "
George Rinchart	SantaFe,N.M.	Nov. 26	" " " " 14
Mitchel T. Brewster	Alton, Ill	June 1	" " " " 9
Fifer.			
Jackson Reed	"	"	
Privates.			
Anderson, William	"	"	
Barnard, George	"	"	
Baker, Perry	"	"	
Braun, Noble J	"	"	
Carter, Benjamin F	"	"	
Cavanaugh, Luke	"	"	
Craig, Samuel	"	"	
Corbin, William	"	"	
Corbin, Elias	Ottawa, Ill	Jan., '48	Joined, a recruit, Aug. 1, 1848
Davis, Gordon	Alton, Ill	June, '47	Left sick at Ft. Leavenworth May 22
Denmick, Harmon	"	"	
Davenport, John	"	"	
Dobbs, Thomas	"	"	

FIRST REGIMENT.

Name and Rank.	Place of Enlistment.	Enrolled	Remarks.
		1847.	
Evey, Joseph	Alton, Ill	June 1	
Ellixson, Lars	"	"	
Ferguson, John	"	"	
Graham, William	"	"	
Gibson, John F	"	"	
Gibson, George	Ottawa, Ill	Feb., '48	Joined, a recruit, Aug. 1, 1848.
Gibson, Theodore	"	"	
Hoxie, Joshua	Alton, Ill	June, '47	
Hayes, James	"	"	
Haight, Josiah	"	"	
Hays, Seeley, Jr	"	"	
Hardin, Elihu	"	"	
Hopper, Dudley	"	"	
Henry, Francis	SantaFe, N.M.	Nov., '47	
Helton, Oliver P	Alton, Ill	June, '47	
Love, Warren	"	"	
McHale, Michael	"	"	
Maxey, Peter	"	"	
Moore, Joseph	"	"	
Martin, Robert N	"	"	
Overacre, Franklin	"	"	
Pheps, Orvill	"	"	
Pratt, Thomas A	"	"	
Seaman, Francis	"	"	
Stone, William	"	"	
Scott, William	"	"	
Tripp, John	"	"	
Thompson, John	"	"	
Tresner, John	"	"	
VanKleeck, Wm. H	SantaFe, N.M.	Nov., '47	
Ward, Harvey B	Alton, Ill	June, '47	
Weeks, Thomas	"	"	
Woodruff, Joseph	Ottawa, Ill	Jan., '48	Joined, a recruit, Aug. 1
Watkins, James	Alton, Ill	June, '47	
Yeigh, John	"	"	

Died:

		1847.	
Corporal.			
Joab Kelly	Alton, Ill	June 1	Died at Santa Fe March 16, 1848
Privates.			
Blackman, David S	"	"	Died at Santa Fe Oct. 1, 1847
Carr, James	"	"	" " Oct. 11, 1847
Cochran, Cornelius	"	"	" " Oct. 27, 1847
Clark, Lewis M	"	"	" " May 1, 1848
Davis, Orson	"	"	" " May 22, 1848
Moore, Peter	"	"	" " April 26, 1848
Martin, Charles	"	"	" " Nov. 18, 1847
McCarty, Michael	"	"	" " Nov. 28, 1847
Watson, James	"	"	" " March 22, 1848
Tresnor, Harvey	"	"	Died on march from Ft. Leavenw'h to S. Fe.

Discharged:

		1847.	
Sergeants.			
John Mosten	Alton, Ill	June 1	Disch. at Santa Fe on expir'n of serv., Aug. 9.
Oscar F. Barnes	"	"	
Corporal.			
John Mosley	"	"	Disch. at Santa Fe on expir'n of serv., Aug. 9.
Drummer.			
Henry Crain	"	"	Disch. at Santa Fe on expir'n of serv., Aug. 9.
Privates.			
Austin, Samuel	"	"	Disch. at Santa Fe on expir'n of serv., Aug. 9.
Anderson, John	"	"	
Barnes, Oliver C	"	"	Disch. on Surg. cert. of disability Mch. 7, '48
Brennon, John	"	"	
Betvey, Joseph, Jr	"	"	" at Santa Fe, expir'n of service, Aug. 6.
Fisher, John W	"	"	" on Surg. cert. of disability Mch. 7, '48
Foy, Michael	"	"	" In disgrace at Santa Fe, June 14, '48
Flick, David	"	"	" at Santa Fe, expir'n of service, Aug. 9.
Harris, Joseph	"	"	" on Surg. cert. of disability July 7, '48

Name and Rank.	Place of Enlistment.	Enrolled	Remarks.
		1847.	
Lawrence, Daniel N.	Alton, Ill	June 1	Disch. at Santa Fe, expir'n of serv., Aug. 9
Littrick, John	"	"	" " " " " " "
Lee, John	"	"	" " " " " " "
McHenry, Thomas	"	"	" " " " " " "
Rood, Daniel L.	"	"	" " " " " " Aug. 14, '48
Smith, William	"	"	" " " " " " 9, '48
Stafford, Jacob E.	"	"	" in disgrace Oct. 16, 1847
Tucker, Henry	"	"	" at Santa Fe, expir'n of serv., Aug. 9, '48
Thompson, William	"	"	" " " " " "
Wilson, James	"	"	" " " " " "

Deserted:

		1847.	
Atkins, John N.	Alton, Ill	June 1	Deserted at Alton June 18, 1848
Adams, Charles	"	"	" on march to Santa Fe July 25, 1847
Bennett, Tolytus	"	"	" at Ft. Leavenworth July 9, 1847
Rogerson, Charles	"	"	" " "
Stilson, Lyman	"	"	" " July 18, 1847
Springstead, Alberon	"	"	" " "
Washburn, Daniel	"	"	" at Alton, Ill., June 19, 1847

This company was mustered out Oct. 17, 1848, at Alton, Ill.

Company "H."

Name and Rank.	Place of Enlistment.	Enrolled	Remarks.
Captain.		1847.	
James Hampton	Alton, Ill	May 29	
First Lieutenant.			
James J. Provost	"	"	
Second Lieutenants.			
John A. Logan	"	"	
James Willis	"	"	
Sergeants.			
Lindorff Osborne	"	"	
Geo. W. Peninger	"	"	Private from enrollment to Oct. 1, 1847
John W. Grammar	"	"	" " " July 10, 1847
Samuel Carlisle	"	"	
Corporals.			
Wm. Hagler	"	"	Private to April 1, 1848
Jordan L. Randall	"	"	
Wm. Brown	"	"	Private to Oct 4, 1847
Wm. Hampton	"	"	" " "
Musicians.			
James Y. Wilkins	"	"	Private to July 15, 1847
Jonas Mangold	"	"	
Privates.			
Alvord, Leroy	Ottawa, Ill	Feb., '48	Joined, a recruit, Aug. 5
Burks, James	Alton, Ill	May, '49	
Bond, Stephen	"	"	
Brandon, Hugh G.	"	"	
Bramlet, John D.	"	"	
Deaver, Eli	"	"	
Broomfield, James	"	"	
Bishop, Thomas	"	"	
Black, George W.	"	"	
Buckles, John J.	"	"	

FIRST REGIMENT.

Name and Rank.	Place of Enlistment.	Enrolled	Remarks.
Beeker, Henry	Ottawa, Ill.	Feb., '48	Joined, a recruit, Aug. 5
Brown, Peter	"	"	" " "
Brunse, Henry	"	"	" " "
Conrad, Geo			
Carlisle, Alex. M	Alton, Ill.	May, '47	
Carr, John	"	"	
Childers, Geo	"	"	
Cuteral, John G.	"	"	
Cable, Michael	"	"	
Christy, David	"	"	
Campbell, John	"	"	
Cotner, Jacob	"	"	
Clark, John			
Doer, Francis	Ottawa, Ill.	Feb., '48	Joined, a recruit, Aug. 5
Diedrock, Christain	"	"	
DeGroat, Wm	Alton, Ill.	May, '47	
Dunn, James	"	"	
Dunn, Absalom	"	"	
Davis, James M	"	"	
Dunn, Wm. E.			
Ehli, Joseph	Ottawa, Ill.	Feb., '48	Joined, a recruit, Aug. 5
Fox, Andrew J	Alton, Ill.	May, '47	
Glen, John E.	"	"	
Grable, John M	"	"	
Grable, Israel	"	"	
Grable, Eli	"	"	Sick in Hospital at Alton from Oct. 8
Goodman, Josiah	"		
Gordon, James P	"		
Herald, John H	"	"	
Hicks, Harrison	"	"	
Hall, James H	"	"	
Lightner, James	"	"	
Mings, James	"	"	
Mings, William	"	"	
Miller, Ezekiel	"	"	
McAnelly, Charles	"	"	
Moor, William			
Miller, James	Ottawa, Ill.	Feb., '48	Joined, a recruit, Aug. 5
Newman, Wm. J	Alton, Ill.	May, '47	
Owens, William	"	"	
Odle, Isaac			
Pike, Seth	Ottawa, Ill.	Jan., '48	Joined, a recruit, Aug. 5
Ramsey, Wm. T	Santa Fe, N.M.	Nov., '47	
Scarlet, John	Alton, Ill.	May, '47	
Sorrels, John	"	"	
Spindler, Frederick	Ottawa, Ill.	Feb., '48	Joined, a recruit, Aug. 5
Strawn, Wm	"	"	" " "
Thompson, John L.	"	"	" " "
Titsel, Wm.	"	"	" " "
Taylor, Charles	"	Mch., '48	
Wimms, Meredith	Alton, Ill.	May, '47	
Walker, Napoleon B.	"	"	
Williamson, John	"	"	
West, Andrew	"	"	
Wagner, Louis	"	"	
Willis, Carroll	"	"	

Died:

		1847.	
Sergeant.			
John W. Pemberton	Alton, Ill.	May 29	Died at Santa Fe, N. M., Oct. 31, 1847
Privates.			
Carr, Wm. A	"	"	Died at Santa Fe, N. M., Oct. 6, 1847
Eakin, James M	"	"	" Las Vegas, N. M., April 9, 1848
Ferguson, John D	"	"	" Santa Fe, N. M., Jan. 14, 1848
Gill, Hardimon	"	"	" " " Oct. 18, 1847
Herron, Samuel M	"	"	" " " Nov. 5, 1847
Hall, David	"	"	" " " Jan. 8, 1848
Jones, Wm	"	"	" Ft. Leavenworth, Mo., July 20, 1847
Keiger, Thomas D	"	"	" Santa Fe, N. M., Nov. 4, 1847
McCarty, Daniel	"	"	" Ft. Leavenworth, Mo., July 5, 1847 9, "
Morrow, Thomas W	"	"	
McCord, Richard W	"	"	" Santa Fe, N. M., Nov. 6, 1847
Morrow, John B	"	"	" Las Vegas, N. M., Feb. 9, 1848
Pearson, Thomas	"	"	" " " Mch. 11, 1848
Penrod, Jacob	"	"	" Ft. Leavenworth, Mo., July 19, 1847
Sitter, Simon P	"	"	" Santa Fe, N. M., Dec. 17, 1847

Discharged:

Name and Rank.	Place of Enlistment.	Enrolled	Remarks.
Musician.		1847.	
Emanuel Penrod	Alton, Ill.	May 29	Disch., Surg. cert. disabil'y, Ft. Leavenworth
Privates.			
Bramlet, Ambrose	"	"	Disch., Surg. cert. disabil'y, Ft. Leavenworth
Carr, James	"	"	" April 26, '48, Las Vegas, disability
Greene, Thomas S.	"	"	" " " " "
Gates, Wm.	"	"	
Hampton, Robt. P.	"	"	" June 10, " " " "
Hampton, Wade	"	"	" " " " "
Jones, Benj. F.	"	"	Surg. cert. disabil'y, Ft. Leavenworth
Keiger, Jacob B.	"	"	April 20, '48, Las Vegas, disability
McAnnelly, John	"	"	June 10, " " "
Robinson, John W.	"	"	April 26, " " " "
Turk, Joseph	"	"	

Transferred:

Name and Rank.	Place of Enlistment.	Enrolled	Remarks.
		1847.	
Davis, Elihu W.	Alton, Ill.	May 29	Transferred to Co. "B," Oct. 30, 1847
Herron, Joseph	"	"	" " " " "
Sanders, Luke R.	"	"	" " " " "

Deserted:

Name and Rank.	Place of Enlistment.	Enrolled	Remarks.
		1847.	
Sipe, Tilman	Alton, Ill.	May 29	Deserted July 22, 1847, at Ft. Leavenworth

*This company was discharged at Alton, Ill., October 16, 1848.

Company "I."

Name and Rank.	Place of Enlistment.	Enrolled	Remarks.
Captains.		1847.	
Franklin Niles	Alton, Ill.	June 2	Died at 110 Creek, near Ft. Leav'th, July 24,'47
John H. Adams	"	"	1st Lieut. from enrollment till July 28, 1847
First Lieutenant.			
Aaron D. Treadway	"	"	2d Lieut. from enrollment till July 28, 1847
Second Lieutenants.			
Thos. McDowell	"	"	2d Lieut. from enrollment till July 28, 1847
Jacob Brott	"	"	Private " " " " "
Sergeants.			
Alexander Craig	"	"	
William H. Starr	"	"	Appointed from private May 1, 1848
Sylvester W. Bell	"	"	
Dan'l W. Henderson	"	"	
Corporals.			
Wm. Harrison	"	"	
Lemuel Southard	"	"	
John Mise	"	"	
David R. Sparks	"	"	
Drummer.			
James Conner	"	"	

FIRST REGIMENT.

Name and Rank.	Place of Enlistment.	Enrolled	Remarks.
Privates.			
Arnold, Lerry	Ottawa, Ill.	Feb., '48	Joined, a recruit, Aug. 15
Caulk, Joshua C	Alton, Ill.	June, '47	
Caldwell, Wm. C	"	"	
Cowell, Benj. F	"	"	
Carter, Daniel	"	"	
Delaney, John	"	"	
Dougherty, John	"	"	
Davis, John	"	"	
Davis, Alfred M	"	"	
Dixon, Ambrose	"	"	
Dush, Geo. S	"	"	
Eldridge, John	"	"	
Evans, Wm. B	"	"	
Elworthy, Walter	"	"	
Fletcher, Paulis E	"	"	
Foster, George J	"	"	
Gaskill, John Q. A	"	"	
Hodgins, Henry	Ottawa, Ill.	Mch., '48	Joined, a recruit, Aug. 15
Herrington, Harris'n	Alton, Ill.	June, '47	
Hodgman, Amos	"	"	
Humphries, Charles	"	"	
Hartman, Louis	"	"	
Haxwell, Ludrick	"	"	
Huntermark, Henry	"	"	
Herrin, Gorden	"	"	
Hocking, Ashberry	"	"	
Herrin, John	"	"	
Hamby, Jacob	"	"	
Hocking, Giles W	"	"	
Herrin, Henry	"	"	
Jett, Benj. F	"	"	
Johnson, Samuel	"	"	
Keho, Joseph	"	"	
Laport, Alonso	Ottawa, Ill.	Mch., '48	Joined, a recruit, Aug. 15
Lamoin, Eloaser	"	"	
Lewis, Richard C	Alton, Ill.	June, '47	
Lawrence, James	"	"	
Loveless, John	"	"	
Little, Wm. A	"	"	
Little, Edward	"	"	Reduced from 2d Sergt. April 27
Marlow, Abraham	"	"	
Merry, Wm. H	"	"	
Pool, Hughy	"	"	
Potter, Theron	Ottawa, Ill.	Mch., '48	Joined, a recruit, Aug. 15
Robbins, Oliver	Alton, Ill.	June, '47	
Sweet, Peleg	Ottawa, Ill.	Mch., '48	Joined, a recruit, Aug. 15
Smith, James H	Alton, Ill.	June, '47	
Seybolds, James	"	"	
Scroggins, Wm	"	"	
Scott, Joseph	"	"	
Sweeney, Nelson D	"	"	
Turner, James W	"	"	
Walden, Frederick	"	"	
Walker, Newton	"	"	
Washburn, Elijah	"	"	
Walker, Andrew	Ottawa, Ill.	Mch., '48	Joined, a recruit, Aug. 15
Wheeler, Wm. E	Belleville, Ill.	"	

Died:

		1847.	
Blevins, Elihu	Alton, Ill.	June 2	Died at Savannah, N. M., Nov. 19, 1847
Cook, John	"	"	Santa Fe, N. M., Nov. 27, 1847
Cowell, Thomas D	"	"	San Antonio, N. M., Dec. 15, 1847
Cave, John	"	"	Santa Fe, N. M., Jan. 19, 1848
Enstein, Balsom	"	"	" Oct. 26, 1847
Evans, Ellis	"	"	Alton, Ill., June 19, 1847
Fetterling, Casper	"	"	Albuquerque, N. M., Nov. 6, 1847
Grant, Daniel	"	"	Secora, N. M., Jan. 6, 1848
Jewitt, John	"	"	Died on march to Santa Fe Sept. 17, 1847
McBroom, John	"	"	Died at Santa Fe, N. M., Dec. 12, 1847
Miller, James C	"	Feb.	" " " Feb. 12, 1848
Ossel, John	"	"	" " " March 3, 1848
Purviance, Samuel	"	"	Died near Secora, N. M., Dec. 1 1847
Scroggins, Jackson	"	"	Died at Santa Fe, N. M., Feb. 7, 1848
Vinson, James	"	"	" " " Sept. 24, 1847

—15

MEXICAN WAR.

Discharged:

Name and Rank.	Place of Enlistment.	Enrolled	Remarks.
Fifer. Robert Weeks	Alton, Ill.	1847. June 2	Disch., Las Vegas, N.M., June 10, '48; disability
Privates. Brown, James	"	"	Disch., Albuquerque, N.M., Apr. 12, '48; disabil.
Cox, Peter H.	"	"	" Las Vegas, N.M., June 10, '48; disability
Grant, Dreury H.	"	"	" Santa Fe, N.M., Aug. 5, '48; term expir'd
Henderson, Benj. J.	"	June 12	" " Oct. 12, '48; disability...
Knight, William	"	June 2	" Ft. Leavenw'th, July 12, '47; disability.
Lager, Gabriel	"	"	" Santa Fe, N. M., Aug. 15, '48; term exp'd
Miller, Jordan	"	"	" Las Vegas, N.M., Aug. 19, '48; term exp'd
Perrin, John	"	"	" Santa Fe, N.M., Aug. 15, '48; term exp'd
Pinckard, Amos G.	"	"	" " Oct. 12, '47; disability...
Weathers, Enoch B.	"	"	" Council Grove, July 29, '47; disability.
White, James A.	"	"	" with disgrace at Santa Fe Feb. 12, '47.

Deserted:

Name and Rank.	Place of Enlistment.	Enrolled	Remarks.
Bankson, Stephen	Alton, Ill.	1847. June 12	Deserted at Ft. Leavenworth July 5, 1847
Gibson, Aaron B.	"	June 2	"
McCoy, Thomas	"	"	" Alton, Ill., June 3, 1847
Stewart, Riley	"	"	" Ft. Leavenworth July 5, 1847
Thornbrough, Wm.	"	"	" " " "

This company was discharged at Alton, Ill., Oct. 17, 1848.

COMPANY "K."

Name and Rank.	Place of Enlistment.	Enrolled	Remarks.
Captains. Israel B. Donalson	Alton, Ill.	1847. May 22	Elected Major of Reg't at Alton June 8. 1847
William Kinman	"	"	2d Lieut. from enrollment to June 8, 1847
First Lieutenant. Manoah T. Bostick	"	"	
Second Lieutenants. Robert E. Hicks	"	"	Suspended 4 months Feb. 1, 1848, sen. G. C.-M.
Constantine Hicks	"	"	3 " 6 " Resi'd Aug. 11
Sergeants. David K. Hobbs	"	"	
Andrew Main	"	"	
Austin W. Matthews	"	"	Appointed from private May 1, 1848
Uriah Thomas	"	"	Promoted from Corporal Sept. 1, 1848
Corporals. Daniel Gray	"	"	
Joseph W. Ingalls	"	"	Appointed from private May 1, 1848
George W. Freeman	"	"	
Jarvis P. Rudd	"	"	" " " Sept. 1, 1848
Musicians. William Kiser	"	"	
John Moore	"	"	
Privates. Arnett, John	"	"	
Atkins, James H.	"	"	
Barthelow, Jasper	Ottawa, Ill.	Jan., '48	Joined, a recruit, July 31
Broadwater, Henry	"	Feb., '48	" " "
Barber, George	"	"	" " " 1848
Beard, Edward	"	Jan., '48	" " "
Beck, Christopher	"	Jan., '48	" " "

FIRST REGIMENT.

Name and Rank.	Place of Enlistment.	Enrolled	Remarks.
		1847.	
Brown, Archibald A.	Alton, Ill.	May 22	
Bobbett, William B.	"	"	
Blair, Alfred I.	"	"	
Bell, Jackson	"	"	
Bristow, Lawrence C.	"	"	
Baldwin, David P.	"	"	
Bulson, Frederick M.	"	"	
Bissell, Alfred	"	"	
Babcock, Robert F.	"	"	
Cram, Ephraim	"	"	
Cooper, John	"	"	
Davis, Calvin	"	"	
Durall, Alney	"	"	
Durall, Duran	"	"	
Fuks, George W.	Ottawa, Ill.	Mar., '48	Joined, a recruit, July 31
Filbert, Sebastian	"	Feb., '48	"
Gray, Burton T.	Alton, Ill.	May, '47	
Hart, Nathaniel P.	"	"	
Hawker, John	"	"	
Heavener, John C.	"	"	
Heavener, Christoph	"	"	
Henry, George	"	"	
Hedrick, Anderson	"	"	
Jennings, Jackson	"	"	
Jordan, Thomas I.	"	"	
Kneeland, John W.	"	"	
Kendall, Hiram G.	"	"	
Kinney, Joseph W.	"	"	
Lewis, James W.	"	"	
Lippincott, Josiah	"	"	
Leeper, James	"	"	
Leonard, Joseph A.	Ottawa, Ill.	Jan., '48	Joined, a recruit, July 31
Main, Philip	Alton, Ill.	May, '47	
Mastin, Benjamin L.	"	"	
Main, Nicholas	"	"	
Meredith, Daniel W.	"	"	
Madison, Franklin	"	"	
Mace, John	"	"	
Main, William	"	"	
McDade, Joseph	"	"	
McDade, Reuben	"	"	
Neely, Andrew J.	"	"	
Neely, John	"	"	
Peterson, Robert	"	"	
Parks, Lemuel	"	"	
Seybold, Jacob	"	"	
Seavers, John G.	"	"	
Smart, Zachariah L.	"	"	
Spencer, Charles A.	"	"	
Spencer, Hiram G. W.	"	"	
Schanck, Samuel	"	"	
Underwood, John L.	"	"	
Wade, Benjamin F.	"	"	
Welch, McDaniel	"	"	
Yorke, Henry P.	"	"	
Yorke, Hezekiel D.	Santa Fe, N. M.	Feb., '48	

Died: -

Privates.		1847.	
Brents, William H.	Alton, Ill.	May 22	Died at Santa Fe, N. M., Oct. 3, 1847
Burland, John	"	"	Killed, affray on m'ch, R'k Corral, N.M., Aug., '48
Crawford, Josiah	"	"	Died en route Santa Fe to Chihuahua, Nov. 4, '47
Hobbs, William M.	"	"	" to " Aug. 31, 1847
Hughes, Hardin	"	"	" at Santa Fe, N. M., Oct. 24, 1848
Howland, Nounan	"	"	" en route San. Fe to Chihuahua, Nov. 15, '47
Smith, Ransom	"	"	" at Santa Fe, N. M., Feb. 12, 1848
Seeley, Gersham	"	"	" en route to Santa Fe, Sept. 4, 1847
String, Thomas D.	"	"	" at Santa Fe. N. M., Oct. 15, 1847
Waller, Aaron J.	"	"	" en route Santa Fe to Chihuahua, Dec. 8, '47
Williams, Elijah W.	"	"	" at Santa Fe, N. M., Feb. 11, 1848

Discharged:

Name and Rank.	Place of Enlistment.	Enrolled	Remarks.
Sergeants.		1847	
Samuel N. Hoyt	Alton, Ill.	May 22	Disch. at Santa Fe, exp. of service, Aug. 11,'48
Richard Lucas	"	"	" " " May 5, 1848, disability
Corporals.			
Samuel P. Mace	"	"	Disch. at Santa Fe, Feb. 19, 1848, disability
Anson Rudd	"	"	" " " April 29, "
Privates.			
Allen, Alfred	"	"	Disch. at Las Vegas June 8, 1848, disability
Chandler, William	"	"	" Santa Fe, March 7, " "
Cavender, James	"	"	" " " " "
Lester, John	"	"	" " " May 5, " "
Nye, Seth S.	"	"	" Alton, Ill., June 21, 1847, "
Powell, Elijah L.	"	"	" Santa Fe, May 5, 1848, "
Seaver, William B.	"	"	" " " " "
Shin, John H.	"	"	
Smith, Hiram	"	"	Left sick at Ft. Leavenworth, July 15, 1847.

Transferred:

Musician.		1847.	
John L. Kiser	Alton, Ill.	May 22	Appointed Fifer Mar. 5, '48; transferred to staff

This company was discharged from service Oct. 13, 1848, at Alton, Ill.

SECOND REGIMENT.

THE FIELD AND STAFF

Of the 2d Regiment of Illinois Foot Volunteers, commanded by Col. Wm. H. Bissell, called into the service of the United States by the President, under the act of Congress, approved May 13, 1846, for the term of twelve months, from the 28th day of February, when last mustered, to the 18th day of June, 1847, when discharged.

Name and Rank.	Place of Enlistment.	Enrolled	Remarks.
Colonel. Wm. H. Bissell	Alton, Ill	1846. June 17	Elected from Captain, at Alton, June 30
Lieut.-Colonel. Jas. L. D. Morrison	"	June 16	[on furl. till expir'n of serv.; ill health; Elected from Captain (in Raith's Co.) July 11;
Major. Xerxes F. Trail	"	June 24	[July 1. Elected f'm Captain (in Miller's Co.) at Alton,
1st Lieut. and Adj't. August. G. Whiteside	"	"	[wounded in bat. at B. Vista, Feb. 23, '47. Appointed (1st Lieut. in Miller's Co.) July 1;
1st Lieut. and A. A. Geo. W. Prickett	"	June 16	Appointed by Col. Bissell, Feb. 28
Surgeon. Edward B. Price	"		Appointed by the President July 7
Sergeant-Major. Christian H. Ketler	"	June 16	[in bat. at B. Vista Feb. 23, '47. App'd f'm 1st Sergt. Co. "H" Jan. 1; wounded
Q. M. Sergeant. Nelson S. Moore	"	June 24	[wounds at bat. of B. Vista, Feb. 23, '47. App'd f'm Sergt. Co. "I"; disch. on account of
Principal Musicians. John Hopkins Reub'n M. Pendexter	" "	June 20 June 17	From Company "A" " "E"
Corp'l and A. C. S. Wm. Fuedlander	"	June 17	

COMPANY "A."

Name and Rank.	Place of Enlistment.	Enrolled	Remarks.
Captain. Elzey C. Coffey	Alton, Ill	1846. June 20	
First Lieutenant. Harvy Nevill	"	"	
Second Lieutenants. William B. Rountree Jackson Dennis	" "	" "	[killed. Promoted from Sergt. Feb. 28, *vice* Rountree,
Sergeants. Geo. W. Hotchkiss James W. Farmer Hugh B. McElhanan Richard M. Clayton	" " " "	" " " "	Furloughed from May 15 Wounded in bat Feb. 23; cert. for full pension

Name and Rank.	Place of Enlistment.	Enrolled	Remarks.
Corporals.		1846.	
James T. Christian	Alton, Ill	June 20	
Thomas M. Reed	"	"	Wounded in battle Feb. 23
Joseph Kinyon	"	"	Left sick at Rio Grande from Oct. 26
Thomas Atchison	"	"	
Musicians.			
John Hopkins	"	"	
Robert W. Fulton	"	"	
Privates.			
Atchison, George W.	"	"	
Auldridge, James	"	"	
Brazel, Robert	"	"	
Burnet, John	"	"	Wounded in battle Feb. 23
Bird, William	"	"	" " "
Bird, Thomas	"	"	" " "
Brown, John W	"	"	
Brown, Jacob	"	"	
Cox, Adison	"	"	
Cooper, Gilbert	"	"	Wounded in battle Feb. 23; leg amputated
Clark, Alfred	"	"	
Castleberry, Mark	"	"	
Chapman, Edw'd R.	"	"	
Chick, Edley A	"	"	
Coleman, Nathan T.	"	"	
Cheek, Robert R.	"	"	
Cheek, James A	"	"	
Davis, James H. H	"	"	
Dempsey, William	"	"	Wounded in battle Feb. 23
Dickerson, Willis	"	"	Detached as Hosp. Attend't in San Antonio
Folson, Thos. D. M.	"	"	
Farmer, John	"	"	
Friend, Isaac	"	"	
Faulkner, Gilbert	"	"	
Gore, Gideon S	"	"	
Green, William L	"	"	
Hodges, James D	"	"	
Hensley, John M	"	"	
Hagans, William H.	"	"	Lost musket in bat'l, retreating, flag to carry
Hutchings, Wes. W.	"	"	
Hall, Jesse	"	"	
Johnson, Archer B.	"	"	
Johnson, Joseph W.	"	"	
Jolliff, James E	"	"	
Jenkins, Louis S.	"	"	
Lee, Abner G	"	"	
Lee, James T	"	"	
Lee, Ephriam W	"	"	
Morris, Joseph	"	"	
Morton, James R	"	"	
Mitchell, William F.	"	"	
Mansker, John G	"	"	Lost musket by being wounded Feb. 23
Myers, Dedrick R.	"	"	
Newman, John	"	"	
Pate, Joseph	"	"	Wounded in battle Feb. 23
Raney, Geo. W	"	"	
Rountree, John M.	"	"	
Redferne, James	"	"	
Robins, John	"	"	Wounded in battle Feb. 23
Ragland, Richard B.	"	"	
Raney, William	"	"	
Stoker, William	"	"	
Sronce, Stephen	"	"	
Slade, Andrew J.	"	"	Wounded in battle Feb. 23
Thomas, George L.	"	"	
Williams, Alexander	"	"	
Wheeler, Allen B	"	"	
White, Willis	"	"	Wounded in battle Feb. 23
West, Thompson C.	"	"	
Williams, Matth'w B.	"	"	

Discharged:

Name and Rank.	Place of Enlistment.	Enrolled	Remarks.
Privates.		1846.	
Boatright, Alex.	Alton, Ill.	June 20	Discharged at Camp Buena Vista May 30
Flanagan, John B.	"	"	" " " " " "
Starkwell, Albert C.	"	"	" " " " " "
Underwood, Wm. T.	"	"	" " " " " "

Died:

Name and Rank.	Place of Enlistment.	Enrolled	Remarks.
Privates.		1846.	
Casnor, Jonas	Alton, Ill.	June 20	Died at Parros Dec. 25, 1846
Penter, George W.	"	"	" " Saltillo March 23, 1847
Stilley, Hezekiah	"	"	" " Buena Vista April 19, 1847

This company was discharged at Camargo, Mexico, June 18, 1847.

Company "B."

Name and Rank.	Place of Enlistment.	Enrolled	Remarks.
Captain.		1846.	
Anderson P. Cordo.	Alton, Ill.	June 26	
First Lieutenant.			
John W. Rigby	"	June 30	
Second Lieutenants.			
Wm. W. Tate	"	"	
James M. Gaunt	"	"	
Sergeants.			
Watho F. Hargus	"	"	
Abraham S. Latta	"	"	Detached service, Hospital Steward, Sept. 29.
Calvin Brown	"	"	
John Delaney	"	"	
Corporals.			
John L. Barber	"	"	
Robt. E. Hall	"	"	
James Cuppin	"	"	
James H. Gorrell	"	"	Absent, sick at Laracco, from Aug. 11
Musician.			
Andrew I. Ring	"	"	
Privates.			
Abbott, John	"	"	
Anglin, Wm. C.	"	"	Taken prisoner at battle of Buena Vista
Bartleson, Edwin	"	"	
Bartleson, Augustus	"	"	
Baccus, Abner	"	"	
Boren, Welbourn	"	"	
Barnett, John	"	"	
Burkhardt, Henry	"	"	
Crippin, William	"	"	
Cole, Robert	"	"	
Cole, Jiles M	"	"	
Curry, John	"	"	Taken prisoner at battle of Buena Vista
Davis, Marion M.	"	"	
Doebeaker, Henry	"	"	
Evans, Joseph	"	"	Taken prisoner at battle of Buena Vista
Echols, Miller	"	"	
Emerick, Daniel	"	"	Wounded at battle of Buena Vista
Goodall, Charles	"	"	
Goodwin, John	"	"	
Harnback, Joseph B	"	"	
Hughes, William	"	"	
Hale, James M	"	"	

Name and Rank.	Place of Enlistment.	Enrolled	Remarks.
		1846.	
Johnson, Reason I..	Alton, Ill....	June 30	....
Johnson, William...	"	"	
Ladd, Elisha.........	"	"	
London, James L...	"	"	
London, Thomas E.	"	"	
Lefler, Pleasant.....	"	"	
McGee, Patrick H..	"	"	
Metcalf, James H...	"	"	
Phillips, Enos A.....	"	"	
Purdy, George.......	"	"	
Parker, Framuel....	"	"	
Russell, John B.....	"	"	
Russell, Pinkney....	"	"	
Russell, John.......	"	"	
Renfrow, David.....	"	"	
Story, Jonathan.....	"	"	
Smith, Columbus C.	"	"	
Scott, Calvin L......	"	"	Absent, sick at Laracco, from Aug. 11.......
Summerville, Jack'n	"	"	
Shepherd, Elijah....	"	"	Absent, sick at Laracco, from Aug. 11.
Stephens, Cyrus....	"	"	
Thorp, James........	"	"	Taken prisoner at Buena Vista.............
Tiner, Andrew J....	"	"	
Tiner, William E....	"	"	
Tiner, Isham L......	"	"	
Thompson, Thomas.	"	"	
Vaugh, Reuben......	"	"	
White, John.........	"	"	
Whittaker, William.	"	"	Absent, sick at Laracco, from Aug. 11.......
Young, H. A.........	"	"	

Died :

Privates.		1846.	
Bankston, Alfred....	Alton, Ill.....	June 30	Died at Saltillo March 21........................
Jones, Thomas......	"	"	" 4.................................
Kelso, Enoch........	"	"	" Laracco, time not known............

Discharged :

Private.		1846.	
Kitchell, John........	Alton, Ill.....	June 30	Discharged on Surgeon's certif. March 20....

This company was discharged from service at Camargo, Mex., June 18, 1847.

Company "C."

Name and Rank.	Place of Enlistment.	Enrolled	Remarks.
Captain.		1846.	
James W. Baker.....	Alton, Ill.....	June 12	Wounded at Buena Vista; absent on furlough
First Lieutenant.			
Turner R. DeButts..	"	"	....
Second Lieutenants.			
John Brown.........	"	"	Wounded in battle of Buena Vista, Feb. 23...
James Smith.........	"	"	
Sergeants.			
North West.........	"	"	
Charles Chaney.....	"	"	
Emanuel Webber....	"	"	
Martin T. Smith.....	"	"	

SECOND REGIMENT.

Name and Rank.	Place of Enlistment.	Enrolled	Remarks.
Corporals.		1846.	
Edward Twaddle	Alton, Ill	June 12	
John Robinson	"	"	
William Austin	"	"	
James Shelby	"	"	
Privates.			
Bings, John	"	"	
Black, Hugh	"	"	
Brown, Cornelius W.	"	"	
Bivins, Clayton	"	"	
Bryant, John M	"	"	Wounded in battle of Buena Vista, Feb. 23.
Bivins, James C	"	"	
Clarage, Francis A	"	"	Wounded in battle of Buena Vista, Feb. 23.
Crabb, John W	"	"	On furlough in Q. M. Departm't, from May 16.
Dimond, John P	"	"	
Deffenbacker, Jacob	"	"	
Easley, William	"	"	Wounded in battle of Buena Vista, Feb. 23.
Foyles, James	"	"	Wounded, and on furl., in Q. M. Dep't May 8.
Fletcher, George	"	"	Wounded in battle of Buena Vista, Feb. 23.
Grace, James T	"	"	
Groves, Jacob	"	"	
Griffith, William	"	"	
Griffith, Joseph	"	"	
Graham, John	"	"	On furlough in Com'sary Dep't from May 17.
Hayse, John	"	"	
Harness, Joseph	"	"	On furlough in Q. M. Departm'nt from May 16
Johnson, Edward H	"	"	
James, Stephen	"	"	On furlough in Q. M. Departm'nt from May 16
McMichael, Obed	"	"	Taken prisoner at Buena Vista, Feb. 23.
Mulligan, James	"	"	On furlough from May 15
McGrau, James A	"	"	
Mansure, Charles	"	"	
Montgomery, Thos	"	"	Wounded in battle of Buena Vista, Feb. 23.
McCann, David	"	"	
Nolland, Jasper N	"	"	
Nolland, John M	"	"	Wounded in battle of Buena Vista, Feb. 23.
Nettelton, James M	"	"	
Parker, James	"	"	
Ricketts, David M	"	"	Wounded in battle of Buena Vista, Feb. 23.
Ryon, John J	"	"	
Stuart, John W	"	"	Wounded in battle of Buena Vista, Feb. 23.
Smith, Henry C	"	"	
Smith, Isaac P	"	"	
Stamps, George W	"	"	
Stratham, Charles H	"	"	
Sidel, Jacob	"	"	
Therman, Jesse T	"	"	Taken prisoner at Buena Vista, Feb. 23.
Torum, Samuel	"	"	
VanCamp, Charles	"	"	On furl'h Q. M. Dep't; wounded, Buena Vista.
Whippill, Laurist'n W	"	"	
Whitmore, Samuel	"	"	On furlough in Q. M. Dep't from May 8

Discharged:

Privates.		1846.		[Mounted Vols. May 29; wounded.
Burk, Robert	Alton, Ill	June 12	Disch. by reason of joining Capt. Meyer's Co.
Coil, Peter	"	"	" " " " "
Kelly, Patrick	"	"	" " " " "
Lanon, Patrick	"	"	" " " " "
Loomis, Ralph I	"	"	" empl't in Ordn'nce Dep't
Luther, Francis	"	"	" at Monterey; wounded at Buena Vista
Maxwell, George R	"	"	

Died:

Name	Place	Enrolled	Remarks
Feak, Nicholas	Alton, Ill	1846. June 12	Wounded, Buena Vista, Feb. 23; died April 25

This company was discharged at Camargo, Mexico, June 18, 1847.

COMPANY "D."

Name and Rank.	Place of Enlistment.	Enrolled	Remarks.
Captain. Erastus Wheeler	Alton, Ill.	1846. June 16	
First Lieutenant. Geo. W. Prickett	"	"	Acting Q. M. for the Regiment from Feb. 28.
Second Lieutenants. Joel Foster	"	"	
Wm. B. Reynolds	"	"	
Sergeants. Geo. T. Cochran	"	"	
Chas. W. Ward	"	"	
Wm. Peel	"	"	
Wm. E. Wheeler	"	"	
Corporals. Constantine Smith	"	"	
Elisha Axley	"	"	Absent, sick at San Antonio, from Oct. 14.
Wm. Calvert	"	"	
Jas. A. Henderson	"	"	
Musician. Joseph Shoemaker	"	"	
Privates. Aker, Stephan	"	"	
Bell, Wiley H	"	"	
Barnrighter, Conrad	"	"	
Blake, Chas. W	"	"	
Bartels, Engelhart	"	"	
Biggerstaff, John W	"	"	
Brown, John	"	"	
Borks, Richard	"	"	
Campbell, Dennis	"	"	
Creed, Colby	"	"	
Douglas, Alexander	"	"	
Davis, Ennels C	"	"	
Duff, Hiram D	"	"	
Davis, Joseph	"	"	
Devine, Charles	"	June 30	
Emmerson, James H	"	June 16	
Fulfer, James	"	June 13	
Gregory, Lisles	"	June 30	
Goodwin, John	"		
Goodwin, Richard	"	June 16	
Glaser, Ludwick	"	"	Absent, sick at San Antonio, from Oct. 14.
Gayler, Joseph E	"	"	
Hays, Andrew	"	"	
Hare, Jephtha	"	"	Absent on furl. f'm May 8; emp. in Q. M. Dep.
Hoop, Philip	"	"	
Jackman, Asborne C	"		
Jackson, Andrew	"	June 30	
Kinder, George	"	June 16	
Keppy, Christopher	"	"	
Lancaster, James	"	"	
Lowdner, Wolf	"	"	
Lewis, Thomas	"	"	
Mings, Uriah	"	June 30	
Murphy, John D	"	June 16	
Murphy, Bonham	"	"	
Muir, Jefferson	"	"	
Massey, Richard	"	"	
Malry, Richard G	"	"	
McCoy, James S	"	"	
Paynter, Robert	"	June 30	
Preg, Andrew	"	June 16	
Paine, Moses R	"	"	
Parker, Wilson	"	"	
Pierce, Mortimer R	"	"	
Robinson, Jesse	"	"	
Ramsey, Gardner	"	"	
Robinson, James	"	"	
Ranson, Wm. F	"	"	
Swain, Andrew, Jr	"	"	
Sobber, Charles	"	"	

SECOND REGIMENT.   235

Name and Rank.	Place of Enlistment.	Enrolled	Remarks.
		1846.	
Squires, James	Alton, Ill.	June 16	
Saunders, Marion	"	"	
Sachse, Lewis	"	"	
Taylor, James H.	"	"	Absent on furl. f'm May 9; emp. in Q. M. Dep.
Tarkinton, Thos. J.	"	"	
Thomas, Leander	"	"	
Updyke, Holcombe	"	"	
VanCamp, Aaron	"	"	Disch. March 24, on Surg. certif.; disability
Van Shaffer, Elworth	"	"	Absent on furl. f'm May 9; emp. in Q. M. Dep.
Warren, Hardy	"	"	
Wingleman, Edward	"	"	

This company was discharged June 18, 1847, at Camargo, Mexico.

COMPANY "E."

Name and Rank.	Place of Enlistment.	Enrolled	Remarks.
		1846.	
Captain. Peter Lott	Alton, Ill.	June 20	Ass't C. S. from July 17 to Sept. 14; then Capt.
First Lieutenant. John A. Prickett	"	June 17	Absent on furl., wounds rec'd in bat'l Feb. 23.
Second Lieutenants. James Catron	"	"	Disch. at Buena Vista May 22; re-enlistment.
Aston Madeira	"	"	Formerly Sergeant
Sergeants. John Roberts	"	June 17	
William Kelley	"	June 20	
John S. Selden	"	June 17	
Corporals. Joseph Quigley	"	"	
Hardy R. Carroll	"	"	
Isaac E. Hardy	"	"	
Privates. Botkin, John B.	"	"	
Burns, Myron S.	"	"	
Carpenter, David M.	"	"	
Clark, Samuel	"	"	
Clark, Thomas	"	June 20	
Cruise, Patrick	"	"	
Duncan, John R.	"	June 17	
Drury, Edward A.	"	"	
Dought, Isaac H.	"	"	
Davidson, John	"	June 20	
Dwyer, John	"	"	
Elwell, Joseph S.	"	"	
Field, Aaron	"	"	Absent on furlough in Q. M. Dept. from May 8
Falkner, William	"	"	
Falkner, James	"	"	
Garrison, John	"	"	
Hutchinson, Pierson	"	"	
Hill, George M.	"	"	
Hatch, Edwin	"	"	
Hunter, Charles	"	"	Absent on furlough in Q. M. Dept. from May 8
Hoffmaster, Chris	"	"	
Hackney, James	"	"	
Hill, Ephraim P.	"	"	
Jenkins, Ezekiel	"	"	Absent on furlough in Q. M. Dept. from May 8
Joice, William B.	"	"	
King, Josephus	"	"	
Keller, John F.	"	"	
Kennedy, William	"	"	
Lovelace, Perry	"	June 17	Absent on furlough in Q. M. Dept. from May 8
Lewis, James	"	"	
Marsh, Caleb N.	"	"	
McGovern, James	"	"	

Name and Rank.	Place of Enlistment.	Enrolled	Remarks.
		1846.	
O'Conner, James	Alton, Ill	June 20	
Prickett, Thomas J.	"	June 17	
Quick, John	"	"	
Roberts, George	"	"	
Roder, John B.	"	"	
Riley, Michael	"	June 20	
Rogers, Andrew F.	"	June 17	
Sprague, William	"	"	Reduced from Corporal from Oct. 2
Stewart, Charles	"	"	
Stanley, John R.	"	"	
Twaddle, William A.	"	"	
Wright, James H.	"	"	
Wiswell, Benj. F.	"	"	
Wright, William R.	"	"	
West, Horace B.	"	"	
Waldron, Elias	"	"	
Wagner, Rufus M.	"	"	
Warnick, Fred'k E.	"	"	

Discharged:

Name and Rank.	Place of Enlistment.	Enrolled	Remarks.
Sergeant.		1846.	
Robert McFarland	Alton, Ill	June 17	Disch. at Buena Vista May 23; re-enlistment.
Privates.			
Bramble, Thomas			Disch. at Buena Vista May 23; re-enlistment.
Brinker, Clark			" " " " "
Graves, Jason			" " " " "
Griffin, John W.			" " " " "
Nettleton, James			" " " " "

Died:

Name and Rank.	Place of Enlistment.	Enrolled	Remarks.
		1846.	
Field, Edwin	Alton, Ill	June 17	Died at Saltillo Mar. 12, of wounds received
Fisher, William	"	"	" " " " 5, " " "
Robinson, John	"	"	" " " " 1. " " "
Ryan, James	"	June 20	Murdered near Saltillo March 26

This company was discharged at Camargo, Mexico, on June 18, 1847.

Company "F."

Name and Rank.	Place of Enlistment.	Enrolled	Remarks.
Captain.		1846.	
John S. Hacker	Alton, Ill	June 25	
First Lieutenant.			
Sidney S. Condon	"	"	
Second Lieutenants.			
Alphonso Grammar.	"	"	
Joseph Martin	"	"	Elected from Corp. Jan. 26, *vice* Selby, dec'd.
Sergeants.			
John C. Hunsaker	"	"	
Alex. J. Nimmo	"	"	
Abram Hargrave	"	"	
John Grammar	"	"	
Corporals.			
Adam Creese	"	"	
Wright C. Pender	"	"	
Henderson Brown	"	"	
Abram Cover	"	"	

SECOND REGIMENT.

Name and Rank.	Place of Enlistment.	Enrolled	Remarks.
Musicians.		1846.	
Jacob Greer	Alton, Ill	June 25	
George H. Hemley	"	"	
Privates.			
Brown, Talbot	"	"	
Bevins, John	"	"	
Brown, John	"	"	
Barringer, Charles	"	"	
Burgess, John Z	"	"	
Cripps, Peter	"	"	
Casper, Peter H	"	"	
Coffman, Elijah	"	"	
Davic, Scipio A. B	"	"	
Davic, John	"	"	
Dougherty, Daniel	"	"	
Fisher, Simeon	"	"	
Findley, Charles A	"	"	On detached service in Q. M. Dept. Dec. 30
Fike, James	"	"	
Gray, Jesse	"	"	
Geargus, Franklin	"	"	
Grammar, James	"	"	
Haugh, Henry	"	"	
Hamby, Wm. N	"	"	
Henry, William	"	"	
Hess, Samuel	"	"	
Hayward, Benj. F	"	"	
Hacker, Henry C	"	"	Hospital Steward from July 25 to Oct. 5, and from Dec. 17 to Jan. 20.
Jones, Fielding A	"	"	
Jones, Silas	"	"	
Kerr, John	"	"	
King, Frederick	"	"	
Lingle, Adam	"	"	
Lewis, Philip	"	"	
Lingle, John	"	"	
Lingle, Henry	"	"	
Lycrley, Daniel W	"	"	
Lemons, Andrew J	"	"	
Lingle, Daniel	"	"	
Langley, Chesterfi'ld	"	"	
Manees, John	"	"	
McCoy, Harrison	"	"	
Maneese, Jefferson	"	"	
Miller, William	"	"	
Milliken, John H	"	"	
Moland, John	"	"	
Martin, Samuel	"	"	
McIntosh, Wash'n L	"	"	
McGinnis, John	"	"	
Phelan, James M	"	"	
Parker, Samuel	"	"	
Resink, Garrett	"	"	
Regan, John W	"	"	
Sprey, Franklin	"	"	
Simons, Amalphus W	"	"	
Springs, Jas. A	"	"	
Thornton, Azel	"	"	
Thomas, LeRoy	"	"	
Toler, Jas. I	"	"	
Thurman, Thos. F	"	"	
Vick, Reuben	"	"	
Walker, James	"	"	

Discharged:

Name and Rank.	Place of Enlistment.	Enrolled	Remarks.
Private.		1846.	
Pless, Martin	Alton, Ill	June 25	Discharged at Saltillo, Mch. 21, on Surg. cert.

Died:

Name and Rank.	Place of Enlistment.	Enrolled	Remarks.
Privates.		1846.	
Anderson, Felix G	Alton, Ill	June 25	Died in Hospital at Saltillo April 9
Davic, Alexander	"	"	at San Antonio, Texas; date not known.
Ledgerwood, Joseph	"	"	in Hospital at Saltillo March 21

This company was discharged on June 18, 1847, at Camargo, Mex.

Company "G."

Name and Rank.	Place of Enlistment.	Enrolled	Remarks.
Captain.		1846.	
Joseph K. Lemen	Alton, Ill.	June 17	
First Lieutenant.			
Jacob C. Hinkley	"	"	
Second Lieutenants.			
Gilb'rt P. McFarland	"	"	
Andrew J. Miller	"	"	Elected from private, Dec. 17
Sergeants.			
William Wastfield	"	"	
John Fincher	"	"	
James L. Roman	"	"	
Joseph Penn	"	"	
Corporals.			
William S. Peck	"	"	
Jas. L. Garretson	"	"	
Jas. G. Abbott	"	"	
John Gaston	"	"	
Musician.			
James H. Beach	"	"	
Privates.			
Benson, Wm. V.	"	"	
Brown, Mathew W.	"	"	
Burnett, Thomas J.	"	"	
Bragg, Solomon	"	"	
Bragg, Thomas	"	"	
Blair, Peter W.	"	"	
Boone, Daniel	"	July 1	
Clark, John	"	June 17	Absent, sick, at San Antonio, from Oct. 14
Evans, John D.	"	"	
Forquer, Eli	"	"	
Fishter, Joseph	"	"	
Friedlander, Wm.	"	"	On detach. serv., Acting A. C. S., from Sept. 4
Green, Mahlon A.	"	"	
Geiwicks, Daniel W.	"	"	
Gleun, Alexander	"	"	
Gallagher, Arthur I.	"	"	On extra duty, Hosp. Steward, from June
Gaskill, Clayton	"	"	
Goree, John C.	"	"	
Holbert, David W.	"	"	
Hammond, Willis M.	"	"	
Hill, Thomas	"	"	
Hornett, John M. O.	"	"	
Hall, Robert	"	"	
James, Langsworth	"	"	
Kertz, Gen. LaFay'e	"	"	
Kennedy, John J.	"	"	
Long, Thomas	"	"	
Lockhart, Gideon	"	"	
Lee, George F.	"	"	
McKenzie, Calvin	"	"	
McLain, Allen	"	"	Wounded in battle of Buena Vista, Feb. 23
Miller, Robert C.	"	"	
Million, Wm. K.	"	"	
McNail, Pierson W.	"	"	
Murray, William	"	"	
McKenzie, Elijah	"	"	
McKinney, Marcus E.	"	"	
Martin, Henry	"	July 1	
Nelson, John S.	"	June 17	
Owing, Washington	"	"	
Parks, Joseph M.	"	"	
Reaves, Samuel	"	"	
Randleman, Joel	"	"	
Stuart, Charles H.	"	"	
Steele, Andrew J.	"	"	
Shall, James	"	"	
Sterling, Henry C.	"	"	
Thomas, Samuel K.	"	"	
Teters, David W.	"	"	

SECOND REGIMENT.

Name and Rank.	Place of Enlistment.	Enrolled	Remarks.
Tunstall, James M..	Alton, Ill....	1847. June 17	
Wood, Alfred H......	"	"	
Wiley, Joseph.......	"	"	Wounded in battle of Buena Vista, Feb. 23.
Walker, James......	"	July 1	

Discharged :

Name and Rank.	Place of Enlistment.	Enrolled	Remarks.
Melton, Aaron B....	Alton, Ill.....	1846. June 17	Disch. at B. Vista; emp. in Q. M. D't f'm May 8
Melton, Guilford M..	"	"	Disch. at B. Vista; joined Capt. Myers' Co.

Died :

Name and Rank.	Place of Enlistment.	Enrolled	Remarks.
Cheek, Allen.........	Alton, Ill.....	1846. June 17	Died at Buena Vista April 21.
Lewis, John.........	"	"	Saltillo May 3.

This company was discharged on June 18, 1847, at Camargo, Mex.

COMPANY "H."

Name and Rank.	Place of Enlistment.	Enrolled	Remarks.
Captain.		1846.	
Julius Raith	Alton, Ill	June 16	
First Lieutenant.			
Nathaniel Niles......	"	"	Discharged at Buena Vista May 31, 1847 ......
Second Lieutenants.			
Adolph Engelmann..	"	"	Absent on furl. f'm May 23 till expir'n of serv.
Louis Stock.........	"	"	
Sergeants.			
Charles A. Fritz	"	"	
Robert Morrison	"	"	Absent on furl. f'm May 31 till expir'n of serv.
Fridolin Schetterer.	"	"	
Corporals.			
Adol. Schlotterback.	"	"	
Charles Gooding	"	"	
Adam Ewing.........	"	"	
H. W. Waldmann....	"	"	
Musicians.			
Gabriel W. Cox......	"	"	
Jacob Kuebli	"	"	
Privates.			
Alexander, Tucker..	"	"	
Becker, John Ph.. ..	"	"	
Becker, Urban.......	"	"	
Berry, John.........	"	"	
Berdoux, Charles ...	"	"	
Buyotte, Louis	"	"	
Bridges, Charles	"	"	
Busch, Herman	"	"	
Brownfield, William.	"	"	
Burg, Valetin.......	"	"	
Clark, John	"	"	
Clemen, Charles.....	"	"	
Doer, Jacob.........	"	"	
Edwards, F. O.	"	"	
Eastes, George	"	"	
Erhard, William	"	"	

Name and Rank.	Place of Enlistment.	Enrolled	Remarks.
		1846.	
Elimger, Augustus	Alton, Ill	June 16	
Funk, Valetin	"	"	
Frank, Jacob	"	"	
Francis, James	"	"	
Feldmeier, William	"	"	
Gerhard, John	"	"	
Gerstenshloeger, J.	"	"	
Gollinger, John	"	"	
Hantz, Joseph	"	"	
King, William	"	"	
Knight, John	"	"	
Kirk, F. M.	"	"	
Lumbert, Caspar	"	"	
Ledergerher, Joseph	"	"	
Mauerer, Nic.	"	"	
Meyer, John G.	"	"	
McDonald, Daniel	"	"	Absent on furl. f'm May 31 till expir'n of serv.
Rice, George	"	"	
Roberts, Charles	"	"	
Rouneberg, Fritz	"	"	
Reeves, William	"	"	
Scheel, Maxmilian	"	"	Absent on furl. f'm May 25 till expir'n of serv.
Schenerer, John	"	"	
Schnebelin, Barth.	"	"	
Sauerwein, Michael	"	"	
Schloesinger, Henry	"	"	
Talbert, James	"	"	
Trautwein, Chas. H.	"	"	
Trautwein, Ph. John	"	"	
Traenkle, Conrad	"	"	
Todd, Jackson	"	"	
Upmann, Hermann	"	July 1	
Voelker, George	"	June 16	
Wedekind, E. O.	"	"	
Wilver, David	"	"	
West, James	"	"	
Wolf, John	"	"	
Weiseborn, John C.	"	"	

Discharged:

		1846.	
Third Sergeant, Charles Sominoky	Alton, Ill	June 16	Discharged at Buena Vista May 31, 1847
Privates. Baker, Daniel	"	"	Discharged at Buena Vista May 31, 1847
Deuker, John	"	"	" " " " "
Kruse, William	"	"	" " " " "
Kurkman, Noble	"	"	" " " " "
Newell, J. H.	"	"	" on Surg. cert. disabil. Mch. 25, '47.
Quenby, Abraham	"	"	" " " " "
Wolf, Philip	"	"	

Died:

		1846.	
Kuchfus, John	Alton, Ill	June 16	Killed bet. Saltillo and Camp Bu. Vista Ap. 15
Sentzinger, John	"	"	Died in hospital at Saltillo May 7, 1847

This company was discharged at Camargo, Mexico, June 18, 1847.

SECOND REGIMENT.

Company "I."

Name and Rank.	Place of Enlistment.	Enrolled	Remarks.
Captain.		1846	
Morrison Miller	Alton, Ill	June 24	
First Lieutenant.			
August. G. Whiteside	"	"	Detached service, Adj't of Regt., order Col Bissell, from July 1
Second Lieutenants.			
John L. Wilson	"	"	
James H. Waddle	"	"	
Sergeants.			
James C. B. Reed	"	"	Absent on furl'h from May 23 till exp. service
Thomas W. Morgan	"	"	Appointed from private March 1
William S. Agnew	"	"	Appointed from Corporal, March 15
Jacob Frick	"	"	
Corporals.			
Isaac Tolin	"	"	
John Agnew	"	"	Appointed from private March 1
Jackson M. Lockert	"	"	" " " " 15.
Samuel McMurtry	"	"	" " " " 1; wounded in battle of Feb. 23.
Musicians.			
John Cook	"	"	Appointed from private
Henry Iman	"	"	
Privates.			
Agnew, Francis	"	"	
Applegate, Aaron H.	"	"	Wounded in battle of Feb. 23
Bruns, Frederic	"	"	
Clark, Felix	"	"	
Clark, Edward	"	"	
Carey, George	"	"	
Divers, Ananias	"	"	
Everett, Edward	"	"	
Fisher, William	"	"	
Finger, Theodore	"	"	Hospital attendant at San Antonio from Oct. 6
Hiltman, Lewis	"	"	Wounded in battle of Feb. 23
Hewett, Jacob	"	"	
Hinkler, Charles	"	"	Wounded in battle of Feb. 23
Hardin, James L.	"	"	
Hill, Samuel G.	"	"	
Harker, Thomas	"	"	
Hobbs, William	"	"	
Iman, Samuel	"	"	
Irmaker, Henry	"	"	
Johnson, William	"	"	
Klinkhard, Joseph	"	"	
King, William	"	"	
Kell, Solomon	"	"	Wounded in battle of Feb. 23
Lacey, William	"	"	
Lilly, James H.	"	"	
McMurtry, Joseph	"	"	
Morrison, William	"	"	
Mummert, Michael	"	"	Wounded in battle of Feb. 23
Mohr, John Jacob	"	"	
Moore, Lewis W.	"	"	
Moore, I. Milton	"	"	
Moore, Nelson S.	"	"	Reduced from Sergt. Mar. 15; transf'd to staff
Murray, Carter	"	"	
O'Brien, John	"	"	
Pilliard, Jacob	"	"	
Sennott, James	"	"	
Sexton, Daniel	"	"	
Stong, John L.	"	"	
Smith, Nicholas	"	"	
Thackeray, William	"	"	
Thompson, James	"	"	
Talbott, Elijah	"	"	
Tope, George W.	"	"	
Wilson, Edward	"	"	
Warnock, Joseph	"	"	
Werhein, Voluntine	"	"	Wounded in battle of Feb. 23

—16

Name and Rank.	Place of Enlistment.	Enrolled	Remarks.
Wallice, George	Alton, Ill.	1846 June 24	
Ward, Philip	"	"	
Helm, William	"	"	Reduced from Corporal March 1 " " Sergeant
Long, John	"	"	

Discharged:

Name and Rank.	Place of Enlistment.	Enrolled	Remarks.
Dains, William	Alton, Ill.	1846 June 24	Disch., Buena Vista, May 30; wounded Feb. 23
Runyan, Courtland	"	"	" " " " " "
White, John M	"	"	

Died:

Name and Rank.	Place of Enlistment.	Enrolled	Remarks.
Leerning, George	Alton, Ill	1846 June 24	Died May 8, at Camp Buena Vista
Squires, Hiram	"	"	" of wounds rec'd at Buena Vista, Feb. 23.
Wilcox, James M	"	"	" at Parros; time not known

This company was mustered out at Camargo, Mexico, June 18, 1847.

Company "K."

Name and Rank.	Place of Enlistment.	Enrolled	Remarks.
Captain.		1846.	
Chas. L. Starbuck	Alton, Ill.	June 26	
First Lieutenant.			
Nath'l B. Dilhorn	"	"	
Second Lieutenants.			
Niccodemus West	"	"	Wounded in battle of Feb. 23.
John D. Rees	"	"	
Sergeants.			
Davidson C. Moore	"	"	
Richard H. Williams	"	"	
Jerome B. West	"	"	
Guilford H. Haggard	"	"	
Corporals.			
John A. Fanin	"	"	
John P. Ford	"	"	
John D. Bourland	"	"	
Elias G. Chappell	"	"	
Privates.			
Armstrong, Robt. W.	"	"	
Anderson, Wm. P.	"	"	
Brown, Isaac M.	"	"	
Brown, Wm. G.	"	"	
Bridges, Wm. W.	"	"	
Campbell, Geo. W.	"	"	Detached service; Ward Master in Camp [Hospital from Jan. 27.
Carmack, Samuel	"	"	
Crawford, Marshall	"	"	
Crawford, Hampton	"	"	
Dailey, Hiram	"	"	
Dry, John M	"	"	
Dry, Edmund	"	"	
Fannin, Wm. P.	"	"	
Foster, Wm. A.	"	"	
Hawkins, Marcus C.	"	"	
Hoge, Marion D	"	"	Wounded in battle of Feb. 23.

SECOND REGIMENT.

Name and Rank.	Place of Enlistment.	Enrolled	Remarks.
		1846.	
Hamilton, Alex. A	Alton, Ill	June 26	
Humphreys, Ford.G.	"	"	
Hammock, Lewis	"	"	
Johnson, Wm. L.	"	"	
Kelley, Uriah D.	"	"	Wounded in battle of Feb. 23.
Lynch, Adam W.	"	"	
Lynch, David G.	"	"	
Lee, George E.	"	"	
Malone, Edwin	"	"	
Marlow, William	"	"	
Marlow, Richard	"	"	
Montague, Cave	"	"	
Montague, Geo. T.	"	"	
Neil, Wm.	"	"	
Pyatt, John W.	"	"	
Pritchett, Levi.	"	"	
Pettit, John D.	"	"	On furlough from May 28; carpenter in Engineer's Dept.
Pettit, Geo. F.	"	"	
Peague, Joshua	"	"	
Robinson, Larkin L.	"	"	
Robinson, John	"	"	Wounded in battle of Feb. 23.
Ramsay, Nathan	"	"	
Ragland, John B.	"	"	Absent sick at camp near Savacca, from Aug. 11; supposed to be dead.
Spong, David	"	"	
Stewart, James	"	"	
Terry, Hansel	"	"	
Taylor, Wm. B.	"	"	
West, Van R.	"	"	
Wells, Giles	"	"	
Wilks, Richard	"	"	

Died:

		1846.	
Delinger, Wm. H.	Alton, Ill	June 26	Died at Saltillo, Mex., May 13.
Higgarson, John P.	"	"	Buena Vista, Mex., May 16.
Terry, Carter	"	"	Saltillo, Mex., March 11.

Discharged:

		1846.	
Ramsey, Eli	Alton, Ill	June 26	Re-enlisted at Buena Vista, Mex., May 28, [and discharged.
Stewart, Robt. W.	"	"	

This company was discharged at Camargo, Mex., June 18, 1847.

SECOND REGIMENT.

THE FIELD AND STAFF

Of the 2d Regiment of Illinois Foot Volunteers, commanded by Colonel James Collins, called into the service of the United States by the President, under the act of Congress approved May 13, 1846, at Alton, Ill. (the place of general rendezvous), organized on the 3d day of August, 1847, to serve for the term of during the war with Mexico. From the 30th day of April, 1848, (when last paid), to the 25th day of July, when discharged. The Regiment was organized by Col. James Collins, at Alton, Ill., in the month of August, 1847.

Name and Rank.	Place of Enlistment.	Enrolled	Remarks.
Colonel.		1847.	
James Collins	Galena	June 22	Elected Col. f'm Capt. Co. F., Aug. 3, '47; discharged at New Orleans July 8, '48.
Lieutenant-Colonel.			
Stephen G. Hicks	Nashville	July 10	Present, commanding the Regiment
Major.			
Thos. S. Livingston			Must'd as Major on day of elect'n, Aug. 3, '47.
Adjutants.			
Henry S. Fitch	Whitehall		App'd Adjt. Aug. 3, '47; elect. Capt. of Co. "D" Feb. 29, '48.
Jas. H. Sampson	Galena	June 21	App'd Adjt. Feb. 29, '48.
A. A. C. S. and A. A. Q. M.			on acct. of prolonged absence f'm reg't.
Elisha Lewis	Belvidere	June 4	App'd Aug. 3, '48; deprived of app't Feb. 16, '48.
Lewis A. Norton	St. Charles	July 1	App'd Feb. 16, '48; must'd out in Co. "I."
Surgeon.			
John L. Miller	Appointed by the President		Present
Assistant Surgeons.			
Nathan H. Ash	Appointed by the President		Disch. at Jalapa, Mex., Dec. 22, '47; disability
Franc's B. Thompson	Appointed by the President		Date of commission, Mar. 29, '48; present

NON-COMMISSIONED STAFF.

Name and Rank.	Place of Enlistment.	Enrolled	Remarks.
Sergeant-Majors.		1847.	
Erasmus D. House	Whitehall	May 12	Appointed from Sergt. in Co. "D" Jan. 17, '48.
James B. Hinde	Mt. Vernon	June 3	Appointed Aug. 3, '47; elected 1st Lieut. Co. "A," Jan. 17, '48.
Q. M. Sergeants.			
Thos. G. Coffy	Galena	June 22	Appointed from Sergt. in Co. "F," Dec. 23, '47.
Wm. G. Taylor	Waterloo		Appointed Aug. 3, '47; died at Jalapa, Mex., Dec. 22, '47.
Principal Musicians.			
Ferdinand Pallaris			Appointed and mustered Aug. 3, '47
Harrison Ramsey	Galena	June 21	Appointed Aug. 3, '47

COMPANY "A."

Name and Rank.	Place of Enlistment	Enrolled	Remarks.
Captains.		1847.	
James Bowman	Alton, Ill.	June 3	Died at Jalapa, Mex., Dec. 28, 1847
Levin H. Powell	"	"	Must'd in as private; app'd 1st Sergt. Oct. 23; elected Capt. Jan. 17.
First Lieutenants.			
Eli Anderson	"	"	Died at Vera. Mex., Sept. 11, 1847; yellow fever
James B. Hinde	"	"	Must'd in as private; app'd Sergt.-Maj. Aug. 3
Willis B. Holder	"	"	Died at Jalapa, Mex., Jan. 2, 1848
Second Lieutenants.			
Hezekiah B. Newby	"	"	Died at Nat. Bridge, Mex., Sept. 16; yell. fever
Jabers J. Anderson	"	"	Must'd in as Sergt.; elec'd 2d Lieut. Mar. 24, '48
Alonzo H. Cox	"	"	" " private; " " Sept. 24
Jacob B. Keller	"	"	Must'd in as private; elec'd Lieut. Sept. 24, '47; resigned March 23, '48.
Sergeants.			
Jonathan Wells	"	"	Must'd in as private; app'd 1st Sergt. Jan. 17 '48
Gilford D. Connolly	"	"	" " corpor'l; " Sergt. Feb. 7, '48
John P. Newell	"	"	" " private; " " Jan. 17, '48
Jonathan S. Cook	"	"	" " corpor'l; " " Mar. 24, '48
Corporals.			
Edward Bond	"	"	Must'd as private; app'd corporal Mar. 24, 1848
Robert R. Ingram	"	"	" " " " " Feb. 7, 1848
Elias M. Holmes	"	"	" " " " " Mar. 24, 1848
William Bullock	"	"	" " " " " Jan. 17, 1848
Drummer.			
John W. Hartley	"	"	
Fifer.			
Thomas Casey	"	"	
Privates.			
Ames, John			
Anderson, Robert C.			
Brown, Calvin			
Cassidy, William			
Cummins, James			
Childers, Richard			
Clark, Martin	Chicago, Ill.	Feb., '48	
Crey, Thomas D.	St. Charl's, Ill.	Mar., '48	
Elee, Julian			
Green, John B.	Alton, Ill.	June, '47	
Godfrey, Caleb	St. Charl's, Ill.	Mar., '48	
Gaston, Newton A.	Alton, Ill.	June, '47	
Hillhouse, Robert S.			
Johnson, Lewis	Chicago, Ill.	Mar., '48	
Kimball, Henderson	Alton, Ill.	June, '47	
Kaltenbach, Peter	"	"	
Kinman, Andrew J.	"	"	
Kennndy, Damon C.	Chicago, Ill.	April, '48	
McCormick, Josiah	Alton, Ill.	June, '47	
McCulloch, Preston	"	"	
McCassilin, William	"	"	
Mullen, Thomas	Chicago, Ill.	Feb., '48	
Messechar, Aaron			
McRorgh, Martin	"	"	
McDonald, James	"	"	
Orton, Job A.			
Osborn, James L.	Alton, Ill.	June, '47	
Root, Welcome			
Rose, John	St. Charl's, Ill.	Mar., '48	
Stephens, Andrew			
Soule, Alonso	"	"	
Safford, Oliver			
Stull, Lawrence	Alton, Ill.	June, '47	
Sanders, Jacob			
Thornton, William A.	Chicago, Ill.	Feb., '48	
Vance, Thomas J.	Alton, Ill.	June, '47	
Wilson, Isaac			
Watts, John D.	"	"	
Weymon, Thomas			
Weldon, Benett M.			
Wood, Sherman D.	St. Charl's, Ill.	Mar., '48	
Wentworth, Henry	"	"	

Died:

Name and Rank.	Place of Enlistment.	Enrolled	Remarks.
Sergeants.		1847.	
James Mathewson..	Alton, Ill......	June 3	Died Oct. 28, '47, at V. Cruz hospital............
Benjamin F. Bogan..	" "	" "	" Jan. 11, '47, at Reg. Hosp., Jalapa, Mex..
Corporals.			
William C. Cook.....	" "	" "	Died Dec. 2, '47, at Reg. Hosp., Jalapa, Mex..
Jonathan Reilley....	" "	" "	" Sept. 14, '47, at Gen. Hosp., New Orleans
Privates.			
Bodine, John........			Died Nov. 13, '47, at Gen. Hosp., New Orleans
Ballard, Mathew ...			" Nov. 22, '47, " " V. Cruz ......
Bruce, Hiram........			" May 17, '47, at Puebla, Mex...........
Cummings, William.			" Dec. 18, '47, at Reg. Hosp., Jalapa, Mex...
Crooms, John.......			" Feb. 1, '48, " " " "
Carter, Dillard B....			" Jan. 15, '48, " " " ".
Clarke, William.....			" Dec. 14, '47, " " " "
Dawson, Isaac.......			" Jan. 2, '48, " " " "
Dorrell, Joseph......			" Sept. 10, '47, at Gen. Hosp., V. Cruz.....
Dornell, Geo. W.....			" Aug. 17, '47, at Reg. Hosp., Jalapa :....
Griffith, James F....			" Dec. 16, '47, " " " "
Goodrich, Robert ...			" Aug. 28, '47, at Gen. Hosp., New Orleans.
Gilbert, John........			" May 4, '48, " " Pueblo ....
Jenkins, John A.....			" Sept. 17, '47 " " V. Cruz.......
Knox, William			" April 21, '48, at Puebla, Mex........
Keller, John			" Jan. 11, '48, at Gen. Hosp., Jalapa......
Inglett, John			" Dec. 16, '47, " " " ".
Leonard, Hiram.....			" Dec. 28, '47, " " " "
Long, Thomas M....			" Nov. 24, '47, " " V. Cruz.......
Lawson, Henry......			" Dec. 1, '47, " " New Orleans..
Light, Reuben......			" Dec. 2, '47, " " Jalapa.......
Marlow, Zedick.....			" Dec. 1, '47, " " " "
Maynor, William R..	Alton, Ill......	June 3	" June 30, '48, at Carrollton, La............
McConnell, James...	" "	" "	" Sept. 12, '47, at Camp Bergara, Mex......
Moss, William N....	" "	" "	" Aug. 16, '47, at Alton, Ill................
McLaughlin, John...	" "	" "	" April 2, '48, at Gen. Hosp., Puebla ....
Piper, Henry........	" "	" "	" Dec. 5, '47, at Reg. Hosp., Jalapa........
Pierce, William.....	" "	" "	" Oct. 12, '47, at Gen. Hosp., V. Cruz .....
Redman, John	" "	" "	" Dec. 29, '47, at Reg. Hosp., Jalapa.......
Reynolds, William R.	" "	" "	" Mar. 5, '48, " " " "
Stewart, William....	" "	" "	" Jan. 23, '48, " " " "
Stull, John H	" "	" "	" Sept. 5, '47, at Camp Bergara ....
Taylor, Wright	" "	" "	" May 6, '48, at New Orleans.............
Worley, William G..	" "	" "	" Sept. 10, '47, at Gen. Hosp., V. Cruz.....
Weston, Charles	Bergara, Mex.	Aug., '47	" Sept. 2, '47, at Camp Bergara ....
White, Thomas A...	Alton, Ill......	June 3	" Feb. 1, '48, at Reg. Hosp., Jalapa.........
Wallace, Daniel	" "	" "	" Feb. 15, '48, " " " "

Discharged:

Name and Rank.	Place of Enlistment.	Enrolled	Remarks.
Sergeant.		1847.	
Jeremiah Morgan...	Alton, Ill......	June 3	Disch. by certificate of disability Feb. 6, 1848..
Privates.			
Baker, William	" "	" "	Disch. by certificate of disability Sept. 27, '47.
Brooks, William C...	Bergara, Mex.	Aug. 31	" " " " Feb. 6, '48 ..
Brown, Clinton......	Alton, Ill......	June 3	" " " " Oct. 10, '47.
Ballard, Robert......	" "	" "	Sent to N. Orleans to be disch. from Jalapa..
Forward, Oliver	" "	" "	Disch. by certificate of disability Feb. 1, '48.
Green, George W....	" "	" "	" " " " Mar. 27, '48.
Hovey, Simeon A....	" "	" "	" " " " Dec. 2, '47..
Leach, Arthur	" "	" "	" " " " Jan. 12, '48.
Osborn, Robert......	" "	" "	Sent to N. Orleans to be disch. at Jalapa, Mex.
Vickory, John	" "	" "	Disch. by certificate of disability Jan. 12, '48..

Deserted:

Name and Rank.	Place of Enlistment.	Enrolled	Remarks.
		1847.	
Porter, Charles......	Alton, Ill......	June 3	Deserted July 6, 1847, at Alton, Ill..............

This company was discharged at Alton, Ill., on July 21, 1848.

SECOND REGIMENT. 247

Company "B."

Name and Rank.	Place of Enlistment.	Enrolled	Remarks.
Captain.		1847.	
Calmes L. Wright...	Alton, Ill...	June 21.	
First Lieutenant.			
Bushrod B. Howard..	"	"	
Second Lieutenants.			
James H. Sampson...	"	"	Appointed Adjutant 2d Ill. Vol., 1848...........
Wm. A. Poillon......	"	"	
Sergeants.			
James McFadden ...	"	"	
George Nolan........	"	"	
Wm. H. Noble	"	"	
Jackson Parks.......	"	"	
Corporals.			
Thomas Sheridan...	"	"	
Samuel Woodhouse.	"	"	
Franklin Ward	"	"	Private to March 22, 1848, then Corporal ......
Thomes R. Waring..	"	"	" May 28, " "
Fifer.			
Cornelius Mellinger.	"	"	Private to May 1, 1848, then Fifer ....
Drummer.			
Oliver P. Welker	"	"	Private to Aug. 1, 1847, then Drummer ....
Privates.			
Adams, John	"	"	
Alexander, Samuel..	"	"	
Author, Robert	"	"	
Baggs, John T	"	"	
Beckwith, Ezra......	"	"	
Casey, Patrick	"	"	
Casey, Francis	"	"	
Carnahan, Thomas..	"	"	
Carr, Wm. L........	"	"	
Childs, Charles......	"	"	
Connor, John.......	"	"	
Cobb, Amasa	"	"	
Depue, Simon.......	"	"	
Ely, Morris M	"	"	
Flanagan, Warwick.	"	"	
Fisher, Thomas.....	"	"	
Funston, John......	"	"	Left sick in Hospital at Vera Cruz, Feb. 6, '48.
Fitzgerald, John	"	"	
Hall, John	"	"	
Higby, Wilder	"	"	
Herrell, James	"	"	
Hare, Henry	"	"	
Jackson, Andrew....	"	"	
Kupser, John.......	"	"	
Kuykendall, Benj...	"	"	
Long, James........	"	"	Left sick in Hospital at Vera Cruz, Feb. 6, '48.
Mathews, Philip....	"	"	
Miller, Christopher.	"	"	
McKinney, Robert C.	"	June 30	
McKinney, John.....	"	June 21	Left sick in Hospital at Vera Cruz, Feb. 6, '48.
McGinnis, Keran....	"	"	
McMillan, John.....	"	"	
Morris, Bluford S....	"	"	
Noble, Albert L......	"	"	
O'Leary, James	"	"	
Posey, David C.....	"	"	
Prickett, James K...	"	"	
Price, Thomas......	"	"	Absent, sick, from Feb. 11, 1848.................
Root, Orwin T.	"	"	
Rogers, Coleman F..	"	"	
Robertson, James...	"	"	
Rossiter, Wm. H....	"	"	...........[Mounted Men, Feb. 1, 1848.
Sample, Thomas	Tampico, Mex	July 8	Joined by transfer from Capt. West's Co.
Sasfield, John	Puebla, Mex.	April, '48	Joined by enlist. at Puebla, Mex., April 18, '48.

MEXICAN WAR.

Name and Rank.	Place of Enlistment.	Enrolled	Remarks.
		1847.	
Shaw, Robert I.	Alton, Ill.	June 21	
Shattuck, Munroc	"	"	
Simms, Jeremiah	"	"	
Sisler, John	"	"	
Spires, Fergus M.	"	"	Absent, sick, from Aug. 23, 1847
Sumner, Alfred	"	"	
Taylor, James E.	"	"	
Tate, Samuel	"	"	Drummer to Aug. 1, 1847, then private
Thomas, John W.	"	"	
Tong, Theodore F.	"	"	
Wade, James A.	"	"	
Wolflnger, Thomas	"	"	
Zuller, John	"	Mch., '48	Joined by enlist. at Puebla, Mex., Mch. 1, '48.

Died:

		1847.	
Corporals.			
McAllister, John C.	Alton, Ill.	June 21	Died at Tampico, Mex., Sept. 27, 1847
Rhodes, Jacob	"	"	" Jalapa, " May 28, 1848
Privates.			
Alvoid, Wm. B.	"	"	Died at Tampico, Mex., Dec. 20, 1847
Barnett, George W.	"	"	" New Orleans, La., June 7, 1848
Benhardt, John J.	"	"	" Tampico, Mex., Dec. 2, 1847
Crankshaw, Peter J.	"	"	" on the Gulf of Mexico, June 25, 1848
Donley, Wm.	"	"	" at Jalapa, Mex., May 20, 1848
Enos, Horace B.	"	"	" Tampico, Mex., Dec. 23, 1847
Ellis, Francis M.	"	"	" " " Jan. 23, 1848
Faherty, Patrick	"	"	" " " Nov. 28, 1847
Hawkins, Stephen	"	"	" " " Sept. 24, 1847
High, David	"	"	" Vera Cruz, Mex., April 2, 1848
Leonard, Wm.	"	"	" Puebla, Mex., Mch. 18, '48; poisoned.
Loyd, John	"	"	" Tampico, Mex., Oct. 3, 1847
McGuire, George	"	"	" " " 25, "
Ramsey, Andrew	"	"	" Puebla, " May 16, 1848
Sumner, Jerome B.	"	"	" Tampico, " Oct. 24, 1847
Stobaugh, Isaac	"	"	" " " Nov. 6, "

Discharged:

		1847.	
Corporal.			
John S. Miller	Alton, Ill.	June 21	Discharged Mch. 22, 1848; disability
Privates.			
John Applebury	"	"	Discharged Mch. 3, 1848; disability
Keyes, Joseph L.	"	"	" Mch. 19, " "
McGregor, Archibald	"	"	" Jan. 19, " "
Murphy, James	"	"	" Mch. 22, " "
Olmstead, John B.	"	"	" Jan. 19, " "

Transferred:

		1847.	
Fifer.			
Ramsey, Harrison	Alton, Ill.	June 21	Trans. to Staff 2d Regt. as principal Musician, Aug. 10, 1847.
Privates.			
Kelley, Wm.	"	"	Trans. to Capt. West's Co., Feb. 1, 1848
Quinche, Fred. L.	"	"	Appointed Hosp. Steward March 23, 1848

This company was mustered out July 20, 1848.

SECOND REGIMENT.

Company "C."

Name and Rank.	Place of Enlistment.	Enrolled	Remarks.
Captain.		1847.	
Harvey Lee	Alton, Ill	July 5	
First Lieutenant.			
Henry W. Good	"	"	
Second Lieutenants.			
William J. Hankins	"	"	
Jesse W. Curlee	"	"	Sergeant to April 1, 1848; then elected 2d Lt.
Richard M. Hankins	"	"	Died at Puebla, Mex., March 28, 1848.
Sergeants.			
Samuel Fortney	"	"	Sergt. to April 1, 1848; then app'nted 1st Sergt
Thos J. Gillenwaters	"	"	Private to Mar. 2, '48; then Corp'l; then Sergt.
Hugh D. Kelly	"	"	" Nov. 1, '47; Corp. to Mar. 2, '48; Sergt
Levi McBride	"	"	" May 2, 1848; then appointed Serg'nt
Corporals.			
James L. Ledbetter	"	"	Private to Feb. 16, 1848; then appointed Corp'l
William Owens	"	"	
Jonathan H. Tucker	"	"	Private to May 28, 1848; then appointed Corp'l
Camm McBride	"	"	
Privates.			
Ashley, William	"	"	
Bryant, William	"	"	
Brown, William	"	"	
Carr, Charles	"	"	
Coy, Stephen	"	"	
Clark, Tillman	"	"	
Caudle, John	"	"	
Deleplain, John	"	"	
Davis, William F	"	"	
Dickman, George H	"	"	Reduced from Sergeant May 28, 1848
Davidson, William H	"	"	
Dorman, Benjamin	"	"	
Dunham, Henry	"	"	Left sick in Gen. Hosp., Vera Cruz, Feb. 6, '48
Elliott, John, Jr	"	"	
Elder, Duma B	"	"	
Elam, William D	"	"	
Funk, Jeremiah R	"	"	
Ginger, John P	"	"	
Gerrick, Christian	"	"	
Gillenwaters, Jas. S	"	"	
Gillespie, Matthew	"	"	
Green, Patrick	"	"	
Gerbot, Frederick	"	"	
Hynkins, Samuel F	"	"	
Harris, Joseph	"	"	
Lane, Joseph	"	"	Left sick in hospital, Vera Cruz, Feb. 6, 1848
Ledbetter, H'nders'n	"	"	
Lecrone, Mathias	"	"	
Loy, James B	"	"	
Loy, George W	"	"	Corporal to Sept. 1, 1847; then resigned
Lee, Andrew J	"	"	
Ludwick, Henry	"	"	
Martin, James	Shelbyv'le, Ill	Jan., '48	
Maxfield, Hiram	Alton, Ill	July, '47	Sergeant to Feb. 16, 1848; then resigned
Miller, Hampton	"	"	Transferred to ranks from Musician
Mills, Jesse A	"	"	
McConkey, George	"	"	
Martin, Eli	"	"	
Perkins, David	"	"	
Parks, William	"	"	
Porter, James	"	"	
Radcliff, Simon	"	"	Corporal to Oct. 31; then reduced
Redfield, Benjamin	"	"	
Rafferty, James	"	"	
Rhodes, Henry	"	"	
Shindle, George S	"	"	
Sears, George	"	"	
Shaw, Andrew	"	"	
Stolle, Ewing	"	"	

MEXICAN WAR.

Name and Rank.	Place of Enlistment.	Enrolled	Remarks.
Smith, Thomas	Shelbyv'le, Ill	Jan., '48	
Tucker, James	Alton, Ill.	July, '47	
Thomps, Thomas H.	"	"	Priv. to Apr. 1, '48; then Sergt.; reduced May 28
Victor, Davis	"	"	
Wicke, Cyrus F.	"	"	Absent without leave; supposed in Q.M. Dep.
Wright, William	"	"	

Died:

		1847.	
Sergeant. Isaac M. Willis	Alton, Ill.	July 5	Died in Hosp., Puebla, Mex., March 1, 1848
Corporal. Joseph C. Sawyer	"	"	Died in Hosp., Tampico, Mex., Dec. 8, 1848
Privates.			
Ames, James	"	"	Died in Hosp., Tampico, Mex., Sept. 25, 1847
Browning, James M.	"	"	" Puebla, " Mar. 12, 1848
Brazil, Robert	"	"	" Tampico, " Nov. 15, 1847
Buradge, John	"	"	" " " Oct. 28, 1847
Crawford, Martin	"	"	" " " Sept. 26, 1847
Clark, Francis A.	"	"	" " " Oct. 29, 1847
Davis, Samuel I.	"	"	" Puebla, " April 8, 1848
Dougherty, Alex. B.	Shelbyv'le, Ill	Jan., '48	Died at sea (Gulf of Mexico), June 28, 1848
Dutton, Abram H.	"	Feb., '48	" at Alton, Ill., July 17, 1848
Frankum, William	Alton, Ill.	July, '47	Died in Hosp., Puebla, Mex., Mar. 31, 1848
Laremore, William	"	"	" Tampico, " Sept. 25, 1847
Moore, Doris	"	"	" " " Oct. 26, "
McMullin, William	"	"	" " " Dec. 25, "
Morgan, James	"	"	" " " Oct. 29, "
Mills, Jesse	"	"	Died at Alton, July 9, 1847
Parks, Samuel A.	"	"	Died in Hosp., Puebla, Mex., April 30, 1848
Parks, Andrew C.	"	"	" " " May 26, 1848
Pomroy, John	"	"	" Tampico, " Oct. 24, 1847
Tanner, Andrew	Shelbyv'le, Ill	Dec. 29	" Jalapa, Mex., June 9, 1848

Discharged:

		1847.	
Privates.			
Baker, John L.	Ewington, Ill.	May 28	Disch., Surg. certif., at Tampico, M., Jan. 27, '48
Collier, James T.	Alton, Ill.	July 5	" " " "
Cronie, Emanuel	"	"	" " " Sept. 28, '47
Edwards, John	"	"	" " " "
Edwards, Adam	"	"	" " " "
Greer, James T.	"	"	" " " "
Lewis, James	"	"	" " " Jan. 27, '48
Philips, Henry	"	"	" " " Sept. 28, '47
Reynolds, Dosin T.	"	"	" " " "

This company was discharged at Alton, Ill., July 20, 1848.

Company "D."

Name and Rank.	Place of Enlistment.	Enrolled	Remarks.
Captains.		1847.	
John Bristow	Alton, Ill.	June 21	Resigned, to take effect March 11, '48.
Henry S. Fitch	"	"	Elected from 1st Lieut. to March 11, '48.
First Lieutenant.			
John H. Hart	"	"	Elected from 2d Lieut. March 11, '48.
Second Lieutenants.			
John Wyatt	"	"	Resigned, taking effect Feb. 5, '48.
Hampton Hunter	"	"	Elected from the ranks, Feb. 5, '48.
Lorenzo E. Carter	"	"	Elected from 4th Sergt., March 11, *vice* Hart, promoted.
Sergeants.			
Ashley L. Sleetman	"	"	Appointed from 3d Sergt., June 18, '48.
Henry P. Garrison	"	"	Appointed from the ranks, Feb. 17, '48.
William Bamber	"	"	Appointed from the ranks. June 18, '48.
Corporals.			
James Bell	"	"	
Samuel Thompson	"	"	Appointed from the ranks, June 13, '48.
Nathaniel Walker	"	"	
Cyrus Little	"	"	Appointed from the ranks, June 13, '48.
Drummer.			
Edward B. Walker	"	July 6	
Fifer.			
Clinton A. Wood	"	June 21	
Privates.			
Bell, John	"	June 2	
Barrett, Jonathan	"	July 6	Appointed Hospital Steward, March 14, '48.
Barr, James	"	June 21	
Brown, Jehu	"	"	
Carroll, Isaiah	"	"	
Crawford, Lewis	"	"	
Conden, Jacob F.	"	July 6	
Davis, John	"	June 21	
Flatt, Dennis	"	"	
Frank, Abraham F.	"	"	
Flagg, William	"	July 6	
Grizzle, James	"	June 21	Reduced from 4th Corporal, June 13, '48.
Gale, William H.	"	"	
Hankins, Andrew J.	"	"	
Harrington, William	"	"	Reduced from 2d Corporal, June 13, '48.
Harrington, Thomas	"	"	
Harrow, Robert	"	"	
Miller, Milton	"	"	
Miller, Joseph A.	"	"	
McClure, William	"	June 28	
McFarland, James	"	Aug. 6	
Nelson, John	"	June 21	
Richards, Thomas	"	July 6	
Roberts, Henry H.	"	June 21	
Stahls, John	"	"	
Scott, Oscar	"	"	
Scott, Robert B.	"	"	
Simmons, Edward	"	"	
Sutton, Joseph	"	"	
Silkwood, Obediah	"	"	
Smith, James	"	"	
Slaton, Jesse	"	July 6	
Thompson, Peter	"	June 21	
Taylor, William	"	"	
Wheeler, Fielding	"	"	
Wilder, Elias	"	"	

Died:

		1847.	
Sergeants.			
John B. King	Alton, Ill.	June 21	Died at Cerro Gordo, Mex., June 17, '48.
George Kain	"	"	Alton, Ill., July 17, '48.

252   MEXICAN WAR.

Name and Rank.	Place of Enlistment.	Enrolled	Remarks.
Privates.		1847.	
Byram, Ephriam	Alton, Ill	June 21	Died on boat *en route* to Mexico, Aug. 17, '47.
Brownlee, David	"	"	" at Jalapa, Mex., Jan. 3, '48.
Bader, Frederick	"	"	" April 7, '48.
Cannon, Andrew	"	"	" Dec. 29, '47.
Carter, Joseph	"	"	Vera Cruz, Mex., Dec. 23, '47.
Crawford, James	"	"	Jalapa, Mex., April 12, '48.
Denny, Bolivar	"	"	Dec. 8, '47.
Dixon, Charles	"	"	Vera Cruz, Mex., Jan. 25, '48.
Day, Henry	"	"	Napoluca, Mex., June 4, '48.
Edwards, William	"	"	Alton, Ill., July 16, '48.
Edwards, Henry L.	"	"	Jalapa, Mex., Feb. 5, '48.
Griffith, Daniel	"	"	Nov. 28, '47.
Hammond, James	"	"	Perote, Mex., April 23, '48.
Henry, Patrick	"	"	En Cerro, Mex., June 12, '48.
Johnson, John D.	"	"	Jalapa, Mex., Jan. 2, '48.
Kasinger, William	"	"	San Juan, Mex., Oct. 28, '47.
Kirgan, Arthur	"	"	Jalapa, Mex., Jan. 18, '48.
Lee, Michael	"	"	Nov. 28, '47.
Phillips, Samuel	"	"	Vera Cruz, Mex., Dec. 28, '47.
Shinautt, Stephen	"	"	Jalapa, Mex., Dec. 20, '47.
Thompson, Thomas	"	Aug. 8	Vera Cruz, Mex., Feb. 7, '48.
Wisely, James	"	June 25	" Oct. 23, '47.

Discharged :

Name and Rank.	Place of Enlistment.	Enrolled	Remarks.
Privates.		1847.	
Brown, Charles	Alton, Ill	June 21	Disch. at N. Orleans, Aug. 23, '47; disability.
Barton, Andrew J.	"	"	Jalapa, Mex., Jan. 8, '48 "
Bryant, Elijah	"	"	" Feb. 6, '48 "
Bowen, Asa	"	"	N. Orleans, date unk'n "
Bowen, David	"	"	" " "
Guthrie, Daniel	"	"	" " "
Colclonzhh, Joseph	"	"	Jalapa, Mex., Jan. 18, '48 "
Harvill, Lewis	"	"	" Feb. 21, '48 "
Hunnicent, John	"	"	N. Orleans, date unkn'n "
Johnson, Moses	"	"	" " "
Johnson, Andrew	"	"	" " "
Logan, John F.	"	"	" " "
Mclvaine, William	"	"	" " "
Powell, Young	"	"	" " "
Quinten, Samuel K.	"	"	Jalapa, Mex., Jan. 18, '48 "
Rountree, John D.	"	"	" " "
Sisk, William B.	"	"	" " "

Transferred :

Name and Rank.	Place of Enlistment.	Enrolled	Remarks.
Second Sergeant.		1847.	
House, Erasmus D.	Alton, Ill	July 6	Appointed Sergt.-Major, Feb. 11, '48.

Deserted :

Name and Rank.	Place of Enlistment.	Enrolled	Remarks.
Privates.		1847.	
Conden, Christian	Alton, Ill	July 6	Deserted at Cape Girardeau, Mo., Aug. 16, '47.
Gibson, William S.	"	"	" Alton, Ill., Aug. 7, '47.
Stevens, John			"

This company was discharged at Alton, Ill., July 20, 1848.

SECOND REGIMENT.

Company "E."

Name and Rank.	Place of Enlistment.	Enrolled	Remarks.
Captain.		1847.	
William Shepard	Belvidere, Ill.	June 4	
First Lieutenants.			
Thomas Oates	"	"	Died at San Juan, Mexico, Oct. 2, 1847
Lyman Andrews	"	"	Elect'd (from 2d Lt.) Oct., '47; resig'd Mar. 11, '48
Thomas D. Timoney	"	"	App'd Dec. 24, '47; elec'd Mar., '47; died Apr. '48.
Sylv'us M. Geotchius	"	"	Sergt. Mar. 22, '48; elec'd 1st Lt. Apr. 25, '48
Second Lieutenants.			
William Haywood	"	"	Supp'd resig'd; left at Jalapa, sick, Mar. 14, '48
Elisha Lewis	"	"	
Sergeants.			
John Pook	"	"	Appointed from Corporal March 12, 1848
John Joel	"	"	" " private February 7, 1848
Moses Doyle	"	"	" " " April 30, 1848
Corporals.			
Leroy Benson	"	"	Appointed from private December, 1848
William Bush	"	"	" " " April 30, 1848
George S. Whitman	"	"	" " " "
John Lower	"	"	
Privates.			
Bowman, Ira	"	"	
Burton, Burwell	"	"	
Cox, Robert L	"	"	
Dewey, George S	St. Charles, Ill	Mar., '48	
Dennis, George	Belvidere, Ill.	June, '47	
Durkin, Frederick	"	"	
Harrison, John C	"	"	
Hanlon, John	"	"	
Irish, John F	"	"	
Judy, Andrew	"	July, '47	
Jones, Thomas C	Chicago, Ill.	April, '48	
Kellogg, Lockwood	"	Feb., '48	
Kingsley, DeWitt C	Belvidere, Ill.	June, '47	
Keenan, John	"	"	
Kasters, Theodore	"	"	
Lynch, William	"	"	
Miller, Reuben	"	"	
Mier, John	"	"	
Murphy, Peter	"	"	
Mullery, John	"	"	
Moore, William	"	"	
Rose, William L	"	"	
Pearsall, Philetus			
Smith, Frank	Chicago, Ill.	Feb., '48	
Shearer, Alvin	Belvidere, Ill.	June, '47	
Shepard, David N	"	"	
Schwatkin, John	"	"	
Thomas, John P	"	"	
Worrell, John	Chicago, Ill.	Feb., '47	

Died:

		1847.	
Sergeants.			
Matthew Smith	Belvidere, Ill.	June 4	Died at Jalapa, Mex., Dec. 21, 1847
Nathan Taylor	"	"	" " " Feb. 6, 1848
Corporals.			
Oliver B. Whitmore	"	"	Died at National Bridge Nov. 5, 1847
Alexander Rice	"	"	" " Jalapa, Mex., Dec. 29, 1847
Henry A. Granger	"	"	" " " Jan. 19, 1848
Musicians.			
Roman P. Holcomb	"	"	Died at Jalapa, Mex., Dec. 21, 1847
Frederick Van Dyke	"	July 1	" " " Dec. 12, 1847

Name and Rank.	Residence.	Enrolled	Remarks.
Privates.		1847.	
Astrop, John	Belvidere, Ill.	June 4	Died at Jalapa, Mex., Jan. 25, 1848.
Allen, Conolly S	"	" "	" " Dec. 29, 1847
Allen, Simon	"	" "	" " Feb. 14, 1848.
Applehoff, Adolphus	"	" "	" " Nov. 27, 1847
Beecham, George	"	" "	" " Dec. 26, 1847
Brown, Charles	Chicago, Ill.	Feb., '48	" New Orleans, La., July 4, 1848
Brenan, Michael	Belvidere, Ill.	June, '47	" Puebla, Mex., May 5, 1848
Cunniman, Froder'k.	"	" "	" " May 28, 1848.
Doyle, Daniel	"	" "	" Jalapa, Mex., Jan. 9, 1848
Fuller, James E	"	" "	" Vera Cruz, Mex., Dec. 4, 1847
Harran, John	"	" "	" " Nov. 11, 1847
Hawes, Solomon	"	" "	" Jalapa, Mex., Dec. 13, 1847
Hyde, William	"	" "	" Vera Cruz, Mex., Nov. 15, 1847
Kraagauger, Wm	Alton, Ill.	Aug., '47	" Puebla, May 19, '48; murd'd by Mexic's
Kodling, William K.	Belvidere, Ill.	June, '47	" Vera Crux, Mex., Nov. 22, 1847
Johnson, Thomas	"	" "	" Puebla, Mex., April 15, 1848
Lewis, James H	"	" "	" Jalapa, Mex., Jan. 7, 1848
Manson, John M	"	" "	" New Orleans, La, Nov. 8, 1847
Mills, John J	"	" "	" Jalapa, Mex., Dec. 17, 1847
Miller, Samuel H	"	" "	" " Dec. 23, 1847
Myers, Abraham	"	" "	" " Dec. 25, 1847
Oswald, William H.	"	" "	" Puebla, Mex., May 19, 1848
Phelps, Alanson H	"	" "	" Jalapa, Mex., Jan. 13, 1848
Phelps, Elisha	Alton, Ill.	Aug., '47	" Puebla, Mex., May 10, 1848
Rollins, Charles	Belvidere, Ill.	June, '47	" National Bridge, Mex., Nov. 10, 1847
Robinson, George	Chicago, Ill.	Mar., '48	" St. Louis, Mo., July 14, 1848; drowned
Reams, John	Belvidere, Ill.	June, '47	" Jalapa, Mex., Nov. 10, 1847
Sullivan, David E	"	" "	" " Dec. 22, 1847
Schwatkin, Gerard H	"	" "	" " Jan. 3, 1848
Swift, Warren	"	" "	" " Dec. 25, 1847
Sponable, William	"	" "	" " Dec. 30, 1847
Ward, John C	"	" "	" " Dec. 12, 1847
Whitback, Jasper	"	" "	" " May 19, 1848
Young, Joseph A	"	July, '47	" Vera Cruz, Mex., Oct. 29, 1847

Deserted:

		1847.	
Burlingame, Rhodes	Belvidere	June 4	Deserted at New Orleans Aug. 24, 1847
Dunsing, Henry	"	" "	" " " "
Koter, Ditherik	"	July 5	" " Aug. 21, 1847
Sutton, Ebbert	"	June 4	" " Jan. 15, 1848

Discharged:

Sergeants.		1847.	
James L. Kennedy	Belvidere, Ill.	June 4	Disch. at New Orleans, La., June, 1848
Matthew McWorter	"	" "	" Vera Cruz, Mex., Jan. 3, 1848
Privates.			
Duvall, Augustus	"	" "	Left at V. Cruz Hosp. Sept., '47; supp'd disch'.
Giese, Henry	"	" "	Disch. at Jalapa, Mex., Jan. 11, 1848
Gilmore, James W.	"	" "	" " "
Loop, Murray	"	" "	" " Dec. 19, 1847
Loop, Edgar S	"	" "	" New Orleans, La., June, 1848
Russell, Francis A.	"	" "	" Jalapa, Mex., Feb. 21, 1848
Rogers, John	"	" "	" " Jan. 11, 1848
Sherwood, Jackson A	"	" "	" New Orleans, La., June, 1848
Towner, Hiram G	"	June 27	" "
Ward, Alfred	"	June 4	" " March 15, 1848
Wheeler, John L	"	" "	" Jalapa Mex., Jan. 11, 1848
Wyde, George	"	July 7	" New Orleans, La., June, 1847

Missing:

		1847.	
John Coleman	Belvidere	June 4	Lost on march from Puebla to Vera Cruz June, '48; supposed captured.

This company was discharged on July 24, 1848, at Alton, Illinois.

SECOND REGIMENT.

Company "F."

Name and Rank.	Place of Enlistment.	Enrolled	Remarks.
Captains.		1847.	
..mes Collins	Galena, Ill	June 22	Elected Col. of regiment, Aug. 3, 1847.
..avid C. Berry	"	"	Elected Capt. (from 1st Lieut.) Aug. 3, 1847.
First Lieutenant.			[died at San Juan, Mex. Sept. 2, 1847.
..hn Boaney	"	"	Elected 1st Lieut. (from 2d Lieut.) Aug. 3, 1847;
..ank Wheeler	"	"	Sept. 25, '47.
..cond Lieutenants.			[resigned, April 23, 1848.
..encer H. Hill	"	"	Elected 2d Lieut. (from priv.) *vice* Van Hook,
..os. J. Andrews	"	"	" " " Aug. 3, 1847
..renzo D. VanHook	"	"	" " " Sergt., Sept. 25, 1847; resigned April 23, 1848.
Sergeants.			
..hn Alexander	"	"	
..raham Leir	"	"	Appointed from Corporal, Oct. 5, 1847.
..nry Conroy	"	"	" private, Dec. 28, 1847.
..os. A. Sanders	"	"	
Corporals.			
..stus Gideon	"	"	
..hn A. Mullen	"	"	
..hn F. A. Eckard	"	"	
..a Stevens	"	"	
Musicians.			
..ller Blair	"	"	
..muel W. Earnest	"	"	
Privates.			
..uder, Audrew	Chicago, Ill	Feb., '48	
..ss, James R	"	"	
..rry, Henry	Galena, Ill	June, '47	
..rker, George	"	"	
..tterfield, Chas. P.	"	"	
..adley, Wm. H	"	"	
..swell, Geo. W	"	"	
..xler, Noah W	"	"	
..rrant, Alpheus	"	"	
..ury, John	"	"	
..dson, James B	"	"	
..egory, William	"	"	
..nry, Theodore	"	"	
..nnon, Patrick	"	"	
..pkins, Vernon J	Chicago, Ill	Feb., '48	
..lcomb, Oscar M	Aurora, Ill	"	
..dges, William A	Chicago, Ill	"	
..hnson, James M	"	"	
..nes, Washington	Galena, Ill	June, '47	
..sure, John B	"	"	
..akley, Thomas	"	"	Left sick at Jalapa; supposed discharged.
..Guire, Henry	Chicago, Ill	Feb., '48	
..Lane, Thomas A	Galena, Ill	June, '47	Left sick at Jalapa; supposed discharged.
..elton, James	"	"	
..ackay, Andrew	Chicago, Ill	Feb., '48	
..ay, John	Galena, Ill	June, '47	
..itchell, John	"	"	
..elson, James A	Chicago, Ill	Feb., '48	
..ice, David	Galena, Ill	July, '47	
..pkins, Jesse	"	"	
..octer, James	"	"	
..ynolds, John	Chicago, Ill	Feb., '48	
..binson, James	Galena, Ill	June, '47	
..ese, Evan	"	"	
..mpson, William D.	"	"	
..nith, Martin	"	"	
..nith, Terrence	"	"	
..ulder, Henry	"	"	

256 MEXICAN WAR.

Died:

Name and Rank.	Place of Enlistment.	Enrolled	Remarks.
Sergeants.		1847.	
J. M. Lichtenberger.	Galena, Ill.	June 22	Died at Alton, Ill., Aug., 1847.
Henry Whysall	"	"	" San Juan, Mex., Oct. 2, 1847.
Corporal.			
James M. Norris	"	"	Died at Jalapa, Mex., Dec. 24, 1847.
Privates.			
Biggs, Henry	"	"	Died at Jalapa, Mex., June 12, 1848.
Brower, John T.	"	"	" New Orleans, La., June, 1848.
Brundige, Hiram	Alton, Ill.	Aug. 1	" Vera Cruz, Mex., Jan. 3, 1848.
Davis, Lewis	Galena, Ill.	June 22	" " Oct. 25, 1847.
Forbes, William	"	"	" Jalapa, Mex., March 23, 1848.
Gentry, Thomas H.	"	"	" New Orleans, La., Nov. 19, 1847.
Gregory, Joel	"	"	" Perote, Mex., 1848.
Hull, Joseph	"	"	" Jalapa, Mex., Dec. 30, 1847.
Helmick, Gerard	"	"	" Vera Cruz, Mex., Oct. 24, 1847.
Henly, William	"	"	Died on Gulf of Mexico June 27, 1848.
Jasper, Francis	"	"	Died at Vera Cruz Sept. 30, 1847.
Long, John	"	"	" Jalapa, Mex., Dec. 16, 1847.
Pogue, William R.	"	"	" " " 8, 1847.
Robinson, Henry W.	"	"	" " " 1, 1847.
Robinson, Henry	"	"	" " " 29, 1847.
Russell, Stephen	"	"	" " " March 30, 1848.
Rundall, Harrison P.	"	"	" New Orleans, La., Nov. 11, 1847.
Seaman, Peter F.	"	"	" Vera Cruz, Mex., Oct. 5, 1847.
Shaw, James	"	"	" Jalapa, Mex., 1848.
Simpson, Robt. K.	"	"	" Puebla, " May 13, 1848.
Swayne, John W.	"	"	" Perote, " April 17, 1848.
Shultz, William	"	"	" Jalapa, " Dec. 19, 1847.
Sanders, David	"	"	" Alton, Ill., July 29, 1847.
Stoner, Jacob	"	"	" Jalapa, Mex., Feb. 24, 1848.
Simpson, Thomas	"	"	" New Orleans, La., Dec. 24, 1847.
Tindall, George S.	"	"	" Jalapa, Mex., Dec. 18, 1847.
Tindall, John	"	"	" " " Nov. 30, 1847.
Truett, Samuel	Alton, Ill.	Aug. 1	" " Dec. 17, 1847.

Deserted:

Name and Rank.	Place of Enlistment.	Enrolled	Remarks.
		1847.	
Collins, John	Galena, Ill.	June 22	Deserted at Alton, Ill., July 10, 1847.
Otis, Ralph	"	"	" " " "
Wood, John W.	"	"	" " " "

Discharged:

Name and Rank.	Place of Enlistment.	Enrolled	Remarks.
Privates.		1847.	
Brown, Samuel	Galena, Ill.	June 22	Disch. at New Orleans, June, '47; disability.
Coleman, Paul E.	"	"	" Jalapa, Mex., Dec. 22, '47 "
Cottle, Orville	"	"	" Vera Cruz, Mex., Jan. 25, '48 "
Duffey, Hugh	"	"	" New Orleans, June, '48 "
Beauchard, Edw. D.	"	"	" Jalapa, Mex., Jan. 7, '48 "
Gibbons, John	"	"	" New Orleans, June, '48 "
Gloder, David	"	"	" " June 8, '48 "
Gaffney, Thomas	"	"	" Vera Cruz, Mex., Dec. 26, '47 "
Harcourt, Gustavus	"	"	" New Orleans, July 8, '48 "
James, Richard H.	"	"	" " June, '48 "
McQuay, John	"	"	" Vera Cruz, Mex., Jan. 15, '48 "
Stiles, Nathan	"	"	" Jalapa, Mex., Jan. 7, '48 "
Shultz, John G.	"	"	" " " "
Vaughn, John	"	"	" " " "
Wilson, Edward	"	"	" New Orleans.

Transferred:

Name and Rank.	Place of Enlistment.	Enrolled	Remarks.
Sergeant.		1847.	
Thomas G. Coffy	Galena, Ill.	June 22	Appointed Q. M. Sergeant Dec. 31, 1847.

Missing :

Name and Rank.	Place of Enlistment.	Enrolled	Remarks.
Corporal. Wm. H. Antis	Galena, Ill.	1847. June 22	Supposed captured by guerillas Nov. 8, 1847.

This company was discharged at Alton, Illinois, July 20, 1848.

Company "G."

Name and Rank.	Place of Enlistment.	Enrolled	Remarks.
Captain. John M. Moore	Alton, Ill.	1847. July 7	
First Lieutenant. Edward O'Melveney	" "	" "	
Second Lieutenants. Wm. C. Starkey	" "	" "	
Austin James	" "	" "	
Thomas James	" "	" "	
Sergeants. James Close	" "	" "	
Lewis I. Eyman	" "	" "	
Solomon Varnum	" "	" "	
William Hillburn	" "	" "	
Corporals. Benjamin Atwell	" "	" "	Appointed from private May 1, 1848.
Peter Dowling	" "	" "	
John Hillburn	" "	" "	
Elijah Adams	" "	" "	
Musicians. Augustus Holley	" "	" "	
Conrad Kimell	" "	" "	
Privates. Abernathy, James	" "	" "	
Alred, Samuel	" "	" "	Left sick in Hospital at Vera Cruz; supposed to be discharged.
Axley, James R	Waterloo, Ill.	June 19	
Burk, Andrew	Alton, Ill.	July 7	
Brant, Jacob	" "	" "	
Butcher, Solomon G.	" "	" "	
Clarke, Samuel C	" "	" "	
Clark, Millington	" "	" "	
Crowley, John	" "	" "	
Criley, Isaac	" "	" "	
Criley, Harman	" "	" "	
Chester, Samuel C.	" "	" "	
Clover, James M	" "	" "	
Coleman, John	" "	" "	
Denton, Liberty	" "	" "	
Dolson, John	" "	" "	
Ellis, Wm	" "	" "	
Frazer, Maxwell	" "	" "	
Glass, Michael	" "	" "	
Hartley, Wm	" "	" "	
Hinton, John	" "	" "	
Husband, Wm	" "	" "	
Hyson, Henry	" "	" "	
Haber, George	" "	" "	
Henley, Washington	" "	" "	
Jackson, Andrew	" "	" "	
Land, Moses	" "	" "	
Lybarger, Henry	" "	" "	
Lasouse, James	" "	" "	
Lakin, John	" "	" "	
Lively, George	" "	" "	

MEXICAN WAR.

Name and Rank.	Place of Enlistment.	Enrolled	Remarks.
McCannah, John	Alton, Ill.	1847. July 7	
McCullock, Wm. G.	"	"	
Murphy, Patrick	"	"	
Mann, Joseph	"	"	
Oman, Martin	"	"	
Peterman, Philip	"	"	
Perry, John	"	"	
Rogers, Wm	"	"	
Reed, Wm	"	"	
Small, Wm	"	"	
Simpkins, Hawkins	"	"	
Swank, John	"	"	
Smith, Wm. J	"	"	
Swear, Charles	"	"	
Willman, Jackson	"	"	
Wilcox, Abraham	"	"	
Wallace, Charles	Puebla, Mex.	April, '48	

Died:

Sergeant. Thomas Spencer	Waterloo, Ill.	1847. July 15	Died in Hospital at Tampico, Mex., Nov. 4, '47
Privates.			
Adams, Edward	"	"	Died in Hospital at Tampico, Mex., Nov., 1847
Blunt, Britain	"	"	" " " " Nov. 4, '47
Bishop, George	"	"	" " " " Nov. 10, 47
Blackstone, George	"	"	" " Puebla, " Apr. 22, '48
Bishop, Evans	"	"	" " Jalapa, date unknown
Burgett, Charles	"	"	" " New Orleans, May 16, '48
Brugel, Nicholas	"	"	" " Tampico, Mex., Sep. 25, '47
Burch, Gustavus	"	"	" " Puebla. " April 24, '48
Dicken, John	"	"	" " Tampico, " Jan. 10, '46
Foshee, Benjamin	"	"	" " " " Jan. 11, '48
Holbrook, John A	"	"	" " Encerro, " June 9, '48
Locum, Wm	"	"	" " Tampico, " Nov. 1, '47
Nixon, James N	"	"	" " " " Nov. 25, '47
Rydenbork, Pasmore	"	"	" " Puebla, " May, '48
Tope, Andrew J	"	"	" " Tampico, " Sep. 21, '47
Taylor, Wm	"	"	" Jalapa, Dec. 22, '47; prom'd Aug. 3, '47
Welch, John G	"	"	" in hospital at Tampico, Mex., Oct. 18, '47
Wetzel, Henry	"	"	" " " " Feb. 11, '48

Discharged:

Musician. John H. Dixon	Waterloo, Ill.	1847. July 15	Disch. at Vera Cruz, Feb. 7, 1848; disability
Privates.			
Beabers, Thomas	"	"	Disch. at Tampico, Sept. 14, 1847; disability
Brewer, Henry	"	"	" " " 28, " "
Biggs, Asa	"	"	" " " 18, " "
Bennett, Franklin	"	"	" " Jan. 20, 1848; " "
Dickerman, Manas'h	"	"	" " " 20, " "
McKinley, Hugh F	"	"	" " Sept. 14, 1847; " "
Morgan, Solomon	"	"	" " " 28, " "
Spots Leonard	"	"	" " " 28, " "
Witmer, John	"	"	" Vera Cruz, Feb. 7, 1848; "

Transferred:

Sergeant. Wm. King	Waterloo, Ill.	1847. July 15	Transferred by order of Col. Gates
Private. Edward Tilley	"	"	Transferred by order of Col. Gates
Corporal. Joseph Wilcox	"	"	Discharged at Puebla, Mex., April 24, 1848

Deserted:

Name and Rank.	Place of Enlistment.	Enrolled	Remarks.
Privates.		1847.	
Heath, Daniel L......	Waterloo, Ill.	July 15	Deserted at Alton, Aug. 13, 1847
Youngman, Jacob...	"	"	" date unknown

This company was discharged at Alton, Ill., July 21, 1848.

Company "H."

Name and Rank.	Place of Enlistment.	Enrolled	Remarks.
Captain.		1847.	
James Burns........	Nashville, Ill.	July 10	
First Lieutenant.			
Malachi Jenkins.....	"	"	Died on Gulf of Mexico June 26, 1848.
Second Lieutenants.			
George W. Walker..	"	"	Resigned at Jalapa, Mexico, Dec. 17, 1847.
James R. Lynch.....	"	"	Died at Vera Cruz, Mex., Sept. 12, 1847
Isaac B. Jack........	"	"	2d Sergt. Sept. 24,'47; prom. 2d Lt. Feb. 28,'48.
Marquis L. Burns...	"	"	Elected Sergt. at San Juan, Mex., Sept. 23,'47.
Sergeants.			
David A. Patterson..	"	"	Appointed from private Jan. 22, 1848
Robert St. Livingston	"	"	Appointed from private Feb. 21, 1848
Thomas W. Anders'n	"	"	
John Robinson	Jalapa, Mex..	Nov. 24	Appointed from private Jan. 17, 1848.
Corporals.			
John C. Burns.......	Nashville, Ill.	July 10	Appointed from private Jan. 1, 1848.
David W. Lowe......	"	"	
Richard P. Carter....	"	"	
James B. Logan.....	"	"	
Musician.			
Matthew M. Curtis ..	"	"	
Privates.			
Anderson, Richard..	"	"	
Aldridge, Peter......	"	"	
Cook, William.......	"	"	
Carter, Emanuel C..	"	"	
Crabtree, James.....	"	"	
Drew, Newton.......	"	"	
Darter, Nicholas H..	"	"	
Franklin, David.....	"	"	
Forbes, David.......	"	"	
Gillen, Owen........	"	"	
Hawkins, Benjamin.	"	"	
Hitt, John B........	"	"	
Hitt, Thomas J.....	"	"	
Jones, Leander......	"	"	
Jordan, Robert B....	"	"	
Losson, John........	"	"	
Livesay, Alfred......	"	"	
Mills, Jesse.........	"	"	
Mathews, William...	"	"	
Moore, Samuel......	"	"	
Morgan, Reuben M..	"	"	
Norris, Alfred.......	"	"	
Newcombe, Levi	"	"	
Pitchford, George W	"	"	
Pitchford, William C	"	"	
Parker, Ellison W...	"	"	

260 MEXICAN WAR.

Name and Rank.	Place of Enlistment.	Enrolled	Remarks.
		1847.	
Pate, Lewis	Nashville, Ill.	July 10	
Rogers, Sylvester	"	"	
Rogers, Horatio	"	"	
Shelton, Cuthbert H.	"	"	
Smithers, Elisha	"	"	
Summers, William	"	"	
Taylor, John C	"	"	
Vanwinckle, Robert	"	"	
Walker, John	"	"	
Walker, Thomas	"	"	
Waldron, George	"	"	
Weaver, James	"	"	

Died:

		1847.	
Sergeants.			
Anderson, James	Nashville, Ill.	July 10	Died at Jalapa, Mex., Dec. 3, 1847
Sanders, Thomas B.	"	"	" Vera Cruz, Mex., Sept. 7, 1847
Privates.			
Carr, Ephriam W.	"	"	Died on Gulf of Mexico, Aug. 28, 1847
Christain, Charles	"	"	" at Vera Cruz, Mex., Oct. 15, 1847
Campbell, Alexander	"	"	" " Sept. 15, "
Field, John	"	"	Killed in action at San Juan, Mex., Sept. 18,'47
Franklin, John F.	"	"	Died at Jalapa, Mex., Dec. 22, 1847
Gore, Thomas	"	"	" " 15, "
Gibson, Josiah	"	"	Died on Dulf of Mexico, Aug. 29, 1847
Hale, Enoch	"	"	" at Jalapa, Mex., Feb. 5, 1848
Livesay, John C.	"	"	" " " May 11, "
Miller, Cyrus	"	"	" at San Juan, Oct. 30, 1847
Miller, Pleasant	"	"	" at Puebla, Mex., April 5, 1848
Owen, William F.	"	"	" " " June 2, "
Pate, Simeon	"	"	" at Camp Encerro, Mex., June 14, 1848
Stoker, Isaac	"	"	" at Alton, Ill., Aug. 3, 1847
Smith, George	"	"	" at San Juan, Mex., Sept. 28, 1848
Summers, Major G.	"	"	" at Jalapa, " Jan. 19, "
Summers, John A.	"	"	" " " 23, "
Thurman, David W.	"	"	" " " Feb. 18, "
Walker, Ezekiah	"	"	" at Vera Cruz, " Sept. 10, 1847
Williams, John	"	"	" " " Nov. 9, "
Wright, James	"	"	" at Jalapa, " Jan. 26, 1848

Deserted:

		1847.	
Manseker, Thos. W.G	Nashville, Ill.	July 10	Deserted from Hosp., New Orleans, Jan. 15, '18
Morrison, Manly F.	"	"	" at St. Louis, Mo., Aug. 13, 1847

Discharged:

		1847.	
Privates.			
Cameron, James D.	Nashville, Ill.	July 10	Disch., New Orleans, June 8, 1848, disability
Craft, John A.	"	"	" Jalapa, Mex., Feb. 4, " "
Edrington, James P.	"	"	" " " " "
Fitzgerald, James	"	"	" New Orleans, Mar. 9, 184\, "
Gaskill, Thomas J.	"	"	" " " Dec. 29, 1847, "
Hutchings, Richard	"	"	" Vera Cruz, Mex., Jan. 2, 1848, "
Harris, Caleb	"	"	" New Orleans, Mar. 13, " "
Harris, Gustavus	"	"	" " " " "
Ingram, Robert	"	"	" " " " "
Jones, John	"	"	" " " " "
Lossom, Thomas	"	"	" Jalapa, Mex., Feb. 4, 1848, "
Livesay, Carter H.	"	"	" " " " "
Martin, John D.	"	"	" New Orleans, Mar. 13, 1848, "
Rice, John	"	"	" Vera Cruz, Mex., Jan. 2, 1848, "
Serance, Peter	"	"	" " " Dec. 29, 1847, "
Thurman, James M.	"	"	" Jalapa, " " "
Underwood, John	"	"	" " " June, 1848, "
Walker, John	"	"	" " " " "

Transferred:

Name and Rank.	Place of Enlistment.	Enrolled	Remarks.
Private. Stephen G. Hicks....	Nashville, Ill.	1847. July 10	Elected Lieut.-Col. of Regiment, Aug. 3, 1847.

This company was discharged at Alton, Ill., on July 22, 1848.

Company "I."

Name and Rank.	Place of Enlistment.	Enrolled	Remarks.
Captains. Edward E. Harvey..	St. Charles, Ill	1847. July 1	Died at Puebla, Mex., March 19, 1848..........
Sewell W. Smith.....	"	"	Elected from private March 22, 1848..........
First Lieutenant. Lewis A. Norton.....	"	"	A. A. C. S. and A. A. Q. M.....................
Second Lieutenants. Hugh Fullerton......	"	"	
William G. Conklin..	"	"	
Sergeants. Nelson, Warner......	"	"	
Chas. E. Merrifield..	"	"	Appointed Sergt., from Musician, Nov. 5, 1847
Phillue Efner........	"	"	Elec'd Corp'l, fr'm priv.; elec'd Sergt. Feb.6,'48
John Spencer........	"	"	Appointed Sergeant Feb. 14, 1848................
Corporals. John A. Patten.......	"	"	
Timothy Ryan.......	"	"	Elected, from private, Feb. 7, 1848.............
Henry Foot..........	"	"	" " 6, 1848.................
George A. Thompson	"	"	" " Nov. 5, 1847.............
Musicians. William H. Lawson.	"	"	
Spaulding Lewis....	"	"	
Privates. Anderson, Joseph R.	Chicago, Ill..	Feb., '48	
Benjamin, Artemus L	"	Mch., '48	
Blowney, Henry.....	"	"	
Boose, George.......	St. Charles, Ill	July, '47	
Brewer, Jacob.......	"	"	
Bennett, Thomas....	"	"	
Brough, David.......	"	"	
Button, Enos........	"	"	
Coreman, Aop.......	"	"	
Chase, Freedom.....	"	"	
Crap, John..........	"	"	
Dunfield, Perry......	"	"	
Ellis, John I........	"	"	
Fouts, Jacob........	"	"	
Finch, Stephen......	"	Mch., '48	
Gorton, Samuel A. I.	"	"	
Hicks, George.......	Alton, Ill.....	July, '47	
Hoffman, Paul.......	St. Charles, Ill	"	
Herrick, Edward....	"	"	Must'd as Corp'l; reduc'd at own request Feb.6
Hill, Asa I..........	"	"	
Johnson, Edward H.	Alton, Ill.....	"	
Jaqusch, Charles....	St. Charles, Ill	"	
Kleyburgh, Charles.	"	"	
Keesar, Sallas.......	"	"	
Leibienstien, Lesser	"	"	
Leligar, John........	"	"	
Lock, LaFayette....	Chicago, Ill	Feb., '48	
Matthews, Peter.....	St. Charles, Ill	July, '47	
Moran, Matthew.....	"	"	
Massey, Robert D...	"	"	

Name and Rank.	Place of Enlistment.	Enrolled	Remarks.
McDonald, Patrick	St. Charles, Ill	Mar., '48	
McGill, Thomas			
Norton, John	Puebla, Mex.	May, '48	
Norris, John S	St. Charles, Ill	July, '47	
Newton, David		"	
Philip, Michael	Alton, Ill	"	
Philips, Orran H	St. Charles, Ill	"	
Paldy, Jacob		"	
Pridemore, Thomas			
Pollard, Thomas	Chicago, Ill	Feb., '48	
Riley, Hugh		"	
Rintew, George W	St. Charles, Ill	July, '47	
Sargeant, Philip H		"	
Stickler, Henry		"	
Sloss, William		"	
Thatcher, Benj. B		"	Originally must'd by name Benj. B. Hampton
Walker, John M		"	
Wilson, Joseph P		Mar., '48	

Died:

Musician.			
Welch, James	St. Charles, Ill	July, '47	Died at Tampico, Mex., Nov. 2, 1847
Privates.			
Austin, Z. C	"	Feb., '48	Died on Mississippi July 10, 1848
Bulson, Warren	"	July, '47	" at Tampico, Mex., Nov. 26, 1847
Brown, Charles P	Tampico, Mex	"	" on march from Puebla June 5, 1848
Courtner, William	St. Charles, Ill	"	" on Gulf of Mexico June 28, 1848
Dorchester, Fred'k	"	"	" at Tampico, Mex., Sept. 27, 1847
Frebert, George	"	"	" " " Oct. 2, 1847
Friend, Asa M	"	"	" Puebla, " March 14, 1848
Freeman, William	"	"	" Tampico, " Nov. 10, 1847
Furgeson, Stephen	"	"	" " " Oct. 25, 1847
Henries, Henric	"	"	" " " Oct. 6, 1847
Lewis, Isaac	"	"	" " " Oct. 29, 1847
McDonald, Samuel	"	"	" Vera Cruz, " Feb. 28, 1848
Mooney, David	"	"	" Tampico, " Dec. 3, 1847
Moore, Nicholas	"	"	" " " Sept. 11, 1847
Marshall, Henry	"	"	" " " Oct. 6, 1847
Mead, John	"	"	" " " Nov. 7, 1847
McColum, Malcolm	"	"	" Vera Cruz, " Feb. 13, 1848
Price, James	"	"	" Puebla, " May 18, 1848
Portord, Stephen B	"	"	" Tampico, " Sept. 28, 1847
Phelps, John	"	"	" " " Sept., "
Phillips, Jedediah	"	"	" " " Dec. 20, 1847
Romine, Alfred	"	"	" Puebla, " April 13, 1848
Scrber, Thomas	"	"	" Tampico, " Dec. 19, 1847
Schoomaker, John D	"	"	" " " Sept. 23, 1847
Smith, Henry	"	"	" near Rio Frio, " March 3, 1848; killed
Tubbs, David	"	"	" at Tampico, " Oct. 6, 1847
Thompson, James	"	"	" " " Dec., 1847
Wilger, Frederick	"	"	" Puebla, " May 11, 1848

Deserted:

Sergeant.		1847.	
Reed Haywood	St. Charles, Ill	July 1	Deserted at Alton, Ill., Aug. 10, 1847
Privates.			
Barnim, George W	"	"	Deserted at Carrollton, La., Aug. 23, 1847
Dortort, Stephen	"	"	" " " "
Eglehough, Alfred		"	
Henry, Thomas		"	" Alton, Ill., Aug. 9, 1847
Johnson, Sween		"	" " "
Koose, John C		"	" Carrollton, La., Aug. 23, 1847
Leet, Niles		"	" Alton, Ill., Aug. 9, 1847
Munster, Augustus		"	" " "
Mahar, John		"	
McLain, Robert		"	" " Aug. 4, 1847
Patrick, Willey C		"	Drummed out, sentence Court Mar. Aug. 2, '47
Pervis, Elisha		"	Deserted at Alton, Ill., Aug. 4, 1847

SECOND REGIMENT.   263

Name and Rank.	Place of Enlistment.	Enrolled	Remarks.
		1847.	
Thompson, Thos. H.		July 1	Deserted at Alton, Ill., Aug. 4, 1847
Wood, Samuel R.		"	" " " " 17, 1847
Zabuki, Fornan		"	" " " " " "
Zahar, Jacob		"	" " " " " "

Discharged:

		1847.	
Sergeants.			
Garfield, Benjamin F		July 1	Disch. at Vera Cruz., Mar. 22, '48; disability
Berry, Smith M		"	" Tampico, Mex., Jan. 19, '48; disability
Corporal.			
Puddleford, Sam'l D.		"	Discharged
Privates.			
Carlisle, Wm. H. S.		"	Disch. at Tampico, Mex., Oct. 14, '47; disability
Christie, Thomas		"	" " " " " "
Ganga, James		"	" " " Jan. 19, '48 "
Kleyberg, George		"	" Vera Cruz, Mex., Feb. 7, '48 "
McNelon, Alexander.		"	" Tampico " Jan. 20, '48 "
Roberts, George D.	Alton, Ill	Aug. 7	

This company was discharged at Alton, Ill., July 24, 1848.

COMPANY "K."

Name and Rank.	Place of Enlistment.	Enrolled	Remarks.
		1847.	
Captains.			
John Ewing	Benton, Ill	July 18	Died at Tampico, Mex., Oct. 3, '49, in quarters
Pierce, James R	"	"	Elect. Capt. Oct.7; died Mch. 28, '48, at Puebla
Mooneyham, Thos. J	"	"	April 4, 1848, from 1st Lieut
First Lieutenant.			
Mooneyham, Daniel	"	"	Elected 1st Lieut. April 4, 1848, from 2d Lieut.
Second Lieutenants.			
William P. Maddox.	"	"	Died in Puebla, Mex., Mch. 28, 1848
William Bates	"	"	Elected 2d Lieut. April 4, 1848, from private
John H. Mulkey	"	"	" " " " " from Sergt
Sergeants.			
William Rogers	"	"	
James S. Rotramel	"	"	Appointed 2d Sergt. April 4, 1848, from private
William Foster	"	"	" 3d " Oct. 8, 1847, " "
Zachariah Young	"	"	" 4th " April 4, 1848, " "
Corporals.			
Dixon Glover	"	"	Appointed 1st Corp'l Mch. 24, 1848
William D. Coin	"	"	
Brunson Daniel	"	"	
Musicians.			
Elijah Rotramel	"	"	
William G. Winn	"	"	
Privates.			
Browning, Joseph	"	"	
Burket, James	"	"	
Burleson, James R	"	"	
Bramlet, Benjamin	"	"	
Briley, Green W	"	"	
Collins, James	"	"	
Connuff, Edward	Chicago, Ill	April, '48	
Dawson, Francis	St. Charles, Ill	"	

Name and Rank.	Place of Enlistment.	Enrolled	Remarks.
Donnis, James H	Benton, Ill	July, '47	
Elkins, Andrew P	"	"	
Elkins, Gasaway	"	"	
Hamilton, Andr'w R.	"	"	
Hopper, Geo. W	"	"	
Isaac, John W	"	"	Discharged June 15, 1848, for disability
Johnson, Nathaniel	"	"	
Kidwell, Johnson	"	"	
Lewis, Jeremiah T.F	"	"	
Martin, Oliver C	"	"	
Maddox, Moses I	"	"	
Maddox, Henry	"	"	
Melvin, John	"	"	
McAmy, William W.	"	"	
Odle, Martin	"	"	
Petty, William A	Tampico, Mex	Aug. 28	
Phillips, John H	Benton, Ill	July 18	
Pitchford, William	"	"	
Parker, Noah	"	"	
Pease, Anson	St. Charles, Ill	Mar., '48	
Reed, John	Chicago, Ill.		
Roberts, Clark W	"	April, '48	
Ryan, Timothy	"	Feb., '48	Died at Alton, July 17, 1848, while making roll
Rotramel, Walter I	Benton, Ill	July, '47	
Redburn, John	"	"	
Roberson, Geo. W	"	"	
Swafford, Emanuel I	"	"	
Shihorn, William	"	"	
Stricklin, Wm. H	"	"	
Shook, Hiram	Chicago, Ill.	Feb., '48	
Williams, Benj. H	Benton, Ill	July, '47	
Wilkinson, James	"	"	

Discharged:

Name and Rank.	Place of Enlistment.	Enrolled	Remarks.
Privates.		1847.	
Burlison, Jonath'n H	Benton, Ill	July 18	Disch. at Tampico, Jan. 19, '48; disability
Cleevaland, And'w J	"	"	Sick at Tampico Feb. 1, '48; supposed disch.
Duff, Daniel	"	"	Disch. at Vera Cruz, March 4, '48; disability
Flint, James	"	"	" Tampico, Jan. 19, '48; " "
Isaac, George	"	"	" Vera Cruz, March 7, '47; " "
Lane, Jacob	"	"	" Tampico, Oct. 2, '47; " "
Price, Wesley	"	"	" New Orleans, June 13, '48; " "
Rice, John T	"	"	" Vera Cruz, May 18, '48; " "
Renche, John	"	"	Jeff. Barracks; reduced to ranks
Summers Elisha	"	"	" Vera Cruz, Mch. 4, 48; disability
Swafford, William A.	"	"	" Tampico, Jan. 19, '48; " "
Towns, Robert T	"	"		

Died:

Name and Rank.	Place of Enlistment.	Enrolled	Remarks.
Sergeant.		1847.	
Cornelius Martin	Benton, Ill	July 18	Died at Puebla, Mex., March 30, 1848
Corporals.			
Lemuel Rancher	"	"	Died at Puebla, Mex., March 18, 1848
Wm. D. McKeoun	"	"	" Alton, Ill., July 14,
Cantrell Bluford	"	"	" Puebla, Mex., March 14, "
Privates.			
Avery, John	"	"	Died at Tampico, Mex., Oct. 21, 1847
Baker, Reuben	"	"	" " " " 20, "
Crawford, George R.	"	"	" " " March 14, "
Crawford, John	"	"	" " " Sept. 29, "
Candle, John W	"	"	" " " Oct. 10, "
Crossner, George H	"	"	" Puebla, " April 13, 1848
Clem, Jesse R	"	"	" Tampico, " Oct. 6, "
Crawford, Joel S	"	"	" " " Sept. 9, "
Corder, Andrew	"	"	" " " " 27, 1847
Clampit, Jonathan H	"	"	" " " " 30, "
Eubanks, John	"	"	" " " Nov. 23, "
Estiss, Thompson P.	"	"	" " " Oct. 4, "
Foster, George E	"	"	" " " " 15, "
Flint, William	"	"	" " " Nov. 13, "
Goff, John	"	"	" " " Oct. 28, "

Name and Rank.	Place of Enlistment.	Enrolled	Remarks.
		1847.	
Giles, John I	Benton, Ill	July 18	Died at Camp Encerro, Mex., June 11, 1848
Maddox, Noah	"	"	" Puebla, Mex., May 21, 1848
Morse, Nathaniel		"	" Camp Encerro, Mex., June 9, 1848
Martin, James		"	" Jalapa, Mex., June 9, 1848
Mooneyham, Heze'h		"	" Tampico, Mex., Nov. 29, 1847
Phillips, Wesley		"	" " " Oct. 20, "
Patton, Thomas I		"	" " " Dec. 24, "
Rice, James		"	" " " Sept. 25, "
Rawlings, Nathan		"	" " " Nov. 19, "
Sweaton, Richard R.		"	" " " Sept. 6, "
Swafford, John L		"	" " " Oct. 17, "
Thomas, Joseph B		"	" " " Nov. 3, "
Walter, James H. O.		"	" " " Oct. 28, "
Ward, Willis		"	" " " Aug. 28, "
Wall, Frederick		"	" " " Nov. 11, "

This company was discharged at Alton, Ill., July 21, 1848.

THIRD REGIMENT.

The Field and Staff

Of the Third Regiment of the Brigade of Illinois Volunteers Militia commanded by Col. Ferris Forman, ordered into service of the United States by the President. From the 30th day of April to the 25th day of May, 1847, when discharged.

Name and Rank.	Place of Enlistment.	Enrolled	Remarks.
Colonel. F. Forman		1846. June 21	
Lieutenant-Colonel. W. W. Willey		June 21	
Major. S. D. Marshall		July 4	
Adjt. and 2d Lieut. C. Everett, Jr		July 8	App. Sergt-Major July 9, '46; elected 2d Lt. and app Adjt. Sept. 2, 1846.
Adjt. and 1st Lieut. J. T. B. Stapp		June 21	Resigned, Sept. 1, 1846
A. Q. M. and Capt. Nath'l Parker			App. Asst. Q. M. July 19, 1846; mustered out of service May 22, 1847.
Surgeons. J. Mahan		Aug. 29	Detached to take charge of hospital; app. by [President.
J. O'Niel		June 23	Left sick at N. Orleans, Aug. 6; died Aug. 13, '46
Assistant Surgeon. D. Turney		Aug. 26	Relieved by order of Gen. Patterson; app. by President.
Actg. Asst. Surg. J. Burch		July 2	Relieved by Asst. Surg. Turney Aug 26, 1846
A. C. S. and Capt. J. S. Bradford		Sept. 17 1847.	Absent by leave Gen. Scott since April 1, '47; app. by President.
S. Hackleton		April 8 1846.	Appointed by President
J. M. Campbell		Aug. 26	Relieved by Capt. J. S. Bradford Sept 17, 1846; app. by President.
Sergeant-Major. Henry Hamilton		July 1	Mustered out of service May 25, 1847
Q. M. Sergeant. J. Wilibanks		June 22	App. July 9, 1846; mustered out May 21, 1847
Principal Musicians Jas. Lamburth		July 2	Tran. to Co. "K;" reduced to private Dec. 9, 1846.
Thos. Mapes		July 4	" Co. "C;" " " Dec. 31, 1846.
W. W. Caton		June 29	App. Dec. 9, 1846; mustered out May 21, 1847
A. Wiley		June 27	" 31, " " " "

THIRD REGIMENT.

COMPANY "A."

Name and Rank.	Place of Enlistment.	Enrolled	Remarks.
Captains.		1846.	
F. Forman		June 21	Elected Col. July 8
Philip Stout		"	2d Lieut. to July 3.
First Lieutenants.			
James T. B. Stapp		"	Resigned Sept. 1. 1846.
James W. Boothe		"	Elected 2d Lt. June 27, '46; 1st Lt. Sept. 1, '46.
Second Lieutenants.			
Richard Hawkins		"	Resigned Sept. 2, 1846.
Cyrus Hall		"	Elected 2d Lieut. Sept. 2, 1846.
Charles Everett, Jr		July 8	App'd Sergt.-Maj. July 9; Adjt. Sept. 2, 1846.
Sergeants.			
Raford B. Reeves		June 21	Corp'l from Jan. 1 to Feb. 12; then 1st Sergt.
James W. Welch		"	
William Terry		"	Appointed Sergeant Sept. 2, 1846.
Lansing B. Mezner		"	Detached as Interpreter; private to Sept. 2, '46
Corporals.			
Jacob Kifer		"	
William Beal		"	Pay due as Corporal from Feb. 12.
Benjamin F. Rees		"	
Josiah Williams		"	Wounded slightly at Cerro Gordo.
Musician.			
Andrew Browning		"	
Privates.			
Arny, James		"	
Bowles, Robert		"	
Briton, Isah		"	
Beal, James		"	
Barringer, Julius		"	
Buniard, James		"	
Chandler, Samuel		"	
Cluxton, Henry J		"	Sick at Matamoras since Dec. 14, 1846
Conner, Sherwood L		"	
Condra, Herod		"	
Cronk, American		"	
Cubbertson, James		"	Sick at Matamoras since Dec. 14, 1846.
Croy, Robin		"	" " " "
Clark, James H		"	
Forbis, William B		"	
Garland, Benjamin		"	
George, John		"	
Haley, George W		"	Wounded slightly at Cerro Gordo.
Hinston, Hardy		"	
Hamilton, Henry		"	Appointed Sergeant-Major.
Ishmael, James M. C		"	
Karney, Arnindith		"	
Leadbetter, Joseph		"	
Larimore, Samuel		"	
Miller, Jacob		"	
Meek, Wm		"	
Nowlin, Pleasant		"	
Nowlin, James		"	
Nowlin, William		"	
Nifong, Joseph		"	
Pennington, Josiah		"	
Prater, Holloway		"	
Roseberry, James		"	
Sears, John		"	
Sears, Joseph		"	
Shears, William B		"	
Stokes, Bird		"	
Stigall, Peter		"	
Tucker, Robert		"	
Thompson, John C		"	Detached in charge of wounded at Jalapa
Whitfield, Elan B		"	
Watwood, Addison		"	Left in hospital at Jalapa; wounded by acc'd't
Wiley, George		"	

Discharged:

Name and Rank.	Place of Enlistment.	Enrolled	Remarks.
Sergeant. John McNicker		1846. June 21	Discharged, disability, Aug. 13, 1846.
Privates.			
Aldrich, Jackson		"	Discharged, disability, Nov. 3, 1846.
Baley, A. G		"	" " "
Baley, John		"	" " "
Daniels, Robert		"	" " " Aug. 13, 1846.
Forbis, Eli H		"	" " " Sept. 3, 1846.
Griffith, William C		"	" " "
Hartman, Benjamin		"	" " "
Jackson, Able		"	" " " March 31, 1847.
Netherby, Andrew J		"	" " " Nov. 3, 1846
Richards, James		"	" " " Aug. 13, 1846.
Shipley, Russell		"	" " " Sept. 3, 1846
Stamps, Lewis		"	" " " Feb. 21, 1847
Smith, Alexander		"	" " " Sept. 3, 1846.
Williams, Thomas C		"	" " " Oct. 28, 1846
Woolsey, John		"	" " " Aug. 13, 1846.
Whitfield, Charles		"	" " " Sept. 3, 1846.

Died:

Corporal. Thomas I. Baley		1846. June 21	Died at Camp Matamoras Dec. 26, 1846.
Privates.			
Bone, Marion		"	Died at Camp Tampico, Feb. 23, 1847
Ballinger, Leander		"	" " Camargo, Oct. 29, 1846.
Donton, John C		"	" " " Nov. 3, 1846.
Hays, Zachariah		"	" " Matamoras, Nov. 6, 1846.
Innman, Robert K		"	" " " Dec 24, 1846
Innman, Joseph O		"	" " Camargo, Oct. 18, 1846.
Johnson, George W		"	" " Point Isabel, Tex., Mar. 3, 1847
Loveless, James		"	" " Camargo, Nov. 5, 1846
Pissen, Nicholas W		"	" " Matamoras, Mex., Nov. 6, 1846.
Price, William		"	" " Camargo, Nov. 13, 1846
Roseberry, William		"	" " Matamoras, Oct. 8, 1846
Smith, David		"	" " Patterson, Tex., Sept. 3, 1846
West, William		"	" " Burcta, Mex., Sept. 14, 1846
White, James		"	" " Camargo, Nov. 21, 1846.

This company was discharged at New Orleans on May 23, 1847.

Company "B."

Name and Rank.	Place of Enlistment.	Enrolled	Remarks.
Captain. James Freeman		1846. June 21	Resigned
First Lieutenants.			
Eli Hooper		"	Resigned
W. L. McNeil		"	Commanding company since Nov. 1, 1846.
Second Lieutenant. David Evey		"	Was 2d Lieutenant.
Sergeants.			
John Casey		"	
Lemuel A. Rankins		"	
Benjamin F. Chew		"	
Orville Robertson		"	

THIRD REGIMENT.

Name and Rank.	Place of Enlistment.	Enrolled	Remarks.
Corporals.		1846.	
William Price		June 27	
L. F. Doyle		"	
Sabin C. Stanwood		"	
Joseph G. Harris		"	
Musician.			
Samuel Bolyjack		"	
Privates.			
Bankson, Arthur C		"	
Brown, James		"	
Beck, Benton		"	
Barns, John C		"	Sick at Matamoras since Dec. 14, 1846
Chatham, Franklin		"	
Chatham, James		"	
Cook, John		"	Sick at Matamoras since Dec. 14, 1846
Clair, Jones C		"	
Cooch, Martin		"	
Dixon, Lawson H		"	
Delap, Grandville W		"	
Griffith, William J		"	
Gordon, Benjamin		"	
Gorden, Abraham		"	
Hooper, Cla'borne R		"	
Hooper, Joseph F		"	
Henderson, Quant'n.		"	Sick at Matamoras
Lang, Elon M. C		"	
Massey, Hezekiah		"	
Massey, Burrel J		"	
Matney, Leonard		"	
Matney, Walter		"	
Matney, Samuel K		"	
McKenzie, George		"	
Mosley, John		"	
Norman, Solomon H.		"	
Phelps, Josiah		"	Sick at Matamoras Dec. 14, 1846
Phelps, Henderson		"	
Row, John R		"	
Renfrow, William B		"	
Ring, Stephen		"	
Riley, Josiah O		"	
Rogers, James F		"	Sick at Matamoras
Smith, William		"	
Smith, Hardin		"	
Story, James		"	
Truitt, David		"	
Templeton, Geo. W.		"	
Tetbrich, William		"	
Turner, Martin L		"	
Walton, Benjamin		"	
Wade, James		"	
Wheat, Levi		"	
Warren, Laborn		"	

Discharged:

Sergeant.		1846.	
Nathaniel Corley		June 27	Disch. Nov. 30, 1846, at Matamoras, Mex
Corporal.			
Enoch R. Vanwinkle		"	Disch. Nov. 2, 1846, at Matamoras, Mex
Musician.			
James Jones		"	Disch. Nov. 2, 1846, at Matamoras, Mex
Privates.			
Armstrong, Joseph		"	Disch. Nov. 2, 1846, at Matamoras, Mex
Banning, Adolph. A		"	" " " " "
Banning, Clark		"	" " " " "
Beck, Benjamin J		"	" Aug. 13, 1846, at Brazos Is., Texas
Branden, James P		"	
Barker, Aaron M		"	" Sept. 18, '46, at Up. Camp Pat'rs'n, Mex.
Classon, Frederic		"	" Nov. 3, 1846, at Matamoras, Mex
Conner, Elijah W		"	" Nov. 2, 1846, " "
Corben, John L		"	" Mar. 3, 1847, " "
Daniels, John		"	
Fanning, Wash'n P		"	" Sept. 18, '46, at Up. Camp Pat'rs'n, Mex.

Name and Rank.	Place of Enlistment.	Enrolled	Remarks.
Farlow, Nelson		1846. June 27	Disch. Aug. 13, 1846, at Brazos Is., Texas......
Jackson, William H.		" "	Mar. 3, 1847, at Matamoras, Mex..........
Killam, William		" "	Sept. 18, '46, at Up. Camp Pat'rs'n, Mex.
Milliken, Jesse		" "	Sept. 6,'46, at Lower Camp Pat'rs'n, Tex.
Pierce, Solomon		" "	Nov. 3, 1846, at Matamoras, Mex......
Reed, Jesse J.		" "	Nov. 2, 1846,
Scribner, Lewis		" "	" " " "
Soales, Burrel		" "	Sept. 6,'46, at Lower Camp Pat'rs'n, Tex.
Stafford, Thomas R.		" "	Sept. 18, '46, at Up. Camp Pat'rs'n, Mex.
Vanwinkle, David C.		" "	Nov. 2, 1846, at Matamoras, Mex........
Webb, Berry T.		" "	Mar. 3, 1847, " " " ....

Died:

Name and Rank.	Place of Enlistment.	Enrolled	Remarks.
Corporal. Michager Holbrook		1846. June 27	Died at Camp Patterson, Tex., Sept. 6, '46.....
Privates. Curry, James S.		" "	Died at camp near Camargo, Mex., Nov. 12, '46
Dixon, Alexander W.		" "	" " " " " " Sept. 15, '46
Goodwin, James		" "	" Matamoras, Mex., Oct. 2, '46 ...
Henderson, Andr. J.		" "	" Camp Patterson, Mex., Sept. 18, '46...
Jayne, John		" "	" camp near Camargo, Mex., Nov. 5, '46.
Moore, Washington		" "	" " " " " Oct. 28, '46.
Myers, John		" "	" Matamoras, Mex., Nov. 4, '46 ....
Williams, Calvin		" "	" camp near Camargo, Mex., Nov. 3, '46.

Deserted:

Name and Rank.	Place of Enlistment.	Enrolled	Remarks.
Private. Spencer Smith		1846. June 27	Deserted July 7, 1846, previous to muster.....

This company was discharged at New Orleans, La., May 23, 1847.

Company "C."

Name and Rank.	Place of Enlistment.	Enrolled	Remarks.
Captain. James C. McAdams		1846. June 26	Died, Jan. 4, 1847, at Matamoras, Mex..........
First Lieutenant. Thomas Rose		" "	In command of company since Dec. 1, 1846...
Second Lieutenants. John Burk		" "	
John Corlew		" "	
Sergeants. Jas. M. Wilford		" "	
Miles Morris		" "	Promoted 1st Sergt. Jan. 31, 1847 ....
Jep. J. McDavid		" "	
Corporals. Wm. Stephenson		" "	
Benj. Blockberger		" "	Appointed Corporal, March 23, 1847............
Chas. H. Rutledge		" "	
Musicians. Joseph Mapes		" "	Left sick at Matamoras since Dec. 14, 1846....
Jas. F. Witherspoon		" "	

THIRD REGIMENT.

Name and Rank.	Place of Enlistment.	Enrolled	Remarks.
Privates.		1846.	
Acres, Claborn		June 26	
Anderson, Jas. B.		"	
Boyd, Wm. R.		"	
Bodkin, John		"	
Bennett, John Q. A.		"	
Bennett, Nelson		"	
Card, Benson		"	
Corlew, Ransom		"	
Craig, John		"	
Cardwell, Lafayette		"	
Davis, Robert W.		"	
Edwards, Wm. A.		"	
Edwards, Mark W.		"	
Frost, Johnson A.		"	
Fullar, John		"	
Finney, Jackson		"	
Garner, James B.		"	
Graf, Daniel		"	
Gunter, Thomas		"	Left sick at Matamoras since Dec. 20, 1846.
Grubbs, Higgason B		"	Reduced to ranks from Corp'l, Mar. 23, 1847
Harman, Stephen		"	
Harman, Achilles		"	
Isaacks, Wilborn		"	
Ishmel, Benj. R.		"	
Kingston, William		"	
Koonts, John		"	
Lerla, Jacob		"	
Loomis, John T		"	
Lyngle, John M		"	
McWilliams, Thos.		"	
McPhail, Joseph		"	
McPhail, James		"	
McPhail, Samuel		"	
Mapes, Thomas		"	
Penter, Joseph		"	
Pruett, John		"	
Pruett, Major		"	
Rose, George W		"	
Starr, Abraham B		"	
Smith, Wiley B		"	
Scott, James M		"	
Turrentine, John		"	
Thomas, Alanson B.		"	
Varner, Wm. H		"	
Wright, Joseph G		"	
Wright, Thomas F.		"	
Williams, James S.		"	
Wright, Jarrett		"	
Wilson, Joseph C		"	Left sick at Matamoras Dec. 14, 1846.

Discharged:

		1846.			
Sergeants.					
Jas. B. McDavid		June 26	Disch. on Surgeon's certificate	March 3, 1847.	
James M. Quellman		"	"	Jan. 23, 1847	
Privates.					
Bishop, Isaac J		"	Disch. on Surgeon's certificate,	date unkn'wn	
Colyar, Wm. D		"	"	"	Jan. 23, 1847
Cress, Martin A		"	"	"	Aug. 31, 1846
Foglemen, Joel N		"	"	"	date unkn'wn
Grubbs, Edwin R		"	"	"	"
King, Samuel F		"	"	"	March 3, 1847
Lewey, Isaac		"	"	"	Aug. 13, 1846
McCaslin, Wm. B.		"	"	"	date unkn'wn
Norman, Thos. A.		"	"	"	Aug. 31, 1846
Peacock, Eli		"	"	"	April 23, 1847
Seymour, William		"	"	"	March 3, 1847
Walker, James		"	"	"	March 3, 1847

MEXICAN WAR.

Died:

Name and Rank.	Place of Enlistment.	Enrolled	Remarks.
1st Sergeant. Robt. Williamson...		1846. June 26	Died Oct. 26, 1846, at Camargo............
Corporal. Elijah Isaacs.........		"	Died March 8, 1847, at Point Isabel..........
Privates. Barnett, William H....		"	Died Oct. 13, 1846, at Matamoras........
Burringer, Moses...		"	" Oct. 22, 1846, "
Burk, Wm. C........		"	" Dec. 26, 1846, "
Briants, George.....		"	" Dec. 27, 1846, "
Card, Levi..........		"	" May, '47, at Jalapa, wo'nds rec'd C. Gordo
Colman, John J.....		"	" Oct. 21, 1846, at Matamoras.......
Gaston, John C.....		"	" Jan. 8, 1847,
Hill, Henry.........		"	" Dec. 27, 1846, "
Halford, Wm. S.....		"	" Sept. 8, 1846, at Camp Patterson......
Knight, Ezra P.....		"	" Jan. 8, 1847, at Matamoras.......
Lazenby, Razin G...		"	" Nov. 25, ——, at Camargo........
Lynch, Charles W...		"	" Oct. 9, 1846, at Matamoras........
Pearson, Alex. W...		"	" Sept. 12, 1846, at Camp Patterson........
Roner, Franklin....		"	" Oct. 26, 1846, at Camargo.......
Williams, John A...		"	" Sept. 24, 1846, at Matamoras........

This company was discharged at New Orleans, May 21, 1847.

Company "D."

Name and Rank.	Place of Enlistment.	Enrolled	Remarks.
Captain. W. W. Bishop........		1847. June 27	
First Lieutenant. John J. Adams......		"	
Second Lieutenants. E. C. Jones...........		"	Died at St. Louis, Mo., March 4, 1847........
H. C. Dunbar........		"	
Sergeants. Burns Harlan........		"	Left at Vera Cruz, in hospital, wounded,
Darius Wiley........		"	[May 7, 1847.
LeRoy Wiley........		"	
James H. Bayley....		"	
Corporals. James C. Robinson..		"	
John Chandler......		"	Appointed Oct. 31, 1846, *vice* Sublett, reduced.
S. W. Ewing.........		"	" " " " McCollister, "
P. P. Miller.........		"	" Mch. 7, " " McDaniel, disch.
Musicians. Arick Sutherland....		"	
Austin Wiley........		"	Transferred to regular Staff Oct. 31, 1846.....
Privates. Brann, George.......		"	
Barney, David......		"	
Benedict, Tera......		"	
Cox, Ulysses D.....		"	
Cox, James.........		"	
Cartwell, George W.		"	
Dyer, James........		"	
Dowling, Thomas...		"	
Downs, Samuel B...		"	
Firis, Jonathan.....		"	Left sick at Matamoras, Mex., Dec. 14, 1846...
Grant, Jesse K......		"	
Griffin, Alexander...		"	

THIRD REGIMENT. 273

Name and Rank.	Place of Enlistment.	Enrolled	Remarks.
		1846.	
Good, Joseph		June 27	
Harmon, Samuel H.		"	
Hoge, Westley		"	
Hays, Tyne		"	Left sick at Matamoras, Mex., Dec. 14, 1846
Hains, John		"	
Henry, William		"	
Ivins, John L.		"	
Kelly, Thomas		"	
Luark, John		"	
Lowthan, Henry W.		"	
Logan, William		"	
Miller, George W.		"	
Miller, Samuel		"	
Marion, Francis		"	
Morgan, James		"	
Moore, Alexander		"	Left sick at Matamoras, Mex., Dec. 14, 1846
Mitchell, Thomas		"	
McKelvy, Patrick		"	
McCollester, Samuel		"	Left sick at Matamoras, Mex., Dec. 14, 1846
Parker, Nathaniel		"	Appointed A. Q. M. July 19, 1846
Romines, George		"	
Rimmer, Nathaniel		"	
Thompson, Fred. G.		"	
Turner, Thomas		"	
Sublett, Jackson		"	Left sick at Matamoras, Mex., Dec. 14, 1846
White, Hiram		"	
White, James		"	
White, Johnson		"	
White, George		"	Left sick at Matamoras, Mex., Dec. 14, 1846
White, William		"	
Winters, James P.		"	
Weston, Isaiah		"	Re-enlisted, May 11, at Vera Cruz
Wiley, James		"	
Wiley, Reason		"	

Discharged:

Name and Rank.	Place of Enlistment.	Enrolled	Remarks.
Sergeants.		1846.	
S. B. Logan		June 27	Discharged Oct. 13, 1846, disability
Alfred Jones		"	" " " "
Corporals.			
Andrew Jeans		"	Discharged Sept. 3, 1846, disability
George Wells		"	" Oct. 13, " "
Joseph Piper		"	" Dec. 6, " "
George McDaniel		"	" Mch. 6, 1847, "
Privates.			
Ashmore, Wm. C.		"	Discharged Oct. 28, 1846, disability
Abbott, John		"	" " 22, " "
Bragg, Alex.		"	" Sept. 3, " "
Bryant, Lewis		"	" " " "
Clements, Thomas		"	" Oct. 22, " "
Carter, Joseph		"	" Sept. 3, " "
Francher, Thomas		"	" Oct. 8, " "
Foster, J. C.		"	" " 28, " "
Grant, Adam		"	" Sept. 3, " "
Harmon, Wm. C.		"	" Oct. 8, " "
Hart, Moses		"	" Nov. 17, " "
Hunt, George		"	" Oct. 13, " "
Lawrence, Robert		"	" Nov. 17, " "
McCollister, Wm. C.		"	" Oct. 13, " "
Owings, James P.		"	" Sept. 3, " "
Pinnell, Henry H.		"	" Nov. 17, " "
Parish, John R.		"	" Oct. 22, " "
Poulten, John D.		"	" " 8, " "
Sublett, William		"	" " 22, " "
Wilson, Marcus		"	

—18

Died:

Name and Rank.	Place of Enlistment.	Enrolled	Remarks.
Privates.		1846,	
Cornwell, Bennett...	....	June 27	Died at Matamoras, Jan. 13, 1847............
Drummond, William	....	" "	" " Sept. 27, 1846.........
Eastin, Harmon......	....	" "	" " New Orleans, Aug. 2, " ....
Fetty, C. D............	....	" "	" " Matamoras, Sept. 27, " ....
Frost, Harvey D.....	....	" "	" " Tampico, Feb. 28, 1847.........
Hart, Thomas.........	....	" "	" " Matamoras, Sept. 27, 1846........
Jarvis, Marion........	....	" "	" " Point Isabel, Mch. 3, 1847........
Winkler, Joseph L...	....	" "	" " Matamoras, Sept. 24, 1846........

This company was discharged at New Orleans, May 21, 1847.
The company was at the seige of Vera Cruz, and at the battle of Cerro Gordo on April 18.

Company "E."

Name and Rank.	Place of Enlistment.	Enrolled	Remarks.
Captain.		1846.	
Benjamin E. Sellers.	....	June 21	....
First Lieutenants.			
James M. Hubbard..	....	" "	Resigned, to take effect Nov. 15, 1846.........
Samuel G. McAdams	....	" "	....
Second Lieutenant.			
Isaac Redfearn......	....	" "	....
Sergeants.			
John A. Washburn..	....	" "	Promoted from 2d Sergeant May 1, 1847.........
Theophilus Short....	....	" "	" " " " private April 4, 1847.........
Felix McGower......	....	" "	....
Richard Roberts	....	" "	" " " " 1st Corporal May 1, 1847......
Corporals.			
Lemuel I. Washburn	....	" "	....
Larkin Jackson	....	" "	....
George Allen.........	....	" "	Promoted from private April 4, 1847.........
William Ray	....	" "	" " " " May 1, 1847.........
Privates.			
Alexander, John.....	....	" "	Left in hospital at Matamoras, Dec. 14, 1846...
Alderman, William..	....	" "	....
Adams, James J.....	....	" "	Reduced from 3d Sergeant April 4, 1847.........
Brown, Calvin.......	....	" "	....
Boothe, Robert C...	....	" "	....
Cruthis, Henry	....	" "	....
Cruthis, James C...	....	" "	....
Diamond, Harvey W.	....	" "	....
Etzler, George P....	....	" "	....
Elmore, Hardin......	....	" "	....
Forbes, William	....	" "	....
Gilbert, Andrew W..	....	" "	....
Gilmore, James H...	....	" "	....
Hillard, Charles	....	" "	....
Harris, James A.....	....	" "	Left in hospital at Tampico, March 1, 1847....
Higginbotham, N. D.	....	" "	....
Kuykendall, James..	....	" "	Left in hospital at Matamoras, Dec. 14, 1846...
Ledbetter, Job.......	....	" "	....
McCracken, John P.	....	" "	Left in hospital at Matamoras, Dec. 14, 1846...
McCracken, Nathan C	....	" "	....
McCollum, Alexand'r	....	" "	....
Padfield, John	....	" "	....
Ray, Henry D........	....	" "	....
Royer, Daniel.......	....	" "	....
Snodgrass, Kilburn M	....	" "	....
Spratt, John	....	" "	....
Smith, Lowell	....	" "	....
Smith, John M	....	" "	....

THIRD REGIMENT.

Name and Rank.	Place of Enlistment.	Enrolled	Remarks.
Simmons, Charles T.		1846 June 21	Left in hospital at Matamoras, Dec. 14, 1846...
Sugg, Josiah F.		"	Same, and reduced to ranks April 4, 1847....
Thorp, Calvin H.		"	
Wade, John T.		"	
White, Stephen		"	
Williford, Robert		"	
Webster, Francis		"	
White, Robert O.		"	

Discharged:

Name and Rank.	Place of Enlistment.	Enrolled	Remarks.
Musician. Joseph Isaacs		1846 June 21	Discharged, disability, Aug. 31, 1846
Privates. Alexander, Henry B.		"	Discharged, disability, Aug. 20, 1846
Amos, Frederic		"	" " Oct. 20, "
Blankenship, James		"	" " Aug. 25, "
Douglas, James A.		"	" " Oct. 20, "
Douglas, John M.		"	" " Aug. 26, "
Ewing, Thomas A.		"	" " Oct. 5, "
Evans, Wilson		"	" " Nov. 3, "
Gray, Samuel		"	" " Aug. 14, "
Gilmore, John M.		"	" " Oct. 20, "
Hignight, James		"	" " Aug. 26, "
Hunter, William M.		"	" " Aug. 20, "
Holland, John		"	" " Aug. 20, "
Jay, Joseph A.		"	" " Oct. 5, "
Larrison, Thomas T.		"	" " Aug. 26, "
Lyttaker, Peter		"	" " Aug. 26, "
Netherly, Nathan H.		"	" " Nov. 3, "
Noland, Enoch M.		"	" " Oct. 31, "
Patterson, John		"	" " Aug. 14, "
Phipps, David		"	" " Aug. 31, "
Reed, Isaac N.		"	" " Aug. 14, "
Reed, George A.		"	" " Aug. 26, "
Steele, Andrew J.		"	" " Aug. 14, "
Sherrod, Joel H.		"	" " Nov. 16, "
Thacker, Henry C.		"	" " Oct. 20, "
Willis, Nathan B.		"	" " Oct. 10, "

Died:

Name and Rank.	Place of Enlistment.	Enrolled	Remarks.
First Sergeant. William S. Allen		1846. June 21	Died at Jalapa, May 1,'47, wounds at Cer. Gor.
Privates. Arnold, Robert		"	Died in hospital, Matamoras, Oct. 12, 1846
Ewing, Samuel J.		"	Died at Camp Patterson, Mex., Sept. 13, 1846
Grigg, Joseph W.		"	" " near Tampico, Feb. 25, 1847
Jett, Thomas J.		"	" " Camargo, Oct. 26, 1846
Jarvis, Henry W.		"	" " hospital, Matamoras, March 2, 1847
Larrison, James		"	" " Camargo, Oct. 9, 1846
Lucas, William		"	" " Matamoras, Sept. 28, 1846
Mackay, John C.		"	" " " Oct. 29, 1846
Madray, William		"	" " " Dec. 27, 1846
Patterson, Robert		"	" " Camargo, Nov. 6, 1846
Seybert, William		"	" " Matamoras, Dec. 24, 1846
Wood, William		"	" " Camp Patterson, Sept. 19, 1846

Deserted:

Name and Rank.	Place of Enlistment.	Enrolled	Remarks.
Privates. Alexander, Rufus B.		1846. June 21	Deserted at Baton Rouge, La., July 29, 1846
Little, John		"	Leave of absence till July 16, 1846, not heard of since.

This company was discharged at New Orleans May 21, 1847.

Company "F."

Name and Rank.	Place of Enlistment.	Enrolled	Remarks.
Captain.		1846.	
John A. Campbell		July 1	
First Lieutenants.			
Jacob Love		"	Died Oct. 5, 1846, at Camargo, Mex.
Ephraim Merritt		"	Resigned Nov. 28, 1846, at Matamoras, Mex.
Samuel Hooper		"	Elec'd 2d Lieut. from Sergt. Oct. 1, 1846; promoted to 1st Lt. Nov. 28, 1846.
Second Lieutenant.			
Samuel J. R. Wilson		"	Resigned Aug. 28, '46, at Camp Patterson, Tex.
Sergeants.			
Austin Organ		"	
William Merritt		"	
James Turner		"	
Warren E. McMackin		"	
Corporals.			
Daniel Simpson		"	
John W. Wallace		"	
William B. Wilson		"	
Joseph J. R. Turney		"	
Musician.			
Jeffers'n W. Barnhill		"	
Privates.			
Armstrong, Wm. R.		"	Sick at Matamoras since Dec. 14, 1846
Barnhill, Rigdon S.		"	
Crews, Nathan		"	
Cox, James E.		"	
Cook, Hiram H.		"	
Cook, Howlett H.		"	
Cook, William M.		"	
Clevenger, Benj. W.		"	
Dorris, John G.		"	
Day, David H.		"	
Ellis, Sterlin C. B.		"	Wounded at battle of Cerro Gordo Apl. 18, '47
Edwards, John Y. C.		"	
Ewing, John		"	
Funkhouser, Benj.		"	
Fitzgerred, Samuel		"	
Frazier, William J.		"	Sick at Matamoras Dec. 14, 1846
Gray, William		"	
Gray, Ellis S.		"	
Harris, Sion		"	
Ham, William D.		"	
Harlin, William E.		"	
Hulshcraft, John		"	
Johnson, Riley V.		"	
Johnson, Silas		"	Sick at Matamoras since Dec. 14, 1846
Kimmel, William		"	" " " Sept. 24, 1846
Lard, Bluford		"	
Lacy, James		"	Sick at Matamoras since Dec. 14, 1846
Matthews, Wm. T.		"	
Morris, Willis		"	
Murphy, Davis		"	
McCullough, Jas. W.		"	
McCollum, David		"	
McCollum, Samuel		"	
Owen, David		"	
Phelps, Hosea C.		"	
Phelps, William C.		"	
Reed, James		"	
Reed, William, 2d		"	
Rusher, Jeremiah		"	
Rusher, Henry C.		"	
Simpson, William C		"	
Simpson, Andrew J.		"	
Simpson, William		"	
Shannon, Rowl'nd H.		"	
Sloan, Jefferson		"	
Taylor, Ninian R.		"	
Taylor, James H.		"	
Tims, John		"	
White, John		"	
West, Alfred		"	

THIRD REGIMENT.

Died:

Name and Rank.	Place of Enlistment.	Enrolled	Remarks.
Privates.		1846.	
Copeland, Joseph	....	July 1	Died Dec. 9, '46, at hospital, Matamoras........
Frazur, John R	....	"	" Dec. 7, '46.
Lockhart, Wm. J	....	"	" Aug. 14, '47, at Brazos Island, Texas.....
Maybry, Wm. H	....	"	" Aug. 10, '46, on ship cross'g Gulf of Mex.
Merritt, Benjamin	....	"	Shot at battle of Cerro Gordo April 18, '47...
Rister, Abraham	....	"	Died Sept. 24, '46, in hospital, Matamoras.....
Reed, William, 1st	....	"	" Oct. 2, '46, at Camargo, Mex.............

Discharged:

Name and Rank.	Place of Enlistment.	Enrolled	Remarks.
Sergeant.		1846.	
Isaac S. Warmouth	....	July 1	Disch. on Surg. cert. of disability, Jan. 10, '47..
Second Corporal.			
James H. Farley	....	"	Disch. on Surg. cert. of disability, Aug. 14, '46
Privates.			
Black, William	....	"	Disch. on Surg. cert. of disability, Nov. 5, '46...
Beech, Benjamin	....	"	" " " " Nov. 28, '46..
Cox, David	....	"	" " " " Oct. 26, '46 ..
Campbell, Moses M.	....	"	" " " " Aug. 31, '46..
Clevenger, Dan'l H	....	"	" " " " Mar. 31, '47..
Fitch, Henry	....	"	" " " " Nov. 28, '46..
Harris, James M.	....	"	" " " " Sept. 2, '46..
Harris, Thomas J.	....	"	
Holmes, John B.	....	"	" " " " Sept. 3, '46..
Linder, Abraham	....	"	" " " " Mar. 3, '47..
McCrary, James	....	"	" " " " Oct. 20, '46...
Matthews, Geo. W	....	"	" " " " Sept. 3, '46 ..
Palmer, Jacob	....	"	" " " " Mar. 3, '47..
Reed, Henry	....	"	" " " " Nov. 28, '46..
Robinson, Tyra	....	"	" " " " Aug. 31, '46..
Trotter, Shirley	....	"	" " " " Sept. 3, '46..

This company was discharged at New Orleans, La., on May 21, 1847.

COMPANY "G."

Name and Rank.	Place of Enlistment.	Enrolled	Remarks.
Captain.		1846.	
W. K. Lawler	....	June 29	....
First Lieutenants.			
Samuel S. M. Proctor	....	"	
Alexander W. Pool	....	"	Resigned Oct. 20, 1846..................
Second Lieutenants.			
William Stricklin	....	"	
James S. Rearden	....	"	Resigned Oct. 1, 1846..................
Sergeants.			
Timothy Ingram	....	"	Promoted 1st Sergt. from Corporal Jan. 1, '47
Patrick Scully	....	"	
Alfred Karnes	....	"	Promoted from Corporal Jan. 13, 1847.........
John Howard	....	"	
Corporals.			
Robert A. Boyd	....	"	Appointed Corporal Jan. 1, 1847...............
George M. Weed	....	"	" " Jan. 13, 1847..............
Edward Jones	....	"	
Isaac M. Sketoe	....	"	
Musician.			
James Creed	....	"	

278   MEXICAN WAR.

Name and Rank.	Place of Enlistment.	Enrolled	Remarks.
Privates.			
Addison, Sir Sidney		June 29	
Baker, David P		"	
Barnett, David C		"	
Bennett, Joseph C		"	
Brazier, Riley		"	
Carpenter, William		"	
Choisser, Attallas		"	
Choisser, Edmund		"	
Crenshaw, Abraham		"	
Cummings, Jacob		"	
Davenport, William		"	
Davis, John B. M		"	
Donovon, James		"	
Duncan, Stephen		"	
Evans, William G		"	
Fugate, John M		"	
Gaston, Wesley W		"	
Grayson, Jesse F		"	
Harmons, George		"	
Hardin, Joseph		"	
Hill, James		"	
Holt, William		"	
Hubbs, James		"	
Hudgins, James		"	
Ingram, John W		"	
Jones, John W		"	
Lewis, Charles		"	
Lowrey, Charles		"	
Lynch, Logan		"	
Manif, John		"	
McChiskey, Hiram		"	
Moore, Ransom		"	
Page, William W		"	
Parker, John		"	
Porter, Robert W		"	
Price, Berry		"	
Reynolds, Thomas		"	
Scarborough, John		"	
Sisk, Albert		"	
Sisk, Benjamin		"	
Sitles, Henry		"	
Skelton, William J		"	
Smith, John		"	
Smith, William T		"	
Sneed, Eldridge		"	
Stiff, Nathaniel		"	
Stricklin, Lewis		"	
Wamack, Sheph'd F		"	
Warren, Chas. M. C		"	
Weddle, Andrew		"	
Weddle, William		"	
Weaver, Stokeley		"	

Discharged :

Name and Rank.	Place of Enlistment.	Enrolled	Remarks.
First Sergeant.		1846.	
Hanson Q. Roberts		June 29	Disch. Sept. 18, '46, Camp Patterson, disabil'y
Corporal.			
Americus Henrick		"	Disch. Aug. 17, '46, Brazos Santiago, disabil'y
Privates.			
Bond, William		"	Disch. Sept. 6, '46, Camp Patterson, disabil'y
Bennett, Thomas Y		"	" Oct. 28, '46, Matamoras, "
Bramlet, Alfred J		"	" Nov. 27, '46, " "
Creed, Robert		"	" Nov. 2, '46, " "
Daws, Edmund		"	" Aug. 30, '46, Camp Patterson, "
Emory, Jacob		"	" Nov. 29, '46, Matamoras, "
Griggs, Hubbard A		"	" Aug. 17, '46, Brazos Santiago, "
Hamilton, James		"	" " "
Karnes, David B		"	" Aug. 31, '46, " "
Moody, John		"	" Nov. 27, '46, Matamoras, "
Proctor, Giles		"	" Aug. 30, '46, Camp Patterson, "
Paisley, Joseph P		"	" Aug. 31, '46, " "
Reid, Johnson		"	" Nov. 2, '46, Matamoras, "
Slavens, A. Calvin		"	" Nov. 29, '46, " "

Name and Rank.	Place of Enlistment.	Enrolled	Remarks.
Stricklin, J. Garner		1846. June 29	Disch. Sept. 6, '46, Camp Patterson, disabil'y
Taylor, Henry		"	" Aug. 17, '46, Brazos Santiago, "
Vinson, Stokely		"	" " " "
Williams, William G.		"	" " " "
Williams, John		"	" Aug. 30, '46, Camp Patterson, "

Died:

Sergeant. Safford B. Eddy			Died at Victoria Jan. 13, 1847
Privates. Baugher, John J.			Died at Camp Patterson Aug. 30, 1846
Cain, James M.		"	Matamoras Dec. 20, 1846
McCauslin, John		"	Vera Cruz April 12, 1847
Oxberry, James		"	Camp Patterson Sept. 1, 1846
Powell, John		"	Matamoras Oct. 24, 1846

This company was discharged at New Orleans, La., May 21, 1847.

Company "H."

Name and Rank.	Place of Enlistment.	Enrolled	Remarks.
Captain. S. G. Hicks		1846. June 4	
First Lieutenants. Lewis F. Casey		"	Resigned Nov. 1, 1846, at Matamoras, Mex.
William A. Thomas		"	Promoted from 2d to 1st Lieut. Nov. 1, 1846
Second Lieutenant. Thos. S. Levington		"	
Sergeants. John Bagwell		"	
Garaway Elkins		"	
Jacob Casey		"	Appointed Sergt. Oct. 18, 1846
Marcus D. Bruce		"	" " July 8, 1846
Corporals. Jos. F. Thomisson		"	Appointed Corporal —— 15, 1846
John Q. A. Bay		"	" " April 30, 1847
William Sumnors		"	" " Jan. 26, 1847
John McConnell		"	" " Jan. 21, 1847
Privates. Atchison, Thomas I.		"	
Bean, Peter		"	
Brown, James R.		"	
Ballard, Thomas H.		"	
Blalock, Eli		"	
Brady, John		"	
Bullock, Samuel		"	
Butler, John		"	
Bateman, James O.		"	
Buckout, Benjamin		"	
Beal, Loring R.		"	
Caldwell, James		"	
Donohoo, James		"	
Dorris, William H.		"	
Fly, Jesse I.		"	
Fields, Abraham W.		"	Left sick at hospital, Tampico, Mex.
Gray, Nicholas		"	Disch. Mar. 3, '47, on Surg. cert. of disability.
Garrison, Jeffers'n I.		"	
Galbreath, James M.			

Name and Rank.	Place of Enlistment.	Enrolled	Remarks.
		1846.	
Hull, James		June 4	
Harlow, Thomas		"	
Hawkins, John		"	
Hawkins, Jesse		"	
Hales, Marcus		"	
Hicks, William		"	
Hales, Albert		"	
Hatfield, Johnson		"	
Knox, George		"	
Kelly, James		"	
Lynch, John B		"	
Lisenby, John R		"	
Lutz, James W		"	
Murphy, James		"	
Milborn, John		"	
Moor, Alexander		"	
McCarver, James		"	
McFarland, Pleasant		"	
McGuire, Andrew		"	
McAtee, Edward		"	Appointed Hospital Steward —— 18, 1847
Overby, James C		"	
Patterson, Benjamin		"	
Poston, John M		"	
Scott, James		"	
Wilkinson, H. H		"	
Wilbanks, Quincy A		"	Left sick in hospital, Matamoras, Mex
Westcoat, James		"	
Warren, David		"	

Discharged:

		1846.	
Sergeant.			
William B. Braden		June 4	Disch. on Surg. cert. of disability Oct. 18, 1846
Privates.			
Atchison, Joseph T		"	Disch. on Surg. cert. of disability Nov. 9, 1846
Arant, Samuel W		"	" " " " Aug. 12, 1846
Foster, William		"	" " " " Nov. 30, 1846
Hill, Alexander M		"	" " " " Sept. 1, 1846
Harvey, Elijah B		"	" " " " Oct. 26, 1846
Ivy, Benjamin		"	" " " " Oct. 18, 1846
Crisel, William I		"	" " " " Sept. 1, 1846
Moss, Lucillus C		"	
McClendon, Wm. R		"	" " " " Oct. 18, 1846
Owens, Sampson R		"	" " " " Dec. 1, 1846
Newby, John E		"	" " " " Oct. 9, 1846
Rankin, Robert B		"	" " " " Dec. 1, 1846
Sterns, Charles W		"	" " " " Jan. 21, 1846
Summors, James E		"	" " " " Oct. 18, 1846
Stephenson, Wm. I		"	" " " " Aug. 15, 1846
Smith, Daniel		"	
Thurman, Patrick T		"	" " " " " "
Teeters, James		"	" " " " Sept. 1, 1846
Veasey, Benjamin		"	" " " " Oct. 9, 1846
Wallace, John A		"	" " " " Aug. 15, 1846
Williamson, Vinc't P		"	" " " " Sept. 1, 1846
Wilkey, Harrison		"	
Yearwood, John		"	" " " " " "
Williams, John			

Died:

		1846.	
Corporals.			
James Bruce		June 4	Died Jan. 16, '47, *en route* to Tampico, Mex
James Wimberly		"	" April 30; killed near Jalapa, Mex
Privates.			
Breeze, Jonathan H		"	Died Dec. 7, '46, at gen. hosp., Matamoras
Harlow, Moses		"	" Oct. 26 at Matamoras, Mex., gen. hosp
Harvy, Joseph		"	" May 13; fell overboard on way to N. Orl's
Newby, James C		"	" Aug. 13, 1846, at Brazos Santiago, Tex

This company was discharged May 21, 1847, at New Orleans, La.

Company "I."

Name and Rank.	Place of Enlistment.	Enrolled	Remarks.
Captain.		1846.	
Jonathan P. Harvey.	....	June 6	....
First Lieutenants.			
Charles Coker........	....	"	Resigned, to take effect Oct. 1, 1846............
Enos A. Lasater.....	....	"	Elected from private, Oct. 1, 1846 ....
Second Lieutenants.			
Warden C. Coons...	....	"	Resigned, to take effect Nov. 15, 1846 ....
John J. Ritchie.......	....	"	....
Sergeants.			
Charles Atchison....	....	"	Appointed 1st Sergt., from private, June 6, '47
Hiram W. Hall.......	....	"	....
Moses Hutson	....	"	....
James Hughes	....	"	Appointed Sergt., from private, Nov. 9, 1846..
Corporals.			
Joseph Koger...	....	"	Appointed from private Dec. 4, 1846 ....
William G. Burnett.	....	"	....
John B. Smith	....	"	Appointed from private Oct. 12, 1846..........
Edward Trammel ...	....	"	" " " Nov. 17, " ....
Musician.			
Thomas Braden	....	"	....
Privates.			
Askey, Jackson	....	"	....
Barnes, Thomas.....	....	"	....
Brill, Solomon S.....	....	"	....
Boster, Jacob.........	....	"	....
Burnett, George.....	....	"	....
Clark, William.......	....	"	....
Cross, John C........	....	"	....
Crisell, George W...	....	"	....
Coons, John	....	"	....
Durham, John W...	....	"	....
Denny, Joseph H....	....	"	....
Davis, Alfred	....	"	Reduced to ranks, from 1st Sergt., Jan. 6, '47.
Estes, William.......	....	"	....
Flannikin, David O..	....	"	....
Ford, Abram.........	....	"	....
Farmer, William	....	"	....
Gibson, James W....	....	"	....
Galliher, James F...	....	"	....
Hays, William........	....	"	....
Heard, Wm. B.......	....	"	....
Johnson, Jesse.......	....	"	....
Lane, James..........	....	"	....
Maulding, John......	....	"	On furlough, at Jalapa, May 6, 1847 ....
Mayberry, Wm. H...	....	"	....
Mayberry, James H	....	"	....
Mayberry, Jacob....	....	"	....
McDaniel, Andrew J.	....	"	....
Shasteen, John K...	....	"	....
Shell, Calvin.........	....	"	....
Stanfield, Thomas...	....	"	....
Starnater, William..	....	"	....
Trammel, Elijah.....	....	"	....
Trammel, Philip	....	"	....
Wheeler, Abner P...	....	"	Reduced to ranks, from Sergt., Nov. 9, 1846...
Webb, John...........	....	"	....

Deserted:

Name and Rank.	Place of Enlistment.	Enrolled	Remarks.
Private.		1846.	
William L. Morris...	....	June 6	Deserted at Alton, Ill., July 8, 1846.............

Discharged:

Name and Rank.	Place of Enlistment.	Enrolled	Remarks.
Corporals.		1846.	
Jasper Ghormley		June 6	Discharged Nov. 17, 1846; disability
Wm. L. Stevens		"	" Dec. 1, " "
Musician.			
William Gross		"	Discharged Oct. 18, 1846; disability
Privates.			
Allen, Dudley R		"	Discharged Aug. 17, 1846; disability
Adaire, Philip		"	" Oct. 17, " "
Biggerstaff, Joshua		"	" Sept. 8, " "
Boyd, Lyle		"	" Oct. 17, " "
Boyer, Anderson		"	" Nov. 17, " "
Cape, Hiram		"	" Oct. 18, " "
Clark, John, Sr		"	" Nov. 26, " "
Coker, Leonard		"	" " " "
Cannada, William		"	" for disability; date unknown
Davis, Thomas P		"	" Nov. 17, 1846; disability
Frazer, John		"	" Nov. 26, " "
Fields, James		"	" Oct. 18, " "
Flanniken, James W		"	" for disability; date unknown
Gibson, Daniel		"	" Oct. 17, 1846; disability
Ghormly, Michael		"	" " " "
Hamilton, Parsons L		"	" Nov. 17, " "
Hayes, John		"	" Oct. 17, " "
Hardester, James		"	" Aug. 31, " "
Lane, James, Sr		"	" for disability; date unknown
Morris, Hiram		"	" Nov. 25, 1846; disability
Mundy, Elias		"	" Oct. 17, " "
Proctor, Saml. H. F		"	" Sept. 8, " "
Sloane, Andrew		"	" Oct. 18, " "
Smiddy, Jeremiah		"	" Nov. 25, " "
Stelle, David		"	" Nov. 17, " "
Williams, William		"	" for disability; date unknown
Williams, Wm. K		"	" Aug. 31, 1846; disability
Willis, Eli S		"	" " " "

Died:

Name and Rank.	Place of Enlistment.	Enrolled	Remarks.
Corporal.		1846.	
David Hutson		June 26	Died at Metamoras, Mex., Sept. 28, 1846
Privates.			
Adams, John R		"	Died at Matamoras, Mex., Oct. 4, 1846
Berry, William P		"	" " " Nov. 30, "
Choice, John		"	" " Rio Grande, " Nov. 22, "
Cook, John		"	" " Camp Patterson, Sept. 3, "
Cheek, Aseur S		"	" " Matamoras, Mex., Oct. 2, "
Clark, John, Jr		"	" " Camargo, " Oct. 28, "
Epperson, James		"	" " Matamoras, " Sept. 29, "
Flannekin, Ewing G		"	" " Matamoras, " Dec. 20, "
Hood, Dempsey		"	" " Brazos Santiago, Mex., Aug. 18, 1846
McGuire, Wm. C		"	" " Camp Patterson, Sept. 6, 1846
McBroom, John S		"	" " Matamoras, Mex., Dec. 3, "
Wright, Elijah		"	" " Camargo, " Dec. 3, "

This company was discharged at New Orleans, May 21, 1847.

Company "K."

Name and Rank.	Place of Enlistment.	Enrolled	Remarks.
Captain. Theodore McGinnis.		1846 July 2.	Commanding company.
First Lieutenant. George Walker.		"	
Second Lieutenant. Green B. Field.		"	
Third Lieutenant. James McDonald.		"	
Sergeants.			
Stephen D. Kennard		"	
William S. Hodge		"	
George F. James		"	On furlough, Vera Cruz, Mexico.
Abraham Gethings		"	
Corporals.			
John F. Johnson		"	
John P. Compton		"	
Elijah E. Trevillon		"	
Huberry G. Glass		"	
Privates.			
Alcock, Edmund		"	
Bolan, Dennis		"	On furlough, Vera Cruz, Mexico.
Belford, Patterson		"	
Boze, Ambrose		"	
Boze, James		"	
Bowman, John A		"	
Craig, Nathaniel		"	
Church, William E		"	
Cranson, Daniel		"	
Cary, Benjamin R		"	
Carr, John		"	
Dyke, David A		"	
Degan, John		"	
Egan, James F		"	On furlough, at Jalapa, Mexico.
Fath, John D		"	
Gray, Thomas S		"	
Green, Isaac		"	
Henry, Willis		"	
Holt, Robert C		"	
Jackson, John T		"	Sick at Matamoras, Mexico.
King, James		"	
Lamburth, James T		"	
Lewis, Joseph		"	
Murphy, Peter		"	
McDaniel, Jacob		"	
McCosland, William		"	
McGary, John		"	
McGuire, James		"	
McElhanny, Moses		"	
McLaughlin, Charles		"	
Pfeninger, John R		"	
Shoemaker, Moses		"	
Sherdon, Daniel		"	
Tomy, Patrick		"	
Wells, John		"	

Deserted:

Name and Rank.	Place of Enlistment.	Enrolled	Remarks.
Privates.		1846	
Foy, Peter		July 2.	Deserted, Alton, July 7, before must'd in serv.
Shaw, William		"	" " 15.

MEXICAN WAR.

Died:

Privates.		1846	
Belford, John		July 2.	Died on Gulf, near Brazos Sant'go, Aug. 12, '46
Boze, Calvin		"	" at Camargo, Oct. 16, 1846
Grim, Martin		"	" Oct. 13, 1846
Lemons, Alfred B		"	" Matamoras, Sept. 22, 1846
Young, Benjamin F.		"	" Camargo, Nov. 5, 1846

Discharged:

Sergeants.		1846	
James C. Hancock		July 2.	Disch. at Camp Patterson, Tex., Aug. 3, 1846
Joseph Brannon		"	" " " " 30, "
Corporals.			
William P. Grace		"	Disch. at Camp Patterson, Tex., Aug. 31, 1846
George Williamson		"	" " " " " "
Privates.			
Bazore, Esau		"	Disch. at Matamoras, Mex., Oct. 20, 1846
Breedlove, James E.		"	" " " " " "
Carrico, Thomas		"	" " " " " "
Corey, Granville		"	" Camp Patterson, Tex., Aug. 31, 1846
Ennis, Thomas		"	" " " " 28, "
Glass, John R		"	" " " " 31, "
Hancock, William F.		"	" Matamoras, Mex., Oct. 20, 1846
Hodge, George D		"	" " " " " "
Keef, Benjamin F		"	" " " " " "
Lamar, John P		"	" " " " " "
Lewis, Thomas C		"	" " " " " "
Moody, Samuel H		"	" Brazos Santiago, Aug. 16, 1846
Modglin, James M		"	" Camargo, Mex., Nov. 18, 1846
Marsh, Josephus		"	" Matamoras, " Oct. 20, "
McDonald, John		"	" Camargo, " Nov. 15, "
Paisley, Andrew J.		"	" Matamoras, " Oct. 20, "
Rubel, Nathan		"	" Camp Patterson, Tex., Sept. 6, 1846
Simpson, Jesse		"	" " " Aug. 21, 1846
Thompson, Rufus L.		"	" Brazos Santiago, Aug. 16, 1846
Welch, Patrick		"	" Fort Polk, March 3, 1847
Musician.			
William Robinson		"	Disch. at Camp Patterson, Tex., Aug. 17, 1846.

This company was discharged at New Orleans May 23, 1847.

FOURTH REGIMENT.

The Field and Staff

Of the 4th Regiment of Illinois Volunteers, 3d Brigade of Volunteer Division commanded by Colonel Edward D. Baker, called into the service of the United States by the President. From the 30th day of April, 1847, to the 29th day of May, 1847.

Name and Rank.	Place of Enlistment.	Enrolled	Remarks.
Colonel. Edward D. Baker...	.	1846 June 6	
Lieut.-Colonel. John Moore...		June 13	Elected from 1st Lieut. in Co. "B," July 4, 1846
Major. Thomas L. Harris...		June 16	Elected from Capt. of Co. "F," July 4, 1846....
Adjutant. William B. Fondey...		June 6	Second Lieutenant........................
Surgeon. Wm. M. P. Quinn....			Regular Government appointee...............
A. C. S. and Capt. Joel Seth Post.......			Regular Government appointee...............
A. Q. M. and Capt. James A. Barrett....		June 6	Appointed from private in Co. "A," Sept. 7,'46.
Sergeant-Major. James H. Merryman...		"	Appointed from private in Co. "A," July 19,'46.
Q. M. Sergeant. Richard F. Barrett... Gilbert E. Winter.... Levi Hite.........		" June 17 June 12	Appointed from private in Co. "A," April 23,'47 Appoin'd; reduc'd; reappoin'd; again reduc'd App'd Dec. 22,'46; reduced Feb. 6,'47...........
Principal Musicians. Samuel Barnes...... Charles Brown		Aug. 10 "	Furl'h May 6,'47, to May 31,'47; to enlist for war

Company "A."

Name and Rank.	Place of Enlistment.	Enrolled	Remarks.
Captain. Horatio E. Roberts..		1846. June 6	
First Lieutenant. William T. Barrett..		"	Absent without leave from April 6, 1847.......
Second Lieutenants. John S. Bradford.... William B. Fondey...		" "	Resigned Sept. 16, 1846.................. Adjutant from July 6, 1846...................

Name and Rank.	Place of Enlistment.	Enrolled	Remarks.
Sergeants.		1846.	
Walter Davis		June 6	
David Logan		" "	
Dudley Wickersham		" "	
Argyle W. Farr		" "	
Corporals.			
Thomas Hossey		" "	
Shelton Ransdall		" "	
Edward Couner		" "	
Lawson Thomas		" "	
Musician.			
William C. B. Lewis		July 5	
Privates.			
Addison, Grandison		June 6	
Ballard, Chris. A.		" "	
Balantine, John J.		"	
Barrett, James A.		" "	Appointed Ass't Q. M. Sept. 7, 1846
Brown, William W.		" "	
Butler, Joshua			
Buel, Abel M.		July 24	Left sick in Hospital at Jalapa, May 6, 1847
Cabaniss, Zebulon P.		June 6	Absent on furl. f'm Feb. 1,'47, till exp'n of term
Capoot, John			
Chapman, John		" "	
Crowl, Upton		" "	
Darnell, Harvey		" "	
Ferrel, William C		" "	
Foster, John E.		" "	
Funk, George W.			
Frink, John S.		July 3	
Gideon, Alfred L.		June 6	
Garrett, Ezra L.		July 11	
Haines, Fletcher		June 6	
Harworth, George			
House, Erasmus D.		" "	
James, George		" "	
Keeling, Singleton		" "	
Marsh, Joseph		" "	
Millington, Aug. O.		" "	
Murray, Mathew		" "	
Peters, Peter C.		" "	
Ransdall, James B.		" "	
Rape, Henry		" "	
Ryan, Jackson		" "	
Spotswood, Jas. H.		" "	On furlough from April 3 to June 6, 1847.
Smith, Joseph H.		July 29	" " May 11 to July 29, 1847
Wickersham, W. H.		June 6	
Wilkinson, Reuben		" "	
Wilcox, Ephriam		" "	
Watson, Charles F.		" "	
Watts, Levi P		" "	
Whitehurst, Thomas		" "	
Weber, George R.		" "	Sent home with sick in charge, Aug. 30, 1846.
Yeakle, Joseph		" "	

Discharged:

Sergeant.		1846.	
William W. Pease		June 6	Disch. on Surg. cert. of disability, Oct. 29, '46.
Corporals.			
Joseph B. Pirkins		" "	Disch. on Surg. cert. of disability
Samuel O. White		" "	
Musician.			
Joseph H. Fultz		" "	Disch. on Surg. cert. of disability, Feb. 28, '47.
Privates.			
Algaire, Nicholas		" "	Disch. Oct. 4, '46, at Matamoras
Butler, John C.		" "	" Aug. —, '46, at Camp. Patterson
Cole, Samuel		" "	" Oct. 4, 1846.
Depuey, John		" "	" on Surgeon's certificate of disability
Dowdell, Silas		" "	
Davis, Isaac		" "	
Goodell, William R.		" "	Disch. Oct. 9, 1846, at Matamoras
Gorley, Levi		" "	" on Surg. cert. of disability, Mar. 3, 1847.

FOURTH REGIMENT.

Name and Rank.	Place of Enlistment.	Enrolled	Remarks.
		1846.	
Hall, George W		June 6	Disch ——, 1846, at Camp Patterson
McDonald, Benj. F		"	" Oct. 29, 1846, at Matamoras
Mathews, Marion F		"	" on Surgeon's certificate of disability
Ransdall, Presley		"	
Ridgely, Vincent		"	Disch. on Surgeon's certificate of disability
Seehorn, Alex. J		"	" Aug. 29, 1846
Whitlock, George C		"	
Waugh, James A		"	
Westbrook, Henry		"	
Wise, Jacob		"	Disch. on Surgeon's certificate of disability

Transferred:

		1846.	
Privates.			
Barrett, Richard F		June 6	Appointed Q. M. Sergt., April 23, 1847
Merriman, James H		"	" " " July 19, 1846

Died:

		1846.	
Privates.			
Conolly, James		June 6	Died at Matamoras, Sept. 27, 1846
Hokey, Daniel		"	" " Oct. 2, 1846
Hardin, William		"	" Camargo, Oct. 31, 1846
Moore, Henry J		"	" Matamoras, Sept. 17, 1846
McCabe, James		"	" Vera Cruz, in hospital, May 4, 1847
Newman, Joseph		"	Killed by the enemy at battle of Cerro Gordo.
Stipp, Joseph		"	Died at Matamoras, Oct. 2, 1846

This company was discharged May 28, 1847, at New Orleans.

COMPANY "B."

Name and Rank.	Place of Enlistment.	Enrolled	Remarks.
		1846.	
Captain.			
Garrett Elkin		June 13	Resignation accepted Oct. 20, 1846
First Lieutenant.			
Andrew J. Wallace		June 26	Died
Second Lieutenants.			
James M. Withers		June 13	Resignation accepted Oct. 20 1846
William L. Duncan		"	Assumed command Oct. 6, 1846
Sergeants.			
B. M. Wyatt		"	
John D. Lander		"	Wounded, Cerro Gordo, Mex., April 18, 1847
E. S. Dukshier		"	
Seaborn Gilmore		June 26	
Corporals.			
Samuel Ogden		June 13	
John G. Crammer		"	
E. W. Nanty		June 26	
A. J. Mason		June 13	Appointed Feb. 15, 1847, from private
Privates.			
Baldwin, William F		"	
Brumfield, William		"	
Baker, Mason		"	
Burnett, William		June 26	

Name and Rank.	Place of Enlistment.	Enrolled	Remarks.
		1846.	
Brown, Isaac		June 13	In hosp., Matamoras, Dec. 12,'46; sup. disch...
Depew, James		" "	Wounded, Cerro Gordo, Mex., April 18, 1847..
Dodson, Ichabod		" "	
Elliott, Edward		June 26	
Good, John		June 13	
Glimpse, Joseph		" "	
Gwinn, William		June 26	
Graham, Joseph		" "	
Graham, Levi		" "	
Guy, R. B. R		" "	
Harbard, William		June 13	
Harris, J. C		June 26	
Harris, A. J		" "	
Hall, John		" "	
Hampton, Felix T		" "	
Jones, John		June 13	
Johnston, Thomas P		" "	
Jenkins, James M		" "	Left in Hosp. as nurse, at Jalapa, April 20, 1847
Lash, William		" "	
Lamer, William		" "	
McIntyre, R. N		" "	
McCarroll, Justus		" "	
Mitchell, Wilson		June 26	
Newton, Anderson		June 13	In hosp., Matamoras, Dec. 12,'46; sup. disch..
Owen, Thomas J. V		" "	Detailed as Hospital Steward July 6, 1846
Palmer, Allen		" "	
Rule, Alexander		June 26	
Series, Julius H		June 13	
Stout, James		" "	
Stockton, Jackson C		June 26	Rejected July 18, 1846, lame ankle
Seaman, Sylvanus		" "	
Smock, Fulcard		" "	
Tennis, John F		" "	
Vanhorn, William M		June 13	
Walker, John		" "	Wounded, Cerro Gordo, Mex., April 18, 1847..
Walker, J. E		" "	
Williams, David		" "	
Withers, Peter		" "	

Discharged:

Name and Rank.	Place of Enlistment.	Enrolled	Remarks.
Sergeant.		1846.	
James E. Park		June 13	Disch. by certificate of disability Sept. 24, '46.
Corporals.			
Nicholas Savage		" "	Disch. by certificate of disability Sept. 24, 46.
Thomas H. Haines		" "	" " " " " "
Musicians.			
Charles E. Fling		" "	Disch. by certificate of disability Sept. 24, '46.
Samuel Hall		June 26	" " " " " " Oct. 13, '46..
Privates.			
Crumbaugh, John I		June 13	Disch. by certificate of disability, Oct. 27,'46..
Davis, William S		" "	" " " " " " Oct. 3, '46...
Daponte, Durant		" "	" " " " " "
Eskew, Jas. W (name, John H. Eskew)		" "	Disch. by certificate of disability Aug. 28, 46..
Gwinn, Alexander		" "	" " " " " " Mar. 3, '47..
Hall, Alfred		June 26	" " " " " " Oct. 3, '46
Hall, Felix		" "	Discharged by Col. Baker for disability
Johnson, John S. W		June 13	Disch. by certificate of disability Sept.
Lash, Henry		" "	" " " " " " Dec. 3, '46..
Little, William I		" "	" " " " " " Oct. 27, '46..
Mahon, David		" "	" " " " " " Oct. 3, '46
Moor, Thomas		June 26	" " " " " " Sept. 24,'46.
Miller, James M		June 13	" " " " " " Dec. 3, '46..
Poindexter, Clinton		" "	" " " " " " Oct. 27, '46..
Palmer, Leroy G		" "	" " " " " " Mar. 3, '47..
Reamer, E. C		" "	" July 23, '46, by Col. Baker
Toppas, William A		" "	" by certificate of disability Dec. 3, '46 ..
Warnuck, Massam'lo		June 26	" by Col. Baker, July 14, '46, disability ..

Died:

Name and Rank.	Place of Enlistment.	Enrolled	Remarks.
Corporals.		1846.	
George Perry		June 13	Died Nov. 3, 1846
John Misner		" "	" Nov. 18, 1846; appointed Corp'l Oct.19,'46.
Privates.			
Hodge, Andrew J		" "	Died Sept. 9, 1846
Ruth, George		" "	" in Hosp., Matamoras, Feb. 12, 1847
Wallace, Marion		June 26	" " Tampico, Feb. 10, 1847
Young, E. B		June 13	" Nov. 30, 1846

Deserted:

Name and Rank.	Place of Enlistment.	Enrolled	Remarks.
Privates.		1846.	
James Pearson		July 3	Deserted from Jefferson Barracks July 4, '46.
Joseph Bozarth		" "	" " " " " "
Stanley S. Foss		" "	" " " " " "

This company was discharged at New Orleans May 26, 1847.

Company " C. "

Name and Rank.	Place of Enlistment.	Enrolled	Remarks.
Captain.		1846.	
J. C. Pugh		June 13	
First Lieutenant.			
R. J. Oglesby		" "	
Second Lieutenants.			
A. Foreman		" "	
John P. Post		" "	
Sergeants.			
Stephen Osborn		" "	
Samuel K. Herrell		" "	
Benjamin F. Oglesby		" "	
James Rea		" "	
Corporals.			
John B. Travis		" "	
William I. Usrey		" "	Hospital attendant in Jalapa, Mexico
John B. Case		" "	
Privates.			
Atwood, John		" "	Wounded in battle at Cerro Gordo, Apr. 18,'47;
Ause, Charles		July 20	[in hospital at Jalapa, Mex.
Barnwell, R. G		June 13	
Butler, Jesse		" "	
Bailor, David		" "	
Bradshaw, Madison		" "	
Braden, George M		" "	
Church, George W		" "	
Chapman, Wm. W		" "	
Chambers, Laban		" "	Wounded in right arm Apr. 18,'47, battle of C. Gordo; arm amput'd, hosp. in Jalapa, Mex.
Carver, George		" "	Wounded severely, battle of C.Gordo, Apr. 18, 1847; in hospital at Jalapa, Mex
Dean, William		" "	
Dial, Davis		" "	
Freeman, James		Aug. 27	
Greenfield, Ambrose		June 13	

Name and Rank.	Place of Enlistment.	Enrolled	Remarks.
		1846.	
Huffman, David		June 13	
Horner, Israel		"	
Henry, Moses M		"	
Henry, William D. B.		"	
Lourie, James A			
Lord, Henry			
Lord, Thomas		June 13	
Lee, Alsa B.		July 3	
Martin, Benjamin		June 13	
Martin, Josiah		"	
McDaniel, William		"	
Muir, Christian		"	
Rice, Etherage		"	
Shepperd, Abram		"	
Sprague, Jason		"	
See, William E.		"	
Spangler, Daniel		"	
Turner, James R		"	
Turner, James		"	
Travis, Finis E.		"	
Ward, Lewis		"	
Warnick, Robert		"	
White, John W		"	

Transferred :

		1846.	
Post, Joel Seth		June 13	Commiss'd June 26, 1846, and transf'd to Field and Staff; appoint'd by President A. C. of S.

Discharged:

Sergeants.		1846.	
George W. Galbreath		June 13	Disch., Surg's certif. of disability, Aug. 27, '46
John B. Brown		"	" " " " "
Lawrence S. Helm		"	" " " " Oct. 6, '46
Privates.			
Bosworth, Miles		"	Disch., Surg's certif. of disability, Oct. 6, '46
Botkin, Amos		"	" " " " "
Greenfield, James		"	" " " " Oct. 18, '46
Hollingsworth, J. H.		"	" " " " Aug. 27, '46
Hawks, William		"	
Ledbetter, James		"	Disch., Surg's certif. of disability, Oct. 6, '46
Malson, George I.		"	" " " " Oct. 18, '46
Martin, Harvey		"	" " " " Oct. 6, '46
Nesbett, William		"	" " " " "
Stevens, Donis		"	" " " " "
Stewart, Robert		"	" " " " "
Travis, John D.		"	" " " " "
Wheeler, William R.		"	" " " " "
Wells, Bazel E.		"	" " " " "

Died :

Corporals.		1846.	
Bennett, L. Martin		June 13	Died at Camp Patterson, Aug. 31, 1846
Nelson, George W		"	" in hosp., Jalapa, Apr. 29, '47; wound rec'd in battle of Cerro Gordo, Apr. 18, '47
Privates.			
Bebee, Pomeroy T.		"	Died in hospital at Matamoras, Oct. 20, 1846
Dillon, Charles W		"	" Camp Patterson, Mex., Sept. 1, 1846
Dickey, John M		"	" " " 18, 1846
Davidson, William P.		"	" in hospital, Matamoras, Oct. 10, 1846
Howell, David		"	" " " 1, 1846
Malson, James C.		"	" C. Gordo, Apr. 22, wound rec'd Apr. 18, '47
Reece, Samuel		"	Died in hospital at Matamoras, Oct. 3, 1846
Robinson, William P		"	" " " " 12, 1846
Shepperd, James A.		"	" " " " Sept. 27, 1846

FOURTH REGIMENT.   291

Name and Rank.	Place of Enlistment.	Enrolled	Remarks.
Saunders, John		1846. June 13	Died in hospital at Matamoras, Sept. 22, 1846.
Souther, Temple		"	" Camp Patterson, Mex., Sept. 19, 1846.
Wheeler, William		"	" in hospital at Matamoras, Oct. 1, 1846.
White, Bazel B		"	" Sept. 26, 1846.

This company was discharged at New Orleans, May 25, 1847.

Company "D."

Name and Rank.	Place of Enlistment.	Enrolled	Remarks.
Captain.		1846.	
Achilles Morris		June 9	Died at Tampico, Mex., Feb. 15, 1847.
Second Lieutenants.			
Alfred C. Campbell		"	Assumed command of company Feb. 15, 1847.
John D. Foster		"	
Sergeants.			
Henry M. Spotswood		"	On furl'h from May 1, 1847, in Q. M. Dep't.
David Meigs		"	
John Davis		"	
Jonathan Morris		"	
Corporals.			
William Campbell		"	
Thomas Higgins		"	
Chris. C. Holyer		"	
Hugh Paul		"	
Privates.			
Alsbury, Edward R		"	
Brannon, Josiah		"	
Bloyd, James B		"	
Cast, Archibald		"	Detailed as wardmaster in hospital, Jalapa.
Cutter, William		"	
Dunlap, James T		"	Left at Matamoras, sick, Dec. 17, 1846.
Daly, John		"	
Darnielle, John C		"	
Dodd, John C		"	
Dillman, David		"	
Duncan, Jerome		"	
Edwards, David		"	
Emmett, Robert S		"	
Foster, Peyton		"	
Foster, William		"	
Henwood, William		"	
Henwood, Henry		"	
Hillyard, James P		"	
Howey, William		"	
Huckleberry, John		"	
Huffmaster, Edward		"	
Huffma-ter, William		"	
Hoskins, John S		July 29	
Jones, T. B			
Kent, Alexander		June 9	
King, John W		"	On furlough in Q. M. Dept. from Jan. 6, 1847, [till June 9, 1847.
Morris, Hamilton		"	
Morris, Randall G		"	
Meigs, Severell		"	Left sick in Matamoras Sept. 15, 1846.
Odell, John		"	
Phelps, Joshua		"	
Rhodes, William G		"	
Shoemaker, Thos. C		"	
Short, James F		"	
Shelton, John		"	
Smith, Alonzo H		July 19	
Skinner, John H		"	

MEXICAN WAR.

Name and Rank.	Place of Enlistment.	Enrolled	Remarks.
Tinker, William		1846. June 9	
Thompson, Saml. M.		"	Left in hospital, Matamoras, Dec. 14, 1846.
Terpin, James		"	
Williams, John R.		"	
Wilcox, Daniel		"	
Workman, Benjamin		"	

Discharged:

Name and Rank.	Place of Enlistment.	Enrolled	Remarks.
Sergeants.		1846.	
Ashley Walker		June 9	Discharged, disability, Oct. 8, 1846.
Chris. R. Pierce		"	" " Nov. 17, 1846.
Privates.			
Bridges, Joseph		"	Discharged by order Col. Baker, July 23, 1846.
Campbell, Levi		"	" " disability, Oct. 5, 1846.
Cross, Riley		"	" " " "
Cross, Daniel		"	" " " Oct. 8, 1846.
Drennan, Samuel		"	" by order of Col. Baker, July 23,'46
Dodd, Newton		"	" " disability, Aug. 29, 1846.
Finger, Jefferson		"	" " " Oct. 8, 1846.
Henwood, Berryman		"	" " " "
Lindsay, David		"	" " " "
Morris, Asa L		"	" " " Oct. 5, 1846.
McCrillis, Lafayette		"	" " " Oct. 13, 1846.
Morris, James		"	" " " Feb. 28, 1847.
Penix, William		"	" " " Aug. 29, 1846.
Pierce, Samuel		"	" " " "
Robbins, Wilson		"	" " " March 7, 1847.
Sullivan, Benjamin		"	" " " Feb. 28, 1847.
Sexton, Calvay		"	" " " Nov. 17, 1846.
Short, Rowan I		"	" " " "
Sampson, William		"	" " " Oct. 5, 1846.
Snyder, Logan C		"	" " " "
Terpin, William		"	" " " "
Vermillion, William		"	" " " "
Walker, Joel H		"	" " " Nov. 1, 1846.

Died:

Name and Rank.	Place of Enlistment.	Enrolled	Remarks.
Privates.		1846.	
Allison, John		June 9	Died at Camargo, Mex., Oct. 28, 1846.
Hellyard, John		"	" " " Oct. 26, 1846.
Harralson, James		"	" " Matamoras, Mex., Dec. 20, 1846.
Jones, James		"	" " Camargo, Mex., Nov. 16, 1846.
Morris, Jacob		"	" " " Oct. 22, 1846.
Morris, Milton		"	" " " Nov. 1, 1846.
McKee, Samuel		"	Killed, by accident, April 16, 1847.
Nation, Wm. F		"	Died at Camargo, Mex., Oct. 18, 1846.
Reed, Henry B		"	" " " Oct. 28, 1846.
Shelton, Morris		"	Killed by Mexicans April 17, 1847.

Deserted:

Name and Rank.	Place of Enlistment.	Enrolled	Remarks.
Peyton Foster, Jr		1846. June 9	Deserted on march to Jefferson Barracks, sick
Wm. Heridith		"	" from Jefferson Barracks July 22, 1846

This company was discharged at New Orleans on May 26, 1847.

Company "E."

Name and Rank.	Place of Enlistment.	Enrolled	Remarks.
Captain.		1846.	
Daniel Newcomb....		June 12	
Second Lieutenants.			
Benjamin Howard..		" "	
Charles Maltby......		" "	
Sergeants.			
William Lowry......		" "	Left sick in hospital. at Jalapa, May 7, 1847...
G. E. Bennett.......		" "	
John Vinson........		July 3	
Absalom Hamilton..		June 12	
Corporals.			
Isaiah Davenport....		" "	
William Allsop......		" "	
William Kinney.....		" "	Hospital attendant at Jalapa, May 7, 1847......
William Davis.......		July 6	
Musician.			
John Mason.........		" "	
Privates.			
Benson, Charles H..		June 12	Left sick at Matamoras Hospital, Oct. 9, 1846..
Brown, Samuel J....		" "	" Jalapa Hospital, May 7, 1847......
Boyer, George M....		" "	
Bobo, Pharlo........		" "	
Clifton, William.....		" "	
Cappenberger, Jos..		" "	
Chack, Adam.......		" "	
Chapman, James F..		July 2	Left sick at Matamoras, Oct. 9. 1846............
Cornell, Samuel.....		July 6	
Davis, Remas.......		June 12	
Farris, Benjamin H.		" "	Left sick at Matamoras, Dec. 14, 1846..........
Glenn, Samuel P....		" "	
Guinn, Darby.......		July 2	............[turned as priv. Feb. 6, 1847.
Hite, Levi..........		" "	Sergt. until Dec. 6, '46; app't'd Q. M. Sergt; re-
Hill, Egbert O.......		June 12	Left sick at Matamoras, Oct. 9, 1846..........
Hutchins, Thomas..		" "	
Harp, William......		" "	
Henry, James.......		July 2	
Innman, James.....		" "	Left sick at Matamoras, Dec. 14, 1846..........
Logan, James A....		June 12	
McDeed, John......		" "	
Martin, James......		" "	
Martin, Benjamin...		" "	
Purdy, William.....		July 2	
Purdy, John H......		" "	
Price, John.........		July 6	
Pennyman, James..		July 2	
Russell, Lowe Z....		June 12	
Stratten, Joseph....		" "	
Star, Conrad........		" "	
Scroggins, Anders'n.		July 2	
Sawyer, Selick......		July 3	
Sawyer, Snowden...		July 6	
Skidmore, Rueben..		" "	
Smith, James.......		June 12	Left sick at Matamoras, Dec. 14, 1846..........
Thornby, Leroy.....		" "	" Jalapa, May 7, 1847................
Tenery, Thomas....		July 2	
Vanate, Isaac.......		June 12	
Welch, Richard D..		" "	
Wright, William W..		" "	
Whillis, Isaac W....		" "	

Discharged:

Name and Rank.	Place of Enlistment.	Enrolled	Remarks.
1st Sergeant. John Hutchins		1846. June 12	Discharged on Surgeon's certif., Aug. 22, 1846
Privates. Brock, Elias		"	Discharged on Surgeon's certif., Oct. 13, 1846
Brock, Andrew		"	" " " " "
Dawson, James B		"	" " " " "
Emland, Alfred		"	" " " " Oct. 18, 1846
Halsey, Solomon		"	" " " " Oct. 13, 1846
Harp, Thomas		"	" " " " "
Hammitt, Joseph		"	" " " " May 8, 1847
King, Daniel		"	" " " " Oct. 13, 1846
Linton, James		July 6	" " " " "
McCuddy, Isaac		June 12	" " " " Nov. 10, 1846
Pomroy, Franklin		"	" " " " Oct. 13, 1846
Richards, Evan		"	" " " " "
Williams, Jared		"	" " " " Aug. 22, 1846

Died:

Name and Rank.	Place of Enlistment.	Enrolled	Remarks.
Privates. Blankenship, Jess		1846. June 12	Died at Camp Matamoras, Oct. 3, 1846
Beebe, David		"	" " Camargo, Nov. 14, 1846
Butler, William		"	" " Matamoras, Dec. 23, 1846
Belford, Owen		"	" " Tampico, Feb. 14, 1847
Clifton, Job		"	" " Matamoras, Dec. 18, 1846
Kinney, Ambrose		"	" " Camargo, Nov. 11, 1846
Johnson, Theophilus		"	" " " Nov. 8, 1846
Jackson, Joshua E		"	Cerro Gordo, April 21, 1847
Murphy, Richard		"	Rio del Plan.
McPherson, Jesse L		"	Patterson, Aug. 25, 1846
Payne, Calvin		"	" Sept. 10, 1846
Richards, Isaac N		"	" " 8, 1846
Wallace, William		"	Camargo, Nov. 3, 1846

This company was discharged at New Orleans, May 28, 1847.

Company "F."

Name and Rank.	Place of Enlistment.	Enrolled	Remarks.
Captain. Asa D. Wright		1846. June 16	
First Lieutenant. Robert C. Scott		"	Elected 1st Lieut. July 8, 1846, from Sergt.
Second Lieutenant. Sheldon J. Johnson		"	Died May 13 of wounds received at Jalapa April 18, 1847.
Sergeants. Franceway Day		"	
William P. Berry		"	
James P. Walker		"	
Cornelius Rourke		"	Left in hosp. at Jalapa; wounded April 18, '47.
Corporals. C. B. Altig		"	
Thomas Watkins		"	
Robert N. Jones		"	
Napoleon B. Greer		"	Appointed Corporal from private Feb. 10, 1847

FOURTH REGIMENT.

Name and Rank.	Place of Enlistment.	Enrolled	Remarks.
Privates.		1846.	
Bishop, Robert		June 16	On furlough April 6, 1847; time not known....
Bond, Bannister		"	
Bell, A. G.		"	Detailed in hosp. as nurse, Jalapa, Apr. 18, '47
Bond, Green		"	
Brown, Jesse		"	
Clary, Daniel		"	
Close, William		"	
Day, Philip S.		"	
Dunton, Geo. W.		"	
Elmon, Elijah		"	
Guernsay, Amos		"	
Garber, John		"	
Goldsby, Richard W.		"	
Goodman, Christian.		"	
Hutcherson, William		"	Detailed in hosp. as nurse, Jalapa, Apr. 18, '47
Haughton, Aaron		"	
Johnson, A. K.		"	Left in hospital at Jalapa, sick, May 6, 1847...
Jones, John		"	
King, Walter W.		"	
Lukins, Jesse		"	
Moore, Robert		"	
Morris, Philmon		"	
Miller, Royal		"	
Nance, George W.		"	
Patterson, James H.		"	
Rhodes, Nathan		"	
Ritchie, Thomas		"	
Smith, John B.		"	Left in hosp., sick, at Tampico, Mch. 11, 1847..
Slaton, Daniel		"	
Senter, William		"	
Tebbs, Samuel		"	
Troxell, James		"	*Left in hosp. at Matamoras, Dec. 14, '46; sick
Wood, McLeu		"	
Wilt, Richard		"	
Wiseman, Enoch		"	
Wiseman, Lewis		"	
Wright, Thomas L.		"	

* Reported on the Regimental Returns for April, 1847, discharged 3d March, 1847, at Matamoras, on Surgeon's certificate of disability.

Discharged :

Name and Rank.	Place of Enlistment.	Enrolled	Remarks.
Privates.		1846.	
Boss, James W.		June 16	Discharged on Surg. certificate, Aug. 29, 1846.
Bond, John		"	" " " Oct. 18, 1846..
Clark, David		"	" " " Aug. 29, 1846.
Clary, Thomas		"	" " " Oct. 8, 1846..
Clary, Robert C.		"	" " " "
Cox, Randolph		"	" " " Nov., 1846...
Ely, Samuel G. W.		"	" " " Oct. 8, 1846..
Estill, Isaac		"	" " " Mch. 7, 1847.
Green, Ivans		"	" " " Aug. 29, 1846.
Gum, Charles		"	ord. of Col. Baker, before service
Hohimer, Elias		"	" July 29, 1846..
Raybourn, Robert A.		"	on Surg. certificate, Oct. 20, 1846..
Smith, O. H. P.		"	" " " Oct. 8, 1846 ..
Stone, William A.		"	" " " Dec. 14, 1846.
Smedley, Richard H.		"	" " " Aug. 29, 1846.
Watkins, James		"	" " " Oct. 8, 1846 ..

Died:

Name and Rank.	Place of Enlistment.	Enrolled	Remarks.
Sergeants.		1846.	
Potter, Robert		June 16	Died at sea, Aug. 5, 1846
Short, David B.		"	Died at Camargo, Nov. 27, 1846
Corporal.			
Hadwick, Michael		"	Died at Matamoras, Jan. —, 1847
Musician.			
Gum, Robert C.		"	Died at Camargo, Oct. 5, 1846

Name and Rank.	Place of Enlistment.	Enrolled	Remarks.
Privates.		1846.	
Atcherson, Lewis C.		June 16	Died at Camargo, Oct. 31, 1846.
Combs, William S.		"	" " Nov. 11, 1846
Durbin, Aaron		"	" " Oct. 11, 1846.
Goldsby, Elias		"	" Matamoras, Sept. 21, 1846
Hamilton, Peter		"	" " Dec. 5, 1846.
Hornback, Alvin		"	Killed in action, April 18, 1847.
King, Joseph M.		"	Died at Matamoras, Oct. 20, 1846.
Miller, John C.		"	" " Dec. 4, 1846
Nance, Henry		"	" " Jan. —, 1847
Nance, Willis T.		"	" Camargo, Oct. 22, 1846
Simpson, Jonat'n H.		"	Died Aug. 6, 1846
Thomas, Owen		"	Died at Camargo, Oct. 19, 1846.
Trust, Anderson C.		"	" " Nov. 6, 1846
Wiseman, Benjamin		"	" " Oct. 28, 1846
Yeokum, James N.		"	" " Oct. 18, 1846.
Yeokum, Geo. N.		"	Died April 23, 1847, of wounds received in action of April 18, 1847.

Deserted:

Sergeant.		1846.	
William C. Phillips			Received furlough from July 18 to Sept. 7, '46; has not since re-joined his company.

This company was discharged at New Orleans, May 26, 1847.

Company "G."

Name and Rank.	Place of Enlistment	Enrolled	Remarks.
Captain.		1846.	
Edward Jones	Springfield, Ill	June 17	
First Lieutenant.			
Leonard A. Knott	"	"	Died at sea, May 22, '47, *en route* to N. Orleans
Second Lieutenant.			
Wm. A. Tinney	"	"	
Sergeants.			
Samuel Rhodes	"	"	
John N. Gill	"	"	
George Burton	"	"	Promoted from Corporal, March 1, 1847.
Corporals.			
Henry I. Heath	"	"	
John G. Hammer	"	"	
Jesse A. Nason	"	"	
John Chandler	Jeff. Barracks Mo.	July 22	Appointed from private, March 1, 1847.
Privates.			
Allen, Bazill	Springfield, Ill	June 17	
Booth, William	"	"	Left sick in hospital at Matamoras, Dec. 6, '46.
Briggs, Thomas	"	"	
Bradstreet, Dudley	"	"	
Billsboro, Henry	Jeff. Barracks	July 23	
Becker, Wm. E.	Springfield, Ill	June 17	
Brown, Wm. H.	"	"	
Cox, Ezekiel	"	"	
Cullen, A. Dillingh'm	"	"	
Drury, John	"	"	
Dixon, Rensalaer H.	"	"	
Fugitt, George W.	Jeff. Barracks	July 22	
Farren, Samuel	Springfield, Ill	June 17	
Flippin, William	Jeff. Barracks	July 22	

FOURTH REGIMENT.

Name and Rank.	Place of Enlistment.	Enrolled	Remarks.
		1846	
Frayer, DeWitt C....	Springfield,Ill	June 17	
Hornbecker, John S..	"	"	Left sick in hospital at Matamoras, Dec. 6, '46.
Hall, Robert.........	"	"	
Hawks, John.........	"	"	
Johnson, Crawford.	Jeff.Barracks	July 22	
Koogin, Daniel......	Springfield,Ill	June 17	Left at Matamoras Dec. 6, '46, to go to Tampico
Kelso, David........	"	"	
Leonard, Zeba.......	"	"	
Miller, Christopher.	"	"	
Mountz, Milton.....	"	"	
Mullen, Samuel.....	"	"	
Merethew, Jonathan	"	"	
Morris, George W...	"	"	
Montgomery, Wm...	"	"	
McMullen, Wm.....	"	"	
McKassen, Thomas..	"	"	
Nicholls, Samuel....	"	"	
Norris, John........	"	"	
Page, Samuel T.....	"	"	
Preddy, Selden.....	"	"	
Preddy, Charles.....	"	"	
Rhoads, John.......	"	"	
Rhoads, Franklin L.	"	"	
Ricketts, James.....	"	"	
Rogers, David.......	"	"	Left sick in hospital at Tampico, March, 1847.
Scott, Peter P......	"	"	
Sullivan, Robert....	"	"	
Sampson, John......	"	"	
Shepherd, Thomas..	"	"	
Thomason, Thomas.	Jeff.Barracks	July 23	
Taney, Marcus D...	Springfield,Ill	June 17	
Town, Hoza P......	"	"	
Walden, Abraham...	"	"	
Weise, Landolen....	"	"	
Winters, Gilbert E..	"	"	Was appointed Qr. Mr. Sergt. July 8, '46; was reduced to private Dec. 22, '46; was re-appointed Qr.Mr. Sergt. Feb. 6, '47, and was again reduced to private April 23, '47.

Died:

		1846.	
Musician.			
Joseph Turner.......	Springfield,Ill	June 17	Died in hospital at Matamoras, Nov. —, 1846..
Privates.			
Bennett, Sylvester..	"	"	Died in hospital at Matamoras, Dec. 8, 1846..
Hammond, James...	"	"	" " Nov. 15, 1846..
Thorp, Joseph.......	"	"	" at Jalapa, April 28, 1847, of wounds received in battle of Cerro Gordo.

Transferred:

		1846.	
1st Sergeant.			
William Campbell...	Springfield,Ill	June 17	To N. C. Staff, July 19, 1846.

Honorably discharged:

		1846.	
Sergeants.			
John W. Page.......	Springfield,Ill	June 17	Disch. on Surg. cert. of disability, Mar. 1, '47.
Richard S. Updycke	"	"	" " May 2, '47.
Privates.			
Dale, Jeremiah......	"	"	Disch. Nov., '46, from gen. hosp., Matamoras
McCracken, John...	"	"	" on Surg. cert. of disability, Aug., 1846..
Martin, Robert......	"	"	" " " "
Snyder, Isaac.......	"	"	" Nov., '46, from gen. hosp., Matamoras
Slaughter, Wm......	"	"	" on Surg. cert. of disability, Dec. 1, '46.
Smith, John.........	"	"	" May 8, '47, from gen. hosp., Vera Cruz.
Searcy, Opian O....	"	"	
Woodrow, Stephen..	"	"	Disch. on Surg. cert. of disability, Aug. 1846.

Deserted:

Name and Rank.	Place of Enlistment.	Enrolled	Remarks.
Corporal. William M. Moore	Springfield, Ill	1846. June 17	Deserted at Tampico, March 6, 1847
Privates. Dunn, John		"	Deserted at New Orleans, July 30, 1846
Wilson, Charles		"	Deserted f'm Jefferson Barracks, July 24, '46.

This company was discharged on May 26, 1847, at New Orleans.

COMPANY "H."

Name and Rank.	Place of Enlistment.	Enrolled	Remarks.
Captain. John S. McConkey		1846. June 20	
Second Lieutenants. J. W. S. Alexander		"	
Albert F. Shaw		"	
Sergeants. Daniel G. Burr		"	
Keefer Laufman		"	Appointed Sergt. March 1, 1847, from private.
Joseph B. McCown		"	
Jira J. Blackman		"	Left sick at Tampico, March 6, 1847
Corporals. Samuel Adams		"	Appointed Corporal Mar. 1, 1847, from private.
Woodruf Rowland		"	
A. J. Shrader		June 21	
Musicians. Johna V. Brown		"	
G. W. Longnecker		June 20	
Privates. Brown, Solomon W.		"	
Ball, Noah C.		"	
Ball, William		"	
Cary, Horace		"	
Cunningham, James		"	
Cunningham, Geo.		"	
Clark, Josiah W.		"	
Downs, Noble		"	
Daughhetee, Joel C.		"	
Ewing, Isaac N.		"	
Evans, Henry B.		"	
Givins, Joseph R.		"	
Givins, William		"	
Gorthwait, Wm. S.		"	
Hill, Wesley		"	
Hogue, William		"	
Hogue, John		"	
King, John P.		"	
Kelsoo, Noah		"	
McConkey, G. W.		"	
McConkey, Leander		"	
Miller, James M.		"	
Mitchell, Samuel		"	
McDavitt, Jas. R.		June 21	
Parish, David C.		June 20	
Pinson, Aaron		"	
Ryon, John W.		"	Left sick at Matamoras, Dec. 14, 1846
Righmier, James		"	
Stephenson, William		"	Left sick at Matamoras, Dec. 14, 1846

Name and Rank.	Residence.	Enrolled	Remarks.
		1846.	
Shoffer, Alexander		June 20	
Smith, James M		June 21	Reduced from Corporal, May 6, 1847.
Welton, John		June 20	
Wright, Bird		"	

Died:

		1846.	
Privates.			
Daughhete, J. W		June 20	Died at Matamoras, Oct. 9, 1846.
Smith, Himelion		" "	Camp Patterson; Sept. 5, 1846.
Smith, Wm. Y		" "	Matamoras, Oct. 24 1846.
Smith, Joseph		" "	" " Dec. 5, 1846.
Wright, H. M		" "	" " Oct. 11, 1846.

Discharged:

		1846.	
Sergeants.			
J. W. McMillan		June 20	Disch. on surg's certif. of disabil., Oct. 13, '46
J. Y. Utter		" "	" " " " Mar. 1, '47
Corporals.			
J. H. Sanford		" "	Disch. on surg's certif. of disabil., Oct. 7, '46
D. J. Connely		" "	" " " " Aug. 31, '46
Privates.			
Buntain, Wm		" "	Disch. on surg's certif. of disabil., Oct. 7, '46
Black, Samuel		" "	" " " " Oct. 21, '46
Blevins, Thomas		June 21	" " " " Nov. 2, '46
Broud, David		July 2	" " " " Nov. 2, '46
Brown, T. B		June 20	" " " " Nov. 2, '46
Culberson, O. E. D		" "	" " " " Oct. 7, '46
Cox, Benard		" "	" " " " Oct. 8, '46
Cusick, Vance		" "	" " " " Oct. 22, '46
Culver, Reuben		" "	" " " " Nov. 4, '46
Duncan, W. S		" "	" " " " Nov. 2, '46
Eaton, R. H		" "	" " " " Oct. 13, '46
Givins, Wm. M		" "	" " " " Oct. 7, '46
House, Samuel		" "	" " " " Oct. 22, '46
Hunsinger, Benj		" "	" " " " Oct. 22, '46
Lawry, J. F		" "	" " " " Oct. 7, '46
Leathers, Wm		" "	" " " " Oct. 8, '46
Lightfoot, J. G		" "	" " " " Nov. 2, '46
Link, David		" "	" " " " Oct. 18, '46
Metcalf, G. W		" "	" " " " Mar. 31, '47
Milburn, Wm. M		" "	" " " " Oct. 21, '46
Morgan, Michael		" "	" " " " Oct. 18, '46
Metcalf, S. R		June 21	" " " " Oct. 18, '46
Pease, S. W		June 20	" " " " Oct. 18, '46
Pease, D. W		" "	" " " " Oct. 22, '46
Reed, B. F		" "	" " " " Oct. 5, '46
Rowland, John		" "	" " " " Feb. 1, '47
Stephenson, Geo. W		" "	" " " " Dec. 8, '46
Tucker, F. B		" "	" " " " Mar. 31, '47
Turner, George		" "	" " " " Oct. 21, '46
Welch, Benjamin		" "	" " " " Aug. 31, '46
Wayne, B. F		" "	" " " " Aug. 31, '46
Young, W. F		" "	" " " " Oct. 13, '46
Wright, J. G		" "	" " " "

Deserted:

		1846.	
Andrew Pulson		June 20	Deserted at New Orleans, Aug. 4, 1846.
H. H. James		" "	

This company was discharged on May 26, 1847, at New Orleans.

Company "I."

Name and Rank.	Place of Enlistment.	Enrolled	Remarks.
Captain.		1846.	
John C. Hurt		June 14	
First Lieutenant.			
Geo. M. Cowardin		"	Killed in battle at Cerro Gordo, April 18, 1847.
Second Lieutenants.			
Jacob P. Shaum		"	Resigned.
David A. Brown		"	Private to June 27, 1846, then took rank as 2d gr. Lieutenant.
Sergeants.			
John M. Handchey		"	
Chris. C. Mason		"	Appointed Sergeant from private, Oct. 21, '46.
John Allison		"	Appointed Sergeant, April 20, 1847.
Corporals.			
Wm. J. Dudney		"	Appointed Corporal from private, Oct. 21, '46.
Wm. Donavan		"	
Hiram A. Bristol		"	Appointed Corporal from private, Oct. 21, '46.
W. J. Allison		"	Appointed Corporal, April 20, 1847.
Privates.			
Ashing, Thomas		"	
Braugher, Fred		"	
Brown, Leroy T		"	
Barnes, Joseph		"	Left sick in hosp. at Matamoras, Dec. 13, 1846.
Brown, Elmore S		"	
Brundage, Sol		"	
Barney, M. W		July 18	
Bentley, John		"	
Chapin, Merrick		June 14	
Downing, John E		"	
Davis, Cyrus		"	
Davenport, John		"	
Fanning, Chas		July 18	
Glenn, Jas		June 14	
Gibson, John W. H		"	
Greenwood, John		"	
Hutchinson, Eli H		"	
McGarvey, Francis		"	
Melton, Austin P		"	
Myers, Leo. W		"	
Milton, Perry		"	
Mason, Thomas		"	
Randolph, Jas		"	
Salmonds, Wm		"	
Sands, Robt		July 18	
Todd, Jas. I. D		June 14	Left wounded in hosp. at Jalapa, May 7, 1847.
Trumbull, Cryl		"	
Wiley, Henry			

Discharged:

Sergeants.		1846.	
Willis Phillips		June 14	Disch. on Surgeon's certificate Aug. 26, 1846.
William H. Young		"	" " " Aug. 26, 1846.
John Cowardin		"	" " " Oct. 18, 1846.
Jas. McGraw		"	Promoted 3d Sergt. from private, Sept. 15, '46, disch. on Surg's certif. Mar. 17, 1847.
Corporals.			
Wm. Loughery		"	Disch. on Surgeon's certificate, Oct. 13, 1846.
Adolphus Vonforull		"	" " " " "
James R. Phillips		"	" " " " "
Privates.			
Collins, Thomas		"	Disch. on Surgeon's certificate, Aug. 26, 1846.
Clark, Peter		"	" " " " Oct. 13, 1846.
Douglass, James		"	" " " "
Davis, Robert		"	" " " " Nov. 2, 1846.
Gregory, L. M		"	" " " " Oct. 13, 1846.
Glenn, G. D		"	

FOURTH REGIMENT.

Name and Rank.	Place of Enlistment.	Enrolled	Remarks.
		1846.	
Lee, Franklin		June 14	Disch. on Surgeon's certificate, Aug. 26, 1846
Lucas, F. A		"	" " " " Oct. 13, 1846
Ray, John G		"	" " " " " " "
Robinson, George W		"	" " " " " " "
Stapleton, James		"	" " " " " " "
Sullins, Wm		"	" " " " Aug. 26, 1846
Turner, Emanuel		"	" " " " Nov. 3, 1846
White, William		"	" " " " Mar. 2, 1846

Died:

Name and Rank.	Place of Enlistment.	Enrolled	Remarks.
Sergeant.		1846.	
Uriah Davenport		June 14	Died of wounds rec'd in action, Cerro Gordo, April 18, 1847
Corporal.			
Nathaniel H. Milton		"	Killed in action at Cerro Gordo, April 18, 1847.
Privates.			
Beason, William		"	Died Sept. 15, 1846, on the Rio Grande
Bowman, John		"	" Nov. 15, 1846, at Camargo
Brown, John E		"	" March 15, 1847, at Matamoras
Cavenaugh, John		"	Drowned in Mississippi, July 3, 1846
Donavan, Joseph		"	Died Sept. 15, 1846, on the Rio Grande
Devault, Abram		"	" Nov. 7, 1846, at Camargo
McGarvey, Alex'dria		"	" July 11, 1846,
Mundy, Henry		"	" Sept. 29, 1846, on the Rio Grande
McGarvey, Henry		"	" Feb. 6, 1847.
Rudder, Thomas		"	Supposed to be killed by Mexicans
Rees, Chas		"	Died Sept. 30, 1846, on the Rio Grande

Wounded:

Name and Rank.	Place of Enlistment.	Enrolled	Remarks.
1st Sergeant.		1846.	
John M. Handchey		June 14	Wounded in action, Cerro Gordo, April 18, '47
Privates.			
Todd, James I. D		"	Wounded in action, Cerro Gordo, April 18, '47
Fanning, Chas		"	" " " " " "

Deserted:

Name and Rank.	Place of Enlistment.	Enrolled	Remarks.
		1846.	
Downing, Robert		June 14	Deserted July 9, 1846, Jefferson Barracks
Wilkinson, Andrew		"	" " 20, " "

This company was discharged on May 25, 1847, at New Orleans.

COMPANY "K."

Name and Rank.	Place of Enlistment.	Enrolled	Remarks.
Captain.		1846.	
Lewis W. Ross		July 4	
First Lieutenants.			
George W. Stipp		July 4	Resigned Aug. 30, 1846, at Camp Patterson
Leonard F. Ross		July 18	Elected 1st Lieutenant from private Sept 4, '46

Name and Rank.	Place of Enlistment.	Enrolled	Remarks.
		1846.	
Second Lieutenant. Joseph L. Sharp	....	July 4	Resigned company at New Orleans May 23, '47
Br't 2d Lieutenants. John B. McDowell	....	July 4	Resigned Aug. 30, 1846, at Camp Patterson....
Robert Johnson	....	" "	" " Dec. 20, 1846, " " Matamoras...
Sergeants. Marvin Scudder, Jr.	....	July 4	
Samuel D Reynolds	....	" "	
Milton C. Dewey	....	" "	
James B. Anderson	....	" "	
Corporals. Tracy Stroud	....	July 4	
James W. Anderson	....	" "	
Edward Brannon	....	July 18	
Simeon Cannon	....	July 4	
Privates. Ackerson, Garrett	....	July 4	
Andrews, Harman	....	" "	
Bennington, George	....	" "	
Bristow, Isaac M	....	" "	
Clark, David	....	" "	---
Crittenden, Uriah	....	" "	
Crawford, James	....	" "	
Collins, David	....	" "	
Carter, Simeon	....	" "	
Coon, Ross	....	" "	
Cannon, John	....	" "	
Dalley, Charles	....	" "	
Ellis, John	....	" "	
Ellis, Jacob	....	" "	
Engle, William H	....	" "	
Foote, Zachariah	....	" "	
Freebourne, P. T	....	" "	
Fitzpatrick, Michael	....	" "	
Gregory, Jesse	....	July 20	
Hoover, Richard	....	" "	
Hammon, Joshua B	....	July 4	
King, Horace B	....	" "	
Kimball, Myran	....	" "	
Lyon, Eli	....	" "	
Land, John	....	" "	
Morton, Richard W	....	" "	
Mayall, Joseph	....	" "	
Millslagle, Elias	....	" "	['47, and left at Hosp. at Jalapa, Mex.
Morris, William	....	" "	Wounded in battle of Cerro Gordo April 18,
Myers, Jonas H	....	" "	Detailed in Hosp. at Jalapa, Mex. April 18, '47.
Murphy, William	....	July 20	
Patton, Hugh	....	July 4	
Powell, Andrew M	....	" "	
Reid, John H	....	" "	
Rigdon, Stephen	....	" "	
Ross, Pike C	....	" "	
Shields, David	....	" "	
Steele, John N	....	" "	Detailed in Hosp., Jalapa, Mex., April 15, 1847
Smith, James H	....	" "	
Smith, Davis	....	July 20	
Stephenson, Thomas	....	July 4	
Taylor, Julius I	....	" "	

Discharged:

Name and Rank.	Place of Enlistment.	Enrolled	Remarks.
		1846	
First Sergeant, Robert Carter	....	July 4	Disch. on Surg. cert. of disability, Nov. 9, '46 ..
First Corporal. Thomas H. Head	....	July 4	Disch. on Surg. cert. of disability, Nov. 25, '46
Privates. Bevord, John	....	July 4	Disch. on Surg. cert. of disability, Dec. 20, '46 .
Beadles, William	....	" "	" " " " " " " " Mar. 7, '47...
Dobson, Joseph	....	" "	" " " " " " " " Feb. 8, '47...
Dobbins, John F. P.	....	" "	" " " " " " " " Nov. 9, '46..
Deiter, John	....	" "	" " " " " " " " Aug. 24, '46..
Deiter, Joel	....	" "	" " " " " " " " Aug. 24, '46..

Name and Rank.	Place of Enlistment.	Enrolled	Remarks.
		1846.	
Kelley, Ephram		July 20	Disch. on Serg. cert. of disability, Sept. 18, '46
Mason, William C		July 18	" " " Aug. 30, '46
McNeil, Malcolm		July 4	" " " Oct. 8, '46
McKee, Patrick		" "	" by order of Col. Baker July 17, '46
Monroe, Thomas		July 20	" Surg. cert. of disability, Feb. 8, '47
Painter, William C		July 4	" " " Nov. 9, '46
Pigg, John		July 20	" " " Sept. 28, '46
Turner, Orren		July 4	" " " Oct. 8, '46
Wilson, Samuel B		" "	" " " Oct. 4, '46

Died:

Third Sergeant. Stephen D. Webb		July 4	Died Oct. 24, '46, at hospital, Matamoras
Second Corporal. James Dunsmore		July 4	" Oct. 1, '46, " "
Privates. Carter, John S. S		July 4	" Oct. 27, '46, " Camargo
Yan, Alonzo A		" "	" Sept. 10, '46, at Camp Patterson

Deserted:

Privates. Ashworth, Chris		July 4	Deserted July 9, Jefferson Barracks, Mo
Barker, James		" "	" July 23, " "
Hamilton, J. R		" "	" " " "
Langford, Asa		" "	Leave of absence 10 days; did not rejoin Co

This company was discharged May 26, 1847, at New Orleans.

INDEPENDENT COMPANIES

Of Illinois Mounted Volunteers, called into the service of the United States by the President, under the act of Congress, approved May 13, 1846, to serve for the term of during the war with Mexico, from the date of enrollment, unless sooner discharged.

Capt. A. Dunlap's Company,

Called into the United States service and mustered in at Alton, Ill., on May 21, 1847. The company was organized by Capt. Dunlap, at Rushville, Ill., in the month of May, 1847.

Name and Rank.	Place of Enlistment.	Enrolled	Remarks.
Captain.		1847.	
Adams Dunlap	Alton, Ill	May 21	
First Lieutenant.			
Samuel Lambert	"	"	
Second Lieutenants.			
Simon Doyle	"	"	
Calvin Jackson	"	"	
Sergeants.			
Samuel W. Boring	"	"	
James B. Wright	"	"	
George O. Backman	"	"	Was private from enrollment to July 9, 1847.
Rich. W. Stephenson	"	"	Appointed from private May 16, 1848.
Corporals.			
Victor C. Putman	"	"	
William Ritchey	"	"	
Newton D. Witt	"	"	
John W. Snider	"	"	Was private from enrollment to Feb. 16, 1848.
Bugler.			
Theodore Smith	"	"	
Charles Hynes	"	"	
Farrier and Bl'ks'ith.			
David Duff	"	"	
Privates.			
Angle, John	"	"	
Allen, Mark	Nauvoo, Ill	Mar. '48	Joined, a recruit, in Mex., May 26, 1848.
Brown, Robert	Vermont, Ill.	Feb. '48	" " " " "
Brown, Alexander	"	"	
Bowen, James F	Alton, Ill	May '47	
Bricklee, Henry	"	"	
Berry, Daniel T	"	"	
Beals, Sam'l O	"	"	
Boyd, David	"	"	
Boyd, Robert	"	"	
Chipman, Seth	"	"	
Chapman, William W	"	"	

INDEPENDENT COMPANIES. 305

Name and Rank.	Place of Enlistment.	Enrolled	Remarks.
		1-47.	
Cumings, Alfred	Alton, Ill.	May 21	
Cuningham, Caleb	"	....	
Chipman, Philip	"	"	
Cram, Henry	"	"	
Carden, Washi'gt'n A.	"	"	
Curtis, Jesse	Rushville, Ill.	Feb., '48	Joined, a recruit, in Mex., May 26, 1848
Corbridge, Thomas	Vermont, Ill.	"	" " " " "
Carter, Rutherford	"	"	" " " " "
Carnes, John T	Warsaw, Ill.	Mar. '48	" " " " "
Duhamell, Benj. F	Vermont, Ill.	Feb. '48	" " " " "
Densmore, James C.	Pittsfield, Ill.	April '48	
Dirickson, Joseph M.	Alton, Ill.	May '47	
Erwin, George W	"	....	
Easley, William	"	"	
Easley, Thomas M	"	"	
Elliott, William	"	....	
Fisher, Jacob	Rushville, Ill.	Jan. '48	Joined, a recruit, in Mex., May 26, 1848
Geiger, Davidson M.	Nauvoo, Ill.	Mar. '48	" " " " "
Gillett, Charles W	"	"	
Gilbreth, Samuel	Alton, Ill.	May '47	
Green, William	"	....	
Gitchell, Calvin L.	"	"	
Green, David	"	"	
Gordon, Franklin	"	"	
Gibson, Isaac W	"	"	
Haverkluft, C. H. C.	"	"	
Holloway, William	"	"	
Hatfield, Abraham	"	"	
Hymer, George	"	"	
Hoyt, Albert	"	"	
Hurry, David	Rushville Ill.	Jan. '48	Joined, a recruit, in Mex., May 26, 1848
Hopkins, Lemuel B.	Vermont, Ill.	Feb., '48	" " " " "
Hopkins, David R.	"	"	" " " " "
Hanson, William B.	Warsaw, Ill.	Mar. '48	" " " " "
Jump, James D	Rushville, Ill.	May '48	
Jones, James B	Alton, Ill.	May '47	
Jones, Levi	"	....	
Kelly, Patrick	"	"	
Lambert, Henry	"	"	
Lamaster, Erwin	"	"	
Lincoln, Jefferson	Rushville, Ill	Jan. '48	Joined, a recruit, in Mex., May 26, 1848
Mullane, Carroll	"	"	" " " " "
Mauck, Abram R.	"	"	
McGee, Elijah	"	"	
Myres, Jacob L.	Vermont, Ill.	Feb. '48	" " " " "
Maynard, Robert H.	Winch'ter, Ill.	April '48	" " " " "
Mars, John L.	"	"	
Martin, George W	Alton, Ill.	May '47	
McKinney, John	"	....	
McNeely, John	"	"	
McMasters, William	"	"	
Murran, James	"	"	
Patterson, Charles R.	"	"	
Parrott, Josiah	"	"	
Puler, Jefferson	"	"	
Presson, William	"	"	
Peirce, George	"	"	
Parker, Oscar J.	Vermont, Ill.	Feb. '48	Joined, a recruit, in Mexico, May 26, 1848
Roberts, Dewitt C.	Winch'ter, Ill.	April, '48	" " " " "
Redmon, William	Matamor's, M.	July, '47	" " " July 9, 1847
Rhodes, Hinman	Alton, Ill.	May, '47	
Scott, George R.	"	....	
Scott, William B	"	"	
Spencer, Elijah	"	"	
Smith, William E	"	"	
Smith, Robert	"	"	
Sidwell, James C	Vermont, Ill.	Feb., '47	Joined, a recruit, in Mexico, May 26, 1848
Seemon, Cornelius	Matamor's, M.	July, '47	" " " July 9, 1847
Stetson, Clinton	Nauvoo, Ill.	Mar., '48	" " " May 26, 1848
Turnbull, Thomas	Rushville, Ill.	Jan., '48	" " " " "
Todd, Simeon S.	"	"	" " " " "
Tucker, William	Vermont, Ill.	Feb., '48	" " " " "
Troy, Jerome S.	Pittsfield, Ill.	April, '48	" " " " "
Thompson, James	Alton, Ill.	May, '47	
Thompson, James D.	"	....	
Throughman, John	"	"	
Vance, John	"	"	
Vancourt, Benj. P.	Warsaw, Ill.	Mar., '48	Joined, a recruit, in Mexico, May 26, 1848
Winsor, Clark	Nauvoo, Ill.	"	" " " " "

—20

Name and Rank.	Place of Enlistment.	Enrolled	Remarks.
Weatherbee, Wm. B.	Carthage, Ill.	Mar. '48	Joined, a recruit, in Mexico, May 26, 1848......
Whitehurst, Willis G.	Winch'ter, Ill.	April, '48	" " " " " ......
Ward, Alfred	Alton, Ill.	May, '47	
Whitlock, George C.	"	....	"
Wright, Isaac S. W.			
Ward, Luke G.	Matamor's, M.	July, '47	Joined, a recruit, in Mexico, July 9, 1847......

Died:

		1847.	
Sergeant. Thomas Tyre	Alton, Ill.	May 21	Died at Matamoras, Mex., July 10, 1847 ....
Corporal. Anthony Porgolio	"	.... "	Died at Matamoras, Mex., Oct. 8, 1847..........
Privates. Beales, Angustus F.	"	.... "	Died at Matamoras, Mex., Sept. 18, 1847......
Biggs, Henry	"	.... "	" " " Oct. 23, 1847........
Burton, George W.	"	.... "	" Point Isabel, Tex., July 18, 1848..........
Castle, Henry	"	.... "	" Matamoras, Mex., Oct. 28, 1847..........
Clark, John	"	.... "	" " " Aug. 1, 1847...........
Cook, William W.	"	.... "	" " " Sept. 28, 1847........
Dyson, Samuel	"	.... "	" " " Oct. 30, 1847.........
Edmonson, N. H. R.	"	.... "	" " " Oct. 18, 1847.........
Fletcher, James C.	"	.... "	" " " Aug. 7, 1847..........
Gipson, Benjamin F.	"	.... "	" " " Oct. 13, 1847.........
Gillett, Plinney P.	Warsaw, Ill.	Mar., '48	" Alton, Ill., Aug. 31, 1848 ....
Ren, Thomas	Alton, Ill.	May, '47	" Matamoras, Mex., July 15, 1847 ....
Smith, John	"	.... "	" " " Sept. 27, 1847........

Deserted:

Brunt, (?) William	Alton, Ill.	May '47	Deserted at Matamoras, Mex., Dec. 1, 1847....
Brooks, William	Rushville, Ill.	July, '48	" Camargo, Mex., August —......
Hoovey, Simeon A.	Alton, Ill.	May, '47	" Alton, Ill., June 9, 1847 ....
Smith, Thomas J.	"	.... "	" June 5, 1847 ....
Wright, David	"	.... "	" New Orleans, La., June 25, 1847...

Discharged:

Sergeant. Marcus Serrott	Alton, Ill.	May '47	Discharged on Surg. certificate, April 27, 1848.
Privates. Cross, Thomas J.	Rushville, Ill.	Feb., '48	Left sick at San Antonio, Tex., Sept. 9 ....
Dickson, Francis	Alton, Ill.	May, '47	Discharged on Surg. certificate, April 27, 1848.
Lansdon, William A.	"	.... "	" " " Dec. 5, 1847 ..
Whitcher, Pat'rs'n V.	Warsaw, Ill.	Mar., '48	" expiration of service, Oct. 3.....

This company was discharged at Alton, Ill., on Nov. 7, 1848.

CAPT. WYATT B. STAPP'S COMPANY,

Called into the service of the United States and mustered in August 10, 1847, at Quincy, Ill
This company was organized at Monmouth, Ill., in month of June, 1847.

Name and Rank.	Place of Enlistment.	Enrolled	Remarks.
Captain.		1847.	
Wyat B. Stapp	Quincy, Ill	Aug. 6	
First Lieutenant.			
George C. Lanphere	"	"	
Second Lieutenants.			
George W. Palmer	"	"	Resigned Oct. 29, 1847
John H. Mitchell	"	"	
Second Second Lieut.			
John G. Fonda	Jeffers'n Bar.	Aug. 17	Elected from Sergt., June 13, 1848
Sergeants.			
John B. Holliday	Quincy, Ill	Aug. 6	
Brice M. Henry	"	"	Appointed from private, Feb. 29, 1849
Thomas H. Davidson	"	"	Elected from private, June 13, 1848
Elias Guthrie	"	"	" " " Feb. 29, 1848
Corporals.			
Robert C. Armstrong	"	"	Elected from private, Feb. 29, 1848
Esau Brown	"	"	" " " Dec. 31, 1847
Joseph D. Mackey	"	"	
Darius Dennis	"	"	Elected from private, Feb. 29, 1848
Buglers.			
Benj. I. Tifield	"	"	
Robert M. Snapp	"	"	
Blacksmith and Farrier.			
Robert C. West	"	"	
Privates.			
Avarill, Wm.	"	"	
Brownlee, David	"	"	
Barnard, Geo. R. A.	"	"	
Berry, Isaiah	"	"	
Barnaby, Wm	"	"	
Beebe, Edward O	"	"	
Backus, Samuel I.	"	"	
Birch, Louis	Perote, Mex.	Jan., '48	
Cowan, David S.	Quincy, Ill	Aug. 6,'47	
Carter, Job L.	"	"	
Daniel, Dickson S.	"	"	
Drain, Charles	"	"	
Dunlap, Nicholas	"	"	
Eads, James D.	"	"	
Furgus, James	"	"	
Gordon, James E.	"	"	
Grover, Alonzo	"	"	
Hatton, Richard	"	"	
Harding, Samuel	"	"	
Honderson, Samuel	"	"	
Howard, John D.	"	"	
King, Michael	"	"	
Kelly, Calvin	"	"	
Lanphere, George	"	"	
Lillard, Augustine	"	"	
Monteith, Wm. H.	"	"	
McWilliams, John T.	"	"	
Moffitt, John	"	"	
Motley, John B	"	"	
Poland, James H	"	"	
Pickenough, Absal'm	"	"	
Parmenter, James S	"	"	
Parmenter, Leinster	"	"	
Rhodes, Job	"	"	
Ruddle, John F.	"	"	
Ruddle, George H.	"	"	
Reed, John	"	"	

308   MEXICAN WAR.

Name and Rank.	Place of Enlistment.	Enrolled	Remarks.
Rodriguez, Janquine	C'y of Mexico.	May 1, '48	
Stanley, Leander	Quincy, Ill.	Aug. 6, '47	
Stigall, Geo. W.	"	"	
Williams, Wm.	"	"	
Wells, Cyrus	"	"	
Watkins, Luther P.	"	"	
Worden, John I.	"	"	
Wilson, James E.	"	"	

Died:

Name and Rank.	Place of Enlistment.	Enrolled	Remarks.
Sergeant. Ishmael H. Holcomb	Quincy, Ill.	1847. Aug. 6	Died at Perote, Mex., March 10, 1848
Corporal. Wm. D. Day	"	"	Died at Perote, Mex., April 3, 1848
Privates. Bartram, Ezra G.	"	"	Died at Perote, Mex., Dec. 26, 1847
Black, John	"	"	" " " Jan. 2, 1848
Cullip, Zachariah	"	"	" " " Dec. 26, 1847
Clannin, Oliver	"	"	" " " Dec. 28, 1847
Fitzpatrick, Michael	"	"	" Vera Cruz, Mex., Dec. 14, 1847
Hatton, William	"	"	" Jalapa, Mex., Feb. 7, 1848
Morgan, Geo. W.	"	"	" en route to Mexico, Sept. 15, 1847
McNeil, Geo. W.	"	"	" Jalapa, Mex., Dec. 7, 1847
Miles, James A.	"	"	" Perote, Mex., Feb. 5, 1848
Nicholas, Ezra H.	"	"	" " " Jan. 2. 1848
Owens, Wm. C.	"	"	" " " Jan. 26, 1848
Porter, Orlando	"	"	" " " Jan. 7, 1848
Sissell, John	"	"	" " " Jan. 16, 1848
Shields, James	"	"	" Jalapa, Mex., April 23, 1848
Webb, Albert	"	"	" Perote, Mex., Dec. 26, 1847
Wilson, Warren R.	"	"	" " " Jan. 4, 1848
Wells, Larkin	"	"	" Jalapa, Mex., Dec. 10, 1847

Deserted:

Name and Rank.	Place of Enlistment.	Enrolled	Remarks.
Private. William Kelley	Quincy, Ill.	1847. Aug. 6	Deserted March 17, 1848

Discharged:

Name and Rank.	Place of Enlistment.	Enrolled	Remarks.
Sergeants. Samuel Douglas	Quincy, Ill.	1847. Aug. 6	Discharged March 11, 1848
James Townsley	"	"	Disch. by certificate of disability Mar. 11, '48.
Nicholas P. Earp	"	"	" " " " Dec. 24, '47.
Corporals. Geo. L. Shippey	"	"	Disch. by certificate of disability, Jan. 3, '48.
James W. Robson	"	"	" " " " Feb. 6, '48.
Privates. Coe, Reuben M.	"	"	Discharged, date unknown
Daniel, Warner I.	"	"	" March 14, 1848.
De LaBar, Joseph M.	"	"	Disch. by certificate of disability Dec. 15, '47.
Foster, Geo. W.	"	"	" " " " Jan. 29, '48.
Hogue, Thomas G.	"	"	" " " " Jan. 3, '48.
Kent, Ezekiel	"	"	" " " " Dec. 15, '47.
Lanphere, Clark	"	"	" " " " Jan. 29, '48.
Mitchell, Jas. W., Jr.	"	"	" " " " Dec. 15, '47.
Pike, Samuel	"	"	" " " " Jan. 29, '48.
Wilson, Isaac	"	"	" " " " Mar. 14, '48.
Weston, Henry	"	"	Discharged, date unknown

This company was discharged at Alton, Ill., July 26, 1848.

INDEPENDENT COMPANIES. 309

Lieut. G. C. Lanphere's Detachment

Of Recruits belonging to Capt. W. B. Stapp's Company of Mounted Volunteers, mustered in on the date of their respective enrollment at Monmouth, Ill. This detachment was organized by Lt. G. C. Lanphere, at Monmouth, Ill.

Name and Rank.	Place of Enlistment.	Enrolled	Remarks.
Privates.		1848.	
Allison, Samuel M...	Monmouth, Ill	April 12	
Allen, William F.....	"	May 13	
Bigelow, Dubois.....	"	Mar. 9	
Butler, Peter.........	"	Mar. 29	
Day, John............	"	Mar. 16	
Dunham, Christ'er N.	"	April 17	
Dargin, John.........	"	May 21	
Elder, William.......	"		
Fitzjerrell, John.....	"	Mar. 11	
Fuller, Limon P.....	"	June 1	Rejected.................
Griffits, Thomas B...	"	April 5	
Hume, Charles R....	"	Feb. 26	
Huddleston, Richard	"	Mar. 6	
Holmes, George B...	"	May 13	
Hurn, George W.....	"	June 1	
Lawrence, Sol. K., Jr.	"	May 21	
Mekemson, John S...	"	Mar. 10	
Meredeth, John J....	"		
Norton, James L.....	"	May 21	
Pratt, Abram, Jr.....	"	Feb. 19	
Peck, James M.......	"	April 1	
Pool, John...........	"	June 1	
Rumpf, Philip.......	"	May 17	
Rennard, John D....	"	June 1	
Shelton, David R....	"	Mar. 14	
Shelton, Samuel.....	"		
Spencer, Franklin...	"	April 14	
Tadlock, Benjamin..	"	Feb. 26	
Tadlock, Edward I..	"	Mar. 8	
Teice, Tandy H......	"	Mar. 13	
Worthen, James.....	"	May 21	

This detachment was mustered out June 28, 1848, at Jefferson Barracks, Mo.

Capt. Michael K. Lawler's Company,

Called into the United States service, and mustered in at Shawneetown, Ill., on August 13, 1847. This company was organized at Shawneetown, Ill., in the month of August, 1847.

Name and Rank.	Place of Enlistment.	Enrolled	Remarks.
Captain.		1847.	
Michael K. Lawler..	Shawn't'n, Ill.	Aug. 13	
First Lieutenant.			
Walter S. Clark......	"	"	
Second Lieutenants.			
Samuel L. M. Proctor	"	"	
John G. Ridgway....	"	"	
Sergeants.			
Howell Sloo.........	"	"	Was private from enrollment to Oct. 25.......
Theod're L. Lockhart	"	"	" " " " Dec. 1.......
George F. White.....	"	"	" Corpl. from " " Mar. 25.......
Robert M. Peebles..	"	"	" private " " June 20.....
Corporals.			
Thomas J. Powell...	"	"	
Samuel H. T. Proctor	"	"	Was private from enrollment to March 25....
Lorenzo W. Stone...	"	"	" " " " May 1........
John C. Mitchell.....	"	"	" " " " June 16......

MEXICAN WAR.

Name and Rank.	Place of Enlistment.	Enrolled	Remarks.
Buglers.		1847.	
William J. Gatewood	Shawn't'n, Ill.	Aug. 13	Was private from enrollment to Oct. 25
Sanford Cockran	"	"	April 1
Farrier.			
Benedict Crandle	"	"	
Privates.			
Baker, William	"	"	
Becraft, John	"	"	
Berry, Charles	"	"	
Bramlet, Sanford	"	"	
Bruce, James	"	"	
Buckner, Edwin	"	"	
Burrel, Mars	"	"	
Burrel, William	"	"	
Calicoat, John	"	"	
Campbell, Chalon G.	"	"	
Catt, Levi B.	"	"	
Catt, Pilate S.	"	"	
Caughman, Charles J	"	"	
Caughman, John	"	"	
Cayton, William W.	"	"	Was Sergeant from enrollment to Jan. 1.
Chapman, Isaac	"	"	
Christian, Rufus	"	"	
Clark, Josiah	"	"	
Conyers, Isaac	"	"	
Crenshaw, Abraham	"	"	
Davis, James B.	"	"	
Eastman, Jacob I.	"	"	
Eaton, William H.	"	"	Was missing from enrollment to April 1.
Ensminger, Stephen	"	"	Hospital Steward from June 19.
Gaston, Robert	"	"	
Gates, William	"	"	
Gillerson, Pat'rson H	"	"	
Greathouse, Tevis	"	"	
Greer, Payton	"	"	Died at Equality, Ill., Oct. 24, 1848.
Hair, James	"	"	
Harget, William	"	"	
Hargrave, Thomas	"	"	
Henson, Elijah	"	"	
Hill, Morris	"	"	
Hood, James	"	"	Absent, sick at Carmi, from Oct. 3.
Hood, William	"	"	
Hughes, Alexander	"	"	
Hughes, Cephas G.	"	"	Was Sergeant from enrollment to March 25.
Hughes, Champ. T.	"	"	
Hughes, George	"	"	
Jameson, John D.	"	"	Was Corporal from enrollment to Sept. 18.
Jones, Richard M.	"	"	
Kennedy, Daniel	"	"	
Leavell, Benjamin	"		
Lynch, John Q. A.	"	"	Sick, in Shawneetown, from Oct. 24.
McClusky, Daniel	"	"	
O'Malley, John	Tampico, Mex	Dec. 8	Joined, a recruit, at Tampico, Dec. 8.
Overbee, John	Shawn't'n, Ill.	Aug. 13	
Perry, Washington	"	"	
Pennell, Willis Y.	"	"	
Pipe, Thomas	"	"	
Rawson, Thomas	"	"	
Renwick, John G.	"	"	
Reynolds, Isaac	"	"	
Ritchey, Williamson	"	"	
Roark, David H.	"	"	
Robison, John	"	"	
Shirley, Nimrod	"	"	
Sinks, Zachariah	"	"	
Stickney, Geo. W.	"	"	Was Corporal from enrollment to Oct. 25.
Trimble, John	"	"	
Turner, John	"	"	
Walters, William	"	"	
Watts, Lewis F.	"	"	
White, Joseph	"	"	
Wolf, Stephen	"	"	

INDEPENDENT COMPANIES. 311

Discharged:

Name and Rank.	Place of Enlistment.	Enrolled	Remarks.
		1847.	
Bozman, Phineas	Shawn't'n, Ill.	Aug. 13	Discharged Jan. 26, 1848; disability
Boyer, Wm. L.	"	"	Reports himself discharged April 1, ——
Brooks, Luke	New Orleans.	Sept. 27	Ordered to N. Orleans to be disch.; fract. leg
Crissup, Thomas	Shawn't'n, Ill.	Aug. 13	Discharged Jan. 26, 1848; disability
Dorsey, Wm.	"	"	Ord. to N. Orleans to be disch. on exp'n term
Eubanks, George W.	"	"	" " " " " for fract. leg.
Fowler, James	"	"	" " " " " on exp'n term
Hill, Edward	"	"	Discharged Jan. 26, 1848; disability
Hudgins, Ambrose	"	"	
Linderman, Isaac	"	"	Ord. to N. Orleans to be disch. on exp'n term
McCarty, Charles	"	"	Discharged Sept. 20, 1847; disability
Miller, John W.	"	"	" Jan. 26, 1848; "
Pool, Thomas	"	"	
Pelham, John	"	"	Ord. to N. Orleans to be disch. on exp'n term
Pillow, Parker B.	"	"	
Reynolds, Thomas	"	"	Discharged Jan. 26, 1848; disability
Ritchey, Francis P.	"	"	Ord. to N. Orleans to be disch. on exp'n term
Sharp, Holmes	"	"	" " " " " " "
Spivey, Lindley M.	"	"	" " " " " " "
Sumpter, William	"	"	" " " " " " "
Vaugh, Thomas B.	"	"	" " " " " " "
Webb, Asa B.	"	"	" " " " " " "
Wright, Robert	"	"	
Wright, Alanson G.	"	"	Discharged Jan. 26, 1848; disability

Died:

Sergeants.		1847.	
Elias Umsnider	Shawn't'n, Ill.	Aug. 13	Died at Tampico, Mex., Oct. 30, 1847
John Cadle	"	" "	" " " " June 19, ——
Privates.			
Burrell, John	"	" "	Died at Baton Rouge, La., Sept 21, 1847
Gaston, John	"	" "	" " Tancasmqui, Mex., May 26, ——
Hudson, Sanford	"	" "	" " Alto Mora, Dec. 10, ——
Jones, Wm. H.	"	" "	" " Tampico, Mex., Oct. 1, 1847
Mahoney, Cornelius	"	" "	" " " " Feb. 11, ——
Morris, Robison B.	"	" "	" " Tancasmqui, Mex., May 31, ——
Mulligan, Thos.	Tampico, Mex	Dec. 18	" " Alton, Ill., Aug. 27, 1848
O'Neil, Peter	Shawn't'n, Ill.	Aug. 13	" " Tampico, Mex., Jan. 12, ——
Rearden, Henry T.	"	" "	" " " " Oct. 15, 1847
Reeves, Jeremiah H.	"	" "	" " " " Oct. 16, 1847
White, Benj. F.	"	" "	" " " " Jan. 1, ——

Deserted:

		1847.	
Harbaugh, Jeremiah	Baton Rouge.	Sept. 20.	Deserted Sept. 21, 1847

This company was discharged at Shawneetown, Ill., Oct. 26, 1848.

Capt. Josiah Littell's Company,

Called into the service of the United States at Alton, Ill., and mustered in on Sept. 18, 1847. This company was organized at Alton, Ill., in month of September, 1847.

Name and Rank.	Place of Enlistment.	Enrolled	Remarks.
Captain.		1847.	
Josiah Littell	Alton, Ill	Aug. 28	
First Lieutenants.			
Charles P. Hazard	"	"	Died at Memphis, Tenn., Oct. 19, 1847
Thomas L. Buck	"	"	Elected from 2d Lieut. Oct. 26, 1847
Second Lieutenants.			
Josiah Caswell	"	"	Elected from 2d 2d Lieut. Oct. 26, 1847
Robert S. Green	"	"	" private Oct. 26, 1847
Sergeants.			
T. D. Linn	"	"	Appointed from private Oct. 26, 1847
James McMahon	N. Orleans, La	Oct. 26	" " " Jan. 1, 1848
John Douthit	Alton, Ill	Aug. 28	
Corporals.			
Jeptha Muer	Alton, Ill	"	
Thomas Bacon	"	"	Appointed Feb. 27, 1848
Jerome Taylor	"	"	
George D.P. Coonrod	"	"	Appointed April 17, 1848
Bugler.			
William Edwards	"	"	
Privates.			
Adams, David	"	"	
Abbott, Howard W	City of Mexico	Feb., '48	
Benson, William	Alton, Ill	Aug., '47	
Blanchard, James W	"	"	
Boyd, George M	"	"	
Buck, Andrew P	"	"	
Bush, Robert	"	"	
Chester, Solomon S	"	"	
Cummings, Jesse	"	"	
Condon, John	"	"	
Carroll, Hardy R	"	"	Reduced from Sergeant Jan. 1, 1848
Denton, Thomas I	"	"	
Darkham, Jonathan	City of Mexico	Jan., '48	
Elwell, Ellis	Alton, Ill	Aug., '47	
Eastep, Joseph R. W	"	"	
Fountain, Pleasant	"	"	
Finney, Clinton	"	"	
Gowen, George A	"	"	
Givinn, John	"	"	
Griffith, Jefferson	"	"	Resigned from 2d Corporal Oct. 26, 1847
Gray, William	"	"	
Hackney, Joseph B	"	"	
Higham, John L	"	"	
Howarton, William L	"	"	
Harris, Rufus	"	"	
Hill, Wyatt R	"	"	
Hoover, Samuel	"	"	
Holley, James H	"	"	
Jones, Joshua	"	"	
Kueffell, Francis	City of Mexico	Feb., '48	
Lancaster, James	Alton, Ill	Aug., '47	
McGraham, Henry	"	"	
McWain, William	"	"	
Moore, John	"	"	
Moore, Samuel W	"	"	
Miller, William E	"	"	
Mott, Sherwood	"	"	
Murphy, James C	"	"	
Noels, William	"	"	
Nettleton, James H	"	"	
Parrish, Isaac	"	"	
Parrish, Samuel	"	"	
Powles, John	"	"	
Phelan, James	"	"	
Rice, Hugh	"	"	
Sprunce, William	"	"	

INDEPENDENT COMPANIES.

Name and Rank.	Place of Enlistment.	Enrolled	Remarks.
		1847.	
Staits, William	Alton, Ill	Aug. 28	
Shelby, James	"	"	
Staggs, Pleasant	"	"	
Staggs, Thomas	"	"	
Tongate, John T	"	"	Resigned from 1st Sergeant Oct. 26, 1847
Tillotson, Willard	"	"	
Tindall, Lewis W	"	"	
Turpin, Calohill	"	"	
Taylor, Jack R	"	"	
Taylor, Jeffrey M	"	"	
Thompson, Daniel E	City of Mexi'o	Feb., '48	Re-enlisted in Mexico
Vestal, Jesse	Alton, Ill	Aug., '47	
Vanhouton, John S	"	"	
Wells, Isaac L	"	"	
Woods, Hiram D	"	"	
Webb, William W	"	"	
Washburn, Coleman	"	"	
Woods, George W	"	"	
Woods, John	"	"	
Weir, Gerd	"	"	

Died:

		1847.	
Sergeant. Isaiah Tetrick	Alton, Ill	Aug. 28	Died near Memphis, July, 1848
Corporal. Jonathan G. Smith	"	"	Died at Rio Frio, Feb. 27, 1848
Blacksm'h & Farrier. John Murphy	"	"	Died Dec. 2, 1847, at Jalapa, of wounds
Privates.			
Barrow, James	"	"	Died on Gulf of Mexico, June 25, 1848
Cameron, Joseph	"	"	Died at Puebla, Dec. 16, 1847
Judd, Corben C	"	"	" Dec. 27, 1847
Jones, William T	"	"	" Rio Frio, Jan. 1, 1848
Kuhn, Herman	"	"	" Alton, July 19, 1848
McWain, William, 2d	"	"	" New Orleans, Oct. 29, 1847
Odell, Allen	"	"	" Vera Cruz, Nov. 17, 1847
Stone, Thomas	N. Orleans, La	Nov. 8	Killed by guerrilas, Nov. 20, 1847
Sullivan, Jerry	Alton, Ill	Aug. 28	Drowned in the Mississippi, Nov. 3, 1847
Schmidt, Hartman	"	"	Died at Camp Encerro, June 16, 1848
Wells, John E	"	"	" Rio Frio, Feb. 12, 1848

Deserted:

		1847.	
Charles Durand	N. Orleans, La	Oct. 28	Absent without leave from Jan. 6, 1848

Discharged:

		1847.	
Corporal. Charles H. Cowden	Alton, Ill	Aug. 28	Discharged on Surg. certificate, April 1, 1848.
Privates.			
Cork, Henry	"	"	Discharged on Surg. certificate, Mar. 1, 1848
Davis, William			" " " "
Fleming, David	N. Orleans, La	Oct. 28	" " " April 6, 1848.
Kuykendall, Peter	Alton, Ill	Aug. 28	" " " April 4, 1848.
Payne, Charles E	"	"	" " "
Taylor, Henry	"	"	" " " Jan. 15, 1848.

This company was discharged at Alton, Ill., July 25, 1848.

REGULAR ENLISTMENTS.

The following rolls of enlisted men were furnished this office by the War Department at Washington, D. C., being of men recruited in the State of Illinois, under the act of Congress, known as "the ten regiment bill." Nothing is known of the particulars of their service further than is already given in the "Historical Memoranda," in the earlier pages of this book. The Adjutant-General of the army, when applied to for data as to the killed, wounded, discharged, etc., stated: "I have the honor to inform you, by direction of the Secretary of War, that the request cannot be complied with, it being contrary to the well established practice of the office, and not consistent with the interests of the public service."

An application was made at the same time for the names of commissioned officers, but the War Department, for some unexplained reason, failed to furnish those also.

14TH U. S. INFANTRY.

Muster roll of the enlisted men of Co. "E," 14th U. S. Infantry, during the Mexican War, who were enlisted in the State of Illinois:

First Sergeants.
William Y. Dillard,
Harrison Q. Roberts,

Sergeants.
Alexander K. Hams,
Benjamin R. Johnson,
William H. Leeper,
Jackson Rushing,
William Willett,
William Waymond.

Corporals.
Reuben Davis,
Robert Green,
John W. Harvey,
Bethuel Hitch,
Henry Irvin,
Lewis Varner.

Drummer.
Thomas Gilbert.

Privates.
Allen, Wm. M.
Burnsfield, William,
Baronett, Zadoch C.,
Baronett, Wm. H.,
Broad, David P.,
Burton, James,
Boyles, Absolem,
Blevens, Warden P.,
Bolerjack, Albert G.,
Culpepper, Joel,
Clubb, Edward A.,
Carbaugh, Simon,
Cowan, Andrew J.,
Davis, Robert,
Dobbs, Elijah,
Durham, James I.,
Dorherty, John P.,
Doyer, Antoine,
French, Hansford,
Franklin, William E.,
Harris, Hardin,
Hoffard, Adam,
Holt, Jesse,
Hilt, Wm. I.,
Hewitt, Samuel R.,
Hutchinson, Phillip S.,
Hopkins, Carley,
Hawks, William E.,
Irick, George,
Irwin, William,
Johnson, William E.,
Jacobs, Bernard,
Jackson, James H.,
Jolleff, Aaron,
Kinnard, Wm. H.,
Kinnard, Simon,
King, James,
King, Robert,
Kelley, William, 1st.,
Kelley, William, 2d.,
Knap, Andrew W.,
Laflure, Ralph,
Lowery, Wm. I.,
Leslie, Wm. W.,
Metcalf, Jackson,
Myers, Wm. C.,
Melton, Joel S.,
Morgan, John S.,
Miller, Arch,
Morris, Jesse C.,
Matthews, Nichols,
Penington, Geo. W.,
Phelan, Gideon I.,
Plunkett, Patrick,
Pate William,
Richey, John,
Rabstock, Anton,
Robinson, George,
Rosser, Peter,
Roswell, Henry C.,
Sharp, John W.,
Stephen, James,
Simes, Thomas M.,
Southworth, Perry,
Smith, John G.,
Swards, David,
Stoker, Gabriel,
Southworth, James,
Trout, Joseph,
Trout, Erasmus,
Trout, John H.,
Turner, Fielding C.,
Thomas, Augustus,
Underwood, Edward,
Williams, Henry M.,
Williams, Reece,
Warren, John,
Williamson, Vincent P.,
Waymond, Edward,
Williams, George,
Withrow, William,
Witzel, Frederick,
Woodsworth, Richard I.,
White, Adam M.,
Wilson, Aaron,
Winter, Geo. W.

16TH U. S. INFANTRY.

Muster roll of the enlisted men of Co. "A," 16th U. S. Infantry, during the Mexican War, who were enlisted in the State of Illinois:

First Sergeants.
Benjamin F. Keys,
Robert B. McDowell.

Q. M. Sergeant.
William F. Peck.

Sergeants.
Charles S. Bagg,
Gilbert W. Dean,
Andrew G. Price,
E. C. Bennett.

Corporals.
Benjamin F. Clark,
Abram Courtright,
Jason Pattee,
Lorence Kern.

Musicians.
Stephen F. W. Lord,
John Van Arnum.

Privates.
Abbott, Henry,
Allen, Andrew,
Anderson, Andrew,
Adderly, John,
Brown, Ephraim,
Boker, John B.,
Bradley, A. St. John,
Benson, A. F.,
Bailey, William,
Bentley, Geo. W.,
Brown, Wm. S.,
Barton, George,
Burger, Robert,
Barber, William,
Bryant, Edward W.,
Bemus, Geo. W.,
Brierton, Sylvester,
Branch, Wheeler,
Boggs, Wm. J.,
Brown, Henry,
Congdonge, Thomas,
Curtis, Jackson,
Crampton, Eli,
Cooper, Thomas L.,
Cole, Samuel C.,
Courtwright, Christopher,
Cottera, Charles,
Charterton, John M.,
Crim, James,
Cunningham, John,
Downs, E. A.,
Davis, Ransom B.,
Doty, Cornelius,
Daley, Edwin,
Ducey, Patrick B.,
Dewitt, Almond T.,
Evans, C. W.,
Estell, John W.,
Edmunds, William,
Flucord, John E.,
Foley, John P.,
Fry, Christian,
Fisher, Hezekiah,
Fager, Henry,
Guthrie, James W.,
Gilbert, Charles M.,
Gordon, Morrison,
Goodwin, Robert,
Hunter, Robert,
Hart, Warren R.,
Hull, Joseph L.,
Heaton, James A.,
Higgins, James H.,
Hoslie, Henry,
Huston, George,
Hicks, Theodore E.,
Hood, Thomas A.,
Johnson, Joseph,
Jackson, Samuel B.,
Klineton, Walton,
Lysle, Matthew,
Miller, Orson H.,
Mahone, Thomas,
Miller, Isaac S.
Moses, Byron,
McNealey, Levi,
McCarthy, Charles F.,
McConnell, John,
Mitts, William H.
Mascrip, William L.,
Mitchell, Joseph B.,
McChesney, John,
Mix, George,
Newcomer, Martin E.
Osterhoudt, Charles H.
Otterson, James,
Peacock, Francis J.,
Phillips, Christian Y.,
Patterson, William,
Roberts, Thomas,
Rosebrook, Lyman,
Read, George D.,
Reed, Elias,
Ramsey, John,
Sherman, A. D.,
Scofield, James,
Steward, Isaac,
Sternes, Daniel A.,
Stacy, Martin C.,
Slaymaker, Wm. A.,
Scott, Jerome,
Secord, George,
Smith, Orange P.,
Stanover, Frederick,
Taylor, William,
Thatcher, John,
Townsend, Philomen,
Taylor, John,
Van Horn, P. H.,
Vest, Wm. H.,
Wright, Pharris,
Whelply, Mangle R.,
Willard, James,
Waddle, Joseph,
Ware, Levi,
Watterbury, James W.
Wiley, William H.,
Wause, David,
Wilkinson, Thomas H.,
Williams, Cornelius,
Youngcourt, Theodore,

Muster roll of the enlisted men of Co. "G," 16th U. S. Infantry, during the Mexican War, who were enlisted in the State of Illinois:

First Sergeant.
Daniel Gregg.

Sergeants.
John C. Parks,
Edwin A. Partridge,
Myron Whipple,

Richard Hudunt,

Corporals.
James S. Porter,
George Watrod,
Levi R. Smith,
John E. Kimberly.

Fifer.
Edwin H. Fay.

Drummer.
Henry E. VanDyke.

Privates.
Amidon, Henry,
Adkin, Valentine,
Butler, Geo. H.
Bennett, William,
Bennett, Elijah C.,
Benson, Bradford,
Blackwell, Geo. W.,
Brown, David T.,
Brown, Edward,
Brown, Henry,
Branch, John F.,
Brockbuler, John,
Babcock, Benjamin K.,
Bowen, David T.,
Birch, Marcellas,
Beecher, Geo. M.,
Bartley, John,
Burnes, Charles B.,
Baldy, Geo. W.,
Beaurgardt, Mathias,
Clark, Lewis P.,
Cecil, George,
Coates, John,
Colburn, William,
Cook, David,
Cluney, James,
Chapman, Bela J.,
Childers, Calvin,
Clark, Geo. W.,
Clasby, Dandridge B.,
Deane, Josiah,
Dewitt, Martin,
Duter, Anthony,
Daskem, William H.,
Dickson, John A.,
Devore, Nicholas,
Dymond, John,
Domback, Godfrey,
Duncan, Joseph W.,
Durell, Charles W.,
Fearrow, William,
Fielding, James E.,
Filley, Timothy,
Fitzsimmons, Hugh D. K.,
Fowler, James,
Fury, William,
Gates, John E.,
Green, Herman,
Godfrey, Scott C.,
Goodman, Thomas F.,
Getzler, Charles H.,
Ghuntley, Andrew,
Haskill, Charles H.,
Hawley, Edward G.,
Horr, John A.,
Holdridge, Luther,
Hefty, Samuel,
Israel, Peter,
Jeffords, Sidney H.,
Johnson, Arthur D.,
Johnson, Ashel C.,
Joslin, Almond,
Link, Anthony,
Lansing, Henry,
Leutz, Geo. F.,
Lake, Nelson P.,
Loe, Fielding,
McAllister, Hugh,
McCombs, John M.,
McDonald, Edward,
McWain, Clark,
May, John,
Martlett, Richard D.,
Morris, John,
Miler, Sylvester,
Murray, John,
Nash, Isaac,
Northcutt, Wm. W.,
Owen, Evan,
Otis, Charles,
Power, Patrick,
Perry, James,
Perry, John,
Plastridge, Francis,
Pfister, George,
Rogers, John W.,
Rogers, Wm. J.,
Skinner, Dempsey,
Smith, Samuel M.,
Smith, Henry,
Smith, Jacob F.,
Synot, Marcus,
Spies, Andrew,
Simpson, James M.,
Sammis, Benj. N.,
Styne, Levi,
Teele, John W.,
Ules, Frederick,
Vogt, Jacob,
Walton, Nicholas,
Wilder, James,
Wickham, Isaac J.,
Wheeler, John L.,
Williams, Ruel,
Wise, Frederick,
Walton, Mark,
Wilson, William A.,
Walls, William R.,
Walker, Henry.

APPENDIX.

WAR OF 1810-'13.

CONTENTS OF APPENDIX.

	PAGE.
Ensign Whitesides Company	319
Massacre of Chicago	320
Captain William Alexander's Company, 1811	320
Campaign of 1812	321
Destruction of Peoria	322

Muster Rolls—1812.

Capt. Thomas E. Craig's Company	323
Capt. Samuel Whiteside's Company	324
Capt. Jacob Short's (first) Company	326
Capt. John Scotts' Company	326
Capt. Samuel Judy or Henry Cooks' Company	327
Capt. William Hargraves Company	328
Capt. Samuel Judy's Spy Company	328
Capt. Absolem Cox's Company	329
Capt. James B. Moore's 1st Company	330
Capt. James B. Moore's 2d Company	330
Capt. Philip Tramell's Company	331
Capt. Dudley Williams Company	332
Field and Staff Roll	333
Campaign of 1813	334

Muster Rolls—1813.

Capt. James B, Moore's (3d) Company	334
Capt. Jacob Short's Company	335
Capt. William Jones' Company	336
Sergt. James N. Fox's Detachment	337
Lieut. Daniel G. Moore's Company	338
Capt. Nathan Chamber's Company	398
Regimental Field and Staff, 1813	339
Capt. James B. Moore's (4th) Company	339
Campaign of 1814	840

APPENDIX.

A RECORD OF THE SERVICES OF THE ILLINOIS MILITIA, RIFLEMEN AND VOLUNTEERS, IN THE INDIAN WARS, 1810 to 1813.

In 1810 a series of massacres and depredations were committed by the Indians of Illinois Territory, upon citizens of Louisiana Territory, which led to a long correspondence between the Governor of Louisiana Territory and Governor Edwards of Illinois Territory. The most daring of these, and which caused great excitement at the time, was committed at Portage du Sioux, on July 19th, which resulted in the killing of four white men and the serious wounding of a fifth. After some correspondence, in which it was made evident to Governor Edwards that the Pottawotamies were guilty of the outrage, and a requisition having been made on him for the murderers, Capt. Samuel Levering, on the 24th of July, 1811, was commissioned by Gov. Edwards to visit the tribes on the Illinois River, and demand of them, the author of the murders which had been committed. (Edwards Ill.)

Of this expedition, Ninian W. Edwards (in his History of Illinois,) says: "Capt Levering departed on that day (July 24, 1811), from Kaskaskia, and arrived at Mr. Jarrot's, in the village of Cahokia, on the next day at 11 P. M. Capt. Ebert had engaged part of the crew for the boat, and on the 25th of July, the boat having been furnished by Governor Clark with the necessary equipments, provisions, etc., they left in the boat for Peoria, with the crew, consisting of Capt. Levering, Capt. Hebert, Henry Swearingen, N. Rector, a Frenchman (who passed as an interpreter but was intended for a spy), a Pottawotamie Indian named Wish-ha, and eight oarsmen, each armed with a gun. The names of the boatmen were, Pierre St. John, Pierre La Parche, Joseph Trotier, Francis Pensoneau, Louis Bevanno, Thomas Hull (alias Woods) Pierre Voedre and Joseph Grammason, all of whom signed the articles of agreement as boatmen and soldiers of the expedition." (Edwards' History Illinois, p. 38). This expedition was met at Portage du Sioux three days afterward by Captain Whiteside and his men, "who had just arrived from a blockhouse near the mouth of the Illinois river."

Of Captain Whitesides company the records of this office show a muster roll of the date of Nov. 13th, 1812. We publish this roll complete.

A muster roll of a detachment of mounted riflemen commanded by Ensign Samuel Whitesides, of St. Clair county, Illinois Territory. By order of his Excellency, Ninian Edwards, Governor of Illinois Territory. From August 7th to August 22, 1812:

Ensign.
Samuel Whitesides.

Privates.
Titus Gragg,
John Swigert,
Henry Taylor,
Azor Gragg,
Abram Howard,
Wm. Pursley,
John Pursley,
Jos. Borough,
Matthew Roach,
John Lacy,
David Porter,
John Howard,
Abram Vanhoozer,
Roland Howitt,
Alexander Biram,
John Davison,
Jacob Smelcer,
David Gragg,
Charles Kitchens,
John Gragg,

The record in Edwards' History continues: "On the morning of the 29th day of July, they arrived at Prairie' Marcot, about nineteen miles above the mouth of the Illinois river, where Lieut. John Campbell was stationed, with seventeen men." The records in this office contain no roll of these men.

On the arrival of the party at Peoria a parley was held between Capt. Levering and a chief named Gomo, of the Pottawotamies. After several conferences Gomo gave up two stolen horses which he found in the possession of his men, but claimed that he could not find the murderers. Little Chief promised to deliver two more horses to Capt. Heald at Chicago, and Gomo promised to deliver the murderers when they could be found. At this conference it was ascertained that the Missouri murderers were near Prophet's town,—Tippecanoe—and hopes were entertained of catching them in the fall. By exposure incurred and disease contracted on this expedition, Capt. Levering died soon after his return to Kaskaskia.

Throughout the whole summer of 1811 the English emissaries kept up, industriously the dastardly work of setting the Indians on the white settlers. Encouraged by their promises, Tecumseh had conceived the plan of combining the Southern tribes into a league with the Northern Indians to make war on the United States until their lands were restored to them.

His attack on General Harrison with a force of over 700 men, under cover of darkness, and his ultimate defeat and flight, with a serious loss of killed and wounded, is a part of the history of our country which concerns us only, as our Illinois troops participated in the victory. This battle, which took place on the 6th day of November, 1811, cost the lives of 37 killed outright and 25 mortally wounded who afterward died, and these were the very flower of the young settlers of Indiana and Illinois Territories. Among the killed in this battle was Capt. Isaac White (for whom White county was afterward named), who commanded a company of Illinois troops raised in Saline county, of which we possess no roll. Here also fell Major Joe Daviess, whose name is also perpetuated in the county of that name; and of the others whose names are not recorded—nor have they be en perpetuated—we can only say they did their duty bravely, and the sacrifice of their own lives saved those of hundreds of women and children who might otherwise have fallen ready victims to the cruelty of the victorious savages.

The rolls of companies of rangers mustered into the United States service during the summer and fall of 1811, are no doubt preserved at the War Department. Of the militia who from time to time were called out by Governor Edwards, there are but few of the rolls preserved. We find, however, a pay roll of militia from July 4th, to July 29th, 1811, as follows:

CAPT. WM. ALEXANDER'S COMPANY.

Pay roll of company of militia commanded by Captain William Alexander, of the county of Randolph, Illinois Territory, by order of Ninian Edwards, Governor of said Territory.

Captain.
William Alexander.

Lieutenant.
Wm. McBride.

Sergeants.
Amos Chaffin,
David Everett,
George Wilson,
John Anderson.

Corporals.
Adam McDonald,
William Dees,
George Cochran,
Joseph Robinson.

Privates.
Joseph Vassume,
George Martin,
James Curry,
James Murtry,
Calvin Laurence,
Idmer Patton,
Drury Stephens,
Leonard St. John,
John Hill,
John McBride,
John Lively, (see campaign 1813)
Daniel Hull,
James McNabb,

Jean B. Iondrow,
Joseph Conway,
Robert Robinson,
Alexander Camudy,
Joseph Petoin,
John Pillers,
Joseph Miller,
Daniel Winn,
Jerome F. Pure,
John F. White,
Arch. Snodgrass,
Amos Robinson,
Edward Lay,
John Crawford,
Daniel Bilderback,
Robert Haggins,
Israel Bailey,
William Welch,
George Creath,
John May,
James Gill,
Robert McDonald,
Edward Rolls,
John Fisher,
John Baptiste Pera,
Joseph Butea,
Louis Dore,
Wiliam Bilderback,
Joseph Eberman,
Henry Null,
James White,
Simeon Brundage,
Eli Lankford,
James Eden.

During the winter of 1811-12 the Indians on the upper Mississippi were very hostile, and committed many murders.

Gov. Reynolds charges in his "Own Times" that the British agent at Prairie-du-Chien —it was reported by Indian traders—"had engaged all the warriors of that region to descend the Mississippi and exterminate the settlements on both sides of the river."

A few marauding parties penetrated far down in the State, killing Andrew Moore and his son on the middle fork of Big Muddy (Moore's Prairie, in Jefferson county, was named for him). Later in the same year they attacked Hill's fort, and were repulsed.

In view of the troubled state of affairs Gov. Edwards, in March, 1812, dispatched Capt. Edward Hebert as a friendly messenger to the Indians living on the Illinois river, inviting them to a counsel, which met on the 16th day of April, at Cahokia, and in which all the tribes in the State were represented. After protracted speech making, in which the Indians rather had the advantage, they came away loaded with substantial presents. Reynolds says:

"The wild men exercised the most diplomacy, and made the Governor believe that the Indians were for peace, and that the whites need dread nothing from them. They promised enough to obtain presents, and went off laughing at the credulity of the whites."

Some of the same Indians who participated in this council were engaged in the Chicago massacre the August following.

The Indians of the North-west, however, did not desire peace. They had been kept stirred up and excited by the British agents, so that when Congress, on the 19th day of June, 1812, declared war against Great Britain, they were ready to take advantage of the fact and throw their aid with the enemy in a general warfare against the settlers on the whole American frontier. In Illinois the militia was thoroughly organized in anticipation of the outbreak, and additional forts were built, one near the mouth of Little Wabash, and another at the mouth of La Motte creek.

MASSACRE AT CHICAGO.

The greatest massacre ever committed in the State occurred on the 15th day of August, 1812, near the site of the present city of Chicago. In 1804 the General Government had erected Fort Dearborn at the mouth of Chicago river, on the site of an old fort built by the French in the 17th century, and maintained in it a small garrison, usually consisting of 50 men and three pieces of artillery. Under this precarious protection there had gathered quite a number of Indian traders and their families, and a few settlers had established their homes in the immediate vicinity. For the eight years of the existence of the fort the history of the garrison had been free from incident. The relations of the officers, the soldiers, and even of the settlers and traders, with the savages were supposed to be of the most cordial nature. At the time of the massacre the garrison consisted of 75 men, few of whom were effective soldiers. The officers were Capt. Heald, Lieut. Helm, Ensign Ronan and Surgeon Voorhees.

On the 7th of August Capt. Heald received an order from Governor Hull, commander-in-chief, to evacuate the fort. The captain and Lieut. Helm, as well as John Kinzie, the principal trader, had families there, and their condition was all the more critical. Mr. Kinzie, who was seconded strongly by the sagacious chief who brought the order, Winnemeg, strongly advised against the evacuation, not believing it to be safe to leave the protection of the block-houses. But the commander, impressed more with his duty of obedience than of fear of danger, which he did not consider imminent, without consultation with his subordinates gave the order to evacuate the following morning. The other officers immediately added their remonstrances, and urged the improbability of being able to make a successful retreat with so small a force to so great a distance as Fort Wayne, through the country of so vigilant and hostile a foe.

The publication of this order for a week previous to the intended evacuation, no doubt added much to the danger.

Capt. Heald called together the Pottawotamies in council on the 12th, and promised them the goods belonging to the government, and in return they promised him to escort his force to Fort Wayne.

Capt. Heald, when too late, found that it was indiscreet to give the ammunition and whiskey to the Indians, so on the night of the 13th he destroyed all the ammunition by throwing it in a well, broke the extra guns and stove the whiskey barrels to prevent them falling into the hands of the Indians. A council of the savages held on the 14th expressed great indignation at this breach of faith on the part of the whites. Notice of the unfriendly attitude of the Indians was given during this day by Black Partridge, but Capt. Wells with 15 friendly Miamis having arrived from Fort Wayne, the despondency of the whites was somewhat dispelled. Capt. Wells was a brother of Mrs. Heald, and hearing of the intended evacuation, had hastened to strengthen the escort with the few men he could command at a short notice.

The reserved ammunition, 25 rounds to the man, was issued, and the baggage wagons for the sick, and women and children, made ready, and on the morning of the 15th of August, notwithstanding another message from a friendly Indian to Mr. Kinzie, warning them of danger, they started on their ill-advised journey, leaving the fort at 9 in the morning, headed by a band of martial music; about a mile and a half from the fort, they encountered the Indians, hid behind the sand-hills which follow the course of the beach of Lake Michigan. The troops fought bravely, but were overborne by numbers; only 28 out of 66 surrendered. Capt. Heald in his report gives them at 54 regulars and 12 militia, of which 26 regulars and all the militia were killed—all the other officers, including Capt. Wells, except the Capt. and Lieut. Helm, and most of the women and children were killed outright, one savage tomahawking 12 children in one wagon alone.

Of all who started out on the fatal morning, was left the Capt., 1st Lieut., 25 enlisted men, and 11 women and children, fortunately including among the latter the brave wife of Lieut. Helm, who herself and Mrs. Heald, who although seriously wounded, escaped most fortunately with her life.

A most notable incident of this massacre was the fact that Mr. Kinzie and family were unharmed, and restored to their house the next day, with the loss of but a small part of their goods; they however ran a close chance of destruction on the day following by a party of Wabash Pottawotamies, who arrived too late for the main attack, and were only saved by the presence of mind of Billy Caldwell, a half-breed Wyandott, who placated them with good speeches in recommendation of Mr. Kinsie's kindness to the Indians, and friendship for them.

Campaign of 1812.

In the meantime Governor Edwards had not been idle. Anticipating for some months the action of the General Government, he had, on his individual credit, thoroughly organized and equipped the militia of the territory, built forts, and made every possible effort.

—21

General Hull having surrendered at Detroit on the 16th day of August, the British and Indians had full sway in the whole northwest, with the exception of Forts Wayne and Harrison. This emboldened them to penetrate further and further into the interior, even encroaching on the settlements in Southern Illinois. The British had descended the Mississippi to Rock Island and were distributing goods to the Indians through their notorious agent, Samuel Girty.

In the latter part of August, General Harrison superseded General Hull in the command of the Northwest.

The State of Kentucky had raised a force of 7,000 men, a portion of which, under the command of General Hopkins and Col. William Russell, was directed to the aid of Indiana and Illinois. On the 11th day of October, Col. Russell with two companies started from Vincennes to join Governor Edwards in an expedition then fitting out at Camp Russell. These companies were commanded by Captains Perry and Modrell. General Hopkins, in command at Vincennes with over 2,000 of the Kentuckians, was to move off the Wabash to Ft. Harrison, pass over into Illinois, march across the prairies on the headwaters of the Sangamon and Vermillion rivers, destroying the Indian villages in the course of his march, and to finally effect a junction with Edwards and Russell on the Illinois, and, combined, to sweep the Indians from the whole length of that river.

Governor Hopkins and his branch of the expedition succeeded very well in their plans, and about the middle of October crossed the Wabash at Ft. Harrison, but the men began to show symptoms of discontent, which on the 20th had assumed so violent a form that the generals were forced to return after having penetrated from 80 to 90 miles into the heart of the Indian country.

In the meantime Gov. Edwards had collected 350 men of the Illinois militia at Camp Russell, by the time Col. Russell had arrived with the U. S. Rangers, as the regular troops were then called. These he divided in two small regiments, commanded respectively by Colonels Elias Rector and Benjamin Stephenson. (Rolls of a portion of these companies are yet preserved, and are published complete in the following pages).

DESTRUCTION OF PEORIA.

It having been reported to Governor Edwards that the French settlers at Peoria were inciting the Indians to attacks on the settlers, he dispatched Capt. Thomas E. Craig, of Shawneetown, with his company (see roll) in advance of the expedition, with two boats on the Illinois river, one boat loaded with provisions, and tools to build a fort, the others armed with blunderbusses and a swivel, as a sort of a gun boat, while both were "fortified so that the enemies bullets could not enter their sides." Craig was to wait at Peoria for further orders from the commander-in-chief, and was to make offensive war on the French inhabitants of that town. The latter instruction was carried out fully, by burning the place and taking prisoners the white inhabitants, who were afterwards sent as prisoners to Camp Russell and from there sent to St. Louis, and discharged some months afterwards. Governor Coles, in a report made to the Secretary of the Treasury, several years afterward, gives the names of these settlers as, Thomas Forsythe, Jacques Mette, P. Larasier, (alias Chamberlain), Antonie Le Claire, Michael La Croix, Francis Racine, Sr., Francis Racine, Jr., Felix Fontaine, Hypolyte Maillet, Francis Banche, heirs of Charles La Belle, Antonie La Pance, Antoine Barbonne and Louis Pencennau. The above list does not include women and children, the number of prisoners in the aggregate numbering 75.

GOVERNOR EDWARDS' CAMPAIGN, 1812.

On the 18th day of October, Governor Edwards and his army took up their march. Their route was up the west side of Cahokia creek, thence to the Macoupin, which they crossed near the present town of Carlinville, thence in a northeast direction, they crossed the Sangamon below the junction of the north and south forks east of the present city of Springfield; passing thence east of Elkhart Grove, they crossed Salt creek near the site of the present city of Lincoln; from thence marching still northward, they came upon a deserted Kickapoo village on Sugar creek, which they set on fire and destroyed. After this, their course was directed to the head of Peoria Lake, where was located the village of Black Partridge, a chief of the Pattawotamies. Having approached within a few miles of the town, Thomas Carlin, (afterwards Governor of the State) and Robert Stephen and Davis Whitesides were sent to reconnoiter the enemy, which they successfully accomplished by passing through and over the town in the night without discovery.

Early on the following morning, the army, with Capt. Judy and his spy company in advance, under the cover of a dense fog moved upon the village, but the troops becoming entangled in the swamps, the Indians were apprised of their approach and fled without fighting or encountering any serious loss. Following the fleeing Indians for several miles across the yielding swamps, a small Indian town was reached and burned. The Indians having all made good their escape, and no news having been received from Governor Hopkins, and a rainy season having set in, the Governor deemed it prudent to retire. As Governor Reynolds quaintly observes in his "Own Times," "Our army returned home with all convenient speed."

MUSTER ROLLS OF VOLUNTEERS—1812.

CAPT. THOMAS E. CRAIG'S COMPANY.

A muster roll of a company of Volunteer riflemen, raised in Illinois Territory, under the command of Capt. Thomas E. Craig in the service of the United States, by order of His Excellency Ninian Edwards, Governor of said Territory. From the 5th September to the 2d December, 1812.

In column headed "date of appointment or engagement," all appear to have been enlisted Sept 5th and all were discharged December 2, 1812.

Captain.
Thoman E. Craig.

Lieutenant.
John Forrester.

Ensign.
Harrison Wilson.

Sergeants.
Walker Skantlin,
Charles Hill,
John G. Wilson,
Phil. Buckner.

Corporals,
Robert Preston,
Joseph Lepan,
Joseph Gordon,
Willis Wheeler.

Music.
John Ormsby, drummer,
Nat. Reeves, fifer.

Privates.
Elias Hubbard
Thomas Hatfield,
Jacob Yocum,
Stephen Fowler,
Moses Rawlings
John Hazelton,
John Woods,
Robert Harris,
William Corn,
Charles Druyer,
Henry Jenna,
Arthur Owens,
James Drake,

Samuel Kimberly,
Richard Hayden,
Robert Cox,
Hiram Higgins,
Randall Davis,
William Gable,
Lewis Young,
Edward Farely,
Sampson Dunn,
David Stanly,
James Wright,
Enoch Brown,
Edmond Stokes,
Jacob Willis,
Elisha Livingston,
John Powell,
Samuel Green,
Dennis Clay,
Russel E. Haycock,
David Johnston,
John Clendenin,
Joel Crane,
Squire Crane,
Alex. Barbour,
Spencer Adkins,
Amos Paxton
John Farney,
George Glun,
Michael Burris,
John Lard,
Lasadore Gander,
Inlam Bart,
Peter Bono,
George Conner,
Richard Hazle,
John Campbell,
David Sipley,
George T. Woods,
Antoine Sander,
Lewis Freedom,
John B. Genam,
Edward Miller,

Although Governor Edwards had several times during the years of 1811 and 1812 recommended to the Secretary of War the enlistment of one or more companies of "Rangers," to protect the frontier, and Congress having, in 1811, passed an act authorizing the organization of ten companies of rangers, which were afterward organized as the 17th United States Regiment, under Col. William Russell, of Kentucky, an Indian fighter of bravery and experience, it does not appear that more than one Company was recruited in the Illinois Territory. Davidson and Stuvé say in their History, in reference to this force: "Four companies were allotted to the defense of Illinois, whose respective Captains were Samuel and William B. Whitesides, James B. Moore and Jacob Short. Independent Cavalry Companies were also organized for the protection of the remote settlements in the lower Wabash country, of which Willis Hargrave, William McHenry, Nathaniel Journey, Capt. Craig, at Shawneetown, and William Boon, on Big Muddy, were respectively commanders, ready, on short notice of Indian outrages, to make pursuit of the depredators." (D. and S. Hist. Ill., p. 249.) We are, however, of the opinion that there must have been some mistake about the fact alleged of four Companies of the 17th Regiment being from Illinois, as, of the Captains mentioned, we have evidence that Samuel Whitesides, James B. Moore and Jacob Short were commanding Companies of Militia at the time, in the service of the Governor of Territory, all belonging to the Regiment which William Whiteside, as Lieutenant Colonel, was then commanding, (the 2d Regiment Ter. Militia.) The organization and size of this command appear from a regimental return, on file in this office, bearing date Sept. 16, 1812, which was no doubt made out at Camp Russell, signed by Lieut. Col. William Whiteside, Commanding, and Elihu Mather, Adjutant, and is as follows:

1st Battalion—MAJOR JOHN MURDOCK.

	Total.
Capt. Jacob Short	80
Capt. John Scott	75
Capt. Abraham Stallions	55
Capt. Edward Ebart	91
Capt. James B. Moore	71
Total, 1st Battalion	372

2d Battalion—MAJOR SAMUEL JUDY.

	Total.
Capt. Amos Squires	64
Capt. Samuel Whiteside	56
Capt. Solomon Pruitt	60
Capt. Henry Cook	79
Capt. Cale Jourango	..
Total, 2d Battalion	259

3d Battalion—MAJOR WILLIAM PRUITT.

	Total.
Capt. Valentine Brazil	30
Capt. Isaac Griffin	30
Capt. Nathaniel Journey	39
Shoal Creek Company	..
Total, 3d Battalion	69
Aggregate	700

In a morning report, also made at Camp Russell, dated Sept. 12, 1812, "of the troops under the command of Major Benjamin Stephenson," we find companies under the command of Captains James B. Moore, W. B. Whiteside, Absolem Cox, Jacob Short, Willis Hargraves, Samuel Whiteside, Nathaniel Journey and Amos Squires, giving an aggregate of 570 men. Two companies on this return, viz: Absolem Cox's and William Hargraves' were probably independent companies or belonged to another regiment, and were reported because present at the same post. These returns were both made out and signed by A. Whitney, Sergeant-Major, and a penman of no mean ability.

In another morning report of "troops under the command of Lt.-Col. Whiteside," dated Oct. 10, 1812,—and also made out by A. Whitney, Sergeant-Major—their appears companies under the command of Captain N. Ramsey, Thomas E. Craig, Willis Hargraves, Absolem Cox and James Trousdale, showing present an aggregate of 316 men. A "staff" return on the same blank shows present 1 surgeon, 1 surgeon-mate, 1 Adjutant, 1 Sergeant-Major, and 1 Judge Advocate. At the bottom of this return is the following: "N. B.—Six company on command, Capt. Moore, S. Whitsid, Short, Whitesid, N. Journey, Squires," Of these companies mentioned in these returns we have rolls of a part only. Those we will now give:

CAPTAIN SAMUEL WHITESIDES' COMPANY.

A muster roll of a volunteer company of mounted riflemen commanded by Captain Samuel Whitesides, of St. Clair county, Illinois Territory, by order of His Excellency Ninian Edwards, Governor of said Territory. Date of enlistment, Aug. 22;—enlisted to Nov. 13, 1812.

Names.	Remarks.
Captain. Samuel Whitesides	
First Lieutenant. Titus Gragg (or Greig)	
Second Lieutenant. John Swigert	

Names.	Remarks.
Ensign.	
Henry Taylor.	
Sergeants.	
Jesse Creek, 1st,	Reduced to the ranks Oct. 10, 1812.
Azor Gragg (or Greig)	
Abram Howard	Reduced to the ranks Oct. 18, 1812.
Wm. Simpson	Reduced to the ranks Oct. 13, 1812.
Corporals.	
John Pursley	Made Sergeant Oct. 18, 1812.
John Waggoner	
William Pursley	Made Sergeant Oct. 18, 1812.
Harmon Gragg	Absented himself without leave Aug. 23, 1812.
Privates.	
Aaron Armstrong	
Benjamin Bishop	
Wm. Burgess	
Jos. Borough	Made 1st Sergeant Oct. 10, 1812.
John Brisco	One horse lost, $30.
Jonas Bradshaw	
Simeon Brundage	
George Barnsback	
Louis Baimmie	
Daniel Cornelius	
William Chelton	
David Carter	
Samuel Davis	
Huber Delorme	One horse lost, $30.
John Ferguson	
John Fulmore	
Joseph Ferguson	
John Gragg	
Wm. Howard	
John Howard	Made Corporal 18th Oct., 1812.
Roland Hewitt	
Matthias Hanlon	
George Hewitt	
John Higens	
Philip Hawk	
George Harmon	
John Jacobs	
James Johnson	
George Kinder	
Charles Kitchens	
John Lacey	
Samuel Lee	
Joseph Lee	
Raphael Langlue	
Batees Labrau	
Walter McFarling	
James Marney	
James McFadgin	
Jesse Million	
Joseph Myars	
Jacob Ogle	
Jubilee Posey	
Pierce Plant	
Wm. Phillips	
John Pixley	
John Powell	
James Pullum	
John Paine	
Wm. Pruitt	
David Porter	
Daniel Pierce	
Matthew Roach	
Wm. Right	
Samuel Stockton	
David Sampler	
Jacob Smelcer	
Robert Stockton	
Moses Sweeten	Deserted.
Thomas Smith	Discharged.
James Tolley	
John Teeter	
Toussant Tramble	
Napees Tuckee	
John Turner	

Names.	Remarks.
Abram Vanhooser	
Joseph Williams	
William Groats	
Joshua Patterson	
Joel Whitesides	
Isaac Lecount	
Joshua Lamotte	
Allan Bridges	
Ellsworth Bayne	One horse lost, $40.
Benjamin Samples	
Benjamin Warren	

I do certify on honor that the foregoing statement is correct, and exhibits a true account of the men under my command. This 13th day of November, 1812.

SAMUEL WHITESIDES, Captain.

Capt. Jacob Short's First Company.

Muster roll of the mounted riflemen detached from the 2d Regiment of militia, Illinois Territory, for a three months' tour, by order of the Commander-in-Chief, March 3, 1812.

Captain.
Jacob Short.

First Lieutenant.
John Murdoch.

Ensign.
Henry Carr.

Sergeants.
Robert Middleton,
Alexander Scott,
George Mitchell,
William Arundel.

Privates.
Adam Clover,
David Kenedy,
Thomas Marney,
Wm. Quigley,
Thomas Porter,
James Hendricks,
Jacob Borrier,
John B. Wisser,
Isaac Carmack,
Daniel Guyee,
Zachariah Hayse,
Samuel Scott,
William Philips,
John Walker,
David Eckman,
Elijah Hoake,
William Ritenhouse,
James Wilderman,
Henry Stout,
Peter Hill,
Peter Wills,
John Bier,
George Wilderman,
Fulden Jarvie,
Hiram Tidwell,
John Brigance,
Daniel McKinney,
John Brigham,
William Steele,
Charles Radclifft,
Henry Walker,
William Middleton,
John Waddle,
Robert Middleton,
Jeptha D. Williams,
Hubard Short,
Peter Risenbough,
William Walker,
Jacob Wilderman,
John Cooper,
John Eastes,
John Myers,
Sam'l Shook,
Andrew Bankston.

Mustered and inspected by me, Elihu Mather, Adjutant 2d Regiment Militia, Illinois Territory.

Capt. John Scott's Company.

A list of the third Company detached from Colonel Whiteside's Regiment, the 3d of March, 1812, as infantry.

Captain.
John Scott.

Lieutenant.
Titus Gragg.

Ensign.
Phillip Roder.

Sergeants.
John Mitchell,
Jacob Randleman,
William Cerns.

Corporals.
Birdett Green,

Christopher Halterman,
James Porter,
John Stallions.

Privates.
Asyl Jerome,
Prior Hogan,
Thomas Todd,
Alexander Wells,
John Robins,
Alexander Jamison,
Daniel Sink,
Jacob Trout,
Geo. Atchison,
Jacob Clover,
Leonard Carr,
Charles Goldsmith,
Joseph Fry,

John Huffman,
Martin Jones,
Patrick Cullin,
Robert Patton,
John Winters,
Isaac Toland,
Absolem Bradshaw,
Jacob Clark,
Abraham Miller,
James Bradshaw,
Thomas Ramey,
James Johnston,

James Whaley,
Robert Hawk,
Jacob Eyman,
George Ramey,
Baker Whaley,
John Moore,
John Porter,
David Whiteside,
Enoch Moore,
John L. Whiteside,
Phillip Cramer,
William Mears.

Mustered and inspected by me, Elihu Mather, Adjutant 2d Regiment Militia, Illinois Territory.

CAPT. SAMUEL JUDY'S COMPANY,
OTHERWISE KNOWN AS
CAPT. HENRY COOK'S COMPANY.

A list of the first Company detached from the 2d Regiment of Militia, Illinois Territory, for a three months tour, by order of the Commander-in-Chief, 3d March, 1812. Inspected at Cohakia.

Captain.
Samuel Judy.

Lieutenant.
Henry Cook.

Ensign.
Christopher Barnhart.

Sergeants.
Samuel Gillham,
Wm. Bradshaw,
Charles Gillham,
Thomas Kitchell.

Drummer.
Hiram Beck.

Fifer.
Bolin Shepherd.

Privates.
Thomas Cox,
David Moon,
Jonas Bradshaw,
Henry Rogers,
Field Bradshaw,
J. Clemont Gillham,
John Hawks,
John Kirkpatrick,
Aaron Linvill,
George Fase,
John Finley,
Meril Ledbetter,
Jesse Bill,
Thomas Rendell,
Joseph Luster,
Thomas Downing,
Abraham Vanhoofer,
Benjamin Samples,

David Samples,
John Talbott,
Ezra Gragg,
James Wilson,
Hardin Wardin,
James McFadgin,
Absolem Wodams,
Wm. Gillham,
John Starkey,
John Arons,
Jacob Linder,
Thomas Blankenship,
Wm. Prewitt,
John Vickery,
Royal Green,
Joseph Ogle,
Davis Waddle,
John McDow,
George Hewitt,
Robert Anderson,
John Adkins,
Willey Willbanks,
Alexander Elliott,
Richard Ackles,
Samuel Hutten,
Robert Whiteside,
Th. Andrew,
Justis Kick,
Jonathan Graham,
Andrew Emert,
John Newman,
Bird Lockhart,
Joshua Diliplain,
Samuel Quigley,
Michael Dodd,
Uton Smith,
John Newman, Jr.,
Wm. Ryons,
John Johnston,
Charles Kitchens,
Jacob Whiteside.

Mustered and inspected by me, Elihu Mather, Adjutant 2d Regiment Militia, Illinois Territory

CAPT. WILLIS HARGRAVE'S COMPANY.

We, the undersigned, being formed into a Company of Mounted Volunteers, under the command of Willis Hargrave as Captain, tender to your Excellency our services, to perform a tour of duty against the Indians on the frontiers of Illinois Territory, and hold ourselves in readiness to march at a minute's warning to any point you may direct.

Captain.
Willis Hargrave.

First Lieutenant.
Wm. McHenry.

Second Lieutenant.
John Graves.

Ensign.
Thomas Berry.

Enlisted Men.
James Long,
William Maxwell,
David Trammel (a spy),
James Wilson,
Thomas McKinney,
John Smith,
Taylor Maulding,
Jeremiah Lisanbee,
James Small,
Thomas Trammel,
James Hannah,
Charles Slocomb,
Edward Covington,
Nathan Young,
Joseph Upton,
James Garrison,
Robt. D. Cates,
Dickason Garratt,
Thomas Boatwright,
Richard Moulding (spy),
Aaron Williams,
John Summers,
Seth Hargrave,
James Trammel,
Lee Moulding,
Morris May,
David Milch,

Henry Wheeler,
Joel Berry,
David Whooley,
Thomas McAllister,
John Love,
James Davenport,
Thomas Stovery,
James Carr,
Daniel Battenhouse,
Gillam Harris,
Abner Howard,
Josiah Dunnell,
Ely Stewart,
Philip Sturn,
Neadham Standlee,
Charles Stewart,
John Lawton,
Alexander Hamilton,
David Snodgrass,
Philip Fleming,
John Morris,
George Morris,
Thomas Upton,
Martin Whitford,
Joseph Lane,
John Dover,
Simon Cannon,
John Mitchell,
James McDaniel,
Adam Winkler,
William Wheeler,
John Bradberry,
Michel Deckers,
Thomas Williams,
Barnabas Chambers,
Ephriam Blackford,
Reubin Blackford,
Rial Potter,
Frederick Buck,
Charles Sparks,
William McCormick,
William Fowler.

CAPT. SAMUEL JUDY'S SPY COMPANY.

Captain.
Samuel Judy.

Privates.
Henry Cook,
Isaac Gilham,
Calvin Adams,
Alexander Waddle,
Ambrose Nix,
Samuel Gilham,
George Moore,
Toliver Right,

Thomas Smith,
Pierre Crossey,
Joseph Newman,
William Griffin,
John Adkins,
Davis Stockdon,
Thomas Cox,
William Going,
William Radcliff,
John Reynolds,
Edward Clark,
Robert Frazure,
Patrick Larner.

APPENDIX. 329

CAPT. ABSOLEM COX'S COMPANY.

Muster roll and inspection return of a detachment of the 1st Regiment of Illinois militia, under the command of Capt. Absolem Cox, at Kaskaskia, the 3d of September, 1812.

(This detachment did not go to Peoria, but was no doubt left behind to protect the settlers.)

FROM CAPT. COX'S COMPANY.

Captain.
Absolem Cox.

Lieutenant.
Thomas Roberts.

Ensign.
Adam Wobrick.

Sergeants.
Robert Foster,
William McDonald,
Richard Robinson,
Samuel Reiner.

Corporals.
John Irwin,
Shadrach Lively,
Amos Lively,
Edward Clark.

Privates.
William Thompson,
William Little,
James Patterson,
James McFarland,
Shadrach Lively,
John McClinton,
John Beatty,
John Smyth,
James Clark,
Thomas McBride,
George Baggs,
John Willson,
Reuben Lively,
Archibald Steel,
John Miller,
Solomon Allen,
John Pillere,
Andrew Ross,
Robert Thompson.

FROM CAPT. ALEXANDER'S COMPANY.

Jesse Boggs,
Matthew Jarvis,
Hugh Robston,
Seth Chalfin,

Wm. McLaughlin,
George Conner,
John Worley,
Chester Marvel.

FROM CAPT. HENRY LEVON'S COMPANY.

George Glenn,
Patrick Lamer,
Benjamin Vermillion,

James Adkins,
Abraham McMurtry.

FROM CAPT. JOHN COCHRAN'S COMPANY.

Jonathan Bowman,
James Steele,
David Johnston.

William May,
John Clendenon,
Squire Crain.

FROM CAPT. M'DINEY'S COMPANY.

James Sleter,
Cyrus Fulton,
Thomas Beson,
Adam Wingate,
Alexander Barber,
James Bail,

William Garver,
Samuel Lard,
Charles Garner,
William Hall,
George Belsher,
David Petel.

From Capt. Greenup's Company.

Ralph Lee,
Joseph Curry,
Francis Toulouse,
James D. Mitchell,
Amos Paxton,
Pascal Lessauree,
Louis Segar,
Jean B. Gendeon,
B. Lachasspell,
N. Beatt,
Louis Lemiene,
George Baker,
Robert St. Pierre,
Manuel Troupa,
J. Chinia,
Alexis Beauvais,
Louis Beatt,
Andrew Charleville,
B. Montrow,
Francis Depreet,
Alexis Beatt,
James Smyth.

From Capt. Gabriel Decoche's Company.

Francis Tongue,
Joseph Tongue,
Andre Barboure,
Alexis Godere,
Andre Roy,
Joseph Godere,
Joseph Vassure,
Ettienne Louglore,
Joseph Pilquer,
Jean Marie Gidier,
Francis Louglore,
August Alter,

Signed: DAVID ANDERSON, Inspector,
Adjutant 1st Ill. Militia.

Capt. James B. Moore's Company.

1st Company—April 15 to May 3, 1812.

Captain.
James B. Moore,

First Lieutenant.
Jacob Ogle.

Second Lieutenant.
John Vaugn.

Ensign.
Simon Wheelock.

Sergeants.
John T. Lusk,
Septemus Mace,
Thomas Piper,
Jesse Miller.

Privates.
J. Milton Moore,
William Biggs,
John Rutherford,
Thomas Talbott,
David Robinson,
James Kirkpatrick,
Henry Mace,
Richard Wright,
Isaac Biggs,
John Davidson,
Israel Robinson,
Cath Wilson,
Aaron Shook,
William Lemon,
Samuel Bonham,
Joseph Bear,
Philip Teter,
Charles T. Walker,
Joseph Ogle,
Francis Kirkpatrick,
John Bloom,
Isham Gillham,
Simeon Vanarsdale,
William Gillham,
Hiram Badgely,
Arthur Morgan,
Joshua Talbott,
Pleasant Goings,
William Goings.

Capt. James B. Moore's (2nd) Company.

A muster roll of a volunteer company of Cavalry, commanded by Capt. James B. Moore of St. Clair county, Illinois Territory. By order of His Excellency Ninian Edwards, Governor of Illinois Territory. From July 27, 1812, to Aug. 11, 1812.

Captain.
James B. Moore.

First Lieutenant.
Jacob Ogle.

Second Lieutenant.
Joshua Vaughn.

Cornet.
Simeon Wheelock.

Sergeants.
John T. Lusk, 1st,
Septemus Mace,
Thomas Piper,
Jem Miller,

Corporals.
Wm. Reed,
James McKinney,
John Davidson,
Pleasant Goings,

Privates.
James Kirkpatrick,
Isham Gillham,
Charles P. Walker,
Aaron Shook,
J. Milton Moore,
David Robinson,
Israel Robinson,
Francis Kirkpatrick,
Daniel G. Moore,
Samuel Bonham,
Philip Teter,
Henry Mace,
Isaac Biggs,
Cath Wilson,
Wm. C. Davidson,
Richard Wright,
Thomas Randle,
Jesse Bell,
John Good,

Wm. Briggs, Jr.,
Thomas W. Talbott,
Ezekial Gillham,
Simon Vadarsdal,
Moses Quick,
Matthew J. Cox,
Arthur Morgan,
Hardy Wilbanks,
Charles R. Matheny,
John L. Whiteside,
George Sanders,
Joseph Ogle (son of B. Ogle)
Isaiah Dunnigan,
Thos. Blankinship,
Bennet Nowlan,
Wm. Talbott,
John Crocker,
William Otwell,
Clement Gillham,
John Deleplain,
Absolem Bradshaw,
Anthony Foucher,
Isaac Clark,
Isham Wright,
Zachariah Hays,
William Porter,
Fielding Jervis,
David Ackerman,
Aaron Whitney,
Guy Beck,
John Huitt,
Charles Gillham,
Wm. Gillham.

CAPT PHILIP TRAMELL'S COMPANY.

Muster roll of a detachment of Mounted Militia, called into the service of the United States, under the orders of His Excellency Governor Edwards, to guard military stores from Shawneetown to Camp Russell, under the command of Philip Tramell, Lieut.-Col. of the 4th Regt. Illinois Militia, acting as Capt. From the 12th day of October to the 31st day of October, 1812.

Captain.
Philip Tramell.

Sergeant.
Morton Ewbanks.

Privates.
James McFarland,
John Murphy,

James Lee,
William Cumins,
Covington Wilson,
John Gillard,
Isaac Sibley,
Wm. Wheeler
John Campbell,
David Sibley,
Solomon Blue,
James Inman,
Pompey, servant to Philip Tramell.

I do certify that the within muster roll exhibits a true statement of the detachment for the purpose mentioned therein, and that James Ratcliff furnished a wagon and team for the purpose of transporting military stores from Shawneetown to Camp Russell, which was employed in the United States service from the 5th day of October until the 31st; the same month with Adam Croach, wagoner. William Morrison furnished wagon, team and driver, for the same purpose, from the 9th October to the 31st of same month, Meed Laughlin and Davis Gillard each furnished wagon, and team, and driver, for the above purpose, from the 31st of same month

PHILIP TRAMELL, Lieut.-Col., 4th Illinois Militia,
now acting as Capt., in place of Leonard White.

Capt. Dudley Williams' Company of the 4th Regiment Militia.

A muster roll of a Volunteer company of Mounted Riflemen, called into service of the United States, agreeable to an order of His Excellency Ninian Edwards, Commander-in-Chief of the Illinois Militia (against the late invasions of the hostile Indians), commanded by Capt. Dudley Williams. From October 14th to November 5th, 1812.

Captain.
Dudley Williams.

Lieutenant.
David Moore.

Ensign.
Reuben Linn.

Cornet.
Alfred Linsey.

Sergeants.
Joseph Ferguson,
John Reed,
Henry Griffin,
James Moor.

Corporals.
Wm. Megee,
James Brown,
Thomas Armstrong,
John Jarrat.

Privates.
Henry Fuel,
John Walker,
Asher Davis,
John Neal,
John Hallin,
Daniel Calhoun,
Allen Barnes,
Furnas Harrison,
Hiram Dikerson,
Matthew Thomas,
Thomas Futral,
Andrew Hallin,
John Show,
Isaac Davis,
Micajah Fort,
Jesse Rascow,
William Cravens,
Elijah Ladd,
Thomas Casten,
Samuel Reas,
Redden Wolf,
Wilbourn Futral,
Joseph Bridges,
Samuel Walker,
William Mathias,
Ezekiel Stevens,
Robert Cain,
Jeremiah Mitchell,
James Woolf,
Hiram Griffith,
Samuel Jennings,
John Matthews,
Richard Clark,
Daniel Coshler,
Joseph Williams,
John Ferguson,
Charles Brownfield,
James Blasingham,
William Armstrong,
John Mabury,
James Randolph,
James Cook,
Harvey Bramlett,
Thomas White.

I certify that the foregoing is a correct muster roll of my company, and that they were mustered into service of the United States Saline, on the 14th day of October, 1812.

Examined and approved,
   B. STEPHENSON, Brigade Major.

DUDLEY WILLIAMS, Capt.

Also endorsed by a certificate of Philip Tramell, Lieut.-Col. of the 4th Regiment Illinois Militia: "That this company found their own provisions from Christian county to the United States Saline and back again, which going and coming may be considered 160 miles."

The foregoing comprises all the rolls of Companies which have been preserved in this office of those who enlisted during and prior to year 1812. As the rolls of many of these Companies of Rangers are no doubt preserved in the archives of the War Department at Washington, and their publication would add much to the resources of the early history of the State, it is to be hoped that the General Assembly may see fit to take some steps to have them transcribed and published.

As to the other most common means of security for families of the settlers in these early days, these consisted of block-house forts, a number of which were built extending from the Illinois river to the Kaskaskia, thence to United States Salines, near the present town of Equality, and up the Ohio and Wabash rivers, and in nearly all settlements in Illinois. Some of these forts were situated as follows: One at the site of the present town of Carlyle, one a short distance above the town of Winston, and two on east side of Shoal Creek, known as Hills and Jones; all these in the limits of the present county of Clinton. One on the west side of Looking Glass Prairie, a few miles southeast of the present town of Lebanon, was known as Chambers' Fort. On the Kaskaskia river were Middleton's and Going's Forts; one on Doza creek, a few miles from its mouth, known as Nat. Hills,; two in the Jourdan settlement, in the eastern part of Franklin county, on the road from the Kaskaskia settlements to the salt works; one at the mouth of the Illinois river, and later John Campbell, an United States officer, erected a small block-house on the west bank of the Illinois river (at Prairie Marcot), 19 miles above its mouth. Larger forts than these were erected opposite the mouth of the Missouri river, to guard the river; and on Silver creek, near Troy. The main fort, however, and military depot of the territory, was at Camp Russell, a mile and a half northwest of the present town of Edwardsville, in Madison county, in honor of the Colonel, the commander of the Regiment of Rangers. (D. and S. Hist. Ill., pp. 249-250.) This fort was protected by the cannon from old Fort Chartres, and under the guns of Louis XIV., under whose protecting muzzles the Territorial Governor was wont to organize his expeditions, gather his military stores, and rendezvous his recruits under the various calls which the necessities of a desultory Indian warfare, of several years' duration, made it obligatory on his Excellency to make.

At this fort, besides the rangers and riflemen mentioned in the various rolls above given, was also a small company of regular troops, under Capt. N. Ramsey, as the return of Lieutenant-Colonel Whiteside on the 10th of October, 1832, hereinbefore published, shows to have contained a total of 33 men. This company was the only company of regular troops in Illinois Territory, during the war of 1812, which reached the headquarters of Governor Edwards, or tested the hospitalities of his fort.

Among these old rolls we find one of perhaps the most interest, in an historical point of view, of any small paper connected with the history of the State. It reads as follows:

GENERAL STAFF.

Muster roll of general and staff officers of a detachment of militia of Illinois Territory, ordered into the actual service of the United States, and commanded by his Excellency Ninian Edwards, Governor and Commander-in-Chief of the Territory aforesaid:

No.	Names.	Rank.	Commencement of Service.	Expiration of Service.	Remarks.
1.	Ninian Edwards	Comm'nder-in-Chief	Sept. 2, 1812.	Nov. 10, 1812.	
2.	Elias Rector	Adjutant-General	Sept. 10, 1812	" "	
3.	Benjamin Stephenson	Brigade Major	Sept. 2, 1812.	" "	
4.	Nath. Pope	1st Aid	Sept. 20, 1812	" "	
5.	William Rector	2d Aid	Oct. 10, 1812.	" "	
6.	Nelson Rector,	Volunteer Aids	Oct. 18, 1812.	" "	
7.	Robert Todd,				

On the back of this roll is the following endorsement:

"NOVEMBER 23, 1812.

"Examined, approved, certified and returned by me according to law, to the Commander-in-Chief.
"ELIAS RECTOR,
"Adjutant General I. T."

CAMPAIGN OF 1813.

Early in this year, the country was put in as good state of defense as circumstances would allow. The forts and blockhouses were strengthened and the settlers in remote and weakly garrisoned blockhouses removed to those that were stronger. New companies of rangers were enlisted and stationed so as to cover the settlements. In addition to the regular forts, from the present city of Alton to Kaskaskia, were twenty-two family forts, scattered along. These precautions, however, did not prevent numerous depredations by the savages. Of these, the following appear to be the most important: In Washington county, four miles southeast of Covington (then the county seat) on the Kaskaskia river, the family of John Lively, an old ranger (see Alexander's company) were attacked ane five persons killed, including Mr. Lively. The bodies of all were shockingly mutilated. The Indians who perpetrated this outrage were supposed to be Kickapoos, and were followed by Capt. Boon and his company, (see roll) but having four days the start, made good their escape. Near the present town of Carlyle a Mr. Young and a minister by the name of McLean were attacked by the savages, Young was killed, and McLean made an almost miraculous escape by swimming the Kaskaskia river, losing his horse and the greater part of his clothing.

Murders were also committed on Cache river within the present limits of Alexander county. Near Fort LaMotte, about 30 miles above Vincennes, Mrs. Houston and four children were killed. In a small prairie near Albion in Edwards county, Mr. Boltinghouse was killed. This prairie was afterwards named for him.

Notwithstanding these, and many other outrages, the general government had provided no means for the support of the rangers and militia, and those in the service, in Illinois, were discharged on the 9th day of June by the Governor.

From a "daily and weekly report of a detachment of rangers of the Illinois Territory, under the command of Benjamin Stephenson, Brigade Major, April 17, 1813," we find that the following companies were included in his command: Capt. B. Whiteside's, Capt. James B. Moore's (3d company), Capt. Samuel Whiteside's, Capt. Jacob Short's, and Capt. Nicholas Jarrott's. Rolls of Moore's and Short's companies at that time, are as follows:

CAPT. JAMES B. MOORE'S (3D) COMPANY.

Captain.
James B. Moore.

First Lieutenant.
David Robinson.

Second Lieutenant.
Arthur Morgan.

Ensign.
John Duitt.

Sergeants.
Thomas Jordan,
Jacob Young,
Benjamin Marney,
James Hutton.

Corporals.
Isaac Basey,
James Talbott,
Henry Randleman,
John Crawford.

Privates.
Enoch Moore,
Jesse Miller,
Joseph Miller,
David Miller,
Abraham Miller,
John Enoch,
Jonathan Knox,
Anthony B. Conner,
Samuel McFarland,
George Lary,
Thomas Johnston,
Hugh Roylston,
Marcus Pelham,
Peter Wills,
Thomas Marney,
Solomon Strong,
Amos Shook,
Francis Pelham,
Fielding Porter,
John Ryan,
Stephen Lacy,
Elihu Axely,
William Ryan,
Job Stallings,
David Porter,
John Waddle,
John Briscoe,
John Moore,
Jacob Clark,
John Clover,
William Harrington,
David Moore,
Thomas J. Mattingly,
Willy Harrington,
Felix Clark,
Stephen Rector,
Joshua Vaughn,
Charles Gillham,
George Richardson,
William Griffin,
Pleasant Going.

APPENDIX. 335

William Forguson,
Hiram Huitt,
Joseph Forgason,
Ornan Beman,
John Finley,
Fleming Cox,
Aaron Whitney,
Martin Wood,
Bennett Newlin,
Henry Mace,
Isaac Smith,
Daniel Winn,
Roland Huitt,
Edward Crouch,
Isaac Carmack,
William Going,
Elisha Taylor,
Andrew Robinson,
William Hogan,
Prior Hogan.

Bartley Cox,
Richard Windsor,
Alexander Biron,
Jude Converse,
George Hawk,
John Hogan,
Eli Langford,
William Chance,
Jacob Luntzford,
Josiah Langford,
John Marney,
John Collins,
Thomas Marney,
Daniel Converse,
John Ferguson,
Robert Hawke,
Benjamin Edwards,
Janus Marney,
Jesse Harrison.

Examined and approved.

B. STEPHENSON,
Brigade-Major.

CAPT. JACOB SHORT'S COMPANY.

Muster roll of a company of mounted rangers commanded by Captain Jacob Short, called into the actual service of the United States, by his Excellency, Ninian Edwards, Governor and Commander-in-Chief,—from the 27th day of February, 1813, to the 31st day May, 1813, inclusive.

Captain.
Jacob Short.

First Lieutenant.
Nathaniel Journey.

Second Lieutenants.
Andrew Bankston.

Ensign.
John Journey.

Sergeants.
John Brigance,
Alexander Scott,
George Mitchell,
James Wyett,
Robert Thomas.

Corporals.
Richard Ackless,
Robert Lynn,
George Soy,
Nicholas Darter,
George Wise,
Samuel Ware.

Privates.
Robert Anderson,
William Adair,
Solomon Allen,
Hugh Alexander,
Elijah Bankson,
Ellsworth Barnes,
Jacob Brimberry,
John Boucher,
Preston Brickey,
Abraham Bateman,
Taphney Brooks,
William Burgess,
Benjamin Cox,
Isaac Clark,
John Corathers,
Jacob Drocker,
Thomas Drocker,
Janus Clark,
Squire Craine,
Isaac Darneal,
John Duncan, Sr.,
John Duncan, Jr.,
James W. Davidson,

Stanley Dodge,
Matthias Edes,
William Edes,
Joseph Fray,
Cyrus Fulton,
Robert Gaston,
Jacob Gragg,
John Hopton,
Nathaniel Hill,
Jesse Hill,
Burrill Hill,
Martial Hawkins,
Robert Huse,
William Journey,
David Johnston,
Jacob Kerns,
David Loyd,
Samuel Lee, Sr.,
Samuel Lee, Jr.,
John Linley,
John Lively,
John Lard,
Rueben Lively,
James Lard, Jr.,
Alex. Mattocks,
Daniel McKinney,
James Moore,
Thomas Morris,
William Moore,
William McElroy,
Edward Miller,
Abel McNeal,
Henry Neele,
William O'Neal,
Aden Posey,
Samuel Patterson,
Field Pruitt,
Joseph Pruitt,
Jacob Pritchard,
John Rutherford,
Francis Scott,
Henry Sealey,
George Swigart,
John Swigart,
Hubbard Short,
John Stout,
John Scott,
Moses Short,
William Stout,
Abraham Smalley,
Abraham Thomas,
William Tilford,
William Virgin,

Charles Wakefield,
George Wakefield,
Henry Watley,
John Woods,
Jacob Wilderman,
John Walker,
John A. Wakefield.

William Walker,
Peter Wright,
Andrew White,
John Whitley,
Mills Whitley,
David White,
Adam Winghart.

Examined and approved.

B. STEPHENSON,
Brigade-Major.

Besides the above which were included in the return quoted, we find the following, which appear to have been under the same command, about the same time, all of which are endorsed as the two foregoing.
"Examined and approved."

B. STEPHENSON,
Brigade-Major.

These following, as well as the two preceding, were evidently the rolls on which these companies were musterd out of the service on June 9th, 1813.

CAPT. WILLIAM JONES' COMPANY.

A muster roll of a company of volunteer infantry, commanded by Captain William Jones, ordered into the service by his Excellency, Ninian Edwards, Governor of the Illinois Territory, May 9, 1813, to June 9th, 1813.

Captain.
William Jones.

Lieutenant.
John Springer.

Ensign.
Thomas Finley.

Sergeants.
Edward Reavis,
John Whitley, Sr.,
David White,
Robert Brazel.

Corporals.
Solomon Pruitt,
Jacob Gragg,
David Smelson,
Andrew Lockhart.

Privates.
Simon Lindley, Sr.,
Simon Lindley, Jr.,
Joseph Lindley,
Benjamin Henson,
John Henson,
William Stubblefield,
Easley Stubblefield,
John Lindley,
John Green,
Ephraim Cox,
John Finley,
James Finley,
Howard Finley,
Moses Finley,
Fields Pruitt,
Martin Jones,
John Jones,
William Roberts,
Abraham Bateman,
William Bateman,

Samuel Lindley,
Mills Whitley,
John Whitley, Jr.,
Randolph Whitley,
Elisha Whitley,
Andrew Robert,
Charles Tetricks,
Valentine Brazel,
Abraham Tetricks,
William Brazel,
Jacob Tetricks,
Richard Brazel,
Peter Tetricks,
Robert White,
David S. White,
John Holt,
James Anderson, Sr.,
James Anderson, Jr.,
Abraham Howard,
James Chilton, Sr.,
William Chilton,
John Giger,
William Howard,
Mathias Chilton,
Isaac Ferguson,
John Higgins,
Aquilla Dallarhide,
Harmon Smelser,
Joshua Chilton,
James Chilton, Jr.,
Byrd Lockhart, Sr.,
George Tayes,
George Hutton, Sr.,
Henry Green, Sr.,
William Lockhart,
George Hutton, Jr.,
Henry Green, Jr.,
John Green,
Bartlett Tayes,
Abraham Van Hoozer,
Jacob Neely,
Joseph St. John,
William Davis,
Henry Walker,
Henry Cox.

APPENDIX.

SERGEANT JAMES N. FOX'S DETACHMENT.

Muster roll of a detachment of rangers, on the frontier of Johnson county, under the command of Sergeant James N. Fox from February 17th, 1813, to March 1st, 1813. This detachment being called into service by order of his Excellency, Ninian Edwards, Governor of said Territory.

Sergeant.
James N. Fox.

Privates.
William Edwards,
James Flanery,
Buckner Harris,
James Buchan,
George Deason,
Daniel Griffin,
Moas Blanc,
John F. Norton,
Shadrack Rawlison,
William Rawlison,
John Davis.

CAPTAIN WILLIAM BOON'S COMPANY.

Muster roll of a company of mounted volunteers of Randolph county, Illinois Territory, commanded by Captain William Boon, and called into service by his Excellency, Ninian Edwards, Governor of said Territory, from the 6th day of March, 1813, to the 5th day of June, 1813.

Captain.
William Boon.

First Lieutenant.
John Lacy.

Second Lieutenant.
William Bilderback.

Ensign.
John Bilderback.

Sergeants.
Robert Gaston,
Louis La Chapelle,
Michael Buyat,
Amos Chaffin.

Corporals.
Joseph French,
Adam Wolrick,
Zophue Brooks,
Henry Barbeau.

Privates.
James Lee,
Charles Garner,
William Tilford,
David Bailey,
Peter Dolin,
Archibald Snodgrass,
Ellis Chaffin,
John Drury,
Erne Godier,
Joseph La Franbris,
Louis Dory,
William Gaston,
John Young,
Adam Winghart,
Stace McDonough,
Gregone DeGognie,
Houry Teabeau,
Charles Bilberback,
William Burnett,
Robert Thompson,
George Cochran,
Elias Roberts,
Andre Roy,
John Gadler,
Levi French,
Samuel French,
Ralph Davis,
John Wootan,
Isaac Glenn,
Thomas Glenn,
Jacob Bowerman,
Francis Garner,
John Robinson,
George Creath,
Jacob Philhart,
Joel Craine,
John Roberts,
Daniel Bilderback,
William Fisher,
Robert Alexander,
James Hughes,
William Garner,
Thomas Wadley,
John Machan,
Benjamin Buyat,
Baptiste Gendron,
Julian Bart,
Francis Montroy,
Peter Pillet,
Henry Connor,
Peter Cossy,
Isadore Godler,
Antoine Barbeau,
Jacob May,
Archibald Steele,
Jacob Honnan,
James Robinson,
Daniel Hull,
Shadrock Lively,
Alexander Clarke,
John Clyne,
Pesio,
Levi Tamaraoa,
Cola,
Poscal,
John Babtiste Tamaraoa,
Jabez Loone,
Jacob Lazadder,

LIEUTENANT DANIEL G. MOORE'S COMPANY.

Muster roll of a company of volunteer infantry commanded by Lieutenant Daniel G. Moore, and called into service by his Excellency, Ninian Edwards, Governor of Illinois Territory, from May 9th, 1813, to June 9th, 1813.

Lieutenant.
Daniel G. Moore.

Sergeants.
Martin Jones,
William P. Rowdon,
Benjamin Stidman,
Zadoch Newman.

Corporals.
George Moore,
James Beaman,
John Russell,
Eli Savadge.

Privates.
John Bows,
John Beck,
John Kirkpatrick,
Thomas Kirkpatrick,
Harrison Kirkpatrick,
Henry B. Riggor,
Joseph Newman,
William Jones,
John Newman,
Jesse Starkey,
Abel Moore,
Jesse Ennis,
William Ennis,
James Beck,
John Braman,
John Fullmore,
Hezekiah Cosby,
William Bartlett,
Burrill Hill,
James Hill,
John Lorton.

CAPT. NATHAN CHAMBERS' COMPANY.

A muster roll of a company of militia in the Illinois Territory, under the command of Captain Nathan Chambers, as foot men. Called into the United States service by his Excellency, Ninian Edwards, from the 12th day of April to the 12th day of May, 1813.

Captain.
Nathan Chambers.

Ensign.
John Savage.

Sergeants.
Henry Carr,
John Nichols,
James Bankson,
Joseph Duncan.

Corporals.
William Scott,
James Crocker,
Charles Cox,
Henry White.

Privates.
George Nichols,
Pleasant Nichols,
Abraham Baker,
Abram Minson,
Francis Swaun,
Malcom Johnson,
William Dunkin,
John Broom,
Robert Farrar,
Thomas Nichols,
Leven Maddox,
William Armstrong,
James Chambers,
Samuel Scott,
Abraham Fike,
Nathan Langston,
Joseph Holcomb,
John Robertson,
Daniel Peek,
Bond Bernett,
Benjamin Hagerman,
Robert Middleton,
Reuben Middleton,
Robert Abernathey,
Miles Abernathey,
Robert Moore,
Arthur Crocker,
William Crocker,
Job Vanwinkle,
Simoon Wakefield,
Henry Hutton,
Jonathan Hill,
Patton Bankson,
John Pea,
John Journey, Sr.,
Robert Dunkin, Sr.,
James McCracken,
Barnet Bone,
Robert Dunkin, Jr.,
James Petty,
Bryant Mooney,
John Crocker,
Hugh Gilbreath,
Paul Gasgill,
Jonathan Gasgill,
William Wakefield.

Following is a Muster roll of regimental and staff officers ordered into service by his Excellency, Ninian Edwards, Governor and Commander-in-Chief of the Illinois Territory, from the 18th day of February, to the 16th day of June, 1813:

APPENDIX.

Names.	Rank.
B. Stephenson	Major
Philip Trample	Major
Nathaniel Jurney	Adjutant
George Fisher	Surgeon
William Reynolds	Surgeon's Mate
Daniel G. Moore	Quartermaster
Aaron Whitney	Sergeant Major

I do certify that the foregoing muster roll exhibits a just statement of the regiment and staff officers as above stated, this 16th day of June, 1813.

B. STEPHENSON,
Brigade-Major.

CAPT. JAMES B. MOORE'S COMPANY (4th COMPANY.)

A muster roll of Capt. James B. Moore's company of mounted rangers of the Illinois Territory, under the command of Major Benjamin Stephenson, from the first day of June to the sixteenth day of the same month, 1813—by order of his Excellency, Ninian Edwards, Governor, etc.

Captain.
James B. Moore.

First Lieutenant.
David Robinson.

Second Lieutenant.
Arthur Morgan.

Ensign.
John Hewitt.

Sergeants.
Daniel Converse,
Jacob Young,
Benjamin Marney,
James Hutton.

Corporals.
Isaac Basey,
James Talbott,
Henry Randleman,
John Crawford.

Privates.
Thomas Jordin,
Enoch Moore,
Jesse Miller,
Joseph Miller,
David Miller,
John Enochs,
Jonathan Knox,
Anthony B. Conner,
Samuel McFarland,
George Lary,
Thomas Johnston,
Hugh Royalston,
Marcus Pelham,
Peter Wills,
Francis Pelham,
Abraham Miller,
Thomas Marney,
Solomon Strong,
Amos Shook,
Fielding Porter,
John Ryan,
Stephen Lacy,
Elisha Axley,
William Ryan,
John Stallings,
David Porter,
John Waddle,
John Brisco,
John Moore,

Jacob Clark,
John Clover,
William Harrington,
David Moore,
Thomas G. Mattingly,
Wylie Harrington,
Felix Clark,
Stephen Rector,
Joshua Vaughn,
Charles Gilham,
George Richardson,
William Griffin,
Pleasant Goings,
William Ferguson,
Hiram Huitt,
Joseph Ferguson,
Orman Beeman,
John Finley,
Fleming Cox,
Martin Wood,
Bennett Nowlin,
Roland Huitt,
Henry Mace,
Isaac Smith,
Daniel Winn,
Edward Crouch,
Isaac Carmack,
William Going,
Elisha Taylor,
Andrew Robinson,
William Hogan,
Prior Hogan,
Bartlett Cox,
Richard Windsor,
Alexander Biron,
Jude Converse,
George Hawk,
John Hogan,
Eli Lankford,
Josiah Lankford,
William Chance,
Jacob Luntzford,
John Marney,
John Collins,
Thomas Ramey,
John Ferguson,
Robert Hawks,
Benjamin Edwards,
James Marney,
Jesse Harrison,
George Glenn,
Simon Vanarsdall,
Samuel D. Davidson,
Elias Roberts,
Aaron Whitney,

340   APPENDIX.

The foregoing company was, no doubt, temporarily called into service to hold the forts and protect the government property from the Indians until some more definite arrangement should be made by the War Department to sustain a military force. The following letter from Governor Edwards to the Secretary of War, will shed some light on the subject:

ELVIRADE, Randolph County, Illinois Territory, May 4, 1813.

SIR: A short time ago I received a letter from Colonel Bond, informing me that you had authorized him to request me to raise and organize three additional companies of rangers. I immediately wrote you, that I supposed what had been done would be sufficient, and that those three companies who, through me, tendered the President their services as rangers, would be accepted.

They have been notified by me that they have been accepted, but lest some accident may have prevented my letters from reaching you, I will here give the names of these officers—all of whom have been chosen by their companies and approved by me:

James B. Moore, Captain.
David Robinson, 1st Lieutenant.
Arthur Morgan, 2d Lieutenant.
John Huitt, Ensign.

Samuel Whiteside, Captain.
Joseph Borough, 1st Lieutenant.
Samuel Gilbaur, 2d Lieutenant.
Arthur Armstrong, Ensign.

Jacob Short, Captain.
Nathaniel Journey, 1st Lieutenant.
Andrew Bankston, 2d Lieutenant.
John Journey, Ensign.

These officers and those of the companies raised here last year, are all exceedingly anxious to be commanded by Benjamin Stephenson as their major, with the exception of an ensign and a lieutenant, who were absent at the time. They have unanimously petitioned me on this subject. The privates comprising the battalion are equally desirous of it, and I can most conscientiously say, that, in my opinion, the territory does not admit of a better choice.

The Legislature of this Territory, at its last session, by the solicitations of certain individuals, was induced to ask for this force and to recommend John Murdock to be authorized to raise and command it.

But I beg leave to observe that the force I have raised has been upon a different plan altogether. Murdock has not raised a man, and has endeavored to throw every impediment in my way. He is not qualified, either by his knowledge or experience, for the command, and those who have recommended him will not pretend to say that his habits do not form a most important objection.

I have the honor to be,

Your obedient servant
N. EDWARDS.

(Edwards' History of Illinois, pp. 347-8.)

SECOND CAMPAIGN 1813.

Large numbers of hostile Indians having gathered among the Kickapoos and Potawotamies at their villages on Lake Peoria, and marauding parties from these being frequently sent out to harass, rout and kill the settlers on the frontiers of both Illinois and Missouri, a joint expedition was projected of the militia of both territories, to disperse them from their convenient location. An army of 900 men was collected and placed under the command of Gen. Howard, who had resigned the position of Territorial Governor of Missouri, for that purpose. The Illinois contingent was ordered to rendezvous at Camp Russell.

One company, however, was ordered to a point on the Mississippi called Piasa, where they remained several weeks and suffered seriously from sickness.

The organization of the Illinois troops at Camp Russell was as follows: Colonel, Benjamin Stephenson, Randolph county; W. B. Whitesides and John Murdock, Majors, and Joseph Phillips, Samuel Judy, Nathaniel Journey, and Samuel Whitesides, Captains. The Missouri contingent was commanded by Colonel McNair, afterward Governor of that State. Both regiments marched up on their respective sides of the Mississippi river, without any adventure, except a slight skirmish by the Illinois troops with straggling Indians in search of wild honey in the present limits of Calhoun county. A junction was formed by the Missourians crossing the river at Ft. Mason, 100 miles above the mouth of the Illinois river, when General Howard took the principal command of the expedition. Passing a recently deserted Indian village on the site of the present city of Quincy, they struck out eastward and reached the Illinois river at the mouth of Spoon river, not far from the present town of Havana, in Mason county.

Here the provision boats arrived and took on board their sick. The march was continued up the Illinois river to Peoria, where there was a small stockade in charge of Capt. Nicholas of the U. S. Army, on which the Indians had two days before made an attack, but were repulsed. But the Indians gaining knowledge of the advance of this force, had, with their usual cunning, fled northward. Of the conclusion of this expedition Davidson and Stuvé, say:

APPENDIX.   341

"The army was marched up the lake to Goma's village, the present site of Chilicothe, and finding that the enemy had ascended the Illinois, two deserted villages were demolished under the shock of its onset, and burned, when it took up its retrograde march. At the outlet of the lake, the present site of Peoria, the troops remained in camp several weeks, building Fort Clark, named in honor of Gen. George Rogers Clark. Major Christy in the meantime, was dispatched with a force, in charge of two fortified keel boats, up the river (Mississippi) to the foot of the rapids, to chastise and rout such of the enemy as might have lodged in that region. Major Boone was sent with a force to scour the Spoon river country, towards Rock river. Both expeditions returned without other discoveries than signs of alarm on the part of the enemy, and his retreat into the interior. The army returned by a direct route to Camp Russell, where the volunteers and militia were disbanded, October 22, 1813. (D. and S., History Illinois, p. 277.)

1814.

The year 1814 was prolific with horrible deeds of savage butchery. The Indians were incited by British agents and were active all along the line of the advancing frontier. Illinois with her large line of explored settlements suffered severely. We will mention only a few of the most aggravated of their outrages. Compiled from Reynolds Times, and Stuve's History of Illinois:

In July, a Mrs. Reagan, living in the Wood River settlement six miles east of the present city of Alton, with her six children, were murdered by the Indians, who were pursued by Capt. Samuel Whiteside and his company of rangers, to the Sangamon river, where all escaped except the leader, who was shot out of a tree top by Capt. Whiteside, with the scalp of Mrs. Reagan fastened to his belt.

In August, Capt. Short's rangers, who were encamped at the Lively cabins in Washington county, discovered the trail of 7 Indians with 14 stolen horses. Capt. Short with 30 men followed them overtaking them on a fork of the little Wabash, near the east line of Fayotte county, and killed them all. The whites lost but one man, William O'Neal, who was killed by an adversary quicker than himself.

The military expeditions in which Illinois participated in this year were by water on the Mississippi. The first was that of Governor Clark (in the absence of General Howard) which left St. Louis on the 1st of May, composed of 200 men, in five barges destined for Prairie de Chien.

Dickson, a British agent, had recruited at that place, a short time previously, a force of 300 Indians for the British army, which he had conducted to Canada, leaving a small garrison of "Macinoe Fencibles" under the command of a British officer to hold the post until his return. These Governor Clark had no difficulty in putting to flight, and quartering his troops in the house of the Mackaw Fur Company, erected a fort which he called Ft. Shelby, and returned in June to St. Louis. But in July a large force of British and Indians under Col. Mackey, coming by water from Mackinaw, via Green Bay, and the Wisconsin river, after a short siege captured the entire garrison, which they paroled, thus leaving the British the gainers of all the material advantages of the expedition.

General Howard having returned to his post in St. Louis in the meantime, and believing it desirable to strengthen the fort at Prairie du Chien, to this end sent 108 men in charge of Lieutenant Campbell of the regular army, in three keel boats up the river, as reinforcements. Of this force 66 men were Illinois rangers under the command of Capt. Stephen Rector and Capt. Riggs, who occupied two of the boats. The remainder of the force with Campbell occupied the other boat. They passed as far as Rock Island, where they laid up for a night without molestation. At the rapids great numbers of the Sac and Fox Indians visited the boats with professions of friendship, yet gave hints to some of the French boatmen, who accompanied the expedition, that all was not right. Lieut. Campbell, however, disregarded these hints, and allowed his force to become scattered, when a gale blew his boat, which was two miles in the rear, over towards the Illinois shore to a small island, when it was attacked by a large force of the Indians from the shore, under the command of Black Hawk.

The strong gale prevented the return of the boats which had gone ahead, and the force on Campbell's boat had been mostly killed and wounded. When Rector, throwing overboard all provisions, with a gallantry deserving of commemoration, came to the rescue of the imperiled men and rescued the survivors, and removed the dying and all to their vessel, leaving Campbell's barge to the enemy, the contents of which furnished them material for a feast as unusual as it was enjoyable.

Riggs' boat was for a time surrounded by the enemy, but toward evening the wind having become somewhat allayed, the boat, under cover of the approaching darkness, and the crew made good their escape without the loss of a single man.

After the two foregoing disasters still another expedition was projected this season for the Upper Mississippi. This latter was fitted up at Cape au Gris, an old French hamlet on the left bank of the Mississippi, a few miles above the mouth of the Illinois. It consisted of 334 men (forty of whom were regulars) in command of Major Zacary Taylor, Nelson Rector and Samuel Whitesides and Captain Hempstead being each in command of a boat. Their principal instruction was to penetrate well up in the Indian country and returning to destroy the corn growing within reach on both banks of the river down to Rock Island, where they intended to establish a fort and leave a permanent garrison.

The expedition passed up as far as Rock Island unmolested, although the country swarmed with the enemy who were aided by the English, who were then in command, with a detachment of regulars and artillery. On the 2d day of August, 1814, the boats were attacked by the combined force of the Indians and English, and turning about began to descend the rapids, fighting with great gallantry, the enemy pouring in a hot fire into their flanks from both sides of the river. A little way above the mouth of the Rock river, near some willow islands. Major Taylor anchored his fleet out in the river out of reach of the rifles, but during the night the English planted a battery of six pieces of artillery at the water's edge, and landed a considerable force of the red skins on the island, to supplement the attack they expected to make. But early in the morning Major Taylor, with all his force except 20 men left in charge of the boats, with great gallantry charged on the savages and drove them with considerable loss from the upper island to the lower one. The fire of the artillery had become to be a serious matter with the boats and they dropped out of range down the stream. After an ineffectual, though partially successful attempt on the part of Capt. Rector to clear the other island of savages, the expedition, with a total loss of 11 men, wounded—of whom 3 afterwards died—continued its retreat down the river. On the site of the present town of Warsaw, in Hancock county, they erected a fort, which consisted of a rough stockade, and blockhouses of unhewn logs. which they named for Governor Edwards. This fort, like Ft. Madison on the opposite bank of the river a little higher up, was a few weeks after (in October) considered untenable—the troops being out of provisions—and was evacuated and burnt, and the expedition continued its retreat to Cape au Gris.

Thus ended the third and last of those ill-fated expeditions, like its predecessors, in defeat and disaster. The rangers and volunteers were discharged Oct. 18, 1814.

With the approach of winter the Indian depredations became fewer, and finally ceased altogether with the peace of Ghent, which closed the war December 24, 1814.

We subjoin a muster roll of a company of mounted rangers, called into service in September, 1814, and which is remarkable as the last body of men enlisted in this State for the war of 1812.

Muster roll of Captain Daniel Boultinghouse's company of mounted volunteers, called into the service of the United States by order of his Excellency, Governor Edwards, Commander-in-Chief of the Illinois militia, to repel the invasions of the hostile Indians. From Sept. 8, to Dec. 8, 1814, inclusive:

Captain.
Daniel Boultinghouse.

First Lieutenant.
John Graves.

Second Lieutenant.
Robert Tavery.

Third Lieutenant.
John Morris.

Ensign.
Thomas Tavery.

Sergeants.
William Nash,
Stephen Stanley,
James Boyd,
James Hopkins,
Tira Robinson.

Corporals.
John Wilson,
Robert Boyd,
David Haney,
William Cummins,
Asa Ross,
Robert Clark.

Privates.
Real Porter,
Edward Pottor,
James Dunlap,
William Trask,
Rolen Lane,
Benj. Kirkendall,
Hiram Jones,
Daniel McHenry,
John Dover,
James Hencely,
Jesse Kirkendall,
George Stumm,
John Morris,
George Martin,
John Burney,
Needham Stanley,
Charles Hencely,
James Paton,
Jonathan Steward,
John Brown,
Eli Selph,
James Boultinghouse,
Charles Burney,
Daniel Boultinghouse,
George Morris,
David Daniel,
John Daniel,
David Brown,
Irvan Wilson,
Charles Steward,
William Vaughn,
John Dennis,
Philip Steward,
John Buckels,
James Corn,
Archibald Clayton,
Nathan Young,
Nathan Harris,
Thomas Pool,
William Meriday,
John Moor,
John Lucus,
William Burney,
Joseph Daniels,
Jesse Boman,
Jarrard Tramell,
Seth Hargrave,
Daniel Snodgrass,
Joseph Lawry,
William Adkins,
James Devenport,
James Wilson,
Robert Stafford,
John Martin,
Robert D. Cates,
Henry Coley,
John Beck,
Moses Sweeton,
Charles Dickerson,
Hugh Collins,
Edward Meloy,
James Hix,
Willis Chambers,
Jesse Adkins,
Wyatt Adkins,
Thomas Chambers,
Joseph Culbertson,
Arvin Wilson,
William Read,
William Chambers,
John Ferret,
Edward Michel,
John Poley,
Thomas McCallister.

APPENDIX.

Alden Henry,
James Martin,
Archibald Rowan,
Joel Metcalf,
Elijah Reede,
Henry Wheeler,
Samuel Davidson,
Moses Lamb,
William McCormick,
Ezekial Hide,
John Gastin,
Charles Lezenby,
James Morris,
Robert Gastin,
Merritt Taylor,
Nimrod Taylor,
Edmond Starks,
William McGehee,

Thomas Gastin,
John McGahan,
William Clark,
Jonathan Hampton,
John Walls,
William McCoy,
John Perry,
Elias Chaffin,
Brice Hannah,
Thomas Wilson,
John McCallister,
Reuben Walden,
James Gastin,
John Hoart,
Henry Stumm,
John Whitaker,
George McCann,
James Haynes.

www.ingramcontent.com/pod-product-compliance
Lightning Source LLC
Chambersburg PA
CBHW020303240426
43673CB00039B/684